Doing Enterprise-Architecture

A Maturity-Model Guide to Architecture Development

Tom Graves
Slade Beard

apress®

Doing Enterprise-Architecture: A Maturity-Model Guide to Architecture Development

Tom Graves
Tetradian Consulting,
Eaglehawk, VIC, Australia

Slade Beard
Ecothought Pty Ltd,
Victoria, 3453, Harcourt, Australia

ISBN-13 (pbk): 979-8-8688-1756-4
https://doi.org/10.1007/979-8-8688-1757-1

ISBN-13 (electronic): 979-8-8688-1757-1

Copyright © 2025 by Tom Graves and Slade Beard

This work is subject to copyright. All rights are reserved by the Publisher, whether the whole or part of the material is concerned, specifically the rights of translation, reprinting, reuse of illustrations, recitation, broadcasting, reproduction on microfilms or in any other physical way, and transmission or information storage and retrieval, electronic adaptation, computer software, or by similar or dissimilar methodology now known or hereafter developed.

Trademarked names, logos, and images may appear in this book. Rather than use a trademark symbol with every occurrence of a trademarked name, logo, or image we use the names, logos, and images only in an editorial fashion and to the benefit of the trademark owner, with no intention of infringement of the trademark.

The use in this publication of trade names, trademarks, service marks, and similar terms, even if they are not identified as such, is not to be taken as an expression of opinion as to whether or not they are subject to proprietary rights.

While the advice and information in this book are believed to be true and accurate at the date of publication, neither the authors nor the editors nor the publisher can accept any legal responsibility for any errors or omissions that may be made. The publisher makes no warranty, express or implied, with respect to the material contained herein.

Managing Director, Apress Media LLC: Welmoed Spahr
Acquisitions Editor: Aditee Mirashi
Development Editor: James Markham
Coordinating Editor: Jacob Shmulewitz

Cover designed by eStudioCalamar

Cover image designed by Ghinzo@Pixabay.com

Distributed to the book trade worldwide by Springer Science+Business Media New York, 1 New York Plaza, New York, NY 10004. Phone 1-800-SPRINGER, fax (201) 348-4505, e-mail orders-ny@springer-sbm.com, or visit www.springeronline.com. Apress Media, LLC is a Delaware LLC and the sole member (owner) is Springer Science + Business Media Finance Inc (SSBM Finance Inc). SSBM Finance Inc is a **Delaware** corporation.

For information on translations, please e-mail booktranslations@springernature.com; for reprint, paperback, or audio rights, please e-mail bookpermissions@springernature.com.

Apress titles may be purchased in bulk for academic, corporate, or promotional use. eBook versions and licenses are also available for most titles. For more information, reference our Print and eBook Bulk Sales web page at http://www.apress.com/bulk-sales.

Any source code or other supplementary material referenced by the author in this book is available to readers on GitHub (https://github.com/Apress). For more detailed information, please visit https://www.apress.com/gp/services/source-code.

If disposing of this product, please recycle the paper

Table of Contents

About the Authors ix

Introduction xi

Chapter 1: The Quest for Effectiveness 1
    The Architecture of the Enterprise 2
    An Architecture for Enterprise-Architecture 5
    Building the Architecture Capability 8
    Into Practice 15
    Summary 17

Chapter 2: Foundations: Making Sense of Change 19
    Core Requirements 21
    Key Concepts and Principles 23
        Effectiveness 23
        Architecture and Design 24
        Organization and Enterprise 25
        Services and Systems 25
        Fractality, Sameness, and Difference 27
        Nature of Change 28
    Into Practice 30
    Summary 31

Chapter 3: Foundations: The Art and Science of Change 33
    The Feel of Change 34
    The Shape of Change 42
    Perspectives, Modes, and Mindsets 47
        The Artist Mode 52
        The Alchemist Mode 53

TABLE OF CONTENTS

    The Analyst Mode 55

    The Agent Mode 56

    The Assessor Mode 58

  The Awareness of Change 60

  Into Practice 62

  Summary 64

Chapter 4: Foundations: The Patterns of Change 65

  A Pattern for Change 66

    Getting Started with the CSPAR Pattern 73

  Into Practice 76

  Summary 79

Chapter 5: Foundations: The Layers of Change 81

  Layers upon Layers 82

  Context in the Change-Layers 90

    Further Notes on Context 95

  Scope in the Change-Layers 96

    Further Notes on Scope 103

  Plan in the Change-Layers 104

    Further Notes on Plan 117

  Action in the Change-Layers 118

  Review in the Change-Layers 123

  Into Practice 129

  Summary 134

Chapter 6: Foundations: The Cycles of Change 135

  Thinking in Fractals 136

    How to Make Fractality Our Friend 137

    How Not to *Lose* Fractality As a Friend 140

  Understanding the Change-Cycle 143

  Context in the Change-Cycle 153

  Scope in the Change-Cycle 156

Plan in the Change-Cycle	159
Action in the Change-Cycle	163
Review in the Change-Cycle	166
Into Practice	169
Summary	173

Chapter 7: Foundations: The Practice of Change 175

The Roles of Change	175
The Uncertainties of Change	182
The Complexities of Change	188
The Scales of Change	197
Into Practice	201
Summary	204

Chapter 8: Step 1: Identify the Enterprise 205

Enterprise As Context	208
Enterprise As Storyworld	210
From Values to Principles	216
Elements of the Enterprise	220
Enterprise Roles and Interactions	223
Organization and Enterprise	229
Positioning the Organization	230
Organization Mission	235
Organization-Vision and Values	237
Organization Value-Propositions	241
Organization Content	246
Organization Structure	247
Set Up for Architecture	252
Creating the Architecture Capability	253
The Sustainment of Change	258
The Governance of Change	260
Documents and Repositories	263
Set Up for Engagement	265

TABLE OF CONTENTS

    Into Practice 266

    Summary 268

Chapter 9: Step 2: Get Ready for Action 269

    From Scope to Plan 271

        From Role to Infrastructure 271

        Set Up for Change 276

    Build the Services 277

        Functions and Systems 278

        From Architecture to Action 288

        Stories of change 314

    Test the Services 321

        From Services to Processes 321

        Checks and Balances 325

    Into Practice 328

    Summary 330

Chapter 10: Step 3: Set Out the Stall 331

    This Goes with That 334

        The Enterprise As a Whole 334

        Strategy Drives Change 339

        Innovation Invokes Strategy 347

    Everything's a Service 353

        The Structure of Services 354

        The Flows of Services 359

        The Effectiveness of Services 363

        The Design of Services 369

    Serving the Enterprise 376

        Promise, Service, and Product 376

        Products 381

        Services 385

    Quality and Compliance 389

        From Values to Quality 389

TABLE OF CONTENTS

    Outsourcing and Quality 396

  Into Practice 402

  Summary 405

Chapter 11: Step 4: Interact with the Market 407

  Outside the Box 410

    Inside-Out and Outside-In 411

    Managing Uncertainty 417

    Skills and Leadership 425

    What's the SCORE? 431

  Design for Flexibility 436

    Design for Escalation 436

    Design for Resilience 440

  From Qualities to Values 444

    Quality in Practice 445

  Service, Trust, and Responsibility 448

    The Architecture of Trust 449

    The Responsibilities of Service 457

  Investors and Beneficiaries 463

  Into Practice 473

  Summary 475

Chapter 12: Step 5: Interact with the enterprise 477

  Facing Hidden Risks 482

    A Problem of Power 482

    Anti-clients 495

    Kurtosis-Risks 504

    Enterprise-Hijack 513

    Assumptions and Myths 518

  Tackling Wicked-Problems 527

    Tame, Wild, and Wicked 529

    Working with Wicked-Problems 533

Disruption and Chaos	540
Business-Continuity and Recovery	541
Fail-Safe and Safe-Fail	545
Coping with Chaos	549
Enhancing Enterprise Effectiveness	554
Enhancing Effectiveness	555
Into Practice	558
Summary	561

Chapter 13: Engaging Others in the Architecture 563

Objections and Engagement	565
Resolving Objections	565
Enhancing Engagement	567
Hands-Off Architecture	570
Preparation for Hands-Off Architecture	573
Project-Gateway Notification and Response	575
Project-Completion	577
Build Architecture-Awareness	578
Conferences	579
Communities of Practice	581
Communication	582
Into Practice	585
Summary	587

Chapter 14: Wrapping Up 589

Into Practice	597
Summary	599

Appendix A: Glossary 601

Appendix B: Sources and Resources 617

Index 623

About the Authors

Tom Graves has been an independent consultant for more than four decades, in business transformation, enterprise-architecture, and knowledge management. His clients in Europe, Australasia, and the Americas cover a broad range of industries including small-business, banking, utilities, manufacturing, logistics, engineering, media, telecoms, research, defense, and government. He has a special interest in whole-enterprise architectures for non-profit, social, government, and commercial enterprises.

Slade Beard is an ICT architect and program manager with extensive experience in the design and implementation of ICT infrastructure environments, including integration with large construction projects. He has knowledge and experience in major IT infrastructure rollouts in the defense, national security, emergency services, health, and secure systems environments.

He has proven experience in supporting the effective design, implementation, and commissioning of complex ICT systems in high-risk environments where considerations such as avoiding disruption of existing operations are crucial to project success. In addition, as a result of his extensive construction design and build experience, he can frame and articulate the integration of complex ICT systems within the services elements of facility build considerations and act as an effective advocate for ICT requirements within construction teams.

You will find him actively blogging on LinkedIn. You can also contact Slade via LinkedIn.

Introduction

Enterprise-architecture is a professional discipline that is becoming ever more important in business and elsewhere. But what do enterprise-architects actually *do*? And what kind of business value arises from that work?

The **role of enterprise-architecture** is to **help each organization to be more effective** in achieving its aims, by ensuring that everything in the enterprise can work better, together, and on-purpose, in an often fast-changing world. To do this, enterprise-architects create and manage a body of knowledge about enterprise structure, story, and purpose that is used to guide all types of change within the enterprise.

It is **a strategic skill** to support organizations of every type, whether commercial, government, or not-for-profit, and of every size from a vast multinational alliance all the way down to a small one-person business. Although an enterprise-architecture may start out with an emphasis on IT, it must eventually encompass every aspect of the entire enterprise, regardless of its size, type, industry, or context.

This book provides a focus on **enterprise-architecture as a business capability** to support the quality and effectiveness of change in the enterprise, much like other whole-of-organization quality-capabilities that support health and safety, sustainability, security, and suchlike. We show how to create and use enterprise-architecture to address the needs of any type of change, and how to extend the capability, competence, and maturity of architecture practice in a step-by-step way. We focus on what needs to be done, and the skills to be added, in what order, and *why* it needs to be done in that way, to support the real business concerns to be addressed at each level of architecture maturity.

This **revised edition** of the book provides a new emphasis on *effectiveness*, and on *context-neutral methods that work the same way everywhere*, for every scope and scale, with every type of content and context, at every stage of the change-process, and for every type of lifecycle and timescale. We show how to use these methods to work with specific needs for particular industries, frameworks, technologies, and governance. We've added many new graphics and illustrations, and now use an airport as our consistent worked-example throughout the book, to show how architecture works in real-world practice. For the Maturity-Model that underpins the whole book, we've updated the model's structure to highlight the underlying dependencies that drive its development of architecture-capability, and expanded our description of architecture-method into a standalone "Foundations" section, as a "Step Zero" that needs to be addressed before tackling the architecture itself.

Whatever your enterprise, this book will show you what to do for its architecture, when and how and why, to make it all work in practice.

Who Should Read This Book?

This book is **for enterprise-architects, strategists, change-managers**, and others tasked with guiding change that can affect the enterprise as a whole. In particular, this book is for you if you now know that you *must* expand the role of your enterprise-architecture, from architectures for enterprise-IT to a whole-of-enterprise scope – a literal "*the architecture of the enterprise.*" This book will provide you with guidance on essential "missing pieces" in current enterprise-architecture practice, and help you break free from the arbitrary assumptions about enterprise-architecture that constrain the *role, scope, and business-value* of your architecture-work.

Previous experience in enterprise-architecture or solution-architecture will be useful, but not essential. Readers with practical experience at an *intermediate to advanced level* are likely to gain the most value, but the book does also provide broader general guidance that will be relevant for newcomers to the discipline.

The book would also be useful for business architects, process architects, security architects, solution architects, software architects, and others working in architecture-related roles, and also as an introduction to what enterprise-architects do, and why they do it.

How to Use This Book

This book deals with **one specific practical concern: what you need to *do*** when doing enterprise-architecture, **to deliver real value to the enterprise as a whole**. Our aim has been to provide you with a compact and easy-to-use reference that you would keep at your desk, to revisit often and to guide you in your architecture development and practice over the years.

To support that aim, there are four main parts to this book.

INTRODUCTION

The first chapter provides an overview of the **business role of enterprise-architecture** as a discipline to **support effectiveness across the enterprise as a whole**. We explore where enterprise-architecture fits within the organization, and the key types of architecture practice. We also introduce the airport worked-example, and the Maturity-Model that we'll use to guide the step-by-step development of capability and competence in the practice of enterprise-architecture.

In the next six chapters, for the new **Foundations** step in the Maturity-Model, we show you how to develop the skills and practices needed to guide any type of change, for any level of complexity, in any type of organization. This includes advice on methods for architecture governance, how to establish repositories for documents and more, and how to embed industry-specific frameworks and standards into the practice.

We then take you through **five distinct steps**, each described in its own self-contained chapter, to enable your architecture to tackle increasing scope, scale, and levels of complexity in your own organization. Each step in development of maturity adds new capabilities to the architecture:

- *Step 1*: How to identify the core business-context and to set up the architecture practice
- *Step 2*: How to establish the key infrastructure and internal services
- *Step 3*: How to bring the organization's services to its market
- *Step 4*: How to address real-world complexities and challenges
- *Step 5*: How to tackle unexpected disruption and large-scale change

In the final main chapter of the book, we show you **how to engage others in the work**, because ultimately architecture is not just for experts, but is *everyone's* responsibility.

Each of these chapters includes practical questions and checklists, and an "Into Practice" section and summary at the end of that chapter. Use these to help you **develop your skills in your own work-context**, and to guide you and others in the work.

The book ends with a summary of the themes covered in the text, and an option for you to review what you have learned from applying the "Into Practice" sections at the end of each chapter.

Throughout the book, we provide worked-examples and real-life experiences to illustrate each theme and provide real-world context. There is also a glossary at the end of the book, together with pointers to books and other resources that can provide you with any further detail you might need.

CHAPTER 1

The Quest for Effectiveness

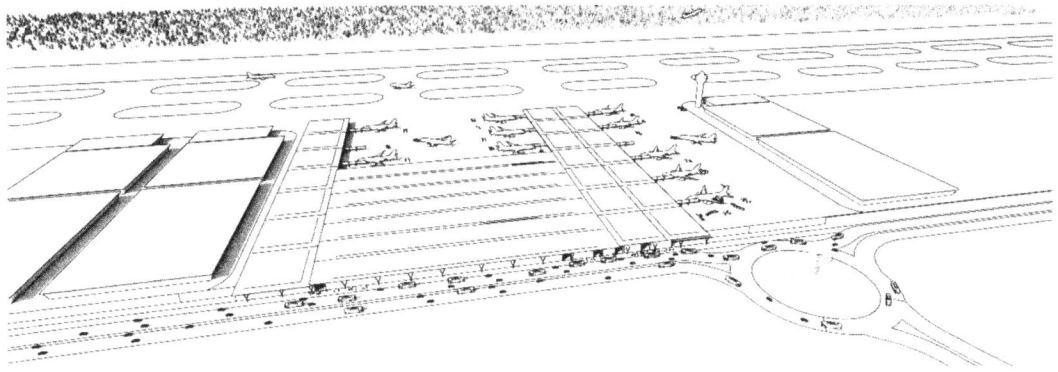

How do we make our organizations more effective?

How do we help our organizations get better at achieving their desired outcomes in a fast-changing world?

And before that, how do we get better at identifying what "effective" and "better" and "desired-outcomes" will mean in our own business-context?

Finding the right answers to those questions could well make the difference between business failure and business success.

This is where enterprise-architecture comes into the picture. Working alongside strategy and change-management, it provides a consistent means to link structure, story, and purpose together across every aspect of the enterprise as a whole. All of this can be summarized in a single motto:

Things work better when they work together, on purpose.

If we think of effectiveness as a quality-concern, much like safety, security, and sustainability, then enterprise-architecture provides tools, disciplines, and professional practices to ensure that every change in the enterprise is "a change for the better," always guiding the enterprise toward greater effectiveness, no matter how much the world may change around it.

The aim of this book is to support you, as an enterprise-architect, in building the disciplines and capabilities that you will need in improving effectiveness across your enterprise, in a world with ever-increasing levels of complexity, uncertainty, and speed of change.

Note As you'll see in a moment, what we'll explore with you in this book is enterprise-architecture, as a literal "the architecture of the enterprise."

If you're a newcomer to enterprise-architecture, or looking at it from elsewhere in the organization, the idea of enterprise-architecture as "the architecture of the enterprise" should seem straightforward enough. We've aimed to keep technical jargon to a minimum, so that you can use these disciplines in whatever aspects of your organization you may need to address.

But if you've been working in the discipline for a while, you may be more used to the idea that it's primarily about the architecture of the enterprise-IT, with everything else as secondary to that focus. If that's the case for you, the fact that we *don't* focus so much as usual on the IT may seem a bit strange at first, maybe even challenging or "wrong." If so, please don't worry about that. Instead, for you, think of this as a "conversion-course" to fill in the gaps and expand the scope of your work onward into business-architecture and beyond, all the way out to the enterprise *as* a whole, connecting everything together all the way. There's a lot to explore here: maybe challenging, at times, yes; but it'll also make your work in enterprise-architecture a lot more exciting and worthwhile too.

The Architecture of the Enterprise

Throughout this book, we'll use the enterprise of an airport as our worked-example. As can be seen in the header-graphic at the start of this chapter, there's a lot going on out there. Some of the things we'd see would include

CHAPTER 1   THE QUEST FOR EFFECTIVENESS

- Passenger-terminal
- Freight terminal
- Runways and taxiways
- Aircraft and other vehicles of many different types
- Connections to road and rail

Down at the detail-level, there's much, much more. And there are flows of people, things, information, and more, too, changes of so many different kinds, all of it happening in many different ways, at different scales, in different places, and over different periods of time. As enterprise-architects, it's our task to help people make sense of all of that complexity, and make the choices needed to keep everything working together, better, on-purpose.

To do that, though, we must first consider the scope that we'll need for our enterprise-architecture. As shown in Figure 1-1, most current enterprise-architecture methods and frameworks are set up to focus mainly on IT:

- "Business-architecture," the business-context for IT
- "Information-systems architecture," including IT-based processes, applications, and data
- "Infrastructure-architecture," including computers, networks, and other physical IT-hardware

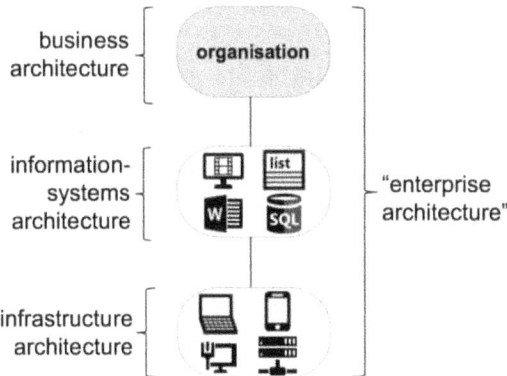

Figure 1-1. Scope of classic enterprise-architecture

CHAPTER 1 THE QUEST FOR EFFECTIVENESS

That emphasis on enterprise-IT will deliver real value: no doubt about that. Yet for the enterprise of the airport, we're going to need **an architecture of the enterprise itself, as a unified whole.** If we focus only on one single theme in that enterprise, such as its IT, and then all but ignore everything else, we risk fragmenting the *overall* architecture, leading to point-solutions that break up the unity of the enterprise as a whole, and destroy overall effectiveness. To avert that kind of risk, we need a ***whole-of-enterprise architecture*** that is able to cover a much broader scope, as shown in Figure 1-2.

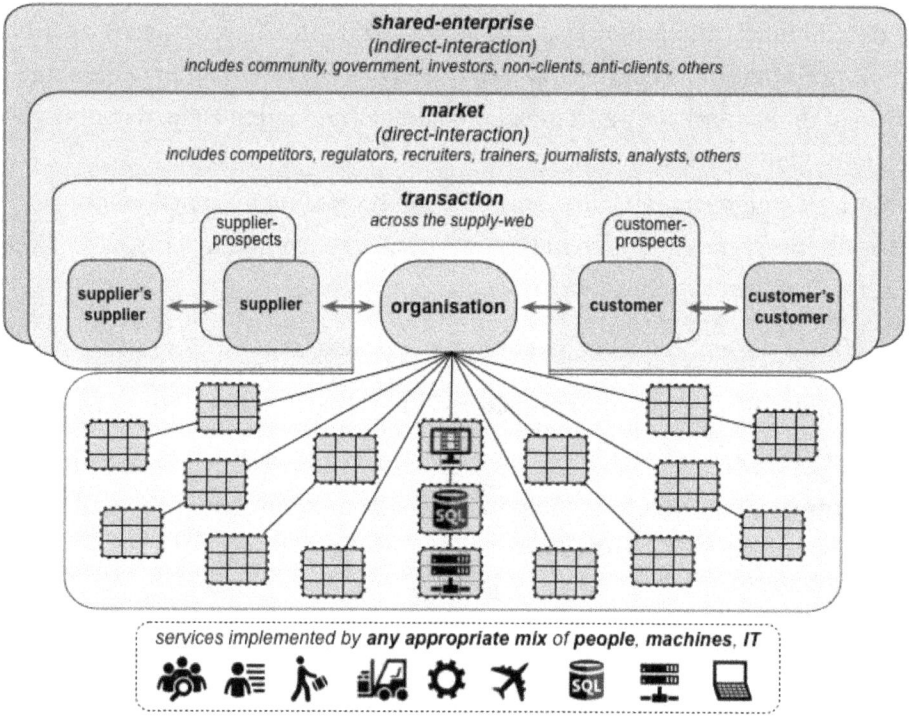

Figure 1-2. *Scope of whole-enterprise-architecture*

For example, the airport's architecture will need to include

- Its IT and other *internal services* to address each type of transaction, direct-interaction, and indirect-interaction

- Its *transactions* such as passenger check-in, security-screening, departure, arrival, baggage-handling, passenger-information, and waiting-areas on landside and airside, and all of the equivalents on the freight-handling side of the airport

- Its *direct-interactions* with recruiters, equipment-manufacturers, service-providers, regulators, and more
- Its *indirect-interactions* with other stakeholders in the overall enterprise, such as employees' families, local communities, and government as a whole

In short, in a whole-enterprise-architecture, we develop an architecture *for* an organization such as our airport, *about* everything within the shared-enterprise that provides its broader context.

An Architecture for Enterprise-Architecture

What kind of architecture would we need for that whole-enterprise-architecture itself? How would it work? What kind of structure would it need: its principles, frameworks, methods, and so on?

To answer that, let's look at the airport in a bit more detail.

From a *business-architecture* perspective, the airport has a very complex multi-way business-model. For example:

- Its *customer-types* include passengers, non-traveling visitors, freight-handlers, airlines, and more.
- Its other *partner-types* include fuel-providers, maintenance-providers, and retailers on both landside and airside who provide food and other services to passengers and visitors, and also pay rent to the airport.

From a *regulatory-architecture* perspective, the airport has a very complex regulatory-environment. For example:

- On the boundaries between landside and airside, the airport must verify *safe-and-legal-to-send* and *safe-and-legal-to-receive* for each passenger and flight-crew member, each item of baggage, and each item of freight.
- The airport must ensure *health-and-safety* throughout the entire airport, with varying regulations applying to different places.

From a *security-architecture* perspective, the airport has a complex security environment. For example:

- The airport must ensure *human-security*, such as access-control, policing, and on-the-spot health-services.

- The airport must ensure *physical-security*, such as preventing items of baggage and freight from being lost, stolen, or sent to or received from the wrong flight.

- The airport must ensure its *information-security*, such as verifying that passengers receive the correct information about flights, locations, schedules, and delays, and also preventing data-loss, data-disruption, data-misrouting, and data-breach.

- The airport must ensure *biosecurity*, such as verifying that passengers do not enter or leave airside with potentially-hazardous plants, fruit, animals, food, and other biosecurity-risks.

From a *complexity-architecture perspective*, the airport is subject to a wide variety of sources for potential disruption. For example:

- Passengers, visitors, flight-crew, and/or staff may *fall ill or be injured*, either in-flight or within the airport itself.

- *Security-incidents* may require closure of part or all of the airport, for any length of time.

- *Flights* may be moved to a different gate, be delayed either on arrival or departure, be canceled, arrive at the wrong airport, or never arrive at all.

- *Weather* may cause delays, cancellations, or other disruptions.

In reality, each of those lists goes on and on, seemingly to infinity at times. There are plenty of other perspectives through which we could view the airport, each with their own near-infinite list of issues. Each of those issues can combine with any of the other issues, sometimes cascading onward throughout the enterprise in unexpected ways. And all of this is changing, all of the time, in different ways, in different places, at different timescales and more.

As enterprise-architects, it's *our* job to help others make sense of all of this complexity, and help them make decisions and take actions that will guide the whole enterprise toward ever-greater effectiveness.

How do we do that?

Classic IT-oriented enterprise-architecture gives us a good start for this. It shows us how to think architecturally, and how to use architecture frameworks, methods, tools, and checklists. It shows us how to guide architecture-driven change, from simple change-projects to large-scale business-transformations. Yet at the whole-enterprise level, there's much more that we'll need to address:

- *It's about more than just IT*: We must be able to address *every* type of content that may be present within the overall enterprise.

- *It's about more than just a predictable world*: We must be able to address both planned *and* unplanned change.

- *It's about more than just project-delivery*: An architecture-task is fully complete only when we have finished the after-action review, and documented its benefits-realized, lessons-learned, and future actions-for-change.

- *It's about more than just the "happy-path"*: We must be able to address all types of events in the context, including exceptions, uniqueness-issues, failure-conditions, business-continuity and disaster recovery, load-balancing, and more.

- *It's about more than just a single change*: We must be able to address interdependencies, interoperability issues, gaps and overlaps between contexts, cross-context synergies, whole-of-context interactions, systems-of-systems or enterprise-of-enterprises issues, across each change, and across the enterprise as a whole.

- *It's about more than just a single project or business-transformation*: We must be able to address complete lifecycles for each type of content in the enterprise, and use our longer-term sustain-architectures to connect the work of change-projects across all of those timescales.

- *It's about more than just the change-plan*: We must be aware of and able to address the whole of each lifecycle in the context, including future migration, platform-refresh, extension of life-of-type, sunset, decommission and disposal, and often more.

- *It's about more than just the organization*: We must always be aware of the overall shared-enterprise and its governance as a whole.

- *It's always about people*: We must always be aware of the roles, responsibilities, commitments, and concerns for each of the players in the enterprise, and the interactions between them that can help or hinder the effectiveness of the organization.

That's a lot of capability that we'll need to add to classic enterprise-architecture that would support the architecture that we'd need for the enterprise of our airport as a whole.

And all of it also needs to be simple enough for anyone to learn and use – because ultimately, as a quality-concern, architecture is *everyone's* responsibility.

That's our challenge. Let's look at how to do that.

Building the Architecture Capability

Before we dive into the "how-to," we first need to summarize what we've seen so far about the role, purpose, and function of enterprise-architecture:

- It is a *quality-support* function – its role is to support the quality of *effectiveness* in the enterprise.

- It's about *effectiveness of outcomes*, for the organization, and for the enterprise as a whole.

- It acts as a *bridge between strategy and change-management*.

- It's about *effectiveness of change itself*, so that every change should be "a change for the better."

- It must be able to address *every aspect of the enterprise* – every scope, scale, and timescale, every type of content or context, every stage in the lifecycle of each element.

- To *support "joined-up-ness" across the enterprise*, the methods we use must be able to work the same way with every aspect of the enterprise, and at every stage of the change-process.

Given all of the above, we will need some kind of roadmap to plan out the sequence in which to build our capability for doing enterprise-architecture. This roadmap must cover a broader scope than most:

- The *purpose* of the work is to build architecture-capability to support continual improvement of effectiveness in the enterprise.

- The *key success-criteria* for the work are to enable the organization to respond appropriately to any type and scale of change, both planned and unplanned, and to do so with the minimum possible disruption of everyday work.

- The *scope* for that work is to embed that architecture-capability into the organization's processes for change, and management of change, for use over indefinite periods of time.

- The *context* for the work is the entire organization – everything the organization is and does – and also some aspects of its interactions with its partners, in relation to the shared-enterprise as a whole.

What we want to achieve is that our organization can respond well to everything that the real-world might throw at it: opportunities, risks, whatever. We also need the organization to be able to do all of that in ways that are effective not just in terms of outcomes, but within itself.

Yet there's almost no way that we'll be able to set up all of those capabilities in one go – especially not across an organization as large as an entire airport. Instead, we'll do it step-by-step, in smaller staged increments that build experience, competence, capability, and maturity by building on the work of the previous steps.

To do this, we first need to map out the respective dependencies, from what we've seen so far in this chapter:

- We want to end up with ***everyone taking responsibility for architecture***, under our guidance as required, supporting overall effectiveness in everything they do.

- To show them how to do that, we ourselves need to be able to ***tackle any kind of change***, planned or unplanned, that the enterprise and wider world can throw at us – any level of complexity, uncertainty, and scale – and still keep everything on-track to purpose.

- To do that, we'll need to ***practice with unplanned change at smaller scale*** – for example, the everyday uncertainties of the market.

- To do that, we first need to ***have something to offer to that market*** that makes sense and works well in that market.

- To support that, we must first ***ensure that the underlying products and services*** are always ***on-purpose and effective for the need*** – efficient, elegant, reliable, adapting smoothly to any change, and all working together in a unified way.

- To get there, we first need to ***know what "on-purpose" and "effective" will actually mean*** within our organization and its enterprise – its vision, values, constraints, success-criteria, and so on.

- To do any of that, for any organization and enterprise, we need to build a solid understanding, capability, and experience about what change *is*, and ***how to work with change*** in any way we might need.

We can then use those dependencies as the basis for our ***roadmap for architecture capability-development***, starting from the first dependency about the need for a consistent capability and capacity for change. Each new capability-increment becomes a step-change in a maturity-model, as shown in Figure 1-3.

CHAPTER 1　THE QUEST FOR EFFECTIVENESS

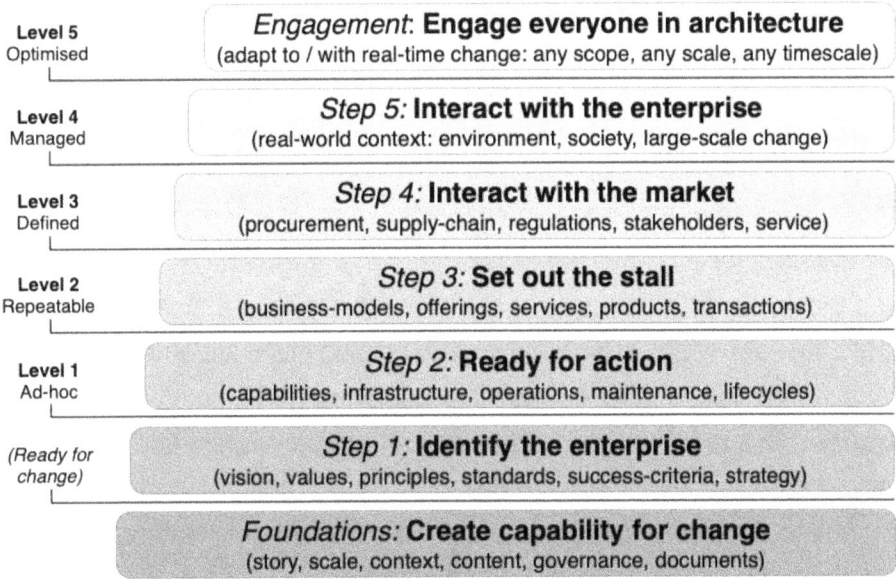

Figure 1-3. *Capability-increments structured as a maturity-model*

Note that we *can* do any of that work "out of sequence," rather than strictly step-by-step – in fact, we sometimes *must* do so, to meet urgent needs. Yet because of those dependencies, doing that may not be all that effective, especially in the longer-term. As in "beginner's luck," we may be able to achieve success once, but not be able to repeat it again – and perhaps more important, it's likely we won't know *how* to repeat it, either. If we want things to work in a reliably-effective way, we do need to respect those dependencies, and build our architecture capabilities step-by-step as summarized above.

Note　Figure 1-3 also shows the steps cross-mapped with the respective levels from version 1 of the well-known CMMI maturity-model: Ad-hoc, Repeatable, Defined, Managed, Optimized. In themselves, though, those levels don't help us all that much: they do indicate the *level* of effectiveness that the respective capabilities should be able to achieve by that point, but that's about it. By contrast, the steps in this Maturity-Model indicate what we need to *do*, and *change*, to extend our architecture capabilities from one level to the next.

Note too that the CMMI levels will also apply to and within each Maturity-Model step: each step will have its own Ad-hoc, Repeatable, Defined, Managed, and Optimized levels. In effect, the capabilities developed in that step will only become fully effective when we reach the CMMI Optimized level for that step.

Warning   Because of those dependencies between the steps, the maximum possible effectiveness at any step will depend on the *lowest* CMMI level currently achieved within each of the previous steps. For example, if the capabilities for Step 1 "Identify the enterprise" are still only at an Ad-hoc level, none of the steps above it will *actually* be able to achieve anything much more than an Ad-hoc level of effectiveness. This is a common reason why enterprise-architecture initiatives that start only at around halfway through Step 2 (such as "digital-transformation") or Step 3 (such as "business-transformation"), without any previous work on Step 1 or Foundations, do tend to fail. Not A Good Idea…

We can also link Steps 1 to 5 capability-increments with the respective part of the whole-of enterprise scope, as shown earlier in Figure 1-2, to be focused on during the work for that capability-increment. We do this via a layered series of perspectives on the relationship between organization and enterprise, such as in the case of our airport:

- *Step 1*: **Boundary** – the boundary between "inside" (the airport as organization) and "outside" (the broader shared-enterprise of air-travel and air-transport)

- *Step 2*: **Inside-in** – the airport looking inward at its internal structures and support-services

- *Step 3*: **Inside-out** – the airport looking outward to customers, suppliers, and other transaction-partners

- *Step 4*: **Outside-in** – the market (or equivalent) looking inward at the airport, as direct-interactions with prospects, competitors, regulators, recruiters, and more

- *Step 5*: **Outside-out** – other indirect-interactions that arise for the airport as a player in the "bold endeavor" of its broader shared-enterprise of flight

Figure 1-4 shows the relationships between the capability-increments and the respective aspects of the organization and enterprise that they each emphasize.

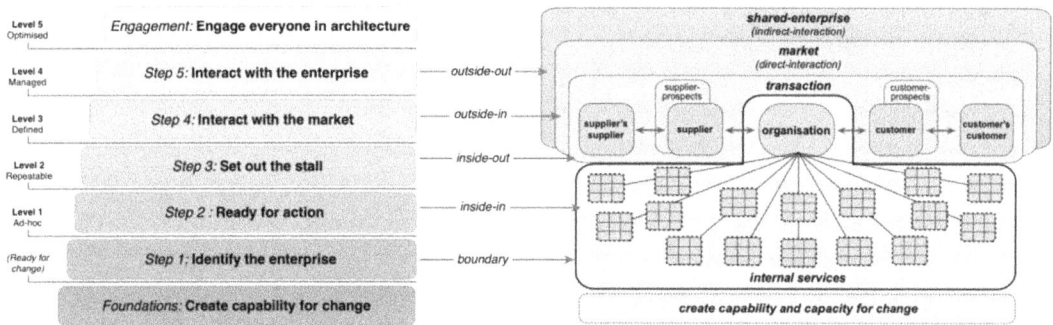

Figure 1-4. Capability-increments, organization, and enterprise

Overall, this gives us the structure that we'll use for the remainder of this book.

In the **Foundations** section, we develop the core capabilities and practices that are needed to do change-work in an effective, disciplined way within our airport, or for any other organization and its enterprise. These will provide the foundations to build upon in the subsequent steps.

In the **Step 1** section, we develop the capability that's needed to identify the effectiveness-criteria and success-criteria for our airport and its enterprise context, and to do change-work within and for that specific context. This will give us enough to guide ad-hoc changes to the airport that have a good chance of working well.

In the **Step 2** section, we develop the capability that's needed to develop and maintain the underlying infrastructure and internal services for our airport, which can support its business-models in a reliable, repeatable, effective way.

In the **Step 3** section, we develop the capability that's needed to define and deliver the business-services, business-products, and business-models that our airport can present to the outside world, and that can adapt well to the needs of the market.

In the **Step 4** section, we develop the capability that's needed to manage the everyday complexities of the real-world, dealing with the airport's concerns around customer-service, recruitment, industry regulations, routine breakdowns, and more, always in ways that are effective and on-track to enterprise-values.

In the **Step 5** section, we develop the capability that's needed to improvise and optimize around major disruptions and unplanned-change. This will include architectures to address reputation-management issues and the like, sometimes at the level of the airport's entire industry and beyond.

In the final section on **Engagement**, we further develop the capability that's needed to support others in taking on the responsibilities of architecture and design for effectiveness, throughout the enterprise as a whole.

To support your development of these skills, the appendixes at the end of the book provide a glossary of terms, and a list of sources and resources that present further detail on specific themes you may encounter on the way.

Note We've said above that this is always about people, which means that it's also always about *you*!

It's quite likely at this stage that you may feel a bit daunted by the scale of the task that lies before you. Don't worry: it won't be as hard as it may seem like right now! A big change, maybe, but one that'll be made up of many smaller and more manageable changes along an overall journey. It's important, though, that you see this not just as a journey that your organization will go through, but also as a journey for yourself. Two things will provide the basis for your part of that journey: the knowledge and skills that you already have, and the skills of observation that you use as you walk around.

In our own practice, we've also had to learn to avoid trying to take responsibility for everything, trying to design, initiate, and manage every part of the change all on our own. As an enterprise-architect, keep your focus on the architecture, and let other people help you with everything else! As we'll show later in this book, you'll identify those allies in the process of observing and exploring the operations of the organization. Cultivate those relationships, and help them to cultivate their own journeys as specialists in their part of the organization and its story.

Remember too to take time for your *own* development of skills and knowledge. Allow time for yourself *as* yourself: time for introspection, time for contemplation, time for mindful relaxation. These things do matter, as you'll see more and more on this journey.

Into Practice

The aim of these "Into Practice" sections at the end of each chapter is to provide you with guidance on how to apply what you've learned here to *your* organization. You'll need a notebook or something similar (perhaps a project-diary, as described in *Everyday Enterprise Architecture*, another of Tom's books in this series), to capture your ideas, experiences, and insights as you go along.

Before you start this exercise, spend some time to **review your own views and assumptions** about the nature, scope, and role of enterprise-architecture as a discipline and practice. This will give you a baseline against which, at the end of the book, you'll be able to assess your own changes in perspective and more, and the progress of enterprise-architecture practice within your organization.

- What, to you, *is* "enterprise-architecture"? What is *not* "enterprise-architecture"? What are the choices and assumptions that guide those decisions?

In the first section here, "The Architecture of the Enterprise," we looked at the **scope of enterprise-architecture**, and why – such as for our airport worked-example – we'll often need to expand that scope outward to a more literal "the architecture of the enterprise."

- What is the *role* of enterprise-architecture in your current organization? What part does it play in the guidance of change, and in improving effectiveness across the organization as a whole?

- What is its *scope*, in organizational terms? Is it considered to be part of the IT-department, or does it have a broader remit, connecting everywhere and anywhere across the organization?

- What are the full set of elements – as in the airport example – that need to be addressed within your organization? If your organization's enterprise-architecture focuses primarily or solely on IT, who is responsible for doing the equivalent work across all the other aspects of the organization, and connecting it with the IT-focused work? If no-one else is doing that non-IT work, what implications will that have for the effectiveness of the organization as a whole?

CHAPTER 1   THE QUEST FOR EFFECTIVENESS

In the next section, "An Architecture for Enterprise-Architecture," we looked at the ***range of architecture-perspectives*** – such as business, regulatory, security, and complexity – that we will need to cover in our whole-enterprise-architecture, and then made a start on identifying requirements for the architecture.

- Using the airport example as a template, what perspectives do you cover within your organization's current enterprise-architecture? Comparing your organization with the airport example, should your architecture cover a different or broader range of perspectives than at present? If so, what implications might arise, in terms of unacknowledged risks or missed-opportunities, *because* those perspectives are not addressed in the architecture?

- Which of those "It's about more than..." themes (such as "It's about more than just project-delivery") are being addressed in your current enterprise-architecture? If they're not addressed there, who else, if anyone, is doing that work, and connecting it with everything else? If there's no-one currently addressing some or any of those themes, what are the implications for the organization, especially in the longer-term?

In the final section, on "Building the Architecture Capability," we mapped out the dependencies to derive a sequence for ***capability-development*** for whole-enterprise-architecture.

- What processes and/or frameworks guide the current capability-development for your organization's enterprise-architecture? Would they cover the full scope and perspectives needed for the whole enterprise of the airport example? If not, what's missing, and what implications does that have for the maximum potential for the architecture?

- Comparing your current processes and frameworks to the Maturity-Model described here, which model's Steps are covered, and which, if any, are not? If some Steps are covered only partially, or not at all, what risks does that imply for your current enterprise-architecture, and for your organization as a whole? In what ways would your organization's effectiveness improve if you *could* and *did* provide the full set of capabilities outlined in those Steps?

Add to your notebook any ideas and insights that may arise from this review. Perhaps show and discuss these notes with your architecture friends and colleagues, and capture any insights that may arise from those conversations. We'll revisit these notes later, in an overall "Into Practice" review at the end of the book.

Summary

In this chapter, we've introduced the role, responsibilities, and purpose of whole-enterprise architecture, using the example of an airport. We've also outlined the capabilities needed to do the work of enterprise-architecture, and the recommended sequence in which to develop those capabilities.

In the next section, we'll start to explore the core foundations for architecture and change-work: the models, methods, mindsets, skills, and structures that we'll need, to work well with any kind of change in any type of organization.

CHAPTER 2

Foundations: Making Sense of Change

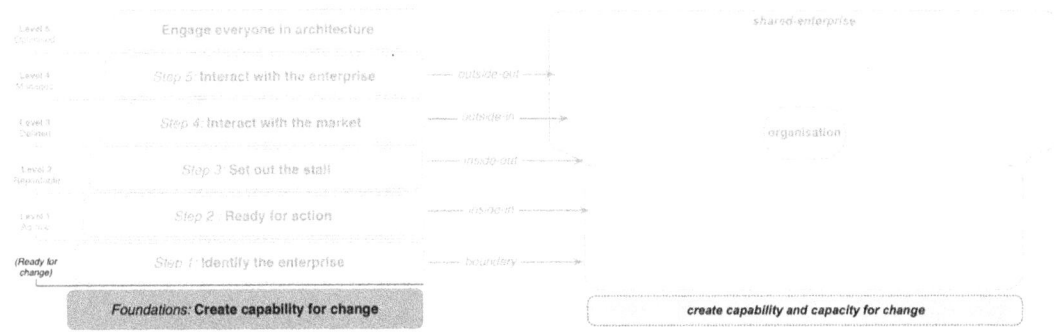

In this "Step Zero" section we'll focus on developing *the capabilities for change*, the foundations to support the disciplines, skills, and competencies that are needed to work well with any kind of change.

As indicated in the graphic above, this Step in the Maturity-Model doesn't address any specific aspect of the organization or enterprise, but instead sets up the capabilities that we'll need within any organization for all change-work on the enterprise and its architecture.

There are six chapters in this Step:

- *Making sense of change* (this chapter): Key concepts needed for sensemaking about change
- *The feel of change*: How to build the disciplines of change-work
- *The patterns of change*: How to describe and plan to do change-work
- *The layers of change*: Step-by-step through the Change-Layers in change-work

- *The cycles of change*: Step-by-step through the Change-Cycle in change-work
- *The practice of change*: How to tackle challenges such as complexity and scale in change-work

Note   Yes, there's a lot of detail to wade through here that may seem a bit daunting at first. But to use a certain famous phrase, **"Don't Panic!"** (in big friendly letters!). There's no test-exam here in this Hitchhiker's Guide to Doing Enterprise Architecture – no-one's expecting you to know everything right from the start!

Instead, on your first pass through this Step, ***it may be best to just skim-read each chapter here to get a sense of where everything is and how it all works***, and then move on to the next Step. Later on, when you've built up a bit more experience with the practice and you realize that you now *do* need that detail, you'll be able to come back here and know where to find the information that you need.

The first of the capabilities we'll need for our whole-enterprise architecture will be a consistent way of seeing and describing the world of change. We'll need this to help us make sense of every aspect of our airport and its enterprise, at every scope and scale, and link each of the multitude of different perspectives on the airport into a holograph-like unified view of the whole.

In this chapter, we'll summarize these key concepts, show why they're needed, and how they work in practice. It'll only be an outline here – we'll see more about the details as we work through the practices in this book – but there'll be enough here to get us started, and provide a basic foundation for what comes next in this Step.

Note   The glossary in Appendix A, near the end of the book, also provides a quick summary for each of the key terms here, and how they're used in whole-enterprise architectures.

We'll tackle this in two parts: first, use a brief reprise of the requirements that arose from the explorations in the previous chapter, to provide the "why" for each of the following concepts and principles; and then an overview of the concepts themselves.

Core Requirements

What are our requirements for the architecture for an enterprise such as our airport? What do we need, to make it all work?

The main **themes** that we saw in the previous chapter were as follows:

- It's about *effectiveness* – continually enhancing effectiveness in the midst of change.

- It's about getting things to **work together, better, on-purpose**, again in the midst of change.

- It's about ensuring that *every change is "a change for the better,"* across the whole of the enterprise.

- Because effectiveness is a quality-concern, it's ultimately *everyone's responsibility*.

From this, the **requirements** for our "architecture of architecture" would include the following:

- It must be able to address *any type of change*, whether planned or unplanned.

- It must be able to address *any scope* – any type of concern, industry, discipline, or whatever.

- It must be able to address *any scale of organization*, from a one-man band to a global concern – our airport is perhaps in the mid-range of that scale.

- It must be able to address *any scale of change*, from the smallest step in any process up to change in the entire enterprise and beyond.

- It must be able to address *any type of context or concern*.

- It must be able to address *any type of content* – whatever mix of things, information, relationships, purpose, and more that might be in the context.

- It must be able to address not just the plan, but *the whole of the change*, from strategy to real-world operations.

- It must be able to address *the whole lifecycle* of each item in the context, from initial idea through to eventual decommission and disposal.

- It must be able to address *any level of complexity, uncertainty, and unpredictability*.

- Because it's ultimately everyone's responsibility, its core methods must also be *simple enough for everyone to understand and use*.

- It must be able to embed and apply any appropriate *frameworks* for the context.

- It must be able to address and embed appropriate *governance* – laws, regulations, standards, cultural-values, and more – for each element in the context.

- To enhance effectiveness and enable real-time adaptation, its methods *must support continual-review and continual-improvement*.

- It must also be able to *respond fast to real-world change*, from minor market-trends to large-scale emergencies.

Example When the COVID pandemic hit, a colleague of ours was working as a business-architect for a large travel-agency. With tens of thousands of its customers at risk of being stranded all over the globe, the company had no real-time CRM (Customer Relationship Management) system capable of tackling the need. Our colleague rose to the urgent challenge: in just ten days, using principles and methods such as described in this book, she designed, implemented, populated, and set in action a new CRM to contact each customer and find them appropriate flights to get them home.

It's unlikely that we'd be able to do all of this right from the start; yet by the time our practice is fully mature, as described in this book, the capabilities that we use for enterprise-architecture must support each of these needs.

Key Concepts and Principles

How do we tackle those requirements? What "ways of seeing" do we need, to be able to make sense of that range of change-work?

Perhaps the best place to start would be by exploring some of the key concepts and terms that we'll need, in order to make this work.

Note Some of the definitions and descriptions that follow may seem noticeably different from those you or others have been using so far for enterprise-architecture. That doesn't mean we're saying that those other definitions are "wrong" – solely that these are ones that we've found to work well for those often more-demanding requirements above.

Here we'll provide a bit of background for each key term and concept, and a working-definition for the term itself.

Effectiveness

As described in the previous chapter, building, maintaining, and enhancing an organization's effectiveness is arguably the real purpose for enterprise-architecture.

- **Effectiveness** is *an assessment of how well something is achieving its intended outcomes*, in terms of a given set of quality-criteria and/or success-criteria. It's about keeping on-track to vision, values, purpose, principles, standards, and so on.

The criteria for effectiveness will depend on the needs of the context. A useful minimum default set of effectiveness-criteria that we could apply to any context is as follows:

- *Efficient*: Makes best use of available resources with the minimum of waste
- *Reliable*: Can be relied upon to deliver the desired outcomes

- *Elegant*: Supports all human factors in the context, such as ergonomics, accessibility, simplicity, and ease of use
- *Appropriate*: Is "on purpose," aligned to the applicable values in the context
- *Integrated*: All elements work together in a mutually-supportive and joined-up way

We'll see more on how to identify effectiveness-criteria for the organization as a whole in Step 1, "Identify the Enterprise," and for individual services in Step 2, "Ready for Action."

Architecture and Design

In enterprise-architecture, we use **architecture** as our main means to guide change that supports the purpose of enhancing enterprise-effectiveness.

- An **architecture** is (a description of) ***the structure and story of the elements in a given context***.

As per the ISO42010 standard, the ***structure*** aspect of architecture is the "fundamental concepts or properties of a system in its environment embodied in its elements, relationships, and in the principles of its design and evolution." There's also a ***story***-oriented aspect to architecture, more about *people*, about process as change, about what it looks like when things work well, and what it looks like when they don't. We'll see more on both sides of this in Step 2, "Ready for Action."

We also need to distinguish between ***architecture*** and ***design***, as different views from the same viewpoint for a context, that lead to different yet interrelated roles about change in that context.

- An **architecture** denotes ***the permissible range of options for any design in that context***, laying out the priorities and trade-offs for each element in the context.
- A **design** denotes (the details of) ***a chosen option for implementation in the real-world***, drawing from the range of options in the respective architecture.

In essence, architecture looks "upward" from the given viewpoint, toward the abstract, more toward purpose, whereas design looks "downward" toward the real-world. We'll see more on this when we look at *Change-Layers* in Chapter 4 and Chapter 5.

Organization and Enterprise

We need to distinguish between these two terms because, as mentioned in the previous chapter, we develop an architecture *for* an organization, *about* the enterprise that denotes its context.

Organization and enterprise are the same kind of thing – an arbitrary region with an identifiable boundary – but the criteria for their boundaries are not the same:

- An **organization** is a *structure* that is ***bounded by rules, roles, and responsibilities.***
- An **enterprise** is a *"storyworld"* that is ***bounded by vision, values, and commitments***.

Another way to describe the difference would be

- An **organization** is about ***the "how" of activity***, about ***preparing for action***.
- An **enterprise** is about ***the "why" of activity***, about ***"a bold endeavor."***

Enterprise is also always about *people*, and their choices, feelings, drivers, and desires – "the animal spirits of the entrepreneur," to quote 18th-century economist Adam Smith. We'll see more on this throughout the book, particularly in Step 1, "Identify the Enterprise," and Step 2, "Ready for Action."

Services and Systems

We can also view the relationship between organization and enterprise as a special-case of a service in relation to its context:

- A **service** is ***a cluster of activities organized to serve an identifiable need***.

In that sense, the organization exists to serve specific needs within the broader enterprise that represents its context. We'll see more on how to use this in Step 1, "Identify the Enterprise."

For most purposes, we'd recommend using a **service-oriented** approach for whole-enterprise architecture:

- In a **service-oriented architecture**, we assume that ***everything is, represents, or implies a service***.

We'll introduce this service-oriented approach in Step 2, and explore services' interfaces with their context in more detail in Steps 3, 4, and 5. (You'll also find more detail on service-relationships, and how to model them in two of the other books in this series, *The Service Oriented Enterprise* and *Mapping The Enterprise* – see Appendix B for more information.)

We can also describe the relationships between a service and its context as a type of ***system***. To paraphrase the ISO42010 standard:

- A **system** is ***a natural, conceptual, and/or man-made cluster of activities and other elements interacting within a given context***.

A system always has some kind of boundary, even if only as "the boundary is where we say it is." A system may also contain or be made up of other systems, intersect with other systems, or be part of larger systems – hence "system of systems" and so on.

The elements that make up a system, or service-as-system, can be summarized as the ***content*** for that system. To again paraphrase ISO42010:

- The **content of a system** may be configured with one or more of the following: ***hardware, software, data, people-based activities and relationships, processes, procedures, facilities, materials, and naturally occurring entities***.

More generally, the content for a service or system is the "what," "where," "when," "who," "how," and "why" for that system or service-as-system. We'll see more on service-content and change-content in the *Change-Layers* chapter later in this Step, and explore it in depth in Step 2 and beyond.

Fractality, Sameness, and Difference

In a service-oriented architecture, we can also describe services and systems as fractal. For our purposes here:

- A **fractal** is *a type of pattern that is "self-similar" for each instance of the pattern, in every context and at every scale*.

Fractal patterns allow us to do like-for-like comparisons across instances that share the same pattern, and connect across an architecture at every scale via fractal patterns that share parameters.

> **Note** Figure 3-2 in the next chapter shows a simple visual example of a fractal relationship, but really all we're talking about here is as described above, namely, a pattern that is a mixture of "same and different" – sameness, to enable like-for-like matching, and different, to carry the specific details for that instance.
>
> For enterprise-architects, fractality is very much our friend. As you'll see elsewhere throughout this book, it's one of the key things that enable architects to make sense of all the huge variance and complexity in a whole-of-enterprise architecture.

For fractal patterns, we need to distinguish between ***context-neutral*** and ***context-specific*** parts of the pattern:

- The parameters for the **context-neutral** part of a fractal pattern's structure *must be the same in every instance of the pattern*, at every scale and in every context.

- The parameters for the **context-specific** part of a fractal pattern's structure *may be different for one or more instances of the pattern*, dependent on varying needs at different scales and/or in different contexts.

In whole-enterprise architecture, we aim to base our models on context-neutral base-patterns, to which we can then "plug in" into that base-pattern any context-specific extensions that we might need. Using base-patterns that share some of the same parameters then enables us to connect cleanly between sometimes very different contexts within an architecture.

We'll see more on how to use context-neutral base-patterns and context-specific "plug-ins" when we look at the *Patterns* chapter later in this Step. This fractal approach to enterprise-architecture also means that even the smallest piece of detail in any item of change-work can help to make the whole picture richer from every perspective and direction, somewhat as in a holograph, but also changing dynamically over time. We'll go into the detail in later parts of the book, particularly in Step 2, where we design and build an organization's core services and explore how to use architecture-repositories for whole-enterprise architecture.

Nature of Change

There are two important concept-pairs that relate to the nature of change itself. The first of these relates to the differences between ***goal-based change*** and ***continuous-change***, and the practical implications of those differences:

- **Goal-based change** relates to *change-contexts that have a defined end-condition* such as time, date, or a specified type of event. Examples include change-projects, larger transformation-initiatives, solution-architectures, and most everyday business-processes.

- **Continuous-change** relates to *change-contexts that do not have a defined end-condition*, and are expected to continue indefinitely. Examples include maintenance-tasks, business-functions such as change-management, finance-management and enterprise-architecture, the organization as a whole, and the storyworld of the broader enterprise.

Both of these are often fractal, such as change-initiatives made up of a swathe of smaller change-projects. Continuous-change functions may also spawn many goal-based changes within the scope of its remit.

These distinctions are important because key terms such as ***vision*** and ***mission*** can have radically different meanings between the two types of context:

- In goal-based change, the **mission** defines the ***desired end-condition for the change***; the **vision** is ***subordinate to the mission***, and provides a description of the ***desired outcomes when the end-condition is met***.

- In continuous-change, the **vision** describes a *storyworld*, defining *the context and governance-conditions* within which desired changes should occur; the **mission** is *subordinate to the vision*, and describes *the scope and remit of activities* within a chosen subset of the respective storyworld.

We'll see more on how to define and use these different types of vision and mission later on, in Steps 1, 2, and 3.

Note The Business Motivation Model standard describes vision and mission in the same way as for goal-based change above, whereas the ISO9000:2000 family of quality-standards define vision and mission in a form that matches continuous-change. Both sets of definitions are correct for the respective type of context, but they're not the same, and it's *really* important not to mix them up!

The other concept-pair relates to the distinction between *planned-change* and *unplanned-change*, and why we need to be able to tackle both types of change in our enterprise-architectures:

- **Planned-change** is *change that we choose to do*, typically to support some part of a broader strategic purpose.

- **Unplanned-change** is *change that is thrust upon us*, usually by events or forces beyond our nominal control.

Most current enterprise-architecture frameworks and standards will focus primarily on planned-change such as large transformation-initiatives, and responses to slower-paced technology-trends and the like. However, few provide much guidance on tackling unplanned-change at smaller scales such as everyday customer-service, and none at all seem to provide any guidance on how to tackle large-scale real-time disruption. We need to remedy that lack, because *both* types of change are very much present in the real-world contexts for our enterprise-architecture.

We can, and generally should, plan to *prevent* any kind of undesirable *unplanned change that we know about*: check that the door is locked, check that the data are properly backed up, and so on. Almost by definition, though, we can't really *plan* for any type of *unplanned-change we've never seen before*. Yet what we *can* do is to build plans and capabilities for *how to respond* to unplanned-change, and test these plans to ensure that we're *ready* for unplanned-change. We'll focus on those themes in particular in Step 4 and Step 5.

Into Practice

Our purpose in this chapter has been to encourage stronger discipline and rigor for the terms we use to describe and understand the world of enterprise-architecture.

- Before you started reading this book, what ideas and assumptions did you hold about the nature, scope, and role of enterprise-architecture?

Revisit that list of requirements for whole-enterprise architecture, as summarized in the section on "Core Requirements" near the start of this chapter.

- To what extent do your current ideas and assumptions about enterprise-architecture align with and support those requirements?
- What, if anything, would you need to change in those ideas and assumptions, for your architecture-practice to fully support and align with all of those requirements?

Revisit the section above on "Key Concepts and Principles," about definitions and uses for terms such as effectiveness, organization, enterprise, architecture, design, service, system, fractality, goal-based versus continuous change, and planned versus unplanned change.

- To what extent do your current assumptions and definitions for these terms align with the descriptions given in this section?
- Where the definitions do not align, what would happen if you were to use your current definitions in the kind of whole-enterprise architecture identified in those requirements earlier above? What problems might arise?
- Where the definitions do not align, what would happen if you were to use the definitions above in your own current context for enterprise-architecture? What might you gain from doing this? What problems might arise? What does this lack of alignment tell you about the way your current organization or context views and approaches change?

- If these definitions have provided you with new insights, how you may consider communicating that awareness across your organization or context? What will it take to put these new insights into practice?

Add into your notebook any ideas and insights that may arise from this review. Perhaps show and discuss these notes with your architecture friends and colleagues, and capture any insights that may arise from those conversations. We'll revisit these notes later, in an overall review at the end of the book.

Summary

In this chapter, we clarified the real-world requirements that a whole-of-enterprise architecture must be able to address, and set out some definitions for key terms that a whole-enterprise architecture must use in order to make sense in real-world practice.

In the next chapter, we'll start to explore that practice, beginning with methods to address the subjective side, or "art," of working with change.

CHAPTER 3

Foundations: The Art and Science of Change

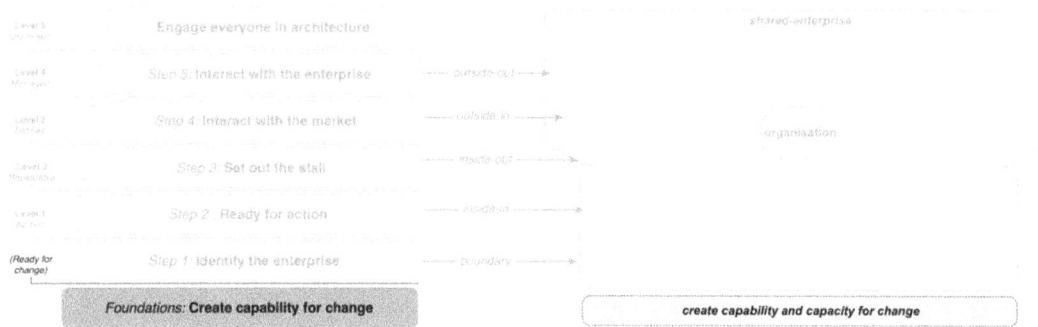

Now that we have some concepts and definitions in place, to help us make sense of whole-enterprise architecture, we next need to put them to use in our day-to-day practice.

At first glance, this may seem to be a straightforward matter of analysis and the like: enterprise-architecture as science. But even science itself isn't always as straightforward as it might at first seem, as William Beveridge describes in his 1950 classic *The Art of Scientific Investigation*:

> *Elaborate apparatus plays an important part in the science of today, but I sometimes wonder if we are not inclined to forget that the most important instrument in research must always be the mind of [the researcher]. It is true that much time and effort is devoted to training and equipping the scientist's mind, but little attention is paid to the technicalities of making the best use of it. There is [a need for a] book which systematises the knowledge available on the practice and mental skills – the art – of scientific investigation.*

Beveridge of course includes chapters on what most people would think of as "science": preparation, hypothesis, experiment, strategy, and reason, for example. Yet he *also* includes chapters on themes that might at first seem surprising: observation, imagination, the role of chance, the role of intuition. Even his chapter on reason is more about its hazards and limitations, which can and so often do lead to difficulties and failures. In that sense, science is much more than just "science."

If we want our enterprise-architecture to be more like a science, we'll need to include *all* of how science actually works – not just the "science-y" parts such as mathematics, analysis, formal-logic, and hard-systems-theory, but also all of those other parts such as intuition and the like. We'll need to balance how we *think* about each change, with how we sense, make sense, understand, and *feel* about that change, as **the art of change itself**.

Yet why do we need those other parts of science in our enterprise-architecture? How do we achieve that balance in our own change-work? As enterprise-architects, how do we help others to achieve that balance in *their* change-work? That's what we'll explore in this chapter.

Caution Much of this part of the work is *necessarily* about more than just mainstream analysis and the like. Given that fact, some parts of the material in this chapter may at first seem a bit strange and uncomfortable, but **don't skip over it** or ignore it! If you want to progress your skills and experience in enterprise-architecture, you *will* need to get a good grasp on all of this, sooner rather than later.

More importantly, understanding how this works in practice will provide you with one of the few ways to support "**defensible uncertainty**" in your work, and mitigate the legal and other risks that arise around some types of inherent-uncertainty. There'll be more on that issue later, particularly in Steps 4 and 5.

The Feel of Change

What do those elements of Beveridge's "art of science" look like from an enterprise-architecture perspective?

Observation is about creating a sense of the world as it is right now. Data can play a useful part in this, of course, but observation is usually more *personal* than that. Expect to use all of the senses: vision, hearing, sight, touch, and even taste. It's often about reading a room more than reading a screen; about listening to the silence; about literally touching the world; about seeing what *isn't* there as much as what is.

It's also about looking *inward*, observing how we feel *within* ourselves. (In that sense, feelings are facts, whereas interpretations and opinions about feelings are *not* facts: too many people seem to get this one the wrong way round…) It's not abstract: it's about a world of *lived* experience, from which subtle skills such as "gut-feeling" and the like can arise. For enterprise-architects in particular, a habit of *curiosity* will also help: be interested in everything, to allow useful insights and observations to arise from unexpected directions.

Exercise Try observing what's happening within you and around you *right now*. Notice where your hands are; the tilt of your head; the tone of your voice; the tension in each of your muscles; what you're thinking and feeling in this exact moment. Then do the same with the next "NOW!", and the next, and the next. Notice, perhaps, how hard it can be to keep the focus on each exact "NOW!", and to distinguish between them; but it does get better with practice.

Once you *can* keep the focus on that "travelling-now," for a few seconds at least, broaden the scope of your listening, your sensing, your observing. Notice the sounds in that space, and beyond it; the temperature, the breeze, the overall feel of the world around you. Then apply the same observing in the place where you work, as you do your various tasks. Allow the noticing to come to *you*, so that insights can arise in their own way.

Imagination is about creating a sense of a *possible* world. Unlike observation, which is about noticing what *is*, imagination is about what *could be*, in the future, the present, or the past, and either in this world or in some other realm entirely.

The skills we use here are much the same as those for observation: we observe the imaginary world, as if it were real. The key difference is that since the imagined world does not yet exist, we'll also need some means to describe it, or make some kind of *image* of it. For example, we might capture it with a sketch, a mindmap, a voice-memo, or a scribbled note.

Note that it's often best to do the initial capture by hand, or on a simple device such as a voice-recorder. The risk here is that if we try to type it out on a computer, for example, or use a sketching app or formal mindmapping tool, we're likely to switch our focus to the technicalities of the process, and lose connection with the imagination itself.

Exercise Imagine a quiet, unhurried breakfast. What is in front of you on the table? What can you see, smell, taste, touch? What is the movement of your arm as you bring the food to your mouth? Who is around you, at the table, or elsewhere in that space? What are sounds that you hear, in this imagined world? And how would you capture this experience, to describe it to others?

Imagine an alternative use – an ***affordance*** – for each object around you in that imagined scene. For example, you could use a plate as a frisbee, a coffee-cup as a ball-catcher, a saucepan as a helmet, or a knife as a splint for the stem of a broken plant. What would the scene look like if people around you start to use those objects in that way?

As an enterprise-architect, imagine all of the elements of your current project as items in a space in front of you, much like in that imagined breakfast. How do all the elements fit together, moving around in that space? What does each element do, in relation to the others? What happens if you change one of the elements for something else? What happens if you combine and recombine elements in unexpected ways, as affordances?

Intuition is literally "teaching from within" that will bypass the conscious mind in some way. There are several distinct types of intuition, including

- *Instinctive or reflex response*, such as the blink-reflex if something moves fast toward your eyes, or the "fight, flight, or freeze" response to stress and danger

- *Decision-habit*, where a previous decision or assumption is used as a substitute for considered sensemaking and decision-making, particularly in fast real-time action

- *Pattern-matching*, often at high speed, such as in proof-reading whole pages in a couple of seconds per page

- *Embodied-knowledge* or "body-learning," where the body moves faster than the brain can directly control, such as in touch-typing and fast ball-games

- *Tacit-knowledge* that arises from within the self, such as in "gut-feel," a sense that something "isn't right" or "feels different," and needs further attention, or as in information, ideas, and insights that arise seemingly from nowhere

All of these will help to build and maintain the speed of action. Instinctive responses are often very fast, but can be almost impossible to control. Because of that, they may not always lead toward the most effective outcomes, and we need to allow for that fact in process-workflows, user-interfaces, and the like.

Decision-habits will typically lead to the most *predictable* actions, but are often embedded through repeated teaching from *outside* the self – the opposite of intuition. The *validity* of the actions will depend on how well the embedded assumptions match up with the real-world context. And changing those decision-habits to align with a new or redesigned process can be problematic, costly, and slow, because the old habits will need to be unlearned before new ones can be embedded.

The quality, reliability, and validity of the other types of intuition – pattern-matching, embodied-knowledge, and tacit-knowledge – will all depend on experience and skill-level, which in turn will rely on practice, observation, self-observation, imagination, practice, and continual-improvement. We'll see more about the role and importance of skill later on in this chapter and throughout this Step.

Exercise There's a well-documented example of operating from embodied-knowledge and/or tacit-knowledge intuition shown in the drama-documentary film *Sully*, about the successful ditching of US Airways Flight 1549 on the Hudson River in January 2009. The script for this part of the film, starting at around 01:19:00, is taken from the transcript of the aircraft's cockpit voice-recorder, so the text and timeline shown should be the same as in the real event. While the pilots are still trying to make sense of what's happened after the birds had hit both engines, Captain Sullenberger says "I'm starting the APU" (Auxiliary Power Unit, a small electrical generator in the tail). He does this *before* asking the copilot to "get out the QRH" (Quick Reference Handbook, with its emergency-checklists); *before* it is confirmed that the engines can't be restarted; and *against* standard procedure (in other words, against trained decision-habit intuition) that says the APU should be used only on the ground, not in the air. If he *hadn't* done this at that point, there would soon have no power available for the aircraft's control-system, and a fatal crash would have become inevitable.

Using that incident as a reference, explore how your own intuitions – particularly pattern-matching, embodied-knowledge, and/or tacit-knowledge – have come into play within your work or elsewhere. What were those intuitions? How did you notice them? How did you use them in the respective contexts? In what ways – if any – did those intuitions help in resolving the respective tasks?

Intuitions may be useful, but that kind of "out-of-the-box thinking" is often hard to explain or justify to others, or even to yourself – especially in the heat of the moment, and even more so if they also go against standard operating procedures or so-called "common sense." How did you overcome those obstacles? How did you make it all work, for the task, and for everyone? Given this, in what ways could you improve your ability to recognize, assess, and use intuitions in your everyday enterprise-architecture?

Chance provides opportunities that we might otherwise miss. They may occur at random, or in relation to probabilities, but in each case it's up to *us* to prepare for them, notice them, and recognize their potential usefulness. "Chance favours the prepared mind," to quote biologist Louis Pasteur.

By definition, chances are outside of our control. If we could predict them, and control them, they wouldn't be chance.

One useful way to frame this is with the classic not-quite-joke of "Murphy's Law": "If something can go wrong, it probably will." This is arguably the only known *real* law – though note the importance there of the word "probably," because that's the part that makes it so much a real-world law. Yet if it *is* a law, then it also has to apply to everything, *including itself* – "If Murphy's Law can go wrong, it probably will." This, we might suggest, is why things *do* seem to work most of the time. In particular, this "inverse-Murphy" also warns us that if we only let things go right in expected ways, we're limiting our chances!

Exercise There's another form of intuition that may be at play in the *Sully* incident, this time coupled with chance. During the climb out from La Guardia airport, Sullenberger comments, to copilot Skiles, "Nice view of the Hudson. I can never get over how beautiful it is up here." "Life's easier in the air," Skiles replies. Some five seconds later, Sullenberger calls "Birds!" as a large flock of Canada Geese appear directly in front of them at their altitude.

That chance encounter with such heavy birds at such a critical point in the aircraft's flight pattern triggers the incident, of course. Yet Sullenberger's chance observation about the Hudson also more explicitly includes the river within the pilots' awareness of the overall context and situation, and may have influenced their choices in handling the incident. As the later investigation showed, any other option than ditching in the river would have led to the deaths of everyone on board, and probably many more on the ground as well – people who happened by chance to be at the wrong place at the wrong time. And chance can work the opposite way, too: people who, by chance, were *not* "in the wrong place at the wrong time," such as those who missed their flights for the aircraft that were hijacked on September 11, 2001, or who were late for their work at the Twin Towers on that day.

Consider how chance – if preferably in less dramatic form! – has played a part in your own work and life. A seat next to a fellow passenger on a plane, for example, or the classic meetup at a water-cooler or a conference, where people from different departments or organizations mix together at random, leading to conversations that at first might seem aimless but suddenly turn meaningful. Or when, to use an example that's occurred surprisingly often in science and elsewhere, the apparent answer to a thorny problem arises in a dream, or "out of the blue" in the midst of other everyday action. How do you *recognize* when useful meaning arises from such a chance event? What do you need to do to *make use of* what you learned from that event? If Pasteur is right, and "chance favours the prepared mind," how do you *prepare* for an event that, by definition, you can neither predict nor control?

Reason is the core of what most people would consider as "science." Good skills in formal-reasoning and the like are essential if, for example, we want to enhance the efficiency of a system. Yet as Beveridge also warns, there are some serious limitations and hazards associated with reason, and we need to be aware of these if we are to achieve effective outcomes for our enterprise-architecture.

The core limitation is that reason is only reliable "*inside the box*," using interpolation and deductive-reasoning inside a frame of logic based on specific assumptions or premises. It is *not* reliable "*outside the box*," using extrapolation and inductive-reasoning in a context where those assumptions may not apply. For example, it is still all too common for enterprise-architects to assume that every problem must have an IT-based solution, and that that solution must be the best one *because* it is IT-based – whereas, as we'll see later, there are many real-world contexts where this assumption is not valid at all. To counter this, we need to be aware of what assumptions we've made, and whether those assumptions are valid in each respective context.

Because reason only works "inside the box" of that frame of assumptions and beliefs, it can lead us into another trap known as Gooch's Paradox: "Things not only to have to be seen to be believed, but also have to be believed to be seen." This gives rise to errors such as "policy-based evidence," in which we not only might dismiss essential information from "outside the box" as irrelevant or out of scope, but may not even be able to see it at all.

Exercise The Airbus series of aircraft, such as that in US Airways Flight 1549, use a "fly by wire" approach in which the controls do not connect directly to any of the aircraft's systems, but instead provide inputs to a sophisticated flight-controller. The computer takes over most the fine detail of flying the aircraft, freeing the pilot to focus on overall guidance and direction of the flight.

In most cases – as it did for Flight 1549 – this works really well. But this can also lead to complacency among pilots, a tendency to think that "the computer is always right": and when the computer *isn't* right, the pilots may become so confused that they won't be able to work out in time what they need to do.

That's what happened just six months later to Air France Flight 447. It was a routine long-haul flight across the mid-Atlantic, from Rio de Janeiro to Paris. At about halfway through the flight, on autopilot at cruise-altitude, the aircraft passed through an icy storm – not unusual out there, at that time of year. But one of the aircraft's airspeed-sensors froze up, sending the wrong speed information to the computer, which then calculated a speed far lower than it actually was, canceled the autopilot, and signaled an automated stall-warning. The junior pilot on duty, suddenly thrown into having to switch to the manual control, misunderstood what was going on, and pulled the stick hard *back*, pushing the aircraft's nose steeply upward – exactly what *not* to do in a stall. The computer, with its parameters now far outside of their expected range, incorrectly turned off the stall-warning, giving the illusion that everything was fine when in reality it was even worse than before.

The captain arrived and tried to take over, from the seat on the other side of the cockpit. He realized that the nose was far too high, and pushed his stick hard *forward* to bring the nose down. But in the Airbus design of that period, the two control sticks are not linked, neither stick had priority, and the junior pilot was still holding his stick hard back. All the computer could do was to use the average between these two conflicting and completely contradictory inputs, leading to a flight-mode that had no real connection to the actual situation in the air. Neither pilot could make sense of what was going on in time to do anything to help the aircraft recover. Now far out of control, the aircraft descended faster than a falling brick, the stall-warning flicking on and off all the way, and crashed into the ocean, with the nose still pointing high into the sky. No-one survived.

Current computers are extreme examples of "reason personified": every decision comes from prefiltered data, following its own strict formal-logic. A lot of value to be gained from that, of course: everyone in business will want that. But as an enterprise-architect, are you *also* aware enough of the "hazards and limitations" of that kind of hardwired reasoning?

How much do *you* rely on computers to do your decisions for you? Do you know, and can trust, the computer's sources for its data? Do you know how its algorithms work? Can you do the same calculations yourself, without using the computer? Can you identify when the computer's decisions are wrong, or invalid? Can you identify when the data are wrong, or incomplete, or misleading? Do you know how to take over when the computer has failed, or isn't there anymore – such as when the power is down? Consider those questions for a while, and their real-world implications at work and elsewhere.

As Beveridge also indicates, we may also need to address themes such as the **_ethics_** and **_politics_** of architecture and change-work, and also architecture not just as a job but as **_a way of life_**. We'll tackle those later in the book; for now, we need to keep the focus on the art and science within change itself.

The Shape of Change

Where does this "art" fit in with the practice of enterprise-architecture? To make sense of this, we'll need a bit of structure, to build a sense of **_the shape of change_**.

We'll start with a simple **_linear view of change_**, with a time-based axis, that we could use to describe _any_ type of change, at any scale. We pick an arbitrary "the moment of change," or "NOW!", and map out what needs to happen before, during, and after that change. For example, in the classic OODA (Observe, Orient, Decide, Act) real-time action-learning loop:

- We **_sense_**, or _observe_, the context of the world that we're interested in.
- We **_make sense_**, or _orient_ ourselves, to that state of the world.
- We **_decide_** how to act to change the world in a desired direction.
- We **_act_** to change the world, in accordance with that decision.
- We loop back to the start, and repeat the cycle for the next change.

The timescale on that vertical axis is whatever we need it to be: it could range from seconds or less – as in the original context for OODA, in air-combat – up to hours, days, years, decades, or beyond.

Figure 3-1 shows what this loop looks like relative to a given "NOW!", an actual moment of change.

CHAPTER 3   FOUNDATIONS: THE ART AND SCIENCE OF CHANGE

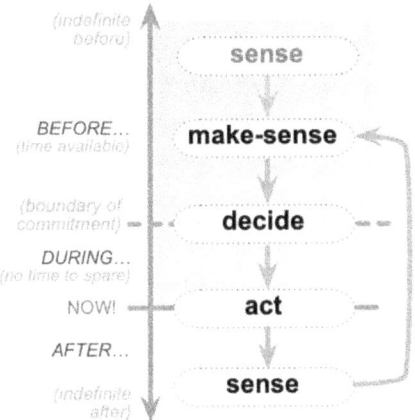

Figure 3-1. Sense, make-sense, decide, act

In the "***before***" part of the cycle, we have time to think, and time to plan how the change-action will work. Yet once we cross over the "***boundary of commitment***" and transition into the "***during***" phase, there's no longer any time to think: all of the focus is on doing the work of the change. As we pass the "NOW!", we move into the "***after***" for the change, where we can review what has happened, and set up for the next change in this linear flow of time.

Note   After the "NOW!", all uncertainties for *this* change-cycle have been resolved, in the sense that this cycle is complete, and we can't do anything more within *this* cycle to change anything.

It's quite likely, of course, that there'll still be *other* issues to tackle, *other* uncertainties to resolve. But we don't know that yet, until we sense what's going on this "new NOW," and loop back to the "make-sense" phase of a *new* change-cycle.

We then continue looping back, and looping back, indefinitely, until we meet up with some kind of end-condition that brings the cycling to a stop.

That linear, somewhat-cyclical concept of change is easy to understand, and it aligns well with those common notions of "science." Hence, classic "scientific management" and the like, where the managers have time to think, while workers do the action, with no time to spare at all.

43

That *does* work well enough with many types of planned change. The catch, though, is that its strict top-down flow can make it slow, and its dependence on assumptions of certainty and predictability can make it fragile and brittle. We can sometimes speed it up with automation, but often at the cost of even further reducing its ability to adapt. It also does *not* work well with unplanned-change – especially if that change comes bottom-upward, as it so often does. And also, as Figure 3-2 reminds us, all of this is fractal, reflecting the same shape of change at every scope and scale.

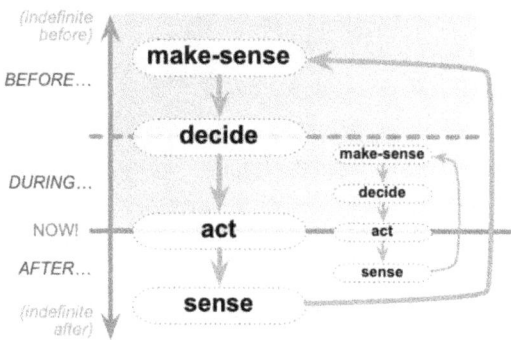

Figure 3-2. *The fractality of change*

To make better sense of what happens there, and to work out how to tackle it, we need to add a separate *horizontal*-axis to our frame. This axis represents increasing levels of **complexity, variability, volatility, ambiguity, uncertainty, unpredictability, and/or uniqueness**, depending on which of those elements we need to assess. The left-hand edge represents a zero-level of variance for those elements, such as absolute certainty, predictability, identicality, and so on. Everywhere to the right of that left-hand edge represents an increased level of variance for the respective element. The scale itself is arbitrary, and often shown with an arbitrary cut-off point at the right, as the scale could potentially extend all the way to infinity.

As with that vertical-axis of time, we can add one or more dividing-lines across the horizontal-axis. The most common divider represents a *boundary of effective-certainty* that the current system would be able to address. To the left of that boundary, we have that phrase often attributed to Einstein: "The definition of insanity is doing the same thing and expecting different results." To the right of the boundary, though, a kind of "Inverse Einstein" would apply: "The definition of insanity is doing the same thing and expecting the *same* results." Beyond that level of uncertainty, doing the same thing may lead to different results, and we may or must do different things to achieve the same effective results.

In practice, the position of that boundary on the horizontal-axis is determined by the ***skill-level and decision-level*** of the respective change-agents. For a change-agent with less skill or capability, the boundary will be more to the left; for a change-agent with more skill or capability, the boundary will be further to the right.

Overall, this gives us two distinct pathways for sensemaking and decision-making, as shown in Figure 3-3. To the left of the boundary-of-effective-certainty, sensemaking and decision-making takes place "inside the box" of nominal predictability and certainty, based on true/false rules, algorithms, analysis, calculation, and other hard-systems methods. To the right of that boundary, sensemaking and decision-making must take place "outside the box," beyond nominal predictability and certainty, and hence must be based more on soft-systems skills and on vision, values, principles, and guidelines.

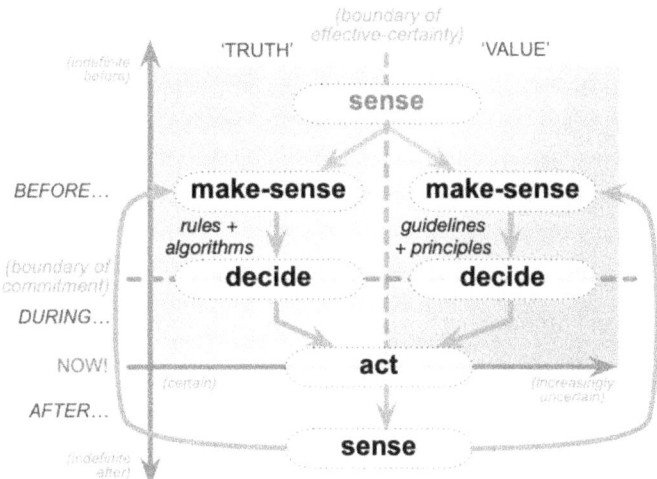

Figure 3-3. *Pathways of change, "inside the box" and "outside the box"*

In effect, this partitions the space above the "NOW!" into four variable-sized domains, as shown in Figure 3-4. This also shows where the classic distinctions between "art" and "science" come into the picture.

45

CHAPTER 3   FOUNDATIONS: THE ART AND SCIENCE OF CHANGE

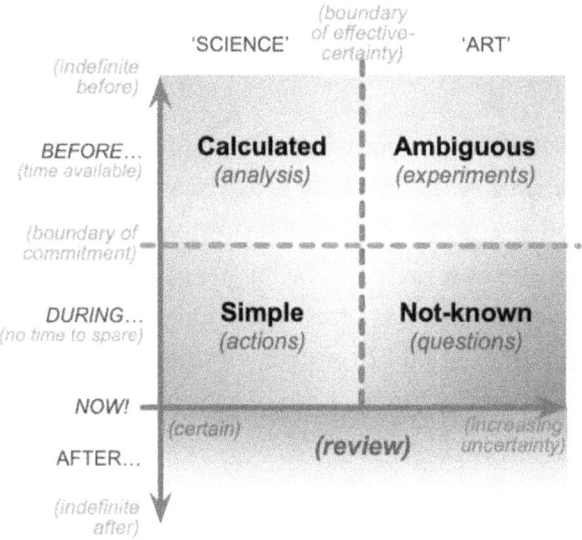

Figure 3-4. SCAN frame – time and uncertainty

The labels we use for these four domains provide the acronym **SCAN**, to describe the frame:

- **Simple** or *Straightforward*: Focused on real-time action; no time to think; can address only low- to mid-uncertainty; decisions rely on rules.

- **Calculated** or *Complicated*: Focused on planning; has time to think, analyze, and calculate; can address only low- to mid-uncertainty; decisions may use algorithms.

- **Ambiguous** or *Actionable*: Focused on sensemaking; has time to explore and assess uncertainties; can address mid- to high-uncertainty; decisions may derive from probabilities, patterns, and guidelines.

- **Not-known** or *the New*: Focused on real-time sensing and ideation; no time to think; can address mid- to high-level uncertainty; decisions depend on principles and experience.

As also shown in Figure 3-4, we need to do a review after the "NOW!", but its main role here is in sensing the differences *after* the change at the "NOW!", to set up for the *next* change. It doesn't take much part in the back-and-forth of sensemaking and decision-making before, during, and at the moment of action.

Perspectives, Modes, and Mindsets

Given that framing above, we now need to see where Beveridge's change-elements will fit within that kind of frame. We'll start with a cross-map between those elements and the SCAN domains:

- We need **preparation** before any action. This places it in mainly the *Calculated* and/or *Ambiguous* domains.

- We develop **hypotheses** away from the action itself, but while things are still uncertain. This places it mainly in the *Ambiguous* domain.

- We **experiment** to attempt to reduce uncertainty. This places the design of experiments in the *Ambiguous* domain, and execution of those experiments mainly in the *Not-known* domain.

- We would usually develop **strategy** and tactics for a task or change before any action will occur. This places it in the *Calculated* domain to guide planning for known tasks, and in the *Ambiguous* domain to guide exploration of the new and unknown.

- We use **reason** only "inside the box," within a realm of the known. This places it mainly in the *Calculated* domain, to develop theory, algorithms, and rules, but also somewhat in the *Simple* domain where we apply those rules in real-world practice.

- We use **observation** to capture information during real-time action, and also after the action itself, to guide reviews and set up the sensing for the next action-loop. This places it mainly in the *Simple* and *Not-known* domains.

- We use **imagination** to refine a theory "inside the box," to explore and invent "outside the box," and also as literal "image-ination" during real-time action. This places it, in somewhat different forms, mainly in the *Calculated*, *Ambiguous*, and *Not-known* domains, but in the *Simple* only when required as part of the task.

- We may watch for **intuition** at any time, but mainly in real-time action. This places it most in the *Not-known* domain, enabling previously-unknown information and insights, quite often in the *Simple* domain as ideas and insights, and occasionally in the other domains.

- We watch for *chance* mainly in real-time action, mostly when looking for new ideas and inspiration. This places it mainly in the *Not-known* domain.

We then view that cross-map from the SCAN perspective, to cluster Beveridge's elements into distinct **modes** or mindsets, one for each SCAN domain:

- The *Artist* or Explorer, as the primary mode for the *Not-known* domain, focused on feeling, observing, sensing, exploring, playing with the world to elicit new ideas, insights, and information, connecting feeling to purpose, always with an emphasis on *value*.

- The *Alchemist* or Engineer, as the primary mode for the *Ambiguous* domain, focused on sensemaking, framing, experimenting, testing, making choices, developing frames of hypothesis, creating something new "like magic" from ideas, information, imagination, and intuition, always with an emphasis on *usefulness*.

- The *Analyst* or Rule-Maker, as the primary mode for the *Calculated* domain, focused on using logic and the like to develop rules and algorithms to control the chosen world, always with an emphasis on certainty and *truth*.

- The *Agent* or Rule-Follower, as the primary mode for the *Simple* domain, focused on making things happen in the real-world, always with an emphasis on *getting things done*.

And also another mode, quiet, calm, and dispassionate, to support review and oversight:

- The *Assessor* or Mentor, as the primary mode for an after-action review *after the "Now!"* but also for general overview, focused on guiding, learning, improving, connecting past and present to future, always with an emphasis on overall *effectiveness*.

As enterprise-architects, **we will need skills in each of these modes**, and know how to switch between them as required. Figure 3-5 provides a visual cross-map between the modes and the SCAN domains, with labels added for the main "edges" or transitions between domains.

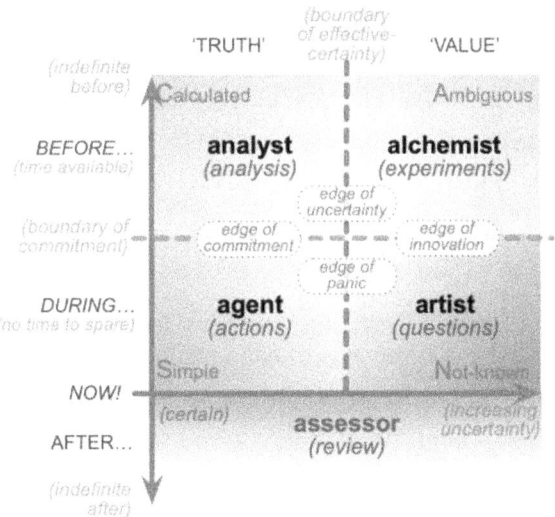

Figure 3-5. *Change-modes and SCAN domains*

We need to remember that all of this is dynamic, not static. In change-work, we'll need to change our perspectives dynamically too, because things tend to work well only when we use the right mode for the respective matching domain. Sometimes this might seem to be a straightforward linear sequence, such as in the apparent progression in scientific research from idea to hypothesis to theory to law. In practice, though, it's often much more complicated, with a lot of non-linear bouncing back-and-forth from domain to domain, refining theories, testing hypotheses, and so on. However, each time we switch between domains, we also have to **switch between mode-perspectives** to ensure that domain and mode will always match up.

Note There'll be more about when, why, and how to use this mode-switching in Chapter 5 and in even more depth in Chapter 6. For now, the main focus is on building a *personal* and *practical* understanding of the modes themselves, and the differences between them, so that you'll be ready to *use* them by the time you get to Chapters 5 and 6.

The catch is that those modes may often be incompatible with each other. For example, imagination and intuition are areas where our skills in thinking can be more of a hindrance than a help. And those clashes between modes will often take place not just between people, but also *inside our own heads*. This is a key reason why change-work can so often be so challenging.

The challenge arises here because the modes are not merely different ways of thinking, they're more like different ways of *being*. For example, in the Artist mode we need to be playful, open, inquisitive, but in the Analyst mode we need to be focused, formal, rigorous – almost exact opposites of each other. Similarities between modes can also trick us into thinking that they're the same, when in fact they're not. For example, both Analyst and Assessor will place an emphasis on thinking, but the Analyst looks more toward the near-future, while the Assessor needs to balance that with a focus on the past.

Caution   To add to the challenge, most people will feel comfortable in only one of the modes, and will be increasingly uncomfortable in each of the others. And yet **the work will often require you to be able to work well in all of them**.

Team-work will help with this, reducing the overall discomfort by sharing the leadership between different people as the team's tasks switch from mode to mode. If you're working on our own, though, you *will* need to take extra care to switch between modes to match up with each domain-change, and *not* fall back to your preferred "comfort-zone" mode as soon as the going gets hard.

The crucial point here is that things tend to go wrong whenever mode and domain *don't* match up. Because of that, it's *really* important to keep track of which phase we're in, and not mix up the modes. However, that's often made harder by the fact that we'll often find ourselves working on multiple tasks within a task-tree at the same moment, often at multiple levels. For example, we may be working on the scope for a sub-task of part of the plan of the parent-task, but need to spin off a nested sub-task of our own to find some new ideas, which will start off in its own Not-known domain. That means that the parent-task needs the Analyst mode, our current task needs the Alchemist mode, and the nested sub-task needs the Artist mode – all at the same time. The only way we'll avoid mixing up the modes there is by keeping careful track about which level of the task-tree we're working in at each moment.

This is where ***the discipline of Context-Adaptive Leadership*** comes into the picture, to help us manage the cognitive and other challenges of real-time mode-switching. It does this by giving us a structured way to keep track of the relationships between task, phase, and mode, such as by continually looping through this real-time checklist:

- Which task in the task-tree am I working on *right now*?
- Which SCAN domain do I need to *be* in for this stage of this task?
- Which domain *am* I in?
- Which mode do I need to *be* in for this domain?
- Which mode *am* I in?
- If mode and domain do not match, how do I switch to the right mode?

To help with those answers, we'll need to know, for each mode

- The key characteristics of that mode
- Where, when, and why you would use that mode
- How you can tell whether you're implicitly using that mode
- Examples of the rules and disciplines that apply within that mode
- The kinds of mistakes that tend to occur within that mode
- Guidance on how and why (or why not) to bridge across to a different mode

The following sections provide a summary for each of the modes.

Example Imagine that you're a farmer with a small arable farm. You're often the only person available to work on the farm – which means that you'll often need to switch between action-modes in real-time as you do the work.

Right now, on the farm, it's getting close to harvest-time out in the wheat-fields, and, as the farmer, you'll need to decide what to do today. The weather-report tells you that it should be a warm, dry day, though there's mild rain elsewhere to the south. The "Example" sidebar after each mode-description below shows you the action-mode you'll need to use for each part of this day's work.

CHAPTER 3   FOUNDATIONS: THE ART AND SCIENCE OF CHANGE

The Artist Mode

We use the ***Artist*** mode in real-time in the initial *Not-known* phase, to search at high speed for ideas and insights, using vision, values, principles, and other criteria as "seeds" to filter the perceived-value of information as it arises.

The ***Artist*** mode is *available during real-time action* and throughout *all of the decision-timescale*. Its role is to observe, to *notice,* to pay attention, to elicit new ideas, new information, new experiences. It manages that which is inherently *unique*, one-off, often with no initial apparent connection to anything else. It responds to the context through a sense of *inner value*, whatever feels right in the moment.

Use the Artist mode when you need to know what you're sensing or feeling; you're working on something for the first time; you want to start afresh, in any sense; or when the context is "one-off" or inherently uncertain.

You're ***in the Artist mode*** when there's a new question or response from the context – especially if the context responds in an unexpected way; an intuitive "side-feeling" comes through; there's an urge to portray what's going on, a desire to create as a way to commit something to memory; or there's a general sense of childlike wonder, of exuberance, energy, excitement, enthusiasm, "in-the-moment-ness."

Rules for the Artist mode include "anything goes" (there is no "right" or "wrong," the feeling or response is what it is); "the response exists only in the moment" (if we wait around, or try to hold onto it, it may be gone); "the response needs some form of expression" (in order to be "realized," made real); and "the response is personal" (it does not necessarily mean anything to anyone else, or "mean" anything at all, but just is).

Warning-signs of a dubious Artist discipline include "this means...," "this proves..." (blurring Artist with *Analyst* or *Agent*); "this has no purpose...," "this feeling gets in the way..." (blurring Artist with *Alchemist* or *Agent*); "I should not feel this...," "I ought to feel...," "this is not what I want to feel..." (blurring Artist with *Agent*); or "the feeling I had here last time was..." (blurring Artist with *Analyst*).

To ***switch from the Artist*** to another mode, see the guidance in the section "Context in the Change-Cycle" in Chapter 6, later in this Step.

Example At dawn, you head out to the wheat-field, and switch to the **Artist** mode to build a **_sense_** of what's going on out there.

It's a lovely, warm autumn day, a farmer's delight indeed! The wheat is a beautiful golden-brown, swaying gently in the breeze. There's a slight heaviness in the air, though, which worries you, even though you don't quite know why.

You reach out to take a stalk of wheat. You feel the texture in your hand, the grains firm and well-rounded. A delicate scent, bringing memories of fresh-baked bread coming out of the oven. You strip the grain off the stalk, and put it into your pocket to look at later.

As you walk through the wheat, a field-mouse skitters away from you in fright. It reminds you of that classic Robert Burns poem, "To a Mouse": "Wee, sleekit, cowrin, tim'rous beastie." You laugh, and move on.

The Alchemist Mode

We use the **_Alchemist_** mode with time-to-reflect in the *Ambiguous* phase to experiment and to seek for patterns, and to distinguish between reducible and non-reducible complexity.

The **_Alchemist_** mode is usually *not available during real-time action*. Its role is to *use*, and to *question* use and usefulness. It manages that which is inherently *ambiguous* – always somewhat uncertain, requiring endless adaptation, and with cause and effect often identifiable only in retrospect. It responds to the context through a sense of *outer value*, experimenting to find whatever feels appropriate for its needs.

Use the *Alchemist* mode when you apply outcomes from other modes to practical use; you need to adapt practice to the specific context; you need to review value, or to question what you're doing in practice – particularly around quality and effectiveness, overall or in a given context; or you need to assess and evaluate any kind of trade-off or risk.

You're **in the *Alchemist* mode** when the focus is on experimentation, testing ideas from the *Not-known*; the focus is on practical, useful results; the focus is on any kind of trade-off or assessment of risk or opportunity – on possibility, probability, and necessity (modal-logic) rather than on supposed certainties ("true/false"-logic); or you're dealing with patterns or clusters of some kind of one-off or special-case.

Rules for the Alchemist mode include "there is no 'truth'" (only usefulness, or not-usefulness); "everything is a tool to a purpose" (beliefs, feelings, objects, facts, whatever); "as above, so below" (everything contains everything else; reality is fractal, self-similar, recursive; and analogy and metaphor are as useful as logic or "proof"); "the LEARN acronym for effectiveness" (is it eLegant, Efficient, Appropriate, Reliable, iNtegrated); "ethics and integrity take priority over 'truth'" (as an Alchemist, I am personally responsible for the consequences of what I do and not-do).

Warning-signs of a dubious Alchemist discipline include "*the* way to do it is..." (blurring Alchemist with *Agent* or *Analyst*); "it'll be the same as last time..." (blurring Alchemist with *Analyst*); "the end justifies the means..." (allowing *Agent* "truth" to override value-assessment); "get the job out of the door any way we can, they won't notice the difference..." (weak handling of value trade-offs, and failure to bridge across to *Analyst* and/or *Artist* to assist in improving quality); or "I'm no good at...," "I'm the best at..." (allowing ego to override the Alchemist's responsibility to test and question everything).

To ***switch from the Alchemist*** to another mode, see the guidance in the section "Scope in the Change-Cycle" in Chapter 6, later in this Step.

Example Walking along the side of the field, you switch to the **Alchemist** mode to *make sense* of what you've just experienced and seen.

Everything looks fine. At a glance, it looks like the wheat should be ready for harvest in just a few days' time. But that heaviness in the air is good reason to worry: despite the weather-forecast, it *feels* like there could be a storm on the way. It's happened before at this time of year, you remember: maybe twenty years ago? It'd definitely be bad if something like that were to hit. You'll need to check the records to help you make that decision.

In itself, the encounter with the mouse was fun, but it could be a worry too. If it's only a few mice, that's fine – nature's tax for the farmer! But if there's more than a few, they could take too much of the crop – and they might encourage snakes to turn up, too, which could be a hazard out here.

Best to head back to the farmhouse: given those worrying hints about weather, it looks like you may need to make a decision right now about whether to harvest today.

The Analyst Mode

We use the **Analyst** mode with time-to-think in the *Calculated* phase, defining the rules needed to work well "inside the box" of a logic, using analysis to break down reducible-complexity, and simplify uncertainties into predictable algorithms and true/false decisions.

The **Analyst** mode is usually *not available during real-time action*. Its role is to *plan* for future action; to *verify* the truth of things in relation to others, within the context of a given frame. It manages that which is nominally *certain*, or "knowable" – a world in which everything is interlinked through connections of cause and effect. It responds to the context through a sense of *outer truth*, measuring, monitoring, and assessing the factors that make up the chains of interrelationship.

Use the Analyst mode when you need to plan for action; you need to verify what is fact, and what is not; you need to compare results from previous tasks or iterations; you need to describe results in ways that can be interpreted in a factual sense by others, and cross-referenced to those of others; or you are creating some kind of theoretical scheme to describe what you've discovered or what you plan to do.

You're **in the Analyst mode** when there's a focus on measurement, fact, and logic; there's a focus on time or location – on *when* or *where* something is happening; there's a focus on verification and assessment against *known* criteria; you're analyzing what's happening or has happened; using interpolation and concepts of causality to connect between elements; or refining the logic on which the analysis is based.

Rules for the Analyst mode include "only facts are real" (opinion is permitted only where vetted and verified by peer-review); "everything must be anchored to everything else" (and ultimately be anchored in shared, agreed standards); "proof depends on repeatability" (especially repeatability by others); "things are true only if verified" (in formal-logic and the like); "experiments should change only one parameter at a time" (*ceteris paribus*, "all other things being equal"); and "all variable parameters must be identified and declared."

Warning-signs of a dubious Analyst discipline include emotional attachment to any supposed theory or "fact" (blurring Analyst with the *Artist* or *Alchemist*); "must be...," "obviously...," "of course...," (failure to bridge across to *Artist* or *Alchemist* for cross-checks against "logic-holes"); "the exception proves the rule..." (blurring the Analyst's true/false logic with the *Alchemist's* modal-logic); or "the only possible truth..." (blurring the Analyst's responsibility for analysis with the *Agent's* "believe the Truth, without question").

To **switch from the Analyst** to another mode, see the guidance in the section "Plan in the Change-Cycle" in Chapter 6, later in this Step.

Example   Back at the farmhouse, you switch to the **Analyst** mode to gather all the other information you need to help you **decide** whether or not to harvest today.

You'll pull the grain out from your pocket, and use the usual meters to check for moisture, density, and the like. Your first guess was good: from *that* data, it would be best to leave the harvest for another couple of days.

But there's that worrying feel about the weather. You dig back into the farm records, and sure enough, there was that same weather-pattern 22 years ago: an autumn day slightly warmer than usual, and mild rain to the south suddenly turning into thunderstorms heading this way instead.

You toss up the trade-offs: there'd be a better yield if you *could* leave it another couple of days, but you'd lose the whole crop if thunderstorms do come through. The latter is just too much of a risk: you'd better do it today.

You make a quick phone-call to get your part-time laborer to come in right now: yes, it'll be an extra cost, but you'll need all the help you can find to get everything done in time today.

The Agent Mode

We use the *Agent* mode in real-time in the *Simple* phase to enact the plan, acting as if everything in the plan is true and correct, with the intent to deliver the desired value from the task. (The validity of that belief will be tested by the Assessor, in the *Review* phase: the belief itself should not be questioned when acting in *this* mode.)

The *Agent* mode is *available during real-time action* and throughout *all of the decision-timescale*. Its role is to *focus*, and to maintain that focus, usually via and in line with predetermined instructions. It manages that which is nominally *known* or believed-certain, turning theory into practical action. It responds to the context through a sense of *inner truth*, acting on the clear certainty of "right and wrong" provided by the work-instructions.

Use the Agent mode when you enact the plan and interact with the real-world; you're holding focus on the task while you're working; you establish a relationship with and responsibility to the real-world context before, when starting, during, at the point of action, and when closing the work-session.

As a person, you're *in the Agent mode* when there is a sense of certainty, combined with a kind of quiet calm; there is a sense of *personal* responsibility for delivering the desired value from the task; there is a sense of "connectedness" with the real-world task and with the context as a whole; there is a subtle sense of heightened perception, such as background sounds seeming clearer; there's a sense of being somewhat "outside of self," of feeling like an outside observer watching what's going on; or characteristic yet personal signals occur, to indicate intuition coming through – for example, a tingling in the hands, or "gut-feel."

Rules for the Agent mode include "follow the instructions" (as specified in the plan for the task); "there is a definite boundary between right and wrong" (as specified in the instructions); "keep the focus on right here, right now" (to whatever "right here, right now" is specified in the instructions); "act local, aware global" (as guided by the instructions, be aware of others around you who may affect or be affected by the work); "be aware that things may not be as expected, nor as they seem" (watch for situations where you may need to move "outside the box" of the instructions); and "I am responsible for the quality of the outcomes here" (quality and expected-outcomes as specified in the instructions).

Warning-signs of a dubious Agent discipline include "what's for dinner?" (focus drifting to a different task and/or away from the specified "right here, right now"); "what am I supposed to be doing?" (loss of connection to instructions); "is this the right way to...?" (must avoid self-doubt here, other than as a bridge to other modes); "this is the right way to do everything!" (blurring Agent with *Analyst*); "this is the best way to do everything!" (blurring Agent "truth" with *Alchemist* value-assessments); "you're doing it wrong!" and/or "it's not *my* job, mate!" (probable failure to manage "act local, aware global"); "yeah, I'm panicking!" (failure to transition cleanly to and/or from *Artist* to manage "outside the box" situations); and "it's not my fault!" and/or "it's all my fault!" (loss of focus on "right here, right now," and blurring Agent with *Assessor*).

To *switch from the Agent* to another mode, see the guidance in the section "Action in the Change-Cycle" in Chapter 6, later in this Step.

CHAPTER 3   FOUNDATIONS: THE ART AND SCIENCE OF CHANGE

Example   The decision has been made: you switch to the **Agent** mode to get into *action* and get the job done. You run to the barn to get the harvester powered up and rolled out into the yard. You complete the full set of system-checks and safety-checks just as the laborer arrives. You go through the plan: you'll drive the harvester; the laborer will drive the grain back to the silo, and also rake up the straw behind you whenever there's a chance to do so.

Go out to the field, get moving; there's no time to waste. Up and down the field with the harvester, the laborer ferrying the grain and raking the straw, hour after hour. By midday, when you take a brief break, you're already past the halfway-mark for the harvest.

You switch briefly into the *Artist* mode: it's still sunny, but that heavy oppressive feeling is even worse than before. You switch into the *Alchemist* mode to make sense of that feeling: yes, despite the weather-forecast, there's a storm brewing all right. The *Analyst* mode agrees: given that updated data, it was the right decision to do the harvest today. So back to the *Agent* mode, to get it all done, as fast as you safely can.

By the late afternoon, the harvest itself is complete – and you can hear the thunder just starting to rumble over there down to the south. The laborer heads home, and you take over to finish raking the straw into rows to give it a better chance to keep dry if it rains. Keep going, keep going, until everything is done.

The Assessor Mode

We use the ***Assessor*** mode after the action at the "NOW!", applying observation, imagination, intuition, reframing, analysis, and synthesis to link together both "inside the box" and "outside the box," and to support continual-improvement in the organization and the enterprise.

The ***Assessor*** mode is *only available after real-time action*. Its role is to *guide* continuous improvement on behalf of the enterprise. It manages the balance between *that which has been* and *that which could be*. It responds to the context through a sense of calm, quiet respect of "that which *is*," and of optimism for the future.

Use the Assessor mode when you need to review what has happened during some action; you need to establish the value gained from that action; you need to elicit any lessons that can be learned from the outcomes of the action; or you want to mentor yourself and others to improve skills and competence.

You're ***in the Assessor mode*** when there's a focus on the past, or bridging from the past toward a new future; there's a focus on melding the objective and subjective, the factual and the personal; a focus on mentoring, on learning from the past, on building new competences and skills, and on quietly striving toward the enterprise and its vision.

Rules for the Assessor mode include "keep things real" (hold the focus on what actually happened rather than on what was expected to happen); "see both the good and the bad" (look for what worked rather than only for what didn't); "pin your stripes at the door" (everyone had their own responsibilities, no-one is either more nor less important than any other); "we're here to learn, not to blame" (because as soon as blame enters the picture, no-one will learn anything); "respect emotion, yet keep it at bay" (feelings are facts in themselves, but allowing emotion to run wild is likely to spiral into blame).

Warning-signs of a dubious Assessor discipline include "you should have…" (demanding that others go back in time to fix something); to Agent, "you didn't follow the rules!" (blurring Assessor enquiry with *Analyst* rule-building); to Agent, "you should have used your imagination!" (Assessor blurring *Agent* role with *Artist* role); anger or other excess emotion (blurring Assessor acceptance of emotion with right to indulge in emotion); "the boss is always right" (failing the "pin your stripes at the door" rule); "it's your fault!" (failing the "no blame" rule).

To ***switch from the Assessor*** to another mode, see the guidance in the section "Review in the Change-Cycle" in Chapter 6, later in this Step.

Example You've finished the raking, and arrive back at the farmyard just as the first raindrops start to fall. Within minutes, the rain turns heavy, and then heavier again, into a full harvest-destroying thunderstorm. Everything done, just in time…

You switch into the **Assessor** mode, to **review** the day and count up the cost – or lack of it, you hope!

Benefits-realized for the farm: You've brought in the entire harvest, a few days earlier than expected. The yield is slightly lower than last year, and it's cost you an extra day's pay for the laborer. But if you hadn't done it today, you would certainly have lost most of it, and probably the lot. So yes, a small bit of bad luck there, but nothing like as bad as it would have been. A definite benefit.

Lessons-learned for the farm: You do need to trust those subtle hints and side-feelings that come up in the *Artist* mode. They may not be right, of course, but you *do* need to capture them so that you can check them in the *Alchemist* mode, and *then* decide in the *Analyst* mode. (And in that order too: don't let the *Analyst* dominate every decision, because, as in this case of today's unexpected weather, the "logical" choice from the predicted data may not always be the right one.)

Suggested-actions for the farm: You write up the farm-records to include a confirmation of this unusual but so-important weather-pattern. And you add a note to check on the field-mice somewhat earlier next year: they're not much of a problem now, but you don't want them to become one in the future.

And now? It's time to rest. For this evening, at least. There's always more work to be done on a farm.

The Awareness of Change

Another role of all that mode-switching is to support building the overall awareness that's needed for this work. In particular, we'll need to develop and maintain

- *Contextual-awareness*: Awareness of purpose, the big-picture, the governing rules and guidelines, the success-criteria, and the boundaries for action

- *Task-awareness*: Awareness of what we and others are doing, right here, right now

- *Situational-awareness*: Awareness of what's happening in the world around us while we're doing the work of the task

- *Self-awareness*: Awareness of ourselves, of our observing, intuiting, thoughts, feelings, and actions in our role as an agent of change

Contextual-awareness comes top-down, such as in the form of "commander's intent" and the like. Situational-awareness comes bottom-up, from Reality-Department. Task-awareness provides the bridge between those two, and connects everything together. Self-awareness, of course, comes from within the self, interacting with the real-world.

We can make a good start on building that awareness, by using checklists such as **the "Architect's Mantra"**:

- "*I don't know*": This opens the door to ask questions about the context.

- "*It depends*": This invites exploration of how things work with each other, and within and between different contexts.

- "*Just enough detail*": This guides the balance between too much information and not enough.

- "*What's the story?*": This helps to keep a focus on the human aspects of the context, and often brings out crucial details that are otherwise "hidden in plain sight."

- "*Why does this matter?*": This helps to keep conversations on-track toward effectiveness and purpose.

"It depends" and "Why does this matter?" are straightforward enough: they're routine concerns that anyone would ask about in business-analysis and the like.

The others, though, can sometimes be a bit more problematic. For example, in many business contexts, saying "I don't know" can feel unsafe, given that many change-work jobs seemingly depend on maintaining an image of "having all the answers." Yet finding the courage to say "I don't know" opens up the space for others to show what *they* know – and that can often be the only way to acquire the information that we really need.

Knowing how to identify "just enough detail," or any other kind of "just enough," is an essential skill in all types of change-work. However, it's also one of the hardest skills to learn, often demanding years of practice, trial-and-error, and too many embarrassing mistakes. Again, though, it *is* essential for everything in enterprise-architecture, and we'll return to this theme often during the remainder of this book.

Story-skills often also play a vital role in change-work. For example, story-building helps us describe the big-picture of a change, while story-listening often elicits information about subtle nuances that may be crucial to the overall success and effectiveness of a change-project. We'll look at this in more detail in Chapter 9, for Step 2, in the section "Stories of Change."

Use this "Architect's Mantra" checklist anywhere, at any time, to start and guide conversations about architecture and change.

Into Practice

Revisit the text above to provide you with guidance on how to build a habit of "***noticing the world***" within change-work. This "habit of noticing" is perhaps *the* core for all change-work, and for all other skills as well: few things will work well without it. Once this habit is ingrained enough that it's running in the background all the time, yet you barely notice the noticing *as* "noticing" anymore, you'll be ready to move on to build the other habits and skills you'll need for the *practice* of enterprise-architecture.

In fact, for a week or two, don't try to do anything more than "noticing the world." Don't worry about the rest of the book for now: it can wait. Instead, within the day-to-day work, just focus on ***allowing yourself to notice***. Using what you've seen in the section "The Feel of Change":

- How can you better notice how you use *observation*, *imagination*, *intuition*, and *chance* at work, and how you avoid those *hazards and limitations of reason*?

- As you start to notice more the importance of these aspects of the work, what difference does that begin to make in how you *do* the work?

- How does that awareness help – or maybe hinder – the *effectiveness* of that work?

Then using what you've seen in the section "The Shape of Change":

- How can you better notice how each of your tasks will go through distinct phases of *sensing, making sense, deciding, taking action*, and *reviewing* the outcomes of that action?

- How can you better notice how this happens simultaneously with tasks at every level, so that you may be sensing in one task, while making sense within one of its sub-tasks, while deciding how to take action in one of that sub-task's sub-sub-tasks, while *doing* the action in yet another sub-sub-sub-task to tackle all of the respective "deciding for the sensemaking for the sensing" in the tasks above.

- How do you keep all of this in balance, and in awareness, throughout all of the layers of tasks all happening at the same nominal time?

And using what you've seen in the section "Perspectives, Modes, and Mindsets":

- How can you better notice how you need to switch between the distinct modes or mindsets of the *artist, alchemist, analyst, agent,* and *assessor* in order to support the different requirements in each of the phases of the work?

- How do you notice *how* you switch between those modes and phases? What leadership (or, better, self-leadership) do you need to help you switch between modes, and keep mode and phase aligned?

- Which of these modes are easy for you to switch to? Which ones are harder? How might you improve on this, to make it easier to switch to and from the modes that feel either more or less "natural"?

- What happens if you *do* manage to keep phase and mode aligned? What happens if you *don't* keep them aligned, particularly in terms of its impact on *effectiveness*? How might you use your real-time "noticing" to help you improve on this?

- How do you keep mode and phase aligned, through all of the simultaneous layering of tasks and their sub-tasks? How might you improve on how you manage that real-time process of alignment?

Wherever you are, whatever you're doing or not-doing, *notice, notice, notice...*

Once you're past that getting-started stage for those "art" aspects of the work, spend perhaps the next couple of months exploring how to **build the disciplines of change-work**, with tools such as the Architect's Mantra and more. Using what you've seen in the section "The Awareness of Change":

- How do you use your "noticing" to help you build and maintain *awareness* of the world within and around you? How would you use that "noticing" to help you distinguish between *contextual-awareness* about the big-picture, *task-awareness* about the current task itself, *situational-awareness* about feedback from the real-world, and *self-awareness* about yourself doing the noticing?

- What do you see, and learn, from using the *Architect's Mantra* in your work on enterprise-architectures and the like? What information and insights arise from the questions? In what ways do they change your working-relationships with stakeholders and others? In what ways do they help – or hinder – your striving toward greater effectiveness across the whole organization and enterprise?

Whenever you're away from the action, grab a moment to apply those checklists to whatever you're working on right now – diving as needed into the detail for each phase of the work, as shown here and, in somewhat different form, in the next chapter. It's often better doing this with colleagues, but you can also do it on your own. Notice what ideas and insights arise from this; reflect for a moment on what you see and learn; then go back to the usual tasks. *Repeat, repeat, repeat...*

Add to your notebook some notes on this, for further review at the end of the book.

Summary

In this chapter, we explored the too-often-ignored "art" aspects of enterprise-architecture, with an emphasis on sensing, feeling, and working *"outside the box."* We also looked at how change-processes work, phase by phase, and the need to switch between modes or mindsets as we move from phase to phase in that type of process. We ended with some practical approaches and tools that could help us get started on this "art of enterprise-architecture."

In the next chapter, we'll complete this picture by providing a systematic, structured approach for working *"inside the box,"* and connect together the art *and* the science that we need for all of our work on change within the enterprise.

CHAPTER 4

Foundations: The Patterns of Change

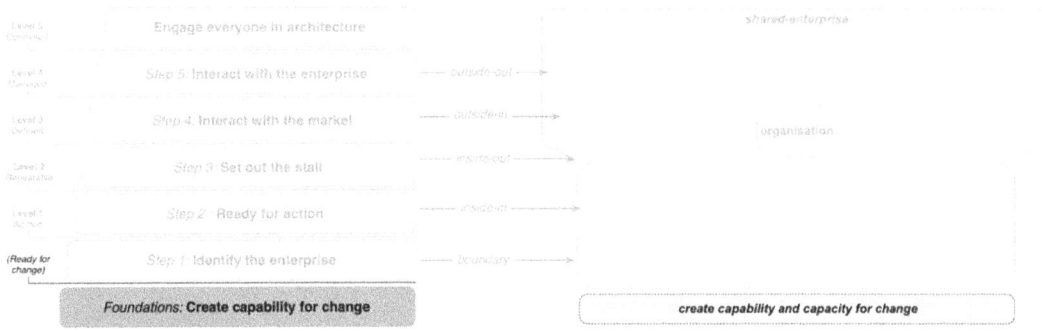

The next thing we need is a consistent method for doing enterprise-architecture and other change-work.

We've previously established that, whatever method we use, it will need to work the same way everywhere in the enterprise. It must work the same way for every type of content or context, at every scope and scale, within every part of a larger change-process and throughout the entire change-lifecycle. It needs to work the same way with both planned and unplanned change, and with both goal-based and continuous change. It needs to support continual improvement and help to ensure that every change will support overall effectiveness. At a higher level, it needs to work the same way within every change-style and framework, and with every type of laws, regulations, standards, and cultures that might apply in that context. Perhaps above all, it needs to be simple enough, not only that everyone can learn and use it, but that they *will* use it, in a disciplined way, for *every* change within every type of change-work.

CHAPTER 4   FOUNDATIONS: THE PATTERNS OF CHANGE

If everyone in our airport is using a change-method that, at its root, works the same way everywhere, then it becomes *much* easier to link everything together in a meaningful, manageable, and more effective way.

Let's see how that works in practice.

A Pattern for Change

Where do we start? The usual place would be with a classic project-management tool such as a Gantt-chart. In essence, it's a structured list of tasks. Above that, we'll often have some kind of framework to tell us what those tasks should be, and a change-style that would tell us what kind of governance to apply to those tasks.

Tasks may run in parallel with each other, as part of a larger task. Tasks may be chained together in sequences, one to the next, to denote the steps in a larger change-process. Tasks may be nested within each other, as sub-tasks and sub-sub-tasks for a task with a larger scope or scale. (There are common labels for those larger-scope tasks, such as "project," "program," or "portfolio.") Tasks may also be linked together in less-structured ways, to identify dependencies and so on.

Note   The term "***task-tree***" will also come up often from here onward. It's a common metaphor used in change-management to describe relationships between tasks and their sub-tasks. The tree starts from one all-encompassing "the Task" that represents all of the activity in the change-project, and then expands outward in ever-smaller but more detailed branches of tasks and sub-tasks.

In a typical Gantt-chart, the task-tree spreads sideways and/or downward, rather than upward as in an actual tree. The standard we've used in this book is that *"upward"* or *"above"* in a task-tree or in nesting means the broader-scope parent for the current task; *"downward"* or *"below"* means a sub-task or child-task of this one; and *"sibling"* means another task with the same parent as this one.

All of this is straightforward enough. Almost everyone will use this kind of approach within their change-work. And at that level, it works well enough. Sort-of.

The catch is that a Gantt-chart is *only* a list of tasks. It tells us what the tasks *are*, but not how to *do* those tasks. And unless we *do* all know how to do change-work in a disciplined way, and actually *do* it in that way, too, then no matter how good our frameworks and styles may be, they risk being more of a hindrance than a help. That's the issue we need to tackle here.

In the Gantt-chart, as shown in Figure 4-1, every task in the task-tree is just a box, with a label.

Figure 4-1. *Gantt-type task*

Outside the task-box, there'll usually be some kind of administrative wrapper, maintained by the change-management team. Depending on the project-management method, the wrapper would typically describe the purpose of the task, the budget in time or money, who's been assigned to do it, dependencies with other tasks, and so on. As shown in Figure 4-2, we'd typically split that wrapper into two parts: *Task-Begin*, to do any checks and setup needed before the task, as above, and *Task-End*, to deal with any governance and other decisions needed after the task.

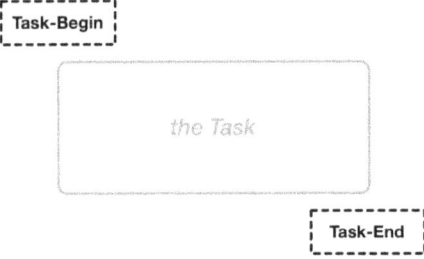

Figure 4-2. *The Task-Begin and Task-End gateways*

But *inside* the Gantt task-box, there's nothing. It's just an empty box, where change somehow just happens, like magic. In practice, the box gets filled with whatever context-specific methods will fill the need: and it's at *that* level where, without a consistent, systematic discipline to hold everything together, things can so easily and so often go horribly wrong.

To support the discipline we need, and prevent that kind of failure, we must make a clear distinction between **context-neutral**, which works the same way everywhere, and **context-specific**, which applies only in that specific type of context or concern. We then build a context-neutral core of methods and tools, used to guide every task, that links everything together across the whole, and plug into that core any context-specific tools, frameworks, and methods that we might need at any given time.

For that context-neutral core, what we've found works best is a sequence of five distinct phases within every task: **Context**, **Scope**, **Plan**, **Action**, and **Review** (CSPAR). As a brief summary:

- *Context*: Establish the **purpose** of the task, where it fits within the broader picture, its guiding vision, values, rules, and standards, and its key criteria for success and not-success

- *Scope*: With stakeholders and other **people**, establish boundaries of impact and influence for the task, its interactions with others, and its requirements for plan, action, and outcomes

- *Plan*: Establish the **preparation** needed for the task, how it is to be done, what resources and records it may need, its start- and end-conditions, and its guidance and governance

- *Action*: Enact the **process** of activities as specified or outlined in the plan, capturing any information, ideas, insights, and artifacts needed for further review

- *Review*: Assess **performance** of the action, to identify benefits-realized and any lessons-learned that could guide continual-improvement for this type of task and across the whole enterprise

All of this is fully fractal, and hence would apply to all types of change-work, everywhere. This means that the CSPAR pattern *must* be present in some form or another within *every* task and sub-task, at every level. For example, the Context and Scope phases for a large change-initiative would each be significant projects in their own right, whereas down at the bottom level, such as writing a single line of code, we'd still need the CSPAR set as a quick checklist for the overall activity.

Warning Because of the dependencies between the CSPAR phases, bypassing any of the phases within any task or sub-task *will* cause problems to occur:

- Without awareness of Context, activities may become purposeless, invalid, unsafe, or even illegal.

- Without awareness of Scope, activities may act in the wrong area, serve the wrong stakeholders, or be based on the wrong requirements or no requirements at all.

- Without awareness of Plan, activities may become pointless, ineffective, and wasteful, use the wrong resources, may never start, or never end.

- Without clear Action, guided by Plan, Scope, and Context, the task would be unlikely to deliver any useful or effective outcomes.

- Without Review, errors may not be caught or corrected, and it could become impossible to support continuous improvement anywhere, or across the enterprise as a whole.

In particular, jumping straight to the Plan or, worse, leaping straight into Action is almost guaranteed to cause failure, either within the task itself or further down the line. Not A Good Idea…

In a mid-range task, the CSPAR pattern might look more like that shown in Figure 4-3. First there'll be a couple of brief checks to confirm that we understand the broader Context and Scope; then a flurry of sub-tasks as we develop and describe the "how" of the Plan; a series of steps for the Action, recording any deviations from the plan; and then a final Review to assess any differences between plan and action, and derive useful lessons-learned, before moving on to the next task.

CHAPTER 4   FOUNDATIONS: THE PATTERNS OF CHANGE

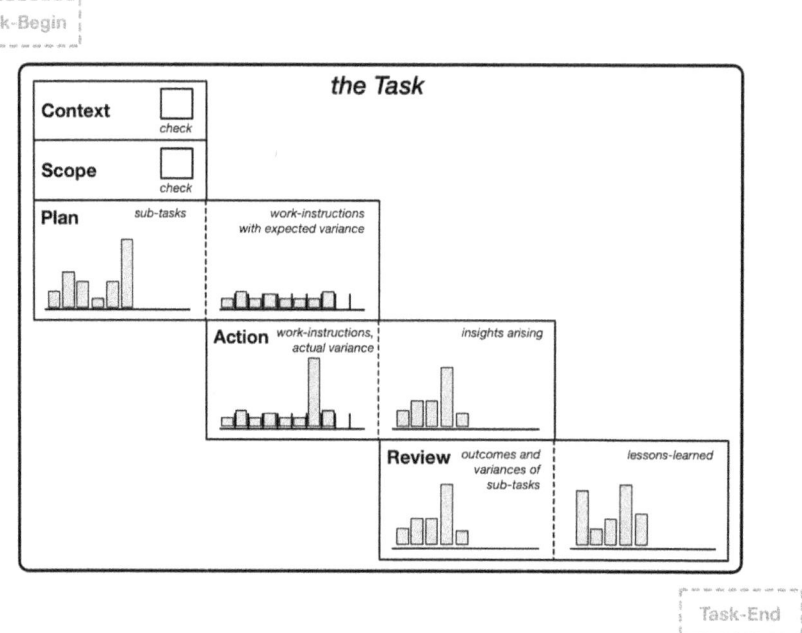

Figure 4-3. CSPAR phases within a mid-range Gantt-type Task

We can use this CSPAR pattern as described above, as a support and cross-check for mainstream project-management and the like.

We can also use CSPAR "vertically" as a Change-Layers pattern, as shown in Figure 4-4, to guide the sequences of the project-lifecycle.

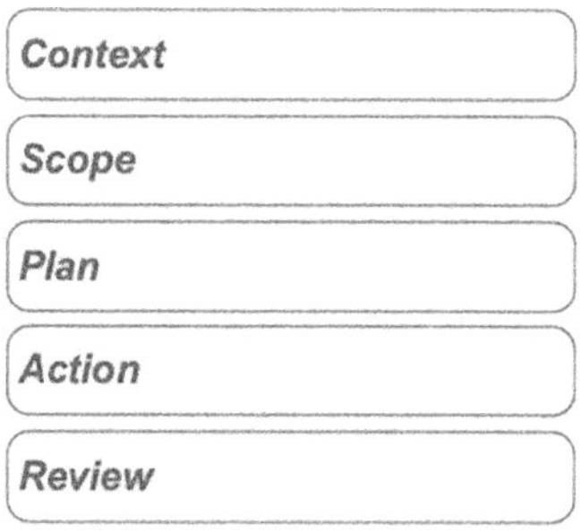

Figure 4-4. CSPAR pattern in "vertical" form as Change-Layers

We'll see more on this later in this Step, in Chapter 5, *"The Layers of Change."*

We can also use CSPAR "horizontally" as a Change-Cycle pattern, to guide the fine-detail of the change-process, and align the activities with the SCAN domains and CALc modes, as shown in Figure 4-5.

CHAPTER 4   FOUNDATIONS: THE PATTERNS OF CHANGE

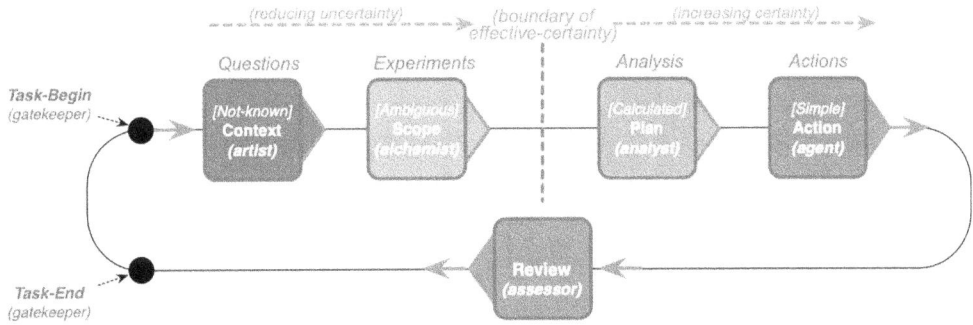

Figure 4-5. *CSPAR pattern in "horizontal" form as Change-Cycle*

We'll see more on this later in this Step, in the Chapter 6, *"The Cycles of Change."*

Each change-cycle takes place within a single change-layer or sub-layer, with the Task-End gateway at the end of each change-cycle making the choice as to whether to move up or down in the change-layers. Figure 4-6 illustrates the relationships between the Task-Begin and Task-End gateways, the Change-Layers and the Change-Cycle.

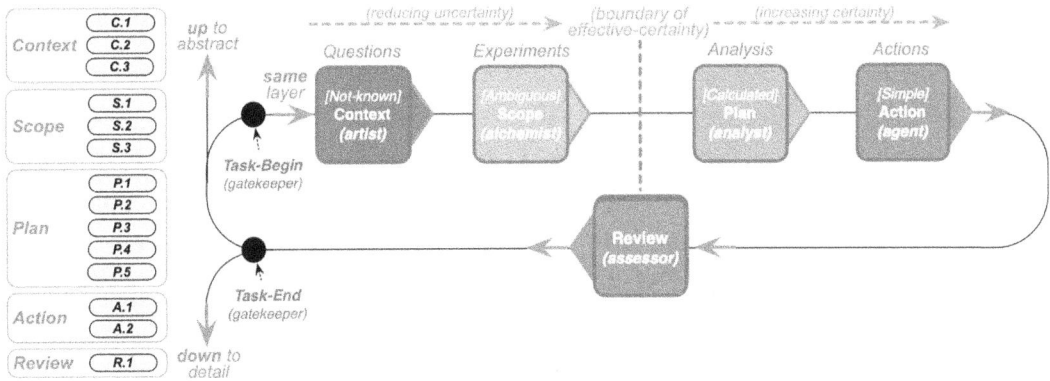

Figure 4-6. *Change-Layers and the Change-Cycle*

To link any **content- or context-specific method or framework** into the plan or action, we use the same core method as described later for the Change-Cycle, drawing on the CSPAR set of phase-labels:

- The *Context* for the iteration is the question or concern that needs a context-specific answer, and also includes everything at and "above" that point in the respective Change-Layers and in the current fractal nesting of tasks and sub-tasks.

71

- The *Scope* for the iteration is the range of tools and methods that we have available to address the question, linked to the skills and capabilities that we have available to us to use those tools and methods, with the question itself as the requirement to be addressed.

- The *Plan* for the iteration would be to find an appropriate tool or method, and then follow whatever instructions and guidelines are associated with the item.

- The *Action* would be to follow that plan, to return the outcomes that we need.

- The *Review* will check whether we *did* get the outcomes we need. If we did, we return back up to the parent iteration. If not, we loop around at the same level, and we try again, with different parameters or other changes to the initial question, or with a different context-specific item.

The aim here is to keep track of how and why and where we've used each context-specific element within the work, and keep them linked together into the whole.

The CSPAR pattern also underpins the related **Change-Mapping** change-guidance methodology. This provides a structured way to keep track of each task and sub-task, the question or concern that each sub-task and change-cycle iteration will address, the outcomes of each iteration, and all of the nesting, chaining, and cross-linking between each of the tasks and iterations. Overall, the Change-Mapping methods

- Address the outside of the Gantt-type task-box with Task-Begin ("Mission-Start") and Task-End ("Mission-End") actions

- Inside the task-box, will keep track of all tasks, paralleling, chaining, nesting, and linking (hence "change-*mapping*")

- Will keep track of the purpose for each task and sub-task, and each call for context-specific plug-in methods and content

- Provide defined sets of roles for project-tasks (Explorer, Guide, Reporter) and cross-project sustainment tasks (Librarian, Coordinator, Architect)

- Provide default templates for each of the Change-Cycle CSPAR phases

The underlying structure of Change-Mapping is fully fractal and fully context-neutral, to support connection and continuity across the entire context-space of an enterprise.

Note The Change-Mapping methods are not described in this book, but have been described in three books so far:

- *Change Mapping* provides a practical introduction to the methods, using a default set of forms and other tools.

- *Tools for Change-Mapping* adds to the Change-Mapping toolkit with a wide array of forms and templates to tackle common questions that arise in change-projects.

- *Advanced Change-Mapping* shows how to use Change-Mapping on larger and more complex change-projects, and in the architectures and methods needed to sustain them over the longer-term.

You'll find details on all three books in Appendix B.

Getting Started with the CSPAR Pattern

To get started with CSPAR, use the *Start Anywhere principle*. Everything in change-work is fractal, and everything is ultimately connected to everything else – which means that we can start anywhere, and doing so will begin to make at least some small difference straight away. In that sense, it really doesn't matter *where* we start, as long as we *do* get started.

We begin with simple **checklists** that we can use anywhere, for any change-work. For example, get into the habit of using this five-word checklist with any change-work that you happen to be working on at that time:

- *Context*: Why are we doing this?
- *Scope*: Who or what will this affect?
- *Plan*: How are we going to do this?
- *Action*: What are we doing right now?
- *Review*: What can we learn from what we've just done?

Even questions as simple as those will help us build that awareness that we need for this work:

- The questions on Context and Scope support ***contextual-awareness***.
- The questions on Plan and Action support ***task-awareness***.
- The questions on Action and Review support ***situational-awareness***.

From there, extend that habit by connecting together the phases of each task, using the dependencies between phases to link the elements of the overall task into a unified whole. For example, we can rework that checklist above into a short ***"how-to" summary*** of what needs to be done to ensure that that task will be able to deliver useful outcomes:

- *Context*: Create a big-picture overview that all stakeholders can understand and agree on, describing the purpose of the task, where it fits within the larger enterprise, its desired outcomes and its governing values, principles, and rules.

- *Scope*: Using the big-picture overview, identify the boundaries for the task, the stakeholders and their concerns, and the interfaces and exchanges beyond the task's boundaries. From this, derive the requirements for the changes to be made via the task.

- *Plan*: Drawing on the big-picture overview and requirements, identify in detail how the task should be enacted, the resources needed for the task, the means to ensure that those resources will be available, the start- and end-conditions for the task, and the records to be created during action. From this, develop the instructions, guidelines, and checklists that will be used to guide the delivery-actions of the task.

- *Action*: As guided by the instructions, guidelines, and checklists from the plan, enact the required delivery-actions of the task, and capture the specified types of change-records as part of that process.

- *Review*: Compare the action-records, and other outcomes from the action, against the instructions from the plan, the requirements from the scope, and the overall vision, values, and constraints from the context. Using these comparisons, and information on any exceptions or incidents that arose during the action, identify benefits-realized, lessons-learned, and issues-arising from the action. From this, derive recommendations for any additional change-tasks that may be required.

Remember that this pattern would apply to *every* task, everywhere:

- It applies "vertically" to an entire change-project, as the Change-Layers pattern.

- It applies "horizontally" within a single task, in a single layer, as the Change-Cycle pattern.

Note You may also have recognized from the descriptions above that the same pattern would also apply to other common types of change-tasks such as classic project-management, enterprise-architecture development processes, and process-mapping for business processes. You'll see more about how that works as we walk you through the detail of the Change-Layers pattern in the next chapter.

A few other points to remember:

- Each phase is a sub-task in its own right, within the frame of the overall task.

- Each phase may be done by different people and/or different systems.

- Each phase may be at any scale, from a single line of code to an entire project in its own right.

- Each phase may be stripped down to almost nothing, but must still always be present in some form within each task and sub-task.

- Each new question or concern implies a need for a new task or sub-task.

- Whether directly or indirectly, each change-task is connected with every other change.

- However small it may be, each change-task will change our entire world.

And that's it: that's all that you'll need to get started on this.

CHAPTER 4   FOUNDATIONS: THE PATTERNS OF CHANGE

Into Practice

Our purpose in this chapter was to establish the foundations for a simple yet systematic way for everyone to design and do change-work, at every scope and scale, everywhere in the enterprise.

Consider just some of the many different kinds of change that would take place in our airport-example:

- Aircraft and people arriving and departing
- Baggage to be sorted, screened, sent to the right flight or conveyor-belt
- Fuel and food to be provided and consumed
- Maintenance and cleaning of all kinds, from aircraft and escalators to tow-trucks and toilets
- Over there on the far side, an entirely new passenger-terminal being designed, built, fitted-out, and readied for action

Different people doing different jobs, everywhere around us, all through the day, all through the night. And every change will affect every other change in some way or other, all across the entire airport.

As an enterprise-architect for the airport, it would be your job to ensure that all of these different kinds of change-work will connect cleanly with each other, support each other, and that everything will *continue* to work together, better, on-purpose.

- How would you do all of that?
- How would you get people to understand *each other's work* well enough that things *can* work together, better, on-purpose?

Now apply this to your own real-world work-context:

- What kinds of change-work take place, at what scope and scale, across the overall enterprise?
- Who or what does each kind of change-work? How do they design and do that work?

- How do you ensure that each type of work connects cleanly with others, works together well with others, continually improves over time in a changing world, and is on-purpose in itself and across the whole context?

- What happens if some form of change-work *doesn't* connect cleanly with others, or work well with others? What, as an enterprise-architect, could you do to improve that?

- What happens if some form of change-work does not or cannot adapt well to a changing world? What, as an enterprise-architect, could you do to improve that?

- How do you discover such issues, across the whole enterprise, in order to be able to resolve them?

It's not uncommon to feel overwhelmed when first faced with questions such as those above. In this chapter, we've suggested that a consistent context-neutral change-pattern such as CSPAR can help to ease that sense of overwhelm. We now need to put that assertion to the test. So choose an upcoming project in your own work-context for which you already have a Gantt-type project-plan, then select any higher-level task from that plan. Use the Change-Layers model – the CSPAR pattern in its vertical form, as shown in Figure 4-4 – as a completeness-checklist for the structure of that task:

- *Context*: How will you identify the purpose of this task, its relationships with other tasks, its desired outcomes, and its governing values, principles, and rules? In what ways will these be used to guide decisions and actions throughout the task?

- *Scope*: How will you identify the boundaries for the task, the stakeholders and their concerns, and the interfaces and exchanges beyond the task's boundaries? How will you derive appropriate requirements for the changes to be made via the task?

- *Plan*: How will you identify how the task should be enacted, the resources it will need, its start- and end-conditions, and the records it needs to create? How will you ensure that this Plan and its Action will align with the criteria from the Context and Scope? What instructions, guidelines, and checklists will you use to guide the delivery-Actions of the task?

- *Action*: How will you use the guidance from the Plan to guide the real-time actions for the task? How will you capture the required records of the action? How will you address, in real-time, any variances and exceptions from the plan?

- *Review*: How will you identify the outcomes from the Action of this task? How will you assess the benefits-realized from these outcomes, and identify any lessons-learned? How should that information about benefits-realized and lessons-learned be used to guide future tasks?

What ideas and insights arise from using this checklist on your planned task? What might you need to change in your current plans for that task? Capture these notes in your notebook for later review.

Now select a lower-level task from that project-plan. Use the Change-Cycle model – the CSPAR pattern in its horizontal form, as shown in Figure 4-5, and its relationship with the Change-Layers model as shown in Figure 4-6 – as a completeness-check on how to tackle that lower-level task:

- *Task-Begin*: What is the question or concern that is to be addressed by this specific task? Which layer within the Change-Layers model will be changed by this task?

- *Context*: How will you ensure that the planned outcomes for this task will align with the broader enterprise vision, values, constraints, and success-criteria?

- *Scope*: How will you ensure that the planned outcomes from this task will align to its requirements and support the needs of its stakeholders?

- *Plan*: How will you ensure that the planned activities for this task will satisfy the requirements and support effectiveness both within itself and across the whole enterprise?

- *Action*: How will you ensure that the activities for this task will align to the respective Context, Scope, and Plan, that they will be able to address appropriately any variances from the conditions expected in the plan, and that they will capture appropriate records of action?

- *Review*: How will you ensure that any benefits-realized and lessons-learned from this task's activities will be appropriately assessed?

- *Task-End*: What decisions will arise from the completion of this task, and how will such appropriate decisions be made?

What ideas and insights arise for you from doing this exercise? Add notes to your notebook for review at the end of the book.

Summary

In this chapter, we introduced the CSPAR pattern (Context, Scope, Plan, Action, Review) as a systematic and consistent guide for all types of change-work, within any context, scope, or scale. We then explored some practical ways to get started with using the CSPAR pattern in real-world change-work.

In the next chapter, we'll expand that exploration to see how the CSPAR pattern works as a set of interdependent Change-Layers, to guide change-work throughout the whole of the project-lifecycle.

CHAPTER 5

Foundations: The Layers of Change

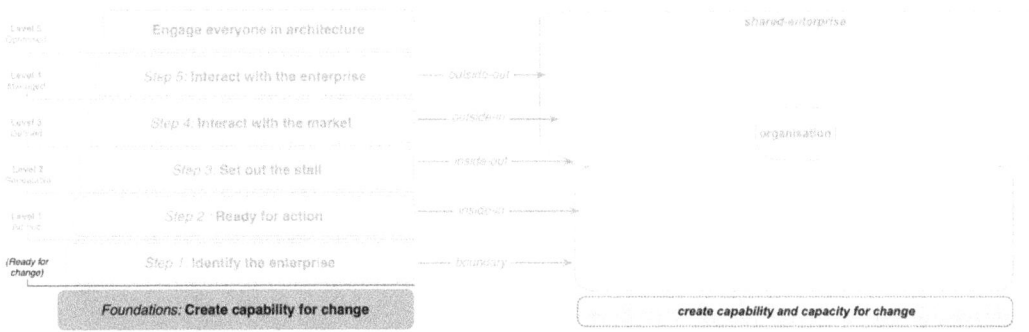

In this chapter, we'll explore how to use the CSPAR pattern in its "vertical" form as the Change-Layers, to guide a larger-scope piece of change-work such as a project, a change-program, or a full-scale business-transformation.

(In the next chapter, we'll do the same with the CSPAR pattern in its "horizontal" form as the Change-Cycle, to guide a single chunk of change-work. In both cases, though, *it's still the same pattern* – just used in a different way.)

Remember that this is still only the "Foundations" step in the Maturity-Model, addressing the skills needed for *all* types of change. We don't get into any of the specific details for whole-enterprise architecture until Step 1, in Chapter 8.

The other catch here is that people do sometimes misunderstand **the fractal nature of the CSPAR pattern**, thinking of it as applying only to a *single* type, scope, and scale of change-work – such as an enterprise-architecture method. Yet as a fractal pattern, it's actually a *generic* context-neutral pattern, to which we can then add context-specific elements to customize it for *any* type of "project-like" change-work, at any scope or scale, to support any purpose we might need. Hence, for example, we can indeed adapt it to

CHAPTER 5 FOUNDATIONS: THE LAYERS OF CHANGE

use as an enterprise-architecture change-process – there'll be more on that in Chapter 9, in the section "From Architecture to Action." In *this* chapter, though, we'll focus on the generic Change-Layers pattern, *before* any of those purpose-specific customizations have been applied.

Note Yes, you'll find that there's a lot to get through in this chapter! We *have* applied the "Just Enough" principle here as much as we can, but this is one case where "just enough" really *does* need to be quite a lot…

Yet although you *will* need every part of this detail somewhen soon, you probably *won't* need all of it right from the start. In your first read-through, perhaps skim-read everything just to get an overall sense of where each part is and what it does. You'll then know where to find whatever Change-Layer detail you may need in the future.

In the next chapter, each CSPAR Change-Cycle relates to just one chunk of change-work, so it'll probably be easier to understand and apply straight away, in a *practical* sense. A Change-Cycle takes place within a single Change-Layer, though, which is why this chapter *does* need to come first.

Layers upon Layers

Why "*layers*" of change? In change-management in general, and perhaps enterprise-architectures in particular, we've long had a concept of "layers" of activities, as distinct stages in how a desired business-change goes from initial intent to realized capability. Each layer represents different types of tasks, typically done by different people with different skillsets.

There are many different models for this – for enterprise-architects, the classic example would be the "rows" of the Zachman framework. In essence, though, most of them would be some variant on this set:

- *Big-picture* ("business"): Detailed overview of desired intent, actions, interactions, and outcomes from the new or changed capability
- *Logical*: "Implementation-independent" design, showing abstract types for each element of the system

CHAPTER 5 FOUNDATIONS: THE LAYERS OF CHANGE

- *Physical*: "Implementation-specific" design, showing real-world types for each element of the system
- *Implementation*: Real-world implementation, including design, installation, and configuration

We connect the layers together through the relationship between architecture and design, as we saw earlier in the "Key Concepts and Principles" section in Chapter 2, earlier in this "Foundations" Step. The design output from one layer – typically as diagrams, models, and specifications – becomes the basis for the architecture at the next layer down.

Yet the catch is that, in practice, all of those classic layers are about various stages of *planning* for change, whereas one of our requirements is that **we must be able to address the whole lifecycle of change** from strategy to operations and back again. As shown in Figure 5-1, those classic layers represent only one part of the whole – and yet for whole-enterprise architectures and the like, we *do* need the complete set of layers, not just that one part.

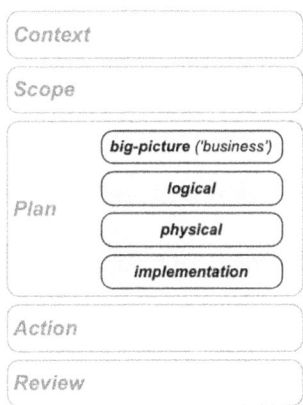

Figure 5-1. CSPAR Change-Layers model and classic change-layers

---

Caution One of the more unfortunate side-effects from that classic framing of layers in mainstream enterprise-architecture, as shown in Figure 5-1, is that it often leads to a conceptual trap: the notion that "architecture" is something that only happens in the early part of Plan, and that everything else is "design" that is done by others. That notion is *sort-of* correct relative to the Plan layer *itself*, but it's *not* correct relative to change as a whole. Don't fall for that trap!

Instead, as described back in Chapter 2, remember that **architecture occurs everywhere**, in *every* part of the overall change-process. Although there'll be many differences in tasks, of course, the only *fundamental* difference between architecture and design is one of perspective. At *every* point in the sequence from initial intent to actual change, "architecture" connects upward to the big-picture, while "design" connects downward toward the real-world.

(Although that notion of "architecture only happens at the start of Plan" will often lead to problems, as above, it can also be *useful* as a cue for sensemaking. For example, wherever you see a role-title of "architect" within your organization, it will usually relate to the tasks for the start-phase of some type of Plan. In which case, what are all the *other* parts of that type of overall change-process, its typical core-question or concern, its Context, its Scope, the rest of the Plan work, the Action, and the Review? Who will do those *other* types of work in that overall change-process? You can find a lot of useful insights about your organization's change-processes from that kind of inquiry.)

Warning That notion that "architecture only happens at the start of Plan" can become *really* dangerous if it gets entangled with another common misperception, that the Change-Layers pattern also represents some kind of social hierarchy in which the people who do the earlier work of a change-process are somehow "more important" than everyone else, and have the "right" to control everyone else "below" them and tell them what to do. This gives rise to disasters such as the dreaded "architecture-police," and all manner of other power-problems that you'll see described later. Not A Good Idea…

Using CSPAR as the base for our Change-Layers model also helps us resolve another confusing complication within change-projects. The classic change-layers only describe change at the level of *the project as a whole* – but because **change is fractal**, the same principles of "layers of change" must also apply to each *fractal-instance* of change, each subproject and sub-subproject within an overall change-project.

In effect, ***each fractal-instance needs its own distinct Change-Layers model***, defining the steps for its own transitions of change, and where its own change-layers are always relative to where this fractal-instance sits in the change-layers model for its "parent" above. For example, imagine a sub-task that's working on part of the "logical-model" for the Plan stage of its parent task:

- The sub-task's ***Context*** is not just the enterprise-as-a-whole as context, but also whatever has been added to the context-description by all of the other tasks nested above this sub-task, eventually including the specific Context of the parent-task.

- The sub-task's ***Scope*** is a layered subset-of-a-subset-of-a-subset all the way back to the Scope of the initial overall change-task or change-initiative.

- The sub-task's ***Plan*** will be about how it works on *this part* of the parent's logical-model – and its own logical-model will be about how it will do *its own* specific sub-task.

- The sub-task's ***Action*** will be about how to change the parent's logical-model.

- The sub-task's ***Review*** will assess what happened as it worked on the parent's logical-model, and what can be learned from this.

Overall, **for each task or sub-task**

- ***Context***-layers refer not only to the parent-task, but also the full layering of all tasks above it in the task-tree.

- ***Scope***-layers are relative to the Context, as applied to *this* task or sub-task. No matter how deep this task or sub-task may be in the nesting of tasks, its ultimate decisions on Scope must not and cannot be completely automated: they are always made by *people*, as an expression of *personal* responsibility.

- ***Plan***-layers are always relative to the Context and Scope for *this* task or sub-task, but may also refer to and/or be dependent on tasks that are "above" in the nesting, or even elsewhere in the task-tree. Some Plan elements may be automated – such as AI interpretation of a pattern – but the final Plan *must* ultimately be authorized by an actual person, again as an expression of *personal* responsibility.

- ***Action*-layers** are always relative to the Plan for *this* task or sub-task. As specified in the Plan, the Action may be automated and/or manual, and executed by any appropriate mix of people, machines, and/or IT.

- ***Review*-layers** are always relative to the Action, Plan, Scope, and Context for *this* task or sub-task, but may reference other tasks that are "above" or "below" in the nesting, or elsewhere in other branches of the task-tree. Certain types of Review may be automated – such as for machine-learning – but any decisions *must* always be subject to oversight by actual people, again as an expression of *personal* responsibility.

We'll need to keep track at all times of where we are in all of these layerings, to ensure that we're always working on the right Context, Scope, Plan, Action, or Review at each moment.

Caution If people don't take enough care to keep track of this fractal layering, then all the chaining, nesting, linking, and suchlike going on between sub-tasks in a typical change-project can turn really confusing, *really* fast. We've seen all too many projects fall apart when that happens. Using CSPAR as a consistent base for all change-layering will definitely help, but ultimately it *is* always up to each of us to get this right.

In practice, the CSPAR set may be at too coarse a granularity, particularly at the whole-of-change level, so we'll often need to add distinct sub-layers as well. Figure 5-2 provides a visual summary of our recommended default set of sub-layers for use at a whole-of-project level.

CHAPTER 5   FOUNDATIONS: THE LAYERS OF CHANGE

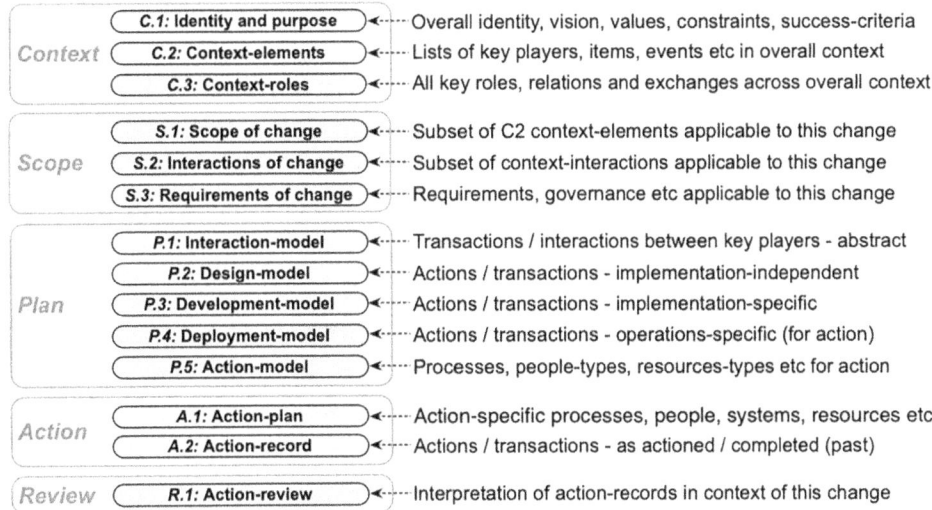

Figure 5-2. *Default CSPAR Change-Layers at whole-of-project level*

In more detail

- **Context** (emphasis on this in Maturity-Model Step 1)

  - *C.1: Identity and purpose*: Overall identity, vision, values, constraints, success-criteria

  - *C.2: Context-elements*: Lists of key players, items, events, and so on within the overall context

  - *C.3: Context-roles*: All key roles, relations, and exchanges across overall context

- **Scope** (emphasis on this in Step 2)

  - *S.1: Scope of change*: Subset of C2 context-elements applicable to this change *(Zachman "row-1")*

  - *S.2: Interactions of change*: Subset of context-interactions applicable to this change

  - *S.3: Requirements of change*: Requirements, governance, and suchlike applicable to this change

87

- **Plan** (emphasis on this in Step 3)
  - *P.1: Interaction-model*: Transactions and interactions between key players and/or systems – abstract *("row-2," "business-model")*
  - *P.2: Design-model*: Actions and transactions – implementation-independent *("row-3," "logical-model")*
  - *P.3: Development-model*: Actions and transactions – implementation-specific *("row-4," "physical-model")*
  - *P.4: Deployment-model*: Actions, transactions, configurations, etc. – operations-specific *("row-5")*
  - *P.5: Action-model*: Processes, agent-types, resource-types, checklists, and suchlike to guide action
- **Action** (emphasis on this in Step 4)
  - *A.1: Action-plan*: Action-specific processes, people, systems, units, resources, etc.
  - *A.2: Action-record*: Records of actions, transactions, and variances from action-plan, as enacted
- **Review** (emphasis on this in Step 5)
  - *R.1: Action-review*: Interpretation of action-records in context of this change

Right down at the bottom of the task-tree, such as at the level of a single execution of a software function, the layering would be much simpler. In that example, the respective Context and Scope are embedded within the design of the software-module; the code itself is effectively the action-Plan; the Action is a single instance of execution, capturing the respective metadata and other action-records; and the Review consists of ensuring that the action-records have been properly logged for later review at a higher level. Note, though, that even down at this level, *all* of the CSPAR layers are still represented in some form or another.

This fractal approach to layering of change-actions may at first seem more complicated than a simple fixed set of layers. Yet by providing a clear separation between "same and different" – context-neutral CSPAR base-layers and context-specific sub-layers – it *does* help to improve consistency across the full scope of the overall enterprise, and *does* help us to avoid getting lost in the layering of tasks and sub-tasks.

The Change-Layers help us maintain an awareness of the *structure* of the work. For each task, we need to know

- *The **Context** of the task*: **Why** it's being done, and how and why the task connects to the big-picture

- *The **Scope** of the task*: **Who** the work is for, who or what will do it and/or be affected by it, and the requirements that arise from this

- *The **Plan** for the task*: **How** the work will be done, what resources it will use, and so on

- *The **Action** of the task*: **What** should or did change, in what ways, by what means, **where**, and **when**, as the work is done

- *How to **Review** the task*: How we can *learn* from what was done, to *improve effectiveness* for this type of task, and across the enterprise as a whole.

This applies in the same way to every type of task and sub-task, at every scale, from a massive multi-year multinational project to change the entire air-transport industry, all the way down to the much simpler task of checking a boarding-pass to confirm that the passenger can go through the boarding-gate at the airport.

Back in the previous chapter, we've seen how to get started in practice with this CSPAR pattern; we've also looked at different types of relationships between tasks, and how to connect content- and context-specific methods and tools into that context-neutral core. We now need to take a deeper dive into the detail of how to use the CSPAR Change-Layers pattern in real-world change-work, such as we see in enterprise-architectures and the like. For each main layer, we'll explore

- The overall *purpose* and *role* of the layer

- The type of *content* to be used or worked on within the layer

- *Who* or what will do the work in that layer

- *Where* the work of the layer will typically take place

- *How* each part of the work will be done

- The *inputs* to be received from other layers

- The typical *process* of the work of that layer, and its intended *outcomes* and *work-products* at each stage, as divided up between the respective sub-layers
- The *outputs* to be sent to other layers
- Any *further notes* about other aspects of that layer

There may sometimes be some back-and-forth between layers, and quite often between sub-layers – particularly in the Plan layer. Overall, though, that kind of movement is far less pronounced in the Change-Layers than it is in the Change-Cycle. As long as we're aware that such back-and-forth *can* and sometimes *does* happen in the Change-Layers, it's safe enough to describe them here as a simple linear sequence, starting with the Context layer.

Note At higher levels in the task-tree, there'll often also be an administrative Task-Begin and/or Task-End between each layer, and even between sub-layers. However, the detail for these will depend on the governance-framework in use for the respective project, so we can't explore that here.

Context in the Change-Layers

The Context phase comes first in the Change-Layers sequence, because ultimately all our decision-making within the task as a whole will depend on this.

Note This section is just an overview of how to identify context in general. There are full worked-examples later, in the section "Enterprise As Context" in Step 1, for the airport as a whole, and in the section "Build the Services" in Step 2, for individual services.

The **role** of this layer is to identify the broader enterprise and storyworld within which this task sits, and verify the task's connection to that broader world. This includes

- The desires and aspirations that drive the need for the task
- The constraints on those aspirations

- What success or not-success would look like
- The core elements, roles, relationships, and exchanges of the overall enterprise

Figure 5-3 provides a visual summary of the **content** that we develop and/or update in this part of the work, showing the effectiveness-criteria and the core elements of the story.

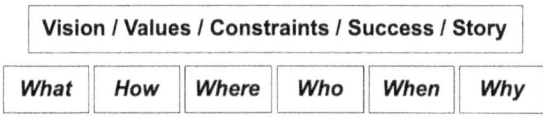

Figure 5-3. *Content developed in the Context layers*

This content for Context will apply not only to this task, but to all of its child-tasks further down in the task-tree. At the top levels of a task-tree, any future changes in its definition of Context may or will affect every other task in its entire task-tree.

Child-tasks will inherit their Context not just from their immediate parent, but from all the other levels above it in the task-tree. Often the only work needed for the Context of a child-task will be to check that we *do* understand it, and only refine it as necessary for the needs of this specific task.

The work for Context is essentially the same for both *goal-based* and *continuing* change. The only difference is that *every* goal-based task must ultimately be anchored by the Context of one or more continuing-tasks, such as the enterprise of the organization, the respective professional-disciplines, or the needs of the nation.

Who does the work for this layer will depend on where the task is in the task-tree. At the whole-of-organization level, this is done by the executive as a whole, supported as necessary by the strategy-team. For a major change-project, it would be done by representatives from all of the change-agent groups: strategy, change-management, architects, designers, operations-teams, and so on. Further down in the task-tree, it would typically be done by the team-lead, assisted by others as required, though we do need to watch out for changes rippling downward from above in the task-tree.

Where we do this work would be in a space that supports the ***artist*** mode. It's best to do it in a space that stimulates the senses; together is usually better than alone; in-person is better than online; outside is often better than inside; and quieter may be better, though even a noisy bar would often be more effective for this than a closed-up

91

cubicle back in the office. It also needs to be a space where we can capture insights as they arise. Classically, this would be a room full of whiteboards, flipcharts, notepads, and sticky-notes – though voice-recorders and camera-apps will also often work well, especially if supported by automated transcription and the like.

How we do this work is iterative, experimental, exploratory, very much in the ***artist*** mode. Although it's classically described as "brainstorming," that's not the right term here. It's not about thinking, nor about argument, but instead more like "heartflowing" or "souldancing"; more art than science, imagining all the possibilities of the broader enterprise within which this task will play its part. What's needed most here is a subtle balance between serious and playful, both at the same time, combining the messiness of creativity with the commitment to get the work done.

The **inputs** for this work will depend on where the task is within the task-tree. At the topmost level – "the Task" – the only inputs will be the question or concern identified in the Task-Begin phase, information about the Context for the organization itself, and maybe some further information about Context from previous and/or related tasks. Below that level, a task will inherit much, most, or all of its Context from the parent-tasks above it in the task-tree, and sometimes also from its sibling-tasks and/or from previous iterations of the same task. Overall, the inputs would typically include

- *From **Task-Begin***: Question or concern to be addressed by the task
- *From **Context***: Aspirations, constraints, success-criteria, and context-elements, as described in this section
- *From **Scope***: Feedback from stakeholders and others regarding purpose, values, and so on
- *From **Plan***: Feedback from architects, designers, and other planners regarding purpose, applicable standards, regulations, and the like
- *From **Action***: Feedback on usefulness and validity of guidelines, and practical challenges on feasibility or viability of purpose
- *From **Review***: Implications for achievability of purpose, and feedback on "what we could do differently next time"

CHAPTER 5   FOUNDATIONS: THE LAYERS OF CHANGE

For **structure**, the default version of the Context layer has three sub-layers, or sets of sub-tasks:

- *C.1: Identity and purpose*: Overall identity, vision, values, constraints, success-criteria

- *C.2: Context-elements*: Lists of key players, items, events, and so on within the overall context

- *C.3: Context-roles*: All key roles, relations, and exchanges across the overall context

---

Note   As mentioned above, see the worked-examples for the airport in the section "Enterprise As Context" in Step 1, and in the section "Build the Services" in Step 2.

In the **C.1 sub-layer**, we need to identify the overall criteria for *effectiveness*:

- The *purpose* for the task

- The overarching *story* for the change

- The overarching *vision*, *values*, *principles*, and *trade-offs*

- The overarching *constraints*, such as laws, regulations, standards, and guidelines

- The overarching *realities* such as geography, weather, politics, and social culture

- The overarching *success-criteria* for the outcomes of the task

Use that list as a reference, then build a conversation around it, to allow ideas and images to arise. Do this iteratively – expect to revisit it at least two or three times – and do it quickly, with each iteration no longer than half an hour at most.

Note   Again, this part is often more art than science, more about feeling than thinking. Yes, deep experience is important, but so is a willingness to let go of it if necessary, and look at the world from a different direction. Don't try too hard, and don't overthink it: instead, allow things to arise in their own way, in their own time.

93

In the **C.2 sub-layer**, guided by what we found or chose in the *C.1* sub-layer, we need to identify

- The overarching *boundaries* for scope, in terms of the core *elements* in the context (What, How, Where, Who, When, Why)

The *C.1* sub-layer gave us the overall frame for a story within which the task will sit: here, we'll start to fill out the elements that would make that story work. Use that list of categories (What, How, Where, Who, When, Why) as a reference, then build a conversation around it, to allow ideas and images to arise, to populate those categories. Note that some items that arise in the conversation may require us to revisit the *C.1* conversation, then come back here to continue this one. Again, do this iteratively, and do it fast, with iterations of around 15–30 minutes at most.

Note Keep this simple, and don't overdo it: typically, no more than a dozen items in each list. This is only a high-level overview: you'll need much more detail later, of course, but that happens in the Plan phase, not here.

In the **C.3 sub-layer**, guided by what we found in the *C.1* and *C.2* sub-layers, we need to

- Map out the overall *roles* and *relationships* between the core types of players in the story behind the change-task – an overview of Who sits Where, How they connect with each other, What is exchanged When between them, and Why those exchanges need to take place for the story to succeed

The *C.1* sub-layer gave us a frame for the context-story, and the *C.2* sub-layer gave us the elements that make that story: we now need to bring this together into a form that others can easily understand and use. We do this by building a map, diagram, or model that shows every element in relation with all of the others, all working together to achieve the overall purpose.

We usually start by placing onto the map all of the Who elements – the players in the overall story – and build outward from there. When the map is complete, it should in some way show *every* element that we identified in the *C.2* sub-layer, and preferably also illustrate everything we identified in the *C.1* sub-layer as well. Note that the process of building the map often suggests other things that we might need to add or change back in the *C.1* and *C.2* sub-layers, rippling back and forth between all three sub-layers as required.

> **Example**   The OV-1 (Operational View 1: High Level Operational Concept Graphic) diagram-type in DoDAF (US Department of Defense Architecture Framework) "provides a graphical depiction of what the architecture is about and an idea of the players and operations involved," to quote the Department's website. A web-search for "*ov-1 diagram*" should bring up a wide variety of examples for you to play with.

The typical **outputs** from Context to the other change-layers will include

- *To **Scope***: Overall boundaries and core-elements (What, How, Where, Who, When, Why)
- *To **Plan***: Overall big-picture and constraints
- *To **Action***: Overall guiding-principles (these should be packaged in Plan as the "chaos-checklist" for the action – see *Plan and uncertainty* later)
- *To **Review***: Overall success-criteria ("What was the expected purpose and the outcomes?")

These "big-picture" parameters from Context will apply not only to this specific change-task, but to *every other possible change-task* within its own task-tree. We may amend or further refine them within sub-tasks in the Change-Layers and/or within other phases of the Change-Cycle, as described in other chapters in this Step and in Step 1, but they *cannot and must not* be ignored, overridden, or superseded.

Once all of the work on Context is complete and available to the task as a whole, we should be ready to move on to the work of the Scope layer.

Further Notes on Context

Do beware of **prepackaged assumptions about context or content**, such as from vendor-driven architectures, or the IT-oriented focus of many current enterprise-architecture frameworks, methods, and tools. Instead, *always* start from context-neutral methods, to identify what the context actually is, and only then select appropriate context-specific methods from that base. (Unless otherwise specified, all of the methods described in this book are designed to work in a context-neutral way.)

If a change is successful in one context, there's often a desire to apply it in other contexts – for example, as a **"best-practice."** When doing this, do be aware of any implications for reusing that change in the new context. The key guideline here is *"**adapt, then adopt**."* In essence, it's a straightforward gap-analysis, followed by making any adjustments implied by the differences between contexts, such as language, laws, standards, technologies, and local practices:

- Identify what the respective context is for the best-practice that is to be reused. If that context is not explicitly defined, derive it by using the methods in this chapter and in Step 2.

- Identify the context, scope, and scale for its reuse, as described in this chapter and in the chapters for the applicable Steps.

- Using a gap-analysis, derive and apply any requirements for change in the best-practice ("adapt"), then roll out ("adopt") the amended best-practice in its new context.

The same principles for "adapt, then adopt" will also apply to reusing context-specific tools, methods, frameworks, processes, and so on in another context.

Scope in the Change-Layers

The Scope phase acts as a bridge between Context and Plan, by identifying the requirements for the desired change.

Note This section is just an overview of how to identify scope in general. There are full worked-examples later, in the section "Organization and Enterprise" in Step 1, for the airport as a whole, and in the section "From Architecture to Action" in Step 2, for individual services.

Each change applies at a specific scope and scale; every change is bounded by its scope. Scope-layers are always relative to the respective Context, as applied to *this* task or sub-task.

The **role** of this layer is to establish the scope, requirements, and intended outcomes for the task. This will include

- The scope of the task, as a subset of the Context
- The stakeholders within that scope, and their needs and concerns
- The concerns arising from any risks, opportunities, and uncertainties within that scope
- How the task should, would, or could address and satisfy those needs and concerns

From these, we would derive and describe

- The requirements and governing policies for the task
- Roadmaps for change

These then provide the starting-point for the work on the task's Plan.

Figure 5-4 provides a visual overview of the **content** that we use, develop, and/or update in this part of the work. In particular, to develop requirements, we need to translate the abstract element-categories from Context into their real-world equivalents: What, How, Where, Who, When, and Why morph, respectively, into Asset, Function, Location, Capability, Event, and Decision.

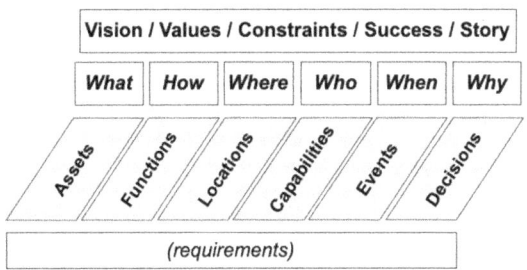

Figure 5-4. Content developed in the Scope layers

This content for Scope will apply not only to this task, but to all of its child-tasks further down in the task-tree. At the top levels of a task-tree, any future changes in its definition of Scope may or will affect every other task in its entire task-tree. Making a high-level change to Scope during the lifecycle of a project is a common cause for major overruns of time and/or budget.

Child-tasks will inherit their Scope not just from their immediate parent, but from all the other levels above it in the task-tree. Often the only work needed for the Scope of a child-task will be to check that we *do* understand the scope and requirements, and only refine or narrow it as necessary for the needs of this specific child-task.

As with Context, the work for Scope is essentially the same for both *goal-based* and *continuing* change. We'll need to ensure that the Scope of each goal-based task is placed somewhere appropriate within the intersection of the Scopes of all relevant continuing-tasks, such as the enterprise of the organization, the respective professional-disciplines, or the needs of the nation.

Who does the work for the Scope layer is much the same as for Context. At the whole-of-organization level, it would be the executive-board. At the major-project level, it would again be representatives from the various change-agent groups, but often other stakeholders too. Further down the task-tree, it would be the respective team-lead and team, often supported by representatives from front-line staff and by others with broader technical expertise. In each case, we again do need to watch out for changes rippling downward from above in the task-tree.

Warning   The scope of impact of a change is usually (much) broader than the scope of action of the change itself; and scope is always a *choice*, made by *people*. This often brings in a lot more "Who" into the picture than you might expect; and failure to properly address those two points can have serious consequences further down the line.

The ultimate decisions on Scope and requirements must always be made by *people*, as an expression of *personal* responsibility. No matter how deep this task or sub-task may be within the task-tree, decisions on Scope *cannot and must not* be completely automated. In particular, *never* allow anyone – including ourselves – to use or attempt to use automation as a means to evade responsibility for decisions on Scope and its impact on others and on the wider world. Not A Good Idea…

Where we do this work can be almost anywhere: in board-rooms, in work-rooms, and wherever our stakeholders may happen to be, from government offices and trade-shows to airport security-lines and down in baggage-handling. Working together with others is often essential here, because we'll need to collect and collate a lot of other people's experiences, opinions, and advice. Wherever we do the work, we'll need notepads, voice-recorders, and the like to capture information, ideas, and insights as they arise, and, back at base, the same whiteboards, flipcharts, sticky-notes, and so on, as in the Context work, to collate and sort that information into the Scope structure that we need.

How we do this work is again iterative, experimental, exploratory, though this time with the emphasis on the ***alchemist*** mode: a balance somewhere between the inventiveness of the *artist* and the formal rigor and disciplines of the *analyst*. We'll need to find a balance between art and science, between theory and practice, between intent and reality, and perhaps above all a bridge between people. We often describe change-work as "relentlessly political" – and it's here, in the work on Scope, that such phrase most often comes to the fore. Technology-based hard-skills will be relevant here, but solid *soft-skills* are often far more important: we'll need to become really good at *listening*, and in being a quiet, calm, patient negotiator, facilitator, arbitrator, referee, umpire, and judge, respectful to all.

Note too that to do Scope-work well, we *must* allow it to take whatever time it needs. If we try to take shortcuts, such as rushing interviews, ignoring conflicts, or stripping the list of stakeholders down to "only the *important* people," the information that we miss by doing so will come back to bite us in the end, costing us far more time than we saved from the shortcut.

The **inputs for this work** depend in part on where the task is within the task-tree. At the topmost level, the only inputs will be the question or concern identified in the Task-Begin phase, the Context information about this task, the organization and the broader enterprise, and maybe some further information about Context and/or Scope from previous and/or related tasks. Below that level, a task will inherit much, most, or all of its Scope from all of its parent-tasks above it within the task-tree, and sometimes also from its sibling-tasks and/or from previous iterations of the same task. Overall, the inputs would typically include

- *From **Context***: Overarching aspirations, constraints, success-criteria, context-elements, and overall scope at the "big-picture" level, and for this task

- *From **Scope***: Constraints on scope from other tasks above in the task-tree, and feedback from other Scope iterations for this task and for sibling tasks at the same layer

- *From **Plan***: Feedback and suggested amendments about policies, complexity, stakeholders, and suchlike

- *From **Action***: Feedback on the usefulness and validity of policies, on complexities and skills-needed, and so on
- *From **Review***: Advice and suggestions about implications for stakeholders and skills, and on "what we could do differently next time"

For **structure**, the default version of the Scope layer has three sub-layers, or sets of sub-tasks:

- *S.1: Scope of change*: Subset of Context-elements applicable to this change *(Zachman "row-1")*
- *S.2: Interactions of change*: Subset of Context-interactions applicable to this change
- *S.3: Requirements of change*: Requirements, governance, policy, and suchlike applicable to this change

---

Note As mentioned above, see worked-examples for the airport, in the sections "Organization and Enterprise" in Step 1 and "From Architecture to Action" in Step 2.

In the **S.1 sub-layer**, we choose the ***scope-boundaries*** for the task. Here, we will

- Verify what the task intends to achieve, and how it will improve effectiveness within its own context and across the enterprise as a whole
- Identify the subset of the Context and its storyworld (from the *C.1* layer) that will be changed and/or affected directly by the task
- Identify the subset of Context elements (from the *C.2* layer) that will be involved in the task
- Identify the subset of Context roles, relationships, and interactions (from the *C.3* layer) that will apply within the scope of the task

These actions identify where the task sits within the broader scheme of things. The process is similar to that in the Context phase, but rather than broadening out our perspective, here we narrow down to the scope and needs of *this* task, and making context-specific adjustments as necessary.

In the first part of the **S.1** work, we ***refine into task-specific form*** the *practical* meaning of the question or concern that originally came in via the Task-Begin gateway, and was then clarified during the Context phase. We bring it out of the abstract, and make it more real. In the other three parts, we essentially apply the same process to what we found in the Context *C.1*, *C.2*, and *C.3* sub-layers, deriving the task-specific subsets for each, and adding quite a lot more detail.

Example   If we think of the airport as one great big continuing-task in its own right, then its Context would be the enterprise of air-travel and air-transport. In Scope, we would then identify the parts of that enterprise that the airport itself will address. The parts of the enterprise that the airport *doesn't* address, and that it trusts to others, would then be classed as "out of scope" – but they still remain part of the overall enterprise picture, and we need to be aware at all times of how they might affect us, and we might affect them.

Note that back in Context, we set the *maximum* range for everything in Scope: vision, values, principles, constraints, boundaries, success-criteria, and so on. We may set task-specific refinements for each of these, but we can't go outside of those limits, nor can we override them. We also start the "translation" from abstract element-categories into implementable real-world equivalents – "What" to "Asset," and so on – ready for the work on requirements in the *S.3* sub-layer. Overall, the process is much the same as for the first part above: revisit what we found in Context, make a task-specific subset, bring it out of the abstract, and make it more real.

In the **S.2 sub-layer**, guided by what we found in *S.1*, we continue the process of "making it real" by finding more detail about ***what the task needs to address***. We'll need to identify and explore:

- The stakeholders for the change, and their respective needs and concerns

- The risks and opportunities implied in or by the scope of the intended change

- The uncertainties in the scope and context of the change, and the skills and experience needed to address those uncertainties

Note that those soft-skills will be absolutely essential to the work we do here, because there can be a lot of "storming" going on. Every stakeholder will be certain that *their* concerns are more important than everyone else's, and hence should be assigned the highest priority. It's also likely that there will be many arguments about risks and opportunities, and about what is or is not uncertain. Finding a good balance that will satisfy everyone can be very hard indeed!

In the **S.3 sub-layer**, we continue the process of making the task **realizable and understandable**, and ready for handing over to the Plan phase. Guided by what we found in *S.1* and *S.2*, we would derive and describe

- The requirements for the change
- The governance and guiding-policies for the task
- Initial change-roadmaps for the task
- Initial communications-strategy for the change

The "storming" may continue for a while during requirements-gathering, but should ease off once we move into the other parts of this sub-layer. (The processes for each of these types of activities should be well-known to most architects, so we won't need to go into them in any depth here.)

The typical **outputs** from Scope to the other change-layers will include

- *To **Context***: Feedback from stakeholders and others about purpose, values, and so on
- *To **Scope***: Feedback on task-specific scope-issues
- *To **Plan***: Requirements, governance, policies, change-roadmaps and communications-strategy, stakeholders for planning, skill-types needed to address uncertainties
- *To **Action***: Action-specific vision, values and success-criteria, stakeholder-types for run-time processes, known-uncertainties for run-time
- *To **Review***: Information about task-specific scope and success-criteria, stakeholders for review ("Who was expected to be involved?")

Once all of the work on Scope is complete and available to the task as a whole, we should be ready to move on to the work of the Plan layer.

Further Notes on Scope

Do beware of **prepackaged assumptions about scope**, such as from vendor-driven architectures or the IT-oriented focus of many current enterprise-architecture frameworks, methods, and tools. Instead, *always* start from context-neutral methods, to identify what the scope actually is, and only then select appropriate context-specific methods and frameworks from that base. (Unless otherwise specified, all of the methods described in this book are designed to work in a context-neutral way.)

If a change is successful in one context and scope, there's often a desire to apply it in other scopes within that overall context – for example, as a "**best-practice**." When doing this, do be aware of any implications for reusing that change in the new scope. The key guideline here is "*adapt, then adopt*," as described in the earlier section "Further Notes on Context."

Identifying the *stakeholders* for a scope can often be hard, yet there are real risks that can arise from failing to find all those who do matter to the task. One useful guideline that can help us to focus on the right people is this phrase: "***A stakeholder is anyone who can wave a sharp-pointed stake in our direction***." If they can cause trouble for anyone in the scope for the task – or help us in that task, for that matter – then they're a stakeholder, and we'll need to engage with them if we're to ensure that everything will work well. (Note too that the term "stakeholder" can apply not just to people, but to any other type of agent, including machines, IT-applications, and other systems.)

Scope may affect **complexity** in a context. For example, complexity tends to increase as scope expands, potentially giving rise to exponential increase in interactions between users and/or other stakeholders, and other emergent-effects. We'll explore various forms of these challenges throughout Steps 2–5. There's also more on this later in this "Foundations" Step, in the section "The Complexities of Change" in Chapter 7.

Scope may also interact with **concerns about scale** in various ways that can affect requirements for the task. For example, increasing the scale of use for an IT-application can be relatively trivial, whereas increasing the use of a skill-based process can be very challenging indeed. As with scope, scale may also be a matter of choice, and care may be needed in making that choice. We'll see more on this later in this Step, in Chapter 7.

CHAPTER 5   FOUNDATIONS: THE LAYERS OF CHANGE

Plan in the Change-Layers

The Plan phase acts as a bridge between Scope and Action, by showing how to realize – make real – those requirements for desired change. This phase, especially at higher levels in the task-tree, will often be deeply iterative, recursive, and fractal.

> **Note** This section is just a general overview of how to do the Plan-type work, because the exact process here will depend on the needs of the task's Context and Scope, the frameworks and standards in use, and the types of content to be described in the various models. There are full worked-examples later, particularly in Step 2, such as in the section "From Architecture to Action."

The **role** of this layer is to identify *how* to do the work of the task, converting requirements into actionable change-processes. ***For each task and sub-task***, this will include

- How we will manage and reduce complexity and resolve run-time uncertainties

- How we will mitigate risks, both during run-time processes and throughout the lifecycle of each entity affected by the task

- How we will identify, source, and manage any resources to be used in the task

- How to train or configure each agent for the task and/or to develop any skills and expertise needed in order to enact the task

- How to set up for Action for the task itself

> **Caution** There's a key point here that's perhaps easy to miss, about the relationship between Plan and Action: What is the Action to which each Plan relates?

Every architect will know that there can be a lot of activity during the planning-process. Yet there's a crucial distinction between the Action where we enact the Plan and the activity we do *during* the Plan process.

In the Change-Layers, the Plan and Action phases are always relative to the initial question or concern for *this* task in the task-tree. By contrast, that activity within the planning-process is taking place within *sub-tasks* of Plan, *lower* in the task-tree, and each called by *Plan-specific* questions or concerns. Each of those sub-tasks has its own Plan, and its own Action: but they're not the same as the Action for which we're developing *this* Plan, for *this* task. Don't mix them up!

The descriptions that follow here focus mostly on planned-change, but the design-sequence for unplanned-change is actually much the same. We'll see more on that later in the book – particularly in Steps 4 and 5, when we work on architectures for tackling small-scale and large-scale disruptions.

For **content** in Plan, we continue the process of translation from Context's abstract elements – "What," "How," "Where," and so on – into real-world entities. We do this by expanding our description of Capability, and adding a new dimension of "segments" to clarify differences in asset-type or entity-type:

- *Physical*: Tangible "thing," such as a printed book or location in a building
- *Virtual*: Intangible "thing," such as data or a web-address
- *Relational*: Connection from person to person
- *Aspirational*: Connection from person to abstract, such as purpose or brand

The segment-types indicate fundamental differences in how we work with the entity: for example, if I give you a physical object, I no longer have it, but if I give you a piece of (virtual) information, I also still have it. An entity can be any mix of these segments, such as a tangible book containing intangible ideas. (We'll see more detail on this in Step 2, in the section "From Architecture to Action," and how to use it with service-design in Step 3, in the section "The Design of Services.") Figure 5-5 provides a visual overview of the content that we reference, develop, and/or update in this part of the work.

CHAPTER 5   FOUNDATIONS: THE LAYERS OF CHANGE

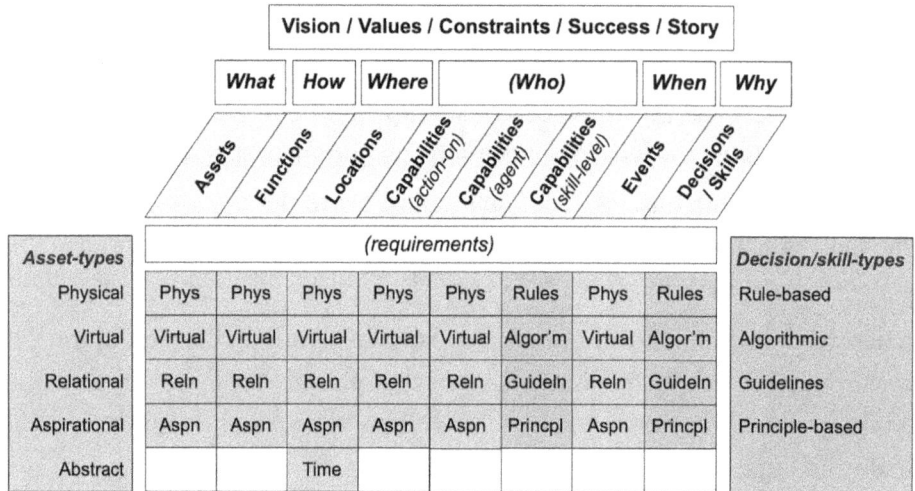

Figure 5-5. Content developed in the Plan layers

What we establish here will apply not only to this task, but to all of its child-tasks further down in the task-tree. We need to be careful about how we set out our Plan at the top levels of a task-tree, because any future changes in that Plan may or will affect every other task below it in its task-tree.

Child-tasks will inherit their Plan not just from their immediate parent, but from all the other levels above it in the task-tree. Often, much of the Plan work for a child-task may have already been done: the only work we'll need to do will be to add task-specific details for this particular child-task.

As with Context and Scope, the work for Plan is essentially the same for both *goal-based* and *continuing* change. There may be differences at the detail-level, but either way it's still just a plan.

Who does the work for the Plan layer will be people like us: this is very familiar territory for architects and designers. A key point we may perhaps need to remember is that this is only *one* phase in the overall work for the task, and since each phase ultimately depends on all of the others, no phase is any more important than any of the rest. A bit of humility and respect for the work of others goes a long way in helping to maintain cohesion across the whole task. Note too that although some aspects of Plan may be done via automated agents, such as in CAD (Computer-Aided Design) or an AI interpretation of a pattern, the final Plan for a task *must* ultimately be authorized by an actual person, again as an expression of *personal* responsibility.

106

Where do we do this work would be in a space that supports the ***analyst*** mode: classically, out in the back-room, or somewhere unnoticeable up in those middle floors of the office-building. In practice, though, almost anywhere will do, as long as it's somewhere that's conducive to thinking and quiet contemplation.

How we do this work is again deeply iterative, recursive, and fractal, with a strong emphasis on *thinking* and the ***analyst*** mode, though the other modes will also play their part. Each iteration tackles a different piece of the Plan puzzle, driving a step-by-step transition from abstract to real-world, though there'll often also be a fair bit of back-and-forth between the sub-layers, and occasional dips down into Action as well. The work needs to be careful, methodical, rigorous, typically guided by context-specific frameworks and standards. Note that to do Plan-work well, we *must* allow it to take whatever time it takes. If we try to take shortcuts, particularly with untested assumptions, the eventual outcomes may well cost far more time than we saved from the shortcut.

The **inputs** for this work depend in part on where the task is within the task-tree. Note that Plan-layers are always relative to the Context and Scope for *this* task or sub-task, but may also refer to and/or be dependent on tasks that are "above" in the nesting, or even elsewhere in the task-tree. At the topmost level, the only inputs will be the question or concern from the Task-Begin phase and as revised in Context and/or Scope; the Context information about this task, the organization, and the broader enterprise; the Scope boundaries and suchlike for the overall task; and maybe some further information about Context, Scope, and/or Plan from previous and/or related tasks. Lower down in the task-tree, a task may inherit much of its Plan from all of its parent-tasks above it within the task-tree, and sometimes also from its sibling-tasks and/or from previous iterations of the same task. Overall, the inputs would typically include

- *From **Context***: Overarching vision, values, and principles; constraints; governance regulations and standards; success-criteria; context-maps

- *From **Scope***: Scope-specific boundaries, governance standards and policies; stakeholder-sets, skill-maps; risk- and opportunity-models; requirements; change-roadmaps; pointers to sources of uncertainty

- *From **Plan***: Feedback from previous Plan iterations, on any plan-specific issues for this type of task

- *From **Action***: Feedback from previous Action iterations of this task, on usefulness and validity of plans, work-instructions, and checklists; ideas and insights about options for improvement; warnings about unexpected uncertainties and variances

- *From **Review***: Feedback from previous Reviews for this type of task, on validity and usefulness of planning-processes *("What was supposed to happen?")*

For **structure**, the default version of the Plan layer has five sub-layers:

- *P.1: Interaction-model*: Transactions and interactions between key players and/or systems – abstract *(Zachman "row-2," "business-model")*

- *P.2: Design-model*: Actions and transactions – implementation-independent *("row-3," "logical-model")*

- *P.3: Development-model*: Actions and transactions – implementation-specific *("row-4," "physical-model")*

- *P.4: Deployment-model*: Actions, transactions, configurations, etc. – operations-specific *("row-5")*

- *P.5: Action-model*: Processes, agent-types, resource-types, checklists, and suchlike to guide action

Note As mentioned earlier, see the worked-examples for the airport in Step 2, in the section "From Architecture to Action," and in Step 3, in the section "Serving the Enterprise."

Most architects and designers will work on only one or two of these sub-layers, but we do all need to be aware of how the overall Plan layer works as a single unified whole. Each sub-layer in Plan works in much the same way with the task's own context- and scope-specific mix of content, but each sub-layer also plays its own part in a series of steps to move from abstract requirements to real, actionable, executable processes, refining and expanding the detail of the task's content at each step of the way to get the task ready for Action.

The sub-layers connect with each other in that the design-output of one sub-layer in the sequence becomes the architecture-input for the next-sub-layer, which then goes through its own iterative, nested Change-Cycles to develop its own more-detailed and more "real" version of the task's content. This process repeats all the way down until we reach the level of an actionable action-model. The most common approach to connecting between the sub-layers is through **documents** – diagrams, models, specifications, and the like – usually as specified by frameworks, standards, and so on. Note, though, that because different groups of people tend to do the work for each sub-layer, the process of connection between the sub-layers will often involve social elements that cannot be covered by documents alone. We'll see more on the role of documents later, particularly in Steps 1 and 2.

Caution We don't do architecture to create documents! Each document is certainly a *connector* in the chain-of-responsibility for the overall work, and perhaps a "*proof-of-work-done*," but it is not the *reason* for the work. That may be a rather important point to explain to managers and the like…

The Plan layer is also where we work to **reduce uncertainty** for the run-time Action, and also mitigate against classic run-time mistakes such as "Just Do It!", "I'll Do It My Way!", and "Ready? Fire! Aim…." We'll only cover the essentials in this section; we'll see more of the detail later in this Step, in Chapter 6, and in the section "The Complexities of Change" in Chapter 7, and also in later Steps, particularly Steps 4 and 5.

Note that in Context and Scope, we in effect set the *maximum* range for all of the **qualitative constraints** in scope for a Plan: vision, values, principles, overarching standards, boundaries, success-criteria, and requirements. We may set plan-specific refinements for each of these limits, but we can't go outside of them, nor can we override them. The only way we can change them is to go back to Context and/or Scope.

This is also where the final **translation from abstract item-categories into their real-world equivalents** must take place: for example, from *abstract* "Asset," to *type* of asset, to actual *real-world* asset. We'll need that translation to be complete by the time we start to work on the Action-Model in the *P.5* sub-layer.

Those issues above apply to all of the Plan sub-layers. We'll now look into the detail of what happens **in each specific Plan sub-layer**.

In the **P.1 sub-layer**, guided by the requirements, roadmaps, governance-rules, and stakeholder-lists from the *Scope* layer, we develop an abstract overview of what we aim to implement in order to support the desired Action and outcomes for the task. We would typically guide conversations with domain-specialists, stakeholders, vendors, users, and others, to identify the types of players in the respective context, the interactions between them, the content for those interactions, and the rules, guidelines, and decisions that would apply in each case. The overall aim here is just to build a broad sense of what the real-world implementation might look like, and of the kinds of issues that might arise, so this phase of the Plan work should be quite quick.

The process is similar to that in the Scope layer, but with more detail, and usually broken into smaller chunks that still need to be kept connected with each other. We would identify each of the main workflows and their key interactions, but only at an abstract level, such as "*Issue boarding-pass to passenger.*"

We would map out the results and outcomes of these explorations as diagrams, models, tables, and other records, and then package these together as an ***Interaction-Model***.

Note In IT-oriented architectures, the Interaction-Model is often referred to as the "Business-Model," but it's best to avoid that term as it has a narrower, more specific meaning in business-architectures.

In the **P.2 sub-layer**, we rework the abstract Interaction-Model from *P.1* into an *implementation-neutral* design. This describes the business-logic for each interaction across the respective scope and context – hence the common term "logical-model" as the outcome for this phase of the work.

This takes us closer toward realization in two ways. The first is by adding more detail: for example, we would split the abstract process "*Issue boarding-pass to passenger*" into distinct steps such as "*verify identity,*" "*verify booking,*" "*create boarding-pass,*" and "*deliver boarding-pass,*" down to any level of detail we might need. The other way is that we specify the general *type* for each of the content-items, in terms of the content-segments – physical "thing," virtual IT-data, people-relationship, or purpose. For example, we might decide that the boarding-pass can be issued by the airline's website, via the airline's mobile-app, via physical-mail or email to the passenger, in-person via a travel-agent, or at the airport via the airline's check-in agent. We decide that the boarding-pass itself may be either digital or physical, and that some of the information must be machine-readable – though we don't yet specify the exact form and format of the pass, nor the code-content or code-type.

We would again map out the results and outcomes of these explorations as diagrams, models, tables, and other records, and then package these together as a **Design-Model**.

In the **P.3 sub-layer**, we rework the *P.2* "logical" Design-Model into an *implementation-specific* form – often described a "physical-model," even though it may be for things that aren't actually physical.

Here, we first expand the detail by doing a full work-breakdown for each task in the Action. For predictable tasks, this will be mapped out step-by-step, or perhaps line-by-line for a code-implementation. Industry-standards and the like will often come into play here. For less-predictable tasks, such as in case-management, we would map out the overall workflows and desired outcomes for each of these, and identify any expected uncertainties and how to resolve them at run-time.

Next, we split the design for implementation into different sections, depending on agent-type:

- For **people** *as agents*: Map out work-flows, task-flows, work-instructions, and ergonomics-issues

- For **machines** *as agents*: Plan to buy and/or build the required systems, and identify their required configuration

- For **IT-systems** *as agents*: Plan to buy and/or build the required software, firmware, and hardware

- For **aspirational-type** *processes, such as in motivation, branding, and commitment*: Identify and plan to develop the required assets, such as logos, design-language, and contract-structure

We'll need to map out the **coordination** and **process-choreography** within and between each of these different elements, between elements with the same type of agent, between different types of agents, and for both predictable and non-predictable elements of each process. We may also need alternative implementations for the *same* process, such as for load-balancing, for business-continuity/disaster-recovery planning, or for regulatory requirements in different jurisdictions.

For each type of content-item in the overall model, we expand the detail even further, using its *P.2* implementation-neutral "*type* of thing" as a guide to help identify the respective implementation-specific "*make and model* of thing," or the equivalent for other agent-types. This may include

- For **people**-*based implementation*: Required skills, skill-levels, certifications and experience, and/or identifiers for training-courses to reach the required competence

- For **machines** *and* **IT-system hardware**: Vendor, product-line, model, and configuration

- For *off-the-shelf* **IT-system software**: Vendor, operating-system, product-identifier, required configuration

This sub-layer of Plan is often intensely iterative and fractal, spinning off its own deeply-nested task-tree to tackle each of the side-issues and requirements that arise. This is particularly true for code-based implementations, where we may well need many separate-but-related child-projects to do the actual design and implementation of the code.

Caution   Beware of the layering here: the Action of the child-task may be the implementation of code, but that's not the same thing as the Action for *this* task! For example, the child-task's Action may *create* new code, so that this task can Plan to *use* that code during its own run-time Action. These are not the same processes, and not the same Actions! It's crucially important to keep track of which *task* we're working on at each moment, and also which *phase* of each task that we're working on, too.

We're likely to build up a lot of **documentation** here: diagrams, models, specifications, tables, and other records. Much of that will be from child-tasks or child-projects, and might not be used in the work for this Plan. However, it may be needed for later reviews and gateway-checks, so it should be stored in the repositories so that it can be available if and when required.

From the documents, we need to derive two sets of **deliverables**.

- The "*deployment-architecture*," to guide the *P.4* deployment-phase, where we'll set up the *work-context* for each type of Action in the task. This will typically include the full specifications for each type of equipment and system to be used in that Action, and guidelines and standards on how to set up each workstation, location, and the like.

- The "*activity-architecture*," to guide the final *P.5* phase, where we'll prepare the setup for the *activities* of each Action itself. This will typically include specifications for Action-requirements, resources, guidance, governance and desired outcomes for actions, and assessments of run-time risks and uncertainties.

Those two deliverables, and the other documentation from those intermediate steps, make up the components of the task's overall **Development-Model**.

In the **P.4 sub-layer**, we expand the "*deployment-architecture*" part of the *P.3* Development-Model into sets of detailed specifications for what needs to go where to support each Action. In principle, this should be relatively simple, because all we would need to do is map out the needs for each type of installation, and everything should be straightforward from there. In practice, though, this process of specification often turns out to be filled with maddeningly variable and context-specific detail, right down to the level of each individual instance of an installation-type – often making this by far **the most complex and work-intensive part** of the entire planning-process.

This also tends to be the point at which **things that were missed earlier in the plan come out of the woodwork**, and force us to go right back to the drawing-board – literally so, at times. And there are a myriad of **regulations and standards** that might come into play here, depending on the particular needs, requirements, and content for each type of installation. Some typical detail-level themes that we might also need to consider here would include

- *Serial-numbers* for machines, physical computers, and other hardware items

- *License-IDs* and *renewal-dates*, for purchased software, leased equipment, and suchlike

- *Configuration-records* for software, firmware, hardware, and any other systems, typically managed in a CMDB (Configuration-Management Database) or equivalent

- *Location-identifiers*, such as mail-address, geographic-coordinates, room-numbers, and IP-addresses

- *Maintenance-records* and *renewal-dates*, particularly for regulated types of equipment

- *Version-identifiers*, *access-controls*, *availability*, and *storage-locations* for manuals, maintenance-certificates, and other context- and/or location-specific documentation

Another theme to watch for here is potential requirements for **redundancy and duplication** in what is nominally a single installation in the Design-Model. For example:

- At the airport, the abstract "*the power-supply*" may actually include connections to the power-grid; solar-panels and batteries for immediate fallback; diesel-generators for medium-term fallback; backup-generators; fuel-storage; and control-system and cabling to manage load-switching.

- In IT-system deployment, an abstract "*the server*" may actually comprise half a dozen production-servers; further production-servers for load-balancing; fallback-servers in case the main servers fail; development-servers; test-servers; and configuration-systems to manage server-updates.

There can be a lot of subtle yet crucially-important complexities here, much of which may be hidden from view unless we make a deliberate effort to search for it.

As in the *P.3* sub-layer, much of the **documentation** we create here will be about what happened during the intermediate steps for this specification-work. This might not be used during the remainder of the work for this Plan, but may well be needed for future reviews and gateway-checks, so again should be stored in the change-repositories.

There are two main **deliverables** here:

- The "*installation-model*": A set of specifications for the installation-engineers that describes the full detail of what will need to be installed and set up at each location, and connected together to form the infrastructure for the overall solution.

- The "*infrastructure-usage model*": A set of descriptions about how to *use* that installed infrastructure during run-time Action, specific to each location or type of location.

We would typically describe that overall package of documentation and deliverables as the **Deployment-Model**. The "*installation-model*" part would typically be handed over to project-management for further development as tasks for a separate installation-team. The "*infrastructure-usage model*" part of that package would continue on to the *P.5* sub-layer, to help guide the development of its *Action-Model*.

In the **P.5 sub-layer**, we combine and expand the "*activity-architecture*" part of the *P.3* Development-Model and the "*infrastructure-usage*" part of the *P.4* Deployment-Model to create one or more *Action-Model* templates on which the action-plans for run-time action will later be built.

An Action-Model should provide the complete guidance for a single type of task at a single type of *locale* – a specific mix of infrastructure, equipment, and context at a specific type of location. Although we would typically be able to adapt the Action-Model to a given locale with simple notes or an addendum-page, some locales may be so unique that we would need a separate locale-specific Action-Model for each of them.

This final part of the Plan phase should be relatively straightforward, though it may involve a *lot* of work in tracking down all the fine-detail, collating it into a suitable structure and order, and deciding the priorities and emphasis to assign to each item. The key content and structure for each Action-Model, as the main type of **deliverable** for this phase, should typically include

- The **Four-Checklists set** (representing the Action's "How," "Why," and "What"), to guide actions and decisions during the Action phase of the task, either via operating-manuals and the like, and/or embedded in software, firmware, and/or hardware. (As we'll see later in this "Foundations" Step, in the section "The Uncertainties of Change" in Chapter 7, these Four-Checklist-types are the *action-checklist*, *preventive-checklist*, *emergency-checklist*, and *chaos-checklist*.)

- Any **expected uncertainties** that will need to be resolved at run-time. (Guidance on these will usually be embedded within the action-checklist and/or preventive-checklist.)

- The **settings** and/or other **constraints** for the Action. (These are also usually embedded within the action-checklist and/or preventive-checklist.)

- The ***resources-plan*** (representing the Action's "Who," "What," and "Where"), to guide selection and availability of agents and assets at each type of locale.

- The ***inputs*** and expected ***outputs*** (representing the "What" that will pass through the Action's interfaces), specifying the assets to be referenced, used, interacted-with, consumed, created, updated, and returned in the task's Action phase.

- The ***sources*** and ***destinations*** for those inputs and outputs.

- The ***start-*** and ***stop-conditions*** (representing the "When" for the task's Action), as the boundary-markers for the "during" phase of the Action.

- The ***setup to capture action-records*** (for the Review phase after the task's Action), specifying which records are to be captured, how they are to be captured, and the expected content for those records.

We use **the same overall structure for all agent-types**: people, machines, and IT-systems. The difference is that people will need to learn how to do the work, whereas for machines and IT it would be embedded within their functionality. For IT-systems, the inputs and outputs will transit through the system's function-interfaces, whereas for a machine the inputs will come through its controls – manual or automated – and the outputs will be the products of the machine itself.

Note also that, for machines and IT-systems, there will often also be people-based Action-tasks for their operation and maintenance, and for training people to do those operations and maintenance tasks. Some of these other tasks may also be locale-specific, each requiring its own variants of the respective Action-Models.

Note As you'll discover in later chapters, we're using a service-oriented approach to architectures here, to help improve consistency and to tackle issues such as alternative implementations for business-continuity and the like. This means that terms such as "input," "output," "interface," "source," or "destination" do not apply solely to IT-based systems, but apply equally to machine-based and people-based services as well. More on that later, anyway.

Once each model is complete, we add it to the **Action-Model** package that would be made available for use in the Action *A.1* sub-layer, as the template for the respective Action-Plan.

At this point, we will have finished all of the work for the Plan layer.

Overall, the typical **outputs** from Plan to the other change-layers will include

- *To* **Context**: Feedback from planners about purpose, values, standards, regulations, and so on

- *To* **Scope**: Feedback and suggested amendments about scope, stakeholders, complexity, policies, requirements, and so on

- *To* **Plan**: Models, documents, feedback on validity, and usefulness of content- and/or context-specific frameworks, methods, and tools

- *To* **Action**: Action-model *(as specified in the P.5 sub-layer above)*

- *To* **Review**: Plan; record-types; project-specific success-criteria ("What was supposed to happen?")

Once all of the work on Plan is complete, documented, and available to the task as a whole, we should be ready to move on to the work of the Action layer.

Further Notes on Plan

Do beware of **prepackaged assumptions about content** in scope for a Plan. The most common source of such assumptions is the frameworks used to guide the planning for the task. For example:

- Vendor-driven architectures tend to constrain the view only to the systems that they provide.

- Industry-specific frameworks will limit the range of content to that used in their own type of context.

- Most enterprise-architecture frameworks specify only particular types of content for assessment.

These constraints on content often lead to a tendency to ignore or exclude anything *not* covered by the framework, making it difficult to connect and integrate everything across the overall context and scope. Instead, *always* start from context-neutral methods, to identify what the content in scope actually is, and then adjust and adapt for the context-specific nature of the methods and frameworks that have been selected for the work. (Unless otherwise specified, all of the methods and tools described in this book are designed to work in a context- and content-neutral way.)

As mentioned above, the Plan may be affected by a wide variety of **concerns about complexity**. We'll see more on this later in this Step, in the section "The Complexities of Change" in Chapter 7.

The Plan may also be affected by **concerns about scale**. For example, as mentioned in Scope, increasing the scale of use for an IT-application can be relatively trivial, whereas increasing the use of a skill-based process can be very challenging indeed. Scale may also be a matter of choice, but care will be needed in making that choice. We'll see more on this later in this Step, in the section "The Scale of Change" in Chapter 7.

Action in the Change-Layers

The Action phase connects between the intent of the Plan and the assessment of outcomes in the subsequent Review, by enacting the desired real-world changes specified in the plan.

Note This section is just an overview of how to guide action in general. There'll be many worked-examples of Action later in the book, starting in Step 1 with the process to identify the context for the airport as a whole, particularly in the section "*Enterprise As Context*."

The **role** of the Action layer is to do the work to deliver the desired outcomes for the task. This will include

- If required, derive an instance-specific action-plan from the provided action-model

- Enact the respective action-plan, using skills as required, and adapting as necessary in response to real-world variances

- Monitor and govern the work in accordance with guidelines from Context and policies from Scope

- Gather action-records and outcome-records as specified in Plan
- Collate and store those records as required for later assessment in Review

For **content** within an Action, we finalize that long process of translation from the initial abstract intent, all the way to *this* moment in *this* real-world context. Some of the content may be inherited from other tasks above or before this one in the task-tree, or from previous iterations of this task, but otherwise the content should be as specified in the Action-Model from the last *P.5* sub-layer of the Plan.

As the Action begins, there may still be some run-time uncertainties to resolve, such as which customer, which workstation, which machine, which settings, and so on. Once that's done, though, the content for the work will be what we have, right here, right now, using *these* assets, *these* interfaces, at *this* location, using *these* capabilities, in response to *these* events, making *these* decisions in line with the rules and guidelines laid out in the Four-Checklists set for this type of Action – particularly the *action-checklist* and *preventive-checklist*. If there are any further unresolved doubts during run-time, we can refer back to the overarching vision, values, and so on, typically via the *chaos-checklist*.

Figure 5-6 provides a conceptual overview of the content that we'll use or change in this part of the work.

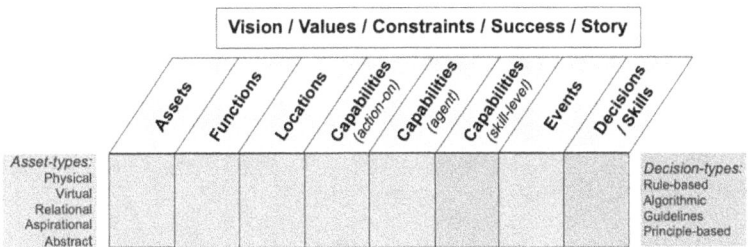

Figure 5-6. *Change-content used in the Action layers*

Remember that Action-layers are always relative to the Context, Scope, and Plan for *this* task or sub-task. As specified in the Plan, the Action may be automated and/or manual, and executed by an appropriate mix of people, machines, and/or IT.

In abstract terms, the work for Action is essentially the same everywhere, both for *goal-based* and *continuing* change, and for *planned-change* and *unplanned-change*. In practice, every action is also different, unique within itself, specific to the exact context in which it takes place.

> **Note** If the purpose of the task is to explore some issue about the initial question or concern, there may not be any apparent Action at this level in the task-tree. Instead, the effective "Action" will have already happened, as the aggregate of the Actions of iterations and child-tasks of its Plan.

Who or What does the work for this layer will be the *agent* as specified in the Action-Model for this type of task. For example, it may be a person, an IT-system, a machine, or a board displaying a brand-logo.

Where the work should be done would again be as specified in the Action-Model. For example, it may be a physical location, a virtual-location within a server, a place of connection between people, the imaginary-space of a brand, or any combination of these.

How the work should be done will again be as specified in the Action-Model – particularly the respective Four-Checklists set – and always with an emphasis on the ***agent*** **mode**, with a clear focus on the work while also, in the background, maintaining *situational-awareness* and *context-awareness*, a constant sensing of the connection between the work and the big-picture. The details will always depend on the nature and purpose of the task, as identified in the respective Context, Scope, and Plan: for example, the task may be unique, or one instance of a myriad of nominally-identical tasks; it may include any number of steps or stages; it may demand strict adherence to the plan, with no allowance for variation; it may instead be iterative, experimental, exploratory.

The **inputs for this work** will depend in part on where the task is within the task-tree. In general, though, it will include

- *From **Context***: Overall guiding-principles, as embedded in the Action-Model's *chaos-checklist*

- *From **Scope***: Stakeholders for run-time context, probable skills required, and guidance on any "unknown-knowns" and "known-unknowns," as embedded in the Action-Model's *preventive-checklist* and *emergency-checklist*

- *From **Plan***: Work-instructions and record-types, sources for materials and assets, start- and end-events, all as embedded in the Action-Model's *action-checklist*

- *From **Action***: Feedback on current issues when enacting this type of task

- *From **Review***: Near-real-time feedback on potential issues when enacting this type of task

For **structure**, the default version of the Action layer has two sub-layers:

- *A.1: Action-plan*: Action-specific processes, people, systems, units, resources, etc.

- *A.2: Action-record*: The outcomes of the work itself, and records of actions, transactions, and variances from the action-plan, as enacted

---

Note In essence, everything in this book describes a worked-example for some form of Action, and/or the outcomes from that Action.

In the **A.1 sub-layer**, the work begins when we receive the start-event signal for the Action. Here, we do the setup for the activity, using the Action-Model created in the *P.5* sub-layer as a template to create an ***Action-Plan*** for the specific content and context for *this specific instance* of the Action:

- Ensure that the Four-Checklists for this type of Action are available to the agent, in whatever form required

- Using the *action-checklist* as a guide, ensure that all resources needed for the work are available

- Using the *preventive-checklist* as a guide, resolve any pre-run-time "unknown-knowns" uncertainties

Before starting, we also need to confirm that the agent has the required skills and experience to do the work. If not – such as in an emergency, or in a "safe-fail" learning-environment – then we need to record that risk in an exception-record for the later Review. We must choose between two options:

- Reject the risk, stop the Action, and move directly to Review

- Accept the now-documented risk, and continue on into the main work for the Action

Once this setup is complete, we should be ready to do the value-creation work of the Action itself.

In the **A.2 sub-layer**, working from the setup created during the *A.1* sub-layer, we will

- Do the work of the action, as guided and governed by the respective Four-Checklists set
- Make the specified changes to the Action-specific content and context, to achieve the desired outcomes
- Address any variances or exceptions that may arise during the activity
- Capture the required information, together with any ideas and insights that may arise during the process

The overall Action will finish when the specified end-event occurs or specified end-conditions are achieved.

The typical **outputs** from Action to the other change-layers will include

- *To* **Context**: Feedback from agents about usefulness and validity of purpose, vision, values, guidelines, standards, regulations, and so on, in relation to this type of task
- *To* **Scope**: Feedback on usefulness and validity of scope-boundaries and policies, and on complexities and skills-needed, in relation to this type of task
- *To* **Plan**: Feedback on usefulness and validity of plan, work-instructions, and advice on unexpected uncertainties and variances, in relation to this type of task
- *To* **Action**: Near-real-time feedback on issues experienced while enacting this task
- *To* **Review**: Action-records, outcome-records, and notices on any exceptions or variances from plan while enacting this task (representing "*what actually happened*")

Once all of the work on the action is complete and documented as above, we should be ready to move on to the work of the Review layer.

Review in the Change-Layers

The Review phase is the last part of the Change-Layers sequence, reconnecting this task back to the rest of the current task-tree.

Note This section is just an overview of how to assess the outcomes of the work, to support continuous-improvement. There'll be several worked-examples later in the book, such as in Step 1, in the section "Enterprise As Context," assessing the outcomes of the process to identify the airport's context.

The **role** of this layer is to focus on *effectiveness*, and on what we can learn from this task to support continual-improvement of effectiveness across the organization and the enterprise as a whole. We explore three distinct themes:

- *Identify **benefits-realized***: Assess what was actually achieved by the task, in terms of its own effectiveness and in support of other tasks

- *Identify **lessons-learned***: Assess what we can learn from what happened, to do better in the future, either in this type of task, or elsewhere

- *Identify **actions for change***: Assess what changes might we make, to improve processes, systems, competence, and skills

The **content** for the Review will be the records and other *assets* from the Action, to assess against the intent from the Context, and the requirements and other *decisions* from Scope and Plan. Relative to each task and sub-task to be assessed, the Review must include

- *All **intent-types** in play*: From *Context*, *Scope*, and *Plan*, including vision, values, constraints, success-criteria, and story

- *All **asset-types** in play*: Physical, virtual, relational, and/or aspirational

- *All **decision-types** in play*: Rule-based, algorithmic, guideline-based, and/or principle-based

The review-process should typically lead to further decisions, linked to any information that may be needed to support those decisions.

Figure 5-7 provides a visual summary of the types of content that we'll reference, review, develop, and/or update in this part of the work.

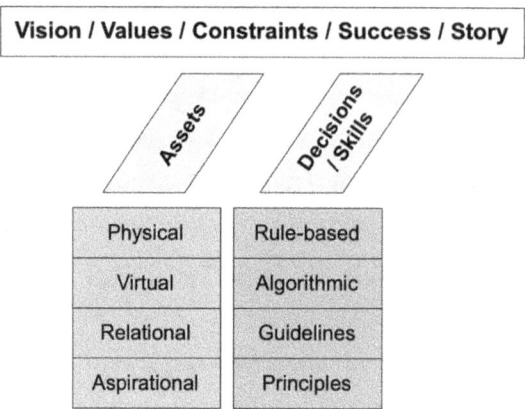

Figure 5-7. Change-content for the Review layer

Each Review is relative to the Action, Plan, Scope, and Context for *this* task or subtask, but may reference or aggregate information from other tasks that are "above" or "below" in the nesting, or elsewhere in other branches of the task-tree.

Who does the work for this layer should be – or at least include in some way – every agent that played a part in the Action, relative to the respective task or tasks in the task-tree.

Analysts and others may also do broader-scope reviews at higher levels in the task-tree. If so, such reviews must take into account not just the information from the lower-level, but *all* asset-types in play within each task's context: physical "things," ideas and information, relationships, and purpose.

Warning   Although some types of review, such as for machine-learning, may be automated in part, any decisions from a Review *must* always be subject to oversight by actual people, again as an expression of *personal* responsibility.

In particular, *never* allow anyone – including ourselves – to use or attempt to use automation as a means to evade responsibility for Review decisions and their impact on others and on the wider world. Not A Good Idea…

Where do we do this work should ideally be at the place where the work was done, immediately after the Action is complete. This is because the memories of the action will still be fresh, and the work-context itself may provide further clues to guide the review. If the review can't be done there and then – for example, if the place is too noisy or too dangerous to do the review there – then it should be done anywhere that is suitable and safe, and as soon after the action as possible.

How we do this work will always use a strong emphasis on the ***assessor* mode**. Although there are many ways to do this, the method we recommend is the ***after-action review*** shown below, based on the classic US Army After-Action Review. This is particularly useful for any task in which skills and experience will play an important part in the work, and where the task itself may provide opportunities for learning and skills-development.

The process is often iterative and recursive, wandering back and forth between the three themes: *benefits-realized*, *lessons-learned*, and *actions for change*. It's also important to allow the process to take whatever time it needs, though it will usually be fast out in the field – often not more than a few minutes at most – and more in-depth back home in the back-office.

The **inputs** for this work depend in part on where the task is within the task-tree, and also whether it is providing an aggregate-Review for other sub-tasks further down in the task-tree. (The latter is a kind of reverse-inheritance, much as with the earlier phases but the other way round, coming *upward* in the task-tree rather than downward from above.) Overall, the inputs would typically include

- *From **Task-Begin***: Initial question or concern for this task and, if required, the trail of provenance and derivation for this task, within the overall task-tree

- *From **Context***: Overall success-criteria ("*What was the expected purpose and outcome?*"), and governance-constraints

- *From **Scope***: Scope-boundaries, relevant requirements, and stakeholders within context ("*Who was [expected to be] involved?*"), and success-criteria for those stakeholders

- *From **Plan***: Action-Model, including action-guidance and action-priorities (in Four-Checklists set), resource-requirements, record-types, and task- and project-specific success-criteria ("*What was supposed to happen?*")

- *From **Action***: Action-plan as derived from the Action-Model, action-records, outcome-records, and exceptions or variances from the plan (*"What actually happened?"*)
- *From **Review***: Feedback about potential issues identified in reviews of previous instances of this type of task

For **structure**, the default version of the Review layer has a single sub-layer:

- *R.1: Action-review*: Interpretation of action-records in context of this change

---

Note As mentioned above, see the worked-examples throughout the text, such as the Review for the airport's context of air-travel and air-transport as described in the section "*Enterprise As Context*" in Step 1.

In the **R.1 layer**, there are three themes that we want to explore in the review:

- *Identify **benefits-realized***: What did we achieve, relative to the task's desired outcomes?
- *Identify **lessons-learned***: What can we learn from what happened, to do better in the future?
- *Identify **actions for change***: What changes might we make, to improve processes, systems, and skills?

To achieve this, we do an **after-action review** that has five main steps, governed overall by ***two rules***:

- *"Pin your stripes at the door"*: Everyone had their own responsibilities; no-one is more important than anyone else.
- *"No blame"*: If blame is allowed to enter the picture, then honesty and openness will evaporate, and no-one will be able to learn anything.

Given those rules, the ***five steps*** are as follows:

- *"What was supposed to happen?"*: To answer this question, there needs to have been some kind of Plan to guide that Action (such as embedded in the Action-Model).

- *"What actually happened?"*: To answer this question, we need to have records of the information, ideas, and insights captured during the Action, and any relevant artifacts from the Action.

- *"What were the sources of difference between plan and action?"*: To answer this question, we need to do critical assessment of the information about exceptions and variances during the Action.

- *"What can I change, to do better next time?"*: To answer this question, each member of the team uses the information, ideas, and insights arising from the overall task to explore options and actions for *personal* improvement.

- *"What can we change, to do better next time?"*: To answer this question, the team as a whole uses the information, ideas, and insights arising from the overall task to explore options and actions for *collective* improvement, and for improvement of processes, systems, resources, and so on.

This review applies to each *agent* in the respective Action, in terms of the Capability: Agent column in the Change-Content model shown earlier. If the agent is an IT-application, it probably won't be able to do its own review, and if it's a machine, it certainly won't be able to do so. In those cases, the review would be done by whoever is responsible for that agent, such as the users, developers, and maintainers. The important point is that even in those cases, the after-action review *does* still need to be done in some way, after *every* task.

In assessing **benefits-realized**, we establish the value of doing the task's change-work, not just for the task itself, but also within its broader context. (Note that for enterprise-architects, this is also one of the few direct means via which to demonstrate and prove the business-value of our work!)

In assessing **lessons-learned**, we provide a key part of the "Why" for business-change – but derived "bottom-up" from real-world practice, rather than "top-down" from ideas that may not yet be anchored in reality.

And in assessing **actions for change**, we identify the "How" and "What" for much of the business-change within the organization – particularly as change for systems, and for individual people, in terms of skills, experience, team-work, and more.

> **Caution** There may also be an important governance-issue here. If there is significant difference between intended and actual outcomes – between Plan and Action – then we may face a *go/no-go* decision here: Can the outcomes still be used as is ("*Accept*"), or will we need to start again ("*Reject*")?
>
> The challenge, of course, will be in identifying exactly what will be considered as "*significant difference*" in outcomes. However we might define it, that needs to be included in the Action Model and/or Action Plan, and used in the respective quality-tests at run-time.

The results of the Review would be stored in the respective repositories for architecture and design, change-management, strategy, governance, and more. The typical **outputs** from Review to the other change-layers will include

- *To **Context***: Implications for future review of purpose and Context for this type of task (also, "*What could I do differently next time?*")

- *To **Scope***: Implications for future review of scope-boundaries, policies, stakeholders, and skills for this type of task (also, "*What could we do differently next time?*")

- *To **Plan***: Feedback for future review of the validity and usefulness of the planning-processes for this type of task (about "*What is supposed to happen?*")

- *To **Action***: Near-real-time feedback on potential issues when enacting this type of task (about "*What could happen?*")

- *To **Review***: Action-notes to guide future reviews for this type of Action

- *To **Task-End*** *(or equivalent)*: Recommended task-management action-decision, such as to do another iteration of this task, do another task at this layer, move to the next layer or sub-layer below, or return to the previous layer or sub-layer above

Once the Review is finished, and documented as above, the work of the task is now complete.

What happens next? If this was a nested-task, we would probably return to the parent-task with the outcomes of this piece of work, and continue the work of the parent-task from there. If this was part of a chained sequence of tasks, and not the last task in that sequence, we would usually move to the next task in the chain. In any other case, we would move to the Task-End gateway – or its equivalent, further down in the task-tree – and follow the action-decisions to be made there.

Into Practice

Our purpose in this chapter has been to use the CSPAR Change-Layers pattern to provide you with a consistent means to make sense of the *structure* of projects and tasks. To put this into practice, we'll use the Change-Layers pattern as a **structural-checklist**, to ensure that

- The task is *structurally-complete*, in that all of the required elements for the task are in there somewhere, in the right kinds of places, and in the right kind of order.
- Everything in the task connects with and supports everything else in the task.
- The task will connect cleanly and clearly with the big-picture of change and change-work across the respective organization and enterprise.
- The task will "do the right things right," in line with overall effectiveness.
- The task will be able to deliver its desired outcomes.
- The task will properly support continual improvement both within itself and across the enterprise as a whole.

For this exercise, you'll need to choose a project to work with: either a real project that you're looking at right now for your own organization, or else imagine any significant-sized project for the airport worked-example. From there, either select a large task within that project, or view the whole project as a task in its own right.

Given that task, go through the Change-Layers in the same sequence as in the chapter above, using the text in the respective section to guide each part of the review.

Start with the **Context** for the task:

- Overall, what is the *purpose* for this task? Why is it being done?
- How and why does this task connect to the *big-picture* of the project, and the overall aims of the organization and enterprise?
- Who will *do* the work of this layer overall, and in each of the sub-layers?
- How will they know *what to do*, and *how to do it*, in each part of their role in this work?
- On *identity and purpose* (the *C.1* sub-layer), how will you establish the overall *vision* for the task? How will you describe that vision for others?
- From that vision, how will you derive the respective *values*, guiding-principles, constraints, standards, and success-criteria for the task?
- On *context-elements* (the *C.2* sub-layer), how will you identify the *core content* for the task – the "what, how, where, who, when, and why" elements of the task, such as key players, items, events, and so on?
- On *context-roles* (the *C.3* sub-layer), how will you map out the *key roles, relations, and exchanges* in play across the overall context for this task?

Move on to the **Scope** layer and sub-layers for the task:

- Overall, *who is this task for*? Whose needs will be supported by it, after the change is complete? Who or what will affect it, and/or be affected by it?
- Who will *do* the work of this layer overall, and in each of the sub-layers?
- How will they know *what to do*, and how to do it, in each part of their role in this work?

- On the *scope of change* (the ***S.1*** sub-layer), how will you identify the ***subset of context-elements*** that apply in this specific task? In particular, how will you identify the respective ***stakeholders*** and ***scope-boundaries*** for this task?

- On ***interactions of change*** (the ***S.2*** sub-layer), how will you identify the ***subset of context-interactions*** that apply in this specific task?

- On ***requirements for change*** (the ***S.3*** sub-layer), how will you identify the ***requirements*** and ***policies*** that will apply in this task? What forms of ***governance*** will you use to ensure that those requirements are understood and complied with during planning and action?

Now move on to the **Plan** layer and sub-layers for the task:

- Overall, ***how*** will the work for this task be done? What types of assets and resources will it use? How will you ensure that those assets and resources are used in the most effective way?

- How will you ensure that everything in ***the plan will connect properly*** to the vision, values, constraints, success-criteria, boundaries, and requirements previously identified in the work on the ***Context*** and ***Scope*** for this task?

- Who and/or what will ***do*** the work of this layer overall, and in each of the sub-layers?

- How will they know ***what to do***, and how to do it, in each part of their role in this work?

- How will you ensure that ***each sub-layer*** supports and connects cleanly to the next?

- For the ***interaction-model*** (the ***P.1*** sub-layer), how will you identify and model the ***abstract interactions*** that should occur during the value-delivery actions of the task?

- For the ***design-model*** or "logical-model" (the ***P.2*** sub-layer), how will you translate the abstract interactions into an ***implementation-independent model*** of the activities and interactions that should occur during the value-delivery actions of the task?

- For the ***development-model*** or "physical-model" (the ***P.3*** sub-layer), how would you translate the implementation-independent interactions into ***implementation-specific models*** of the activities and interactions that should occur during the value-delivery actions of the task?

- If the interactions are to be implemented by people, what ***training and skills*** will they need for the respective actions, and how will you ensure that they *do* have the ***required competencies*** before attempting to do those activities?

- If the interactions are to be implemented by physical machines, how will you ***configure and test those machines*** to do the respective actions?

- If the interactions are to be implemented by computer-based automation, how will you ***develop and test the software*** to do the respective actions?

- If the interactions are to be implemented by a mix of people, machines, and computer-based systems, how will you develop and test the ***coordination and choreography*** between those different implementations?

- For the ***deployment-model*** (the ***P.4*** sub-layer), how will you develop, test, and guide the ***installation of the infrastructures*** needed for those respective implementations?

- For the ***action-model*** (the ***P.5*** sub-layer), how will you specify the processes, agent-types, resource-types, instructions, checklists, start- and end-events *for the real-time use* of those respective implementations?

- How will you ensure the ***required availability of resources*** for run-time use?

- How will you identify the ***action-records*** that the Action-agents must, could, or should capture at run-time?

- On ***managing uncertainty***, how will you identify and make sense of any ***uncertainties*** that may arise within the task's scope and context?

- How, in your plan, will you *mitigate and/or manage* those uncertainties? How will you enable them to do such mitigation?

- What *skills and skill-levels* will you need to plan how to mitigate and/or manage those uncertainties?

- What skills and skill-levels will the Action-agents need, to be able to *resolve run-time uncertainties*?

- Via what means – such as a Four-Checklists set – will you plan to *guide the Action-agents* to resolve those run-time uncertainties?

Next, move on to the **Action** layer and sub-layers for the task:

- Overall, *what should or did happen* in the value-delivery actions for the task? What will change, or be changed, when and where, while the work for the task is being done?

- Who and/or what will *do* the work of this layer overall, and in each of the sub-layers?

- How will they know *what to do*, and how to do it, in each part of their role in this work?

- For the *action-plan* (the *A.1* sub-layer), how will your Action-agents translate the Action-Model from the plan into an *action-plan* that supports and guides the required actions within the specific conditions that will apply at run-time?

- For the *action-records* (the *A.2* sub-layer), how will the Action-agents *capture the required records* during the action, including records of any run-time variances from the prescriptions of the Action-Plan? How will the agents register and store these records, and also the outcomes of the action itself?

Move on to the final **Review** layer for the task:

- Overall, how can you *learn* from what was done in the task, to improve effectiveness for this type of task, and across the enterprise as a whole?

- Who will *do* the work for this layer?

- How will they know *what to do*, and how to do it, in each part of their role in this work?

- In the ***action-review*** itself (the ***R.1*** sub-layer), how will you ***interpret the action-records*** from the action?

- How will you identify and verify the ***benefits-realized and value-returned*** from the action?

- How will you identify and assess any ***differences and variances*** between "what was supposed to happen," as per the plan, and "what actually happened" during the action?

- From those assessments, how will you derive any ***lessons-learned*** that could be used to guide future improvements in planning, action, and overall effectiveness?

- From those assessments and lessons-learned, how will you derive any recommended ***actions for change***, particularly for skills-development for individuals, change-teams, and larger groups?

- If differences and variances between plan and action trigger a requirement for a ***go/no-go decision***, how will such a decision be made, and who will make that decision?

And finally, looking back at **the task or project as a whole**:

- How might you improve on your current structure, guidance, and connection of tasks, in the sense described here in this exercise?

- What else might you do to improve the effectiveness of change-work in your organization?

Note any ideas and insights that arise for you during this exercise. Add these to your notebook as you go along, for review at the end of the book.

Summary

In this chapter, we did an exploration of how to use the CSPAR change-pattern as a systematic sequence of Change-Layers, to guide the development, actions, and review, from start to finish, of an entire change-project.

In the next chapter, we'll explore how to apply the same CSPAR change-pattern as a Change-Cycle to guide, step-by-step, the process and progress of a single chunk of change-work.

CHAPTER 6

Foundations: The Cycles of Change

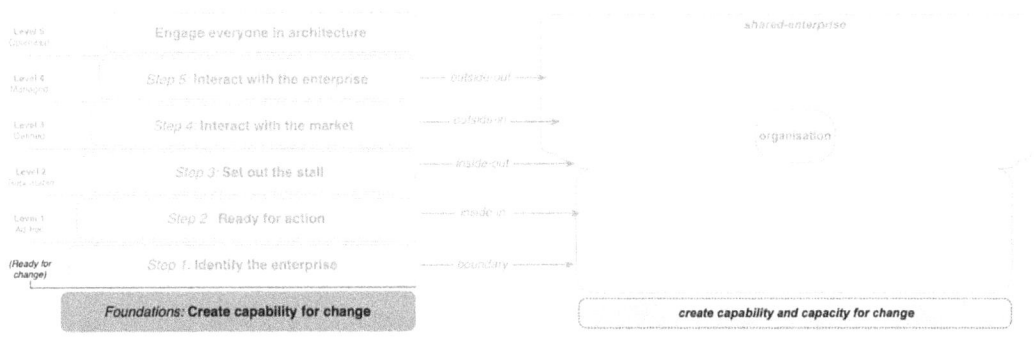

Every task, every chunk of change-work, will start from some kind of question or concern. At the airport, for example, the question may be a significant challenge ("How do we adapt our screening-processes to match these new security-regulations?") or something at a much smaller scale ("How do I ensure that this passenger is meant to be on this flight?"). Yet the underlying principle is always the same: by the end of each task and sub-task, we want our world to be different in some way from when we started.

In the previous chapter, we explored how to do this for larger project-like tasks with the Change-Layers pattern, all the way up to major transformations at the whole-of-organization level and beyond. Here, we'll do the same for tasks at a smaller scale, using the Change-Cycle pattern.

Remember, though, that as described back in Chapter 4, **each task traverses through the same fractal CSPAR pattern**. Although the Change-Layers and Change-Cycle may look different, and have different emphases, the CSPAR labels that we use for the layers and the phases indicate that it's the *same* pattern underlying both of them. In fact, the only real difference, as shown in Figure 6-1, is one of perspective: in the

CHAPTER 6   FOUNDATIONS: THE CYCLES OF CHANGE

Change-Layers we were looking "vertically" at a project-like task *as a whole*, whereas in the Change-Cycle we'll look "horizontally" at only *one* specific chunk of work at a time, usually as a sub-task within that overall task.

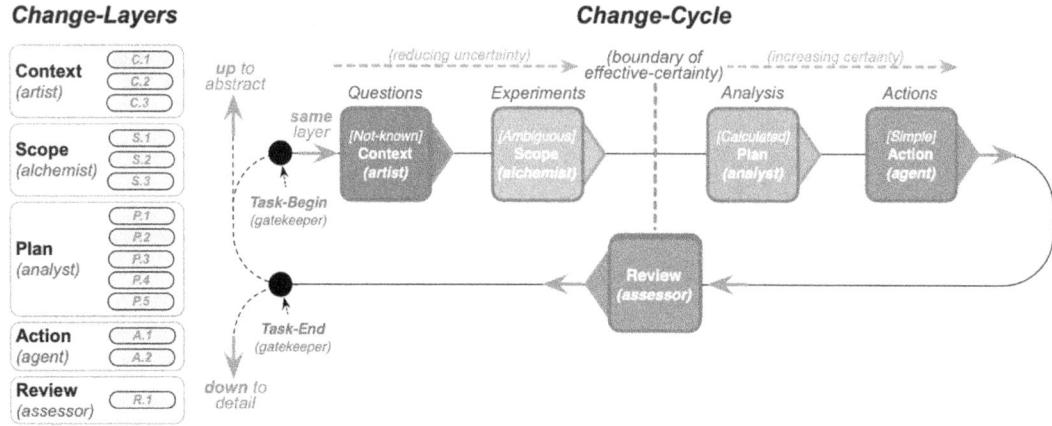

Figure 6-1. Change-Layers ("vertical") and Change-Cycle ("horizontal")

It's fractal: always the same, yet always different, at every scope and scale, for every type of content or context, everywhere.

To help make sense of this, and to avoid some specific traps that can cause real problems further down the line, we'll need to do a brief detour to look at working with fractals in change-work.

Thinking in Fractals

The term "**fractal**" can mean different things in different contexts. In mathematics, for example, it's the outcome of an algorithm that repeats the same variations of a pattern at every scale. For our purposes, though, as we noted back in Chapter 2, it's best to define "fractal" as ***a type of pattern that is "self-similar" for each instance of the pattern, in every context and at every scale*** – a pattern with an *identifiable and repeatable mix of* "same" and "different."

In that sense, there's a ***spectrum of fractality***. If we map this out in SCAN terms, as the horizontal-axis, then at the left-hand edge there'll be "all-sameness," such as in simple-recursion – repetition of the exact same pattern at multiple scales – while far over on the far right-side it'd be "all-different," near-absolute uniqueness. Between those two extremes, there'll be ***useful-fractality***, from the kind of basic parameter-driven recursion that's often used in software-designs, to contexts where the parameters *themselves* can be different but there's still *enough* "sameness" to keep things connected together, at a conceptual level at least.

We said earlier that in all types of change-work, and especially in architectures, ***fractality can be very much our friend***. This is because that ***fractality helps to make complexity more manageable***:

- It ***provides "just enough simplicity"*** – simple but not simplistic – to enable us to keep track of what's going on throughout all of the real-world complexity.

- Fractals are ***self-similar at every scale*** – a mix of "same and different" in which the "sameness" parts are the same not just at a single scale, but at *every* scale.

- The **"sameness" part** of a fractal pattern ***provides "just enough sameness"*** to enable "sort-of-like-for-like" comparisons, across any scale in a given context, and often across different contexts.

- The **"difference" part** of a fractal pattern is ***always specific to that exact context***.

For change-work, the trick with fractality is to ***find as much "sameness" as possible*** while still ***respecting the "difference" part***. The more context-neutral sameness that we can find, the easier it will be to work with; yet we do still need to keep track of all the finer context-specific detail, otherwise it risks being literally unrealistic. In other words, it's a classic "Goldilocks" challenge: not too little, not too much, but just the right amount.

How to Make Fractality Our Friend

As we saw back in Chapter 4, a project-planning map such as a **Gantt-chart** provides an everyday business-example of a fractal pattern.

The **"sameness"** part of that pattern is that every task and sub-task will be described in the same way, using the same metadata-parameters in each case: label, start-date, end-date, resource-requirements, and so on. There'll also be metadata to indicate connections between tasks, such as interdependencies and parent-child relationships. Those relationships give rise to the task-tree map for the project – its "work-breakdown structure."

However, there's also the **"*difference*"** part of any fractal pattern. In this project-planning example, that would be the set of context-specific activities for the respective task or sub-task. This usually starts out as just an empty box containing nothing more than vague intentions and "Magic Happens Here." That's why we use CSPAR to extend the "sameness" part of that fractal pattern, to give some consistent structure *inside* the box as well as outside of it. There'll always be *some* difference between each instance of the pattern, though – otherwise it would be merely repetitive, rather than fully fractal.

In change-work, the simplest way to make fractality our friend is to map out the work *in real-time* in terms of the Change-Cycle, as shown in Figure 6-1. It's the *same* work-pattern everywhere, seen from multiple same-and-different perspectives, including

- *CSPAR **activity focus***: Context, Scope, Plan, Action, Review
- *SCAN **sensemaking focus***: Not-known, Ambiguous, Calculated, Simple, then after-action review
- *CALC **mindset focus***: Artist, Alchemist, Analyst, Agent, Assessor

Metaphorically, we dance between these different perspectives within each element of change-work, **switching back and forth between context-neutral sameness and context-specific difference** at every step of the way. As also shown in Figure 6-1, we'll see this play out in three main types of back-and-forth conversations within the Change-Cycle itself:

- Between the **Artist** *sensing the world* and the **Alchemist** *framing the world*, to resolve Gooch's Paradox that "things not only to have to be seen to be believed, but also have to be believed to be seen"
- Between the **Alchemist** *framing the world* and the **Analyst** *framing the action*, to separate reducible-complexity from non-reducible complexity, and to identify the types of levels of skills needed to resolve any non-reducible complexity
- Between the **Analyst** *framing the action* and the **Agent** *doing the action*, to act on and change the world in an intentional way, to decide when to stop the action, and to confirm that plan, action, and outcomes do all align

Also, during the action, there can be some other brief forays from **Agent**-mode into **Artist**-mode to resolve any context-specific differences that cannot be predicted in advance – the difference between the *planned versus unplanned* aspects of change, the *type* of change versus the exact change *itself*. For example, in a typical customer-service context, we should know what we would be able to sell, and how to sell it, but we can't know in advance who the next customer will be, nor what their exact requirements would be.

Note For more detail on how this dance between "planned" and "unplanned" plays out in real-world practice in customer-services and the like, see the worked-examples in the section "The Complexities of Change" in Chapter 7.

In the last part of the fractal CSPAR change-pattern, such as in the Review phase of the Change-Cycle as also shown in Figure 6-1, there's yet another kind of perspective-switching that's used within the **Assessor**-mode to guide the after-action review. There, we would bounce back and forth between *looking at the past*, at what *has* happened, versus *looking toward the future*, at what we want to do about what has happened. On the basis of that internal conversation, we would either loop back to restart the same task with its new status and context, or move on to a new task based on the same CSPAR pattern.

Alongside CSPAR, there are a wide variety of other types of fractal patterns that we can use in change-work, as components, checklists, templates, methods, frameworks, and suchlike. We've come across a few of these already: for example, the Organization-Context Map and the Maturity-Model in Chapter 1, and the SCAN complexity-map, CALc decision-modes, and Architect's Mantra in Chapter 3. There'll be others coming up in later chapters, such as the Enterprise-Context map, the Service-Canvas and Service-Cycle, the Service-Content map, the SCORE strategic-options map, and so on.

There's also the fractality about *"meta-,"* as used in metamodels, metamethods, metaframeworks, and more. The "meta-" prefix here indicates that this thing can be used as a template for the same kind of thing at the next detail-level down:

- A *metamodel* provides a template for a detail-level model.

- A *metamethod* provides a context-neutral template for a context-specific method.

- A *metaframework* provides a context-neutral template for a context-specific framework.

It's also fractal in that a *metametamodel* is a template for a metamodel, a *metametametamodel* is a template for a metametamodel, and so on. We'll often come across that in various aspects of the IT-oriented world: one well-known example is the MOF (Meta-Object Facility) standard that provides the metametamodel template for all of the OMG (Object Management Group) modeling-standards such as UML (Unified Modeling Language), BPMN (Business Process Management Notation), and more. For architects, there's a terrible pun here about "I never met a 'meta-' that I didn't like," but there's no doubt that this kind of fractality can help us a lot as well.

We can also use the same type of "*same and different*" mapping to connect different fractal-patterns and create new ones, in a process called **context-space mapping**. We use the "*sameness*" aspect between patterns to provide connection: one example we'll see later is that we use the "before/during/after" structure of SCAN's vertical-axis to connect with the "before/during/after" phases of the Service-Cycle and the matching child-services in the Service-Canvas. Once we've connected two or more fractal-patterns together, we can use the *differences* between those patterns' own "samenesses" to create a deliberate *mismatch* between them, which then provides a new frame through which new and often unexpected insights about that context can arise.

Note There'll be more on context-space mapping in various places throughout this book, but it's covered in more depth in another of Tom's books, *Everyday Enterprise Architecture* – see Appendix B for the publication-details.

Whatever we do in change-work, the habit of thinking in fractals will make everything so much simpler, and help to bring out hidden patterns and hidden information. In that sense at least, fractality is very much our friend.

How Not to *Lose* Fractality As a Friend

As we've seen from the above notes, the "same and different" mapping in fractality can be enormously useful in all types of change-work, including enterprise-architecture. Yet **to use fractality well depends on a particular way of looking at "same and different"** – and the catch is that it's one that *doesn't* always mix well with some of the common assumptions in the classic analytical approaches to change-work. It's really important to keep track of which perspective we're using at each point, and take care to *not* mix them up. The risk is that if we allow ourselves to get lost within all of this switching between perspectives, we not only lose all of the advantages of a fractal approach, but things can get very confusing, very quickly,

For example, classic **Gantt-style project-mapping** can itself be **a direct cause of that type of confusion**. In terms of the CALc modes, we might think of the **analyst** and **agent** modes as working "inside the box," while the **artist** mode always works "outside the box," and the **alchemist** mode creates the framing for "the box" itself. But in Gantt-style task-mapping for project-management, the whole thing is actually back-to-front or inside-out: the analytic metadata is all on the *outside* of the task-box, while all of the context-specific "Magic Happens" bit has to take place *inside* the task-box.

And the catch there is that, as we've seen in the previous section, much if not most of that "Magic Happens" stuff is *not* analytic at all. Yet that task-mapping part of the analysis is only the *start* of the work, not the end of it. The real work happens *inside* the task-box that is actually *outside* of the box framed by the task-mapping metadata.

Warning This back-to-front aspect of Gantt-charts can lead to real confusion if you're not careful about it. For example, one of the huge booby-traps hidden within **classic project-management** is that it **can create the delusion that the act of mapping out the work-breakdown structure** of tasks and sub-tasks and sub-sub-tasks **is the only real work that needs to be done**, and that the rest of what happens inside the task-box is "mere detail." As one of our colleagues put it, it treats the common bad habit of playing "Somebody Else's Problem" not as a mistake but as a *methodology* – and managers then wonder why it doesn't work out as well as expected? Not A Good Idea…

Another way that fractals get misunderstood is by **applying an arbitrary framing such as categories** to particular instances or contexts of use, even though a fractal is always the *same* underlying pattern in each case. For example, we might decide that it's easiest to categorize the Change-Layers as change-decomposition, versus the Change-Cycle as change-design. In practice, that's actually a misframing trap, much like that assertion that "architecture" only happens at the start of the Plan-layers, and that everything else after that is "design."

Again, *it's not an "either/or," but a "both/and"* about *"same and different,"* both at the same time. In that example above about "decomposition versus design," it's true that the Change-Layers do represent a kind of coarse decomposition of change-tasks – *but the same is true for the phases of the Change-Cycle*. It's true that purpose of the Change-Cycle is to design some way to respond to a question, and use that design to reach toward the required answer or outcome – *but the same is true whenever there's a move "downward" through the Change-Layers*. Both assertions are true for both Change-Layers and Change-Cycle, because it's the *same* fractal CSPAR pattern that's behind both of them.

If we over-focus on the difference, we risk ending up with mistakes such as arbitrary categories; but if we over-focus on the sameness, we risk losing track of the context-specific detail that allows it to work with the real-world. It's a Goldilocks-like balance: always same, always different, always just the right balance of each.

Another variant of that categories-error is a **mistaken assumption** that **the Change-Cycle describes only the "Action" part of the Change-Layers**, and that its content and unknowns are simpler than elsewhere in the Change-Layers. Again, although the Change-Layers and Change-Cycle do provide us with somewhat different views into the sequence of work within a task or sub-task, it's the *same* fractal CSPAR pattern underlying both of those views.

The CSPAR pattern gives us a structured way to describe the action-learning loop: Sense, Make-sense, Decide, Act. In that sense, it's not just about making sense of Action, but about a continual loop of making sense of *anything*, then taking appropriate action based on that sensemaking. Given that, we'll typically use a Change-Layers view at a larger whole-of-task scale, and a Change-Cycle view for a sub-task that's triggered by a **question** that has arisen in *any* part of *any* of the CSPAR Change-Layers. But do remember that it's the *same* pattern in both cases, covering the *same* overall range of enquiries and activities. At the end of the respective task or sub-task, regardless of whether we've used a Change-Layers or Change-Cycle view of the activity, we'll return the outcome of that enquiry to the caller as the respective "answer" to that question.

Finally, yet another related problem is **the "all-or-nothing" mistake**: the assumption that a framework or suchlike can be either context-neutral *or* context-specific, but cannot be a mix of both. This mistake is what has led to the current situation in enterprise-architecture, where we have

- A handful of abstract frameworks that can sort-of cover everywhere, but cannot reach down to the real-world

- A morass of industry-specific frameworks that address the real-world detail, but can't connect with each other

- A myriad of mini-frameworks for small specific issues such as event-logging and issue-tracking that have to be addressed in isolation even though they recur in many different contexts

The "same-*and*-different" approach used in fractal-type frameworks gives us the only workable way out of that mess:

- There's a "sameness" part in *every* framework that is context-neutral, enabling us to identify what each context *is*, and to connect everything together.

- There's a "difference" part to each framework that addresses the context-specific needs for that particular industry or context.

- A framework may include fractal, context-neutral "plug-ins" to address needs that are common across some but not all types of context.

Again, the usual approach to frameworks for enterprise-architecture and the like does sort-of work well as long as we only need to work with a *single* type of concern, industry, technology, or domain. However, it falls apart in a heap of random fragmentation as soon as we try to connect *across* concerns, industries, technologies, and/or domains, making a literal "architecture of the enterprise" all but impossible. In short, we *cannot* do whole-enterprise architectures and similar whole-of-context change-work without using a fractal-based approach. And we cannot do that without being able to "think in fractals," and *not* fall into the "all-or-nothing" traps which so easily arise from classic analytics-only methods.

Anyway, we'll see more about fractality later; for now, let's get back to working with the CSPAR pattern and the Change-Cycle.

Understanding the Change-Cycle

The **role** of the Change-Cycle pattern is to help ensure that, however small it might be, ***every task is effective and "on-purpose"*** toward its intended aims.

The core **structure** of the work is that, as shown earlier in Figure 6-1, ***the Change-Cycle follows the same overall CSPAR pattern as in the Change-Layers***. Each task goes through the *same* CSPAR pattern as before, this time as a fractal iteration of the Change-Cycle.

Each Change-Cycle *starts with a new question or concern*. Or to put it the other way round, every time we come across a new question or concern, we'll probably need to start a new Change-Cycle to address it.

Caution Even if we're not answering a new question, it's probable we're already in the process of answering another one – or maybe several of them, all at once. One of the challenges of change-work is keeping track of *which* question we're actually answering at each moment: don't mix them up!

The new Change-Cycle iteration is either chained from or nested within the task or sub-task in which the question arose. In turn, the iteration may chain and nest its own sub-tasks as needed – often giving rise to a fractal "cloud" of nested Change-Cycles – and also link to other tasks if required.

Note also that, in general, *all of the phases of a single Change-Cycle iteration will take place within a single layer* or *sub-layer* in the Change-Layers. By default, this will be the same layer as in the parent-task, though it may be above or below that layer as required. For example:

- The question *"Which stakeholders are likely to be affected by this change?"* would typically be tackled by a change-cycle in the *S.1* "Scope of change" change-layer.

- The question *"How should I model those stakeholders in our architecture modeling-language?"* would typically be tackled by a change-cycle in the *P.1* "Interaction-model" ("business-model") or *P.2* "Design model" ("logical-model") change-layers.

The iteration's sub-tasks, if any, must likewise each run at a single layer, but that layer may be "below" or "above" that of its parent task if required.

At higher levels in the task-tree, **Task-Begin** and **Task-End** will usually be separate and distinct gateways, and run by change-management rather than the change-team itself. Lower down in the task-tree, though, the Task-Begin activities will usually be subsumed into the Context phase, and Task-End into the Review phase.

The task-*content* to be worked on or with during a Change-Cycle will depend on the Change-Layer in which it takes place. In essence, its content will represent some intermediate stage or state of all the transformations that should be made between the inputs and the outputs for that overall Change-Layer. For example:

- Work on a *context-overview model* would typically be done in a change-cycle in the *C.3* "Context-roles" change-layer.

- Work on mapping out the *detail for a code-module* would typically be done in a change-cycle in the *P.3* "Development-model" change-layer.

- Content for a change-cycle in the task's *"value-delivery" activity* in the *A.2* "Action-record" change-layer would be as specified in the *P.5* "Action-Model" from the Plan layers, and amended or adapted to this *specific* context in the *A.1* "Action-plan" layer.

Who or what does the work in a Change-Cycle will depend on the task, the current Change-Layer, and the needs of the current context. Within the Change-Layers, particularly with larger tasks, each layer may be done by different groups of people. By contrast, and particularly in the lower levels of a task-tree, **the entire work of a Change-Cycle will usually be done by the same group of change-agents** associated with that respective layer or sub-layer. For example:

- *Strategists* in a C.2 "Context-elements" layer

- *Process-designers* in a P.2 "Design-model" layer

- *Front-line staff* or an *IT-application* in an A.2 "Action-records" layer

Where this work is to be done will again depend on the task, the current Change-Layer, and the needs of the current context. It could also take place in at be ***any type of location*** – any mix of physical, virtual, relational, and/or aspirational – again dependent on the needs of the task and context.

How we do the work of any given Change-Cycle **will always be a mix of context-neutral and context-specific**. We address the *context-specific needs* of the task by using context-specific frameworks, tools, and methods, in accordance with the respective context-specific standards and requirements. The Change-Cycle, and the other context-neutral tools and methods described later in this book, then provide a *context-neutral frame* in which to place all of those different and disparate context-specific elements, and connect them together into a unified whole. We "plug in" that context-specific content via a variant of the CSPAR pattern, as we saw earlier in Chapter 4.

So far, this is much the same as in the Change-Layers. However, there are some crucial differences that we need to address, arising from two key points noted above:

- All of the phases of a single Change-Cycle iteration will take place within a single Change-Layer or sub-layer.
- The entire work of a Change-Cycle will usually be done by the same group of change-agents associated with that respective layer or sub-layer.

In the Change-Layers, each CSPAR layer tackles its own specific types of tasks, and requires its own distinct set of perspectives, skillsets, and mindsets. Each phase also has its own role within the overall challenge of reducing and managing complexity. Earlier in this Step, in Chapter 3, we categorized those mindsets and perspectives in terms of the five "*modes*" (Artist, Alchemist, Analyst, Agent, Assessor) of Context Adaptive Leadership (CALc), and explored the complexity issues with the SCAN complexity-map, each of its domains cross-mapped to the respective CALc mode.

For the Change-Layers model, the CSPAR phases are largely *separate* from each other, done by different groups of people who each need to tackle only one type of task. The Change-Layers sequence flows step-by-step, usually with little back-and-forth between the steps, rarely requiring much need for active Context-Adaptive Leadership to switch between modes.

But in the Change-Cycle, the opposite is true for each of those themes:

- The CSPAR phases are not separate, but deeply interlinked with each other.
- There is often a *lot* of back-and-forth bouncing around between phases.
- The different types of work within each phase must all be done by the *same* people.
- In moving back and forth between phases, those people must switch to the CALc mode for the respective phase on each transition between phases.
- All of the task's complexity-issues must be resolved within the task itself.

CHAPTER 6   FOUNDATIONS: THE CYCLES OF CHANGE

To help make sense of this, it can be useful to imagine the Change-Cycle in terms of people moving between rooms or departments. Each of those rooms are places that enable different types of activities to happen, using the respective CALc mode. There's also a central atrium that holds the core-question that drives the Change-Cycle, and a space for Context-Adaptive Leadership to guide the coordination and choreography of the overall process. Although people can move between rooms in any way that the task might need, there *is* an overall sequence or flow that starts in the Context-room and finishes at the end of the work in the Review-room. Figure 6-2 provides a visual summary of this "rooms" metaphor.

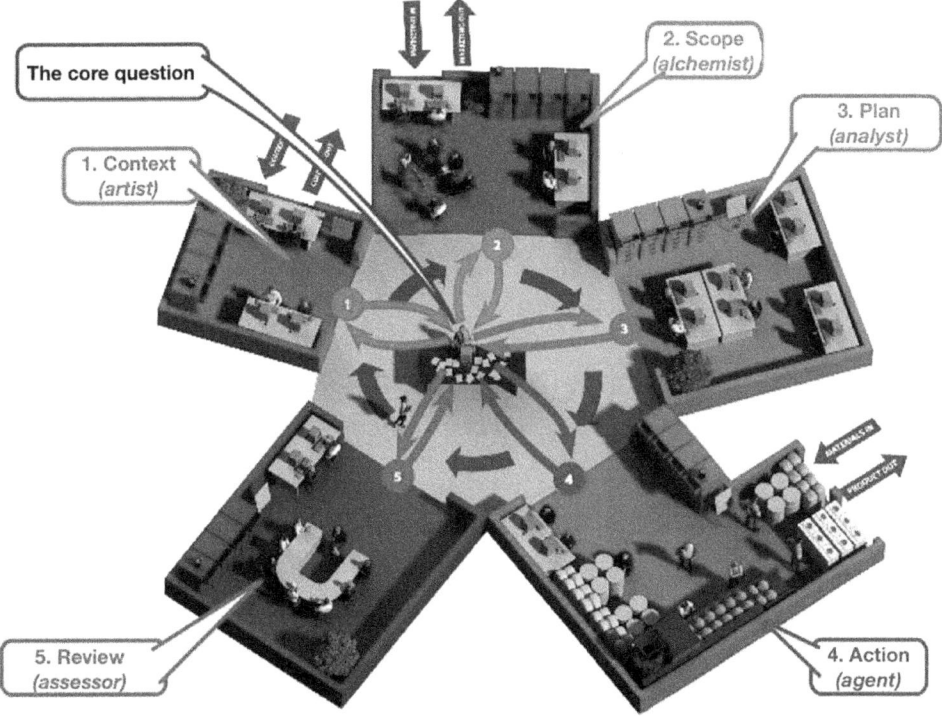

Figure 6-2. Change-Cycle phases and CALc modes: the "rooms" metaphor

Back in Chapter 3, earlier in this Step, we saw a cross-map between the CALc modes and the **uncertainty-domains** from the SCAN complexity-map – *Simple, Calculated, Ambiguous, Not-known,* and *Review*. Given that we've also cross-mapped the same modes to the CSPAR phases above, we can combine these two cross-maps to link all three themes together: CSPAR activity-phases, SCAN complexity-domains, and the CALc modes. This set of relationships is illustrated in Figure 6-3.

147

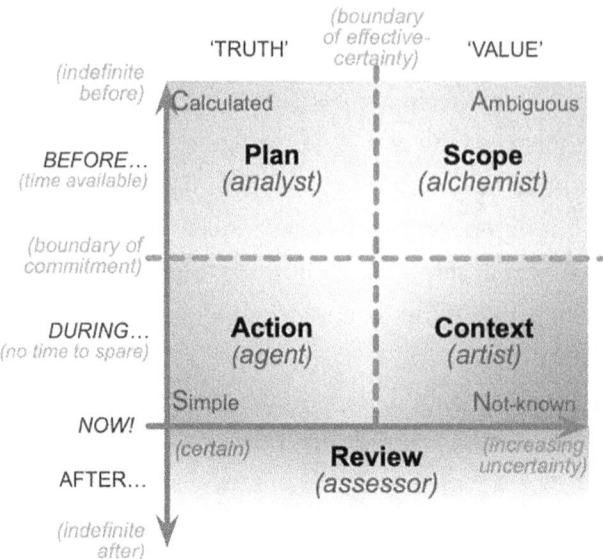

Figure 6-3. CSPAR, CALc modes, and SCAN

Note It may at first seem a bit strange to place Context and Not-known together here, especially as, in the Change-Layers, the Context and Action spaces might seem about as far apart in time as it's possible to be.

In the Change-Cycle, though, it *does* make practical sense to describe it this way. In part this is because both Context and Not-known use the CALc "*artist*" mode, and for similar reasons. For example, both need the playfulness and willingness to explore that is really only available to the artist.

The other main reason relates to the real role of Context in change-work. It's about establishing vision, values, and guidance that apply *everywhere* and *everywhen* within the scope and enterprise of change. It's also where we obtain the content for the "*chaos-checklist*" that forms an essential part of the Four-Checklists set developed in the Plan phase for use during Action. At the beginning of a Change-Cycle, these are "not-knowns" that we need to establish as "knowns," before we start any other work at all. Without that connection to Context, we'd have no guidance for exploration, nor for when things go wrong in unexpected ways: Not A Good Idea...

We'll see more on this mode-switching as we explore each of the Change-Cycle CSPAR phases, but we can summarize it here as follows:

- In the **Context** room, we tackle the "***not-known***" of the question itself. We act like an ***artist***, connecting feeling to purpose, linking the task "upward" to the big-picture and "downward" to real-world intent. There's an emphasis here on value and values, and on meaning and purpose.

- In the **Scope** room, we tackle the ***ambiguous*** and uncertain aspects of the task. We act like an engineer or ***alchemist***, constructing frames for sensemaking, and working our magic with experiments and the like to create a *usable* "something" out of the initial "nothing" of the question. There's an emphasis here on usefulness, on *people*, and on setting boundaries and making choices.

- In the **Plan** room, we work in a ***calculated*** way, using logic like a scientist or ***analyst*** to extract the truth from the question, and develop rules and algorithms to connect it to the rest of the known world and set up for action. There's an emphasis here on certainty, predictability, efficiency, and "truth."

- In the **Action** room, we (or a computer or machine) will follow ***simple*** rules and guidelines as an ***agent*** to deliver value and resolve the question or concern. There's an emphasis here on the "NOW!" and on getting things done to the best of ability.

- In the **Review** room, we act like an ***assessor***, reviewing the value gained from the changes achieved in the task, and connecting past to future by deriving new questions to explore. There's an emphasis here on realism, respect, and learning, to improve overall effectiveness.

With these cross-maps between CSPAR, CALc, and SCAN, the Change-Cycle looks as shown earlier in Figure 6-1, and again here in Figure 6-4. As also shown in the upper part of this figure, the Change-Cycle sequence systematically reduces uncertainty so that the action can be as simple as possible and always aligned to purpose.

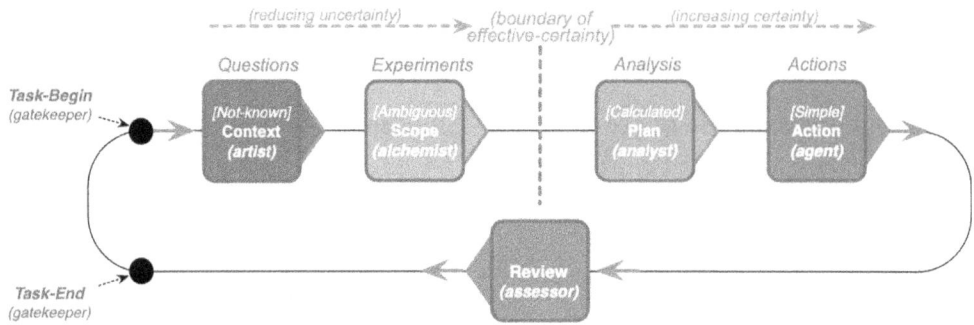

Figure 6-4. *Change-Cycle – a single fractal-instance*

The **inputs** for a Change-Cycle will again depend on the context from which the initial question was asked. The ***one essential input for a Change-Cycle is the initial question or concern***: everything else in the cycle will be anchored in some way to that question.

Beyond that, the Change-Cycle could, would, or should have access, as appropriate, to any or all of the available task-content from above it in the task-tree, from its siblings, from its own child-tasks, from previous iterations of the same task, and/or from linked-tasks elsewhere in the task-tree or in the broader repositories. This needs to include any contextual guidance, constraints, and boundaries from the parent Context and Scope, such as vision, values, standards, and success-criteria.

Within this overall frame, the **process** for the work of a Change-Cycle will depend on the question or concern from the parent-task, the overall requirements for the respective Change-Layer, the inputs for the task as described above, and the nature of the task itself. The process itself will move through each of the phases of the Change-Cycle, as described below. Note that there may be quite a lot of back-and-forth between the phases, until the final exit from the overall cycle after the end of the Review phase. We'll continue to use the term "phase" here, because that does describe the overall flow of the work; yet in practice these are more like *modes* than step-by-step-phases, because it's usually the *same* people or other agents doing each part of the overall work.

These interactions between phases tend to fall into the following patterns:

- Normal ***supply*** to the next phase in the sequence, such as Context (*artist*-mode) providing new ideas to Scope (*alchemist*-mode)

- Routine ***request*** back to the previous phase in the sequence, such as Scope (*alchemist*-mode) asking Context (*artist*-mode) for further new ideas

- Potential ***disruption*** between phases two steps apart in either direction, such as Context (*artist*-mode) telling Plan (*analyst*-mode) that "I've just had a great new idea, so let's change everything!"

- Abnormal ***exception*** usually between phases more than two steps apart, such as Action (*agent*-mode) urgently asking Context (*artist*-mode) for new ideas when things have gone wrong at run-time

In each case, the focus of activity in the Change-Cycle will move from the source-phase to the target-phase. For example, while working on an experiment in the *Scope* phase, we realize that we need some useful new insights and perspectives about a question that has just arisen in our results. We then move briefly to the *Context* phase, as a space that's more conducive to that part of the work, and then return to *Scope* when we have the information that we need to help us continue with our experiments.

- The ***supply*** and ***request*** interactions between the phases are part of the normal iterative back-and-forth within the Change-Cycle.

- Any ***disruption*** interactions typically arise whenever an intermediate phase is skipped: for example, throwing an Ambiguous "It depends…" into run-time Action can easily cause serious disruption and delay. Instead, the ambiguity first needs to be resolved into Simple instructions or checklists via Plan, before passing it on to Action.

- An ***exception*** interaction will typically arise only when something has gone wrong, and needs to be resolved or addressed in some non-standard way.

The main **outputs** of the overall Change-Cycle will be the elements of the task-content that have been changed during the work of the cycle. For example, these may include

- Changes to physical things, such as a component for a product
- Changes to data, such as a sales-record
- Changes to relationships, such as bringing two people together
- Changes to purpose and motivation, such as the mutual commitment represented by signing a contract

CHAPTER 6   FOUNDATIONS: THE CYCLES OF CHANGE

Other typical outputs would include various work-records created during the process, particularly from the Action and Review phases.

At the ***Task-End*** gateway for the Change-Cycle iteration, there is a choice to be made. We can either return back to the same place in the ***parent-task*** in which the question or concern for this Change-Cycle arose, with the respective answer or other outcomes from this overall chunk of work; or else continue working on the same question:

- Start a new Change-Cycle iteration ***at the next level up*** in the Change-Layers, to broaden the range of options that can be assessed at the current level

- Start a new Change-Cycle iteration ***at the same level*** in the Change-Layers, to work on another step of a step-by-step process at the current layer, or to explore a question that arose during the *Review*

- Start a new Change-Cycle iteration ***at the next layer down*** in the Change-Layers, to move closer toward full realization of the overall change

Figure 6-5 provides a visual reminder of this relationship between Change-Cycle and Change-Layers.

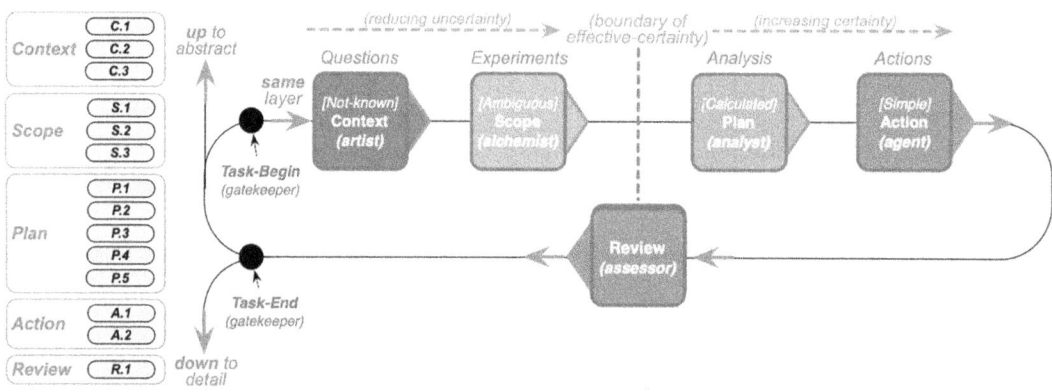

Figure 6-5. *Change-Cycle and Change-Layers*

Once all of the outputs have been set up, and stored in repositories as required, we would continue on with the work of the parent-task.

152

CHAPTER 6   FOUNDATIONS: THE CYCLES OF CHANGE

Given this background, we can now explore what happens in each of the Change-Cycle phases. For each of these, we'll address

- The *role* of the respective phase in the overall Change-Cycle
- Its *inputs* from other phases, and CALc mode-transitions, in terms of those interaction-types described just above
- Its *process*, the kinds of activities that occur in that phase, to drive the overall Change-Cycle onward
- Its *outputs* to other phases, and CALc mode-transitions, again in terms of those interaction-types

As in the Change-Layers, we'll start with the Context phase.

Context in the Change-Cycle

The **role** of the Context phase in the Change-Cycle is to *elicit new ideas, insights, and information about the question*, in context of everything else that's been done so far in the overall task. As shown in Figure 6-6, it's always the first phase in the cycle because, by definition, the arrival of any new question places us in the "Not-known."

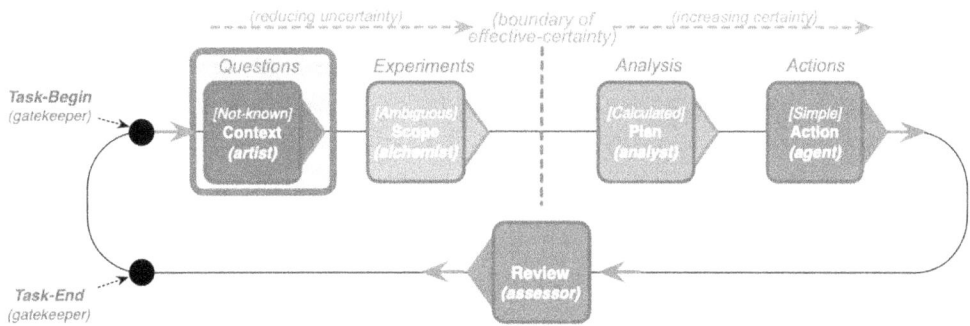

Figure 6-6. *Context phase in the Change-Cycle*

In the Change-Cycle, as also shown in Figure 6-6, the Context phase is associated with the **"Not-known" uncertainty-domain** and the CALc **"Artist" mode**. There'll be an emphasis here on *value and meaning* rather than "truth," and often on speed rather than "time to think."

153

The **inputs** for this phase and CALc mode-transitions, from the parent-task or other phases, will typically include

- *Initial **supply** from **Task-Begin**, or direct from the **parent-task***: The question or concern to be addressed, and any information and other content from the parent-task that may help in making sense of the question. This content should include the respective guiding values, principles, standards, constraints, and success-criteria.

- *Routine **request** from **Scope** (alchemist)*: Request for new ideas, insights, and/or perspectives, usually in relation to an experiment or test. The content should include context, scope, and other contextual information.

- *Potential **disruption** from **Plan** (analyst)*: Unhelpful rule-based assumptions and assertions such as "You're wrong!" or "Stop playing around and get back to doing real work!"

- *Abnormal **exception** from **Action** (agent)*: Urgent request for ideas after something has gone wrong at run-time that cannot be resolved by any of the means or methods immediately available. The content should include context, scope, plan, real-world responses, and other contextual information.

The **process** for this phase is perhaps best described as ***"having a conversation,"*** either *with* the question, *about* the question, or both. We use "just enough" of the methods and guidance from the Context layers as will satisfy the need. The aim here is to find enough ideas, insights, and information on which to base an experiment or test.

By definition, every question drops us into the Not-known domain, and we need to respect the fact that, at the start, ***we do not know what the outcome will be***. We need the playfulness and *principles-based* decision-making of the ***Artist*** here: child-like, but not childish; inquisitive, but not "The Inquisition." Other themes to watch for here will include

- As with Context in the Change-Layers, ***we need to make use of all of the senses***. Visuals, touch, movement, open space, and other sensory triggers will often help here.

- The process is often quite subtle and delicate, so ***don't try too hard***: provide conditions under which ideas and insights can arise, but allow them to do so in their own way.

- Maintain a *quiet focus on the question* or concern – often supported by the respective *chaos-checklist* – to provide an anchor around which appropriate ideas, insights, and information can coalesce.

- To get the best value from this phase, *this process will need to take its own time*. Demands from change-management that we should be able to invent on schedule are literally unrealistic here.

- It *is* also useful to *keep an emphasis on speed*, though more for playfulness than for panic, nor as a response to management pressure. Doing this will help to keep at bay any tendency to try too hard, and also to dissuade us from falling into that habitual reflex of trying to *think* our way through every challenge, when it's actually the wrong mode for *this* phase of a task.

Note   As with the Context layer, remember that this phase is *about "feel," not "think."* Being dropped into the Not-known can sometimes feel very uncomfortable, but it's essential to *not* give in to the desire to switch immediately into the supposed certainty of the *Analyst* mode, and then grab at the first "The Answer" that comes up, to get away from here as fast as possible. Instead, we need to sit with that discomfort, and give this space whatever it needs from us – just enough time, just enough detail – until *it* tells *us* when it's the right time to move on.

The **outputs** from this phase and CALc mode-transitions to other phases will typically include

- *Normal* **supply** *to* **Scope** *(alchemist)*: Ideas, insights, sensemaking, and perspectives about the initial question or concern that could be used as the basis for an experiment or test. (The content will include a summary of the work done to elicit those insights from the question and the source-material.)

- *Routine* **request** *to* **Task-Begin**, *or direct to the* **parent-task**: Request for clarification on some aspect of the initial question or concern, and/or for further information about the respective context and background for the question.

CHAPTER 6   FOUNDATIONS: THE CYCLES OF CHANGE

- *Potential **disruption** to **Plan** (analyst)*: Unhelpful value-based assertions and distractions such as "I've just had a really great new idea about this, so let's change everything!"

- *Potential **exception**-response to **Action** (agent)*: Values-based guidance on how to tackle a situation that is not covered by the plan's work-instructions and checklists.

- *Abnormal **exception** to **Review**, to **Task-End** or direct to the parent-task*: Notification that the task will have to be abandoned or restarted because no way forward could be found. (The content will include a description of the apparent reasons and/or context for the "stuckness," and a summary of all work done on the task to date.)

Scope in the Change-Cycle

The **role** of the Scope phase in the Change-Cycle is to ***make practical sense of the question***, and to ***map out a frame for options to tackle the question***, in context of everything done so far. As shown in Figure 6-7, we need to do this only *after* we've made some sense of the question itself.

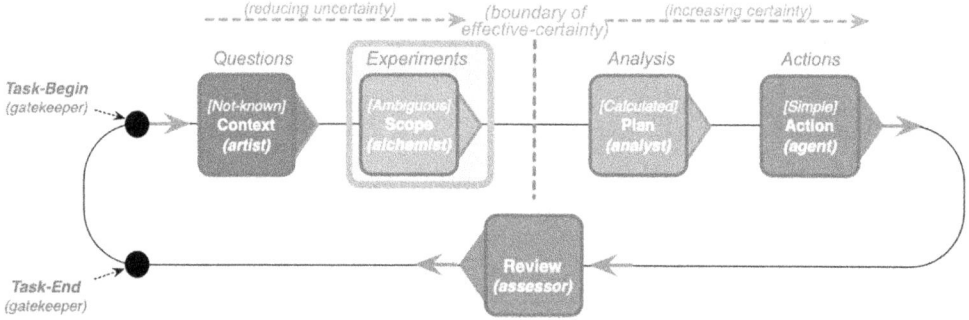

Figure 6-7. *Scope phase in the Change-Cycle*

In the Change-Cycle, as also shown in Figure 6-7, the Scope phase is associated with the ***"Ambiguous"* complexity-domain** and the CALc ***"Alchemist"* mode**. There'll be an emphasis here on *usefulness* and actionability, rather than perceived "truth," but also with appropriate time to do any required explorations or experiments.

The **inputs** for this phase and CALc mode-transitions will typically include

- *Normal **supply** from **Context** (artist)*: Ideas, insights, sensemaking, and perspectives about the initial question or concern that could be used as the basis for an experiment or test. The content will include a summary of the work done to date, and also access to the initial question or concern, the respective guiding values, principles, standards, constraints, success-criteria, and any other Context-related content.

- *Routine **request** from **Plan** (analyst)*: Request for further information on implementation-options, scope, stakeholders, skills, requirements, and the like, for reframing, for assistance in resolving ambiguities that have arisen in Plan, or to conduct experiments and/or tests in relation to some point of uncertainty. The request should include access to any other Plan-related content that may be useful in explorations.

- *Potential **disruption** from **Action** (agent)*: Unhelpful complaints such as "Don't say 'It depends,' just tell me what to do!"

- *Abnormal **exception** from **Action** (agent)*: Urgent escalation-request for guidance on how to handle an unexpected ambiguity or special-case. The content should include context, scope, plan, real-world responses, and other contextual information.

The **process** for this phase is perhaps best described as "*creating something from nothing*," like a magician, an *alchemist*, or a more everyday engineer. The "nothing" that we start from is an idea, insight, or other item of information that we receive from Context/Not-known, together with the initial question or concern, and the related values, principles, constraints, success-criteria, and so on that came in at the start of the cycle. We prod and poke at that idea, developing framings and hypotheses, devising experiments to test them, looking for ways to make the ideas more *useful* and more real. Much of this is what we would do in a Scope layer, adapted for the specific needs in *this* context in *this* specific part of the task-tree. Yet there'll often also be an emphasis on addressing complexity, uncertainty, ambiguity, and the dynamics of the context:

- Reducing ambiguity and uncertainty by experimenting to identify **what does and doesn't work**

- Reducing complexity by addressing the **human issues**, both within the context and scope, and also in the team-dynamics within the work

- Distinguishing between **non-reducible complexity** such as wicked-problems that can only be addressed here, **reducible-complexity** and reducible-uncertainty that can be addressed in Plan, and specific types of **inherent-uncertainty** such as weather or client-requirements that can only be addressed during Action

Skills will usually be essential here, in part because so much of the work for this phase takes place *before* we've crossed that "boundary of effective-certainty," as shown in Figure 6-7. Other themes in play here will include

- A focus on **usefulness**, in terms of the respective context

- A focus on the default effectiveness-dimension of **"elegance,"** in whatever form that may apply in the respective context: mathematical simplicity, for example, or design-quality, ergonomics, maintainability of code, clarity of user-journeys, and so on

- Acknowledgment and respect of people's **emotions** about the concern, and the importance of *soft-skills* to address those emotions

The **outputs** from this phase and CALc mode-transitions to other phases will typically include

- *Normal* **supply** *to* **Plan** *(analyst)*: Potential options for implementation, including information on scope, boundaries, stakeholders, skills, requirements, reducible-complexities, and inherent-uncertainties such as weather and customer-identity that can only be resolved at run-time.

- *Routine* **request** *to* **Context** *(artist)*: Request for new ideas, insights, and/or perspectives, usually in relation to an experiment or test. (The content of the request should include context, scope, and other contextual information.)

- *Potential **disruption** to **Action** (agent)*: Unhelpful distractions such as "It depends...", or bringing up uncertainties and ambiguities that have not been passed through *Plan*.

- *Potential escalation-**exception** response to **Action** (agent)*: Contextual guidance on how to handle an unexpected ambiguity or special-case.

- *Abnormal **exception** to **Review** (assessor), to **Task-End** or direct to the parent-task*: Notification that the task will have to be abandoned or restarted because of non-resolvable uncertainties or ambiguities. (The content will include a description of the apparent reasons and/or context for the "stuckness," and a summary of all work done on the task to date.)

Plan in the Change-Cycle

The **role** of the Plan phase in the Change-Cycle is to ***identify and define specifications and models for action***, in context of everything done so far in the cycle. As shown in Figure 6-8, this needs to happen *after* a Scope phase, because the aim of the model is to show how to implement an option previously identified as "in scope."

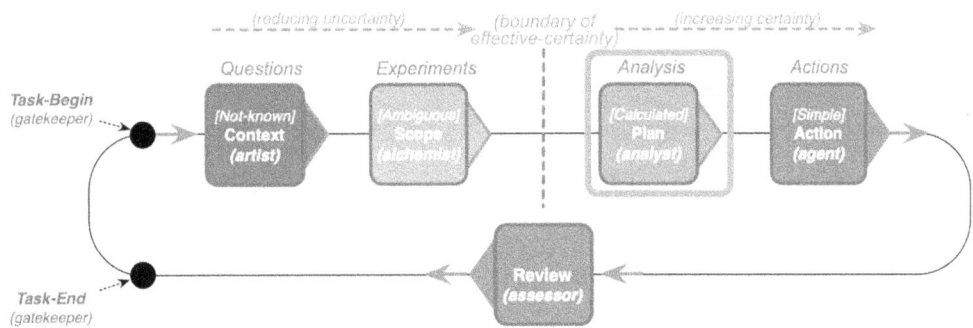

Figure 6-8. Plan phase in the Change-Cycle

In the Change-Cycle, as also shown in Figure 6-8, the Plan phase is associated with the **"Calculated" complexity-domain** and the CALc **"analyst" mode**. There'll be an emphasis on finding the respective "truth," though also requiring appropriate allowance for "time to think."

CHAPTER 6   FOUNDATIONS: THE CYCLES OF CHANGE

Caution   Most of this should be familiar territory for anyone in enterprise-architecture. The catch is that this can be *so much* "familiar territory" that we might try to jump to here straight from the start, and skip over all of that essential work on the "uncertain" side of the boundary-of-effective certainty. If we do that, we risk falling into the trap of "doing the wrong thing righter": a plan that may provide an excellent solution to a *different* question, and/or that can only work well with the "happy-path," ignoring the possibility of any real-world variance from what we expect to happen. We need to do the *whole* of the Change-Cycle each time – not just the comforting and comfortable "easy bits!"

The **inputs** for this phase and CALc mode-transitions will typically include

- *Normal **supply** from **Scope** (alchemist)*: Scope and potential options for implementation, including information on scope, boundaries, stakeholders, skills, framings, requirements, reducible-complexities, and inherent-uncertainties such as weather and customer-identity that can only be resolved at run-time.

- *Routine **request** from **Action** (agent)*: Pre-run-time request for clarification on availability of equipment, resources, skills, and suchlike.

- *Potential **disruption** from **Context** (artist)*: Unhelpful value-based assertions and distractions such as "Let's change everything, because I've just had a really great idea!"

- *Potential **disruption** from **Review** (assessor)*: Unhelpful challenges about the quality of the plan or planning.

- *Abnormal **exception** from **Action** (agent)*: Urgent escalation-request for guidance on how to resolve a run-time issue not covered in any of the provided work-instructions or checklists. The content should include context, scope, plan, real-world responses, and other contextual information.

The **process** for this phase is perhaps best described as "***setting the rules for Action***," developing theories to solve technical problems like a scientist or ***analyst***, but often also doing preparation like an administrator, getting everything in place for the action.

This is a world filled with rules, laws, and standards; a world of algorithms, formulae, theory, the desire for certainty and control. There's often still a lot of complexity to reduce here, making full use of technical knowledge and the hard-systems toolkit. All of that will be coupled with a relentless focus on "truth," on predictability, and a continual quest to improve on that effectiveness-criterion of "*efficiency.*" All of this work should take place on the "more-certain" side of SCAN's "boundary of effective-certainty": any complexity that *isn't* on the "certainty" side of the edge will need to be passed back over that edge to the alchemist-mode in *Scope*.

The aim here is to create the right Action-Model for *this* chunk of work, with the right work-instructions, checklists, methods, tools, and so on – much as described for Plan in the Change-Layers, but scaled and adapted to match the needs of *this* specific task. The action-outcomes we need to plan for, the content to be created or changed in the action, and the resources to be used there, will all depend on the needs of the overall project, and where this specific chunk of work sits within the Change-Layers and the task-tree. Some themes to watch for here would include

- Ensure that everything we do here is **linked back to the initial question or concern** for this chunk of work. We need to remind ourselves about what this plan is *for*, and to beware of scope-creep, untested assumptions, technical bias, and the like.

- Be careful **not to over-plan**. The task is not about creating "the perfect plan," but to provide simple-as-possible instructions and guidance for the subsequent Action.

- Be careful **not to mix up the roles of Plan and Action**. For example, it may be necessary here to spin off a sub-task to develop code to support the planning; but if the role of the overall Action itself will be to develop code to resolve the needs of the initial question or concern, then *we should not be writing that code here.* If we did so, we would risk doing it from the perspective, mode, mindset, success-criteria, and focus of the *Analyst* rather than the *Agent* – a mismatch that could lead to serious problems at run-time.

- Beware of reaching out too far toward **the wrong kind of "control."** No matter how hard we might try, the reality is that not everything can be reduced to a simple algorithm or a predictable set of business-rules. Some things are *inherently* unique, *inherently* uncertain, and can only be resolved during the run-time action.

Caution Be careful about the fractality here! – about where things happen in which part of the task-tree. Also, in particular, take care not to confuse the role of each *phase* in the Change-Cycle with that of the matching *layer* in the Change-Layers. (The same issues apply in each of the other Change-Cycle phases, but Plan is perhaps the phase where those confusions most often arise.)

In the Change-Layers, the Plan layer is decidedly complex, with its five distinct *P.1* to *P.5* sub-layers, and usually with different people tackling different parts of the overall task of that layer. Here in the Plan phase in the Change-Cycle, though, we do the equivalent of that *entire* set of Plan-layer activities for the respective task, all in one go, but usually in a way that's focused on a much simpler question that's also much smaller in scope and scale, and with a much simpler output.

For example, in Plan in the Change-Layers, we should worry about resource-estimates, dependencies, risk-management, constraints, boundaries, and so on. Yet in the Change-Cycle, we would tackle just *one* of those concerns at a time, each via *its own Change-Cycle*, within which the Plan phase would be solely about how to set up the Action to tackle that *one* concern. Once the *overall* Change-Cycle task is complete, after its own Review-phase, we would return the overall outcomes from that enquiry back to where the question first arose in the respective part of the Change-Layers.

Hence, as shown below, the output from the Plan-phase to the Action-phase in the Change-Cycle would be the respective Action-Model, and usually nothing more than that. If there *are* specific concerns such as risks that need to be addressed within the Action rather than the Plan, they need to be described and included in the work-instructions in the Action-Model.

The **outputs** from this phase and CALc mode-transitions to other phases will typically include

- *Normal **supply** to **Action** (agent)*: Action-Model, including work-instructions, checklists, locale-requirements, settings and constraints, resource-plan and resource-availability, inputs and expected outputs, required action-records and means of capture, start- and stop-conditions, and known inherent-uncertainties to be resolved at run-time.

- *Non-routine **supply**-response to escalation-request from **Action** (agent)*: Broader rules- or algorithm-based guidance on how to handle an unexpected run-time issue.

- *Routine **request** to **Scope** (alchemist)*: Request for further information on implementation-options, scope, stakeholders, skills, framing, requirements, and the like, for assistance in resolving ambiguities that have arisen in planning, or to conduct experiments and/or tests in relation to some point of uncertainty. The request should include access to any other Plan-related content that may be useful in explorations.

- *Potential **disruption** to **Context** (artist)*: Unhelpful rule-based assumptions and assertions such as "You're wrong!" or "Stop playing around and get back to doing real work!"

- *Potential **disruption** to **Review** (assessor)*: Defensive arguments about the quality of the plan and/or planning, such as "The plan was perfect, it was the execution that was bad!"

- *Abnormal **exception** to **Review**, to **Task-End** or direct to the parent-task*: Notification that the task will have to be abandoned or restarted because of non-resolvable issues related to the plan, such as non-availability of essential equipment or resources. The content will include a description of the apparent reasons and/or context for the "stuckness," and a summary of all work done on the task to date.

Action in the Change-Cycle

The **role** of the Action phase in the Change-Cycle is to ***deliver appropriate outcomes in response to the initial question or concern***. As shown in Figure 6-9, this needs to happen *after* a Plan phase, because the aim is for the action to enact the respective plan.

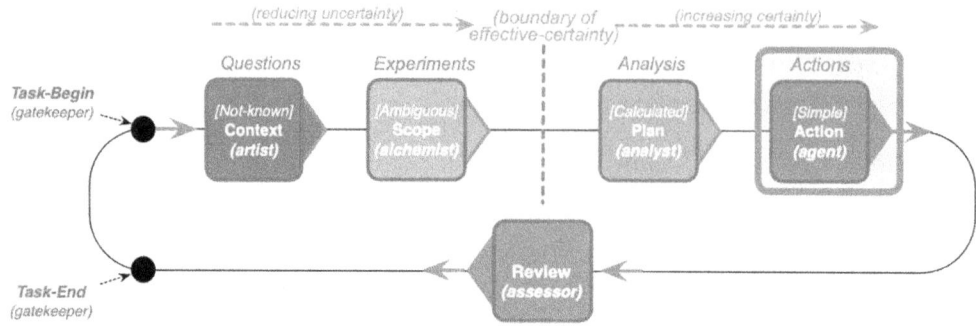

Figure 6-9. Action phase in the Change-Cycle

In the Change-Cycle, as also shown in Figure 6-9, the Action phase is associated with the *"Simple"* **complexity-domain** and the CALc *"agent"* **mode**. There'll be an emphasis on the presumed "truth" of the Plan (though with an awareness that Reality Department may have other views on that...), and on keeping everything moving at "production-speed."

The **inputs** for this phase and CALc mode-transitions, from other phases, will typically include

- *Normal* **supply** *from* **Plan** *(analyst)*: Action-Model, including work-instructions, checklists, locale-requirements, settings and constraints, resource-plan and resource-availability, inputs and expected outputs, required action-records and means of capture, start- and stop-conditions, and known inherent-uncertainties to be resolved at run-time

- *Non-routine* **request** *from* **Review** *(assessor)*: Request for clarification and/or further details about some aspect of the action or its outcomes

- *Potential* **disruption** *from* **Scope** *(alchemist)*: Unhelpful distractions such as "It depends...," or bringing up uncertainties and ambiguities that have not been passed through *Plan*

- *Potential* **exception**-*response from* **Context** *(artist)*: Values-based guidance on how to tackle a situation that is not covered by any of the Action's work-instructions and checklists

The **process** for this phase is perhaps best described as "***Get it done!***," with all of the focus, commitment, and determination that an actor or ***agent*** may bring to the matter. This is actually where the question will be answered, the concern resolved; where value is delivered, designs documented, code completed, or whatever else the concern might need to be done.

Unlike in the often-imaginary world of the Analyst, and the sometimes-stranger worlds of the Alchemist and Artist, this is where we meet the ***real-world*** of the question, in real-time, right here, right now. There'll be an emphasis on speed, on precision, and on the effectiveness-criterion of ***reliability***; an emphasis on following the rules and algorithms set out in the plan, yet also watchful for variances, exceptions, things that don't fit the plan's expectations but are undoubtedly part of the real-world picture. Some themes we may need to watch for here will include

- The plan's Action-Model may need to be ***adapted*** into a real-world action-plan that we can use in *this* moment, at *this* place, with *these* resources, for *this* client, to meet *these* specific needs.

- Capture not only the artefacts and ***action-records*** as specified in the plan, but also any ***ideas and insights*** that may arise during the action.

- ***Follow the plan*** as if it is "the law," "the truth," yet also ***remain aware*** in the background that it possibly isn't.

There's also a subtle and often difficult trade-off here, about levels of uncertainty, unpredictability and uniqueness, and the skills needed to resolve those issues. There's often a strong desire to keep everything as ***Simple*** as possible here, so that this work can be done by a physical machine, an IT-system, a robot, or a low-skill trainee. Given that desire, the plan will have usually been developed to match the level of *expected* certainty or uncertainty that the respective agent will have to address. The catch is that the expected-certainty may be based on untested assumptions or unrealistic tests, and the actual skill-levels needed to reach the required real-world level of *effective*-certainty for the task may be much higher than those specified in the plan. This *may* be resolved by enabling escalation to other people with *apprentice*-level or *journeyman*-level skills. But doing this always takes time, and slows things down, and in practice the only higher-level skills that may be available at run-time would be those of the *master*. If we want to keep things moving fast, and still be able to resolve run-time uncertainties in real-time, we'll need to have someone with *master*-level skills available right there on the floor at all times – and doing so will often be *less* expensive than trying to do everything with *trainee*-level skills alone.

The **outputs** from this phase and CALc mode-transitions to other phases will typically include

- *Normal **supply** to **Review** (assessor)*: Outcomes of action, action-records, and any other ideas, insights, and information that arose during the action.

- *Routine **request** to **Plan** (analyst)*: Pre-run-time request for clarification on availability of equipment, resources, skills, and suchlike.

- *Non-routine escalation-**request** to **Plan** (analyst)*: Run-time concerns about variances, needs for resources, and/or about instructions that don't seem to make sense in the real-world context.

- *Potential **disruption** to **Scope** (alchemist)*: Unhelpful complaints such as "Don't say 'It depends,' just tell me what to do!"

- *Abnormal **exception** to **Context** (artist)*: Urgent request for ideas after something has gone wrong at run-time that cannot be resolved by any of the means or methods immediately available. The content should include context, scope, plan, real-world responses, and other contextual information.

Review in the Change-Cycle

The **role** of the Review phase in the Change-Cycle is to ***verify the validity and appropriateness of the response to the initial question or concern***, and also ***identify any options for improvement***. As shown in Figure 6-10, this needs to happen *after* an Action phase, because otherwise there would be nothing to review.

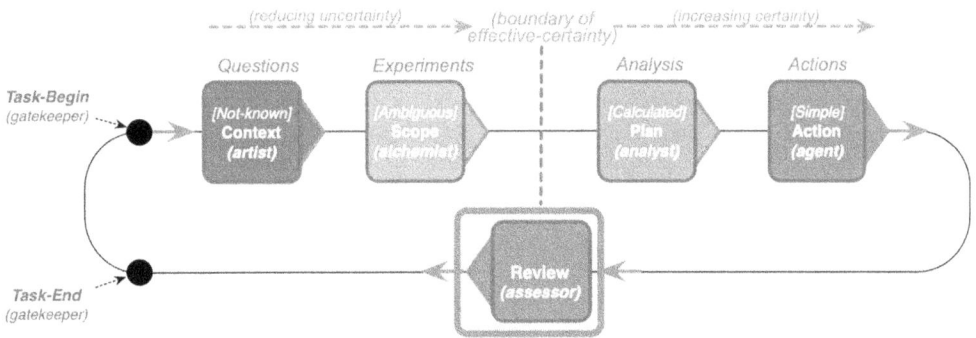

Figure 6-10. *Review phase in the Change-Cycle*

In the Change-Cycle, as also shown in Figure 6-10, the Review phase is associated with the *"Review"* **uncertainty-domain** and the CALc *"**assessor**"* **mode**. There'll be an emphasis on integration between the "truth" of the action and the value derived from doing the work, and also on integration between the past of "what has happened" versus the potential future of "what should happen next."

The **inputs** for this phase and CALc mode-transitions, from other phases, will typically include

- *Normal **supply** from **Action** (agent)*: Outcomes of action, action-records, and any other ideas, insights, and information that arose during the action.

- *Non-routine **request** from **Task-End**, or direct from the parent-task*: Request for clarification about some aspect of the review-assessment and/or the overall task.

- *Potential **disruption** from **Plan** (analyst)*: Defensive arguments about the quality of the plan and/or planning.

- *Abnormal **exception** from **Scope** (alchemist)*: Notification that the task will have to be abandoned or restarted because of non-resolvable uncertainties or ambiguities. The content will include a description of the apparent reasons and/or context for the "stuckness," and a summary of all work done on the task to date.

- *Abnormal **exception** from **Context** (artist)*: Notification that the task will have to be abandoned or restarted because no way forward could be found. The content will include a description of the apparent reasons and/or context for the "stuckness," and a summary of all work done on the task to date.

The **process** for this phase is perhaps best described as *"What can we learn from what we did?"* – reviewing the records and outcomes of the work, calmly reflecting on the past like an ***assessor***, a historian, a biographer, or a documentary-maker. In the background, there'll be a quiet emphasis on that effectiveness-criterion of ***integration***.

What we do here is essentially the same as in the Review layer in the Change-Layers, as described in the previous chapter. The only difference is that it may be tailored to the purpose and scale of this chunk of work, and also to its position in the task-tree and its location in the respective Change-Layers. The overall aim is the same as in the Change-Layers:

- Assess action-records and outcomes to identify ***benefits-realized*** and value returned by the work

- Compare the Plan's "what was supposed to happen" with the Action's "what actually happened," to derive ***lessons-learned*** – about what went unexpectedly-right as much as about what went unexpectedly-wrong

- If required, do an ***accept/reject*** test to decide whether the work needs to be done again

- From the benefits-realized, lessons-learned, and accept/reject test, derive any suggested ***further actions***, for the project and/or for individuals and teams

This review should, if at all possible, be done immediately after the action, and can be adapted as appropriate for the scale and nature of the work. We may sometimes need to remind ourselves, though, that if we want to support continuous-improvement, ***this type of after-action review is not optional***. At a minimum, we do need to ensure that the action-records are safely stored, and that they *will* be reviewed as soon as possible.

The single most important rule here is ***"No blame!"*** If blame comes into the picture, people will instantly become defensive and guarded, and we will lose any opportunity for anyone to learn anything from the action.

The **outputs** from this phase and CALc mode-transitions to other phases and elsewhere will typically include

- *Normal **supply** to **Task-End**, or direct to the parent-task*: The answer or response to the initial question or concern, in the form of new and/or changed content, together with the review-assessment of benefits-realized, lessons-learned, and suggested further-actions.

- *Non-routine **request** to **Action** (agent)*: Request for clarification and/or further details about some aspect of the action or its outcomes.

- *Potential **disruption** to **Plan** (analyst)*: Unhelpful challenges about the quality of the plan or planning.

- *Abnormal **exception** to **Context** (artist)*: Restart a new iteration of this Change-Cycle, from the beginning, with the same question or concern, but with the content from this iteration as additional guidance and context.

Once the outputs are complete, this iteration of the Change-Cycle comes to its end, and we start again with the next chunk of work to be done.

Into Practice

Our purpose in this chapter has been to explore how to use the CSPAR Change-Cycle as a consistent **structure-template** and **structural-checklist** to guide each individual chunk of change-work. The practice-issues for the Change-Cycle here are essentially the same as those we worked with in the previous chapter, on the Change-Layers, but this time we'll do it in a somewhat simpler way.

For this exercise, select a project that you've worked on recently, and then choose some suitable chunk of work from that project, as a task in its own right.

We want to focus here on the underlying *structure* of the work, rather than the *content* of the work. To do this, we'll use the Change-Cycle as a checklist on how you did that task, in the actual process of change. Refer back to the text above as necessary while doing this review.

CHAPTER 6   FOUNDATIONS: THE CYCLES OF CHANGE

In the **setup** for this task

- What was the ***question*** or concern to be addressed in this task?

- What was this task's ***parent-task***? Where did this task sit within the overall ***task-tree***?

- In which ***Change-Layer*** did this task sit? *(if necessary, see the previous chapter on change-layers)*

- ***Who*** did the work of this task? What ***skills and experience*** did they need to do this work?

- What ***content on context and scope*** – vision, values, standards, success-criteria, boundaries, stakeholders, and so on – was carried through from the parent-task, to connect this task to the bigger picture? How did you ***maintain that connection*** throughout the work of this task? *("act local, think global")*

- What ***other content*** – things, information, relations, and more – did you bring in from the parent-task, sibling-tasks, child-tasks, and/or previous iterations of this task? How did you use, reference or change that content during this task?

In any **Context** or **Not-known** phase in this task

- How did you ***feel*** when you first faced the question? *("feel," not "think")*

- To what extent were you able to face it *as* a ***real question***, rather than something to which you already knew "The Answer"? *(i.e., an implicit immediate jump to Plan)*

- What process and workspace did you use to ***elicit ideas and insights*** about the question? *("fishing for facts")*

- How did you ensure that those ideas and insights were ***appropriate*** for the initial question or concern?

- What ***approach and mindset*** did you need, to do this part of the work? In what ways, if any, did this differ from the approach you usually use in your work?

- How did you *capture* those ideas and insights, and *package* them into a form that others could use?

In any **Scope** or **Ambiguous** phase in this task

- What did you need to *explore*, to find ways to realize those ideas and insights about the initial question? What *ambiguities and uncertainties* arose during those explorations? How did you address any *further questions* that arose during this process?

- What process and workspace did you use to *develop experiments and tests* to identify and resolve those ambiguities, uncertainties, and questions?

- How did you ensure that your suggestions for action could be *easy and elegant* to do, in delivering the solution to the initial question?

- What *approach and mindset* did you need, to do this part of the work? In what ways, if any, did this differ from the approach you usually use in your work?

- How did you *capture* the results of those experiments and tests, and *package* them into a form that could be used in the Plan/Calculated phase?

In any **Plan** or **Calculated** phase in this task

- How did you *prepare* for the value-delivery action of the task? What *instructions and checklists* did you need to develop? Which *reducible-uncertainties* did you need to address and resolve? Which *resources* did you need to find and make available for the action? What *deliverables* and *action-records* did you need to specify, to satisfy the initial question?

- What process and workspace did you use to *build the plan and preparation* for the action of the task?

- How did you ensure that the action would be as *efficient* and reliable as possible?

- What ***approach and mindset*** did you need, to do this part of the work? In what ways, if any, did this differ from the approach you usually use in your work?

- How did you ***capture*** those plans and preparation for action, and ***package*** them into a form that could be used during the Action/Simple phase?

In any **Action** or **Simple** phase in this task

- What did you need to ***do***, in the action for the task? What type of ***value*** did you create, as the main ***deliverables*** for the task? What ***form*** did that value take? *(physical "thing," virtual information, relational-asset, aspirational-asset, or any mix of these)*

- What process and workspace did you use to ***enact the plan***? What were the overall ***outcomes*** of that work?

- How did you ensure that the action would deliver a ***reliable answer or response*** to the initial question?

- What ***approach and mindset*** did you need, to do this part of the work? In what ways, if any, did this differ from the approach you usually use in your work?

- How did you ***capture*** the action-records, ideas, and insights, and ***package*** them into a form that could be used during the Review phase?

In the **Review phase** for this task

- How did you ***verify*** that the action, and the task overall, did satisfy the initial question or concern? What ***themes*** did you cover during the review-process? *(such as benefits-realized, lessons-learned, further-actions, accept/reject)*

- What process and workspace did you use to ***review the outcomes and records*** from the task?

- How did you ensure that the review would bring together and ***integrate*** all the elements and phases of the task?

- What ***approach and mindset*** did you need, to do this part of the work? In what ways, if any, did this differ from the approach you usually use in your work?

- How did you ***capture*** those review-outcomes, and ***package*** them into a form that others could use?

In the **completion** for this task

- What ***gateway-review***, if any, did you do after completing this task? If that review was done, what were its outcomes?

- Which task did you move on to, after completing this task?

Now select a project you're working on right now, or about to start work on, and choose a similar chunk of work from that project. Review what you're aiming to do there, in terms of your answers to those questions just above. In what ways, if any, would you now change how you had planned to do in that work?

Note any ideas and insights that arise for you during this exercise. Add these to your notebook as you go along, for the final review at the end of this book.

Summary

In this chapter, we explored how to apply the CSPAR change-pattern as a Change-Cycle to guide, phase-by-phases, the process and progress of a single chunk of change-work, and its transitions between SCAN complexity-domains, and between the various modes and mindsets needed within each part of the work.

In the next chapter, we'll see these how these themes connect with the different change-roles and their responsibilities and relationships, and the architectural challenges of uncertainty, complexity, and scale.

CHAPTER 7

Foundations: The Practice of Change

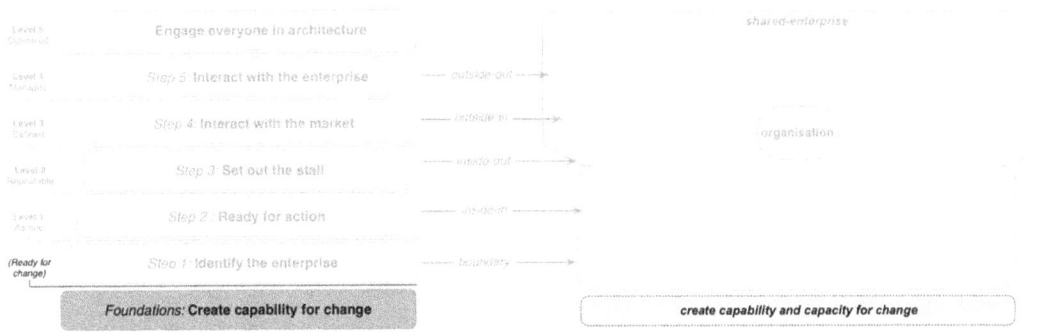

The Change-Layers and Change-Cycle provide us with a consistent method and frame that can link together all of the context-specific content that we need for each individual change, and for architecture as a whole. Once we have that method in place, though, there are a few other core concerns that we need to watch for in our practice of change-work. In particular, these relate to the different change-roles and their responsibilities and relationships, and the architectural challenges of uncertainty, complexity, and scale.

The Roles of Change

The key aim in this Foundations step in the Maturity-Model is to build *a capability for working with change in a disciplined way* that we can then use within any organization and enterprise. An essential part of that is to understand the *roles for change-agents*, clarify the relationships between them, and connect them to the responsibilities, authority, and support that they'll need in order to do their change-work.

In a sense, ***everyone in the enterprise is a "change-agent,"*** because in practice everyone will be working on *some* kind of change within their own work-area. Here, though, we need to sort those agents into five distinct ***roles***:

- ***Change-guides*** such as strategy and tactics teams, who read the dynamics of the context, and then choose the right *positioning* for the change

- ***Change-creators*** such as architects, designers, and implementers, doing their change-work at each of the respective change-layers, who *create* the conditions for the actual change

- ***Change-managers*** and suchlike, who *administer* the change-work, and enable availability of whatever resources that the creators and users may need

- ***Change-users*** such as front-line staff, who *enact* the changed processes and suchlike, and who *deliver* on the promise of the intended change

- ***Change-integrators***, who ensure that everything links together, support continual-improvement, and apply *governance* to help keep everything on-track toward value and effectiveness

Note that ***these are roles, not job-titles.*** Some people do work only in a single role for much of their working life, of course, but in practice, as architects, we're likely to find ourselves switching between those roles from time to time, just as part of the work. This is much the same as with the mode-switching of Context-Adaptive Leadership, but at the level of work-role and work-tasks rather than mindsets and perspectives.

Caution When switching between roles, always remember that they *are* different, with different tasks and different responsibilities, and take care not to mix them up. For example, change-management do often *administer* many of the processes for governance, but in that role should not attempt to take control of *governance itself*. Architects, designers, and others do *create* value, and create conditions for *others* to create value, but in that role do not determine what value *is*. These types of distinctions may seem subtle, perhaps even pedantic, but can be extremely important in practice!

We can map the relationships between the first three roles – change-guidance, change-creation, change-management – in terms of the three core themes from classical building-architecture: *desirability*, *feasibility*, and *viability*. Figure 7-1 provides a visual summary of the relationships of those roles and themes with each other and with the integration of change, and the change-user role also shown as responsible for enacting, delivering, and achieving that desirable, feasible, and viable change.

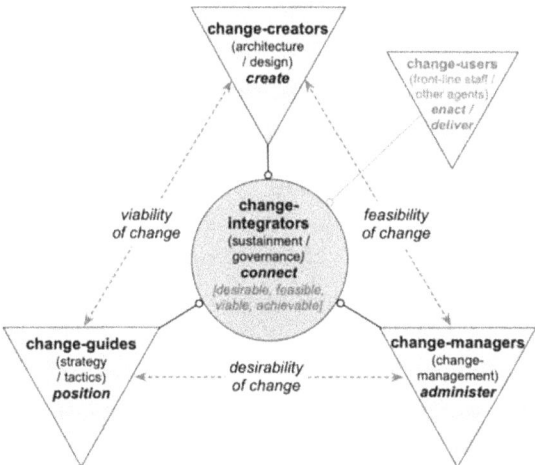

Figure 7-1. Change-roles and themes of change

We can summarize those three themes as follows:

- *Desirability*: Will align with values and success-criteria

- *Viability*: Will align with effectiveness-criteria (reliable, efficient, maintainable, etc.)

- *Feasibility*: Can be brought successfully into actual existence (i.e., completes a full traverse through the change-layers from ideation to realization)

This implies the following relationships between the respective roles:

- **Strategy-and-tactics** work with architecture-and-design to validate the *viability* of a positioning, and work with change-management (in their governance-role) to validate the *desirability* of a positioning, but must rely on architecture-and-design and change-management to establish a positioning's *feasibility*.

- ***Architecture and design*** work with change-management to establish an idea's *feasibility*, and work with strategy and tactics to establish a positioning that would ensure its *viability*, but must rely on strategy-and-tactics and change-management (in its governance role) to establish its *desirability*.

- ***Change-management*** work with architecture-and-design to establish the *feasibility* of a change, and with strategy-and-tactics to establish the *desirability* of that change, but must rely on strategy-and-tactics and architecture-and-design to determine its *viability*, to indicate whether it would be worthwhile for that change to be done.

This has important practical implications for enterprise-architecture:

- On their own, *architecture-and-design do not determine desirability*. If we want to be more than mere "order-takers," we *need* to engage with strategy-and-tactics and change-management to ensure that our voices are heard in that conversation.

- As architects and designers, *we need to be aware of when we switch roles*, either to strategic choices about positioning, or into change-management of others' work, particularly in its governance-role.

Caution Some form of role-switching is actually *mandatory* in most enterprise-architecture frameworks. For example, in the TOGAF ADM, we act as change-guides in Phase A, as architects in Phases B to D, as designers in Phase E, change-managers in Phase F, as change-integrators in Phase G, returning to the role of change-guides again in Phase H. To do that kind of enterprise-architecture, people will need to have solid experience in *all* of those often mutually-exclusive skillsets, and also the skills needed to bounce between them. As one colleague put it, "the range of skillsets needed to do what I do can sometimes be daunting" – and building all those skills can be daunting, too.

Yet if those skills are not present, and/or the role-switching is not managed correctly, things can *and do* go badly wrong, without people being able to understand *why* they're going wrong. Far too often we see change-managers trying to do architecture and architecture-governance, architects and designers trying to do change-management and procurement, people who only know architecture trying to do design, and people who only know design trying to do architecture. It's a mess...

In short, keep track of that role-switching, hold tight to the tasks and responsibilities of each respective role, and don't mix them up!

There are also distinct differences in the coverage of various types of architecture. First, some architects are specialists who focus only on a subset of content or context; others are generalists who focus more on how everything connects across the whole of a context. Most will work on a subset of scope, scale, or timescale, within a project or change-initiative; a few will work on *sustainment-architectures*, connecting everything together at a whole-of-enterprise scope, scale, and timescale.

As shown in Figure 7-2, this gives us four types of architecture-work:

- *Module-architecture (project specialism)*: How all the elements within a selected subset of a change-project will work together

- *Solution-architecture (project connect)*: How all the subsets of a change-project will work together as a whole

- *Domain-architecture (sustain specialism)*: How a broader specialism such as application-architecture, security-architecture, business-architecture, or brand-architecture will apply within a change-project, and between the scopes and timescales of different change-projects

- *Enterprise-architecture (sustain connect)*: How all changes will link together across the full scope, scale, content, context, and timescales of the overall enterprise

	specialism (subset of scope)	connect (whole of scope)
sustain (continual)	domain	enterprise
project (task-bound)	module	solution

Figure 7-2. Four types of architecture-work

CHAPTER 7   FOUNDATIONS: THE PRACTICE OF CHANGE

> **Warning**   The connect-architectures are "above" the respective specialism-architectures in that they need to link all of the specialisms together across the respective context and scope. However, this does *not* mean that enterprise- or solution-architects have the right to play "architecture-police" and to tell others how to do their work!
>
> Architecture is about management of quality and effectiveness, not administrative "control." ***Architects provide decision-support for others, not decision-making.*** And as generalists, architects will usually know much less about the fine-detail of a context and its content than the specialists do – so a bit of humility and respect toward others will usually go a long way to keep things working well!

The *role* of architecture is to support effectiveness across the whole of the enterprise, in response to any kind of change, whether planned or unplanned. We develop an architecture *for* an organization, *about* the shared-enterprise that is its context.

We may enact this role by assisting others with their projects, doing change-projects ourselves, and in maintaining a ***sustainment-architecture*** that will address broader needs throughout longer timescales and across the scope of the overall enterprise.

The ***relationship between architecture and design*** is that at each of the layers of change, architecture looks "upward" toward the abstract, toward new possibilities, whereas design looks "downward" toward the concrete, toward real-world implementation. We need to keep track at all times about which way we're looking: "up" or "down."

We depend on the ***fractality of change*** to support methods that can work the same way everywhere, within every task. Fractal-instances of tasks and sub-tasks may chain, link, and nest to any depth, but the core methods we use will still remain the same, across every type of context.

The ***change-layers*** also represent stages of change, where new information is added to the design at each step further downward toward implementation and use, and different sets of stakeholders may be engaged in the work of architecture and design.

The ***content*** for architecture and design is the set of elements that may be created, referenced, amended, used, or discarded within the context and scope for any change. These elements will comprise any mix of assets, functions, locations, capabilities, events, and decisions. For enterprise-architecture especially, the elements in scope may be physical, virtual, relational, and/or aspirational, and may require decisions or skills for any level of complexity.

The ***deliverables*** of architecture-work may include artifacts such as diagrams, reports, work-instructions, and activity-lists. However, the real value of architecture-work is not solely in the deliverables themselves, but always in the *conversations and explorations* from which those deliverables arise.

Our ***frameworks*** for architecture typically provide *context-specific guidance and checklists* on typical content, methods, artifacts, and deliverables that are applicable for the respective type of context. We do need to note, however, that context-specific frameworks may not work well or at all outside of that type of context, and that we should always use *context-neutral methods*, such as the Change-Layers and Change-Cycle, to link together the disparate context-specific methods and content-checklists.

Architects and designers, and all of the other change-agent roles, will also need to work well with both ***planned-change*** and ***unplanned-change***:

- **Planned-change** is "*change that we choose,*" about which we would typically seem to have control, and for which we would usually have time to prepare.

- **Unplanned-change** is "*change thrust upon us,*" arising either from interactions with others, or from factors outside of our control, and about which we may have little to no time to prepare.

The latter can be a challenge for enterprise-architects, because almost all current frameworks are designed around planned-change, with little to no built-in support for working with unplanned-change. Some of the frameworks and methods relevant for handling unplanned-change in IT environments can be found in IT Service Management, specifically within technology monitoring and change-management functions. The methods described in this book, though, *are* designed to work equally well with both planned and unplanned change.

There's also the point that in terms of the change-layers, planned-change is usually top-down, whereas any response to unplanned-change tends to start bottom-up. This can be problematic, because both strategy-and-tactics and change-management naturally tend to look "downward" from the top of the change-layers, and hence would agree with each other that anything coming bottom-upward would have "low desirability," in terms of those relationships shown in Figure 7-1. The same would be true for design, who, as we've seen, look downward from each of the respective change-layers, and would likewise tend to regard anything moving back upward as an unwanted conflict with their chosen solution-design. That often leaves architects, whose role requires them to look upward through the change-layers, as the only change-agents who *are* well-equipped to work with unplanned-change, and hence find themselves responsible to present it to the other change-agents in ways that seem less threatening to them.

Even so, it generally *is* best for architects to build some solid experience with planned-change before trying to tackle unplanned-change, especially at larger scale. In the Maturity-Model used here, Step 1, Step 2, and Step 3 focus mostly on capabilities for planned-change, with capabilities for working with unplanned-change added later in Step 4 and Step 5.

The Uncertainties of Change

How do we make sense of **uncertainty**? How do we plan for **inherent-uncertainty** – things that cannot be known until the exact moment of action? Where do **skill** and **experience** come into the picture? These questions become increasingly important when we dive deeper into the detail for Plan, as we try to reduce the uncertainties that must be faced in the Action.

This is part of the role of the Change-Cycle, particularly during the Plan phases in the Change-Layers. As we saw in Chapter 6, the process for reducing uncertainty during a change-cycle goes roughly as follows:

- Within the **Not-known** phase, check if the question is already understood; if not, explore the Context of the question, and look for potential patterns to pass on to the *Ambiguous* phase.

- Within the **Ambiguous** phase, check if the Scope is already understood, and "effective-certainty" already achieved; if not, use patterns and experiments to identify reducible-uncertainty to pass to the *Calculated* phase, and/or, for non-reducible uncertainty, prepare checklists to be passed onward to the *Simple* phase.

- Within the **Calculated** phase, use analysis and other Plan(ning) methods to derive predictable formulae and step-by-step processes to pass to the *Simple* phase for use in action.

- Within the **Simple** phase, use the provided formulae, processes, and checklists in real-world Action.

- Within the ***Review*** phase, assess and validate the outcomes of the action, to identify what types of uncertainty still remain to be resolved.

In that sequence, we used the cross-map between the CSPAR phases and the SCAN complexity-map. Here we need to revisit that complexity-map, this time with more of an emphasis on that "***boundary of effective-certainty***," as shown in Figure 7-3.

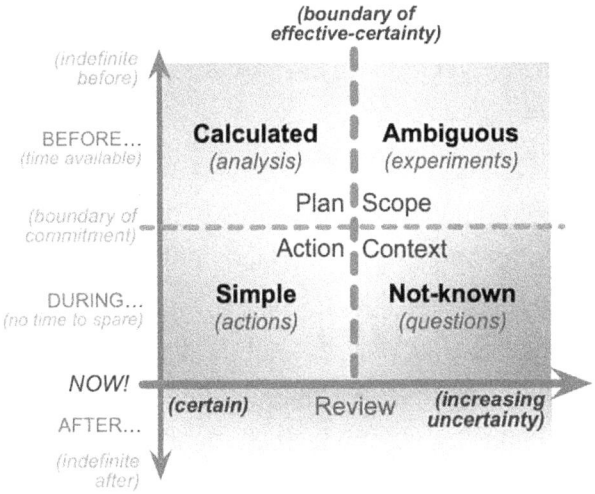

Figure 7-3. *SCAN, CSPAR, and the "boundary of effective-certainty"*

As described earlier in this "Foundations" Step, in the section "The Shape of Change" in Chapter 3, the "*boundary of effective-certainty*" is an indicator of the level of *uncertainty* that we can address within the respective context. For a system that can only follow simple rules, the boundary will be right up against the left-hand side of the SCAN frame. A rules-engine that can work with known exceptions will push the boundary some way to the right, but there are limits to how many layers of exceptions-to-exceptions a rules-engine can handle before it collapses under its own weight. Different people with different skills can push the boundary further, and further, but again there are real-world limits to that, depending on context and the like. The one-line summary, though, is that ***the more adaptable the system is, the more the boundary will be pushed rightward on the frame***.

On the far side of that boundary, we're in a different world, where achieving the desired-outcome is at best a matter of probability, not certainty. As described earlier in this Step, in Chapter 3, it's a context where ***Inverse-Einstein*** applies: "doing the same thing may lead to different results, or we may or must do different things to achieve the same effective results." It's also where we *need* the skills of the **artist-mode** and **alchemist-mode**, and all of their associated techniques and focus-themes again described earlier in Chapter 3.

The reason why all of this will matter to our Plan for change is that ***the only way to manage run-time uncertainty is through skill and experience***. We can embed *some* of that skill and experience into the design of a physical machine, and often quite a bit more into an IT-based system, such as through machine-learning and AI. Yet there is always a limit as to how far those options can go; and beyond that limit – the boundary of effective-certainty – the only option we have left is to rely on *the skills, experience, and adaptability of the people in that context*.

Warning With current technology it's possible to design and implement IT-based systems that can show an impressive simulation of human intelligence. However, it's essential always to remember that it's only a *simulation* of intelligence, not the real thing: useful for decision-*support*, but not for decision-*making*. That distinction is crucial, and if it is ever forgotten or ignored, it can easily lead to a situation where things go very badly wrong, but with no means to work out how it happened or what to do about it. Not A Good Idea…

There's more on this later in the book, particularly in Steps 4 and 5.

Given this, it's useful to cross-map the classic four skill-levels onto the SCAN frame:

- *Trainee*: "Follow the instructions" – can address *Simple* challenges via rule-based decisions; the minimum skill-level required for *Action*

- *Apprentice*: "Learn the theory" – can address *Calculated* challenges via algorithmic decisions; often the minimum required for a viable *Plan*

- *Journeyman*: "It depends…" – can address *Ambiguous* challenges via guideline and pattern-based decisions; may be the minimum required to make sense of uncertainties in *Scope*

- *Master*: "Just enough detail…" – can address *Not-known* challenges via principle-based decisions; may be the minimum required to make sense of big-picture *Context*

Figure 7-4 provides a visual summary of that Skills-Model cross-map.

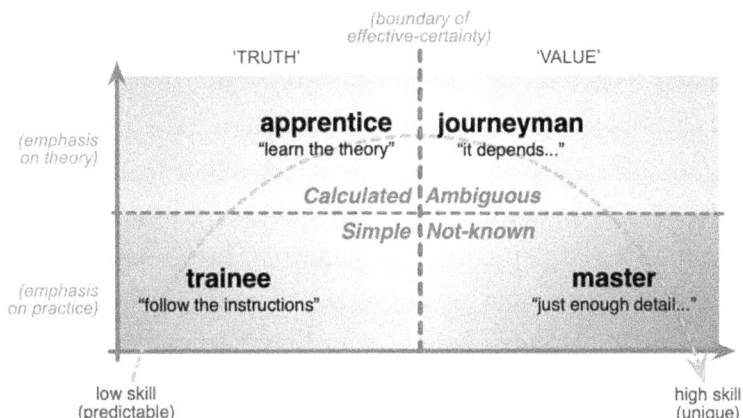

Figure 7-4. CSPAR, SCAN, and skill-levels

This also tells us what types of **agents** we're likely to be able to use for implementations:

- Physical ***machines*** must follow *Simple* laws of physics and the like, and will have only limited direct access to *Calculated* means of control, such as a centrifugal-governor or a safety-valve on a steam-engine.

- The algorithms of ***IT-applications*** can provide control for *Simple* machines and *Calculated* systems, and some limited ability to work with *Ambiguous* patterns, but cannot yet make principle-based decisions for working in the *Not-known*.

- ***People*** may be capable of tackling any or all *Simple, Calculated, Ambiguous,* and/or *Not-known* challenges, though sometimes with lower speed and/or capacity than may be available with equivalent machines or IT-systems.

In order to have available the skills and experience needed for complex tasks – especially those with high inherent-uncertainty, unpredictability, or uniqueness – we need a clear ***skills-development-path*** from Trainee to Apprentice to Journeyman to Master, as also shown in Figure 7-4. Where necessary, that development-path should be included as part of the overall Plan.

CHAPTER 7   FOUNDATIONS: THE PRACTICE OF CHANGE

However, there's an important trap here, which becomes visible when we compare the Skills-Model back to the original SCAN map: ***development of Apprentice- and Journeyman-level skills is only possible when we make time available for it***, away from the front-line. If there's no time made available, or allowed – for example, if the airport becomes obsessed with short-term "productivity" – then there ceases to be any path to reach the Master-skills that are essential for resolving deep-uncertainty. The result is that in that airport's example, the airport does some minimal training to get new people able to do the job at all, and then relies on what few Masters that are still available to fix any problems or mistakes that are beyond a Trainee's ability to resolve. When those Masters later move on, the airport would be left with no Apprentices or Journeymen to take over, and *no* way to fix any problems, yet also have no means to understand *why* those problems cannot be fixed.

Once that kind of chaos starts to arise, it can spiral *very* fast into a situation from which there is no possible recovery. This is why we *must* address this type of skills-related risk in every Plan. There's more on this later in the book, particularly when we look at hidden-risks and wicked-problems in Step 5.

A follow-on point is that in some cases, particularly during run-time, ***a Trainee will need to know how to be their own Master***. The keyword there is *"during"*: in SCAN terms, that tells us that there may not be any time available to stop and think about what to do. If that happens, we won't be able to escalate the issue to someone with Apprentice-level skills, let alone more experienced Journeyman-level skills, because there isn't enough time to do that. The only other skill-level that might be available at run-time is Master – but if there's no-one around with that level of skill and experience, the Trainee has to be able to solve it on their own, in real-time. If they can't do that, then things can go badly wrong for someone or something, very quickly indeed.

This is where the ***Four-Checklists set*** comes into the picture, as mentioned in the description of the Plan phase in the Change-Layers. As shown in Figure 7-5, these checklists are used to guide run-time action, where the boundary of effective-certainty might well be described as *"the edge of panic."*

CHAPTER 7   FOUNDATIONS: THE PRACTICE OF CHANGE

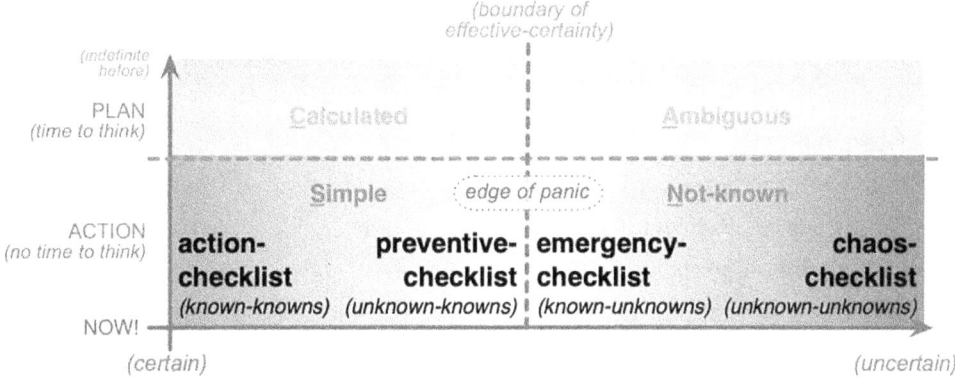

Figure 7-5. The Four-Checklists set

The first of these is the **action-checklist**, typically in the form of *work-instructions* or *standard operating procedures*. This covers *rule-based* decision-making for the "known-knowns" of the task: what to do, how, when, why, and where, in the expected context and conditions. It can be any length at all, from a scribbled note to a thick, heavy, thousand-page manual: whatever level of detail may be needed for the task. We would usually begin to develop this during the *P.2* to *P.3* phases of Plan, once the detail of the Action for the task starts to become clear.

Next is the **preventive-checklist** – the first of two types that would be commonly recognized as "a checklist." This covers decision-making for the "unknown-knowns" of a task: things that the agent needs to be certain about, but can't be known until run-time. The purpose is to help prevent known-risks from happening, and to keep operations within Simple bounds. The checklist will be sorted by task, with a list of essential checks for each task. Each list can be of any length, because it will be used *before* commitment to the full real-time action of the task takes place. We would usually start to develop this during the *P.2* to *P.3* phases of Plan, in parallel with the action-checklist, as awareness of inherent-uncertainties for the task begins to arise.

Next is the **emergency-checklist** – the other type commonly recognized as "a checklist." This covers decision-making for the "known-unknowns" of a task, to give immediate advice on what to do when things have gone wrong at run-time, but have gone wrong in a known way – the type of checklist we need when we've crossed over into the Not-known and need to keep the panic at bay. Each section of the checklist will cover a single known type of failure, and each list itself will be as short as possible – rarely more than five to seven lines – covering only the items that agents tend to forget in that type of emergency. We would usually develop this during the later phases of Plan, after real-world tests had shown up any serious hard-to-prevent issues that *did* arise during real-time Action.

Finally, we have the **chaos-checklist** – already in common use in business and elsewhere, though rarely recognized *as* a type of checklist that we need to include in the Plan. Its purpose is to provide immediate yet *general* advice to support *principle-based* decision-making to tackle "unknown-unknowns" – those "none-of-the-above" Not-known situations that are way over on the far side of the edge of panic, and that are not covered by anything in the existing emergency-checklist. The whole checklist needs to be very short – rarely more than seven items or so. It should preferably be easy to memorize, and even in printed form should be small enough to fit on the back of a business-card. The ultimate source for this checklist is the set of principles and priorities that we developed way back in the early stages of Context, so we should be able to start work on it even in the *P.1* phase of Plan, though we may well need to refine it on the basis of real-world testing of the task in the *P.4* and/or *P.5* phases.

Note In principle, there's also a "fifth-checklist" used for the Review phase of the task. What that would need to cover, though, is generally regarded as part of the regular "known-knowns" and/or "unknown-knowns" of the Action, and hence in practice it's usually bundled in with the main action- and preventive-checklists.

All of these checklists need to be included in the package of the *P.5* Action-Model, to be used as the template for each respective instance of the task's Action.

The Complexities of Change

Complexity is always a key concern for enterprise-architecture, and for all other ways of working with change. Yet some kinds of complexity we need to eliminate, some forms of complexity cannot be avoided; and some other forms of complexity we will actually want to keep:

- Some people argue that we should eliminate all complexity – yet it's inherently unachievable in practice, and may cause us to miss crucial nuances and special-cases.

- Others argue that we should instead embrace complexity – yet that can lead to needless inefficiency and endless complications.

- Both are right, in the right context; both are wrong, in the wrong context; and the fractal nature of complexity means that both can be both right and wrong at the same time.

Caution   Even in itself, complexity is complex: finding the right balance can be hard. A paraphrase to Reinhold Niebuhr's "Serenity Prayer" might be useful here: "Grant me the serenity to accept the complexities that I cannot reduce, the courage to change the complexities that I can reduce, and the wisdom to know the difference…"

In short, the simplest summary is that some elements of complexity are reducible to simplicity, and some elements of complexity are non-reducible; we need to know and respect the differences. Don't mix them up!

To make it easier, we first need to make sense of what complexity *is*, and how to work with it. Probably the best place to start is by assessing the ***dimensions of complexity***. These include

- Physical "hard-systems" complexity, such as feedback-effects, damping, and delay-loops

- Social "soft-systems" complexity, such as wicked-problems, information echo-chambers, and compounding-effects of crowds

- Chaotic-systems complexity, such as weather-patterns, catastrophic-collapse, and "attractors" in pseudo-stable systems

- Systems-of-systems complexity, such as misalignment of guidance and governance

- Inherent-uncertainty or unpredictability, such as in nuclear fission or earthquake-events

- Mass-uniqueness complexity, such as in microclimates and patients' needs in healthcare

- Emergent-systems complexity, arising from interdependencies within and/or between any of the above, especially at scale

> **Note** A chaotic-type "pseudo-stable system" is actually *more* stable than we might expect, but suddenly breaks down, often without any apparent warning, and falls into a fully-chaotic state until it can find a new way to become stable again. This kind of system is made resilient by its built-in "*attractors*" that push back against disruption. Yet there's a limit to how much the attractors can push back: and once that limit is overreached, the system can't hold itself together any more, and flails around for a while until it can find a new equilibrium.
>
> This seems to be true for most markets and other social, political, and economic systems: they may *look* stable, when seem from the outside, but they're actually pseudo-stable in exactly this way. Hence why this type of complexity can be *very* important for enterprise-architects and others working in large-scale change.

All of this complexity is also fractal, with different types of complexity intersecting with each other, nested inside each other, and so on. The challenge for enterprise-architects and other change-agents is to reduce the complexity as much as we can, to make things simple enough to use, but without making them so simplistic that they can't cope with the unavoidable complexities of the real-world.

A useful metaphor here is "tame versus wild":

- A ***tame-problem*** is one in which its "wild" complexity has been reduced to true/false answers and predictable calculations.

- A ***wild-problem*** is one which retains all of its original complexity, unpredictability, and uniqueness.

The advantage of "taming" a wild-problem is that doing so simplifies it into to a form that is amenable to processing by computers, machines, and predefined processes. That fact underpins much of the huge success and increase in productivity of industrial development over the past few centuries.

The catch, though, is that a tame-problem is still only that subset of the original issue that *can* be reduced to true/false answers. No matter how "tame" it may seem, its original "wild" nature is still there in the background, often as subtle nuances hidden deep within nested layers of surface sameness and simplicity. If we're not careful, that hidden complexity can come back to bite us, in the form of "unpredictable" failure and the like. There's a fundamental warning here: ***some forms of complexity cannot be reduced to simple algorithms or true/false answers.***

For example, there is a class of wild-problems known as a ***wicked-problem***. Often encountered in social-contexts such as sales and customer-service, their characteristics include

- Each instance of a wicked-problem is essentially unique.
- A wicked-problem cannot be solved, but only "re-solved" for the context of each unique instance.
- Re-solving a wicked-problem will lead to outcomes that can only be described in terms of "better or worse" rather than a binary "right or wrong."
- There is no identifiable end-point to a wicked-problem.
- Every wicked-problem is a symptom of another unresolved problem.

Yet because of the fractal nature of complexity, within even the most complex wicked-problem there will be some elements that *are* reducible to simple true/false answers. Again, this does not mean that the wicked-problem can be "solved"; but it *does* mean that it could at least be made somewhat more amenable to resolution.

Caution Don't try to do this all on your own! For the more complex wild-problem situations in particular, you *will* need to work with the respective stakeholders who are responsible for managing those sub-worlds. For example, the system and context "owners" and "custodians" should be able to help you to scope and descope options for stabilization and boundaries for change.

There'll also be more on tame-problems, wild-problems, and wicked-problems in Step 5, in the section "Tackling Wicked Problems" in Chapter 12.

Once again, it can be useful to map out the context on a SCAN frame such as that shown earlier in Figure 7-3. We can cross-map various themes previously discussed onto that SCAN frame as follows:

- ***Tame-problems*** can only be addressed efficiently in the left-side domains (*Simple* and/or *Calculated*).
- ***Wild-problems*** may be addressed within any appropriate mix of domains (*Simple, Calculated, Ambiguous, Not-known*).

CHAPTER 7 FOUNDATIONS: THE PRACTICE OF CHANGE

- *Machines* can only address low-uncertainty, close to the left-hand edge (*Simple* and some *Calculated*).

- *IT-systems* can address contexts with low- to mid-uncertainty, though may need more time for the latter (*Simple, Calculated,* some *Ambiguous*).

- *People* may address any level of complexity at any timescale (*Simple, Calculated, Ambiguous,* and/or *Not-known,* dependent on context and skill-level).

- *Planned-change* can be addressed in real-time in *Simple* or *Not-Known.*

- *Unplanned-change* can be addressed initially only in *Not-known.*

- *Hard-systems assessment-methods* typically apply in the *Calculated* domain.

- *Soft-systems assessment-methods* typically apply in the *Ambiguous* domain.

To *use SCAN to help make sense of complexity in a context,* map out the elements of that context on the SCAN frame, in terms of how distant in time they are from the "*Now!*", the moment of action, and in terms of the level of uncertainty. For example, Figure 7-6 shows a SCAN-type map with the elements of a surgical-operation sorted in time-order, and, in this case, split into *three* categories of complexity: "*must be certain,*" "*reasonable-uncertainty,*" and "*inherently-uncertain.*"

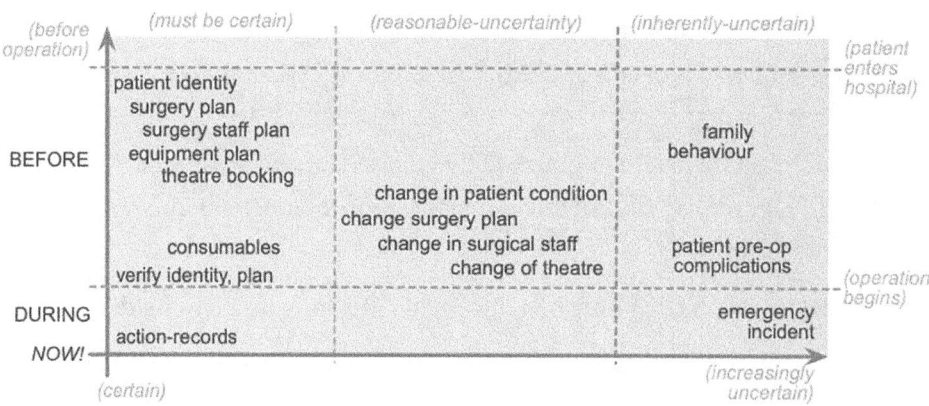

Figure 7-6. Mapping complexity for surgical-operation

For the "***must be certain***" category, we would need processes that can be relied upon absolutely, and that allow either no variation, or only as much variation as is absolutely necessary. IT-systems will provide real value for this category.

All of these are *planned-events*, following a predictable pattern. For example, the patient would be assigned an identifier on arrival at the hospital, and issued with a bar-coded wristband to be worn at all times until discharged from the hospital. All interactions with the patient would be tracked in a data-record, linked to that identity-tag. The surgery plan would allow for some variation, but both patient-identity and surgery-plan would be checked and verified on entry to the operating-theater. Records would also be created for all actions and consumables-used during the operation in the operating-theater.

In the "***reasonable-uncertainty***" category, we would require standard procedures built upon guidelines and patterns that can be adapted to the respective need. These would usually follow a case-management model, often based on personal-responsibilities but with IT-support in the background.

All of these are *unplanned-events*, but common enough that standard procedures can be built for them. They also often trigger follow-on events, some of which end up in the "*must be certain*." For example, the patient's condition changes in an unexpected way at some point between arrival and the planned operation-time; this triggers a change in the surgery-plan, which must be recorded as a validated amendment to the original plan. Later, but also before the operation, one of the surgical-staff falls ill, and must be replaced on the roster for the operation. At the last minute, the intended operating-theater becomes unavailable: an alternative must be found, or the operation postponed, following standard procedures for this kind of unplanned-event.

In the "***inherently-uncertain***" category, we would need predefined protocols that would draw on the respective values, laws, and standards, but in essence responding to these events would always rely on human skill, experience, and adaptability. IT-systems would have little to no place here, other than in recording of actions taken and results achieved, and in supporting the clean-up actions after the event.

All of these are *unplanned-events* in the "none-of-the-above" category: some of them rare, barely-imaginable, or even completely unprecedented. For example, the patient's family break into the ward, and make fear-filled demands that the operation be stopped: the hospital's chaplain would be called, or the security-guards if this happens just as the patient is being wheeled out to the operating-theater. As the surgical staff go through pre-op, the patient has sudden complications from an unrelated and previously-undiagnosed illness: instant decisions need to be made to either cancel the operation, or rewrite the surgical-plan on the spot to deal with both the planned and unplanned issues. And during the operation itself, the surgeon has a heart-attack: all parts of the initial plan must be changed in real-time, to ensure that *both* patients can have the best possible outcomes.

A complete system that must be able ***to tackle all types of real-world complexity*** within its context ***will need to incorporate all of those types of design-elements*** within its overall structure and operation.

To give a more everyday example, Figure 7-7 illustrates how these principles might be applied in the design of a partly-automated customer-service system, to be used by customers themselves:

- Start **Simple**: Provide a quick-search FAQ, and/or first-level checklists, optionally backed by a basic chatbot geared toward speed of response

- In case that can't satisfy the immediate need, shift to **Calculated**: Provide an option-tree or and/or a more-capable chatbot to search for more-targeted checklists and context-linked information

- In case the required answer cannot be found there, switch to **Ambiguous**: Provide searchable worked-examples, patterns, and more in-depth manuals that illustrate potentially-relevant nuances and special-cases

- If all else fails, or the question is too urgent to go through *Calculated* and/or *Ambiguous*, switch to **Not-known**: Provide skilled experts on-call for immediate in-person problem-assessment and problem-solving

CHAPTER 7   FOUNDATIONS: THE PRACTICE OF CHANGE

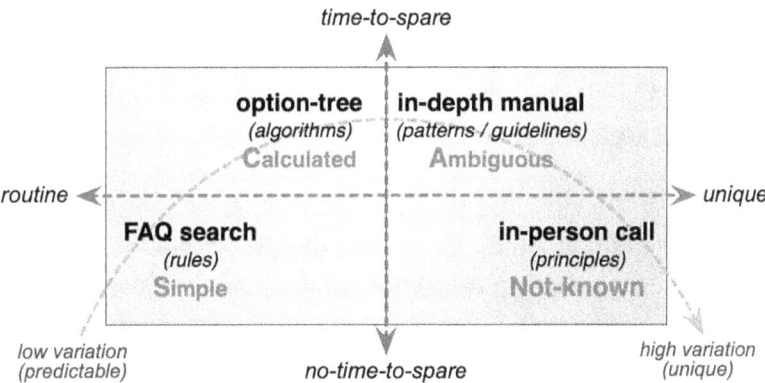

Figure 7-7. Customer-service methods

Alternatively, much the same structure could be implemented via the classic operator-based call-center, though with one important difference:

- A trainee-level call-operator answers a call, working from **Simple** scripts.

- If the call-operator cannot resolve the query, they will escalate the call to an apprentice-level specialist who knows more about the **Calculated** technical issues, and/or to a journeyman-level expert who understands the various **Ambiguous** nuances.

- If this still does not resolve the query, it will be escalated again to a master-level deep-expert who has the experience to tackle any **Not-known** "none-of-the-above" issues.

- However, the classic escalation process takes time – sometimes a *lot* of time; therefore at least one master-level expert must be embedded within the call-center, to be able to tackle urgent **Not-known** queries in real-time.

195

> **Warning** The structure of SCAN also warns us why that last point is so essential, especially in contexts that will need real-time support, such as first-responders and other emergency-workers.
>
> In the classic call-center, call-operators will work only from Simple scripts, and, as above, would escalate anything more than that to the higher levels of either *Calculated* or *Ambiguous*. During real-time Action, though, those two domains are not available: the only domains that *can* be accessed are *Simple* and *Not-known*. So if a master-level expert is not present in the call-center at that time, and the issue must be resolved without delay, call-operators who are faced with any issue not covered by their scripts would themselves be forced into the *Not-known* domain, but without the expertise to work at that level – unintentionally creating very real risks from random guesses and misguided misinformation. Not A Good Idea…

SCAN also provides us with a structured means to identify and tackle **reducible-complexity**, through which a wild-problem may be at least partially tamed. This is much the same process as used in the Change-Cycle to reduce uncertainty:

- By definition, every new question starts in the *Not-known* domain.

- Within the **Not-known**, use *reframe* and *rich-randomness* to identify potential patterns to pass to the *Ambiguous* domain for further assessment.

- Within the **Ambiguous**, use fractal "same-and-different" patterns such as *recursion* and *reflection* to identify elements of reducible-complexity in the context, and pass these to the *Calculated* domain for further evaluation.

- Within the **Calculated**, use "hard-systems" methods such as *reciprocation* and *resonance* to isolate out and extract the controlling factors in the respective complexity, then derive predictable formulae to pass to the *Simple* domain for final tests.

- Within the **Simple**, test the provided formulae in real-world practice; if any issues arise, iterate around the same loop in either direction as appropriate.

Note Remember always that a tame-problem solution will only be able to address a *subset* of the underlying wild-problem – the part that has no significant non-reducible complexity. If we do need to address the whole problem, the tame-problem elements will not be enough, and we will need some kind of fall-back to tackle the remainder of the complexity by other means.

There's an everyday example of this that we've seen in a well-known café chain. Like most organizations, they use an IT-based application – a *tame-problem solution* – to track their sales-transactions. But when the network fails, the real underlying complexity of the overall problem resurfaces. By law, they must always have *some* means to record their sales-transactions – but the IT-application is not available right now to do that. To resolve that part of the wild-problem, and keep trading, they have an old-fashioned pen-and-paper ledger below the counter, ready for use. They record the transactions there; and then later, when the network comes back up again, they copy those transaction-records back into the regular IT-system, using a manual-override to adjust the system's automatically-generated date and time as required.

The Scales of Change

The relationships between **complexity and scale** provide another common theme for enterprise-architects. For example, when a change proves successful, there is often a desire to apply that change elsewhere at a larger scale. We need to be aware of complexity-issues that may arise when we do that. Common sources of complexity related to scale include

- *Context*: Any context with high inherent-uniqueness or inherent-uncertainty such as healthcare or emergency-services is likely to have increasing complexity with increasing scale.

- *Scope*: An organization that expands its reach from local to regional to national to multinational must address increasing complexity from different laws and standards that apply in each part of the scope.

- *Agent-type*: Increasing the availability of an IT-application is relatively easy; increasing the availability of a given type of machine can be hard; increasing the availability of more people with the required skills and experiences is *always* hard.

Again, the first task here will be to identify and eliminate as much as possible of the reducible-complexity, as described above. As before, use fractal patterns in *Ambiguous*-mode assessments to identify and distinguish between reducible and non-reducible complexity, and then pass the reducible elements over for *Calculated*-mode analysis, deconstruction, and simplification. We can also use the same tactics to survey change "at scale" to help identify subtypes and supertypes of the same kind of change.

Typical non-reducible elements arising from scale that would still remain would include

- *Exponential increase of interactions* between elements in a system
- *Emergent-effects* arising from issues such as communication-delays
- *Compound-delay effects* arising from lead-time issues at larger scale
- *Breakdown of situational awareness* arising from hierarchical layering of systems

On **exponential increase of interactions** between elements, the most common issue arising is an overload of the system's capacity to respond. Communications will then be missed, and process-stages skipped or not even started, eventually triggering a chaotic-collapse breakdown of the system.

The simplest way to manage this is to identify, simplify, and eliminate any unnecessary interactions. An everyday example of this is an organizational habit of using a "Reply-All" function in email-chains, leading to many unnecessary distractions, and a vast increase in both size and volume of mail to deliver and store. By teaching staff to be more selective about who to reply to, the risk of overloading the system can be significantly reduced.

On **emergent effects** from issues such as communication-delays, this is a common theme that occurs as change-projects increase in scale. Human-systems do not mesh together like gears inside an enormous clock: miscommunications, misinterpretations, and misunderstandings are an inherent fact of the system, and will cause delays, errors, unintentional failure-demand, and more. As scale increases, the effects of these misinteractions can increase exponentially, again with the potential to trigger a chaotic-collapse breakdown of the overall change-project.

There is no simple way to tackle this, although a first requirement would be to acknowledge that it is an inevitable fact of human-systems at scale, and hence no-one's fault as such. For enterprise-architects, a good strategy would typically include

- Embed a soft-systems approach into the architecture of the project-management itself, to identify any potential sources for miscommunication and to resolve inter-group clashes

- Ensure availability of knowledge-management support such as a "jargon-buster" glossary and thesaurus, to minimize any potential sources for misinterpretations and misunderstandings

- Use a time boxed approach to cover at least the breadth of the change, with further exploration of depth as appropriate

On **compound-delay effects** from lead-time issues, this is about the time and complexity to get something done, and how these delays multiply and interact with each other at increasing scale. This is another variant of the exponential-increase and emergent-effects issues as above, but its intensity and impact will vary dependent on agent-type and task to be done. For example, consider the lead-time issues for roll-out of a web-based e-commerce application:

- Creating a new instance of a back-end **IT-application** takes little to no perceivable time.

- Manufacturing, procuring, and installing **IT-hardware** to host the back-end application takes a significant amount of time.

- *Training a staff-member* to operate and maintain the IT-application on the IT-hardware will take an even more significant amount of time.

- Inducing *a potential end-user* to successfully *self-train* to learn and use the front-end interface of the back-end IT-application on their own browser and IT-hardware will take a yet more significant amount of time.

- *Recruiting and training a customer-service agent* to be able to support end-users of the IT-application will take a *very* significant amount of time.

Because the lead-times are different in each case, and interact with each other as the roll-out scales, building a commercially-viable community of end-users of a new e-commerce application can be very complex indeed. Again, there is so simple way to tackle this: for enterprise-architects, we first need to acknowledge that this is an unavoidable fact of scaling these kinds of systems, and do what we can to minimize these effects.

On ***breakdown of situational-awareness***, this arises as an interaction between organizational-architecture, information-architecture, and the dynamics of human systems. Functionally, the maximum viable size for a single organizational unit is around 10–12 people – the classic "two-pizza team" – each of whom is in direct touch with both the unit's purpose and the real-world. Above that size, the overall group needs to be split into sub-units, each with that same maximum team-size, and with a layer of management above to guide and link the teams. The managers' situational-awareness is maintained by proxy, via conversations with their respective teams.

Yet once the scale of the organization rises above a team-of-teams – a maximum size of around 150 people, described in social-systems as the "Dunbar Number" – the management-team will itself need to be split into sub-units, adding another layer to the hierarchy. From this point onward, situational-awareness will become dependent on the quality and reliability of communication between the layers, giving rise to new emergent risks:

- Senior management will risk losing contact with the real-world.

- Front-line-staff will risk losing contact with the organizational purpose.

- Middle-managers will risk living in an imaginary world, depicted only by the information that they receive from elsewhere.

The potential for breakdown from these risks will then get worse with each increase in the number of layers in the organizational hierarchy. Again, though, this is no-one's fault: it is a direct and inevitable outcome of how human-systems work.

The best way to tackle this is by focusing on the quality and flow of information up and down through the hierarchy. Ideally, this would be anchored by ensuring continuity of person-to-person communication across all of the layers, but that can often be non-feasible in large multi-layered organizations. As a fall-back, enterprise-architects and information-architects can reduce the risks by focusing on elements of the information-system:

- Link the logical information-model both downward to the physical data-model, *and* also upward to the business knowledge-model.

- Beware of over-simplifying information and losing sometimes-crucial nuances (a particular concern for relational-databases that require predefined data-structures).

- Ensure that each item of information traveling through the hierarchy can be linked downward to the respective action-task, *and* upward to the initiating purpose for that task.

- Ensure that full drill-down to the original source-data for any derived information is always available.

These tasks can often be challenging, especially in contexts such as finance, litigation, surveillance, and defense, where tracing the various information-flows up, down, sideways, and across the hierarchies will often be subject to more formality and controls, and require authorization for appropriate access to the information. Overall, though, enterprise-architects *can* and *should* find ways to work well with this type of complexity, no matter how challenging the context may be. The summaries above should provide a usable start-point for this, but there is always more to learn.

Note There'll be more on this theme of complexity throughout the remainder of this book. For example, as mentioned earlier, the Change-Cycle also acts as a method to identify and reduce complexity in a context. There's also more about emergent-effects from scaling of systems in Step 2, and scaling of markets in Step 4.

See also Appendix B at the end of the book. We've included references there to other sources of information and guidance on tackling complexity, such as Donella Meadows' classic "Leverage Points: Places to Intervene in a System."

Into Practice

For this final part of this Step, you'll work with others to set up the capabilities that will provide foundations for change within the organization, and sometimes also shared with the broader enterprise. Enterprise-architects will only be responsible for some of these capabilities, but you'll still need to ensure that all the other responsibilities are fully addressed elsewhere, and do all connect together across the whole context. Use the ideas in this chapter and the questions below to help you guide those conversations.

On the *roles* of change

- Who in your organization is responsible for ***strategy, tactics, and operations*** – the *choices* for change? How do they do this? To which contexts do their choices apply? Who ensures that these choices align with and support each other, in terms of nesting, dependencies, and links across the whole?

- Who in your organization is responsible for ***architecture, design, and implementation*** – the *creation* of change? How do they do this? In which contexts do their actions apply? Who ensures that these actions align with and support each other, across the whole?

- Who in your organization is responsible for ***change-management*** – the *administration* of change? How do they do this? To which types of change would this administration apply? Who ensures that these forms of administration align with and support each other, across the whole?

- Who in your organization is responsible for ***maintaining the balance*** between choices, creation, and administration? How do they do this? Where and with whom do they do this? How do they ensure that everything does balance, dynamically, in terms of nesting, dependencies, and links across the whole, over whatever timescales may apply in that context? What does it look like if things *are* in appropriate balance, or *not* in balance?

On the *uncertainties* of change

- Who is responsible for ***identifying inherent and/or unavoidable uncertainties*** in the organization's operations-context – particularly those ***uncertainties that can only be resolved at run-time***? How and with whom will they do this?

- Who is responsible for ***identifying the skills, resilience, adaptability, and experience*** needed to ***resolve those run-time uncertainties*** in an effective way? How and with whom will they do this?

- Who is responsible for ***developing methods, plans, and processes*** to ***address and resolve those run-time uncertainties***? How and with whom will they do this?

- Who is responsible for ***ensuring that the respective agents*** (people, machines, and/or IT-systems) will be able to ***embed, acquire, and/or develop*** the requisite skills, resilience, adaptability, and experience to resolve those run-time uncertainties? How and with whom will they do this?

- For people as agents, what ***skills-development pathway***, from trainee to apprentice to journeyman to master, would be needed to ***ensure that they <u>will</u> have the requisite levels of skills*** and so on available to them at run-time? Who is responsible for ***developing and/or delivering*** the requisite ***training, education, and/or experience-building*** for those people-as-agents? How and with whom will they do this?

- Who is responsible for ***developing appropriate guidance for agents*** (such as in work-instructions and other elements of the Four-Checklists set; for people as agents, configurations for machines, or embedded in software for IT-systems) to ***support effective outcomes*** from resolving uncertainties that may arise in run-time action? Who is responsible for ***ensuring that this guidance will be available*** for use by the respective agents ***during run-time action***? How and with whom will they do this?

- Who is responsible for ***assessing and validating the effectiveness of the use of skills*** and so on at run-time? Who is responsible for ensuring that these assessments are used in appropriate ways to ***guide continuous-improvement*** across the organization and enterprise? How and with whom will they do this?

On the ***complexities*** of change:

- Who is responsible for ***identifying complexities*** arising from changes in the enterprise? How will they distinguish between reducible and non-reducible complexity – between that which can be simplified or eliminated and that which will remain inherently-uncertain? How and with whom will they do this?

- Who is responsible for identifying *systemic-complexities* that arise from interactions or non-interactions between distinct elements across the whole context? How and with whom will they identify this?

- Who is responsible for identifying *emergent-complexities* that arise over time – such as via wear in machines, equipment failure, or loss of tacit-knowledge when someone moves on? How and with whom will they identify this?

- Who is responsible for *mitigating each type of complexity* – reducible and/or non-reducible, systemic and/or emergent – identified within the enterprise? How and with whom will they do this?

On the *scale* of change:

- Who is responsible for *identifying issues arising from changes of scale* within the organization and/or the broader enterprise – whether increase or decrease of scale of the organization or enterprise? How and with whom will they do this?

- Who is responsible for *identifying issues arising from scale of changes* within the organization and/or the broader enterprise – whether increase or decrease in scale of change? How and with whom will they do this?

- Who is responsible for *mitigating those scale-related issues*? How and with whom will they do this?

Summary

In this chapter, we first explored the roles and responsibilities of enterprise-architects and the other change-groups, and the relationships between them. We then completed this Foundations step with a review of some practical concerns such as inherent-uncertainty, complexity, and scale, and how these may influence what we'll need to address in our work on enterprise-architectures.

In the next chapter, we'll begin to apply to our enterprise-architecture what we've learned in this set of Foundations chapter, starting in Step 1 by building the capabilities we'll need in order to construct and maintain a clear understanding of the context and scope of our organization and its enterprise.

CHAPTER 8

Step 1: Identify the Enterprise

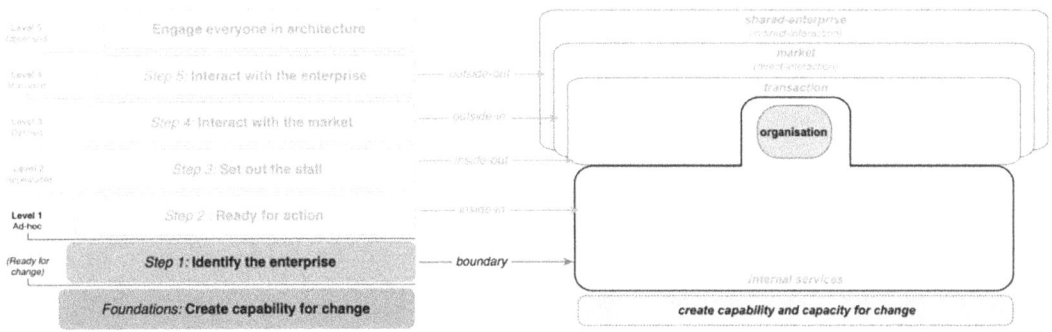

In this Step, we'll focus on identifying and establishing the ***core context and scope*** for the organization and its business, and the capabilities and setup needed to support effective change throughout the organization.

The previous chapters in "Step Zero" were about how to do effective change-work in a generic sense, anywhere. This is where we start to explore the architecture for a *specific* organization, such as the airport, or your own work-context.

Most of what's currently called "business-architecture" fits in more with Step 3, setting up for transactions and the like. By contrast, what we tackle here in Step 1 is the actual *foundations* for that business-architecture: what the business *is*, why it exists, where it fits within the wider world, what governs how it works, and what it believes success to be. In CSPAR terms, what we identify here is the core Context, the first part of Scope, and the very first level of Plan for the organization as a whole. This then gives us the basis on which we can develop our services and products, and define and monitor the effectiveness of the organization.

> **Note** You'll also find this type of assessment useful as part of due-diligence for a proposed merger or acquisition. Once you've had some practice at doing this Step for your own organization, you can apply the same process to review a different one. This could, for example, elicit essential information to guide a gap-analysis on values, culture, and background. That in turn would provide the basis for a crucial go/no-go decision, because the degree of alignment between the respective organizations is a known key criterion for future success or failure.

As indicated in the graphic above, this Step in the Maturity-Model also identifies the ***boundary between the organization and the broader shared-enterprise.*** Among other things, that's the boundary between "inside," where our own rules can apply, and "outside," where they probably won't – and those kinds of differences *really* matter in real-world practice. We don't need to do all of this in one go – in fact, it's generally better to develop it iteratively, first moving back and forth between the first two parts of this Step, and then making minor adjustments later from what we learn while working on Steps 2 and 3. Yet because of the dependencies between the Steps, we *do* need to start here, and we do need to have at least *some* clear grasp of this before we try to do anything else.

> **Warning** One unwise approach we've seen too often in business, especially in startups, is to begin from something like "I've just had a great idea for a new product! – let's sell it!" and rush off to get it all going as fast as possible. They then discover that even defining the product turns out to be surprisingly hard; setting up processes that can reliably deliver that product is even harder; finding people who actually *want* to buy that product is harder still; and making any real profit out of the idea seems impossibly hard. After a lot of futile struggle and wasted effort, the whole thing gets abandoned, even though it actually *was* a good idea. It happens again and again, in business and elsewhere. Oh well.
>
> It *looks* like it should work: so why doesn't it? The core reason is that this approach in effect tries to run the Steps backward: start at Step 3, then Step 2, then Step 1. This goes counter to the actual dependencies between Steps, relying on all manner of untested assumptions in Step 3, before those assumptions collide with

Reality Department in Step 2, and again in Step 1. Because each change in earlier-level Steps necessarily ripples back upward to the later ones, this leads to a vast amount of extra rework, and ends up being insanely expensive in every possible sense. Not A Good Idea…

As architects, another aim for us in this Step is to ***show why an architecture capability would be useful for the organization and its enterprise***. Here, we would demonstrate that usefulness by producing, quickly and at minimal cost, a set of architectural artifacts that have ***immediate practical value for the business***. These would include

- *Strategic description of the broader enterprise context*, including its shared vision, values, purpose, markets, legal and regulatory milieu, and overall success-criteria

- *High-level business-description*, outlining the mission and role that the organization will play within that broader context

- *Core content for the architecture framework*, including assets, functions, locations, capabilities, events, and decisions

- *Core Function-Model* or "organization on a page," summarizing how the organization will serve its business role

Another essential task here would be to do the formal setup for the enterprise-architecture-capability within the organization. Typically, this would include some kind of Architecture Charter, documenting the capability's formal role, responsibilities, fund, staffing, activities, deliverables, and reporting-relationships across the organization as a whole.

There are three sections in this chapter:

- *Enterprise as context*: Identify the overall context, scope, and storyworld that the organization will choose to work within

- *Organization and enterprise*: Choose how the organization will position itself within that shared-enterprise, to define its own purpose and scope

- *Set up for action*: Set up the capabilities to support the organization's effectiveness in its chosen position in the enterprise

We'll end this chapter with a brief review of what you've learned during this Step, and how to apply it within your own organization.

Enterprise As Context

As mentioned in the definitions at the start of the Foundations step, we need to draw a clear distinction between the organization and its context or *"enterprise."* In essence, if the organization represents a "how," then the enterprise represents a "why." The organization does have its own enterprise, of course – its own business-"why," as we'll see later. But the enterprise we need to explore here is one with a broader scope, which the organization *shares* with others, and provides the *reason* for it to do business with those others.

Warning   It's essential to understand here that **the shared-enterprise comes as a complete package**. If the shared-enterprise is to be effective, its vision, values, constraints, success-criteria, and so on *will and must* apply in some way to *every player* within its boundaries.

Yes, the organization does have choices about which shared-enterprise it will work within: that part is important. But once it *does* commit to working in that enterprise, and establishes its role and position within it, the organization can't then arbitrarily choose to work only with the parts of the enterprise that it likes, and ignore the rest. Among other things, playing that kind of game *will* damage or destroy the organization's reputation and "social license to operate," and can kill its viability very quickly indeed. Not A Good Idea…

From an architectural perspective, we need this because the shared-enterprise determines what "effective" and "good" look like *when seen from outside of the organization*. This then becomes the basis for business-architecture and more. For example, without clarity on those themes, the organization could not safely do business with others at all. That's also why we need to do this part first, *before* we look at the organization itself.

In this section of Step 1, we identify that shared-enterprise in terms of its ***vision***, ***values***, ***constraints***, and ***success-criteria***. From these, we can derive its ***effectiveness-criteria*** and ***guiding-principles***, and identify the essential elements of its ***content*** – the what, how, where, who, when, and why that are needed to make the enterprise work well as a unified whole.

We'll tackle this in three parts:

- Identify the key *characteristics* of the shared-enterprise or "storyworld," as summarized in the first row of Figure 8-1

- Identify its key *elements* or components of the enterprise, as shown in the second row in Figure 8-1

- From those elements, identify the key types of *players* in the enterprise, their respective *roles and relationships* with each other, and the key *interactions* between them

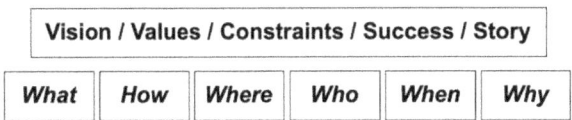

Figure 8-1. *Shared-enterprise content*

In practice, the enterprise-architects would typically do this part of the work with the executive-team, not least because those are the only people who would have the authority to make these kinds of decisions. A first cut at this shouldn't take long: if it takes much longer than half a day, they'd almost certainly be overthinking it.

Note Most of the work in this part of Step 1 is *in Context/Not-known* territory. This means we'll need to engage the "serious play" of the ***Artist-mode*** here: exploratory, creative, light-hearted, fast-moving. Make it tangible, make it playful; later on in this Step, when we look at the organization and its place within the shared-enterprise, we'll need to make it personal, too.

Story-based approaches also work well here, though there's more on that in Step 2, particularly in the section "Stories of Change."

CHAPTER 8   STEP 1: IDENTIFY THE ENTERPRISE

Enterprise As Storyworld

Perhaps the easiest way to understand the shared-enterprise is as a ***storyworld*** – a space where stories happen or, maybe more accurately, where stories are *lived*. Each interaction within that storyworld is a story in its own right, with its own purpose, its own beginning, middle and end; but the storyworld itself continues onward, always slightly changed, yet also, at its core, staying essentially the same.

A simple example of a storyworld is a TV series, or a regular news-show. All manner of stories can take place within that storyworld, at all different levels, all of them different yet all of them related in some way to the same shared set of themes. For example, the TV-series may fit more into a specific genre, such as crime, romance, sci-fi, comedy, or documentary; may focus on character, action, relationships, challenges, or imagination; its setting may be bright or dark, grimy or hyper-clean, realistic or fantastical. The news-show may focus on more fact, or on interpretation; more on short summaries of current events, or on longer pieces exploring how those events fit into a big-picture. Overall, as shown in Figure 8-2, the core types of themes that define an enterprise are its vision, values, constraints, and success-criteria, which in turn define the types of stories that will fit well within its storyworld.

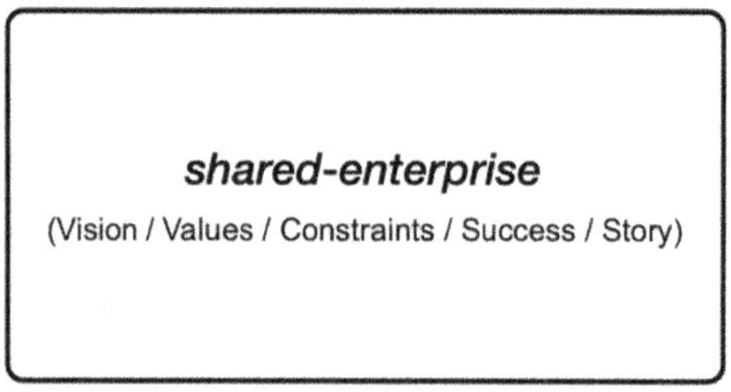

shared-enterprise
(Vision / Values / Constraints / Success / Story)

Figure 8-2. *The enterprise as a bounded storyworld*

The first and most important theme that sets the boundary for the enterprise is its shared ***aspiration***, or "***vision***," that defines its core "what," "how," and "why."

Caution   A quick reminder here that, as described in the "Key Concepts and Principles" section in Chapter 2, *vision and mission are not the same.* In the terms we're using here, an enterprise has a vision, but no mission as such, because it merely *is*, as an aspiration: it doesn't *do* anything. An organization, however, *should* have a distinct mission, and probably also a vision of its own, in context of the enterprise-vision.

There'll be more about those distinctions later in this chapter. In the meantime, don't mix them up!

A few shared-enterprises do have a vision that is goal-based, such as in the vast storyworld created by US President Kennedy's assertion in 1961 that "this nation should commit itself to achieving the goal, before this decade is out, of landing a man on the moon and returning him safely to the earth." The catch with that, though, is that once the goal is reached, the enterprise and its purpose will cease to exist, leaving the organization in urgent need of a new enterprise in which to place itself. For most organizations, it's probably best to look instead for an enterprise that continues onward indefinitely, such as in the storyworld of continual improvement implied by the Olympics slogan of "faster, higher, stronger."

For enterprise-architecture, a **vision** is a single brief phrase or one-line sentence that outlines the purpose of the enterprise. This should consist of three distinct parts, separate yet interrelated with each other:

- *The **focus** or concern*: The "what" that everyone in the enterprise is concerned about

- *The **action***: The "how," what everyone in the enterprise is *doing* about that concern

- *The **driver***: The "why," why doing this is *important* to everyone in the enterprise

This should be expressed in a single phrase or sentence that is easy to remember, and as brief as possible. An extreme example of a vision-statement is the one used by the TED conferences, which consists of just three words: "ideas worth spreading." Each word there encapsulates one of the three parts of a vision: everyone is concerned about *ideas*; everyone is *spreading* those ideas; and everyone is doing this because these are ideas that are *worth* spreading.

Example   For the airport, everyone in its shared-enterprise is concerned about *transporting people and things* around the world. The airport wants its business to include both air-travel, for people, and air-freight, for things, and hence will need to align with an enterprise that will cover both.

Everyone in its shared-enterprise will be involved in some way in *enabling transport via air*. This narrows the scope of its own enterprise, but it does also mean that it will need to connect with other modes of transport, via land and/or via sea.

This is important to everyone in the enterprise because transport via air is often *the only way to transport people and things quickly over medium to longer distances*, especially over barriers such as seas or mountain-ranges.

We could summarize all of that so far with a basic vision-statement such as "*transporting people and things via air over medium to longer distances.*" This doesn't give us much of a strong "why" as yet, but we should be able to fix that after we look at the enterprise's values.

The **values of the shared-enterprise** define its **quality-systems**, which in turn **indicate the meaning of "effectiveness" within the enterprise**. These values would apply to *every player* in the shared-enterprise. Individual players may well need additional values to guide their role in the enterprise, and to support their own business-purpose. However, each player's values *must* align overall with those of the shared-enterprise; otherwise, they cannot act as a viable player *within* that enterprise, and may put the enterprise at risk for *all* of its players.

We can derive the enterprise values in a somewhat back-to-front way by exploring the implications of the enterprise-vision, using questions such as these:

- What would be valued if the enterprise was working well for all of its players?

- What value or quality would be absent if the enterprise was *not* working well for its players?

- What does "effectiveness" look like in this enterprise?

- What values would guide the players in the enterprise toward that picture of effectiveness?

- What values would or might steer players *away* from shared-effectiveness in this enterprise?

It's probable that every enterprise would include, in some way or other, each of the values implied by that default set of effectiveness-criteria: efficient, reliable, elegant, appropriate, integrated. Most enterprises, though, would also need to include other values and effectiveness-criteria that would be essential for guiding players toward success in each interaction at every level within the respective storyworld.

We also need to identify the respective ***priorities*** between each of the values. For example, the classic Agile Manifesto assigns its priorities in a set of comparative left-to-right statements such as "We value individuals and interactions over processes and tools," and adds "While there is value in the items on the right, we value the items on the left more." (These priorities are typically described via ***principles***, which we'll look at shortly.)

Note that although players in the enterprise may adjust *some* of the relative priorities between the values, others of the values may be considered so essential to the viability of the whole enterprise that their relative priorities are not negotiable at all. For example, the Agile Manifesto asserts that "Our highest priority is to satisfy the customer through early and continuous delivery of valuable software." We need to capture those relative priorities as a core part of the architecture.

Example For the airport, the key additional values for its shared-enterprise would include safety, security, timeliness, and management of cost, particularly in a human sense. Of these, by far the most important are safety and security, with safety as the highest priority of all.

Given this, we could amend that vision-statement to include those two values: "*safe and secure transport for people and things via air over medium to longer distances.*" Note, though, that "security" in particular may mean different things to various players, potentially giving rise to further implications for the enterprise that will need to be explored later in this chapter and elsewhere.

There are likely to be various **constraints** imposed on the enterprise, either from outside by other enterprises, from within by the enterprise itself, and/or from the nature of what the enterprise is and does. These constraints would again apply to *every player* in the shared-enterprise. Individual players may well face additional constraints that apply to their specific role in the enterprise, and/or from their specific business-context.

However, such additional constraints *must* align overall with those of the shared-enterprise – or rather, the whole-enterprise constraints must in some way encompass *all* additional types of constraints that may apply within the overall context.

We can again identify the enterprise constraints by exploring the implications of the enterprise-vision, using questions such as these:

- Which *rules, laws, and regulations* would apply to this overall enterprise? How might these vary across different *jurisdictions* and the like?

- Which *standards and guidelines* would apply to this overall enterprise? How might these vary between different player-roles and/or jurisdictions and the like?

- Which *social and/or cultural constraints* might apply to this enterprise, potentially affecting "social-license-to-operate" for specific types of players, or for the enterprise as a whole?

- Which *real-world constraints* might or would apply to this enterprise, potentially affecting the operations and/or viability of specific players in the enterprise, or of the enterprise as a whole?

Real-world constraints could include any of a wide variety of things, such as physics, chemistry, geology, weather, and availability of natural services or resources.

Example For the airport, a vast array of local, national, and international laws and regulations would apply to various parts of and/or roles within the enterprise, and to the enterprise as a whole. A vast array of standards and guidelines would likewise need to be used within various parts of the enterprise, and/or across the whole enterprise.

Factors for the enterprise's social-license-to-operate include noise, pollution, disruption of traffic and social-life, safety-concerns for people on the ground, and social-unfairness challenges if air-travel is viewed as only available to "the elite."

Real-world factors include weather, availability of fuel and other resources, and physical space large enough to accommodate aircraft of the required size and performance.

Next, we need to identify the **success-criteria** for the enterprise. These are signals that would indicate whether the enterprise is or is not working well for its players.

In general, ***an effective enterprise is also a successful one***, and vice versa. Given that fact, we can derive the success criteria from the practical implications both of the effectiveness-criteria – from enterprise vision and values – and of alignment, or non-alignment, with the enterprise constraints. We do this via questions such as these:

- Given the enterprise vision, values, and constraints, what would *success* look like, across the enterprise as a whole? What markers, signals, events, or metrics could you use to identify and/or measure enterprise success? In what ways might these markers vary between different players in the enterprise?

- Given the enterprise vision, values, and constraints, what would *not-success* look like, across the enterprise as a whole? What markers, signals, events, or metrics could you use to identify and/or measure enterprise failure or not-success? In what ways might these markers vary between different players in the enterprise?

- In what ways might *priorities* between values and/or between constraints affect success, particularly for different players? In what ways might the *different priorities* of players affect effectiveness and success for other players, and/or for the enterprise as a whole?

Document these criteria as a set of simple one-line statements, in a similar format to that used for the vision-statement.

Example For the airport, its central success-criterion would be much the same as its vision-statement for the shared-enterprise: that *people and things arrive at their destination safely, intact and on-time, at acceptable cost to all players, and in accordance with all applicable law.*

There would also need to be success-criteria for the players in the enterprise: for example, that *all participants in the enterprise of air-transport support its effectiveness of the enterprise through their actions within their role in that enterprise.* A follow-on success-criterion from that might be that *all participants have enough support from each other to enable them to enact and continue in their role in the enterprise.*

The enterprise of air-transport is also part of the larger enterprise of transport in general, which will have a larger-scope end-to-end concern that "people and things transit *from their point of origin to their final destination* safely, intact and on-time" and so on. Given this, the airport will need its shared enterprise to include success-criteria that focus on its interfaces with other modes of transport, to satisfy that larger-scope requirement.

From Values to Principles

The **principles** for governance of an enterprise provide *practical, actionable guidance* on how to address and align with enterprise vision, values, constraints, and success-criteria within everyday action. The values must pervade throughout every layer and function, downward into the fine detail of systems designs and individual actions. We use principles to help make that happen, and make the values real in everything the enterprise is and does.

In some ways, principles are *above* the law – or rather, they are what law is drawn *from*. Each law, regulation, standard, or suchlike is actually a prepackaged *interpretation* of a principle, specifying how things supposedly *should* work, in theory, in a given context, "in a perfect world" – in other words, "inside the box." Yet principles should apply *everywhere* within the enterprise. In effect, whenever Reality Department forces us "outside the box," and the law or standard or whatever no longer makes practical sense, we'll still have the respective underlying principles to fall back on, to guide our decision-making in whatever we need to do within the enterprise. That's what the "chaos-checklist" is for, for example: it provides a reminder of core principles that can provide *useful* guidance when we're faced with some outside-any-box "unknown-unknown" in run-time action.

Given that, we do need to recognize the priority of principles, above laws or standards or anything of that kind. Principles really *do* come first. That's why, in enterprise-architecture, often the first principle we'll need to write will be about the primacy of principles. Yet in turn the principles express the enterprise values; and the values themselves express the shared vision that defines what the enterprise *is*. That's why none of this work is abstract, and why it *does* need to be done even before we start to look at the organization itself: it's because without this, the enterprise, and thence the organization, would have no identifiable or *practical* purpose.

Warning There's also another core-principle that may be easy to miss here, from an architectural perspective, yet is actually *essential for every enterprise*: that **no player in the enterprise is inherently "more important" than any other**. The assertion might at first seem a bit "political," but it arises directly from the nature of "enterprise" itself: all of the players in an enterprise are inherently interdependent with every other player in some way or another. In that sense, a useful test-guideline at a whole-of-enterprise level is that *either everyone wins, or everyone loses*.

In practice, as architects, we'll no doubt see all manner of attempts to create exceptions to that principle. This can perhaps be seen most easily in the enterprise of politics, such as in "All animals are equal, but some are more equal than others," to quote George Orwell's *Animal Farm*, for example, or Francis Wilhoit's description of one strand of politics, that it "consists of exactly one proposition, to wit, that there must be in-groups whom the law protects but does not bind, alongside out-groups whom the law binds but does not protect." But that kind of imbalance doesn't occur only in politics: it can happen *anywhere*, in any enterprise – including our own enterprise, if we're not careful.

As in most systems, imbalance will also impact the effectiveness of the enterprise: in general, the more unbalanced it is, the less effective it can be. It's true, though, that most enterprises can and do survive *some* degree of imbalance. And some enterprises – such as governments almost everywhere, perhaps – can limp along for quite a long time despite high levels of imbalance, low effectiveness relative to their vision and purpose, and very low levels of satisfaction among some or even all of their players.

The useful test there is "*satisfaction*," or literally "making enough." As long as the players are making enough in some sense from their engagement in the enterprise, they'll probably continue to stay around. But "*enough*" is always somewhat subjective, and it's unwise for any player in the enterprise to try to push it too far. If they do, some or all of the other players will walk away; the entire enterprise will come apart in a chaotic-collapse; and then *everyone* will lose. Not A Good Idea…

Principles form hierarchies as they devolve down into the deeper detail. Yet ultimately every one of those principles needs to be anchored back into one or more values; and in turn every value needs to be expressed in explicit, actionable principles. We'll also need to test the validity of each principle via keywords such as *understandable, robust, complete, consistent, stable, measurable,* and *verifiable*.

By their nature, principles will also often compete or conflict with each other: transparency versus privacy, for example, or innovation versus the safety of "the known." We need to document such clashes, and, wherever practicable, assign priority to one or other of the respective principles – such as in the Agile Manifesto, as mentioned above – so as to simplify decision-making in the field.

Given that, there's another essential principle that we'll need that comes in two interrelated parts. The first would be an assertion that every person in the enterprise is *personally responsible* for acting in accordance with all respective principles in their context. The other would be an acknowledgment that while, in "a perfect world," that mandated responsibility *is* the requirement, few if any people will ever be able to achieve it – not in the real-world, anyway. The appropriate test there would not be a demand for an impossible perfection, but more that all applicable principles were taken into account, and that all reasonable efforts were made to resolve any conflicts, under the constraints of the context.

We can explore the requirements and content for principles via questions such as these:

- What principles apply in the enterprise? In what ways are these principles expressed and documented?

- What value or values does each principle express? How would you confirm that those values are expressed by the principles?

- Are there any principles – explicit or implicit – that do *not* seem to be anchored in any espoused enterprise value? If so, what values are implied by such principles? Do any such "shadow" values conflict with the espoused values of the organization? If so, how, and which values "win"?

- What principles express each value? Is every espoused value expressed within at least one hierarchy of principles which devolves all the way down to the operations layer? If not, what principles would be required to express that value?

- In what ways are each principle applied, in theory, and in practice? What evidence exists to identify that they *are* applied, or *not* applied? If not applied in practice, what needs to be done to ensure that they *are* applied? What metrics would be needed to monitor and confirm this?

- What conflicts exist between principles? What guidance is provided to help people resolve such conflicts between principles in their own work?

There are many ways to define principles, but the format that we recommend for whole-enterprise architecture would be as follows:

- *Name*: Represents the essence of the principle in a form that is easy to remember, and may be embedded in checklists and the like

- *Statement*: Presents a succinct, unambiguous summary of the principle

- *Rationale*: Anchors the principle back to the business reasons and business-benefits arising from the principle, and ultimately to the core value or values that it represents

- *Implications*: Describes how the principle should be expressed in everyday actions or in influence on practical decisions

- *Consequences*: Describes what the respective part of the context would be expected to look like if the principle *is* applied, or is *not* applied.

Document each principle in the enterprise section of the requirements repository, as linked trails of decomposition and derivation linked back to the respective enterprise-values.

Example For the airport, the principles for its enterprise of air-transport would include all of the essential ones described above: the primacy of principles, that no player is more important than any other, and that everyone is personally responsible, to the best of their ability, for appropriate compliance with all applicable laws, regulations, standards, and principles for the respective context.

Beyond that, the enterprise would also need actionable principles to support each of the values and their respective priorities as described earlier. These would include the primacy of safety, for example, the importance of ensuring all required forms of security, and the importance to the enterprise as a whole of timeliness and end-to-end connection and coordination.

Elements of the Enterprise

Having established the *characteristics* of the enterprise, we now need to identify the essential components or "**elements**" that would be needed in this enterprise, to enable it to reach toward its desired vision in real-world action. We can summarize these elements in terms of the content-categories described in the previous *Foundations* Step:

- *What*: Key "things," items, assets, and resources
- *How*: Key actions and activities
- *Where*: Key locations
- *Who*: Key roles and responsibilities
- *When*: Key events
- *Why*: Key decision-types, rules, standards, laws

We'll need to make a brief list of elements for each category and, as shown in Figure 8-3, add them to our overall picture of the shared-enterprise.

shared-enterprise
(Vision / Values / Constraints / Success / Story)
(What / How / Where / Who / When / Why)

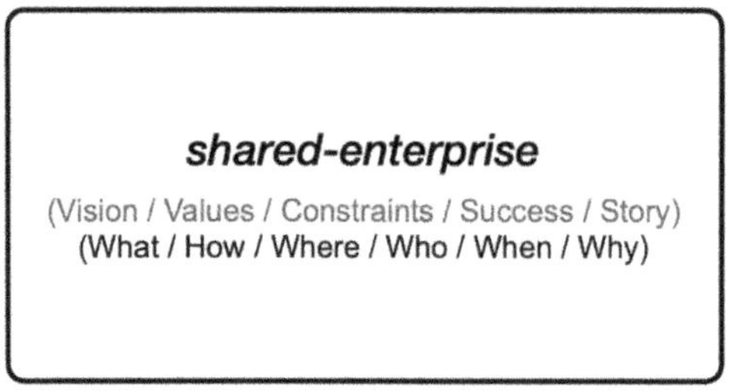

Figure 8-3. *The elements of the shared-enterprise*

We use those six categories to help us identify and list the most essential and characteristic elements that apply across the overall enterprise. For example, the lists for *What, How,* and *Why* would expand on and provide more detail for, respectively, the *focus, action,* and *driver* sections of the enterprise vision-statement.

Note As described in Chapter 5, these abstract element-categories will eventually morph into their real-world counterparts, as *Asset, Capability/Process, Location,* Agent, *Event, Decision/Reason,* and so on. For here, though, the emphasis will need to be on those more abstract versions of the categories.

Each element will be a major focus for at least *some* of the players in the enterprise. In turn, *all* players will be part of an enterprise in which these elements will apply and are important, either directly or indirectly. For the enterprise-story to succeed, as per its success-criteria above, all of the elements we identify here *must* exist and/or be supported *somewhere* within the overall enterprise.

For the *What, How, Where,* and *When* lists, the **value-segments** set – *physical, virtual, relational, aspirational,* and also *temporal,* as described in Chapter 5 – can also be useful for identifying items in those element-categories. For example:

- *Physical*: (What) tangible "thing"; (How) action on tangible "thing"; (Where) physical location; (When) physical event

- *Virtual*: (What) data or idea; (How) action on data; (Where) identifier for location; (When) information-based event

- *Relational*: (What) connection between people, inference between information-items; (How) bringing people together; (Where) relative positioning, such as in a reporting-hierarchy; (When) change in relationship

- *Aspirational*: (What) souvenir, talisman, brand, logo; (How) morale-boosting; (Where) tourist-destination, sports-stadium, or other "sacred place"; (When) purpose-linked event

- *Temporal* ("Where"-only): Location in terms of a particular date, time, or interval, often associated with a specific "When" or event

CHAPTER 8   STEP 1: IDENTIFY THE ENTERPRISE

Overall, across that set of element-lists, each of those value-segments should be represented by at least one enterprise-element. Note, though, that some real-world elements may well be made up of composites of these categories. For example, a boarding-pass would always include virtual-information, but may also take the form of a physical card that carries that virtual information.

To identify these key elements, explore the implications of the enterprise vision, values, constraints, and success-criteria identified earlier above, in terms of those categories of *What, How, Where, Who, When,* and *Why*. Optionally, note and annotate any essential relationships and/or dependencies between elements in the same category-list, or between different categories. Aim to collect around *six to ten elements* per category.

Example   For the airport, the initial *What* list for its shared-enterprise would include transit-entity (passenger, baggage, freight), vehicles, buildings, transit-documents, status-information, flight-information, position-information, people-relationships, and public-relations.

The *How* list would include process-for-outbound, process-for-inbound, schedule flights, manage aircraft-movement on ground, manage aircraft-movement in air, manufacture aircraft, fly aircraft, and maintain aircraft.

The *Where* list would include on-the-ground, airport as node, airport-to-ground, airport-to-air, in-the-air, manufacturer facilities, maintenance facilities, air-traffic control facilities, and nation.

The *Who* list would include aircraft-manufacturer, aircraft-operator, airport, passenger, freight-shipper, ground-transport, air-traffic control, maintenance-provider, fuel-provider, and regulator.

The *When* list would include ground-arrival, outbound-process, air-departure, take-off, in-flight, landing, air-arrival, inbound-process, ground-departure, and in-maintenance.

The *Why* list would include aircraft-safety, transit-safety and security (passenger, baggage, freight), flight-safety, ground-safety, information-security, national-security, biosecurity, social-license-to-operate, and quality of service.

Enterprise Roles and Interactions

Next, we'll need to identify the player-*roles* across the entire enterprise. From those, we'll establish the *relationships* and *interactions* between them, their individual and mutual *responsibilities*, and their respective expectations and drivers. Given those, we'll also be able to identify the various forms of *governance* that would need to apply across the whole of the enterprise.

This expands on the "Elements of the Enterprise" section above, with an emphasis on the *Who* part, as roles, and aspects of the *Why* part, as governance.

Note Remember that this is still about *the enterprise as a whole*, regardless of whether or not the organization is present within that overall enterprise. It's in the next section, "Organization and Enterprise," that you'll identify where to position the organization within this mesh of roles, responsibilities, and relationships.

In effect, the *Who*-category elements provide us with the list of **roles** in play in the enterprise. If we then cross-map those with elements from the other categories, we can build a picture of those roles' respective **relationships** and **interactions**. We do that cross-map through questions such as these:

- *Who + What*: What assets and resources are used by and passed between players?

- *Who + How*: What do individual players and groups of players do with and to those assets and resources?

- *Who + Where*: What is the location of each player and item at each moment, in terms of geographic or physical location, virtual identifiers, relative to each other, or relative to shared-purpose?

- *Who + When*: What events, physical or otherwise, that guide the actions of each player, and what coordinates those interactions between players?

- *Who + Why*: What decisions guide what players do? What guides those decisions?

As we build the map, we need to confirm that each item in the *What, How, Where, When,* and *Why* element-lists can be associated with at least one role or player-type from the *Who* element-list. We may also identify items that we'll need to amend or add into one or more of the element-lists. Continue the mapping-process until *all* content from all of the element-lists has been accounted for in the map.

It's usually best to start the mapping on a whiteboard or with sticky-notes on a large sheet of paper, because the relative positions of the various players in the space are likely to move around until a natural structure becomes clear. Once the structure of the map starts to stabilize, rework it into a more visual form that can be shared with others. A complete map should ideally show every element in the enterprise context, although that can become cluttered and too hard to read. Figure 8-4 provides a basic Enterprise Context map for the airport's enterprise, simplified to show only the enterprise roles and relationships.

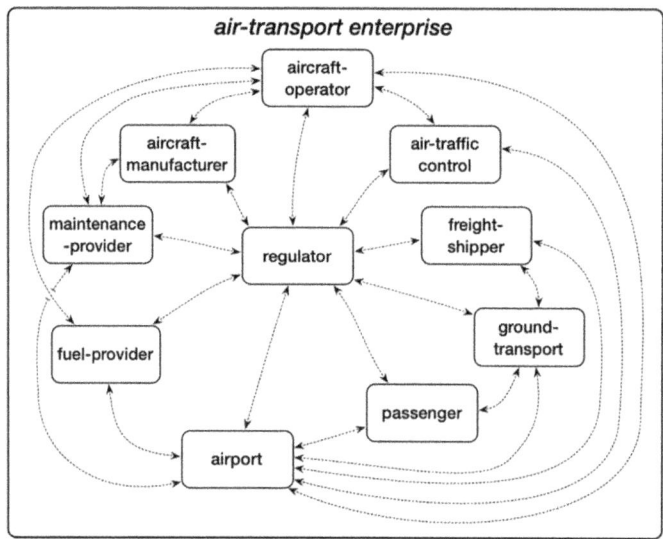

Figure 8-4. *Enterprise-Context map*

For each action, interaction, and outcome across the enterprise, we should also map out the **responsibilities** for each *Who*-element in the enterprise, and in relation to each other *Who*-element. We'll need this in order to identify what forms of governance and regulation will be required for the various parts of the enterprise. It's simplest to do this mapping in terms of the classic **RACI** or *Responsibility Assignment Matrix*:

- Who is *Responsible* for the action and/or outcome?
- Who is *Accountable* for the action and/or outcome?
- Who needs to be *Consulted* before, during, or after the action, or about the outcome?
- Who needs to be *Informed* before, during, or after the action, or about the outcome?

Note In using RACI, there's often some confusion about "Responsible" versus "Accountable." In some versions of the RACI frame, only one person is considered Responsible for the outcomes of actions in each context, while everyone else directly involved in the action is considered Accountable. However, we prefer and recommend the model which describes the responsibilities the other way round: everyone Responsible for their actions in that context, with only one person Accountable as the "approver" or "approving authority."

You can use either of those two models for this purpose. Do be clear, though, about which model you're using, and use it consistently throughout this work. Don't mix them up!

In the next task here, we need to identify and describe the forms of **governance** that should apply across the enterprise as a whole. Note that some of these forms of governance that we identify here may not apply directly to *all* roles, but would still imply *Consulted*-type and/or *Informed*-type responsibilities even for those roles for whom the respective forms of governance apply only indirectly. Regulators and the like would typically have the responsibility to define enterprise-scope regulations and standards, and to verify compliance to those requirements. Ultimately, though, it's still the responsibility of *everyone in the enterprise* to take the respective actions that will make compliance happen, and support effectiveness across the enterprise as a whole.

To do this, we link the responsibilities for each *Who*, as identified above, back to the enterprise-definitions from the previous section. The question we need to answer here is

- What governance and compliance do we need, to ensure that each player in the enterprise does everything they can to support the vision, values, and success-criteria for the shared-enterprise as a whole?

CHAPTER 8   STEP 1: IDENTIFY THE ENTERPRISE

There are three parts to this.

First, review the vision, values, constraints, and success-criteria from the "Enterprise As Storyworld" section earlier, to identify **governance-themes** that would imply **governance-requirements**, so as to ensure alignment to those values, and support continual-improvement overall. For each of those themes, identify

- The requirement or governing-*principle*
- The implications if the requirement *is* met
- The implications if the requirement is *not*-met

Next, identify appropriate **governance-models**, such as defined within laws, regulations, standards, guidelines, and checklists, that could be used to specify **governance-tests** for any given governance-requirement. For *each* governance-requirement derived above, identify one or more sets of

- *Governance-model*: Type of law, regulation, standard, or suchlike.
- *Governance-positioning*: Relative to the enterprise, the governance-model is internal, "self-policed" by the overall enterprise, or external, "externally-policed" by some other agency such as a government regulator.
- *Governance-tests* that would indicate compliance or non-compliance to the requirement.
- *Governance-supervisor*: Typical agency that assures that the governance-model is appropriately applied.

Finally, link those requirements to each role in the enterprise in terms of **mutual-responsibilities**, using the same RACI frame as per earlier. For *each* governance-requirement derived above, identify

- Who is *Responsible* for ensuring alignment and/or compliance to the requirement? What actions do they need to take to support that responsibility?
- Who is *Accountable* for ensuring alignment and/or compliance to the requirement? What actions do they need to take to support that accountability?

- Who needs to be *Consulted* about ensuring alignment and/or compliance to the requirement? What actions do they need to take to verify that they have been appropriately consulted about that requirement?

- Who needs to be *Informed* about ensuring alignment and/or compliance to the requirement? What actions do they need to take to verify that they have been appropriately informed about that requirement?

Caution Do remember the earlier note about Responsible versus Accountable: be clear which way round of that pairing you'll use, be consistent, and don't mix them up!

Note also that this exercise may bring up further roles for the enterprise-context, which might otherwise be regarded as "outside" of the enterprise, but are still relevant *to* the enterprise. Some government-regulators, for example, may now be seen here as active players "inside" the enterprise as a whole, and the broader community may be an important stakeholder in how governance for the enterprise should be applied.

Using the questions above, derive the **governance-themes**, **governance-principles**, **governance-requirements**, **governance-tests**, and **governance-models** for the enterprise. Map out the respective **governance-responsibilities**, from the regulators, to develop, tests, and verify compliance to the governance-models, and from everyone, to ensure their own compliance with those requirements and models. If necessary, update the enterprise-elements and/or enterprise-roles lists to reflect any necessary changes identified in this action. Document the results of this work in the respective risk and compliance architecture-repositories.

> **Example** For the airport, its shared-enterprise will need governance for each of its roles or player-types, both within their own operations, in each of their interactions with other roles as shown in Figure 8-4, and in relation to the broader community and others affected by this enterprise, in relation to each of the values-themes such as safety, security, timeliness, and so on that may be applicable in each case.
>
> It's a lot – far too much to define here. But one that may be useful to explore on your own, perhaps?

Before we finish this section, it may be useful to do a quick **After-Action Review**.

What was supposed to happen? We intended to develop a picture of the shared-enterprise, to gain a clear understanding of the context in which we would place our organization.

What actually happened? We explored and mapped out

- The enterprise-context, in terms of its vision, values, constraints, success-criteria
- The key elements, in terms of What, How, Where, Who, When, and Why, that would be needed to enable the players in the enterprise to reach towards its shared vision
- The key roles, relationships, and responsibilities required in order to make that happen
- The types of governance needed to help all of the players keep on-track to the shared purpose

We illustrated each of these with our worked-example of an airport, seeking to understand its own business-context.

What was the source of any difference?

- We've achieved everything that we set out to do here, in terms of describing and identifying the overall range of elements that would form the anchor for a whole-of-enterprise architecture.
- The worked-example for the airport is still incomplete, though one or two further passes through the same process should provide enough information to fill in any remaining essential gaps.

What can we learn from this?

- We really *can* identify and map the core elements of a shared-enterprise in not much more time than it takes to read this "Enterprise As Context" section of the book.

What are the benefits-realized from this?

- We have the core of a whole-enterprise-architecture, in a process that *can* be done with executives and others in half a day and that delivers its outcomes and information in a form that can be used directly by others for whole-enterprise architecture and more.

We'll do a similar After-Action Review when we complete the next section, on viewing the shared-enterprise from the organization's perspective.

Organization and Enterprise

In this overall section, we'll explore how to identify the key **strategic anchors** for the organization – about where and how it positions itself within the enterprise, and how it will deliver value to its customers, to its suppliers, to itself, and to the enterprise as a whole.

There are several parts to this process, which we'll base on the well-known sequence *Vision, Role, Mission, Goal*, as shown in Figure 8-5.

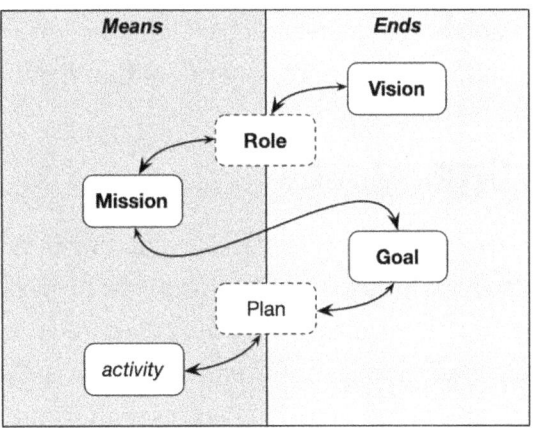

Figure 8-5. Vision, Role, Mission, Goal

For this purpose, we'll use a variant of that structure, because we don't yet need to go as far as Goals, but we do end up sort-of going through the Vision/Role/Mission part twice to capture a bit more about content and structure:

- *Enterprise-vision*, including values, constraints, and success-criteria
- *Enterprise-content*, the "elements" of the enterprise
- *Enterprise-roles*, including relationships, responsibilities, and governance
- *Organization-role in the enterprise*, including positioning and differentiation
- *Organization mission*, describing how it will serve the enterprise as a whole
- *Organization-vision*, including its role-specific values, constraints, and success-criteria
- *Organization value-propositions*, as its "missions" for other roles in the enterprise
- *Organization-content*, the "elements" of the organization in its enterprise role
- *Organization structure*, as a set of *internal* roles

In effect, we've already done the first three steps in that list, in the overall section "Enterprise As Context" above. Using that as a base, we can move straight to the point where the organization chooses its position and role within the shared-enterprise.

Positioning the Organization

The organization has a **strategic choice** about its positioning in the enterprise, in terms of its role and differentiation. It's one of the most important types of choice that the organization will ever make. The strategy-team can adjust and tweak that choice in small ways over time, following the dynamics of the enterprise, but that initial commitment to a positioning is so fundamental that it will affect *everything* that the organization is and does. As enterprise-architects, this process allows us to support the organization's executives in making *more conscious and considered choices* about what they want that positioning to be.

Start by reviewing the list of roles in the enterprise that we mapped out in the section "Enterprise Roles and Interactions." Choose a **role** from that list that you want to explore as a possible positioning for the organization.

Optionally, you may instead invent a role that does not yet exist in that enterprise – such as you might do if you see a gap in the market that has not yet been addressed, and that presents an opportunity to disrupt the market. If you do so, though, this new role *must* still align with the vision, values, constraints, success-criteria, and so on of the overall shared enterprise, as identified in the "Enterprise As Context" section above.

Use these questions as a cross-check that this would be a good positioning for the organization:

- What role or roles does the organization *want* to play within the enterprise, to contribute toward the vision?

- What roles does it *not* want to play – hence leaving open for other stakeholders?

- Who are those other stakeholders, and what roles do *they* play within the overall enterprise?

- What relationships and transactions are implied by these different roles within the enterprise?

- How would you verify that each role – especially the organization's own chosen role – *does* support the enterprise vision?

If that role seems a good fit for the organization, continue on. If not, loop back, and choose and test another role in the enterprise. If there are no roles that seem to fit, you'll need to go back to "Enterprise As Context," and map out a different shared-enterprise that looks like it may offer at least one role that could provide a suitable position for the organization.

Example For the airport, it already knows that it will take on the *Airport* role in its shared-enterprise of *air transport*.

Next, we'll need to map out, from the organization's chosen position in the shared-enterprise, its relationships with other roles and players in that enterprise.

231

CHAPTER 8 STEP 1: IDENTIFY THE ENTERPRISE

From the previous work in the "Enterprise Roles and Relationships" section, we already have the full list of enterprise roles, and summaries for the *What, How, Where, When,* and *Why* of the relationships between them. Given that, we can categorize the other players' roles in terms of their "distance" from the organization's own role:

- *Transaction* ("trade"): Typically, the organization's customers, suppliers, and other active partners

- *Direct-interaction* ("market"): Typically recruiters, trainers, regulators, and others with whom the organization will have direct yet non-transactional relationships

- *Indirect-interaction* ("enterprise"): All other roles previously identified as necessary to the overall shared-enterprise

This gives us the basis for an Organization-Context Map – sometimes nicknamed a "holomap" because it provides a view of ***the whole shared-enterprise as seen from the organization's perspective***.

Example For the airport, the set of roles and relationships for its shared-enterprise as a whole are as shown in the Enterprise-Context Map in Figure 8-4.

In its role as an Airport in that shared-enterprise, its main *transactions* are with the Aircraft-Operators and Freight-Shippers, who are its visible customers. It also needs to connect continually with Air-Traffic Control. Its relationship with Passengers and their baggage is somewhat transaction-like, so it does belong in this category, though in reality it's more like they're just passing through the system, rather than active customers as such. Other less-visible customers or partners, not shown in Figure 8-4, would include retail-stores and similar service-providers inside the airport itself.

It has non-transaction *direct-interactions* with Ground-Transport, moving people and things in and out of the "landside" of their airport, and also working-interactions with a myriad of different Regulators. It coordinates with Maintenance-Providers and Fuel-Providers to support its Aircraft-Operator customers. Not shown in the Enterprise-Context Map here, but likewise belonging in this category, would

CHAPTER 8   STEP 1: IDENTIFY THE ENTERPRISE

be others such as funders, insurers, auditors, and probably local, regional, and/or national government as providers of grants and subsidies.

It has only *indirect-interactions* with Aircraft-Manufacturers, and with the broader community on which its social-license-to-operate will depend.

Figure 8-6 shows the Organization-Context map for the airport's relationships with other roles in its "*air-transport*" shared-enterprise.

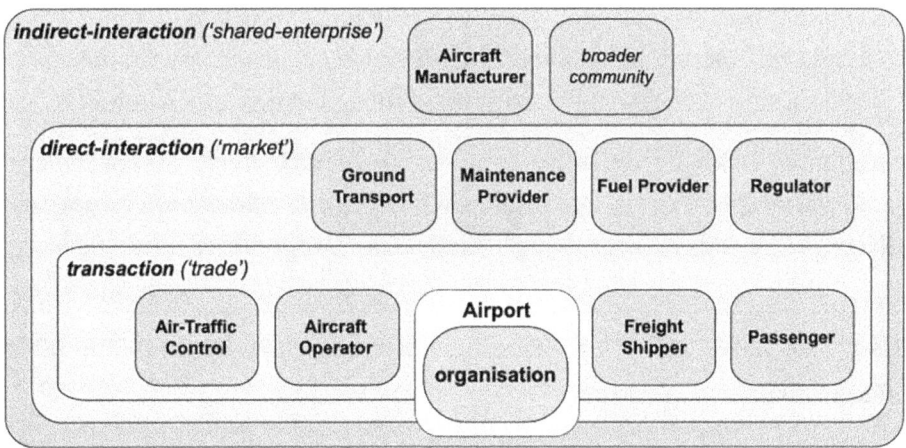

Figure 8-6. Organization-Context Map for the airport

The next step is to use **differentiation** to refine the organization's positioning in the enterprise. In other words, how it will distinguish itself, in the market and elsewhere, from other players who occupy the same nominal enterprise-role.

Note   If you position your organization in the exact same place within the enterprise as other players in that role, your options for differentiation may be limited to price and volume, with a risk of getting trapped in the wrong kind of competitive race-to-the-bottom.

For that reason, it's worthwhile exploring those questions below in some depth. For commercial-organizations, the right kind of use of the *Artist*-mode's outside-the-box thinking can provide a differentiation such that it might have no real competition at all.

233

CHAPTER 8   STEP 1: IDENTIFY THE ENTERPRISE

To do this, note first the enterprise vision, values, constraints, and success-criteria, and how these and the respective enterprise-elements apply to the enterprise-role that you've selected for the organization. From there, ask these questions:

- What does the enterprise require *everyone* in this role to do?

- Within those bounds, what can the organization do that could be different from others in the same role, in terms of *What, How, Where, Who, When,* or *Why*?

- Given those options, what does the organization *want* to do that could be different from others, and that also brings it closer to the vision, values, and success-criteria for the enterprise as a whole?

The organization's ***differentiation*** should ***change only slowly, if at all, over time***. Note that ***any change here*** may and often will ***imply and require major changes in capabilities and services*** at the strategic, tactical, and operational levels.

Example   For the airport, it will seek to differentiate itself from other airports in three main ways.

The first is a *Where*, about its physical location. It will be the main airport for a major regional city, giving it a broad catchment in an area that is not served by high-speed trains – its only potential competitor for fast medium-distance transport.

Next is a *What*, about its services. Although there are other airports within reach of the city, this will be the only one equipped to handle the larger aircraft needed for medium- to long-haul flights.

Finally, there is a *How*, about how it relates with its customers. This is a new modern airport, with full support for major airlines. It also wants to commit itself to the challenge of making the transit process as seamless and painless as possible for its passengers and freight, with a strong emphasis on customer-service in all of its forms.

Organization Mission

The next task is to identify the organization's **mission**, relative to other players in the overall enterprise. Before we move on, though, we need to clarify where "mission" fits into the greater scheme of things, from an *architectural* perspective.

First, **the mission does not stand on its own**. As shown earlier in Figure 8-5, it's *one* link in the "vision, role, mission, goal" chain that describes the architecture of how motivation works in real-world practice.

As also shown in Figure 8-5, the mission is more of a "How" than a "Why" – **a means, not an end** in itself. It's about services and capabilities and so on, and *how* the organization intends to use them to deliver value to everyone in the enterprise. The *why* for that mission comes more from the enterprise itself, via the enterprise-vision. This is another reason why, in architecture at least, it's crucially important to *not* confuse "mission" with "vision."

Much like a vision, though, **a mission usually describes a continuing-task** rather than a *goal-based task*. If the mission is only goal-based, the motivation to *do* anything for the mission will vanish as soon as the goal is reached. If we want the motivation to continue, the mission needs to be continuing too.

The mission describes how the organization will perform its role in the enterprise, so there should be **only one mission per role**. We should *not* have separate "missions" for each relationship with other roles in the enterprise – that's the task of *value-propositions*, which we'll explore after this. The only cases where an organization should have more than one mission is if it plays more than one role in an enterprise or, as in a business-conglomerate, it has business in more than one shared-enterprise.

Also, note that **a mission is literally a "sending"** – someone has sent the organization on that mission, to fulfill its role in the enterprise. In most cases, of course, the one doing the "sending" will be the organization itself. Yet it somehow often *feels* better, in a motivational sense, if it seems to be someone greater than just the organization that's doing the sending, as a "pull" from outside rather than a "push" from within. (See Hagel, Brown, and Davison's book *The Power Of Pull* for more on that – though note that their emphasis is more on how the same "pull" mechanism can be used to pull people *toward* the organization, rather than pushed *at* by the organization.)

Given all of this, we'll need to frame a **mission-statement** that links the organization, via its role, to the broader shared-enterprise. This needs to summarize what the organization does for the enterprise, and how and why its differentiation encapsulates the unique elements of its chosen role within the enterprise.

> **Warning** Although, as with value-propositions, all of the organization's marketing should ultimately be anchored in the mission, the mission-statement itself is *not* solely a tool for marketing. As indicated above, the mission's architectural-role is much broader than that, both within the organization itself, and in the organization's relationships with the other players in the shared-enterprise.
>
> Far too often, we'll see a supposed "mission" framed as some kind of a grandiose marketing-puff: "We will be the greatest airport in the world!" or something like that. That might appeal to the marketing-team, perhaps, and may help the executive-team feel a bit better for a while. But to everyone else, both inside and beyond, it just makes the organization look vain, stupid, bombastic, and with no real clue about what they actually need to do. Not A Good Idea…

The mission-statement needs to embody only the most essential points about who the organization are, what it does, and why it does that *for others in the enterprise.* We can make a useful start on that with the *What, How, Where, Who, When,* and *Why* questions:

- *What* does the organization do?
- *How* does the organization do what it does?
- *Where* does the organization do what it does?
- *Who* does the organization work with, to achieve its outcomes?
- *When* does the organization do what it does?
- *Why* does the organization do what it does, and how is it different from what others do?

We then link that with what we've gleaned earlier above about the organization's role in the shared-enterprise:

- What is the organization's *role* in the enterprise?
- Who does the organization *serve* in that role?
- *In what ways* does the organization serve those others in that role?
- What *tests and metrics* would the organization need to confirm that its mission is "on purpose" and *effective* in supporting its role in the enterprise?

We derive the mission-statement from the answers to all of those questions above. By convention, the mission-statement would begin with something like "At this airport, our mission is...," with an emphasis on what the organization *does*, rather than what it *is* or wants to be. The statement should, again, be brief – ideally, no more than perhaps two to three sentences.

Note also that, as with the organization's enterprise-role, the organization's mission should change only slowly over time. That's because any amendment here is likely to require significant changes in capabilities and services, particularly at the tactical and operational levels.

Example For the airport, the initial mission-statement its executive-team arrive at is *"At this airport, our mission is to serve the people of this region by providing them with safe, secure, reliable, and friendly access to air-transport, with quick connections throughout the country and across the world."*

It's only a first try, of course, but it's short, it's easy to understand, and it does indeed encapsulate what they do, where they do it, who they do it for, and the core values they espouse. Good enough, anyway, to *use* straight away in their business-relationships with others.

Organization-Vision and Values

At this point, we loop back to the start of the *Vision/Role/Mission/Goal* sequence, but at the next level down, viewing the organization as its own enterprise in relation to the broader shared-enterprise that denotes its Context.

Because the organization's enterprise is "within" the shared-enterprise, it automatically inherits all of the latter's vision, values, value-priorities, constraints, success-criteria, and so on. What we need to do here is to identify what aspects, if any, of that list we would need to amend or add, to better support the organization's chosen role and mission in the shared-enterprise.

We would identify and derive these in much the same way as for the enterprise, using the same processes described earlier in the section "Enterprise As Storyworld." Note that the enterprise values and so on have priority here: we can amend or add to those aspects from the enterprise, but we can't simply overrule or ignore any of them for the organization.

> **Example** For the airport, it accepts all of the vision, values, and other aspects identified for its "*air-transport*" shared-enterprise, including safety, security, timeliness, and management of cost.
>
> It does also add some refinements to the default "*Elegant*" or people-oriented category, such as friendliness, comfort, mutual-respect, and "creating a sense of service." Safety and security, however, still remain as the highest priorities of all.

If we're doing this process for an existing organization, there are two additional cross-checks we'll need here. The first is about **values** and, specifically, any potential or actual mismatch between ***required-values***, ***espoused-values***, and/or ***actual-values***, within the organization itself, and/or in its relationships with other players in the shared-enterprise:

- What shared values are required from every player in the overall enterprise, in order for that enterprise to achieve success within the terms of its vision?

- What individual and collective values – either implicit or explicit – are required to support each of the relationships and transactions in the organization's roles within the enterprise?

- What values does the organization espouse, both in its relationships with others and its relationships within and to itself?

- What actual values does the organization express in its actions and relations with others and within itself?

- Are there any misalignments between required, espoused, and actual values? If so, what impacts do these differences have on the effectiveness of the shared enterprise, of the organization in relation to and with the enterprise, and the organization's internal functioning and relationships within itself?

Identify ***required-values*** from an assessment of what "effectiveness" would look like in relation to the enterprise and its vision. For example, fairness and trust will usually be required in almost any functional enterprise.

Identify ***espoused-values*** from the organization's Annual Report or other public sources, such as an "About Us" or "Our Values" section on a website, or publicity material provided to prospective customers, investors, or employees.

Identify ***actual-values*** from the behaviors or phrases actually used within the organization. Note especially how these may vary at different levels or in different parts of the organization.

Document the required and espoused values as core requirements in the requirements repository. Document each values-mismatch as a priority item in the architecture-risks register (though see the "Caution"-note on this later).

The other cross-check is about the organization's **business-purpose**. The previous parts of the assessment should have identified what the organization believes its business purpose to be; we now need to check that against the reality. To *see* the difference can sometimes be painful, but nonetheless important to know...

Perhaps the best guide for this is a phrase coined by the cyberneticist Stafford Beer: *"the purpose of a system is [is expressed in] what it does."* In systems-theory terms, the organization is a system in its own right, interacting with the larger ecosystem of the overall enterprise. The vision, values, and principles define what the organization's purpose *should* be, in theory. By contrast, Beer's phrase, usually known by its acronym "**POSIWID**," indicates the organization's effective purpose *in practice*, and hence its *actual* principles, values, and, probably, vision. For example:

- The organization states that health and safety are key values, but the reality is that there are high rates of accidents, illness, and absenteeism. From POSIWID, we can be fairly certain that those themes are *not* valued in practice.

- The organization's website asserts the primacy of quality above everything else in its products. But POSIWID shows us that the managers believe the only thing that matters is "the numbers" – and their bonuses also reflect that fact. Notice what impact this has on product-quality, and on overall effectiveness.

Values *matter*. Yet we need to be clear which values *actually* apply in the enterprise; otherwise, we have no means to identify when what we do really *is* "on purpose."

Any values-mismatch will lead to ineffectiveness. Each mismatch is something we'll need to address as an organization, and hence needs to be documented in the architecture gap-analysis:

- If "the purpose of the system is what it does," what *real* principles and values are implied in what happens in the organization and in its relations with the overall enterprise?

- Comparing the results with the values and principles already documented, what conflicts can be identified? In each case, do the espoused values have priority, or the actual "shadow" values? What is the impact of each values-mismatch on overall effectiveness?

As before, document each mismatch of values or principles as a high-priority entry in the architecture-risks register.

Caution From an architecture perspective, you *do* need to document any values-mismatch between required, espoused, and enacted values, and misalignments between espoused and actual POSIWID-derived business-purpose, because these can, and usually will, have huge impacts on concerns such as enterprise-effectiveness, trust-issues, and the organization's social-license-to-operate. However, it's wise to document such issues in a secure for-architect-eyes-only part of the architecture-repositories, and **be very careful about where, when, why, and with whom you discuss these issues**. In general, *only* discuss these issues with others when you have been explicitly asked to do so, and usually *only* when you have authority to do so from the executive as a whole.

The reason why it can be so dangerous for architects even to talk about values-mismatches is that it can trigger and/or expose all manner of hidden risks that can be very hard to resolve, including power-issues, anticlient-risks, enterprise-hijack risks, assumption-mythquakes and more. The blunt reality is that most people do *not* like to hear about this – especially if they're the ones who are causing the problems in the first place…

There'll be more on this later, particularly in Step 5, in the section "Facing Hidden Risks" in Chapter 12. In the meantime, though, **do beware of the politics here** – because those politics can bite!

Organization Value-Propositions

Next, we'll identify the organization's **value-proposition** – literally, ***the value that it proposes to deliver*** to its customers and others. Or rather, its value-*propositions*, plural, because the organization will need at least one value-proposition for *each role* that it may interact with in the enterprise.

In effect, a value-proposition is ***a promise about service***, and quality of service. In a classic business-model, we might only be interested in the relationships and interdependencies within its immediate supply-chain, from supplier's-supplier to customer's-customer. In a whole-enterprise architecture, though, we recognize that a shared-enterprise can only succeed when *all* of its dependencies are fully supported, directly or indirectly, by *all* players in the enterprise. This means that we'll also need to have value-propositions for regulators, recruiters, and many others, all the way across the entire enterprise. In our worked-example, the airport will need distinct value-propositions for and with each of the roles in its "*air-transport*" enterprise as shown in Figure 8-4.

From the work we did in the "Enterprise Roles and Interactions" section above, we'll have already identified the key roles in the enterprise, the respective responsibilities for each role, and the relationships between those roles. By choosing a role and mission within the enterprise, the organization also takes on the responsibilities and relationships of that role, both directly with certain other roles and then indirectly, via *those* roles' relationships and responsibilities, onward to all other players in the enterprise.

To identify what needs to go into the value-propositions for each interaction, we'll need to categorize the respective role-relationships in terms of their "distance" from the organization. We would use the same categories that we did when positioning the organization into the shared-enterprise: *transaction*, *direct-interaction*, and *indirect-interaction*. We also need to add another category, "*self*," to represent the organization's side of each value-proposition. This would be to ensure, for example, that the organization receives enough from other players in the shared-enterprise that it *can* continue to play its role within that enterprise.

Note Some role-relationships may turn out not to be as straightforward as they might at first seem. The airport, for example, has transaction-type interactions with the Passenger role, but they aren't actually direct customers of the airport itself. Instead, they're in a close customer-of-customer relationship with the airport as it acts on behalf of its *actual* direct-customers, such as the Air-Operators who operate the flights that connect to the airport, and the shops, restaurants, and other services that rent the retail-space within the airport.

Given that example, you may find that you'll also need to add further roles and players into the overall enterprise, such as the communities and countries within which the organization operates and where its members' families live. Where appropriate, return briefly to the "Elements of the Enterprise" section to add those roles to the "*Who*" element-list, and to the "Enterprise Roles and Interactions" section to amend the role-details and governance-implications for those roles. Other roles such as the airport's shops and services may more properly belong to the "*Who*"-elements for the organization rather than for the enterprise: see the sections "Organization Content" and "Organization Structure" below for more detail on that.

Note too that the details you find here may also suggest the need for further tweaks and amendments to the organization's mission and/or vision. If so, go back to the sections "Organization Mission" and/or "Organization-Vision," respectively, to make the necessary adjustments. You may need to iterate back and forth a few times between mission, vision, and value-propositions before moving on to explore the requirements for governance.

Do apply the "Just Enough Detail" principle here, though! For an initial version of this, you probably need only the most basic detail for the "transaction"-type interactions with customers, suppliers, and partners – much as in a classic business-model – and also perhaps a one-line overview for each of the direct-interaction roles. By the time you're doing this for real, though, you *will* need the full detail for all of the interaction-types, including all of those indirect-interactions with the more-distant players in the enterprise.

For each of these role-relationships, we identify what needs to be exchanged between the organization and the respective role. We'll already have some suggestions about this, from the "*What*"-element list derived in the work we did in the "Elements of the Enterprise" section, and about exchanges between roles as derived from the "*Who + What*" exploration in the "Enterprise Roles and Interactions" section. From that, we can identify the value that each party obtains from that interaction, typically in terms of one or more of the enterprise-values and/or success-criteria from the "Enterprise As Storyworld" section.

Map out the details for each of these value-relationships as follows:

- *Role*: The other party in the interaction – either the abstract role as per the set of previously-identified "Enterprise-roles" or, optionally, the name of a specific organization that takes on that role

- *Interaction-type*: Either "transaction," "direct," "indirect," or "self"

- *Value provided to <role>*: The "*What*" proposed to be provided by the organization, such as physical goods or services information, person-to-person connection or brand-connection

- *Value to <role>*: Why that "*What*" would be perceived as "valuable" for that role's activities in the enterprise

- *Value for <role>*: How the transaction or interaction supports that role's mission within the enterprise

- *Value created by "self" for <role>*: How the organization will create and/or deliver the "*What*" to be provided to the other role

- *Value provided to "self"*: The "*What*" proposed by the other role to be provided in return to the organization

- *Value to "self"*: Why that "*What*" would be perceived as "valuable" for the organization's own role in the enterprise

- *Value for "self"*: How the transaction or interaction supports the organization's mission within the enterprise

- *Value for enterprise*: How the transaction or interaction supports the vision, values, and success-criteria of the enterprise as a whole

From those details, derive a brief statement that summarizes the mutual value-propositions between the organization and the respective enterprise-role.

> **Note** You may find it useful to cross-check your work here with the approach popularized in Alex Osterwalder's book *Value Proposition Design*.
>
> Do note, though, that contracts, warranties, service-level agreements, and so on are always a two-way street: value-propositions need to work the same way. However, the approach described in that book addresses only *one* side of the relationship, the value-proposition to be made by the organization to some other "customer"-type party. You may need to adapt that approach somewhat to align with the more symmetrical two-way model of value-proposition that's being developed here.

Document each value-proposition and its underlying source-information in the architecture-repository. Also, optionally, rework the respective Organization-Context Map, such as shown in Figure 8-6, to include connection-lines that illustrate each of the interactions and exchanges, and the value-proposition that underpins that relationship.

> **Example** For the airport, its value-proposition to the Passenger role is that it will provide a space for connection with air-travel that is clean, comfortable, easy to navigate and use, and friendly and stress-free. In return, it asks the Passenger-role to treat all others in the same way, including other Passengers, and the staff of the airport, the security-staff, the staff of the Air-Operators at the airport, and the staff of the various vendors who provide food and goods throughout the airport.

In the next step, we explore in more depth how **enterprise-governance** would apply to ***the value-propositions*** that the organization will use, as above, to guide its relationships with other players in the shared-enterprise.

In essence, this is the same process as with governance for the overall enterprise, but adapted to fit organization-specific concerns. As before, this also needs to link with each role in its Organization-Context Map, such as shown in Figure 8-6, and again back to the vision, values, constraints, and success-criteria as identified earlier in the "Enterprise As Storyworld" section. The question we would aim to answer here is

- What governance and compliance will the organization need, to ensure that each player in the enterprise with whom it interacts, and everyone within the organization, will act in accordance with the respective value-propositions, and that they will do everything they can to support the vision, values, and success-criteria for the organization and the shared-enterprise as a whole?

Again, these concerns are always *everyone's* responsibility. What we look for here are the forms of governance that can help everyone involved engage appropriately with that responsibility.

For this purpose, we'll employ the same process that we used to explore governance at the whole-enterprise-level, as described earlier in the "Enterprise Roles and Interactions" section. We'll capture the same types of items as before:

- Governance-principle
- Governance-requirement
- Context for governance
- Implications if the requirement is met or not-met
- The governance-model to be used
- Its positioning relative to the organization (self-governance, or governance by others)
- Person or governance-body that would assure that the governance-model is appropriately applied and complied with by all relevant parties

The process is somewhat simpler this time, because most of this merely extends the work that we did back there. We also won't need to do a full RACI mapping for each governance-requirement here, because at the whole-of-organization level, by definition, the organization declares itself to be *Responsible* for each of the principles that it chooses to apply to itself. We do need, though, to pay particular attention to any *other* governance principles for which the organization's enterprise-role is listed as *Responsible* or *Accountable*. We may also be able to derive further guidance-principles from the organization's *mission* and *differentiation*, as described respectively in the "Organization Mission" and "Positioning the Organization" sections above.

> **Example** For the airport, it will need governance for each of its role-relationships, as outlined in Figure 8-6, and for their respective value-propositions. Each of these will need to be assessed in terms of each of the values and suchlike that it mapped out in its work in the "Organization-Vision and Values" section.
>
> As with enterprise-governance, it's a lot – far too much to define here. Again, though, it might be something that's useful to explore on your own.

Organization Content

As a cross-check on the organization's role, positioning, mission, and value-propositions, we'll need to identify the subset of the enterprise-elements – *What, How, Where, Who, When,* and *Why* – that would apply to that role within the overall shared-enterprise.

We would identify and derive these in much the same way as we did for the shared enterprise, using the same processes described earlier in the section "Elements of the Enterprise."

> **Example** For the airport, it identified its relevant subsets of enterprise-elements, mapped out in terms of *transaction, direct,* and *indirect* concerns, as follows:
>
> For the enterprise *What*-elements, the airport would have a transaction concern about *transit-entities* such as passenger, baggage, or freight; about *vehicles* and *buildings*; about *transit-documents, status-information, flight-information,* and *position-information*; and about *people-relationships* and *public-relations*. There are no enterprise *What*-elements for which it will have only a direct or indirect concern.
>
> For the enterprise *How*-elements, the airport would have a transaction concern about *process-for-outbound, process-for-inbound,* and *manage aircraft-movement on ground*. It will have a direct concern about *schedule flights* and *maintain aircraft*, and also *manage aircraft-movement in air* where it relates to the airport itself. It will only have an indirect interest in *manufacture aircraft* and *fly aircraft*.

For the enterprise *Where*-elements, the airport would have a transaction concern about *airport-as-node, on-the-ground, airport-to-ground, airport-to-air*, and *nation*. It will have a direct concern about *maintenance facilities* and *air-traffic control facilities*. It will only have an indirect interest in *manufacturer facilities* and about what happens *in the air* beyond the airport itself.

For the enterprise *Who*-elements, the airport would have a transaction concern about *aircraft-operator, passenger, freight-shipper*, and *air-traffic control*. It will have a direct concern about *ground-transport, fuel-provider, maintenance-provider*, and *regulator*. It will have only an indirect relationship with *aircraft manufacturers*.

For the enterprise *When*-elements, the airport would have a transaction concern about *ground-arrival, ground-departure, inbound-process, outbound-process, air-arrival*, and *air-departure*. It will have a direct concern about *take-off, landing*, and *in-maintenance*. It will have only an indirect interest in what happens *in-flight* beyond the airport itself.

For the enterprise *Why*-elements, the airport would have a transaction concern about *aircraft-safety* when the aircraft is on the ground, on the apron, or connected to the airport itself; about *transit-safety and security* for passengers, baggage, and freight; about *ground-safety, information-security, national-security, biosecurity, social-license-to-operate*, and *quality of service*. It will have a direct concern about *aircraft-safety* during taxiing, take-off, and landing. It will only have an indirect concern about *aircraft-safety* or *flight-safety* in the air, beyond the airport itself.

We'll also need to map out the equivalent enterprise-elements for the organization when looking *inside itself* as an enterprise in its own right. It's a task that more properly fits into Step 2, though, so we'll leave it until then, in the next chapter.

Organization Structure

With the Enterprise-Context Map, such as in Figure 8-4, and the Organization-Context Map, such as in Figure 8-6, we have a usable overview of the structure of the shared-enterprise and of the organization's position and role within that structure.

Yet that's only looking *outward* from the organization's perspective. We now need to begin to look *inward*, mapping out the structure of the organization itself in terms of its own internal roles and interactions. We do that with a **Function-Model** of the organization.

In essence, the Function-Model is a visual map of "***the organization on a page***." As we'll see later, it's one of *the* most valued and valuable artifacts of enterprise-architecture. We can use it in its own right as a single-page summary of the business as a whole; we can use it as a base-map for all manner of other cross-references, from project-touchpoints to costings to information-systems and process-flows; we've often seen managers use it as a way to show new recruits where their own work will fit in with that of everyone else. We'll go into that in more depth in Step 2, though. For now, we only need to make a start on it, to give us a foundation for what happens next.

The terms "*function*," "*capability*," and "*service*" do tend to get blurred together at times, and we'll need to clarify the distinctions between them. We'll do that in Step 2, though. For here, the key is that a function is where something *happens* in the business – where something is changed, where something is *done*. In that sense, a Function-Model is a visual summary of what the enterprise *does*, organized as nested hierarchy with up to four tiers of functions:

- *Tier-1*: Major categories of business functions, the key aspects of what the organization as a whole actually *does*

- *Tier-2*: Clusters of related activities, the major support-missions for the tier-1 functions

- *Tier-3*: "Activities" or clusters of related tasks, typically the emphasis of a team's or a person's work

- *Tier 4*: The detail for individual tasks within business processes, the actual delivery-processes

The aim here is to create a model that remains much the same as long as the organization does that kind of work. Given that, it needs to be *independent of any current assumptions about business structure*. We usually start with the "to-be" model, as the description of the idealized enterprise, and then later work backward to the "as-is" to give us our gap-analysis.

A Tier-1 model would typically split up the organization's work into around five to ten blocks of major business-functions, as in the example for a generic retail-organization shown in Figure 8-7. A Tier-2 model would partition the Tier-1 blocks into around 20–40 smaller blocks of types of work. For a first-cut version here, we'll only need to model down to Tier-2 at most; we'll do the rest in Step 2.

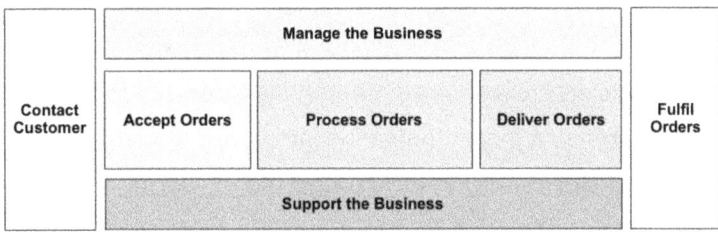

Figure 8-7. *Generic Tier-1 Function-Model*

Remember that we're working here on the organization's Context and high-level Scope. That means that we need to take care not to overthink it too much: this is more an exercise in *feeling* and connecting, rather than anything else. It also means that we'll need to engage the playfulness of the **artist-mode**, coupled with a bit of the **alchemist-mode**'s experimentation and people-oriented view of the world. For example, we'll often get the executive-team to draw out a first-cut of the model by hand, and to place photographs of themselves onto the respective parts of the map to show the relationships between each other and to make the organization's enterprise their own.

At this level, the information we need for the Function-Model should not be hard to find. If we're working with a team that has any significant real-world experience within the organization itself, most of what we need here will arise anyway just from the conversations between them. In practice, the whole thing should take no more than a couple of hours to build.

Example For the airport, they start from the generic Tier-1 model, and quickly realize that its simple one-way flow doesn't match with what they do. An airport is like a giant switchboard, connecting between different modes of transport, and sending people and things onward into the various directions that they need to go.

The airport will have their own "Manage the Business" and "Support the Business" functions, of course – every organization does. But beyond that, the crucial distinctions for their business are the various boundaries across their context-space. The main legal boundary is between "airside," where air-operations happen, and "landside," which is basically everything else. For example, passengers transition into airside at the moment they move through the flight-gate into the boarding-tunnel for the aircraft. For the airport, though, their definition of "landside" is a bit more complicated. There's the everyday landside beyond the airport; then a more controlled version of "landside" inside the airport's borders; and a secure version of "landside" for people and things that have gone through the required security-checks, and are safe and legal to transit into "airside." The airport's job is to make sure that people and things are always in the right place at the right time as they move through the context-space. Given that, they frame their Tier-1 model as shown in Figure 8-8.

They then move on to add the detail needed for their Tier-2 model. Their key focus here is on the main flows, passing through the various boundaries from landside to airside, and in the reverse direction from airside to landside. Some people do an "air-to-air" transit, staying within the secure-area to connect between flights. Others such as visitors and friends do an equivalent "land-to-land" transit, because they don't need to go into the secure-area. In each direction, there are different pathways for vehicles, for people, and for things.

For "Support the Airport," they map out the main categories of tasks needed to keep the airport running, and for "Manage the Airport," they settle for an overview of those tasks that's based on the Enterprise Canvas model to be explored in more depth in Step 2. From all of that, they frame their initial Tier-2 model as shown in Figure 8-9.

Figure 8-8 shows the airport's initial version of its Tier-1 Function-Model.

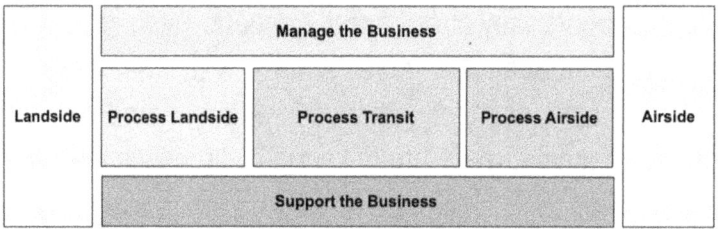

Figure 8-8. *Tier-1 Function-Model for the airport*

Figure 8-9 shows the airport's initial version of its Tier-2 Function-Model.

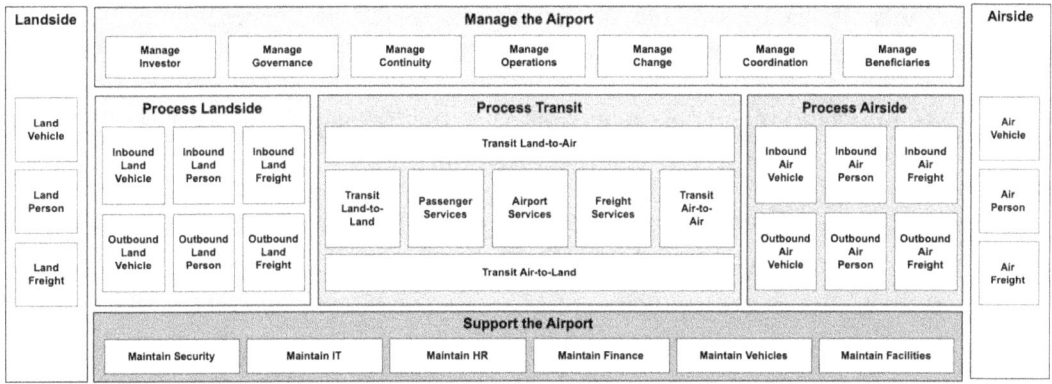

Figure 8-9. Airport Tier-2 Function-Model

Completing the Tier-2 model is enough for now. As mentioned above, we'll fill in the further details for Tier-3 and beyond in later work.

At this point, we'll have completed all of the architecture-work we need for Step 1, identifying the core architecture of the organization's Context and the initial high-level overview of its Scope. In an architecture sense at least, we're ready to move on to Step 2, to fill in more of the details and to map out the key functions and services that will be needed to support the organization's mission.

As with the previous main section, let's finish this one with a quick **After-Action Review**.

What was supposed to happen? We intended to develop a picture of how the organization positions itself within the shared-enterprise, to gain a clear understanding of the context in which the organization would work.

What actually happened? We explored and mapped out

- The organization's *role* in the enterprise, including its positioning and differentiation

- The organization's *mission*, describing how it will serve the enterprise as a whole

- The organization's *vision*, including its role-specific values, constraints, and success-criteria

- The organization's *value-propositions*, as its "missions" for other roles in the enterprise

- The organization's *content* in an abstract sense, as the "elements" of the organization in its enterprise role
- An initial outline of the organization's *structure*, mapped as a set of *internal* high-level roles and business-functions

We again illustrated each of these with our worked-example of an airport, seeking to understand its own business-context and scope.

What was the source of any difference? We've again achieved everything that we set out to do here, in terms of describing and identifying the overall range of elements that would form the anchor for an organization's *business-architecture* within its whole-of-enterprise architecture. The worked-example for the airport could perhaps be improved with one or two further passes through the same processes, but it's usable enough right now as a base for the work to be done in Step 2.

What can we learn from this? We really *can* identify and map all of the core elements of the "What," "How," and "Why" of an organization's business within not much more than a single day.

What are the benefits-realized from this? We now have the core of the Context and the high-level Scope for the organization's whole-enterprise-architecture, in a process that *can* be done with executives and others in a single day, and delivered in a format that can be used directly by anyone in the organization.

Set Up for Architecture

As noted above, by this point we'll have completed all of the architectural work for Step 1. If we've done it right, the organization's executives and others should now have a better sense of purpose, of their interconnection and interdependence with others beyond the organization itself, and of what "success" actually *is* within an enterprise. They'll also have a better understanding of what value actually is – and that there are some forms of value that are far more valuable than money.

In a Maturity-Model sense at least, they should now have enough understanding of their organization, and its place in the broader world, on which they could base **ad-hoc decisions** that have a reasonable chance of success.

Before we move on to Step 2, though, there's one more task that we need to do here. We need to set up the support for *our* role within that picture – **our own positioning and mission** and so on as enterprise-architects for the organization. If we don't get all of that set up right now, then we probably won't be able to repeat the work we've just done above – and *repeatable* is the test for the next level of maturity, for our own work as much as for everyone else.

There are several distinct parts for this setup, which we could summarize under the following headings:

- Creating and positioning the architecture-capability
- Setting up architecture-processes for projects and for sustainment
- Setting up governance for architecture and change
- Setting up knowledge-management and document-management for architecture
- Setting up the engagement-strategy for architecture

There are various other things that we'll need, such as choosing the right toolsets and frameworks and the like. But those can wait until later – these we need to do now.

Creating the Architecture Capability

In that one brief piece of work above, we'll have proven the value of architecture as a way to make *practical* sense of connection, structure, and story, throughout the organization and its enterprise.

That's also the ***mission*** of architecture: to provide guidance on connectedness, structure, and story, and how they link everything together on-purpose to support effective outcomes across the whole enterprise.

Right now, if we've done this right, people really *will* be listening to us as architects.

If we want that to continue, we need to move fast.

Yet what do we need to do? And how do we do it?

The first task is to establish where we fit in relation to the other "change-agents" that we looked at in the previous chapter, and with strategy and change-management in particular. We need to be seen and recognized as their direct peers – the third leg in a tripod of capabilities that the organization will use to tackle its complexities of change.

Given that, we next need to establish the ***positioning*** of architecture within the organization.

Much like strategy and tactics on the one side, and change-management on the other, architecture is layered and fractal, from small-scale projects, to larger-scale ones, to whole-of-organization transformation-initiatives, to vast nation-scale changes, and also long-term sustainment across all of those and more. As we saw in the previous chapter, there are at least four distinct categories of architecture: module-architecture, or project-specialism; solution-architecture, connecting everything across a single change-project; domain-architecture, as specialisms that would apply across almost every scope and scale; and enterprise-architecture, connecting everything together across the entire organization and its relationships with the broader enterprise.

As shown in Figure 8-10, those four categories form a matrix: *single-project* versus cross-project or "*sustain*," and *specialism* versus whole-of-context *continuity* and synthesis. Note, though, that **all of these are "architecture."** That emphasis on connection, structure, story, and *practicality* is the core theme that they all share, and that links them together across the organization.

	specialism (subset of scope)	connect (whole of scope)
sustain (continual)	domain	enterprise
project (task-bound)	module	solution

Figure 8-10. *Project-type and sustain-type architecture tasks*

Given that, where do we place those different forms of architecture? How do we get the funding and suchlike that we need for our work? Who do we report to, within the organization? For all of us, the **setup for architecture** must include

- Formal status as a distinct discipline

- Where required, formal status as a distinct business-unit

- Operating charter and reporting-relationships

- Defined service-offerings for others

- Defined service-relationships with others

- Continuing funding and access to any required resources

- Role-definitions and job-descriptions

> **Note** Although it's beyond the remit of this book, architectures also *need* a distinct **code of ethics**. A discipline only becomes a *profession* when it has an explicit code of ethics that is *mandatory* for all of its practitioners, and that guides their *actual* real-world decisions and actions. Most forms of business-oriented architecture don't have that yet. (Nor do managers, for that matter – but that's another story…)
>
> A profession is an enterprise in its own right; its code of ethics is a declaration of the principles that link back to its values and its vision. In practice, though, that code of ethics will only have meaning, and teeth, when the profession's practitioners *prove in action* that they're serious about it. In essence, to *be* professionals, they must show that their commitment to the enterprise of their profession is *necessarily* greater than their commitment to the enterprise of any single organization in which they may be employed.
>
> For example, at a research-lab we worked at, a project-manager insisted that the safety of the test-article had the highest priority of all, above even the safety of the people working on the test. The engineers warned him that if he put that in writing, *every professional engineer in the lab would have to resign immediately*, because any engineer who continued to work in a place that allowed that kind of breach of their profession's code of ethics would permanently lose their professional registration and license. The senior executives acknowledged this, and forced the project-manager to back down.
>
> A code of ethics needs to be central to any profession's training and education, and needs to come *before* any system for certifications and the like. If, as architects, we want to be viewed as real professionals, we need a real code of ethics right now that all of us will follow in our actions.

For the **module-** and **solution-architecture** roles, their situation is relatively straightforward. Most organizations by now will recognize that unless there *is* at least one person on a project who'll focus on keeping everything linked together, things tend to fall apart in expensive ways.

Given that, their funding will usually come from the projects within which they're placed. They'll report, respectively, to their team-lead, or to the overall project-lead or technical-lead. Solution-architects may also support the project-lead by acting as a bridge between the project-sponsor, who provides the desires and requirements for that change, and project-management, who provide the administration for the change.

Those two architecture-roles also provide some degree of continuity for architecture as they move from project to project. The catch is that, like the hermit-crab, they risk being somewhat exposed to the political winds whenever they move *between* projects. For that reason, they're sometimes funded directly by the change-management group, who then assign them to projects as appropriate from a common pool of architects.

Warning All this "people-stuff" *matters*. For example, *never* underestimate **the politics of architecture**. Whatever type of architecture you do, remember always that its role is to provide decision-*support*, not decision-*making*. As architects, we need to be viewed as people that others *want* to see, as "the folks from The Department of Yes-And" who really *do* help in getting things to work better, together, on-purpose.

If we as architects don't take enough care about that kind of business-politics, we'll risk being disparaged and dismissed as "Ivory Tower Idiots," or as the dreaded "architecture-police from The Department of No." Not A Good Idea…

The more specialist **domain-architectures** would be placed somewhere within the matching business-units, and would ultimately report to the respective senior-executive. For example, business-architecture would often report to the CMO; data-architecture and information-architecture would typically be placed under the CIO; IT-infrastructure architecture reporting to the CTO; financial-architecture to the CFO; process-architecture perhaps under the COO. Security-architecture might not have their own board-level executive, but would instead be attached to a broader security-management team. Their role in each case would be to ensure that the voice and architectural concerns of the respective department will be heard and respected everywhere around the organization, and sometimes beyond.

For **enterprise-architecture**, though, getting the positioning right can be more of a challenge. This arises in part because it has to connect *everything* together. All of the project-architectures, all of the domain-architectures, and all of strategy and change-management too. Everything about purpose and change in the organization and its relationships with broader shared enterprise. Everything needed for support of the sustain-architectures and sustainment in general. And all of this across whatever timescales may be involved: business-folks rarely deal with timescales much beyond minutes to months, whereas enterprise-architects may have to cover a time-range anywhere from microseconds to millennia, and sometimes more.

On top of that, we're still stuck with that common myth that enterprise-architecture is primarily about IT. Yes, the IT is important, no doubt about that; yet the reality is that, as can be seen just from the architecture-work we've done during this Step, even the IT is merely one small part of the much broader scope that a whole-enterprise-architecture *must* address.

Warning Because of that requirement to be able to address any aspect of the enterprise, enterprise-architecture *must* also have the authority to talk with anyone, anywhere in the enterprise, as required. Reporting to the executive as a whole, rather than only to a single executive, is usually the only way to gain and maintain that authority – and the work *cannot* be done well without it.

We have first-hand experience of the expensive disasters that can arise when an enterprise-architecture unit is trapped several layers below the CIO, with no authority to talk with anyone else outside of that silo. Not A Good Idea…!

All of this can at times make enterprise-architecture very "political," in the business-politics sense at least. So yes, challenging indeed.

To resolve that challenge, we need to look again at the actual requirements:

- Because it must connect between the scope and scales of every change-project, it cannot *itself* be set up with a scope any smaller than that of the entire enterprise.

- Because it must support sustainment and connect across every timescale, it cannot *itself* be set up as a one-off-project.

- Because it must connect everything to everything else across all of the silos, it cannot *itself* be placed within a single silo.

- Because it must support all projects, all timescales, all silos, and all types of sustainment, it must have *some* staff that are permanently assigned to itself.

All of this tells us that enterprise-architecture *must* be set up as a distinct business-unit in its own right. It also indicates that it *must* be positioned such that it can work with every silo and executive. As shown in Figure 8-11, the only positioning that works is when enterprise-architecture is treated as a direct peer of strategy and change-management, reporting to the entire executive-board.

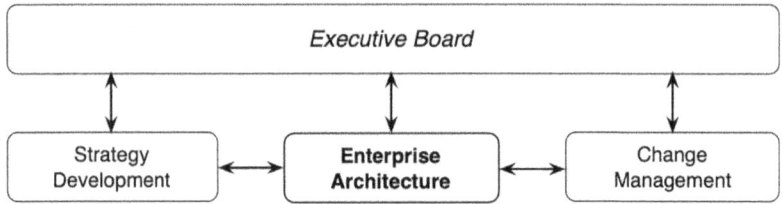

Figure 8-11. Positioning enterprise-architecture within the organization

The summary here is that *enterprise-architecture can only do its required work* when it has that kind of positioning within the organization, interacting with everyone, and reporting directly to the executive as a whole. Despite all of the problems and business-politics, it really *is* as simple as that.

The Sustainment of Change

What do enterprise-architects actually *do*? And how do they do it? What *are* their work-processes and suchlike?

On **project-type** work, we don't really need to cover that here. Almost every architect would already know how to do this, at least for the standard models and methods in the usual architecture-frameworks and change-management manuals. Earlier in this book, we've also described some useful extensions for those methods, such as with the *Change-Layers*, in Chapter 5, and the *Change-Cycle*, in Chapter 6. In the next chapter, for Step 2, we'll explore a few more suggestions to improve business-infrastructure initiatives, and in the chapter after that, for Step 3, we'll do the same for business-transformations. But other than that, yes, the roles and practices for architectures in project-type work are basically understood by everyone.

For ***sustainment-type*** work, though, it's a different matter. At the time of writing, there still seems to be almost nothing on it in any of the standard architecture-methods, nor in the change-management manuals. For enterprise-architects, and for whole-enterprise architecture in particular, we're pretty much on our own. We'll look at this in more detail later, in Step 2 and beyond, but we do at least need to make a start here by exploring the core requirements about sustainment.

In some ways, sustainment is the exact opposite of the usual project-type change-work: it's often more about ***continuity*** than about change as such. Or rather, like an automatic-pilot, it's about the vast number of changes, often quite subtle and small, that are needed to keep things on-course *overall*, toward effectiveness, toward the aims of the organization and enterprise, and always toward "*better*," via continual-improvement across all relevant scopes, scales, and timescales.

Sustainment also ***connects everything beyond and between the specific scopes of single change-projects***. For example, a typical change-project would have a narrower scope and timespan than that of the overall organization and/or enterprise, and, as we've seen earlier, the architecture for a typical project will address only the "*Plan*" phases of the work, leaving everything else for others to do as best they can.

By contrast, sustainment-type architecture must **bridge the gaps** between each specific project and every other project, and ensure that all the changes will work together as a whole. As shown in Figure 8-10, the "project" and "sustainment" architectures represent different sets of tasks – and yet the *overall* architecture must cover *all* of those tasks, not just the project-type ones.

In essence, the **role of sustainment-architecture** is to ***keep everything working together***, not just at the design-stage for each new capability and service, but throughout the entire lifecycles of those capabilities and services, all interacting with each other in different ways over time as they themselves change, along with the organization, the market, the broader enterprise, and the wider world.

With that in place, typical **tasks for sustainment-architecture** would include

- Identify gaps, overlaps, and synergies across the whole context

- Identify opportunities for management and reduction of technical-debt

- Identify architectural-implications of lifecycle-events such as platform-migration, platform-refresh, sunset and replacement, and decommission and disposal

CHAPTER 8   STEP 1: IDENTIFY THE ENTERPRISE

Each of these tasks would follow the fractal CSPAR pattern as summarized in the chapters of the previous "Step Zero" *Foundations* section. Each assessment should end with a list of recommendations for change, if any, with matching proposals for change-projects that would be coordinated and administered by the change-management team.

Note   You'll also need some way to map out the respective scope and content covered by each project, and then cross-map that onto the scope and content that you want to assess.

The simplest way to do this is by mapping everything onto an organization-wide Function-Model – which you've already started to build during this Step. In Step 2, in the next chapter, there'll be more detail about how to refine and extend the Function-Model, and how to use it in a wide range of other architecture-related tasks.

Later again, in Chapter 13, you'll discover how to use the Function-Model to support a "hands-off architecture," in which the project-teams do much of the architecture administrative-work automatically, as a background part of their routine change-management processes. That does make sustainment-architecture a lot easier to do!

Sustainment-related architectural reviews may be triggered on a per-project basis, and/or at regular scheduled intervals as a general whole-of-context review. We'll see more on how to do this in Step 2 and beyond.

The Governance of Change

Supporting governance is a central part of our role as enterprise-architects. We'll need to identify and set up here the processes that we need for that task.

In essence, ***an architecture is a form of governance***. For example, the architecture at each Change-Layer represents a set of governance-parameters for all design-work at that layer. As we've seen earlier, those parameters would include vision, values, constraints, success-criteria, and more, depending on how we are in the task-tree.

The ***purpose of governance*** is to ensure that each change will help to keep everything on-track and aligned with enterprise values, enterprise success-criteria, and better effectiveness overall.

By definition, governance must apply everywhere, for everyone, in every item of change-work, at every level, and at every scale. In that sense, **governance is fractal**: always the same overall patterns, but always somewhat different in each context and at each scale.

Although it may at first seem somewhat abstract, in practice **governance is always about people**. Governance is about the enterprise: people define the enterprise, and in turn, governance helps to keep people connected with purpose and effectiveness in the enterprise.

For our architectures to support effectiveness, and to keep each change on-track toward greater effectiveness overall, we're going to need several forms of governance, across several distinct scopes and scales:

- Governance of the *processes of change*, at the project-level

- Governance of how *architecture* is applied to each change-project and change-initiative

- Governance of *sustainment-architecture*, across the overall organization and its enterprise, and across all relevant lifecycles and timescales

- Governance of the *management of architecture*

- Governance of *architecture itself*, including the "architecture of architecture" that we explored in the "Step Zero" *Foundations* section

In the CSPAR method that we'd explored earlier, the Review phase at the end of each fractal instance of a task provides a basic form of governance, doing a cross-check on benefits-realized, lessons-learned, and actions for improvement. That type of informal after-action review – or "post-mortem," to use the Agile phrase – is usually enough when working on the detail-level of an architecture-project or change-project.

At the larger scale, though, and especially at a whole-of-project level or a subproject within a broader change-initiative, the project's sponsors, funders, and regulators will almost certainly want a more formal kind of governance. Probably the most common approach is a call for a "*gateway-review*" at each major transition-point, such as at the transitions between Layers in the *Change-Layers* pattern. If the project needs a finer-grained approach to governance, the transitions between the sub-layers in the *Change-Layers* pattern would usually suffice.

The same principles for governance would apply at each gateway, to confirm that the work of the previous stage has been properly completed, and everything is ready to move on to the next stage.

Note Different industries and contexts will often have their own specific governance-frameworks, though, and if we work in those contexts, we'll need to follow those rules. This would certainly apply to our airport example.

We'll also need ***governance for the sustain-architectures*** – the domain-architectures and enterprise-architecture. Unlike projects, these are continuous processes, so we won't have the same clear phase-boundary transitions at which to insert governance-reviews. Instead, it's simplest to use the Review phase of each piece of architecture-work as a micro-scale governance-review in its own right. We can then consolidate and review these at regular intervals, such as the typical quarterly-review period of most organizations.

In essence, ***enterprise-architecture is a quality-function***, so we can also use whole-of-scope governance-methods from service-management or quality-management. Quality-governance on architecture-services would need to cover themes such as architecture-support for projects; identification of gaps, overlaps, and synergies; management of the architecture-related information; whole-of-context and longer-timescale concerns such as technical-debt; and how architecture provides a bridge between strategy and change.

As described earlier, the key role of enterprise-architecture is to ***support effectiveness as a quality***. The governance for those quality-related themes will need to cover the processes to build awareness of what effectiveness means to the organization and why it's important, to build people's ability to support effectiveness in their work, to review the effectiveness of work itself, and to review the actions taken to improve effectiveness.

Reports and other documents arising from governance reviews would typically be stored and maintained in the architecture-administration repository.

Documents and Repositories

As mentioned at various points in the earlier explorations, each task will create, read, refer to, update, or maybe delete a wide variety of documents and other records. We'll store these in the ***architecture-repositories***, which we'll need to set up at this stage. These would include

- *Architecture-engagement repository* (often linked to project-management), to record requests for enterprise-architecture work, statements of work, resourcing, and delivery plans

- *Requirements repository* (often linked to project-management), to document requirements, tests for confirmation of those requirements, and relationships between them

- *Architecture-products repository*, for diagrams, models, specifications, reports, and other deliverables from architecture-work

- *Architecture-administration repository*, for change-project identifiers and key project-information

- *Architecture-registry* – architectural-elements, including information on lifecycles

- *Architecture-records repository* – usages of architectural-elements, including project-scope

- *Risk and opportunity registers* – broader-scope issues, including lifecycle-events

- *Dispensations register* – technical-debt from dispensations and waivers

- *Glossary and thesaurus* (often linked to knowledge-management), to provide standard definitions and cross-references between acronyms, synonyms, homonyms, heteronyms, and the like

Our planning and preparation here would need to consider the ***role of documents***:

- Documents convey decisions between change-layers and between actions, often over long periods of time. How will we make that happen?

- Documents are used as inputs for work. Who will use each document, for what purpose?

- Documents are stored in repositories. What repositories and repository-types will we need?

- What categories of documents will we need? How, why, and for how long should we maintain them?

We also need to be conscious about the ***users of documents***:

- What standards should we use? How should we prepare for changes in those standards over time and/or across contexts?

- What language, language-style, and visual-language should we use?

- How should we plan and design for reuse across contexts and over time?

- What access-control will we need, both for "need to know" and "need to not-know"?

Other **document-management** themes that we need to consider now would include

- What record- and repository-management will we need? Who will do that work?

- What versioning and version-management will we need?

- What tracking will we need for use of documents, including alternate-uses in affordances and the like?

- What lifecycle-management will we need for each type of document, and for document-context?

- How would we use documents in continual-review processes such as for management of technical-debt?

- How will we manage ownership of documents, including the migration of ownership over time?

- How will we manage the dynamics of access-control, where access-rights change over time?

We'll see more on these document-related themes as we move through the other Steps in the Maturity-Model.

Set Up for Engagement

For architecture to be useful, people have to be willing to *use* it. And they'll only be able to use it if they know it exists – which is why it's essential for us as architects to communicate what we do. Hence why, at this point, we need to set up our strategy for communication and engagement with others, and also set up the tools and processes that we'll need when we put that plan into practice.

As we've seen throughout this Step, an enterprise is about *shared* goals, *shared* vision. Given that, we need to acknowledge that although we may have the nominal responsibility for the architecture, we don't *possess* it: instead, **the architecture belongs to everyone in the enterprise**. The architecture will only happen when people feel that they "own" it – not imposed on them from above, but something in which they themselves are co-authors, co-creators. That's what engagement is about, and what it's *for*.

The challenge is that, by definition, engagement is mostly about *people* – and it's true that for many of us in architecture, that kind of "people-stuff" can be *hard*. Yet all of our previous work on analysis and the like may be in vain unless we *do* tackle this. Remember, then, that architecture is a conversation: a *dialogue*, not a monologue. Perhaps most of all, listening is more important than talking; people are more likely to listen to us if they feel they've been heard *by* us. And the real architecture, the place where the architecture is literally "real-ized," is always through people.

An enterprise is a storyworld, a place where stories happen, so story-based approaches will often help here. The Function-Model can help us in this because it describes the organization in a way that includes *everyone* – the organization as a whole, as an ecosystem, in context of its enterprise.

Each business-process is the thread of a story; each use-case is a story; each transaction is a story. We can use the Function-Model to show how those stories weave their way across the organization and the enterprise, touching different business functions and services and capabilities, using enterprise assets in different ways and in different locations, triggering other business events for different business reasons. The architecture *itself* is a story, so to help others make sense of the architecture, tell it *as* a story, a narrative which includes them *in* the story. We'll also see more on how to use story in architecture-work in the next chapter, in the section "Stories of Change."

Communication creates engagement with people. In turn, engagement supports governance, or, more precisely, it creates the kind of governance in which people *want* to be involved, because the work and its governance have meaning for them.

Typical techniques for engagement would include publishing models and documents on an in-house architecture-website, and running seminars and workshops to engage operations-staff and others in exploring the architecture. We also need to maintain a "watching-brief" relationship with senior staff and with the strategy and change-management teams, and build working-relationships with people working on other values-related themes such as security, privacy, quality, health and safety, ethics, and environment. We probably wouldn't need to use all of these approaches straight away, but we *do* need to start the planning and preparation for them right now. There'll be more on these themes in other Steps, and also in Chapter 13, in the section "Build Architecture-Awareness."

In practice, enterprise-architecture only becomes "the architecture *of* the enterprise" when the enterprise in general is engaged in every aspect of its creation and use. That's what we must aim for here.

Into Practice

In the section "Enterprise As Context," we explored how to identify the key information about the shared-enterprise that acts as an organization's Context. Using what you saw there, apply the same methods and checklists to your own organization.

- Does your organization already have a clear picture of its *"enterprise as storyworld"* – the vision, values, priorities, constraints, success-criteria, principles, and so on of the shared-enterprise(s) that form its Context? If not, what impact does that have on the organization's architectures and effectiveness? How would you mitigate that impact?

- Does your organization have a clear picture of the *"elements" of the broader shared-enterprise* – its "What," "How," "Where," "Who," "When," and "Why"? If not, what impact does that have on the organization's architectures and effectiveness, and what, as an architect, could you do to mitigate that impact?

- How do you map out the *enterprise roles and interactions* – the roles, relationships, interactions, responsibilities, and governance across your organization's shared-enterprise? If you have that information, how do you use it, and how could you improve it?

In the section "Organization and Enterprise," we explored the Scope of the organization's positioning and interactions within its shared-enterprise. Using what you saw there, apply the same methods and checklists to your own organization.

- What is your *organization's role* within the shared-enterprise – its positioning, relationships, and differentiation? How is that described? How might you improve that description?

- What is your *organization's mission* – who the organization is, what it does, who and how it serves? How is that described at present? How might you improve that description?

- What are your *organization's vision and values*? How are these described? How do they relate to the shared-values of the broader enterprise? What mismatches are there, if any, between required, espoused, and actual enacted-values? What does a POSIWID comparison show you about your organization's enacted business-purpose? What, as an architect, could you do about any mismatches?

- What are your *organization's value-propositions*? Who are those value-propositions for, and what value will be exchanged? From what you've read here, how might you improve the descriptions and definitions for those value-propositions?

- What are the "elements" of your *organization's content*? How are these elements used within your architecture-descriptions for the organization? How might you improve on this?

- What is your *organization's structure*, relating to the external enterprise, and within itself? How do you describe this at present? Try reframing the description in terms of a Function-Model: Does this make it easier to describe the structure to others, and if so, how and why?

In the section "Set Up for Architecture," we explored the requirements and actions needed to set up an enterprise-architecture capability within an organization. Using what you read in that section, apply the same methods and checklists to your own organization.

- What is the *positioning of enterprise-architecture* within your organization? From what you've read here, would you need to change that positioning? If so, how would you set about doing that?

- What support do your organization's architecture-capabilities provide for *sustainment of change*? From what you've seen above, would you need to improve that? If so, how would you do it?

- What support do your organization's architecture-capabilities provide for *governance of change*? From what you've read above, would you need to improve that? If so, how would you do it?

- What *documents* and other records do you create, maintain, and use in your architecture-work? What *repositories* do you use, in which to store those documents? What governance do you apply to the access, use, and maintenance for those documents, especially over the longer-term? How might you improve on any of those concerns?

- How do you, as an architect, *create engagement* from others in the processes of architecture? What might help you in improving and maintaining that engagement?

Summary

In this chapter, for Step 1 in the Maturity-Model, we explored how to identify the core of the organization's Context, and the first stages for its Scope. We also worked through what we would need to do to set up the enterprise-architecture capability within the organization.

In the next chapter, for Step 2, we'll fill out more of the internal Scope for the organization, and make a start on identifying, designing, and setting up the core services that will provide the "backbone" infrastructure for the organization's business.

CHAPTER 9

Step 2: Get Ready for Action

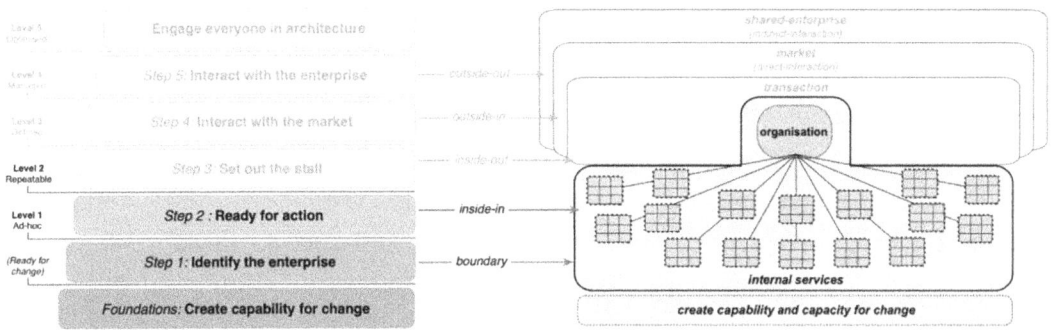

In the previous Step, we focused on identifying the *core context and scope* for an organization and its business, its underlying "*Why*." We also explored how to establish architecture-capabilities within the organization, so that we will have the continuing support that we'll need to do this work.

In this Step, we'll shift the focus to the underlying "*How*," identifying and establishing the **core capabilities and services** that the organization will need across the entirety of its functional scope. These will provide the **business-infrastructure** that, in the next Step, we'll put to use to underpin the organization's business-models and delivery of its value-propositions.

In CSPAR terms, what we identify here is the practical detail for the organization's Scope, and we also make our first complete high-level forays through the Plan, Action, and Review for the organization's architecture. This is also where we start to apply those "Step Zero" architecture-foundations practices in a more visible and tangible way, to guide effective real-world change for a specific organization such as the airport, or for your own work-context.

As indicated in the graphic above, this Step in the Maturity-Model also focuses on ***the "inside-in" of the organization*** – all of those parts that are essential to its operations yet aren't really visible from the outside. All the architecture-development we do here will work in much the same way for a "greenfield" context such as for a startup, or a transformation for an existing organization – the only real difference, in fact, is that there won't be much if any "as-is" infrastructure in a startup.

For any significant organization, there'll be a lot to do here – and to do it, we'll need an architecture-team of an appropriate size to match the organization's needs, too. Yet as in the previous Step, we won't need to do all of this in one go – instead, it's generally better to develop it iteratively, first moving back and forth between the three parts of this Step, and then making adjustments later from what we learn while working on Steps 3 and 4. Yet because of the dependencies between the Steps, we *do* need to start the organization's functional-architecture here, and we do need to have at least *some* implementation of this before we try to do anything else.

Whatever we do here, it must align and support everything we established in the previous Step: all of the vision and values and so on of the organization and its shared-enterprise, and the organization's role and positioning and value-propositions and all that. We'll also need appropriate governance and sustainment to ensure that alignment and support, over whatever timescales the organization might need.

By the end of this Step, we want the architecture to be able to bring the organization to the ***CMMI "repeatable" level*** of business-maturity. In practice, this means that our aim here is to create a business-infrastructure that is adaptable, reliable, efficient, elegant, integrated, and everything else that would support the organization's ***effectiveness***.

Note There'll be a lot of documents created during the process, of course, which would be stored in the repositories set up in the previous Step. Most of these would be of little interest to anyone other than architects, designers, developers, and implementors, yet the updates to be done here to the Function-Model and its various overlays would be of immediate *practical* use for just about everyone in the organization. As architects we need to make use of that fact to help maintain our credibility as useful allies in the business of the business!

There are three sections in this chapter:

- *From Scope to Plan*: Explore how to identify and model the business-infrastructure that will be needed for the organization's chosen role and positioning within the shared-enterprise

- *Build the services*: Plan, design, build, and implement the services and service-relationships that will provide and deliver that business-infrastructure

- *Test the services*: Define and run tests and scenarios, in parallel with the build, to assess and improve the reliability, adaptability, and resilience of that business-infrastructure

We'll end this chapter with a brief review of what you've learned during this Step, and how to apply it within your own organization.

From Scope to Plan

What will the organization need to have and do, to support its chosen role and positioning in its shared-enterprise?

As enterprise-architects, our answers here will define the business-infrastructure that the organization will use to underpin its business-offerings. In this section, we'll explore how to set about doing that process.

From Role to Infrastructure

How do we identify what infrastructure we'll need, to support the organization's role in the shared-enterprise?

From an architecture-perspective, there *is* one really simple way to do that. To get there, though, we'll first need to do a sort of two-step shuffle, to set up how we think about how an organization actually works.

First, we make an assertion that, from an *architectural* perspective at least, **everything in the enterprise is, represents, or implies a service**. Or, to put it another way round, we'll use a *service-oriented* approach as the core basis for our enterprise-architecture.

> **Note** Don't worry! We're not saying that a service-oriented approach is the *only* way to do enterprise-architecture. It isn't, of course. And anyway, whatever approach we might choose to use, there'll always be some exceptions for which we'll need to use a different approach.
>
> What we *are* saying is that, in our experience, a service-oriented approach provides the *simplest, easiest, and most reliable way* to make consistent and meaningful sense of, and design for, the vast, sprawling, tangled fractality of what goes on within any real-world enterprise. Or, arguably, it's perhaps the only chance we have to stay even *somewhat* sane while working across the entirety of a whole-enterprise-architecture!
>
> Hence, from now on, unless otherwise indicated, we'll use a service-oriented approach for all of the architecture-work described in this book. Do remember, though, that other approaches to architecture-tasks are always available, and may well be better than a service-oriented one in some specific circumstances.

Given that assertion, the underlying structure for the organization's business would then consist of a set of distinct yet interdependent **services**. Every workflow or process consists of a sequence of service-invocations, linked together to provide and deliver the overall functionality required for that particular type of task.

This leads to the second step in our sideways-shuffle. We start by noting that architecturally, as we saw back in Chapter 5, we translate each "How" into a *function* for a service. A service comprises many different elements, for which its functions represent only one part – specifically, the service's interfaces to the world beyond itself, and that will be used by workflows and processes and so on to invoke the work of the service.

Yet as shown in Figure 9-1, although function and service are different, *the function is the only part of the service that is visible from the outside*. In practice, this means that it will often seem that the function *is* the service – that they're the same thing, even though they're not.

CHAPTER 9 STEP 2: GET READY FOR ACTION

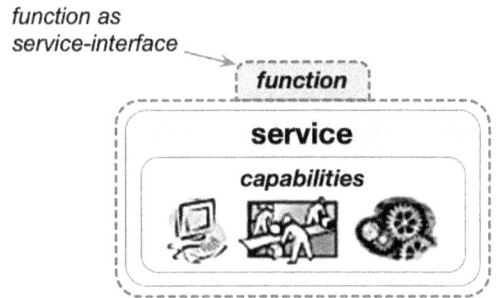

Figure 9-1. Function as outward-facing interface for a service

That confusion between "function" and "service" can sometimes be a real problem, as we'll see later. For our purposes *here*, though, we can turn that confusion to our advantage – because it means that we can identify the organization's business-structure in terms of its business-functions. And in the previous Step, we'd already made a start on mapping those business-functions, with the Function-Model.

At the abstract level at least, the organization's Function-Model *is* a multi-tiered map of the organization's business-structure.

For the airport, for example, its tier-1 Function-Model provides a high-level overview of its business-structure, partitioned in terms of what it needs to do *as* an airport. In the same way, its tier-2 Function-Model, as shown in Figure 9-2, provides a mid-level view of the types of tasks it will need to address.

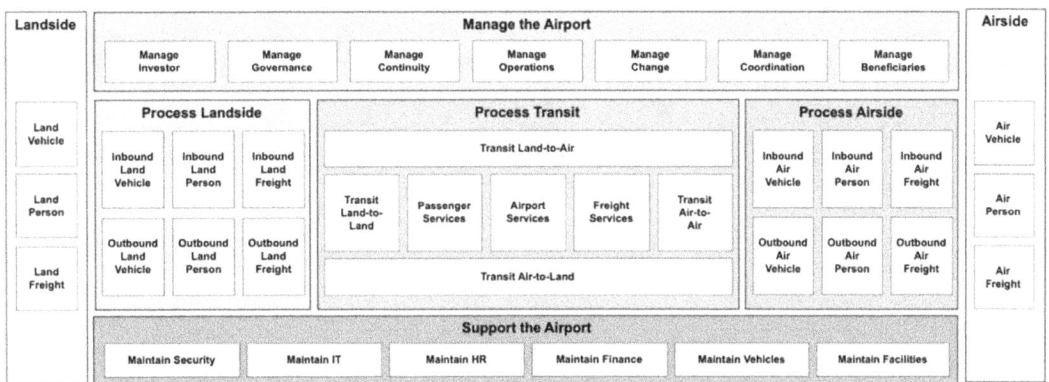

Figure 9-2. Airport tier-2 Function-Model as overview of its functional structure

For what we'll need for this Step, we'll have to develop the Function-Model down to a tier-3 level – "boxes within boxes within boxes." We'll see how to do that in the "Functions and Systems" section later below. We'll also see there how to develop, from

273

the Function-Model, the business-systems and information-systems overlays that can *really* help us to make sense of how the architecture and governance will need to work.

For now, though, that tier-2 Function-Model will be enough to get us started. We won't need to do anything new to identify the business-structure because *we've already done it*, with the Function-Model we developed back in Step 1.

There's one more task we need to do here first, before we dive into the rest of the work. We need to separate out the *business-infrastructure* from the rest of the operational-level business-structure, because what we need *as* "infrastructure" are the functions that are *stable*, and that can be relied upon by the other business-functions to not change much, if at all.

We can do that by applying to the Function-Model a bit of SCAN-type thinking about uncertainty. This will enable us to sort the various functions in terms of a pattern we describe as "**backbone and edge**," as summarized in the example shown in Figure 9-3.

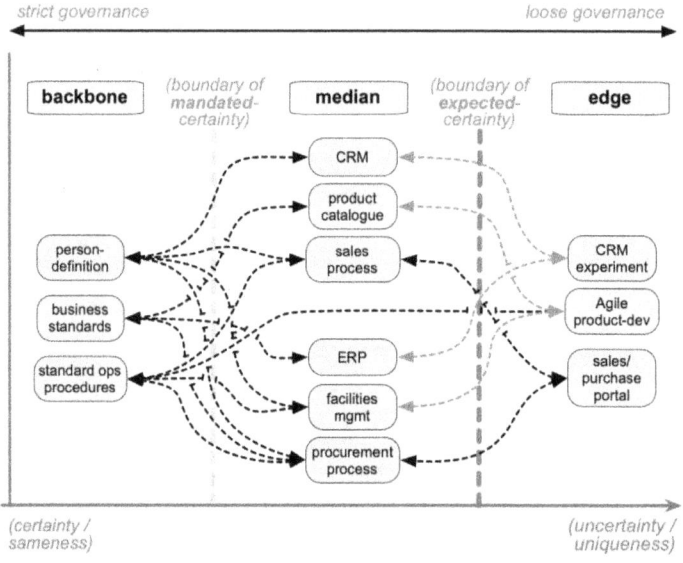

Figure 9-3. "Backbone and edge" example

In SCAN, we have a horizontal-axis of certainty and sameness versus uncertainty and uniqueness, with highest-certainty to the left, and lowest-certainty to the right. For backbone-and-edge, we note that that SCAN axis also matches the levels of certainty and reliability that we'll need from the various services, and hence the types of governance we'll need over their usage and change. Aligning with SCAN, we would map the services that need stricter governance more to the left, and those needing only looser governance more to the right. (There's no real vertical-axis here: we can use the vertical dimension of a backbone-and-edge governance-map in any way that would aid in meaning, such as grouping related services into appropriate clusters.)

Again, as with SCAN, that governance-axis is actually a spectrum, but it does have two distinct transition-points, as also shown in Figure 9-3: a boundary of *mandated*-certainty, and a boundary of *expected*-certainty. This partitions the governance-spectrum into three distinct regions: *backbone*, *median*, and *edge*.

- *Backbone*: Core business-infrastructure, used by many if not all teams; trusted, certain, "official," "single-source-of-truth"; functions, interfaces, and content under strict governance; change would require "Waterfall"-type notification and governance

- *Median*: Services used by a large group such as a department, but shared with others; tested and trusted for departmental use; functions, interfaces, and content under departmental governance; change would require intermediate-type notification and governance

- *Edge*: "Shadow"-type developments used by a single team, and not meant to be shared with others; unproven, untrusted, only local source-of-truth; functions, interfaces, and content under local and often minimal governance; change could take place at any time, often without notice and maybe without any real governance

---

Warning   As architects, we do *want* "shadow"-type developments to happen, because that's where new ideas are created and tested out on the edge. It may also be the only way to respond to a real-time urgent need. What we *don't* want, though, is people using some system or service that *looks* like it can be trusted, but actually can't – and they don't know that.

The basic rule for edge-developments is that low-to-no-governance is sort-of-okay for anything as long as it's used only by a small team of people who *know* how fragile it is, who *do* understand and acknowledge the risks that they're taking, and who *do* know what to do if the risks eventuate. But once anyone outside that team wants to use it, it *must* come under appropriate governance. That rule needs to be understood by *everyone* who does any kind of edge-development work.

If people don't follow that rule, then bad things can and do happen, often seemingly "without warning." Far too often, we've seen quick-hack spreadsheets, jury-rigged equipment, or apps developed in some obscure and forgotten language, all ending up as the hidden "backbone" behind services used by almost everyone, with no actual security, safety, reliability, governance, or anything. Not A Good Idea…

Over time, systems and services may need to move back and forth along that spectrum of governance. For example, people start seeing the usefulness of some edge-development, and want to use it elsewhere, so it needs to move toward the median. A system used by a single department gets adopted for use organization-wide, and becomes part of the backbone. The opposite can also happen: the organization withdraws from a particular market, so the backbone-services to support it become redundant, and move toward the "edge"-type governance of the customer-service team for those old products. As architects, we do need to plan for those changes of governance and the like.

The other key point here is that the services directly behind business-offerings will tend to be more volatile, to follow the needs of the market. We need to keep them separate from the business-infrastructure, which needs to be stable enough to support *any* likely business-offerings within the organization's chosen role in the shared-enterprise. Given that, in this Step we'll focus mainly on services that will belong in the backbone. We'll explore governance for the more-volatile business-offerings in Step 3, and for edge-developments in Step 4.

Set Up for Change

Drawing on everything that we've explored in this section, we can now build a plan for how to tackle the work needed to establish the organization's business-infrastructure:

- In the "Functions and Systems" section of the work, we'll identify candidate services for the business-infrastructure. To help us in this, we'll expand the **Function-Model** to a tier-3 level, and then derive the **business-systems** and **information-systems** overlays from that model. We'll use these later, in the architecture-process, to support a ***"backbone-and-edge" assessment*** to clarify which services should or should not be included within the "backbone" business-infrastructure.

- In the "From Architecture to Action" section of the work, we'll develop the architecture for the change, and guide its design, implementation, and use. We'll use the **CSPAR** pattern to guide the process of change, as represented by the **Change-Layers** and **Change-Cycle** change-models. We'll use the **Service-Content** model and content-transitions to help us identify the content-elements needed for each "backbone"-service. We'll also use other tools such as **SCAN** to resolve any other issues that may arise.

- Optionally, we may also use **narrative-oriented methods**, as described in the "Stories of Change" section, to help in eliciting requirements and in identifying hidden opportunities and risks.

As mentioned earlier, the overall process will be essentially the same for every type of business-context, whether we're working on the "greenfield" of a startup, or a larger-scale transformation of the business-infrastructure for an existing business. The only real difference is that assessment of the "as-is" for a greenfield is much simpler, because there won't be much already existing that needs to be assessed.

Build the Services

What do we, as enterprise-architects, need to *do* to help the organization build the business-infrastructure that it will need for its chosen role and positioning in its shared-enterprise?

It's here that we'll first need to put into practice everything that we'd learned from the "Step Zero" *Foundations* work: the terms and definitions for whole-enterprise architecture, the art and science of change, the Change-Layers and Change-Cycle, and the tactics to tackle uncertainty, complexity, and scale.

We'll start, though, by refining the Function-Model, to help us identify the scope of the work that we'll need to do.

CHAPTER 9   STEP 2: GET READY FOR ACTION

Functions and Systems

We already know how to develop a Function-Model down to the tier-2 level. For example, as shown in Figure 9-4, we've already done so for the airport example.

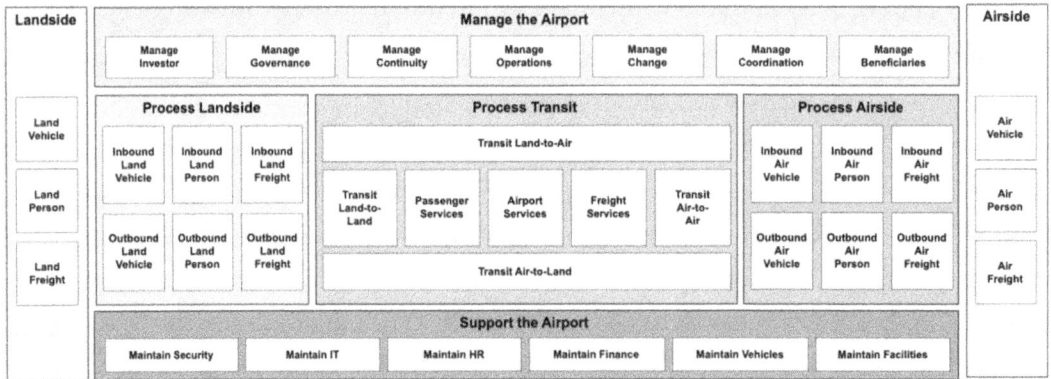

Figure 9-4. *Tier-2 Function-Model for the airport-example*

We now need to extend that down to the next level, as a tier-3 model with occasional forays into the finer-detail of tier-4.

Tier-3 activities are clusters of related tasks that typically represent the main focus of a smaller group or even a single team. We would aim to include around five to ten key tier-3 functions per tier-2 function, with a total of perhaps 250–300 across the overall Function-Model. (We typically limit it to that number of tier-3 functions because that's about the most that can fit on a single page and still remain readable as "the organization on a page.") Information that we might capture about other functions or child-functions would need to be relegated to tier-4.

To identify candidate functions and activities, trawl through any available sources for information about points where business processes start and end, or wherever something is changed:

- *Org-chart entries*: Each role implies one or more business functions, though they may overlap, or be repeated in multiple locations, or aggregate several distinct functions.

- *The organization's **Annual Report***: Almost by definition, this is supposed to list every major category of business activity.

- *References to **projects***: Each project is likely to imply a new or upgraded capability, which again implies a function.

- *References to phone-numbers or other **contact-points** for business-units*: These imply business-functions behind the points of contact.

- *Business **information-models***: Look for the implied functions that would create, read, aggregate, update, or delete the information-items.

- ***Conversations** with appropriate staff throughout the organization*: Use these to elicit information about distinct clusters of business-activities and functions.

Caution When you're gathering those suggestions from staff, do beware that they're likely to want you to list every one of their tasks as a top-level business function! That way, insanity lies…

Instead, work with them to summarize their tasks down to perhaps half a dozen tier-3 activities per tier-2 cluster, and record all the other details as tier-4 tasks.

- Every business function *does* something, so each function-label on the Function-Model should include a verb. For tier-1 and tier-2 functions, we can usually get away with abstract verbs such as "Provide" or "Manage." For tier-3, though, and especially for tier-4, we do need to use more-descriptive verbs such as "Receive," "Assess," or "Monitor."

Example For the airport, doing a full tier-3 Function-Model would definitely be worth the effort, but would also be a lot of work. As a real-world comparison, we needed a team of about ten people over a couple of months to map out the first full text-and-graphics draft of a tier-3 model for a 50,000-person national logistics organization. The airport would be all at one location, but would still employ perhaps a third of that number of people, with all of the complexities that an organization of that size would imply.

CHAPTER 9   STEP 2: GET READY FOR ACTION

For simplicity's sake, the airport decides to do a test-run first with just the tier-2 "Transit Land-to-Air" function, and then aim to build outward from there on that experience.

From here on in this section, we'll use as our worked-example the airport's test-run with its tier-2 "Transit Land-to-Air" function. This should describe the business-functions to be used when bringing a "transit-item" – Passenger or Freight – from "airport-landside" inside the airport boundary or building, through the various checks to pass into "airport-airside" inside the secured areas of the airport, and onward through the flight-gate into "airside proper" to board the aircraft for the flight itself.

In essence, the core purpose of the "Transit Land-to-Air" function is to bring the correct people and items of freight to the correct point at the correct time for the respective flight, and also to confirm that each of these is *valid, legal, safe, and secure* to board that flight.

It's easy to see that the transit-processes for people and for freight are functionally the same at the tier-2 level, and are essentially the same at the tier-3 level. However, the two pathways would come under different rules and regulations and are processed in different ways within different parts of the airport. We would model these as near-identical sets of tier-3 functions, to be shown in linked-yet-separate tier-2 boxes, to be labeled as "Transit Land-to-Air (Person)" and "Transit Land-to-Air (Freight)."

We would also notice two minor issues that would need to be addressed here. The first is that, in practice, the people who will travel on the flight will include not just the passengers, but also the aircrew, and occasionally other airline staff as well. For this we would use the role-label "Person" rather than "Passenger" in function-descriptions at this level, although at the detail-level these different groups would often transit through the various checks via somewhat different paths.

The other point is that all of those people may also take on the Freight-Shipper role, in that they would typically be allowed to bring not just "carry-on" items with them onto the flight, but also checked-baggage to be carried separately as regular freight on the same flight. This means that there would need to be some kind of process to separate that checked-baggage from the person and move it to the freight-transit path.

We might also note that, at a *functional* level, there's no real difference between the transit-paths for domestic and international flights. The implementations may need to be somewhat different, with additional roles in some cases, but the respective tier-3 functions are essentially the same.

Given this, we could model the respective tier-3 functions as follows:

- *Confirm Validity of Flight-Booking* (*Person*-path and *Freight*-path): Verify that the respective person or item has a valid and appropriate booking for travel or transport. A confirmation-docket should be issued, such as a boarding-pass for a passenger.

- *Move Checked-Baggage to Air-Freight Transit* (*Person*-path only): Transfer any checked-baggage of a validated traveler to the freight-transit path, to be handled as freight booked for the respective flight.

- *Confirm Valid to Travel* (*Person*-path and *Freight*-path): Confirm that the person or item has the appropriate identity and booking-confirmation, and if so to move on to the next stage of the secure-area boundary-checks.

- *Confirm Legal to Travel* (*Person*-path and *Freight*-path): Confirm that the person or item has the appropriate legal authority to travel by air and arrive at the specified destination, and if so to move on to the next stage of the secure-area boundary-checks.

- *Confirm Safe to Travel* (*Person*-path and *Freight*-path): Confirm that the person and/or item has passed all required physical-security, health, and other checks, and if so to move on to the staging-area.

- *Provide Staging-Area* (*Person*-path and *Freight*-path): Use the staging-area (including seating, food, and shops for persons) to await the respective flight, and to access the respective gate for that flight.

- *Provide Travel-Information* (*Person*-path and *Freight*-path): Provide passengers, aircrew, and freight-handlers with real-time information about flight-gates, onboarding-times, and routing to the respective gates.

- *Reconfirm Valid for Travel on Flight* (*Person*-path and *Freight*-path): Exit-gate check (valid to travel on this flight).

- *Provide Access to Flight Air-Vehicle* (*Person*-path and *Freight*-path): Provide the person or freight-item with some means to move from the "airside"-boundary to the aircraft, such as a boarding-tunnel, bus, and/or marked-pathway for a person, or a container-loader or a baggage-trolley for a freight-item.

Note that each of the "Confirm" or "Reconfirm" stages may or will be handled by different agents. For example, on the *Person*-path, "Confirm Booking" would be done by airline-staff, "Confirm Valid to Travel" by airport-staff, "Confirm Legal to Travel" by police or border-staff, "Confirm Safe to Travel" by airport or official security-staff, and "Reconfirm Valid to Travel" again by airline-staff.

Figure 9-5 provides an excerpt from the airport's tier-3 Function-Model that shows the two pathways for the tier-2 function "Transit Land-to-Air," with the pathways for people and for freight laid out as separate left-to-right workflows.

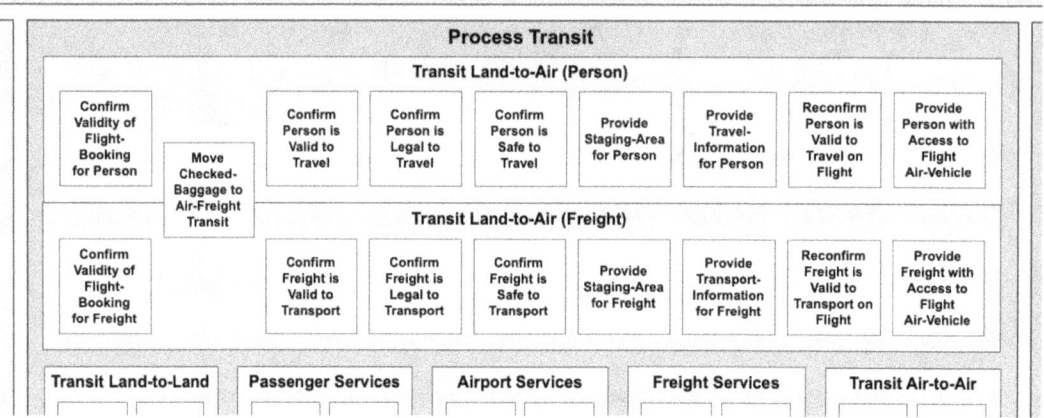

Figure 9-5. *Airport tier-3 Function-Model – Transit Land-to-Air*

The Function-Model provides us with a base on which to build a variety of valuable overlays for the organization's architecture. The first of these is the **Business-Systems Model**. In principle, the Function-Model ought to be complete and approved before we do this work, but for the airport there *is* enough in their current Function-Model to make it worthwhile to do an initial pass at this.

The aim here is to identify potential duplications and/or options for reuse of functions and services. Once we have that, we should be able to identify and describe the core decisions for the ideal "to-be" of the overall structure of support for the activities of the business – particularly its information-systems, because they're so often the source of so much immediate business pain. This would then provide an agreed base for all future decisions.

Caution Do explore "information-systems" in its broadest, most generic sense – *not* solely the information that's in computer networks and system-databases.

Much of an organization's core information is word-of-mouth, or held in individual or collective memory, or built into work-instructions for machines and the like. IT would play an important role, of course, but it's by no means the only part of the story!

Note too that at some point, you'll also need to model the equivalent systems that support the physical flows, the people-relationships, and so on. It may even be necessary to do some of those mappings straight away for an organization that, like the airport, is in a logistics business, or in a recruitment or sales-oriented context. Do those other assessments in much the same way as for the information-systems: adapt the questions below to suit, and create the models accordingly.

The aim here is to identify groups of activities that perform the same kinds of functions and share similar kinds of information and other assets, and hence should be supported by similar systems even though their operational processes may be different. This should help us to ensure that any systems developed or purchased to manage these assets don't overlap in function or in the information that they store.

The simplest way to describe this kind of mapping is by using color-coding for the tier-3 activities on the Function-Model. Each color-code would represent a different "business-system," or clustering of related activities. For example, we could split some of the business-systems by service-category-type:

- Is it about developing the business, changing the business, or routine management of the business?
- Is it about a specific value-chain or type of delivery-service?
- Is it about funding, or people-management, or customer-relationships?
- Is it operated and managed by a group of people from a specific domain of expertise?

And so on, and so on. The most appropriate split will depend on the nature of the organization. There are no standard guidelines for this, but aim to identify some 10–20 distinct shared areas of functionality. To ***identify business-systems***, particularly in terms of information-flows, ask

- Which tier-3 activities, whether in the same part or different parts of the organization, have similar functions and share much the same information and other assets?

- What IT-systems or other information-systems should these activities use? In IT terms, what applications are or should be used to store and access this information?

- If a tier-3 function does not seem to use any identified IT-systems to support its specific activities, how do they manage the information needed for their work?

- As a cross-check, what existing business-information, information-systems, applications, or business-processes do *not* seem to be used by any activity on the Function-Model? What changes would this suggest to the Function-Model itself?

Note that we may also need to rethink the leveling or structure of the Function-Model somewhat if we can't assign an activity to a business-system, or if we seem to be forced to split an activity between two or more business-systems. That may also be a reason to rethink the business-system boundaries – which would also be the case if we end up with a business-system that seems to have only one or two members.

At the end of this process, we should have a color-coded version of the Function-Model diagram, in which every tier-3 activity has been assigned to just *one* business-system. In the airport's case, they assign the "Transit Land-to-Air" tier-3 functions in terms of "responsible agency," as follows:

- *Air-Operator*: "Confirm Validity of Flight-Booking" for *Person*, and "Reconfirm Valid to Travel on Flight" for both *Person* and *Freight*

- *Freight-Shipper*: "Confirm Validity of Flight-Booking" for *Freight*

- *Freight-Handling*: "Move Checked-Baggage to Air-Freight Transit," and "Confirm Valid to Transport," "Provide Staging-Area," and "Provide Access to Flight Air-Vehicle" for *Freight*

- *Passenger-Services*: "Confirm Valid to Travel," "Provide Staging-Area," and "Provide Access to Flight Air-Vehicle" for *Person*

- *Border-Services*: "Confirm Legal to Travel" for both *Person* and *Freight*

- *Air-Security Services*: "Confirm Safe to Travel" for both *Person* and *Freight*

- *Information-Services*: "Provide Travel-Information" for both *Person* and *Freight*

Figure 9-6 shows the "Transit Land-to-Air" section of the airport's Function-Model color-coded for the respective business-systems.

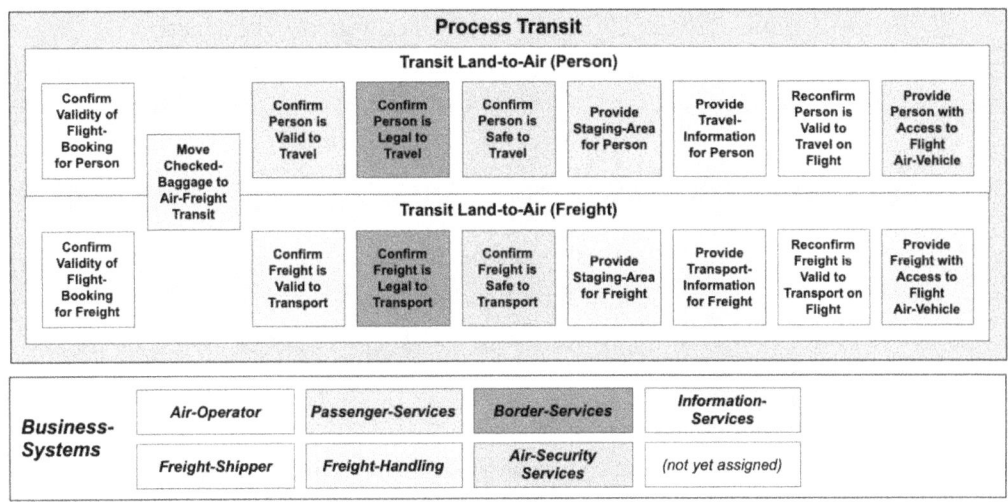

Figure 9-6. *Airport Function-Model – business-systems overlay for "Transit Land-to-Air"*

It can be useful to make up a set of **Business-Systems Detail** diagrams, one for each of the business-systems, together with an appropriate text-description. There's no standard layout for these individual system diagrams, but a typical approach would be to place all of the respective tier-3 activities in the middle, with connections between each other, and to other business-systems and external actors shown on the outer edges.

To **map out individual business-systems**, we note that all activities are also *functions*: something happens, something is changed. Each function uses *assets* of different types – physical, virtual, relational, and/or aspirational. For the Information-Systems Model that follows after this, we need to focus on the virtual-asset data-flows, but in the Business-Systems Model, it's important to also take note of flows of the other asset-types. For each tier-3 activity in this business-system

- What, if anything, is passed between this activity and each of the other activities in this business-system?

- What, if anything, is passed between this activity and any of the other Business-Systems? What asset-types are involved in this transfer? Summarize each connection between the activity and Business-System to a *single* description, as a single flow of one or more asset-types.

- What, if anything, is passed between this activity and other actors outside of the scope of the Function-Model? What asset-types are involved in this transfer? Summarize each connection between activity and external actor to a *single* description, as a single flow of one or more asset-types.

Identify the *asset-types* involved in each transfer, then summarize each connection between activities to a *single* description of a one-way or two-way flow of one or more asset-types. Add symbols for other Business-Systems and for other outside actors to the diagram only if they are referenced by activities within this Business-System.

Another overlay for the Function-Model that is likely to be of immediate value is the **Information-Systems Model**. By now, we should already have a summary of the information flows between the activities within each Business-System. To **identify the information-systems**, we also need to assess the information used *within* each activity. We need to review the business activities to verify the "chunks" of IT-type systems and other information-related services that would be required to support those business activities. We then summarize these chunks of functionality and related storage as abstract "information-systems."

Note It's usually best to define these information-systems in "business" and/or "logical" terms, at the whole-of-organization or even whole-of-enterprise level, *without reference to existing IT-applications* or the like. Strictly speaking, it's not even a "to-be" — a picture of what actual systems the organization would have at a particular future time — but more an *idealized* view of what ought to exist to support the needs in a perfect world.

This type of mapping should ensure that, overall, the activities and information-systems each perform functions that make sense to perform together, that there are no overlaps in functionality, and that all of the required functionality is covered.

The resultant Information-Systems Models would consist of an overview-diagram showing all of the information-systems together, then a more detailed diagram for each of information-systems, and a textual explanation of the content and role of each system. At the end of this process, each Business-System should be aligned with just *one* matching Information-System.

There would usually be a variety of information-applications that might draw on and manipulate that information, but preferably a *single* shared data-store in each case. That's certainly the ideal for any "to-be" design, though it may not work out that way in practice – especially not in the "as-is" setup.

Yet what we're really aiming for here is that, for each business-system, there is just *one* "database of record": a "***single source of truth***," in the information sense of the term. To ***identify single-source-of-truth***, we would look at each identified business-system and its information-system in turn, and ask

- What are the sources for transaction-data, information, and knowledge for this system?

- Who or what may create, read, update, or delete transaction-records for this system? For what purposes?

- Who or what may collate transaction-records into aggregations or transformations such as counts-of, trends-of, averages-of, and suchlike? For what purposes? Via what transform-processes? Where and in what systems are such transforms maintained? Who or what may create, read, update, or delete these transforms, or the means by which the transforms take place?

- What audit-trails exist for changes and aggregations of data, information, and knowledge for this system?

- What services does each information-item provide or support?

- Is there a "single source of truth" for information in this system? If not, what are the consequences of having more than one source of truth?

We may need to reassess the Information-Systems Models, the Business-Systems Models, and even the Function-Model, in the light of the results of this "single-source-of-truth" review.

CHAPTER 9   STEP 2: GET READY FOR ACTION

From Architecture to Action

It's now time to get started in the process of designing and building the actual systems that the organization will use in its real-world enterprise.

We'll use the Function-Model and its overlays as an initial map and overview of the work that will need to be done.

Example   For the airport, they've already decided that for now they'll work only on the tier-3 functions that they identified within the tier-2 function "Transit Land-to-Air," and may take only one of those down to the level of a full real-world simulation. Later, they'll use the experience gained from this exercise to start tackling a full business-transformation of their business-infrastructure functions.

We'll need ***governance*** in place, as described in the "Set Up for Architecture" section in the previous chapter. This will include governance for architecture, for change, for the specific industry (in this case, aviation, air-travel, airports, and air-freight), and for national and other concerns such as health-and-safety and security.

We'll need ***architecture sustainment*** processes in place, as described in the same section in the previous chapter. This project will give us a chance to experience how sustainment processes interweaves with regular goal-based change.

We'll need the full set of ***document-repositories*** in place, as also described in the "Set Up for Architecture" section in the previous chapter. A purpose-built toolset for enterprise-architecture could also be useful here, though note that few at present can cover much more than the mid-range of Plan.

We'll use the ***Change-Layers*** model to guide the overall project. It may be useful to revisit Chapters 4 and 5 to do a quick refresh on how that process works. Figure 9-7 provides a visual summary of the layers and usual sub-layers of that model.

CHAPTER 9 STEP 2: GET READY FOR ACTION

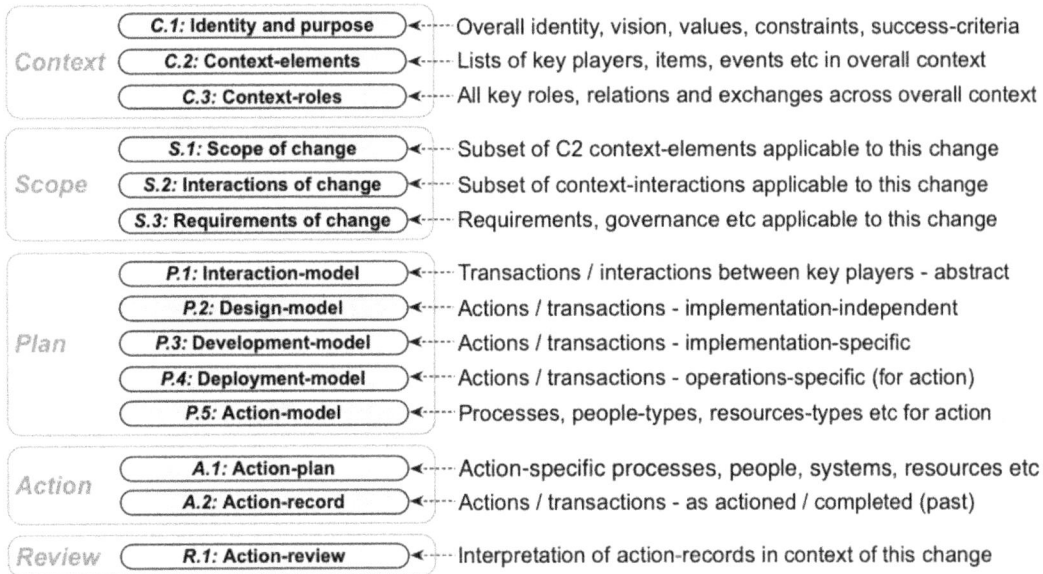

Figure 9-7. *CSPAR Change-Layers*

We'll use the **Change-Cycle** model to guide each smaller chunk of work within the project. It may be useful to revisit Chapter 6 to do a quick refresh on how that process works, and the mode-switching that needs to take place between phases in the cycle. Figure 9-8 provides a visual summary of the cycle, the modes, and the relationship with the Change-Layers.

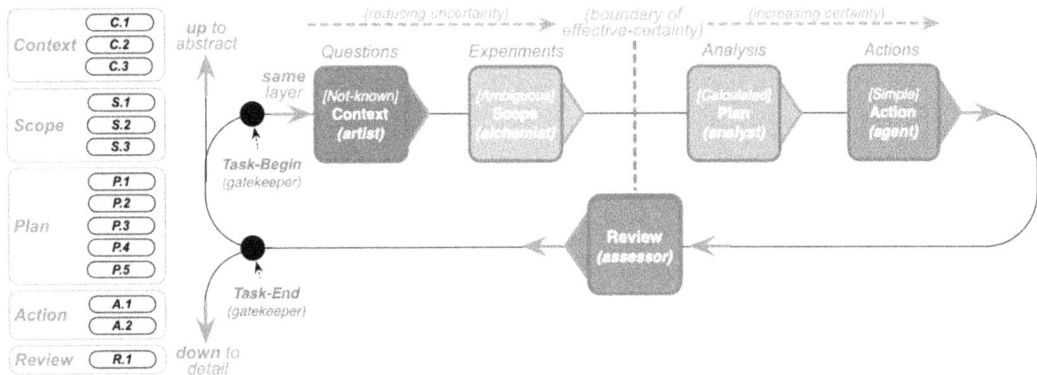

Figure 9-8. *CSPAR Change-Cycle and relationship with Change-Layers*

We'll use the **Service-Content** model that we developed throughout the Change-Layers as a visual-checklist for the structure and content for each function, and the transitions of that content through the change-process. It may be useful to include a quick refresh on this in your revisit of Chapter 5. Figure 9-9 provides a visual summary of this model.

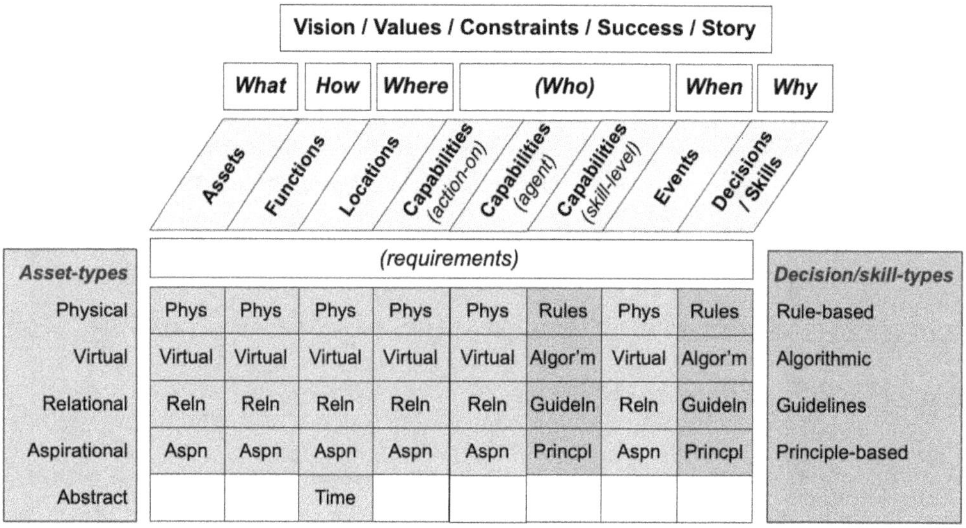

Asset-types	What Assets	How Functions	Where Locations	Capabilities (action-on)	(Who) Capabilities (agent)	Capabilities (skill-level)	When Events	Why Decisions /Skills	Decision/skill-types
				(requirements)					
Physical	Phys	Phys	Phys	Phys	Phys	Rules	Phys	Rules	Rule-based
Virtual	Virtual	Virtual	Virtual	Virtual	Virtual	Algor'm	Virtual	Algor'm	Algorithmic
Relational	Reln	Reln	Reln	Reln	Reln	Guideln	Reln	Guideln	Guidelines
Aspirational	Aspn	Aspn	Aspn	Aspn	Aspn	Princpl	Aspn	Princpl	Principle-based
Abstract			Time						

Above the table: Vision / Values / Constraints / Success / Story

Figure 9-9. *Service-Content model*

While doing this work, we'll also need to sort the functions in terms of their respective positions on the ***"backbone-and-edge" stability-spectrum***, as shown in Figure 9-3. Given the nature of the "Transit Land-To-Air" worked-example, we would expect that all of those functions and their implementations would fit somewhere on the *backbone* to *median* part of that spectrum. We would not expect any edge-type implementations there other than for test-purposes.

Note As described back in Chapters 5 and 6, for the Change-Layers and Change-Cycle, respectively, this part of the work will often be deeply iterative – particularly in the Plan phase, for architects.

For example, some iterations will focus on functional-decomposition and the like; other iterations will then do the development for each element of that decomposition, leading to further Action and Review as required. Remember, though, that **_all of this is fractal_**; each iteration will need its own Context, Scope, Plan, Action, and Review, and probably also its own governance-checks and gateways, as summarized below.

Context Layer

In this layer, we establish the connection to the big-picture. For details on this layer and its three sub-layers, see the section "Context in the Change-Layers" in Chapter 5.

We would derive the Context for a tier-3 business-function from a layered-hierarchy of contexts. In order of priority, these would include

- From Step 1, the Context of the shared-enterprise, the organization as a whole, and the respective tier-1 and tier-2 functions.

- From Step 2, the Context of the tier-3 function itself.

In the **C.1 sub-layer**, we need to identify the overarching criteria for **_effectiveness_** from themes such as purpose, story, vision, values, principles, trade-offs, constraints and realities, and success-criteria. For the upper layers of the context-hierarchy, we would use the respective methods as described earlier:

- *Shared-enterprise*: See the section "Enterprise As Storyworld" in Chapter 8.

- *Organization as a whole*: See the section "Organization-Vision and Values" in Chapter 8.

- *Respective tier-1 and tier-2 functions*: See the section "Organization Structure" in Chapter 8.

We would adapt the same methods for each of the tier-3 functions to match their respective roles, such as identified via the process described in the section "Functions and Systems" earlier in this chapter.

Example   For the airport, the values of its "air-transport" shared-enterprise include the default set of *efficient*, *reliable*, *elegant*, *appropriate*, and *integrated*, and also *safety*, *security*, *timeliness*, and *management of costs*.

As an organization, it added some people-oriented values such as *friendliness, comfort, mutual respect*, and *creating a sense of service*.

Its tier-1 "Process Transit" function adds no more values of its own, but must address a broad array of national and international laws, regulations, and standards that relate to the tests of "valid, legal, safe, and secure to travel." Many of these can, and often do, create value-priority conflicts between values such as *safety, security*, and *timeliness* versus *friendliness, comfort*, and *mutual respect*, which must be addressed and resolved within the respective functions and processes.

Its tier-2 "Transit Land-to-Air" functions must also address constraints such as capacity and staff-availability, and uncertainties such as weather, cancellations, land-transport issues, and late passengers needing to push through as fast as possible while still going correctly through each of the respective checks and tests.

The tier-3 functions within "Transit Land-to-Air" may each have their own additional constraints and success-criteria, depending on where they sit within the respective workflows.

In the **C.2 sub-layer**, we need to identify the ***core elements*** within the boundaries implied by the respective context: *What, How, Where, Who, When,* and *Why*. For the upper layers of the context-hierarchy, we would use the respective methods as described earlier:

- *Shared-enterprise*: See the section "Elements of the Enterprise" in Chapter 8.

- *Organization as a whole*: See the section "Organization Content" in Chapter 8.

For the functions at tier-1, tier-2, and tier-3 levels, we would adapt and use the same methods by treating each function at the respective level as an "organization" in its own right, with the level above representing its "enterprise."

Example For the airport, most of the tier-2 "Transit Land-to-Air" function consists of a series of barriers and gateways for physical "transit-items" – people and freight – with various capabilities attached to those gateways to conduct the respective tests. There'll also be facilities to move or park those items, and information to track where they are and where they next need to be. It's fairly straightforward to map all of this, down to the tier-3 functions, in terms of *What*, *How*, *Where*, *Who*, *When*, and *Why*.

In the **C.3 sub-layer**, we need to map out the overall **roles**, **relationships**, and mutual **responsibilities** between the core types of players in the story behind each function. In essence, we need an overview of *Who* sits *Where*, *How* they connect with each other, *What* is exchanged *When* between them, and *Why* those exchanges need to take place for the story to succeed. For the upper layers of the context-hierarchy, we would use the respective methods as described earlier:

- *Shared-enterprise*: See the section "Enterprise Roles and Interactions" in Chapter 8.

- *Organization as a whole*: See the sections "Positioning the Organization" and "Organization Mission," and also "Organization Value-Propositions" in Chapter 8.

For the functions at tier-1, tier-2, and tier-3 levels, we would adapt and use the same methods by treating each function at the respective level as an "organization" in its own right, with the level above representing its "enterprise."

Remember that there's often a fair bit of rippling back and forth between all three sub-layers here, because the process of building the *C.3* models often suggests other things that we might need to add or change in the higher *C.1* and *C.2* sub-layers.

Example For the airport, Figure 8-4 in the previous chapter shows its Enterprise-Context map of the "*air-transport*" enterprise, and Figure 8-6 shows the Organization-Context map for its *Airport* role in that shared-enterprise.

Its Function-Models give some idea of *Who* sits where, in terms of relationships between the various functions, though further work will need to be done to flesh out more about the full set of relationships for the respective *Where*, *How*,

What, *When*, and *Why*. Its tier-1 and tier-2 models are shown in Figures 8-8 and 8-9 in the previous chapter. Its tier-3 model for the "Transit Land-to-Air" function is shown in this chapter in Figure 9-5, with the respective business-system groupings shown in Figure 9-6.

We store the results of the Context-work in the architecture-repositories previously set up during Step 1.

Before leaving the Context-layer, we'll need to pass a ***gateway governance-check*** to verify the overarching purpose, principles, laws, standards, decision-criteria, effectiveness-criteria, and success-criteria. We can only move on to the next layer if the work so far does satisfy those tests.

Scope Layer

In this layer, we set up the boundaries and requirements for action. For details on this layer and its three sub-layers, see the section "Scope in the Change-Layers" in Chapter 5.

In the sub-layers of the Scope layer, we essentially apply the same respective processes that we used in the Context *C.1*, *C.2*, and *C.3* sub-layers, deriving the *function-specific* subsets for each, and adding more detail.

Example   If the airport's architecture-team think of the airport as one huge continuing-task in its own right, then the airport's Context would be the enterprise of air-travel and air-transport. In Scope, the team would identify the parts of that shared-enterprise that the airport itself will address. The parts of the enterprise that the airport *doesn't* address, and that it trusts to others, would then be classed as "out of scope" – but those will still remain part of the overall enterprise picture, and the team will need to be aware at all times of how those "out-of-scope" items might affect the airport, and the airport in turn might affect them.

We derive the Scope for a tier-3 business-function from a layered-hierarchy of scopes, each itself derived as above from that layered hierarchy of Contexts. In order of priority, these would include

- From Step 1, the Scope of the shared-enterprise, the organization as a whole, and the respective tier-1 and tier-2 functions.
- From Step 2, the Scope of each tier-3 function itself.

In the **S.1 sub-layer**, we choose the ***scope-boundaries*** for each function, to identify where it sits within the broader scheme of things, and the types of tasks it will need to undertake. We verify what the function must achieve and how it will support overall effectiveness, and identify the subsets of the *C.1* Context and storyworld, *C.2* Context-elements, and *C.3* Context roles, relationships, and interactions that will apply within the scope of the function.

The process of exploration here is much the same as in the Context phase. The difference is that rather than broadening our perspective outward to the big-picture, as in the Context phase, here we narrow it downward and inward in each case to the scope and needs of *this* function, making adjustments for the context of each function as necessary.

In the first part of the **S.1** work, we **refine into function-specific form** the *practical* meaning of the question or concern that we clarified during the Context phase.

To do this, we revisit what we found in Context, make a function-specific subset, bring it out of the abstract, and make it more real. For that reason, it's here that we also start the "translation" from abstract element-categories into implementable real-world equivalents – "*What*" to "*Asset*," and so on, as shown in the Service-Content model in Figure 9-9. We'll need to use those real-world "translations" for the work on requirements in the *S.3* sub-layer.

Example For the airport, the purpose, role, and processes for the tier-2 "Transit Land-to-Air" function all seem well understood.

Given that, the team decide to focus on the practical implications of those people-oriented values such as *friendliness*, *comfort*, *mutual respect*, and *a sense of service*. Two themes quickly emerge, from the team's own experiences of air-travel: the relentless pressures to "hurry up and wait!" that seem to pervade everywhere, and the feeling of utter confusion, panic, and despair that arises as soon as something goes wrong in any way at all.

It's clear that if the architecture-team can do anything to reduce those miseries, it would be a practical expression of those people-oriented values, and should help to establish the airport's reputation as one that *does* care about its passengers. The team decide to keep aware of those two themes in the explorations for each of the tier-3 functions on the passenger-side of "Transit Land-to-Air."

In the **S.2 sub-layer**, guided by what we found in *S.1*, we continue the process of "making it real" by finding more detail about ***what each function needs to address***. We'll need to identify and explore the *stakeholders* in scope with their respective needs and concerns, the *workflows* that would be in play, the *risks and opportunities* in scope, the *uncertainties* in scope, and the *skills and experience* needed to address them.

Do be aware, though, that there's good reason why this part of the work is described in Tuckman's "Group Dynamics" project-lifecycle as the "storming" phase. As mentioned back in Chapter 5, people-oriented "soft-skills" will often be more important here than the analyst's usual technical "hard-skills," because there can be a *lot* of arguments here, sometimes coupled with a lot of emotion. Those kinds of explosions should generally be unusual elsewhere, but are *normal* here: we do need to be ready for that, respect it, and work with it as best we can.

Example   For the airport and its "Transit Land-to-Air" functions on the passenger-side, the core responsibilities, processes, actions, and flows are all easy to model and map, with the only complication that some parts, particularly in the "safe-to-travel" checks, do tend to undergo change and redesign every few years in response to changes in regulations and technologies. For the most part, though, they're all well understood.

What is *not* so well understood is why passengers' experience of those processes is so often extremely unpleasant, creating a lot of unnecessary stress for travelers. Looking at their own experiences of travel, the architecture-team identify two key issues: inherent-uncertainty about the time needed to transit through the checks from landside departure-gate to lounge, and lack of real-time information about this and similar concerns. In essence, it seems that the only way for passengers to get through on-time without wasting time is if they have better skills and understanding about the airport's systems than the airport has about itself.

(A strange requirement, of course, though one that also seems common in some other "service"-type industries such as banking and insurance.) Anyone who *doesn't* have that knowledge would be condemned automatically to the miseries of "hurry up and wait." The architecture-team decide to use this concern as their priority test-case for the remainder of this exercise.

In the **S.3 sub-layer**, we continue the process of making each function and its tasks ***realizable and understandable***, and make everything ready to hand over to the Plan phase. Guided by what we found in *S.1* and *S.2*, we would derive and describe the *requirements* for each function, the respective *governance* and *guiding-policies*, and the initial *change-roadmaps* and other communications-strategies for any changes to its internal flows and operations.

Note The processes for each of these types of activities should already be well-known for most architects, so we'll presume we won't need to go into them in any depth here.

Everyone has their own preferred methods for this part of the work. For example, one of our own favorites for requirements-gathering is the Robertsons' *Volere* process, as described in their book *Mastering the Requirements Process*. Andrew Campbell's *Operating Model Canvas* has also been useful for sketching out high-level structure and workflows. In essence, though, use whatever works well for you, and follow the guidance of the standards and frameworks for the respective industry and context.

Those soft-skills will be important here too, because the "storming" from the previous sub-layer may well continue for a while, particularly during the requirements-gathering process. It should ease off once we move into the other parts of this sub-layer, but we do again need to respect it while it lasts.

> **Example** For the airport architecture-team, the scope for their architecture-development exercise has been narrowed somewhat, to just the passenger-side of the "Transit Land-to-Air" function. In part, this is because much of the freight side of that function is handled in a separate part of the airport, by the Freight-Shipper organizations and their agents.
>
> They're still looking to identify which functions should be considered "backbone," but the detail-focus has shifted somewhat to that theme of using the architecture to help minimize the miseries of "hurry-up-and-wait."
>
> They identify a couple of conflicts-of-interest around "hurry-up-and-wait" that they'll need to address. One is that most of the slowdown occurs in the security-checks, and there'll probably be considerable pushback against any attempts to speed these up, unless these can make the work of the security-staff easier too. The other is that the vendors in the staging-areas will *want* the passengers to be waiting around doing nothing; otherwise, there won't be enough time to sell them anything. Since the vendors represent one of the airport's two major customer-groups (the other being the airlines), this may be a hard challenge to resolve…
>
> For the Plan phase of the work, the requirements they've agreed on are that they'll map out the full workflows and pathways to at least the level of the "business-model" or Interaction-Model, and then go into more depth on the functions that seem to be involved in the "hurry-up-and-wait" issue. As this is still only an experience-building exercise, it's not yet certain as to how deep they would go, but they do want to take at least a simulation all the way to build, deployment, Action, and Review.

We would again store the results of the Scope-work in the respective architecture-repositories. This would include the *requirements-repository* shared with project-management.

Before leaving the Scope-layer, we'll need to pass a **_gateway governance-check_** to verify the scope-boundaries, stakeholders, requirements, and any scope-specific amendments to purpose, principles, standards, and so on. We can only move on to the next layer if the work so far does satisfy those tests.

Plan Layer

In this layer, we establish how the work will be done. For details on this layer and its five sub-layers, see the section "Plan in the Change-Layers" in Chapter 5.

> **Note** Throughout the Plan layers, but particularly in *P.1* to *P.3*, it's generally a good idea to support architecture-sustainment by looking for potential conflicts and synergies, and opportunities to reduce technical-debt. The Function-Model will be a valuable ally in that, particularly through the implied relationships between functions as highlighted by its Business-Systems and Information-Systems cross-maps.
>
> There's more detail on that exploration-process later in the book, in the section "Hands-Off Architecture" in Chapter 13.

In the **P.1 sub-layer**, we develop an overview of what would need to be done to support the desired Action and outcomes for the task. The overall aim here is to build a broad sense of what the real-world implementation might look like, how it would work, and of the kinds of issues that might arise.

The process is similar to that in the Scope layer, but with more detail, and usually broken into smaller chunks that still need to be kept connected with each other. We would identify each of the main workflows and their key interactions, but only at an abstract level, a barebones description of what needs to happen within and between each respective function.

We would map out the results and outcomes of these explorations as diagrams, models, tables, and other records, and then package these together as an ***Interaction-Model***.

> **Example** For the airport, the tier-2 "Transit Land-to-Air" function in their Function-Model shows the overall workflow, with each of the services delivered by different providers – airline, airport-staff, security-staff, and so on. They'll need to add detail about what needs to happen outside of that "happy-path," though, such as when passengers fail any of the tests, or equipment breaks down.

Even for the "happy-path," some of the details can be different for domestic versus international because of jurisdiction issues. For example, "valid to travel" and "legal to travel" could be combined in domestic, run by airport-staff with regular security-staff available in the background. But in international these tests must be separated because the "legal-to-travel" test must be run by border-control under the rules of international law rather than in-nation law. Some countries also require a further "legal-to-travel" check at the flight-gate, run by their own country's border-staff rather than the border-staff of the airport's nation.

There may also be some outsourcing issues, ensuring that organizations and staff from outsourced services will support the airport's values such as *friendliness*, *comfort*, *mutual respect*, and *creating a sense of service*. Some means to negotiate these issues will need to be included in the airport's architecture. The negotiation may be easier with organizations that are the airport's customers, such as airlines and vendors, but could be challenging with services that must be outsourced by law, such as police and border-control, and the security-agencies for the "safe-to-travel" checks.

We would store the results of this work in the respective repositories, such as the *architecture-products* and *architecture-records* repositories and the *architecture-register*. We would also track any issues related to technical-debt and the like via the *dispensations-register*.

Note that we may need to pass a ***gateway governance-check*** to verify and validate the Interaction-Model before moving on to the *P.2* tasks.

In the **P.2 sub-layer**, we rework the abstract Interaction-Model into an *implementation-neutral* design. This describes the business-logic for each interaction across the respective scope and context.

Here, we split each tier-3 function into child-functions, to help us model the interactions in more detail. For example, we would split the abstract process "*Confirm validity of flight-booking for passenger*" into distinct steps such as "*Verify identity,*" "*Verify booking,*" "*Create boarding-pass,*" and "*Deliver boarding-pass,*" down to any level of detail we might need.

We also specify the general *type* for each of the content-items, in terms of the content-segments – physical "thing," virtual IT-data, people-relationship, or purpose. For example, a boarding-pass could be issued by the airline's website, via the airline's mobile-app, via mail to the passenger, via a travel-agent, or at the airport via the airline's check-in agent. However, at this stage we're still working at an *abstract* level: the full implementable details for the boarding-pass would be identified in later sub-layers of the Plan layer.

To help us make sense of how to tackle the "backbone-and-edge" issues at this layer, it's probably easiest to turn to the ***ISO9000 quality-system*** and its four-layered structure of *Vision, Policy, Procedure*, and *Work-Instructions*:

- The ***Work-Instructions*** provide guidance on what should be done in the real-world. We typically start to work on these in the *P.3* sub-layer of the Plan, and they represent a key part of the deliverables from the *P.5* sub-layer. They are specific to a given implementation, and may be specific to a single instance of that implementation. If the implementation changes, we will need to rework the Work-Instructions in line with the respective Procedure.

- Each ***Procedure*** provides guidance on what must be included within a given type of implementation, and in the Work-Instructions that match that implementation. We typically start to work on these in the *P.1* sub-layer of Plan, and they form a key part of the Design-Model deliverables of the *P.2* sub-layer. They are specific to a given *category* of implementations. If the category needs to change, we must rework the Procedure in line with the respective Policy.

- Each ***Policy*** provides agreed decisions and trade-offs that must be addressed within any applicable Procedure. We typically work on these within the Scope layer, and they form a key part of the deliverables for the *S.3* sub-layer. They are specific to a given range of scopes for Procedures. If those scopes need to change, we must rework the respective Policy in line with the organization or enterprise Vision.

- The ***Vision*** is the ultimate anchor for the quality-system, and – as we've seen in Step 1, back in the previous chapter – provides guidance on overall aims, values, constraints, and success-criteria for everything that happens in the organization and its broader shared-enterprise. We typically work on these within the Context layer, and they form a key part of the deliverables from those sub-layers.

In those terms, we'll often discover here that what we'll need for a backbone "infrastructure-function" is actually the respective *Procedure*, or even a *Policy* in some cases, rather than the operable *Work-Instructions* and the like. The respective real-world functions, as implemented, are "backbone-like," but will sit closer to the median on that spectrum because they'll undergo quite frequent updates with each change in regulations and the related technologies.

Overall, we would map out the results and outcomes of these explorations in diagrams, models, tables, and other records, and then package these together as a **Design-Model**.

Example For the airport, the team map out the workflows and other flows for each of the tier-3 functions in "Transit Land-to-Air." They start to recognize the relevance of the ISO9000 layering for identifying where things fit on the "backbone-and-edge" spectrum. At an abstract level, each of these tier-3 functions is "backbone," but their *implementations* are likely to change quite often, and hence cannot themselves be considered "backbone."

For these functions, what's needed in the backbone are the ***policies*** and ***procedures*** that define what needs to be done within each of those functions, but allow their actual run-time operations to be separate – not least because those operations will often be done by outsourced agents or agencies. There are then further backbone-policies and procedures that identify what to change for each of the functions, how to do each change, and who to contact for authorization and guidance on the change. The only ***work-instructions*** in the backbone would be those on how to do the respective changes for the underlying service or function – not the operations of the functions themselves.

The team map out the operations-procedures for each of the functions, and then move toward creating more-detailed plans to help the airport respond as quickly as possible to change-requirements coming from elsewhere, such as regulatory changes and updates to other nations' travel-rules. This includes relationships with other groups in the airport, such as rapid procurement and installation of any new equipment that may be required.

They also map out procedures and processes for fast onboarding of new vendors and other service-providers in the various staging-areas, both inside and outside the secure-area, and for new airlines involved in the functions "Confirm validity of flight-booking" and "Reconfirm valid to travel on flight." They define and design similar procedures and processes to address how airlines will be able to switch between air-gates at run-time, when aircraft need to be diverted to a different gate.

The one function within this set that is under the airport's direct control is "Provide travel-information." The team assess what might be done there to reduce the stress of "hurry-up-and-wait," and realize that they could provide not just the information about flights, gates, and boarding-times, but also *how long it would take to get there* from each respective point in the airport, from check-in to staging-area to gate. This should be valuable to all passengers, yet also relatively simple to implement. The team decide to focus on this theme for the remainder of this exercise.

As in the *P.1* sub-layer, we would store the results of this work in the respective repositories, such as the *architecture-products* and *architecture-records* repositories and the *architecture-register*. We would also track any issues related to technical-debt and the like via the *dispensations-register*.

Note that we may need to pass a **gateway governance-check** to verify and validate the Design-Models before moving on to the *P.3* tasks.

In the **P.3 sub-layer**, we rework the *P.2* Design-Model into an *implementation-specific* form – though note that this part of Plan is often intensely iterative and fractal, with many sub-tasks within the overall planning task. We expand the detail by doing a full work-breakdown for each task in the Action, either step-by-step, for routine predictable tasks, or the overall workflows, desired-outcomes, and uncertainties for case-management and the like.

We'll need to define separate implementations with different skill-levels for each of the agent-types – people, machines, IT-systems, and aspirational-elements – and map the *coordination* and *process-choreography* between the various steps and implementation-elements. In many cases, we'll also need alternative implementations for the *same* process, such as for business-continuity and disaster-recovery planning, or for regulatory requirements in different jurisdictions.

CHAPTER 9   STEP 2: GET READY FOR ACTION

It's also here that we'll need to tackle the full "translation" of service-content from the abstract *What, How, Where, Who, When,* and *Why* into their real-world expressions as *Asset, Function, Location, Capability, Event,* and *Decision,* as illustrated earlier in the Service-Content model shown in Figure 9-9. The *content-categories* are as follows:

- **Assets** ("What") are resources for which the organization will or must assume responsibility. These may include physical "things," virtual data and information, relations between people and other real entities, links to purposive or "aspirational" content such as a nation or a brand, or any combinations of those themes.

- **Functions** ("How") represent how things are done, or, in service-design, the surface-level *interface* to how things are done, with capabilities and suchlike hidden behind it to do the actual work. Functions may work on or apply to physical things, virtual data and information, relational assets, aspirational-assets, and/or any combination of those asset-types.

- **Locations** ("Where") represent points or positions within some kind of schema. These may be physical, such as the airport's geographic location, or somewhere within the airport-building or on a conveyor-belt; virtual, such as a room-number or an IP-address; relational, such as within the airport's management-hierarchy; aspirational, such as in the airport's brand-architecture; or a location in time – events take place *in* time, but are not "time" *itself*. Locations may also be any combination of those themes: for example, a space in the airport has a physical location, will typically be assigned a virtual identifier, be associated with particular people, and may be a place where something famous happened.

- **Capabilities** are a bit more complicated: they are always composites, combining the underlying *How* behind a Function with the *Who* for action and more. They can also include other capabilities or complete services, embedded or linked inside each other in a fractal nesting. We typically divide the structure of capabilities into three parts: *action-on, agent,* and *skill-level*.

- ***Capability: action-on*** represents the Asset(s) to be worked on by the Capability. As described above, these Assets would be described in terms of the asset-types set.

- ***Capability: agent*** represents the entity or entities that will do the actions on the respective Capability "action-on" assets. This is a broader sense of *Who*: the agent may be a physical machine to work on physical-assets, a computer-application to change virtual-assets; an actual person working on relational-assets, a brand or live-event to change aspirational-assets, and/or any combination of these.

- ***Capability: skill-level*** denotes the type and level of competencies and skills needed by the Capability's agent to work appropriately on Capability's "action-on" assets. The required skill-levels will be as described in Chapter 7, in the section "The Uncertainties of Change": *Trainee, Apprentice, Journeyman,* and *Master*.

- **Events** ("When") denote potential or actual triggers for change. These may be physical, virtual, relational and/or aspirational, as per the asset-types. Events may also be composites of these types: for example, in the classic "a man walks into a bar" scenario, the event is physical, in that the door is opened; the event is virtual, in that there will be some kind of signal as the door is opened; the event is relational, in that the man wants someone to serve him a drink; and the event is aspirational, in that the man desires a drink.

- **Decisions** ("Why") in the Plan, Action, and Review phases of a task usually denote the responses or *answers* to a previous "Why" – rather than the *questions* that represent the "Why" itself, as we would more often see in the Context and Scope phases. These Decisions would typically take the form of simple rules; specifications for or outcomes from more-complicated algorithms; heuristics, patterns, and the like as guidelines for action in uncertain, ambiguous, or unique contexts; principles and values to guide action in unknown situations; and/or any combinations of these.

As indicated above, there are two sets of *content-segment* types that apply to these content-categories:

- The **Asset-types** are *physical, virtual, relational,* and *aspirational*. These apply to *Asset, Function, Location, Capability: action-on,* and *Capability: agent*.

- The **Decision-types** are *rule-based, algorithmic, guidelines,* and *principle-based*. These apply to *Capability: skill-level* and *Decision*.

The Asset-types are fundamentally-different from each other in several key ways:

- Physical assets are *alienable* – if I give it to you, I no longer have it – whereas virtual-assets such as data are *non-alienable* – if I give it to you, I still have it.

- Relational assets connect between real people and the like, whereas aspirational assets connect a real-person to something abstract such as a memory, a purpose, or a brand.

- Physical and virtual-assets are *discrete* and *intrinsic* – they exist in their own right – whereas relational- and aspirational-type assets connect *between* entities, and will cease to exist if dropped from either side of the connection.

Warning That last point about "relational-assets cease to exist if dropped from either side of the connection" highlights a fundamental error in the concept of a CRM or Customer Relationship Management system.

The usual model captures and maintains information about the organization's relational-assets – its relationships with customers, prospects, and the like – *but views the relationship only from its own perspective*, as if it were a *physical* asset or "thing" that they possess. That isn't how relational-assets work: they can vanish if dropped by the *customer*, not just by the organization. Many CRMs are stuffed full of information about relational-assets that no longer actually exist, and annoy former customers who no longer want that "relationship" at all. Not A Good Idea...

We're likely to build up a lot of *documentation* here that should be stored in the repositories so that it can be available if and when required. From those documents, we would derive two sets of **deliverables**: the "*deployment-architecture*" for the *P.4* deployment-phase and the "*activity-architecture*" for the final *P.5* phase. Those deliverables and the related documentation from any intermediate steps should be packaged together as the task's **Development-Model**, as described in the section on the *P.3* sub-layer in the Change-Layers in Chapter 5.

Example For the airport, the team explore what would be needed for the more people-friendly information-system. They map out what information would be needed, where and how they could obtain that information, what transforms would be needed to create the actual information required, and how it could be displayed.

The airport's information-systems already provide a "single-source-of-truth" for information about flights, boarding-gates, boarding-times, and departure-times, as shown on display-boards throughout the airport. Beyond that, the key elements are the display-boards themselves. Their locations are known, so it's easy to calculate the distance from there to each gate, and the typical time that it should take for people to travel the respective distance. Adding that information to the displays should be straightforward, as the displays themselves are modern freeform screens that can display anything required. The distance-and-time information can be attached to the existing flight-data. This would also help to reduce the sense of panic that can occur with a gate-change, as passengers would immediately know how long it should take them to get from the current gate to the new one.

The main uncertainty is the time it takes to get through the three main checks: valid-to-travel, legal-to-travel, and safe-to-travel. There can be huge variations here, depending on time of day and flight-schedules. The team consider that their best option will be to track random de-identified individuals through the process at each step, using existing camera-sources in those areas. They map out where they can source that data, obtain the requisite privacy and other permissions to use it, and how to process it to derive the effective time to reach each transition-point. If they can do this, then no new technology would be required: it could all be done with existing equipment and systems.

They also identify an additional benefit for late-running passengers and for the airport as a whole. Since the time for departure and time to get to the gate at each point for each flight would now be known, late passengers could be diverted through the faster VIP-only channels, to give them a better chance of reaching the gate on time. Passengers trying to "game" the system by falsely claiming that they were late for their flights could easily be identified and sent to the back of the queue again. The only system requirement for this would be an update to the operator's display at the entry to the VIP lane, and an old-fashioned ticket-dispenser for the operator to hand to late-running-passengers to help them move faster through the travel-checks.

The team decide to build a simple physical simulation of this as a proof-of-concept to show to executives and change-managers, and to test ideas and gather real-world information.

As in the previous *P.1* and *P.2* sub-layers, we would store the results of this work in the respective repositories, such as the *architecture-products* and *architecture-records* repositories and the *architecture-register*.

Note that we may need to pass a **gateway governance-check** to verify and validate the Development-Models before moving on to the *P.4* tasks.

In the **P.4 sub-layer**, we expand the *P.3* "Deployment-Architecture" into detailed specifications for what needs to go where to support each Action, sometimes all the way down to the level of each individual instance of an installation-type.

There can be a lot of subtle complexities and traps in this part of the planning work, many of which may be hidden from view unless we make a deliberate effort to search for them. One such theme to watch for here, and to check in governance-reviews in each iteration, is that a myriad of different regulations and standards that might come into play, again sometimes varying down to the individual-instance level. Another theme is the potential need for *redundancy and duplication*: for example, an abstract *"the power-supply"* might need to include connections to mains-electricity, solar systems, diesel backup-generators, and controllers to manage the load-switching.

As mentioned back in Chapter 5, there are two main **deliverables** from this work: the "*installation-model*" specifications that will be sent to project-management for the installation-engineers, and the "*infrastructure-usage model*" that will move onward to the *P.5* sub-layer to guide the development of the *Action-Model* for run-time Action. We would typically describe that overall package of documentation and deliverables as the **Deployment-Model**.

Example   For the airport, the team obtain the official scale-drawings of the airport, and identify the locations of each display-screen. They also discover that the distance between the furthest gates apart is almost a kilometer, or around a thousand yards – not a distance that most people could easily run while carrying a gaggle of small children and a full load of carry-on baggage!

The team gain permission to walk through the airport and measure the typical time it takes to go from point to point. They also measure the typical transit-times through the travel-checks on a quiet day, and at a busy time. This gives them a baseline on which to build a basic software-driven experiment.

They plan to take over a large conference-room for a day. They'll first build a simple scale-model of the key points of the airport, based on the official drawings, and marked out with tape and sticky-notes on the conference-tables. They'll then run a simulation of how the timings would work, with stick-figures to move around and stand in for the passengers. A set of laptops would run the software for each point, and be used to emulate the airport's displays. To minimize the time needed to set up the scale model in the conference, they document their build-instructions in a Deployment-Model, and develop the spreadsheets and interfaces on which the simulation would be based.

As in the previous *Plan* sub-layers, we would store the results of this work in the respective repositories, such as the *architecture-products* and *architecture-records* repositories and the *architecture-register*.

Note that we may need to pass a **gateway governance-check** to verify and validate the Deployment-Models before moving on to the *P.5* tasks.

In the **P.5 sub-layer**, we combine and expand the *"activity-architecture"* part of the *P.3* Development-Model and the *"infrastructure-usage"* part of the *P.4* Deployment-Model to create one or more *Action-Model* templates on which the action-plans for run-time action will later be built.

The Action-Model is the main type of **deliverable** for this phase, and should provide the complete guidance for a specific type of task or related set of tasks at a specific type of locale. The typical content for an Action-Model should include the respective *Four-Checklists* set, lists of potential uncertainties to resolve at run-time, any machine-settings and similar setup-conditions, the resources-plan, the inputs and outputs through the function-interfaces, the start- and stop-conditions, and the setup to capture the required action-records.

Once the work is complete, the ***Action-Model*** package would be made available for use in the Action *A.1* sub-layer, as the template for the respective Action-Plans.

Example For the airport, the team plan out the work-instructions for their simulation. Because it's only a basic "low-fidelity" simulation, they won't need a fully-detailed Four-Checklists set for this, but they're well aware that that *would* be needed for any real-world operational environment.

The work-instructions describe the tests they want to do, how they will capture the information they need, and then process that information to pass to the respective displays. They've included checklists for a variety of situations where things could go wrong, and they also want to capture any insights and exceptions that might come up during the simulation process. In particular, although the focus will be on how the information-system would work, they also want to identify how other contexts or events might affect or be affected by the information-system.

They document all of this as an Action-Model that they'll bring out as soon as they've built the scale-model in the conference-room.

As in the previous *Plan* sub-layers, we would store the architecture documents from this work in the respective repositories, such as the *architecture-products* and *architecture-records* repositories and the *architecture-register*. The Action-Models would typically be passed to the respective project-management, change-management, or line-management teams to guide the run-time action.

At this point, we will have finished all of the work for the Plan layer. Before leaving this layer, though, we may need to pass a ***gateway governance-check*** to verify and validate the Action-Models and confirm the availability of any required resources.

Action Layer

In this layer, we do the work needed to deliver the desired outcomes. For details on this layer and its two sub-layers, see the section "Action in the Change-Layers" in Chapter 5.

In the **A.1 sub-layer**, the work begins when we receive the start-event signal for the Action. Here, we do the setup for the activity, using the *P.5* Action-Model as a template to create an ***Action-Plan*** for the content and context for *this specific instance* of the Action.

Once the pre-start setup and checks are complete, we should be ready to do the value-creation work of the Action itself.

Example For the airport, the team move into the conference-room that's been set aside for their simulation. They use the Deployment-Model to guide their simple model of the airport, and set up the laptops that would play the part of the respective information-displays.

They then bring out their Action-Model, adapt the details to match the exact situation in the conference-room, and start their simulation.

In the **A.2 sub-layer**, working from the *A.1* setup, we do the specified work for the action, changing the content and context to achieve the desired outcomes. We address any variances or exceptions that may arise during the activity, and capture the required information, ideas, and insights.

The overall Action will finish when the specified end-event occurs or specified end-conditions are achieved.

Example For the airport, the team run their simulation of the time-to-gate information-updates for the airport-displays.

The software works as intended, adjusting the times correctly at each one-minute iteration. However, the member of the security-team they brought in for the test shows them a much broader range of error-conditions than they'd expected. For example, they'd assumed they could track a single passenger through the travel-checks – but that passenger might be turned away or detained at any of the checks. The passenger may also take much longer than expected because their carry-on baggage had been set aside for a manual search at the "safe-to-travel" check. From this, the team realize that they would need to derive a dynamic average by tracking multiple passengers at each iteration, drop any passenger-avatar that didn't make it through the checks after a load-adjusted time-out, and perhaps show separate times for those who did or did not need a manual-search.

The team store their Action-Records and other insights for a subsequent After-Action Review, and then clean up the conference-room for the next users.

The results of the Action should be stored as specified in the respective Action-Model and Action-Plan.

Before leaving the Action-layer, we may need to do a brief ***governance-check*** to verify the completeness of all tasks within the Action, and that all required records are available. We can only move on to the Review layer if the work so far does satisfy those tests.

Review Layer

In this layer, we assess the outcomes of the work in relation to the initial intent. For the details on this layer and its single sub-layer, see the section "Review in the Change-Layers" in Chapter 5.

In the **R.1 layer**, we want to identify *benefits-realized, lessons-learned*, and *actions-for-change* arising from all of the previous work. To do this, we would typically run an *after-action review* as described in the section "Review in the Change-Layers." The "benefits-realized" establish the value of doing the task's change-work, while the "lessons-learned" and "actions-for-change" will support continual improvement of effectiveness within the organization and the overall shared-enterprise.

Example   For the airport, the architecture run a full After-Action Review, not just of the simulation, but of the whole exercise from starting with the Function-Model to map out the "backbone-and-edge" situation for each of its tier-3 functions.

The ***benefits-realized*** include the first-hand experience of whole-enterprise architecture gained by going through the full CSPAR Change-Layers process, from Context to Scope, Plan, Action, and, here, Review. From this experience, they feel much more comfortable about rolling out architecture-guided change-processes for any part of the airport, rather than solely for the airport's IT.

The ***lessons-learned*** include a much better awareness of how architectures work across the overall organization and its enterprise, and a better appreciation of why it's important to architect and design for more than just the "happy-path" in operational processes. They also now recognize the value of focusing on values, because that was the initial trigger for the time-to-gate project, and also how that experiment showed that useful innovations could be built on top of existing systems without requiring any new equipment at all.

The suggested ***actions for change*** for the team itself include setting up a systematic process of engagement with experienced operations-staff throughout the airport, as these people would be the most likely to know about real-world exceptions and special-cases that would need to be addressed in the respective architectures. The team would also provide feedback to change-management about strategies needed to improve architecture governance of "backbone" functions, and also recommend that the time-to-gate experiment be developed into a full change-project, based on the results of the simulation and tests.

The results of the Review would be stored in the respective repositories for architecture and design, change-management, strategy, governance, and more. Any suggested actions-for-change would be passed to change-management and others as appropriate.

Before leaving the top-level Review-layer, we'll need to do an ***end-of-project governance-check*** for the architecture work, in context of the current strategies and requirements of the organization as a whole. We can only mark the project as complete once that governance process has been done.

CHAPTER 9   STEP 2: GET READY FOR ACTION

Stories of change

Enterprise is always about *people*. Everything we do in enterprise-architecture will change people's lives. There is often a tendency in enterprise-architecture to over-focus on the technology: we need to counter that tendency, to instead keep the focus where it actually belongs, with people. For example, we can use that common phrase "*people, process, technology*" as a reminder that, in every architecture, **people always come first**.

When working with people, one of the most useful tools we have is *story*. It's especially important in the "Not-known," where story-based practices can help us to elicit tacit-knowledge and experiences about the context. We've already seen one example of this back in Chapter 3, in the section "The awareness of change," where a story-based question is a key part of the **Architect's Mantra**: "I don't know," "It depends," "Just enough detail," *"What's the story?"*, and "Why is this important?"

Stories are everywhere, if we take care to notice them. For example, **every change implies a story**: each instance of a process is a story in its own right, with its own purpose, beginning, middle, end, and outcomes. These stories are also fractal, always "same and different," small stories nesting within larger stories, chaining together in steps and sequences, with connections to other stories elsewhere in the enterprise.

In enterprise-architecture, we can use this connection between story and change as a unifying theme to help us make sense of what happens in the enterprise, and to guide us towards improving overall effectiveness across the enterprise as a whole.

Story-listening and story-capture come first; and then, perhaps, story-building and story-telling. For example, consider **the value of visuals** in helping people to understand and explore a story of change. All of the diagrams in this book do that, in one sense or another. Many of those diagrams, such as the Change-Layers in Figure 9-7 earlier above, the Change-Cycle in Figure 9-8, and the Service-Content model in Figure 9-9, also provide visual-checklists to guide and validate various aspects of change-processes and system-design.

Back in Chapter 5, in the section "Context in the Change-Layers," we talked about using the DoDAF *OV-1* operational-view diagram to provide a visual overview of an overall context or system, and to guide people through the various elements and interactions of that system. Many of the diagram-types here can serve the same kind of purpose: the Organization-Context Map back in Figure 8-6, for example, provides an overview of an organization's relationships with the other players in its enterprise-context, and an organization's Function Model, such as shown in Figure 9-4 above, provides a base on which to do walkthroughs of workflows and other interactions across the organization itself.

Warning   Don't use technical diagrams with a non-technical audience! One of the authors learned that lesson the hard way, trying to use a BPMN diagram to explain to the executive-board a set of relationships between projects that the architecture-team needed to change. It did not go well... Fortunately I was able to talk my way out my own mess – literally so, by building a verbal picture rather than a visual one, enough for them to invite me to come back later with a diagram they could understand. I duly returned the next day with the same story reframed in real-world terms, with graphics of people, trucks, machines and conveyor-belts rather than as abstract symbols – and they immediately gave their approval for the change.

Those non-technical audiences aren't stupid: far from it! If we throw a technical-diagram at them, then in effect we're expecting them to instantly learn yet another arbitrary set of abstract symbols, translate their own real-world experience into those specific terms, get a grasp of what the diagram is trying to say, and then translate it all back again into the actual real-world context. In many cases, they simply won't have the *time* to do that, let alone anything else. As an architect, *you* are responsible to match your diagrams to the respective audience: mismatches of that kind are Not A Good Idea...

Remember to engage ***the other senses*** too: hearing, touch, texture, scent, and sound. Scents can bring images from the past or present: even mentioning the smell of an airport will trigger memories of the reek of aviation-fuel pervading every part of the place. Including sound can also help people make sense of a workspace: the eerie quiet of an empty woodland, compared to the clamor of a manufacturing-workshop or the howl of aircraft-engines out on the tarmac.

Remember, too, ***the importance of playfulness***, especially when exploring the Not-known. Even everyday toys can be useful in this. For example, we (the authors) have used a toy train to illustrate service-dependencies and service-conflicts, mini-figures and a toy-theater to model process-flows and process-interactions, and wooden building-blocks to map out system-units, system-structures, and system-relationships. As mentioned earlier, we've also got clients to map out their organization's Function-Model using their own photographs to indicate their roles within the organization's business – creating a space for much-needed conversations that had never happened before.

Another useful tactic is **role-play**. This can take many forms, such as modeling service-interactions with mini-figures or playing the roles in person, or using **improv** improvisational-theater methods to play out, for example, the interaction between an angry customer and a customer-service agent. As in the airport-example above, we could take the Stanford Design School's IDEO approach and build a simple simulation of a workspace with tables and chairs and other items as props, to map what actually happens in a real-world workflow. Or we can go the computer route, build a CGI model of some future workspace, and then use VR or the like to explore that virtual-world. As long as it will support that kind of story-oriented role-play in some useful way, anything goes.

Note Don't be put off by any potential costs here! Full computer-based or real-world simulations can be expensive to set up, of course, but most of the simpler tools are much cheaper and much more easily available. A wooden toy-train, a set of building-blocks, or a set of mini-figures can all be picked up at any toy-store for pocket-money prices. The toy-theater that we've used in some of our client-work – Pollock's "Cinderella" theater, with a working stage and backdrop, and wires to move mini-figures around on the stage – can be ordered online, takes just minutes to assemble, and costs less than an evening meal out. Purpose-built kits such as "Lego Serious Play" can be somewhat more expensive, but still well within the range of any department's discretionary-budget. With the right audience, willing to let go into "serious-play," they all work *really* well.

Books that we've found useful as guides for serious-play include Dave Gray's *Gamestorming*, IDEO's *The Field Guide to Human-Centered Design*, Keith Johnstone's *Impro: Improvisation and the Theatre*, and the anthology *This Is Service Design Doing* edited by Marc Stickdorn and others.

You'll find links and details for all of these in Appendix B.

We can also use a structured approach to story as a business-sensemaking tool in its right. This gives us a people-oriented checklist and cross-check for business-analysis and the like. To do that, we start from this well-known quote from Shakespeare's play "*As You Like It*":

All the world's a stage, and all the men and women merely players. They have their exits and their entrances; And one man in his time plays many parts.

Given that, we can reframe "*people, process, technology*" as "***actor, scene, stage***." We can then describe everything that happens within and between organizations as scenes within stories, each scene with its own players and interactions, and its own stage, setting, and background within the theater of life itself. Each scene plays its part in driving a larger story forward, with story itself as a fractal element: small stories interweave with other stories within larger stories within yet larger stories.

In turn, we can also connect that reframe to other tools such as the concept of the enterprise as a shared "bold endeavor," and the CSPAR change-process model, the Change-Context model, and Change-Content model. This gives us a story-based approach through which to make sense of any business context.

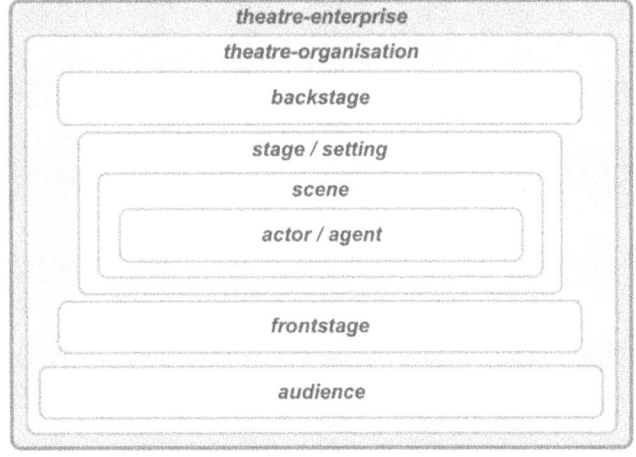

Figure 9-10. *The theater-metaphor – "actor, scene, and stage"*

Using the visual-checklist shown in Figure 9-10, we start on the theater-stage with the ***actors***, and move outward from there:

- Who or what are the players in the scene – the **actors or agents**? What *is* each player – a person, machine, or IT-application?

- What is the **role** of each player in the scene? How does their presence in the scene support the overall story?

- What are the "**things**" or props used by the players in the scene? How are those things used to drive the story onward?

- What **information** is conveyed, or hidden, within this scene? In what ways does its presence, absence, or change drive the story onward?

- What are the **relations** between each of the players, within the scene, and within the broader story? What are the *politics* of those relations, such as power, status, or responsibilities?

- For each player, what is their own **purpose** or intent within this scene, and in the overall story? What denotes their own vision, values, drivers, standards, and success-criteria? How do they show, or not show, these criteria to others, or even to themselves?

- What are the **interactions** between the players in the scene? What is their interface or *function* relative to other players? What is the overall experience of each player in the scene, in the sense of "user-experience"? What is the emotive mode or *mood* of those interactions, such as supportive, disruptive, controlling, or other?

Next, we look at the **scene** itself, as a story-fragment within a larger story:

- What is the **context** of this scene, in terms of the overall story, and other larger stories beyond this one? What are the values, constraints, and success-criteria for the story as a whole?

- What is the **scope** of this scene, relative to other scenes in the overall story?

- What is the **plan** or script for this scene? How will it drive the story forward, for each of the players, and for the enterprise as a whole?

- What is the **action** in the scene? What happens? What is done? What is changed?

- What are the ***events*** of the action? What are the start- and end-points of the scene, and for each "beat" of the scene such as the entry or exit of a player?

- What are the ***outcomes*** of the action in this scene? How will this serve the story as a whole? Whose needs will be served, or not served?

And then that ***larger story*** in which this scene plays its part

- From whose ***perspective*** is the overall story seen? In what ways, if any, are the perspectives of some players prioritized as "more important" than those of others, such as that of a specific protagonist?

- What, if any, are the ***story-outcomes*** for the overall story? If there is a specific protagonist, are their desired outcomes achieved, or thwarted?

- What, if any, is the ***story-arc*** of benefits-realized or not-realized, and/or lessons-learned or not-learned, as the story moves toward its outcome? What transition-events and/or intermediate outcomes denote each point of change in that story-arc?

- What, if any, is the ***character-arc*** of benefits-realized or not-realized, and/or lessons-learned or not-learned, for each of the players, as the story moves toward its outcomes? What transition-events and/or intermediate outcomes denote each point of change in that character-arc?

We then shift our focus to the ***stage*** on which this action is happening:

- What is the ***stage*** on which the action takes place?

- What is the ***structure*** of that stage? What type of actions and changes does that structure invite or dissuade, allow or not allow?

- What is the ***setting*** for that stage and scene, such as time and place? What elements set the emotive mood, such as sights, sounds, scents, or textures, or "extras" in the background who play no active role for the scene itself?

CHAPTER 9 STEP 2: GET READY FOR ACTION

Moving outward on that visual-checklist

- What, if anything, will happen *front-of-stage* for this scene or story? Will there be an orchestra, perhaps, or a narrator, compere, or MC (Master of Ceremonies)?

- Who are the *audience* for the story, intended or otherwise? What vision, values, principles, and standards do they bring to their observation of the story? What are their criteria for quality, for effectiveness, and for success or not-success?

- What happens *backstage*, hidden out of sight, to make the action possible, and to set up the setting for the stage?

- What *organization* is needed to enable to the story to happen, with those actors, scenes, and stage? Who runs the theater? What do they do, and with whom, for what purpose, over what timescales?

- What is the *enterprise* of the overall story, and of the places where these stories are told? What vision, values, principles, and standards does this story present? What are its criteria for effectiveness, and for success or not-success?

Moving outward again, to view the overall story as something created by others

- Who *creates* the story? What vision, values, principles, and standards do they bring to the creation of the story? What constraints do they face? What are their criteria for quality, for effectiveness, and for success or not-success?

- Who *directs* the creation and/or execution of the story? What vision, values, principles, and standards do they bring to the direction of the story? What are their criteria for quality, for effectiveness, and for success or not-success?

- Who are *stakeholders* in the creation, direction, and execution of the story? What stake do they each hold? Why do they hold that stake, in context of the story? What vision, values, principles, and standards do they bring to the story, in context of that stake? What are their criteria for success or not-success, in relation to that stake?

- Who *judges* the story, in terms of its creation, direction, execution, and/or outcomes, both in itself and in its impacts or implications for any broader context or shared-enterprise? What vision, values, principles, and standards do they bring to their observation of the story? What are their criteria for quality, for effectiveness, and for success or not-success?

- In what ways, if any, do these various perspectives of creators, directors, stakeholders, observers, and judges *align* and/or *conflict* with each other? If conflicts exist, what can we, as architects and/or designers for the story, do to learn from, mitigate, and resolve each conflict, to make it work better for everyone next time?

Always remember that *people*, not technologies, are the actual reason and basis for all enterprise. To support that point, use this metaphor of "actor, scene, stage" as a counterpoint and cross-check for the phrase "people, process technology" in business-analysis and in enterprise-architecture and design.

Test the Services

What we've worked on so far in this Step are the core functions and infrastructure for the organization – the *backbone* of its business. Everything else will depend on them: they *must* work. So how do we test that? How do we verify that we do have the right business-infrastructure for the organization? How do we ensure that it will be robust and resilient enough to act *as* the business-infrastructure?

As enterprise-architects, what we do here to answer those questions may well be crucial for the organization, its business-strategies, and its business-operations.

From Services to Processes

What's the difference between a service and a process? The simplest answer is that a process is sort-of a service in its own right: it has a definite boundary, with inputs and outputs, a value-proposition of its own, and value of some kind that it aims to deliver by the time the process reaches its end. Going the other way, though, it's clear they're *not* the same: a service can *contain* processes, or play a *role* in processes, but they're not really processes as such. There *is* a difference here.

The real risk of treating processes as standalone services is that we can end up with an overall system made up of "monolithic" chunks that may not interface well with anything else – as is all too often the case with prepackaged "best-practices" brought in from elsewhere. Even worse, that type of system can be extremely fragile and brittle, in which any needed change in the workflow will require the entire chunk to be rebuilt from scratch, often causing everything to break all over again.

Warning   Don't roll out a new process or workflow into live operations unless it's already been tested and proven at full load and full scale under real-world conditions. If you *haven't* done those tests well enough, then Murphy's Law will test it for you, right out there in public where everyone can see and experience your mistakes…

A few years back, one of our colleagues was caught up in that kind of mess at a major airport. Someone had had the bright idea that the "safe-to-travel" checks for international passengers and their baggage should be combined, sending scans of checked-baggage to the passenger-check so that passengers with any questionable baggage could be more easily found and taken aside. Our colleague had the misfortune to travel through that airport on the morning that they first rolled it out.

It didn't work. At all. The software was still riddled with bugs, and the network crashed repeatedly under the data-load of the huge image-files. There was no link to the previous identity-checks, so staff were reduced to shouting passengers' names to get them to come through to the baggage-check. The process slowed to less than a crawl, and the area was soon crammed with hundreds of worried, angry passengers, all watching the displays show their flights departing without them…

Eventually, the security-staff gave up, and shut down the whole system to reinstall the proven old process. Yet all of those stranded passengers first had to be brought back into the "landside" area, through the international-arrivals side of the airport – where further chaos ensued because, of course, none of them could be matched to any incoming flight. Our colleague eventually arrived at his destination two days late for his meeting.

Rolling out a new workflow without fully testing it? Not A Good Idea….

A better way to view this is that ***a process is a sequence of invocations of services***, with each service adding its own actions and value to the overall changes called for by the process. This gives us a metaphor of "boxes and lines," in which the services are "boxes" enacting discrete chunks of work, while the processes and workflows traverse the "lines" between the boxes to connect those chunks together to deliver the workflow's broader-scope outcome. (We'll see more on this "boxes and lines" metaphor in the next Step.)

The workflows travel "horizontally" at what we might call the *surface* level. However, the services themselves will often call on *other* services to help them deliver their required outcomes. As shown in Figure 9-11, these connections are more "vertical," following essentially the same pattern of relationships as in "backbone and edge," but this time in a more layered form.

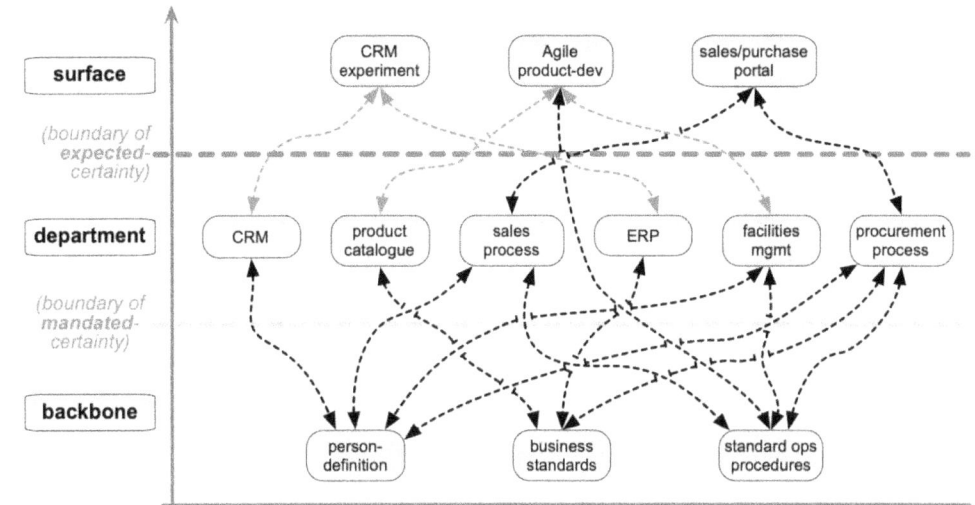

Figure 9-11. *Vertical "layering" of interdependencies between services*

This means that we can use surface-level processes and workflows to test the organization's backbone-level functions, and also at least identify the types of information and other content that would need to be managed at a more departmental or "median" level of the backbone-and-edge structure.

From what we've done here so far, the obvious way to do this is to start from the Function-Model, and map out various workflows from what we can see there. For example, as we've seen earlier, the airport's tier-2 "Transit Land-to-Air" function has an implicit workflow from a passenger's perspective, which starts at the airline's check-in, and ends when they board the aircraft.

Given a suitable workflow to play with, we build the test as follows:

- Identify the steps in the workflow. For example, map them out as discrete scenes in a story, in which the nominal protagonist – the passenger, in this case – meets specific sets of actors to do specific things with them to drive the overall story forward.

- For each step, map out what needs to happen, and change, within that chunk of the story. Notice anything that needs to be brought in from elsewhere – in other words, to be provided by a dive down to a deeper service, a hidden scene in the background. Also, identify any "foreshadowing," where something is done or something is carried forward – such as the boarding-pass, in this case – to be used again in a later scene in the story.

- For each "downward dive," identify what service is required, from which level. For example, in the backbone-and-edge mapping, the depth from surface to backbone can be identified by the amount of certainty we need about something such as a person's identity, and how close we need to be to "single-source-of-truth" to obtain that level of certainty.

- For each item or foreshadowing-action carried forward, identify *how* it will be carried forward, and where it will be brought back to the surface. For example, the boarding-pass may be in physical or virtual form, but it must be carried somehow by the passenger as a "product" that travels between the steps. (We'll see more on this relationship between *product* and *service* in the next Step.)

Use this process to identify what each function at each level in the Function-Model must receive, do, and return.

Example For the airport, the architecture-team create a table-sized print of their Function-Model, and use it to simulate a range of different airport-workflows, using mini-figures to "walk" across the model to represent the various steps of each flow. They identify and map out the interactions not only between the surface-level services that do the work at each node of the workflow, but also between those services and the deeper backbone-services that keep everything stable in the background.

They identify some issues, both with the surface-level services and the background ones. Most of the issues relate to gaps, missed steps, or misconnections, but the nature and structure of the service-interfaces make it relatively easy to track down the underlying problems and resolve them. For the team, that principle of separating backbone from edge and building all of the flows through distinct service-connections does add a bit to the design-work, but makes the overall workflows *much* easier to test and adjust in real-world practice.

Checks and Balances

For the final part of this Step, we need to build the capabilities that we'll use to **confirm correctness and completeness** for each of our services.

We already know how to do this, in a general sense, by using the cross-checks built into the CSPAR pattern. For example, we identify the requirements in *Context* and *Scope*, and resolve any uncertainties and other issues in Change-Cycle iterations in the *Plan* phase. After the *Action*, we use the *Review* phase to identify any issues that arose there, and then loop back through *Plan*'s "Model," "Design," and "Build" as appropriate to fix anything that needs to be done.

The challenge, though, is to know *what potential issues to look for* in those checks and assessments in Scope, Plan, and Review. For those, a good place to start is that set of "*It's more than just...*" checklists that we saw back in Chapter 1. For example, as we've also seen throughout this step, **it's about more than just the "happy-path"** – we must be able to address all types of events in the context, including

- Exceptions
- Uniqueness-issues
- Failure-conditions
- Business-continuity and disaster recovery
- Load-balancing

CHAPTER 9   STEP 2: GET READY FOR ACTION

As we also saw in Chapter 1, ***it's about more than just a single change*** – for each event or change, we must also be able to address

- Its interdependencies
- Its interoperability issues
- Any gaps and overlaps between contexts
- Any cross-context synergies
- Any whole-of-context interactions
- Any systems-of-systems issues, across the enterprise as a whole

---

Warning   Always ensure that every step of an end-to-end process remains fully connected at all times, particularly if the process moves between departments or organizations. This is especially important to help in recovery when things have gone wrong in a multi-organization workflow.

Some years back, I had a first-hand experience of what happens when this *isn't* done, and the chain of connections is allowed to break. I'd been booked on a long-haul flight that included an intermediate stop at an international hub-airport. For various technical reasons, the flight took off five hours late, and we eventually landed at the hub-airport, somewhat after midnight, tired, weary, and worried. At which point, we discovered that we had good reason to worry, because the airline hadn't bothered to tell anyone that we were running that late. No-one at that airport was set up and ready to tackle the avalanche of issues that arise from an entire aircraft's worth of transit-passengers arriving without warning in the middle of the night, almost all of whom had missed their connecting flights.

Under the circumstances, the local crews did a brilliant job. There were only three airline staff at the night-desk, who somehow managed to prevent any fights breaking out for the few available seats they could find immediately on other airlines. None of us transit-passengers had visas for that country: the border-control staff waved us through anyway, without any comment at all. The airport hotels somehow found beds for all of us in the middle of the night – though I was called out of bed just three hours later to get ready for a flight that they'd found for me. And the baggage-crew must have done a herculean job of sorting out the mess, because my checked-baggage did arrive with me when I finally got to my destination. But I was lucky that I arrived only a full day late: many of the others missed out on most of their vacations, and one of the passengers eventually arrived more than a week late for her own wedding. *Not* fun.

Yet it would have cost the airline a fortune in fees and fines and more – certainly far more than they would have made from the original flight-bookings. Carelessly breaking the chain of connections? Not A Good Idea….

At the project-level, ***it's about more than just a single project*** or business-transformation – we must also be able to

- Address complete lifecycles for each type of content in the enterprise
- Use our longer-term sustain-architectures to connect the work of change-projects across all associated timescales

And also at the project-level, ***it's about more than just the change-plan*** – within that plan, we must be aware of and able to address the *whole* of each lifecycle in the context, including

- Future migration
- Platform-refresh
- Extension of life-of-type
- Sunset
- Decommission
- Disposal

As we've seen throughout the past two chapters, we'll also need to check for ***alignment to Context and Scope***, including

- Enterprise and organizational vision and values
- Constraints such as laws, regulations, standards, and real-world limits
- Effectiveness-criteria and success-criteria

- Boundaries of scope and responsibility
- Value-propositions and promises

Example   For the airport, as described throughout this chapter, the architecture-team have applied these checklists to guide assessments, system-designs, and development practices. For example, their focus on the airport's values of comfort, friendliness, and mutual-respect was the start-point that eventually gave rise to the project to create a "more people-friendly" flight-information-system that included time and distance to the departure gate for each flight, and would help to reduce the "hurry-up-and-wait" stress on everyone.

Once the checks and balances such as these are all in place, we should be able to ensure that our business-functions, services, processes, and workflows are **repeatable**, in the CMMI sense. In the next Step, we'll explore how to reach the CMMI **defined** level for all of our services, products, and other business-offerings.

Into Practice

In the section "From Scope to Plan," we explored what our organizations will need to have and do, and how we as enterprise-architects can help to identify and resolve those needs. Using what you saw there, apply the same methods and checklists to your own organization.

- How would you identify and, where appropriate, design your organization's *business-infrastructure*? How might a service-oriented approach to architecture help in this? How will you ensure that the infrastructure will support the organization's needs in a reliable and *repeatable* way? What might you learn from applying a "backbone-end-edge" mapping to your organization's systems and infrastructure?

- What frameworks, models, and methods might help you as you *set up for change* in your organization's infrastructure? What do you use at present in your organization? How might you change that, from what you've learned in this Step?

In the section "Build the Services," we explored what we as enterprise-architects need to *do* when working on the organization's infrastructure, and how to put into practice what we learned earlier in the "Step Zero" Foundations section. Using what you saw there, apply the same methods and checklists to your own organization.

- What methods and models do you use at present to map out your organization's *functions and systems*, and the relationships between those various architectural elements? Are you able to derive appropriate cross-checks for those elements, such as a Business-Systems Model and Information-Systems Model? How might a Function-Model approach assist you in doing this?

- What methods, frameworks, and processes do you use within your organization to guide the transitions *from architecture to action*? How might the descriptions in this section, on the CSPAR sequence and the like, help you to improve how you do that work, and guide others in doing their parts of that work? How might you apply the airport-examples in your own organization's business?

- As an architect, what *stories of change* do you use within your organization? For example, how do you use visual-storytelling, with graphics and diagrams, to explain what you do and what needs to be done? How might a narrative-oriented approach to business-analysis, such as in "actor, scene, stage," help as a counterpart to the usual "people, process, technology"? What further insights might you gain by using those narrative-oriented methods?

In the section "Test the Services," we explored how to test and validate an organization's "backbone" infrastructure. Using what you saw there, apply the same methods and checklists to your own organization.

- How do you test the reliability, repeatability, and validity of your organization's backbone infrastructure-services? How do you test the connections *from services to processes*? In what ways might the approach used here, using a Function-Model to link from surface-level workflows to backbone functions, help you in doing and validating those tests?

- What checklists do you use to help you validate and verify the completeness of your *checks and balances* for these tests? From what you've seen in this section, what might you add to your organization's existing checklists and tests?

As usual, capture into your notebook any ideas and insights that arise from exploring these questions, to include in your final review at the end of the book.

Summary

In this chapter, for Step 2 in the Maturity-Model, we explored how to use a Function-Model and the CSPAR Change-Layers to identify, design, set up, and test the core services of the "backbone" infrastructure for the organization's business. We also worked through how to design and run a simple simulation, and use story-based approaches as a counterpart and cross-check for classic "people, process, technology" analysis-methods.

In the next chapter, for Step 3, we'll see how to use the same methods to define and design the services that will run on top of that infrastructure, to deliver the organization's value-propositions to its market.

CHAPTER 10

Step 3: Set Out the Stall

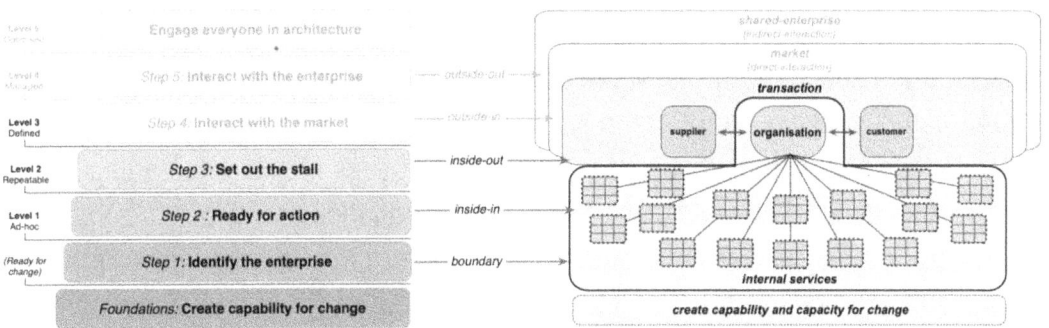

Back in Step 1, we first focused on how to identify the differences and *boundaries* between enterprise and organization, and establishing the underlying "*Why*" for an organization in terms of the *core context and scope* for its business and the *core policies and principles* that it will use in decision-making within that business. This alone gave us enough to support *ad-hoc* decision-making within the organization that had a good chance of proving *effective* in real-world practice.

In Step 2, we extended that by looking "*inside-in*" at the organization's *core capabilities and services* for the organization's *business-infrastructure*, the underlying "*How*" for all of its business operations. We also explored how to architect, design, build, and run services and change-projects that can support *repeatable* processes for repeatable business outcomes.

For this third Step in the Maturity-Model, as indicated in the graphic above, we'll shift to an *"inside-out" perspective*, about the organization's *outward-facing* relationships with its broader shared-enterprise. We'll focus on the "***What***," "***Where***," and "***When***" of the organization's business-models and the delivery of its products, services, and value-propositions. We also need to extend our architecture to include defined mechanisms to cope with *change* – at this stage to respond to variances in strategy, law, and the like, though later also able to react to real-time events as well.

Much of what we do here will have "***top-down***" emphasis, moving from strategy down into action, though there'll be some movement "bottom-up" as well. In CSPAR terms, we'll work mainly in the upper part of ***Plan***, particularly the *P.1* and *P.2* sub-layers. And in SCAN terms, we'll still be on the left-hand "certainty" side of that frame, but pushing hard to move the "***boundary of expected-certainty***" further and further to the right.

Note If you're an experienced enterprise-architect, much of this should seem familiar at first, because this is where classic EA frameworks such as TOGAF, FEAF, DoDAF, and Frameworx would come into their prime, and deliver real business-value. Do beware, though, that some of their assumptions may be misleading here, and at times you'll *need* those "Step Zero" foundations-practices to counter them. For example, for this work, you'll need to be able to cover the *whole* of the enterprise scope, rather than only the architectures for its IT.

Bear in mind, too, that while this is where classic enterprise-architecture stops, we don't. There's a lot of valuable work to do here, but at Step Three this is still only the halfway-point of the Maturity-Model. As you'll see in the later Steps, you can still develop your architecture, and its business value, much further than just this level.

By now, the architecture should be fully established as an ongoing strategic capability for the business, with the sections in this Step showing the kinds of tasks that we would expect to undertake at this point. Whatever we do here, though, it must align with and support everything we established in the previous Steps: all of the vision and values and so on of the organization and its shared-enterprise, the organization's role and positioning and value-propositions, and the Function-Model and all that. As before, we'll also need appropriate governance and sustainment to ensure alignment and support, over whatever timescales the organization might need.

One point to reiterate here is that *every item of architecture work starts with an explicit business purpose, for explicit business value* – and defining "business-value" would also include defining any required timetables, milestones, deliverables, and so on. By the end of this Step, we want the architecture to be able to bring the organization to the ***CMMI "defined" level*** of business-maturity, with business-offerings that others elsewhere can understand, use, and rely on in *their* roles in the shared-enterprise.

Caution In this Step, you'll start to need access to people with a *much* broader range of skillsets and experience. These will again include the domain-architects and suchlike, as before, but would now encompass the strategists, business-intelligence, market-analysts, and others at the business level; the process-architects and any number of domain-specialists at the integration and detail-levels; the "value-evangelists" who deal with the qualitative themes such as security, safety, governance, efficiency, and ethics; and operations teams as well.

As the architect, it's *your* task to coordinate and communicate between all of these different areas of expertise. The phrase "herding cats" may come to mind at this point...

Yet don't worry about that too much: it *does* get easier with practice. And this is one of the most engaging and exciting areas of all of the architecture, so it *is* well worth all the agony and the effort!

There are four sections in this chapter:

- *This goes with that*: Explore how everything connects with everything else across the organization and enterprise

- *Everything's a service*: Explore the structures, flows, interdependencies, implementations, and trade-offs for services

- *Serving the enterprise*: Identify the organization's choices about the products and services that it offers to the enterprise, and the value-propositions and promises that go with them

- *Quality and compliance*: Identify how the organization will maintain its values and quality within itself and in its relationships with others in the enterprise

As usual, we'll end this chapter with a brief review of what you've learned during this Step, and how to apply it within your own organization.

CHAPTER 10   STEP 3: SET OUT THE STALL

This Goes with That

How do we connect everything together, across the organization and its enterprise? How do we connect strategy to execution, and back again? How do we respond to change, and how each change ripples back and forth across the enterprise?

As enterprise-architects, we'll be responsible for ensuring that everything behind the organization's business-offerings *does* work in a well-defined, reliable, efficient, and effective way. In this section, we'll explore how to set about making that happen, using the Change-Layers and Change-Cycle to guide the architecture-work.

The Enterprise As a Whole

In an architecture, everything connects with everything else; everything depends on everything else; and things work better when they work together, on purpose. Yet before we can "connect everything together," we first need to ensure that we *can* address everything, rather than solely an arbitrarily-selected subset of "the everything."

This is where we hit a problem.

If you read about enterprise-architecture, you're likely to get the impression that it all started a few decades ago, is all about IT, and really only about IT. Almost all EA standards focus on IT; almost all EA toolsets are focused on IT; almost all advertised "enterprise-architecture" roles are oriented toward some form of IT – and often only detail-level IT at that. Most of the big consultancies in the EA space seem to suggest that its only real purpose is to support the IT-industry in rolling out the latest IT fad, to give large organizations quick short-term gains before the next IT fad comes along.

Unfortunately, almost all of that is almost completely wrong, in almost every possible way. This can cause a *lot* of problems...

Note   We don't need to go into the details about how and why it's so wrong and so misleading, because that alone would be a book in itself – and we have other things to do here!

As a quick summary, though, an enterprise is, in essence, "an ecosystem with a purpose." If that enterprise is to succeed, it will need the *systemic* support of an appropriate "architecture of the enterprise" that will connect the structure, story, and purpose across the whole scope, scale, context, content, and lifecycles of that enterprise. Hence, enterprise-architecture is actually not new at all: as a discipline, it's already been around in some identifiable form or other for hundreds and even thousands of years, almost everywhere around the world.

Every time there's been a huge multi-year, multi-decade, multi-century project, from choirs and cathedrals to the organizations of empires, there'll have been some kind of architecture behind it, to help make it happen and make it work. Every time there's been a rollout of a new technology, from radar to railways, from canals to cotton-mills, there's been an architecture behind it. Every time there's been a rollout of a new cultural or commercial concept, from universal-mail to universal-healthcare, from double-entry bookkeeping to mass-manufacturing, there's been an architecture behind it.

In short, the current IT-oriented version of enterprise-architecture is neither particularly new nor particularly special: it's merely one relatively-recent iteration of something that's been quietly around in the background almost everywhere for a very long time. So don't ever forget that fact and get lost in all the IT-centric hype – because if you do, you'll risk causing a lot of problems, not just for others, but for yourself as well.

The reason *why* this is a problem is because of a fundamental rule for all architectures: ***in an architecture, everywhere and nowhere is "the center," all of the time***. This is why, for example, the generic Organization-Context Model or "holomap," as shown in Figure 10-1, asserts that services may be *"implemented by any appropriate mix of people, machines, IT."*

CHAPTER 10 STEP 3: SET OUT THE STALL

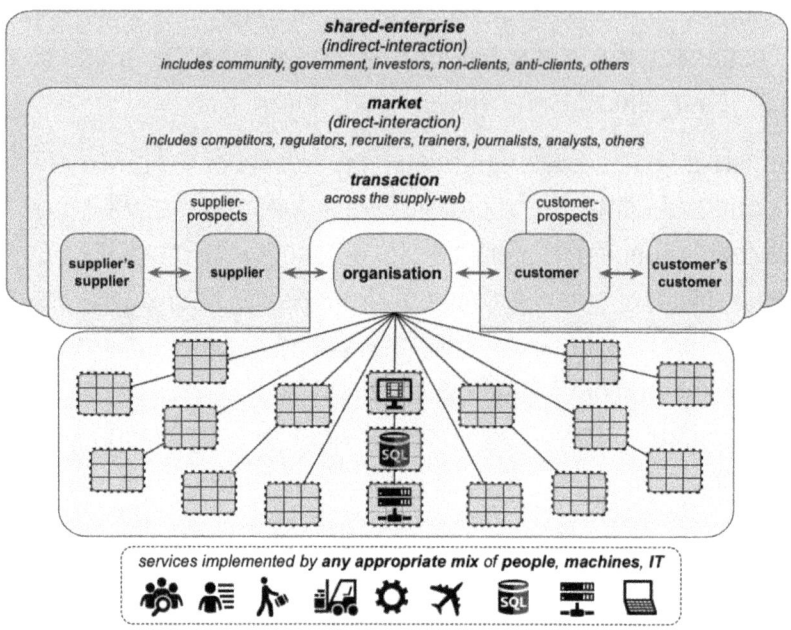

Figure 10-1. *Generic Organization-Context Model*

It's also why the Service-Content model for CSPAR, as described in Chapter 5 in relation to the Change-Layers and shown in Figure 10-2, can likewise support *any* appropriate mix of people-based, machine-based, and/or IT-based implementations of services.

Asset-types	What Assets	How Functions	Where Locations	Capabilities (action-on)	(Who) Capabilities (agent)	Capabilities (skill-level)	When Events	Why Decisions/Skills	Decision/skill-types
	(requirements)								
Physical	Phys	Phys	Phys	Phys	Phys	Rules	Phys	Rules	Rule-based
Virtual	Virtual	Virtual	Virtual	Virtual	Virtual	Algor'm	Virtual	Algor'm	Algorithmic
Relational	Reln	Reln	Reln	Reln	Reln	Guideln	Reln	Guideln	Guidelines
Aspirational	Aspn	Aspn	Aspn	Aspn	Aspn	Princpl	Aspn	Princpl	Principle-based
Abstract			Time						

Figure 10-2. *CSPAR Service-Content model*

The moment we assert that something – such as IT-systems, in this case – is "*the center*" of the architecture, we risk losing track of everything else. For example, in most organizations, IT represents at most around 5-10% of total spend – so if our enterprise-architecture focuses only on the IT, and all but ignores the other 90-95% of the organization, we'd risk having an "enterprise-architecture" that would be so skewed and so misleading that it could actually be worse than useless.

Note It's perhaps important to reiterate here that, in IT-centrism, it *isn't* the IT itself that's the problem. Far from it: we *need* an appropriate focus on IT in our enterprise-architectures – no doubt about that at all.

Instead, ***it's the "-centrism" that is the problem***, because it breaks that fundamental rule about "everything is the center, all at the same time." The IT in this case is merely the type of content that's been arbitrarily selected as "the sole center of everything." So while IT-centrism is often the immediate problem here, the same exact issue is equally true for business-centrism, security-centrism, shareholder-centrism, or any other form of "the-bit-that-I'm-interested-in-is-the-sole-center-of-everything-ism."

There will often be a *lot* of pressures, from all manner of different directions, to promote or enforce some or other arbitrarily-selected "centrism," in terms of technology, ideology, society, culture, politics, economics, or whatever. As an architect for the respective enterprise, you'll need to resist those pressures as best you can, to protect and maintain the balance of the architecture as a whole.

This problem of "something-centrism" is a particular issue *here*, in *this* Step, because it's here that enterprise-architecture becomes most visible (or, for many people, often the *only* time that it becomes visible). Unfortunately, as soon as an architecture becomes visible, it seems to entice certain architecturally-illiterate stakeholders to demand that their own particular set of presumptions, preferences, and priorities should be framed as "the sole center of everything" in that architecture – regardless of the impacts that doing so will have on everything else.

To counter those pressures, we need to ensure that we can **expand the scope-awareness** to whatever extent is actually needed for the *overall* architecture. The simplest way to do that, in an IT-oriented world, is to note every point where an IT-related element touches a non-IT space. We then follow the trails of connections *for at* *least one or two steps beyond the initial contact-point.* This will provide us with "hooks" from which to explore further. For example, we'll use those "hooks" in the next section, when we start to look at the impacts of strategy.

At each contact-point with a non-IT space, questions we might ask would include

- At which *Change-Layer* does this touch-point occur? What are the implied responsibilities and time-perspectives here?

- What are the *transactions* at this touch-point? What types of *functions*, *assets*, and *locations* are involved – *physical, virtual, relational*, or whatever? If as patterns or composites, what are their underlying primitives?

- What types of *events* – as *physical, virtual, relational*, or whatever – trigger each transaction? If as patterns of composites – perhaps with specific types of assets – what are their underlying primitives?

- For each transaction, what *capabilities* are required – *physical, virtual, relational*, or whatever? What competencies and skill-levels are required for these capabilities – *rule-based, analytic, pattern-based, principle-based*? In what ways are these capabilities and skill-levels clustered into roles? In what ways do these roles intersect with the functions, assets, locations, and events of the transaction?

- What *decisions* or *reasons* guide the interactions and transactions at this touch-point? How would you categorize the form of each decision – as *rules*, as outcomes of *analysis*, as *guidelines* or heuristics, or as *principles*?

- What *business-principles* and other constraints apply in the context of this touch-point and its transactions? How does the touch-point ensure compliance with those principles? How and in what ways do these context-specific principles anchor back to the core principles, values, and vision of the enterprise, and by what means could this compliance be verified?

Document the results in the architecture-repositories, as models, architecture-records, and the like. Include any namings, risks, opportunities, issues, or requirements in the respective registers.

Caution Be careful to keep this within realistic bounds. Don't let yourself be accused of arbitrary "scope-creep," because that would *really* start to hurt in terms of architecture's credibility and perceived value. Focus on establishing "hooks" for future explorations, but don't go further than that unless someone is willing to pay for it!

Strategy Drives Change

In this section, we'll make use of all those cross-dependencies and connections mapped out in the background during the work in the previous section, by using the architecture to identify the impacts and opportunities arising from changes in strategy.

We start from a single high-level ***strategic theme or driver***, such as

- Potential changes in law or regulation
- Introduction of a new technology or process-design methodology
- Market disruption from new or existing competitors
- Potential for the organization to enter into a new market
- Supply-chain opportunity and/or disruption
- Social and/or political change within the broader enterprise scope
- Emergent effects from interactions between strategic themes or drivers

Given that theme or driver, we then work our way downward through the framework to assess and design for its impact anywhere and at any level in the enterprise. We ***follow the impact-trails***, using the implied connections to trace and identify the theme's impact on the architecture as a whole. We'll use the *Change-Layers* to guide the assessment, and also the Service-Content model, as shown in Figure 10-2, to provide a map for the respective types of content. We'll also use the Function-Model and the Business-Systems Model and other systems-models developed in Steps 1 and 2 as higher-level base-maps for impact-trails.

We'll document the results of this assessment in the architecture repository in terms of impact and "bindedness" of relationships between vision, values, and principles and the respective aspects of the theme. Any required changes to the theme itself, and also any implied risks, opportunities, or issues go into the respective registers.

Caution   By this stage, you *must* also have a proper architecture-toolset in place and in use. The sheer complexity of all the interconnections between entities, requirements, risks, and so on is far beyond the capability of standard office software. Don't even *think* of trying to limp along here with a couple of spreadsheets and a home-made database, because it'll drive you mad in days!

If you don't yet have a toolset, you'll need one that can follow the trails of relationships and dependencies in either direction, top-down or bottom-up – or any direction, really. The toolset will also need good support for "what-if" scenarios, and also good version-management to keep track of all those different scenarios and options.

If you don't know where to start, one popular option is the free-and-open-source multi-platform toolset **Archi**. It does have some limitations, but it does its job well, and should provide you with enough experience to help you identify the appropriate requirements for your own architecture context. You'll find a link to the *Archi* website in Appendix B.

We start at **Context**, to compare the theme against the defining "universals" for the organization – its overarching vision, values, principles, constraints, success-criteria, and so on:

- In what ways does the theme align, or not align, with the enterprise vision, values, and principles?

- If the theme represents an internal choice – such as a proposed change in strategy – what do the vision, values, and principles indicate or imply about the theme? Since these, in principle, would have higher priority than a strategy, in what ways might they imply changes to the strategy itself?

- If the theme is imposed from the wider environment – such as a potential change in standards or regulations – what do the vision, values, and principles indicate or imply about organizational response to the theme? Since the vision, values, and principles represent the organization's core choices in relation to the wider environment, does the theme imply a requirement to review any of those core choices? Since these choices are fundamental to the organization's self-definition in relation to the wider enterprise, what impact would any such changes have on the overall structure, focus, and direction of the enterprise?

Note In each subsequent level, you should again recheck each impact and implication for alignment against the vision, values, principles, constraints, and success-criteria. In general, you would do this by comparing against the qualitative-themes – reliability, security, privacy, safety, and so on – which devolve from that topmost layer. If that comparison highlights a significant issue or misalignment, you may need to go back up a layer or two – perhaps even to the topmost layer – and restart the assessment with all the amendments identified to date. You never actually lose anything by going back up again, but it can be invaluable in helping you avoid intractable "wicked problems" further down the track.

In the *Scope* layers, we identify the key "items of interest" for the enterprise:

- What impact would the (amended) theme have on the core assets, functions, locations, capabilities, events, and decisions of the organization?

- What impact would it have on the organization's roles, missions, and overall services and service-relationships within the enterprise?

- What impacts would it have in relation to the organization's values and other qualitative-concerns that need to pervade everywhere ("pervasives")?

- In what ways might any of these change the theme itself?

At the **Plan P.1** sub-layer, for the **Interaction-Model** or abstract "business-model," we assess the relationships between those key items identified in *Scope*:

- What impact would the (amended) theme have on the *relationships* between the core assets, functions, locations, capabilities, events, and decisions of the organization?

- What impacts would it have on relationships and transactions with other entities – other players – within the enterprise?

- What impacts would it have in relation to the organization's "pervasives"?

- In what ways might any of these change the theme itself?

At the **Plan P.2** sub-layer, for the **Design-Model** or "logical-model," we expand those entities and their relationships out to "logical" design-patterns that are independent of any specific implementation:

- What impacts would the (amended) theme have on the *types* – physical, virtual, relational, aspirational, abstract, composite – of assets, functions, locations, capabilities, and events that would apply within the organization's services?

- What impacts would the theme have on the *skill-levels* – rule-based, analytic, pattern-based, principle-based – required for the capabilities needed within the organization's services?

- What impacts would the theme have on the *form* and *bindedness* – rules, analyses, emergence, context-unique – required for reasoning and decision-making within the organization's services?

- What impacts would these have on *structures* of composites and design-patterns for implementations?

- What impacts would these have on *trade-offs* between implementation choices?

- What impacts would these have on *reporting-metrics* that should be consistent for all implementations of a given design-pattern?

- What impacts would these have in relation to the organization's "pervasives"?
- In what ways might any of these change the theme itself?

At the **Plan** *P.3* sub-layer, for the **Development-Model** or "physical-model," we extend the abstract "logical-model" designs more toward the real-world, with implementation-specific patterns:

- What impacts would the (amended) theme have on the *types* of assets, functions, locations, capabilities, and events that would apply within an implementation?
- What impacts would the theme have on the *skill-levels* needed within an implementation?
- What impacts would the theme have on the *form* and *bindedness* for reasoning and decision-making within an implementation?
- What impacts would these have on *structures* of composites for implementation-patterns?
- What impacts would these have on *trade-offs* between and within implementations?
- What impacts would these have on *reporting-metrics* and other controls within implementations?
- What impacts would these have on *transactions* and other applicable factors and concerns within implementations?
- What impacts would these have on the structures and handovers in *end-to-end processes* that use specific implementations – especially where implementations must transition between people-based, machine-based, and IT-based segments of end-to-end processes?
- What impacts would these have in relation to the organization's "pervasives"?
- In what ways might any of these change the theme itself?

At the **Plan** *P.4* and *P.5* sub-layers, for the **Deployment-Model** and **Action-Model**, respectively, we need composites that are "complete" across all of the framework columns: "with *<asset>* do *<function>* at *<location>* using *<capability>* on *<event>*

because <decision>." The decisions about types – physical, virtual, relational, and so on – for assets and the like should all have been resolved in the *P.3* layer; here, the questions focus more on operational issues such as configuration, shift-rosters, logistics, and backup-plans:

- What impacts would the (amended) theme have on planning for routine real-time *redundancy* and *variance* – overflow, underflow, task-balancing, task-mix, and the like?
- What impacts would the theme have on run-time *configuration*-issues such as development versus test versus production versus fallback?
- What impacts would the theme have on planning for *maintenance* and other scheduled downtime?
- What impacts would the theme have on planning for *business-continuity*, repair, disaster-recovery, and other unscheduled incidents?
- What impacts would the theme have on planning for *substitution*, rostering, and other scheduled and unscheduled transfers of operational and personal responsibility?
- What impacts would the theme have on run-time *resource-management* and *reporting*?
- What impacts would the theme have on run-time *transactions* and other interactions, for what reasons, and in what ways?
- What impacts would these have in relation to the organization's "pervasives" – particularly run-time quality-management, security-management, and legal-compliance issues?
- In what ways might any of these change the theme itself?

At the **Action A.1** and **A.2** sub-layers, the "complete" composites shift to the present-tense (*A.1* sub-layer and the action itself) or past-tense (*A.2* sub-layer). Questions here need to address not only what is being done and has been done, but also in what ways these differ from the scheduled plan:

- What impacts would the (amended) theme have on *performance-reporting* and performance-metrics?

- What impacts would the theme have on *audit* and *verification* of run-time activity?

- What impacts would these have in relation to the organization's "pervasives" – particularly post-run-time quality-management clean-up such as correction, corrective-action, and information for process-improvement?

- In what ways might any of these change the theme itself?

At the ***Review*** layer, we do the usual assessment of *benefits-realized, lessons-learned,* and *suggested-actions* in relation to the work that's been done above. Once everything has been documented and stored in the repositories, we prepare an appropriate report for whoever it was that requested the impact-assessment.

Example For the airport, one of their airline customers has said that they'd like to run a regular service – initially, one flight each way per week – to a country not yet served by the airport. The airport's marketing and strategy groups are keen to support this opportunity, but also need to understand the costs, risks, and other implications of doing so. They ask the architecture-team for their advice on this. The team use the Change-Layers and Function-Model to guide their exploration.

For the ***Context*** layer, the team obtain the nominal requirements from the airline and the country's embassy, and check them against the airport's "backbone" Vision and other high-level "universals." They find no particular issues at this stage, but keep all of the information on-hand for further cross-checks.

For the ***Scope*** layer, the team start by identifying the scope of change in terms of the Function-Model. The main difference is a requirement to move the visa-check for that country, from the standard checkpoint at "Confirm Person Is Legal to Travel" to the exit-gate check at "Reconfirm Person Is Valid to Travel," with the visa-check to be done by that country's border-control staff rather than those of the airport's country. The team retrieve the "backbone" Policy and Procedure documents for those two functions, and cross-check the country's requirements against the standard list of stakeholders, tasks, and architecture-elements. No changes would be required for the standard visa-check prior to entry to the airport-airside staging-area, but there would be significant changes at the exit-gate. From this, they develop a variant of the standard change-Procedure for the exit-gate Function that matches that country's specific requirements.

For the *P.1 **Interaction-Model*** ("business-model") sub-layer, the team use the context-specific Procedure to map out the new interactions, workflows, and other content for the exit-gate. The gate area would need to be sealed off, with a boundary controlled exclusively by the country's own border-staff, using their own equipment and security-staff – in effect, creating a country-specific region inside the airport. This would also mean that that gate could not be used for any purpose other than services to that country. The final valid-to-travel gate-check would still be done by the airline's staff as per the standard procedure, but inside that sealed-off area.

For the *P.2 **Design-Model*** ("logical-model") sub-layer, the team map out the details for the change. The main issues would be the structures needed to seal off the boarding-area and to provide the boundary-gates, work-desks, and network-connections for the country's border-staff, and also the procedures to bring any rejected passengers and their carry-on baggage to the airport's security-team to be escorted back out to airport-landside. The team also identify a possible need for a small seating-area *outside* the sealed-off area at the gate, to align with the airport-values of "friendliness," "comfort," and "service," to allow some passengers to rest while waiting for the border-check.

For the *P.3 **Development-Model*** ("physical-model") sub-layer, the team belatedly recognize that this "legal-to-travel" border-check at the gate means that passengers' checked-in baggage cannot be loaded into the aircraft until each respective passenger is cleared to travel. This also occurred with the regular "legal-to-travel" check, but much earlier in the overall workflow, giving the baggage-team time there to respond without causing delays. This much later check will require a new real-time information-link between exit-gate and the baggage-team at the aircraft, and *will* increase the risk of the aircraft departing late from the gate.

For the *P.4 **Deployment-Model*** sub-layer, the team prepare only a summary of the probable requirements for the build, because some of the details such as the materials to be used to seal off the area and the exact structures for the border-control gate are not yet known. One potentially-significant issue relates to the network-connection: if that country requires its own dedicated network separate from the airport's existing system, this could add considerable costs to the overall change-project.

For the *P.5 **Action-Model*** sub-layer and ***Action*** layers, the team note that the new actions at the gate would be handled solely by that country's border-staff, and hence are out of scope for the airport itself.

For their own ***Review*** layer, the team prepare a report for the strategy and marketing groups that maps out all of their findings. This also provides the detailed models and other documentation that the airport would need to support any final decision about whether or not to go ahead with the proposal.

Innovation Invokes Strategy

All of the above assumes that the theme to be considered in this kind of analysis is already known. But we also need to keep an eye open at all times for useful ideas and suggestions that we *don't* know about beforehand. Such innovations could well come from *anywhere* – from the industry, the market, from new technology, and from within the organization itself, to name just a few of the possible sources. They're often more likely to arrive "bottom-up" than "top-down." Given that, we'll need systematic processes to find them and to assess their value and implications for the enterprise, as part of the architecture-team's routine work on maintaining its sustainment-architectures.

Note   Text-messaging on cell-phones arose from a classic example of a "bottom-up" affordance of this kind. It was always part of the technical-standard, but wasn't designed for public use at all. Instead, it was intended as a hidden means to allow technicians to send brief status-messages to their base in real-time, about signal-quality and the like, using very little bandwidth and able to work with even the smallest signal-strength. However, the messages could be sent not just to a central base, but also to *any* cell-phone that used that standard. The technicians soon started using this hidden channel to chat with each other about whatever issues they needed to address.

This went on for some years, quietly unnoticed by anyone outside the technical-community. Until the day that someone from a telco's marketing department apparently heard about it – and made the connection that this kind of messaging could be useful not just to technicians, but to *everyone*.

And it didn't even need any new technology. It was already part of the standard, and every cell-phone built to that standard was capable of supporting it. The only thing that needed to be done was to bring it out of hiding, and let everyone know it was there. The rest, as they say, is history…

This kind of search might need to be done in any of a whole variety of ways – top-down, bottom-up, sideways-in, and so on. In practice, though, we can tweak the standard architecture-cycle to give us a workable process for the purpose, whichever way round we would want to do it. Strictly speaking, it's always sort-of top-down, but it comes out the same in the end.

The initial **question or concern** for this type of architecture-work is always the same: the search for appropriate innovations to enhance enterprise effectiveness. The intended **business-value** to be derived from the search would be in terms of reduced risk, reduced time-to-market, and suchlike.

As usual, we start at the **Context layer** in the Change-Layers, to refresh our overall sense of the organization and its shared-enterprise. In essence, this is a quick, simplified version of the explorations we did back in Step 1, to identify the drivers, concerns, constraints, content-types, roles, and interactions across the shared-enterprise as a whole.

- What is the overall *vision* for the shared-enterprise, and for the organization within that enterprise?

- What *values* are shared by every player in that enterprise? Which values of its own does the organization add to that list? How does the organization prioritize that full set of values?

- What *constraints* apply to the enterprise as a whole, either man-made, such as laws, regulations, and standards, or natural, such as weather, geography, and distance? What additional constraints apply to the organization?

- What are the *success-criteria* for the shared-enterprise? What additional success-criteria apply for the organization? What are the respective priorities for those success-criteria?

- From all of the above, what are the *effectiveness-criteria* for the enterprise, and for the organization?

- What are the *roles* within the shared-enterprise? Which role does the organization take within that enterprise? Which other organizations, if any, take on the same role in that enterprise, as potential allies or competitors? How does the organization differentiate itself from others, in its positioning within that enterprise-role?

- What are the key *content-elements* of the shared-enterprise – its What, How, Where, Who, When, and Why? Which aspects of this apply to the organization, in its role within the enterprise?

We would then do a brief gap-analysis to identify any differences between the current records and this new information, and to derive suggestions for where to set the scope for this inquiry.

At the **Scope layer**, we choose the scope for the architecture-iteration. This choice would usually be straightforward and uncomplicated. In principle, the scope *should* always be "the everywhere," within the enterprise and even beyond, but in practice we'll need to apply *some* limits on scope in order to return useful results within a reasonable timescale and realistic budget.

Caution Don't automatically ignore anything interesting that's outside of that preset scope! Remember that one of the key aims for this exercise is to *allow the unexpected to emerge.*

Instead, the chosen scope-boundary for the search merely provides a known, certain reference-point for the investigation. If you seem to be straying too far from it, perhaps it's time to come back to that anchor and rethink where you're going. That shouldn't prevent you from finding what you need to know about, but it *does* protect you against getting lost in the uncertain seas of innovations and ideas.

At the *P.1 **Interaction-Model*** sub-layer for *Plan*, we explore the "as-is" architecture in terms of the scope, allowing new ideas to emerge:

- What are others doing at present, in the same industry, the same overall enterprise, in other enterprises entirely? What could we learn from this?

- What technologies, business-processes, business-models, and so on are others using at present? What could we use or adapt from this?

- What does benchmarking against competitors, partners, or other industries suggest?

- What gaps exist within the current architecture? What gaps do these suggest in terms of potential for innovation?

- What options and needs for innovation are indicated by risks, opportunities, issues, and dispensations currently recorded in the respective registers?

- What risks, opportunities, and issues do all of *these* imply for the architecture, and for the enterprise as a whole?

We repeat this process for one or more future time-horizons. We ask the same questions as in the previous phase, but with more of a future-oriented emphasis, such as about upcoming technologies, known trends in the industry, and brainstorming for possible "wildcards" that could create or change a whole industry.

We then do a variant of the standard gap-analysis, in which we not only compare between the "as-is" and the one or more "to-be" views, but also record and assess any gaps, overlaps, and other issues that we've found within each view. From this, we derive a list of ideas or themes or questions that we could then bring to others for their opinions.

Caution   Remember that a so-called "solution" is not a strategy! A prepackaged "solution" is something that a vendor wants to sell, and is almost invariably designed to fit *someone else's* needs – sometimes only the vendor's needs, to be somewhat cynical about it…

Remember the rigid rule here: if anything purports to be a "solution" to something, it *must* be shelved until the *P.3* Development-Model phase at the earliest in any architecture-iteration. Prior to that point, you're *only* assessing requirements. When you do come across a purported "solution" in this type of work, note it down, place it ready to go into the *P.3* phase of a suitable iteration, and search for the real needs and issues *behind* that "solution" that it would aim to address.

The relevant strategic theme to use as the initiating business-question for any architecture-work would typically be at least two or three steps back from any would-be "solution," and will usually be much broader in scope. That business-question is what you should be looking for in this part of the review.

At the *P.2* **Design-Model** sub-layer for *Plan*, we share and explore this list with solution-architects, process-architects, and high-level designers. Although we're not doing any solution-design as such, these are the same people that we would work with in developing solution-architectures and the like, so we can reuse the same stakeholder-lists and governance-rules for this purpose. What we're looking for here are potential innovations in the solution-architecture space, as per the chosen scope but across the whole organization. Examples would include new design-patterns, new development-processes, new technologies, and so on. We're also looking for their views on risks and other issues, as seen from their own communities of practice that bridge beyond the enterprise itself. Document these in the respective risk, opportunity, or issues registers, and also add them to the discussion-list as appropriate.

At the *P.3* **Development-Model** sub-layer for *Plan*, we do the same with developers, detail-level designers, and project-managers – again, much the same groups of people with whom we would usually work in this phase of a normal architecture-development iteration. Here, we look for innovations in planning and preparation, and new combinations of ideas and options that have direct practical applications. We'll also ask for those stakeholders' views on risks, opportunities, and other potential issues. Again, document these as appropriate.

For the final part of the search, at the *P.4* **Deployment-Model** and *P.5* **Action-Model** sub-layers for *Plan* and the **Action layer**, we move much closer to the real-world processes and transactions within and between the organization and the enterprise. Typical themes that would arise with the people who work in these contexts would include new ideas in workflow-management, quality-management, business-continuity, and disaster-recovery. Again, they too have their own communities of practice both within and beyond the organization. Their hands-on experience also makes them more likely than most to spot any potential for *practical* "bottom-up" innovations.

We end at the ***Review layer***, to pull together all the different strands that have come up during this search, and from there produce a prioritized list of strategic, tactical, and/or operational themes that can then be explored in more depth by the strategy-teams and others as required.

Example For the airport, the architecture-team have already done something like this with the "time-to-gate" experiment in the previous Step. As described in that chapter, they forwarded the report on that experiment to project-management. The idea was taken up, and is now being implemented, both on the display-boards and, in a simpler form, in the airport's public smartphone-app.

During *this* search, the team notice that the information-infrastructure group are in the process of installing cell-phone-repeater units throughout the airport, to reduce the frequent overload on the existing cell-masts beyond the airport boundary. One member of that group casually mentions that, by using triangulation from the repeaters' locations, it would be possible for a cell-phone to identify and track its own position within the airport, continually, down to just a few meters.

This immediately sparks the idea of using the airport-app to help people navigate their way around the airport. The app already has an embedded map of the airport, and also knows the passenger's current flight-booking, flight-number, and the respective boarding-gate. If the position-data is added, the "time-to-gate" information could also include step-by-step real-time *directions* to that gate, from any point in the airport. This would be of huge value for transit-passengers and late passengers, and for any passengers needing to deal with a gate-change. The airport could also add data to provide directions to other key points already shown on the map, such as the airport's help-desks and airlines' airport-airside support-desks, which again would help people such as transit-passengers who might need new onward connections after arriving on a late-running flight.

This aligns well with the airport's values of "friendliness" and "being of service," and the promise to minimize the stress of air-travel. However, tracking people's locations in real-time could clash with values and regulations on themes such as privacy. This could be resolved by having the calculations for real-time location and direction-finding done only within the app, and switching off that part of the app's functionality as soon as the passenger boards their flight or leaves the airport via a landside exit.

The architecture-team include full details on this suggestion in their end-of-search report to the strategy-team.

Everything's a Service

We've often talked already about services in this book, right from the start, then throughout the *Foundations* chapters, and in much of the work for Steps 1 and 2. We've also gone into some detail on *service-content*, as summarized in Figure 10-2. Yet if a service-oriented architecture asserts that "everything is a service," then some further questions still arise:

- What *is* a service, to make it work *as* a service?
- How do services *connect* with each other, to create supply-chains and value-webs?
- How do we ensure that a service will be *effective* and "on-purpose"?
- How do we *design* a service, to support all of that?

In this section, we'll start to answer those questions by exploring the structure of services, their flows and interactions, and their relationships with various support-services. From there, we'll move on toward *service-design*, about how to match the implementation to the need, and manage the trade-offs and technologies for each implementation of a service.

CHAPTER 10   STEP 3: SET OUT THE STALL

The Structure of Services

First question: **What is a service?** Back in Chapter 2, we gave a preliminary definition that "*a service is a cluster of activities organized to serve an identifiable need.*" That still *is* valid enough, but there are a few tweaks and nuances that we need to take note of here, before moving on.

The first is that the boundary around that cluster of activities, which makes it identifiable *as* "a service," is almost entirely arbitrary. In essence, **a service is what we say it is**; the boundary, the content, the structure, the purpose – each of these is a *choice*.

Next, once we put a boundary around a service, we need to put some kind of interface – a *function*, per the terminology we've been using here – onto somewhere on its outer surface. Without that interface, we would have no way to access the functionality inside the box defined by that boundary. Inside the box, there's the **service-content**, as shown in Figure 10-2 and in the previous Step: *assets, functions, locations, capabilities, events,* and *decisions*. As shown in Figure 10-1, we can use any type of capability or agent to deliver the service itself, any appropriate mix of people, machines, or IT-systems, as long as it satisfies the request described via the function-interface.

Another point is the fundamental difference between services and products: **a service does, a product is**. A product can help set up a service, or provide a template for the content and action of a service, but it doesn't actually *do* anything on its own. In the terminology we've been using here, a product is a type of *asset* that's passed between services. It's an *output* from one service, to be used as an *input* for another.

And lastly, like tasks and enterprises and so much else, **services are fractal**. Services can contain services, be contained by other services, interact with other services, nested to any level that we might need. In that sense, to paraphrase an old adage, it's services all the way down.

On to the second question: **How does a service work?** On the inside, it's a set of interactions between the various elements of the service-content, responding to the request coming in through the function-interface. Those interactions may all be predetermined and programmed, or be allowed to resolve each request in a more freeform way: that's set up in the service's design, in whatever way we might need. On the outside, though, it's just *a box that does something*. Input, process, output: that's it.

But if each box does something, *changes* something, then we can **link services together to serve a larger-scope need**, within a process, supply-chain, or value-web. For example, at the highest level, we can think of the entire organization itself as one gigantic service: it has inputs, it does things with or to those inputs, and it provides outputs that other people will need.

We can illustrate this with a variant of that generic tier-1 Function-Model from Step 1, shown back in Figure 8-7. For the moment, let's ignore the "Support the Business" functions, because in essence they're just services-to-other-services. Let's also ignore the "Manage the Business" functions for now, for the same reasons. If we do that, then from left to right, as shown in Figure 10-3, *everything else is one simple end-to-end chain of services* that, collectively, deliver the overall service of "providing customers with the organization's products and services."

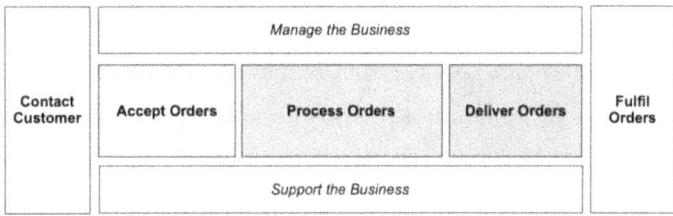

Figure 10-3. *Whole-organization as a service*

In a *supply-chain* of connections, each of the services in the chain will have one or more *suppliers* or service-providers. Given that, the service will need a set of interfaces or *supplier-channels* through which it can connect with those suppliers, and receive the required goods or services. The service then does its own *value-creation*, to play its own role within the chain. Once that's done, it places the results into the respective *customer-channels*, to send them onward via the supply-chain to the appropriate *customers* or service-consumers. Figure 10-4 provides a visual summary of this overall process-flow, for "the organization as a service."

CHAPTER 10   STEP 3: SET OUT THE STALL

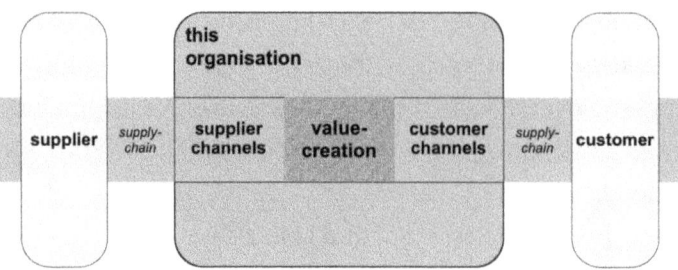

Figure 10-4. *Service and supply-chain*

Yet all of this is fully fractal. The whole organization is a service, but in turn **each individual service is an organization in its own right**, with its own structure, its own suppliers and customers, and so on. Likewise, **each service is also part of its own broader shared-enterprise**, with its own role, positioning, mission, and stories, and with the other roles as its stakeholders within that shared-enterprise.

For the same reasons, it also has its own distinct Context and Scope of operations, exactly as we explored in Step 1. From this, we can now see the reason *why* its suppliers and customers would want to do business with the service: it's because at least some of their respective concerns and values will align, through that shared connection with the broader enterprise. This is where **trust** comes from, which is central to all business. This is what the **value-propositions** with suppliers, customers, and other enterprise-stakeholders are for, as we again explored in Step 1. This is why the service will need **value-governance**, to keep everything aligned to values and purpose.

Overall, as shown in Figure 10-5, the service's **value-creation** sits at an intersection of **value**, as a flow through the supply-chain, and **values** coming down from the shared-enterprise. The various services connect with each other because, even if only for a brief moment, their values and respective value-propositions align well enough to provide a *reason* to connect. That intersection and alignment is actually what drives the *What*, *How*, and *Why* of every service, and every interaction between services.

356

CHAPTER 10   STEP 3: SET OUT THE STALL

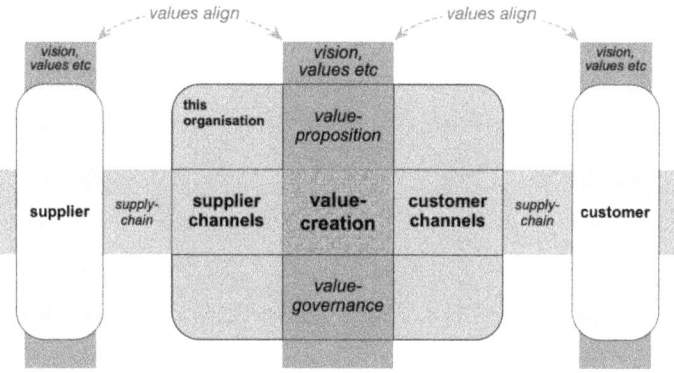

Figure 10-5. Service at the intersection of values and value

In what we've done so far on this above, we've already split the inner workings of the service into a set of "child-services," particularly in a "horizontal" direction in terms of which way those child-services need to face: *supplier-facing*, internal or "*self*," and *customer-facing*. We can now apply a bit of SCAN thinking to add more detail, and more child-services, by also dividing the service in a "vertical" direction in relation to time: interactions *before* the main value-flow transaction, interactions *during* the main value-flow, and interactions *after* the main transaction.

As shown in Figure 10-6, that matrix of horizontal and vertical split gives us *supplier-relations*, *supplier-channels*, and *value-outlay* on the supplier-side, and *customer-relations*, *customer-channels*, and *value-return* on the customer-side. In the middle, for "self," it's clear that a *value-proposition* needs to be present before any transaction or *value-creation* can take place, and *value-governance* to keep everything on-track by, among other things, maintaining the balance between value-outlay and value-return. This provides us with the core for a "Service-Canvas" checklist and template for service-design.

CHAPTER 10   STEP 3: SET OUT THE STALL

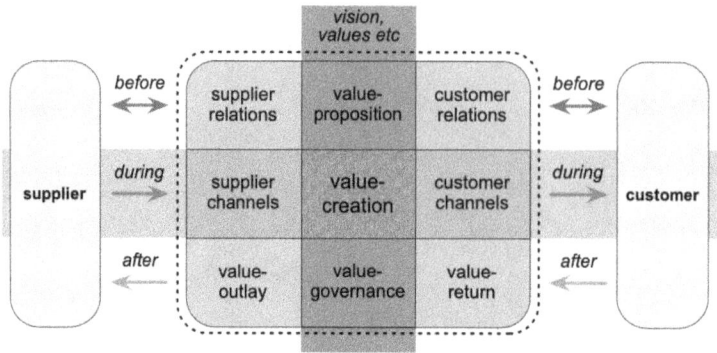

Figure 10-6. *Service-Canvas core – before, during, after*

Note   If you know Alex Osterwalder's Business Model Canvas, as popularized in his book *Business Model Generation*, then yes, this might seem a bit familiar... Don't worry, though, because that similarity *is* intentional: the two types of Canvas *are* significantly different, as will become clear later, but if you're working with business-architects, you'll need to be able to translate between their work on Business Model Canvas and your work here. (We won't cover that translation-process in this book, but there are full details on how to do the round-trip conversions in another of Tom's books in this series, *Mapping the Enterprise*, in that book's Appendix B.)

Business Model Canvas has long proven its value for business-architecture – no doubt about that. It can be more problematic, though, for service-design – and that's where this Service-Canvas comes into the picture. In particular, there are key differences in how the two model-types handle the fractality, symmetry, and viability of services – but that's something that can be left to explore some other time.

Although nominally abstract, that structure of child-services *does* appear quite often in the real-world. For example, "*supplier-relations*" is what the procurement-department does, and receives the procured services or products via "*supplier-channels.*" Over on the customer-side, "*customer-relations*" is the classic role of marketing, compared to sales as "*customer-channels.*" On the far side of each transaction, there's accounts-payable as "*value-outlay*" on the supplier-side of the organization, and accounts-receivable as "*value-return*" on the customer-side. It does all fit, in each fractal instance of a service, with equivalent child-functions often easy to identify even in the smallest services down at the very bottom of the service-hierarchy tree.

There's another useful twist that can come up here when we remember not only that a value-proposition is a *two-way* relationship, as we noted in Step 1, but we also recognize that the *value-proposition* and *customer-relations* child-services sit right next to each other within the overall service. This means that, if we plan it right, we would have a way to capture unexpected affordances that customers create with our products and services, and turn them into new value-propositions for other customer-types. The classic example of this, as we saw in the previous section, is in how cell-phone text-messaging began, and how it became such a core function in every cell-phone today.

The Flows of Services

Next question: **How do services connect with each other**? To answer this, we'll need a means to model the interactions and transactions *between* services, and that will also align with the service-structure we've explored above. In short, we'd need a pattern that applies fractally to *all* identifiable interactions and transactions that take place between any pair of services.

That's what the **Service-Cycle** model will provide. As shown in Figure 10-7, this is a structured visual-checklist that maps out the overall content-types and flows of *mini-interactions* between the customer-facing side of a service in a supplier-role, and the supplier-facing side of a service in a customer-role.

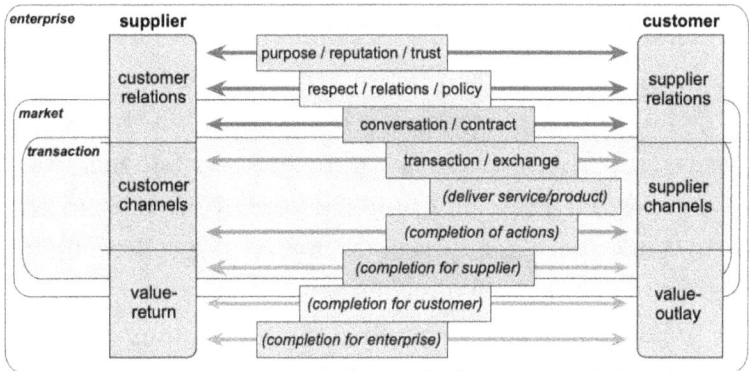

Figure 10-7. Service-Cycle

CHAPTER 10   STEP 3: SET OUT THE STALL

In Figure 10-7, the three layers for the services' Organization-Context Map are also shown in the model's background. This is a reminder that the respective Supplier and Customer services may not be the only stakeholders in a transaction or interaction. There may be others in the market-space and/or enterprise-space, as per the respective Organization-Context Map, who could have a direct or indirect concern that we may need to address. For example, as a supplier, others may watch how we treat our customers, and change our broader reputation from what they see, even though they played no active part in the transaction at all.

The overall cycle here follows much the same pattern as in the marketer's classic acronym **AIDA**: *Attention, Interest, Decision, Action*. Yet not only does this pattern occur in the lead-up to the main delivery-part of the interaction or transaction, but also *in reverse order* on the way out, to close the whole cycle. This ensures that each interaction is fully aligned with the respective Context, Scope, Plan, and Action, both on the way in *and* on the way out.

Note   The Service-Cycle shows a simple left-to-right interaction from Supplier to Customer, mapped out as a set of mini-interactions. In practice, the complete "the interaction" may go back-and-forth quite a few times, with the two (or more) players switching between Supplier and Customer roles. In that kind of case, you may find it helpful to map out the overall interaction using a separate Service-Cycle template for each stage of the role-switching.

In line with the structure of the customer-facing and supplier-facing sides of the Service-Canvas, we split the sets of mini-interactions into three distinct phases: *before*, *during*, and *after*. Note that, as indicated by the arrows on the Service-Canvas, the overall flows tend to be different in each phase: in the *before* phase, a mostly-symmetric back-and-forth; in the *during* phase, a mostly rightward flow from Supplier to Customer; and in the *after* phase, a mostly leftward flow from Customer to Supplier. In the Service-Cycle, all of the flows are shown as bidirectional, but the respective emphasis is indicated by the size of the arrowheads in each direction.

For the *before* phase of the cycle, between the Supplier's *customer-relations* and the Customer's *supplier-relations*

- In the first step in this phase, the focus will be on *purpose*, *reputation*, and *intent*, and other Context-related themes. There'll be an emphasis on *aspirational-assets*, guided by themes such as identity and brand. By the end of this step, **Attention** will have been achieved.

- In the next step, the focus will be on *respect*, *relationships*, and *policy*, and other people-oriented Scope themes. There'll be an emphasis on building and maintaining *relational-assets*. By the end of this step, **Interest** will have been achieved.

- In the final step for this phase, the focus will be on information and conversation, leading toward a Plan for further action, such as an agreement or contract. There'll be an emphasis on *virtual-assets* such as information and data. By the end of this step, **Decision** will have been achieved.

For the *during* phase of the cycle, between the Supplier's *customer-channels* and the Customer's *supplier-channels*:

- In the first step of this phase, the details for the transaction are set up through the Supplier-service's *customer-channels* functions. The **Action** will begin, ultimately enacted through real-world *physical-assets*.

- In the next step, behind the Supplier's *customer-channels*, the *value-creation* activity of the service takes place. The products of that Action, as *assets* of some kind, will be sent to the Customer's *supplier-channels*.

- In the final step for this phase, the service itself signals that the **Action** is complete.

For the *after* phase of the cycle, between the Customer's *value-outlay* and the Supplier's *value-return*

- In the first step of this phase, the Customer signals that it has received the products, and returns to the Supplier, via its *value-outlay* services, the appropriate value specified in the agreement. At this point, *from the Supplier's perspective*, the agreement or **Decision** is complete.

- In the next step, the Supplier signals that it has received the appropriate value via its *value-return* services, and verifies that the Customer is also satisfied with the outcomes of the interaction. At this point, their mutual **Interest** in the interaction is complete.

- In the final step for this phase, the Supplier and Customer verify that all other interested stakeholders are satisfied with the progress and outcomes of the interaction. At this point, the **Attention** of the shared-enterprise is also complete, and the Service-Cycle comes to an end.

The CSPAR *Review* phase should also help to verify that the appropriate "benefits-realized" have been received by all stakeholders in the interaction.

Warning   Yes, there's a lot going on in the Service-Cycle, which means that, especially in today's business-culture, there'll often be a *lot* of pressure to take shortcuts. If so, beware: there are real traps there...

It's true that *some* of the steps – particularly the outer ones – *can* be skipped *some* of the time. For example, with repeat-customers, it's probable that the Attention and Interest would already exist – so it may well be possible to jump straight to the conversation, Decision, and contract, and then into Action from there.

Yet it's essential to realize that that kind of shortcut will only work *some* of the time – not *all* of the time. Attention and Interest are fickle, and need frequent refresh, which can only be done by going through the *whole* cycle, step by careful and respectful step. As enterprise-architects, we've now seen far too many organizations get greedy and fall into the "***quick-profit failure-cycle***" trap, dropping all attention on the customer as soon as they've paid. This *looks* more "efficient" in the short-term, but in practice is often disastrously *ineffective*, especially over the longer-term. There's nothing there to maintain relationships with customers or the broader-enterprise, so all reputation and trust will slowly fade away, causing the whole thing to suddenly collapse into nothingness, "without warning." Not A Good Idea...

The Effectiveness of Services

This brings us to that third question: **How do we ensure that a service will be effective?** This is where the "Manage the Business" services come into the picture, as shown in Figure 10-8.

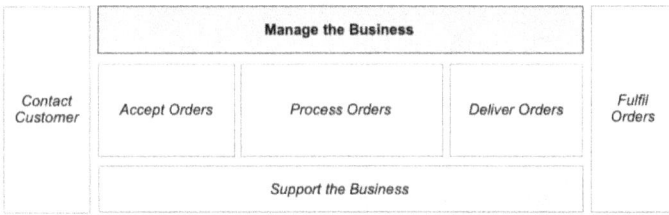

Figure 10-8. *"Manage the Business" services for the organization as a whole*

There's a bit more to it than "it's management stuff," though. That's because it's not something separate from services, but needs to be *interwoven* with the way that every service works.

In part, this is also about the ***validity and viability of a service***, particularly over the longer-term. One of the classic models for this is Stafford Beer's **Viable System Model** [VSM], first used in the design of the whole-of-nation *Cybersyn* system in Chile in 1971, and described in his 1972 book *Brain of the Firm*. The model is fully-fractal, and aligns well with the fractal concept of services that we're using here.

To align with VSM, we can then simplify the core of the model down to a set of "systems": a *delivery-service* that represents the service that's our current focus of attention; and three types of guidance-services, described as *direction-services*, *coordination-services*, and *validation-services*. Figure 10-9 provides a visual summary of the relationships between these various types of services.

CHAPTER 10 STEP 3: SET OUT THE STALL

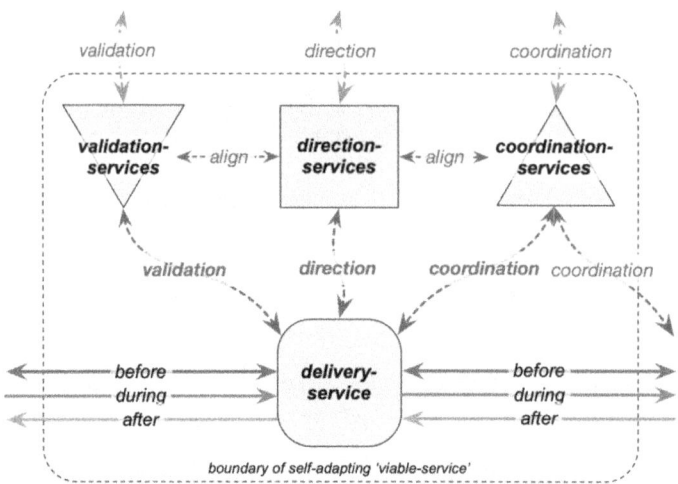

Figure 10-9. *Service viability*

In VSM, the **delivery-services** are known as *system-1*. In CSPAR terms, this is a service that provides Action, in response to the respective Plan, Scope, and Context. In essence, since every service should deliver *some* kind of action, and *some* kind of value, this could represent any service at all – including the ones that provide direction, coordination, and validation, whenever we want to assess those too *as* services in their own right.

The **direction-services** would be provided by the "Manage the Business" functions as shown in Figure 10-8. In line with VSM, we would split these into three distinct groups that align well with the respective CSPAR phases at enterprise, organizational, and service-specific levels:

- *Identity and purpose* (VSM *system-5*): Services that identify and maintain the connection of the service-in-focus with its Context

- *Outside and future* (VSM *system-4*): Services that identify and maintain the strategic connection of the service-in-focus with its Scope and with the wider world, and also identify, maintain, and implement the Plan for that service

- *Inside and now* (VSM *system-3*): Services that, as "line-management" and the like, define, mandate, and enforce the delivery-service's Action on that plan

The ***coordination-services*** (expanded VSM *system-2*) provide guidance and process-choreography for the interactions *between* delivery-services, and also, at a higher level, for changes to the organization itself:

- *Develop the business*: Services that coordinate portfolios of longer-term change across units, and also provide a cross-functional bridge between Direction's "*identity and purpose*" and "*outside and future*"

- *Change the business*: Services that coordinate cross-functional change-projects, and also provide a cross-functional bridge between Direction's "*outside and future*" and "*inside and now*"

- *Run the business*: Services that coordinate cross-functional interactions between delivery-services, to support load-balancing (as per VSM *system-2*) and connections along a supply-chain, and also provide a cross-functional bridge between Direction's "*inside and now*" and the delivery-services

The ***validation-services*** (expanded VSM *system-3**) support alignment and adaptation to the big-picture of Context and Scope – the vision, values, principles, constraints, success-criteria, and so on. (The validation-services are sometimes called the "*pervasive-services*," because what they do must pervade everything.) For *each of the values and principles in the respective Context*, we'll need

- *Develop awareness*: Services that promote and evangelize to create awareness of the importance of the respective values and their practical implications

- *Develop capability*: Services that educate in practices and metrics to enact and monitor compliance to the values and principles

- (The service-in-focus would use that developed awareness and capability to take action at run-time, to support the value as an embedded part of every activity.)

- *Verify and audit*: Services that review action-records (as per VSM *system-3**), and identify benefits-realized and lessons-learned, to assure compliance with the values and to support overall effectiveness

In the background, the validation-services also support the organization's any-to-any "*algedonic*" (literally, "pain-pleasure") links, such as a suggestions-box or a whistleblower line, that can, if necessary, bypass the official hierarchies to report unaddressed opportunities or risks.

Note As mentioned above, there's a lot more to VSM, but that's probably all that's needed for here. VSM has a lot to offer for enterprise-architects: it's rigorous, coherent, consistent, and fully fractal. Its only real problem is that it can be so "technical" that people sometimes drift off into long theory-based discussions that may lose any connection with the actual real-world challenges.

To counter that, we'll continue to keep everything as simple as possible, and focus only on what's needed for immediate practice. If and when you do need to know more about using VSM in service-design, though, it's described in depth in Tom's book *The Service-Oriented Enterprise*.

Another way to make sense of those service-roles and relationships is to extend the old "*boxes-and-lines*" metaphor into "**boxes, lines, and glue**." Figure 10-10 shows a visual summary of this metaphor.

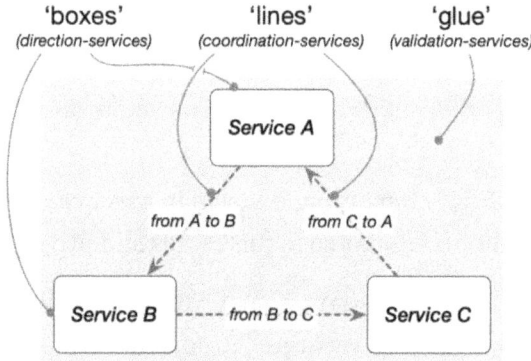

Figure 10-10. *The "boxes, lines, and glue" metaphor*

Every service is a "***box***" that contains "a cluster of activities organized to serve an identifiable need." The ***direction-services***, typically represented by the respective service-manager, will bring the respective Context, Scope, and Plan into that box and, in the classic "scientific-management" sense, control what happens inside that box.

Every interaction between services is a *"line"* that carries the required service-products between the respective services. The **coordination-services** will guide negotiations between the respective services and service-managers to ensure that the appropriate exchanges and choreography will take place across the connection-lines between the services.

Behind everything is a kind of amorphous *"glue"* that fills every empty space in a fluid yet sticky way, even *inside* the boxes, and holds everything together, even while things are changing and moving around. Among other things, it represents and supports connection to and alignment with the overarching purpose and Context for the organization and for the enterprise as a whole. The **validation-services** will ensure that that Context is fully understood and applied everywhere, in every Action.

A complete service-architecture must cover all of this: not just the boxes, but also the lines, *and* the glue as well.

Warning The *direction-services* and *delivery-services* do fit well with the classical strict-hierarchy notions of "scientific-management": "managers tell the workers what to do, the workers do what they're told" and all that. However, the *coordination-services* and, even more, the *validation-services*, do *not* fit well with those classic notions, because coordination-services will require dual or multiple reporting-relationships, and validation-services may need to bypass the management-hierarchy entirely. Because of this, some managers will absolutely *hate* them, and do everything they can to get in their way.

As enterprise-architects, we've had much painful first-hand experience of the problems that such hatred can cause. Yet no matter how disliked those services may be, they are *essential* to the viability, validity, and connectedness of the service as a whole. If they're absent, disconnected, or shut out of the story, the overall system cannot be effective or viable, and often *will* fail as a result. Not A Good Idea…

We now need to add these support-service connections to our generic service-template, to complete our **Service-Canvas** as a visual-checklist for the structure and relationships of a *"viable-service."* As shown in Figure 10-11, the guidance-services will connect and pervade through every part of the service-in-focus, as represented by the small black ball connected to the dashed-line that represents the service-boundary. The *value-governance* child-services within the service-in-focus will also help in connecting the guidance-services downward to the next levels in the service-hierarchy.

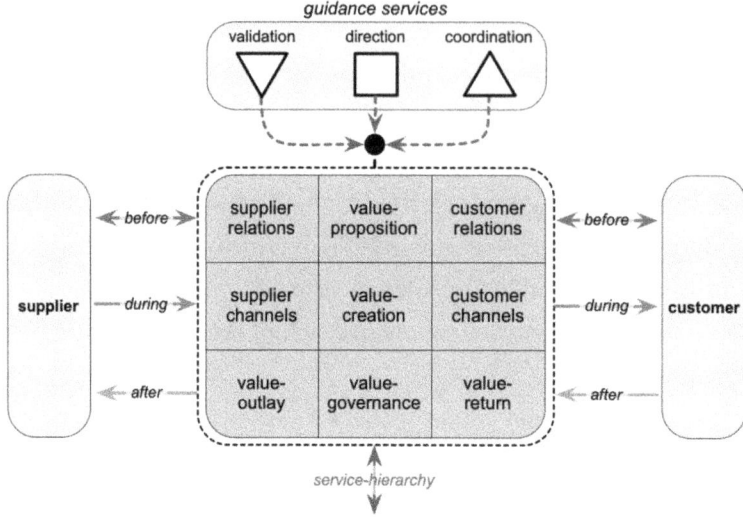

Figure 10-11. Service-Canvas service-structure model

We'll use this Service-Canvas, together with the Service-Cycle, as a completeness-checklist for service-design and service-delivery.

Note The *Service-Canvas* can also be extended into an **Enterprise-Canvas** form, which adds checklist-items and links for *investor* and *beneficiary* relationships. This variant of the Service-Canvas is mainly used for services at or near the whole-of-organization level, to help address some specific issues that can arise there. There's more on that in the next chapter, on Step 4, in the section "Investors and Beneficiaries."

There's also more detail on these investor/beneficiary relationships and issues in Tom's book *Mapping the Enterprise,* in its Chapter 11.

CHAPTER 10   STEP 3: SET OUT THE STALL

The Design of Services

This brings us to the last in that set of questions for this section: **How do we design a service** to enable its required functionality? How do we ensure that the appropriate structures, service-content, interactions, flows, and connections with support-services are all in place?

For this, we'll again use that architectural principle that *everything in the enterprise is a service*. Each of the business-functions delivers a service; coordination of end-to-end processes is a service; change-management is a service; management itself is a service. *Everything* is a service.

As shown in Figure 10-12, we can summarize a service as a composite of *function* as a point where an identified change can take place, and *capability* as a set of competencies to enact the required change.

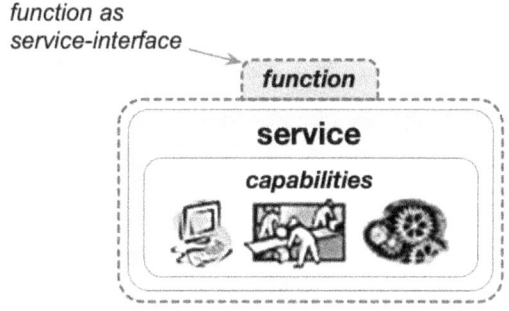

Figure 10-12. *Service, function, and capability*

A service may be implemented by any appropriate combination of machine-based, IT-based, or people-based capabilities. We can combine function together with a different capability or *technology* – a "clustering-together" of a specific set of capabilities – to deliver a different service. Or, conversely, the same function can be implemented in many different ways and with different technologies.

Given that, we'll need to identify the best fit of technology, capability, and function for each different context, using different *trade-offs* as required. We'll do this in two parts:

- Assess the "*service in the abstract*," to identify the abstract **common requirements** that *all* possible implementations of the service must be able to address. Common factors for implementations would also include reporting-metrics that would enable like-for-like comparisons under different operating conditions.

369

- Explore **options, technologies, and trade-offs** for **real-world implementations** for that service. These implementations must *each* address all of the common-requirements, but also, *as a set*, successfully address the full range of operational scenarios that may apply in that context.

Typical examples of scenarios that may need to be addressed would include

- Variances in *complexity*, such as escalations, exceptions, and special-cases
- Variations in load or *scale*, such as rush-hour versus night-shift, harvest-time, or holiday-season at the airport
- Variations in *uniqueness* or other special conditions, such as locality, culture, age, health, disability, or resource-quality
- *System-disruptions* and other emergencies, such as system-failure, unit-failure, partial-failure ("graceful-failure"), communication-failure, machine-blockage, or machine-breakdown

In architecture terms, all of this work would take place in the earlier parts of the CSPAR *Plan* layer. We presume that a **P.1** "*Interaction-Model*" for the respective services and service-relationships is already available, based on the *Function Model, Business-Systems Model,* and *Information-Systems Model*, and their equivalents for the other asset-types and asset-flows.

Note To do this part of the work, you'll need to have the Function-Model developed down to at least tier-3 across the whole organization, and down to tier-4 for each function on the Function-Model that you want to explore in depth.

Note also that if you haven't already extended the Business-Systems Model to include the flows of physical "things" and other non-information assets, you should probably do that before starting this exercise.

You'll probably also need those equivalents of the Information-Systems Model for each of the other asset-types. It's unlikely that for those there would be an exact analogue of the information-management "single source of truth," but otherwise the principles, and the questions that need to be asked, are all much the same.

We start by exploring ***services in abstract***, viewing the service from the *outside* where, as shown in Figure 10-12, the function-interfaces will seem to *be* "the service." We would do this exploration at the CSPAR abstract-level **P.2** "*Design-Model*" sub-layer of **Plan**, by asking questions such as these:

- What does the service *do*? What is its purpose within the overall enterprise? What value does it deliver?

- What *assets* would be used or referenced within the abstract service, that would be common to *every* implementation of the service? Are these assets physical, virtual, relational, aspirational, abstract, and/or other composite forms?

- In what *locations* would the abstract-service be delivered? What types of locations are involved in delivery of the service? Are these locations physical, virtual, relational, aspirational, abstract, and/or other composite forms?

- What *events* trigger or are triggered by the abstract-service? What types of events are involved in delivery of the service? Are these events physical, virtual, relational, aspirational, abstract, and/or other composite forms?

- What *decisions* and *business-rules* apply to and within the abstract-service? What types of decisions are involved? Are these decisions rule-based, analytic, pattern-based, principle-based, and/or other composite forms?

- What *capabilities*, and *competencies* of those capabilities, would be required to deliver the abstract-service? In what ways do the asset-types, location-types, and event-types – physical, virtual, relational, aspirational, abstract, and composite – and decision-types – rule-based, analytic, pattern-based, principle-based – determine the capability-types and competencies that would be required in every implementation of the service?

- In *interfaces* to the abstract-service, either as "requester" for the service or "provider" to the service, what would be required that is common to every implementation of the service? What are the assets, events, and information-flows that would be required in each transaction or interaction through those interfaces? What content would be required to define templates for a service-agreement and/or service-level agreement for each interface?

- In what business-processes is the abstract-service used? By what means is the use of the service *coordinated* or choreographed with other services to deliver the results of each business-process?

- In what way is the overall abstract-service managed? What *control-information* and *performance-metrics* would be common to every implementation of the service?

- What determines *quality* within the abstract-service? How would such quality be monitored and maintained within every implementation of the service?

From the results of this inquiry, we would derive requirements that should be common to *all* implementations of this abstract business-service. We would document these as descriptions of entities, attributes, and links within architecture models, and as requirements, risks, opportunities, and issues in the appropriate repositories, with any names and cross-references entered in the glossary and thesaurus.

Note The required competencies for the capabilities, as skill-levels or equivalent, which are captured here, will be critical later in helping to determine choices for trade-offs between implementations.

In practice, machines can only be used to implement rule-based capabilities, and IT only for rule-based and analytic capabilities. In general, IT can also be used for decision-*support* in emergent and principle-based contexts, but not for decision-*making* – a crucial distinction which is all too often forgotten in practice!

Conversely, although people *can* do work which is solely rule-based, the presence of *some* scope for personal skill is usually essential to engagement, because personal effectiveness will suffer without it. Wherever practicable, rule-only components of work should be implemented by machines or by IT.

Using what we've found above, we next shift to exploring ***services for real***, looking at the capabilities and suchlike *inside* the service, as also shown in Figure 10-12. This work takes place at the CSPAR **P.3** "*Development-Model*" sub-layer of **Plan**.

For *each potential implementation* of the abstract-service, we need to ask:

- What does the implementation *do* internally that implements the abstract-service? What additional value – if any – does it deliver?

- What additional *assets* would be used or referenced within the service-implementation that would be specific to *this* implementation of the service? Does the implementation itself impose constraints on the assets and asset-types that can be used? Are these assets physical, virtual, relational, aspirational, abstract, and/or other composite forms?

- In what additional *locations* would the implementation be delivered? What additional types of locations are involved in delivery of the service? Does the implementation itself impose constraints on the locations and location-types that are involved? Are these locations physical, virtual, relational, aspirational, abstract, and/or other composite forms?

- What additional *events* trigger or are triggered by the implementation? What types of events are involved in delivery of the service? Does the implementation itself impose constraints on the events and event-types that are involved? Are these events physical, virtual, relational, aspirational, abstract, and/or other composite forms?

- What additional *decisions* and *business-rules* apply to and within the implementation? What types of decisions are involved? Does the implementation itself impose constraints on the decisions and decision-types that are involved? Are these decisions rule-based, analytic, pattern-based, principle-based, or other composite forms?

- What additional *capabilities*, and *competencies* of those capabilities, would be required to deliver the implementation? In what ways do the asset-types, location-types, and event-types – physical, virtual, relational, aspirational, abstract, and/or composite – and decision-types – rule-based, analytic, pattern-based, principle-based – determine the capability-types and competencies that would be required? Does the implementation itself impose constraints on the capabilities and competencies that would be required to deliver the service?

- In *interfaces* to the abstract-service, either as "requester" for the service, or "provider" to the service, what else would be required that is specific to this implementation of the service? What additional assets, events, information-flows, and decisions would be required in each transaction? What constraints, if any, would the implementation itself impose on transactions? In what ways, such as response-times, service-volumes, and service-quality guarantees, would the definitions for a *service-level* agreement for each interface need to be amended specific to this implementation?

- In what business-processes is this implementation used? By what specific means is the use of the implementation *coordinated* or choreographed with other services to deliver the results of each business-process?

- In what ways might the *management* of this implementation vary from that for the overall abstract-service? What additional *control-information* and *performance-metrics* would be required for this implementation? In what ways does this implementation ensure that the common control-information and performance-metrics are appropriately supported?

- What additional factors determine *quality* within this implementation? How would such quality, including all the shared quality-parameters for the abstract-service, be monitored and maintained within this implementation?

Finally, viewed as a set:

- What are the *trade-offs* between each implementation? In what contexts would one implementation be preferable – more effective – than others, and for what reasons?

We would document the results as described above for abstract-services. On completion of the assessments for both the abstract-services and the real-services, we would use gap-analysis and so on to derive requirements for change-projects, to pass on to project-management and the like as appropriate.

Note Many of the trade-offs, and factors within the trade-offs, are context-dependent, and themselves may force changes elsewhere.

In some disaster-recovery scenarios, for example, a people-based implementation of the service may be essential, because the IT is out of action or no longer exists. The details of the *service-level* agreement (SLA) will need to change, such as response-time or volume of transactions that can be handled in a given period, but as far as practicable, the *parameters* of the SLA should remain the same.

Another complication there is that the *asset-type* of some assets in the transaction may also need to change. For example, in that disaster-recovery scenario, the "pure" virtual-asset-type managed by IT would not be available, because the IT-system is itself unavailable. If that's the case, the information will need to arrive as a composite, bundled with a physical-asset such as a paper form, or relational-asset, as in a person-to-person message.

Conversely, changing the main implementation-mechanism may force other competency-changes elsewhere. Converting from a paper form into something that a physical machine or an IT-system could use would speed up the processing, but would still require someone to pre-interpret the information into a structure that that system can handle. In a human-only implementation, it's possible to work with low-competency input – just ask the Post Office how to handle badly-scrawled hand-written addresses! In a machine-based or IT-based implementation, though, the required "intelligence" must often be moved elsewhere in the process-chain: hence "please mark the boxes in black ink only," and so on. The *overall* competencies required by the service don't change, but they can be moved around a bit as appropriate within different implementations.

CHAPTER 10   STEP 3: SET OUT THE STALL

Serving the Enterprise

How does the organization play its part in the shared-enterprise? What does it have to offer? How does it create its value and deliver on that offer? And, also important, what are its responsibilities in relation to that offer?

We've talked earlier about value-propositions, though so far mostly at a whole-of-organization level. It's here that we need to dive down into more of the detail, in terms of ***products and services***, looking inside-out from the organization to the wider world.

Promise, Service, and Product

For the organization, what's the difference between a product and a service? What are the architecture implications of offering a product, versus offering a service?

The fundamental difference between products and services is that ***a product is, a service does***:

- A service brings together its various functions and capabilities to *do* something useful, to deliver something or an outcome of value.

- A product just sits there, waiting, until someone wants to use it. On its own, it doesn't, and in fact can't, do anything at all.

A product doesn't just appear from nowhere. Always, ***a product is an output from a service*** – literally, something that is "lead outward" from that service.

Also, always, ***a product is a static asset of some kind***. It will always be some *combination of asset-types* – physical, virtual, relational, and/or aspirational. It may itself be a *composite* of many such assets, nested to any appropriate depth. It may include *embedded functionality*, such as in a computer-program or the components of an electric drill – yet if so, always in a static or "frozen" form that cannot do anything on its own until it is awakened by the capabilities of some other service.

In service-oriented terms, ***the purpose of a product is to bridge a gap between services***. A gap may be created by any kind of boundary or transition: a gap in time or distance, for example, or a change of ownership, responsibility, or jurisdiction. Wherever such a gap exists between services, as shown in Figure 10-13, at least one product *must* exist to provide a means to bridge that gap.

CHAPTER 10   STEP 3: SET OUT THE STALL

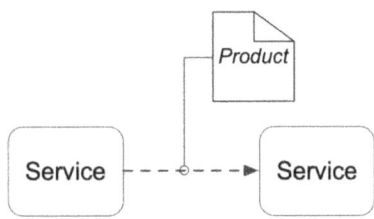

Figure 10-13. Product as bridge between services

Conversely, whenever a product exists, there *must* always have been some kind of a service that produced it, and in principle at least *one* service that would, should, or could use it as an input.

Note   A product that *doesn't* seem to have any service that would use it is otherwise known as "**waste**." This has real implications for business-effectiveness: for example, to quote Ray Anderson, former CEO of carpet-manufacturer Interface Inc., "every scrap of waste is something I've paid for that I cannot sell."

If you want to improve the effectiveness of your organization, one good place to start would be to identify any items that are currently considered to be "waste," and then look for affordances in other services that might be able to use those items. That's how a circular-economy is built. In Interface's case, Anderson created processes and services to recycle all waste-carpet materials into new carpet, reducing their dependency on inputs of imported oil and plastics, and greatly cutting costs all round.

Given that a service always implies the existence of a product, and a product always implies the existence of a service, it doesn't really help us to regard them as fundamentally-separate things. Instead, as shown in Figure 10-14, **each process or supply-chain consists of a continuous alternation between "product" and "service,"** as different views or modes of what is essentially the *same* thing.

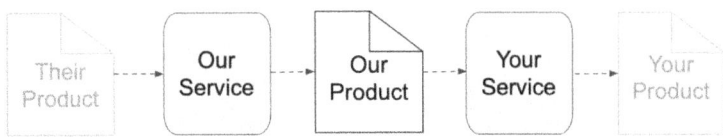

Figure 10-14. Service, product, service

377

CHAPTER 10   STEP 3: SET OUT THE STALL

For example, at the airport, consider the role of a boarding-pass. It's a product of the check-in service behind the "Confirm Validity of Flight-Booking for Person" function, as shown in Figure 9-5 in the previous chapter. This is then used as an input to the "valid-to-travel" test within the service for the "Confirm Person Is Valid to Travel" function, and again later as an input to the second "valid-to-travel" test within the service for the "Reconfirm Person Is Valid to Travel" function at the departure-gate.

Caution   The distinction between "*logical*" (Design-Model) and "*physical*" (Development-Model) is also relevant in that example.

The term "*boarding-pass*" there represents a "logical" or abstract entity that would be realized in the real-world as one or more "physical" *assets* in any appropriate mix of formats and asset-types. For example, it may take a literally physical form, as a printed cardboard object; it may exist only in virtual form, as data either embedded in a scannable code on a passenger's smartphone, or associated with the identity-card of a crew-member; it may even include a relational-asset element, with a physical or virtual boarding-pass carried by someone else on behalf of a disabled passenger or a child.

Be careful not to mix up "logical" and "physical" in architecture-models: they're not the same!

Note, though, that *a service may produce or consume many other products* than just the nominal "The Product" presented by that service. For example, in a commercial context, even if what is delivered is "The Service" rather than "The Product," there'll still be visible products in the form of the bill for payment, and the receipt in return. In the airport, a cleaner will fold over the ends of the toilet-roll to signal that the cleaning has been done.

In the Service-Cycle, as shown in Figure 10-15, every arrow represents a back-and-forth of products in the respective phase of the cycle. Every one of these products will be used *somewhere*, either in one or other of the child-services within one of the main services in the interaction, or else in a monitoring or auditing service or suchlike either elsewhere and/or at some other time.

CHAPTER 10   STEP 3: SET OUT THE STALL

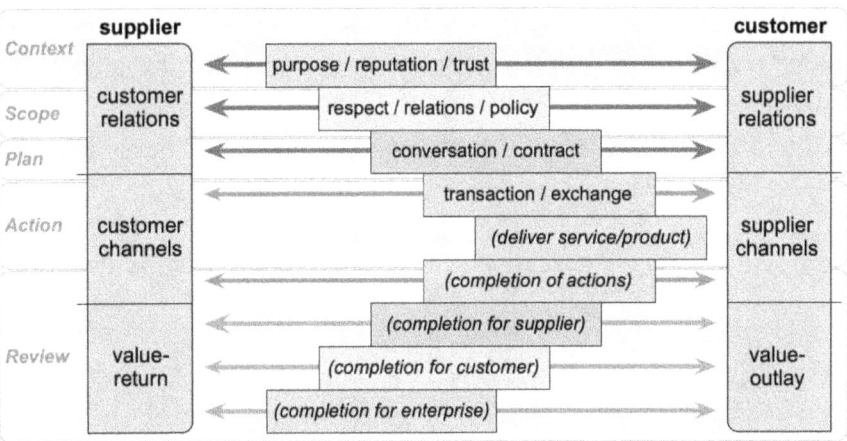

Figure 10-15. Products in the Service-Cycle

The typical asset-type of the products at each phase will align with the nature of the phase itself: aspirational-assets in the Context or AIDA "Attention" phase; relational-assets in the Scope or "Interest" phase; virtual-assets in the conversations about requirements, specifications, and contracts in the Plan or "Decision" phase; physical or other real-world assets in the Action phase; and then in reverse order through the various steps in the Review phase. The relative size of the arrowheads on each arrow indicates the typical proportion of products moving in one direction or the other between the respective services.

Caution   Remember that although interactions between services should follow the general pattern of the Service-Cycle, the cycle itself can be iterative and fractal, giving rise to a wide range of possible variations.

One common example is that payment – "completion for supplier" – may in some cases occur *before* delivery of the product or service. In practice, this is only feasible when there are no variations to the product or service itself – no add-on purchases, or "extras" during a meal-service. For the customer, the perceived-value of the product or service will also depend on whether they believe that the supplier has delivered on their value-proposition and promise of service. If the latter does *not* occur, and yet payment had already been made before delivery, expect many arguments at the "completion for customer" stage of the cycle!

CHAPTER 10   STEP 3: SET OUT THE STALL

The first products in the Service-cycle will usually be *aspirational-assets* that relate to **the supplier's value-proposition and promise of service**. In effect, the only thing a salesperson ever sells is a promise: everything else follows on from that. As shown in Figure 10-16, a receipt of that promise is what starts off the chain of services in a process, or the Service-Cycle for a single segment in that chain.

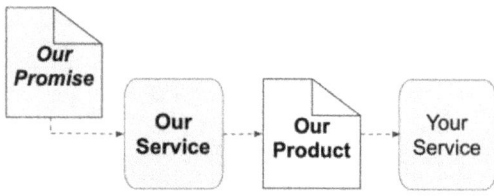

Figure 10-16. *Promise, service, product*

In AIDA terms, the customer's Awareness of this promise, and then **trust** in that promise either through reputation or past experience, is what creates enough Interest from the customer to want to move to the next and more relational stage of the cycle. It's only later on, in the conversation-stage that takes place before the AIDA Decision, that the customer provides their own response to the supplier's value-proposition and promise.

This is particularly important when the "product" is itself a promise about *future* service, such as in an "insurance-product." Trust in those promises, and trust that the respective services will or even can be delivered, is a foundational concern for that type of enterprise – especially when we view it in the sense of "enterprise as service." Some form or other of non-recoverable "waste" will be created within the shared-enterprise as a result of the loss of the promise or the loss of trust in that promise.

Note   Those summaries above should be enough to get you started on the planning for product-delivery and/or service-delivery.

Although it is enough for that purpose, we'll admit that it *is* only an introduction. As you delve deeper into the practice on this, you'll find that there can be many other subtleties, nuances, and complications in those relationships between value-proposition, promise, service, and product – far more than we can cover in this book. If and when you do need it, though, there's a lot more detail on this in Tom's weblog-anthology *Making sense of services in EA* – see Appendix B for more information on that ebook.

Products

In this section, we'll focus on the "*product*" part of the "service-product-purpose" relationships, as shown in Figure 10-17.

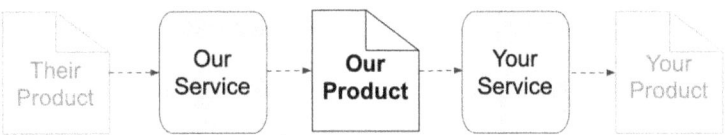

Figure 10-17. Service, product, service – product-supply

Let's start with some quick **definitions**.

First, a product can only exist as such in a gap between services. In that sense, from the supplier's perspective, ***products are assets for others to use in their own services for self and/or others***. The customer, not the supplier, will do the work that uses that product.

As an asset, ***a product will comprise any appropriate mix of asset-types***: physical, virtual, relational, and/or aspirational. A product may also itself be a composite of assets, nested to any appropriate depth.

A product also ***represents the promise of future service*** for self and/or others, via the use of that product. That point about "*future* service" is important: a product can only be used *after* it has been released by the supplier-service into that gap between services. This is one reason why a Service-Cycle will always take an identifiable time to execute: time is expended not only in the execution of the services that process each step on either side of the boundary, but also in the time that it takes for each of the myriad of intermediate products to cross the gaps between those services.

Example   Few of the airport's products are instantly recognizable as such. Most of them can be identified, though, via a reminder that it's the *customer*, not the supplier, that does the work with a product, and also that "a product represents the promise of future delivery of *self*-service via use of that product."

Given that clue, the most obvious product is the information shown on the flight-status displays, which passengers use for the self-service of making choices about when to undertake their various actions within the airport. There are also the water-fountains that produce water for passengers to drink, and seating that enable passengers' self-service of rest. Technically speaking, the various points of access to the areas of the airport, such as the entry-doors, security-gates, staging-area, vendors, and departure-gates, are also products because they enable the self-service of entering and leaving the respective area. The perceived quality of these products would depend on how well the airport succeeds in holding to its own values: worn-out seats, broken water-fountains, and display-panels stuck in a reboot-loop would not be a happy experience for passengers...

Those products are virtual and/or physical, of course. More subtle, yet equally real, are the changes to relational and/or aspirational assets, which may be amended in ways similar to the CRUD pattern for information-assets: Create, Read, Update, Delete. Relationships between passengers, airport-staff, and others – relational-assets – can be affected in interactions within the airport and/or during the airport's processes. In the same way, changes to aspirational-assets such as the airport's reputation and the desire to engage (or not!) in the enterprise of air-travel are products of passengers' interactions with the airport as a whole. Again, the quality and value of these products will depend in part on how well the airport succeeds in holding to its own values.

Next, we need to explore the **quality-implications** for each product, such as those around "fitness for purpose" and the like.

In the same way that a principle is an *expression* of a value, ***quality is the experience of a value***. As in the classic phrase, "quality is in the eye of the beholder," this experience of value is *not* something that the organization can control.

However, the organization can *influence* its customers' experience of product-quality. For example, it could do this by showing how its products each align with the values of the organization and shared-enterprise, and how these also express the organization's choices about priorities and trade-offs between those values.

Marketers and product-designers would typically address this by using ***value-proposition and promise***, as above, to ***describe expected-quality*** for a product. Customers' expectations and experiences about what is considered "good," "bad," or indifferent quality also tend to be ***relative to their needs***, rather than in absolute terms. For example, with "fast-food" at the airport, speed of service can be more important to the customer than other qualities such as taste, texture, or size of portions. Likewise, all flight carry-on bags have the same core *value-proposition*, as a bag that will fit airlines' rules for carry-on baggage, but there'd be a difference in *promise* and *expected-quality* for a rough-and-ready bag that would only be used once or twice a year, versus one that needs to look good every day in a business-meeting, or one used to carry climbing-gear up a mountain.

Enterprise-architects can support this by helping to ensure that every step in the path from idea to delivered product can *and will* support the required values and expected-quality, using the methods and checklists described earlier.

Product-quality issues may also connect with **product-liability issues**. In principle, responsibility for a product would be passed from supplier to customer along with ownership of the product. In practice, it isn't quite as simple as that, because the product's promise will also make various claims about quality and **fitness-for-purpose**, which would be subject to the **regulatory-regime** of the respective nation, region, and/or market. These regulatory-regimes tend to sit somewhere on a spectrum between extreme *inside-out*, where the customer has sole-responsibility, and extreme *outside-in*, where the supplier has sole-responsibility:

- *Extreme **inside-out***: A supplier may sell anything, of any quality, to anyone, unless someone can prove that that product is *not* fit-for-purpose or *not* safe for a prospective buyer to use.

- *Extreme **outside-in***: A supplier may sell anything only if that organization can prove that that product *is* fit-for-purpose and safe for a prospective buyer to use or consume.

Products that are designed to align with a particular regulatory-regime may hit problems if they're offered into a new market with a different regulatory-regime. For example, the organization may find that its product cannot be sold there because it can't meet the regulatory requirements, or it cannot compete because the costs of producing its quality makes it too expensive for that market.

A whole-enterprise architecture can help to identify and expand the range of markets that can be addressed, by mapping out the requirements of regulatory-regimes to the values of the organization and the types of quality that the organization can produce via its existing and future systems. We'll see more on this in Step 4, in the section "Design for Flexibility" in the next chapter.

CHAPTER 10   STEP 3: SET OUT THE STALL

Before a customer obtains a product, they need to ***trust that the product will deliver on its promise of future service-delivery*** not just in terms of quality, but also at the required time, and for the entirety of its lifecycle. In many cases, they will also need to ensure that it will *not* create other side-effects or affordances, such as corrosion, pollution, or health-hazards.

Note   One of the sadder examples of such side-effects of products relates to military hardware. On the former battlefields of the First World War, French and Belgian farmers face what they call "the Iron Harvest" of unexploded shells still buried beneath their fields, and that kills or injures some of them every year, more than a century after that war had ended. All over Europe, construction crews still have good reason to fear unexploded bombs buried deep below ground during the Second World War, and hope that they won't hit one that will blow them up before they can call for help. All over the world, long-forgotten minefields and cluster-bombs still maim hundreds of children and adults every year. Old sea-mines finally break free from their moorings and eventually wash up, deadly as ever, on present-day tourist-beaches. That's what happens when dangerous goods *don't* deliver their desired services at the required place and time…

Even everyday waste can be serious problem. Rubbish-tips pile higher and higher each year, becoming breeding-grounds for flies, rats, and birds that spread dirt and disease wherever they go. The old gold-fields around where we authors live are still littered with unstable mine-shafts, lethal arsenic, and cyanide from gold-processing and tetanus-inducing rusty old iron. Plastics-manufacture produces deadly dioxins that last forever, and microplastics are *everywhere*.

For enterprise-architects, industrial waste isn't just Somebody Else's Problem. As a profession, we have ***a professional responsibility to minimize all waste in our industries***, and help our organizations find better and more effective uses for *all* of the products that they create, and to manage the resources-chain all the way through to final disposal or reuse of any waste.

We also need to explore the **customer-support implications** for each product. For example, appropriate use of a product may be the *customer's responsibility*; but without good advice from the supplier, they'll have no way to know whether a potential usage *is* appropriate or not. That's the *supplier's responsibility* – and it may be mandated and enforced by the respective market's regulatory-regime, too, much as for the products themselves.

For enterprise-architects, part of our role here would be to define an appropriate ***architecture for customer-support***. We need to identify all of the support services and support-products that customers might need, much as described earlier in the notes about customer-service in the section "The Complexities of Change" in Chapter 7. Typical items might include a "Getting started" guide packaged in with the product itself, an online FAQ, an online search-engine or query-engine, an in-depth manual and other usage-guides, and facilities to support in-person advice-calls. All of these would need to align well with enterprise and organizational values and product-promises.

Other issues relate to ***longer-term promises for products***, such as product-warranties, maintenance-services, availability of consumables and spare-parts, and end-of-life issues. For enterprise-architects, the challenges here would center not only around potential usages and affordances, as above, but also the overall lifecycle and future of the product, from delivery to disposal and beyond. We'll need to define support-services for each of these needs, and update the guidelines for these throughout the lifecycles and overall lifetime for each product.

Warning   Product-warranties and the like can be a thorny issue for enterprise-architects and everyone else, but above all *don't* allow anyone to hide booby-trap betrayals of promises in the small-print of the contract, the warranty or the manual. These might *seem* like they'll benefit the organization, but in practice they *will* create kurtosis-risks and anti-client issues that can be extremely expensive and potentially fatal for the organization as a whole.

There'll be more on this in Step 5, in the section "Facing Hidden Risks" in Chapter 12. For now, what you *do* need to know for certain is that playing games in the small-print is Not A Good Idea…

Services

In this section, we'll focus on the "*service*" part of the "service-product-purpose" relationships, as shown in Figure 10-18.

CHAPTER 10   STEP 3: SET OUT THE STALL

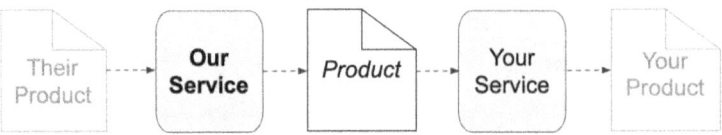

Figure 10-18. *Service, product, service – service supply*

Let's start with some quick reminders about **definitions**.

First, as before, ***a service is a cluster of activities and other elements organized to deliver some kind of identifiable value.*** The expected value created for the customer by the service would be outlined in the value-proposition, and defined in detail in the service-agreement and service-level agreement. The supplier, not the customer, will do the work of that service.

As a means to create value, ***a service would comprise any appropriate mix of assets, functions, locations, capabilities, events, and decisions.*** A service may also itself be a composite of any number of subsidiary services, nested to any appropriate depth.

A service also ***represents the promise of immediate outcomes*** for the customer, either in the present, or at some time in the future in accordance with specified conditions. For example, a flight-booking conveys a promise that the required services of the airport *will* be provided when it's time to catch that flight.

Example   The airport is primarily a "service-organization," acting as a node for transitions between land-transport and air-transport. The main services that it offers are shown on the Function-Model as the "transit" functions "Transit Land-to-Air" and "Transit Air-to-Land," and also as "Transit Air-to-Air" for transit-passengers who don't leave airport-airside, and "Transit Land-to-Land" for passengers' friends and other visitors who stay only on airport-landside.

Many of the airport's services are actually outsourced via others, such as the airlines, freight-handlers, and vendors, and also to border-staff, security-agencies, cleaning-agencies, and so on. The various additional issues that may arise in outsourcing-relationships are explored in the section "Outsourcing and Quality" further below.

Next, we need to explore the **quality-implications** for each service, such as those around "fitness for purpose" and customer-experience.

Most of these are much the same as for products: ***perceived-quality*** as the ***experience of a value***, we address this by using ***value-proposition and service-promise***, we help to define ***expected-quality***, and so on. For a flight-booking, for example, these themes would help us clarify and define the differences between "economy" and "first-class" seating and other services on the aircraft.

The issues around ***service-responsibility and service-liability*** are a bit different from those for products, because the supplier does the work, rather than the customer. There are various ***values-related concerns*** such as safety and so on, particularly whenever the other party is present or involved in the delivery of the service – as is the case with many of the airport's services, for example. Each of these has similar ***supplier-liabilities*** as we saw with product-liabilities, and would be subject to the same kind of ***regulatory-regimes*** as for products – with all of the same challenges for architects and others when services need to switch between regulatory-regimes.

Note One of the most challenging tasks for enterprise-architecture is to assist an organization in transitioning **from a product-oriented business to a service-oriented one**.

There are good business reasons why an organization would want to do this. For example, Rolls-Royce changed from selling the *product* of aircraft-engines to providing the *service* of thrust-hours and flight-cycles for aircraft, because it gave them better control and information about how their engines were used. Once Interface Inc. had perfected their processes for recycling carpet-materials, they changed their business-model from selling the *product* of carpet-tiles to selling the *service* of carpeted floors, because doing so reduced the costs of raw materials and overall waste in their business and supply-chain.

It doesn't work for everyone, though, and in certain contexts it can be *really* hard to make it work, with all manner of hidden-assumptions and unexpected issues popping up out of the woodwork. One infamous example of this came up when carmakers started to experiment with providing the service of self-driving cars. It dawned on them that if they *did* succeed in making the car fully autonomous, then it would be they, and not the "driver," who would be legally responsible for all traffic-violations, including parking-fines!

We also need to explore the **customer-support implications** for each service, such as those around service-level agreements and promise of future service.

The general support-issues are much the same as for products, although there's often less for architects to deal with there because most of the work will be done by the supplier rather than the customer. There can be some complications when the customer or other party is present or involved in the service – as may be the case with services such as house or garden maintenance or, again, as with many of the airport's services. As with products, the same kind of regulatory-regimes and regulatory issues would apply.

For enterprise-architecture, there's often an important difference here between *service-agreement* and *service-level agreement*. The **service-agreement** outlines *what* the service will do, and what the overall *expected-quality* and *expected-outcomes* would be: in essence, the inputs and outputs for the customer-facing functions of the respective service. This should be basically the same for every implementation of the service, as described earlier in the section on "The Design of Services." The **service-level agreement** extends the service-agreement to include quality-related themes such as bandwidth, capacity, speed of response, availability, uptime, mean-time-between-failure, recovery-time, and so on, relative to the *individual* implementations of the service that may need to be switched in and out under different load-conditions, failure-conditions, and others. We explored that too in the section "The Design of Services": this is where we put that work into real-world use.

The more difficult concerns relate to ***longer-term service-issues***. These are not just about longer-term availability of the service – though this can be a particular problem, sometimes with legal consequences, if the customer has built their own business around it. Other types of concerns, often more difficult, are the liability and intellectual-property issues that can arise from any potential need, such as ***escrow*** and ***service-substitution***, to support the customer when the organization is no longer able or willing to continue to provide the service.

Another key point here arises from the question "What is the lifetime of a service?" On the surface, it might seem self-evident that the service begins when the order is received, and ends when the last part of the action is completed. If so, remember what the Service-Cycle shows us, back in Figure 10-15. What we think of as "the service" actually starts when someone first thinks about the potential need for that kind of service – way back in the aspirational-assets realm of purpose, reputation, and trust. And that ending of the action is only the first part of the completions: there are three more completion-steps beyond that. The *actual* end of the overall service occurs after the last step, "completion for the enterprise," with its focus again on aspirational-type assets. The *perceived-quality and value of a service* – whether "good" or "bad" – **will last as long as people still remember it**. In short, the real lifetime of a service is *much* longer than most people seem to think it is – and will have an impact on the organization's reputation and trust for that length of time, too. We need to be aware of that fact in all of our work on service-architectures.

That's probably enough here for now. Later on, in Step 4, in the section "Service, Trust, and Responsibility" in the next chapter, we'll do a deeper dive into the underlying notion of "***being of service***" – one of the core values for the service-oriented business of the airport. In particular, that will include a focus on **responsibility as "response-ability"** and responsibility *as* service, working on the architecture with RACI responsibility-mapping and the like.

Beyond "being of service," we'll also need **an architecture of trust and reputation** – because without trust, the organization won't have any business! We'll explore that in the same section in Step 4.

Quality and Compliance

In the previous section, we identified the kinds of quality-issues that would apply to our organization's value-propositions, products, and services. In practice, though, those issues are not only outward-facing. To make those outward-facing functions work well, the same quality-issues will also ripple onward throughout *every* part of the organization and its enterprise.

Here, then, we'll explore how to connect values and suchlike into the real-world actions that are needed to support quality in all of its forms. We'll also address the additional challenges around how to keep those values and quality-concerns fully connected and maintained across supply-chains and outsourcing-relationships.

From Values to Quality

Quality of output, compliance-certifications, and the perceived-worth and reputation of the organization as a whole will all depend on the ability to connect everyday action all the way back to the respective vision and values. As enterprise-architects, we need to ensure that those **connections between values and quality** can be identified, defined, and maintained at all times.

The core methods here would be similar to those we'd used to link strategy and innovation in the section "This Goes with That" earlier. The main difference will be that it'll be driven mainly from the enterprise and organizational core values and principles, rather than from a description of new strategy or legislation. We'll also need to make extensive use of the links and gap-analyses that we've been collecting in the architecture repository, because much of the work here will be about looking for what *doesn't* yet exist.

The key point here is the distinction between ***functionality*** and ***quality***. In standard business-analysis, the requirements are split into two categories: "*functional*" versus "*non-functional*." The risk is that the latter term can be misleading, because it implies that so-called "non-functionals" have no function, and therefore don't matter – which is certainly *not* the case. While the functional-requirements describe *what needs to be done*, the non-functional requirements are about the *quality* of what is done, in all its different forms.

This brings us back to the enterprise *vision, values, constraints, success-criteria, and effectiveness-criteria* for the respective context, because it's in those that the *meaning* of "quality" is defined for that enterprise and the various players in its shared story.

Note The anchor-point for all of this is the set of values, principles, and so on that were identified back in Step 1, right at the start of the architecture-work. You may find it useful to go back and review that before starting work here.

These represent *quality-decisions* that should apply in each context, typically expressed in practice as rules, laws, regulations, standards, guidelines, and principles. (For simplicity's sake, we'll use the term "***principle***" from here on in this section as a generic label for all of those types of actionable-decisions.) We also need to note the relative ***priorities*** to apply between each of those principles, and how those priorities may vary within each context.

Every *principle* implies the need for a ***quality-system*** through which to implement it in practice. Of these, probably the best-known quality-system is the Deming and Shewhart ***"Plan, Do, Check, Act" cycle*** (PDCA) that provides part of the underlying basis for the ISO-9000 family of quality-standards. The ***After-Action Review*** that we use in the CSPAR *Review* phase aligns exactly with this, though half a step onward in each case:

- *Plan*: Precursor to "What was supposed to happen?"
- *Do*: Precursor to "What actually happened?"
- *Check*: Precursor to "What was the source of each difference?"
- *Act*: Precursor to "What can I/we learn from this, to do differently next time?"

We then need a way to embed those principles into everyday practice and everyday quality-management. For a service-oriented architecture, we can resolve this by again rotating the PDCA cycle around a bit more. This then aligns exactly with the structure of **validation-services** as described earlier:

- *Develop awareness* of the principle: Aligns to "*Act*"
- *Develop capability* to enact the principle: Aligns to "*Plan*"
- *Enact* the requirements of the principle: Aligns to "*Do*"
- *Verify compliance* to the principle: Aligns to "*Check*"

Since the values need to permeate throughout the enterprise, these pervasive validation-services need to touch *everywhere*. The core responsibility for making this happen will lie with the respective "value-evangelists," but as architects *we* are responsible for embedding appropriate support for it throughout the architecture.

Bear in mind that there can be an impossibly huge scope here. By definition, it covers *every* aspect of the entire enterprise, many times over – at least once for each core-value, in fact, and often more, where multiple distinct principles devolve from a value. It's like the Function-Model, only worse: there's no way we're going to be able to do all of this all in one go.

Instead, as with the Function-Model, we tackle it systematically, piece by piece. In fact, the easiest way to do this is to work our way down through the tiers of the Function-Model. By now, this should have been developed to a full tier-3 level everywhere; this also gives us another chance to identify all the tier-4 functions in the respective areas, and perhaps more detail than that if required.

We would usually select just one principle or set of principles to work on at a time. In turn, this also identifies the set of "value-evangelists" with whom we'd need to work. We would then build outward from there.

CHAPTER 10   STEP 3: SET OUT THE STALL

In each case, we also need to decide whether we're going to go "*broad*" or "*deep*." A "broad" view would follow the trails across all of the functions at a specific tier. A "deep" view would go all the way down from root-value to operations, starting from a single higher-tier function, and then devolve downward through its "child"-functions in the next tier, then the "children" of each of those, and so on. That choice of view is important, because we may not have enough time to do anything useful if we try to do both at once.

Caution   If the aim of the exercise is to gain a compliance-certification, such as for the ISO-14000 standards on environment, for example, or ISO-27000 standards on security, then you're almost forced to go deep. If you do that, you *can* perhaps still also cover the breadth by running assessments in parallel at the same time.

The "best" way, though, is *whatever works well in your context*. If you use the methods shown here, you'll eventually cover it all anyway, but just not all at once!

In the validation-services, the "*Enact*" part for the principle would be embedded within the work of the function itself. The other three parts – "*Build awareness,*" "*Build capability,*" and "*Verify and audit*" – would each need their own distinct functions and services. These sets of services would often be run by the same teams, though in some cases such as financial audit or regulatory compliance, the "*Verify*" parts may need to be kept separate, either by custom or by law.

To identify *how* a given principle or compliance-requirement should be promulgated throughout the enterprise, we start from an initial function at any level on the Function-Model, and then ask

- How does this principle apply in the context of this function?

- What actions need to be taken within the function to enact this principle?

- What metrics would be needed to monitor and report on the application of this principle within the function?

- What needs to be done to ensure ongoing and increasing *awareness* of the relevance and application of this principle within the development, management, and operation of this function? What business-services would be required in order to support those needs? What capabilities and competencies would be required in those business-services? With what assets, at what locations, in response to what events, and in accordance with what business-rules?

- What needs to be done to ensure ongoing and increasing *capability* to apply the principle within the development, management, and operation of this function? What business-services would be required in order to support those needs? What capabilities and competencies would be required in those business-services? With what assets, at what locations, in response to what events, and in accordance with what business-rules?

- What needs to be done to *verify* and audit the application of this principle within the development, management, and operation of this function? What business-services would be required in order to support those needs? What capabilities and competencies would be required in those business-services? With what assets, at what locations, in response to what events, and in accordance with what business-rules?

On completion of the assessment for this function, we select the next function to be assessed:

- *"Broad" assessment*: Choose the next "sibling" function at the same tier, and optionally move down a level when all functions at this tier have been assessed

- *"Deep" assessment*: Choose the first available "child" function at the next tier, and continue down the tiers until all functions on this thread have been assessed; then move back up to the starting-level and work downward again for each unassessed function.

We then loop back to ask the same set of questions with this newly-chosen function, and repeat until all functions in scope have been assessed.

We would document the results as links and dependencies in the architecture repository, together with any requirements, risks, and the like in the appropriate registers. Typical artifacts would be process-models and value-models and, in conjunction with the "value-evangelists," detailed work-instructions and requirements-tests to implement the value-principles in practice.

Next, we need to explore **interdependencies between services**, to help us assess how each quality-concern will be addressed across the enterprise as a whole.

As described earlier, we can summarize the *roles* for services in terms of four distinct categories: *delivery-services, direction-services, coordination-services,* and *validation-services*. So far, we've viewed these as if they are separate *types* of services. Yet we also need to note that, at a conceptual level, ***every service is a "delivery-service"*** that delivers some kind of value of its own.

Whatever its role might be, *every service has exactly the same structure*, with the same sets of ***relationships and interdependencies*** such as those shown in the Service-Canvas back in Figure 10-11, and in the Service-Cycle as shown in Figures 10-7 and 10-15. We can use that fact as a means to verify "service-completeness" in any part of the organization, and across the enterprise as a whole.

The simplest way to do this assessment is to go back to the Function-Model, and start the verification process from there. Note that some of the key services, such as those that provide coordination-service and validation-service support for other functions, may be represented by business-units so small that they may not be visible even at the tier-3 level of the model, so we may need to look for them explicitly in this assessment.

In many cases, the required support-services or links will in fact exist, but are not recognized as such. Instead, they may only be implied in what is done in practice, or be subsumed into "general responsibilities of line-management." The catch in such cases is that there may be no explicit means to ensure that the work required for the inter-service link is actually done.

In other cases, the links may be erratic, or absent altogether. The *symptoms* of the disconnect will usually be all too evident, but the cause may not. One common quality-management example is a confusion between "correction" – "fix it up to get the job out of the door" – versus "corrective action" – "make sure it doesn't happen again." All of the links need to be fully present and fully working before the service, and, in turn, the enterprise itself can be said to be "viable."

We apply the ***completeness-checklist*** to each function-interface and service in scope, at each tier of the Function-Model:

- *Policy*: What is the service's *purpose*? Who or what defines its *policy*? From where are these policy-services obtained?

- *Strategy*: What is the current *strategy*? In relation to what outside *relationships*? Who defines these? From where are these strategy-services obtained?

- *Manage*: How are the service's *tasks defined, managed*, and *monitored*? From where are these services obtained?

- *Verify*: What random checks or *audits* are used to *verify* performance? From where are these services obtained?

- *Coordinate*: How is the service *coordinated* with other services? From where are these coordination-services obtained?

- *Tasks*: What does the service *do*? How does it do it? How does it support its "child" delivery-services (if any)? From where are these child-services obtained?

- *Exceptions*: How does the service apply *correction* to identify, escalate, and resolve any *run-time exceptions*? From where are these escalation-services obtained?

- *Quality*: What *corrective-action* does the service undertake for *causes* of issues? From where are these services obtained?

- *Track*: How does the service *track* and manage *quality-issues* and other issues? From where are these services obtained?

- *Improve*: How does the service manage *improvement* of its *processes*? From where are these services obtained?

- How are all of these links and interdependencies identified, modeled, managed, and maintained?

That checklist above provides a minimum default set of tests to apply in each case. We may need to add further context-specific tests to that list as appropriate.

Each link should reference services that this service would consume either from other services elsewhere in the organization or broader enterprise, or from subsidiary functions and tasks within its own service-decomposition tree. In principle, every one of these linked services must exist *somewhere*; otherwise, the organization would be unable to operate – or operate well, at least.

Document any identified gaps, and resolve these gaps wherever practicable.

Note The Service-Canvas can also be used as a service-completeness checklist in a similar way. The full details on this are in Tom's book *Mapping the Enterprise*, in Appendix D.

CHAPTER 10   STEP 3: SET OUT THE STALL

Outsourcing and Quality

We now know how to track and maintain the quality-connections *within* the organization. Yet how do we do the same in **outsourced business-relationships**, in which some other organization does the work on the organization's behalf, and often in the organization's name? The same applies in **supply-chain relationships**: everyone's reputation depends not only on their own work, but on the quality from *everyone else* in the chain.

If you're involved in planning any kind of sourcing-relationship – from call-centers to cloud-computing, from cleaning to catering to conferencing, and anywhere in between – then you *need* to know about this one. This is about looking closely at the *whole* context – about interactions and interdependencies across the whole enterprise, about understanding the full implications of a customer-centric view, about maintaining consistency of service across *all* insource and outsource relationships, and so on. We'll need to use our enterprise-architecture to help identify the *hidden costs and risks* of outsourcing and to mitigate the *risks to quality, trust, and the organization's and others' reputations* that might be created in such relationships. All of these issues will also arise in customer-journey modeling, process-mapping, business-continuity planning, anticlient-risk management, and anything else that must address these types of business-relationships.

Warning   In business-politics terms, it's quite easy to frame these issues as operational concerns that are identifiably within the scope of a whole-enterprise architecture. In that sense at least, *these* issues should be reasonably safe for architects to tackle.

Note, though, there are *other* key architectural issues that can come up in outsourcing-relationships that are politically *much* less safe for architects to tackle. These include the risk of loss of knowledge or capability for innovation, or the loss of the skills-development pathway from trainee to master, as described in Chapter 7. However, these are *strategic* concerns rather than *operational* ones. They're somewhat within the scope of sustainment-architecture, but *only* at an advisory level – nothing more than that. So yes, you might find that the executives may be making a mistake in their outsourcing choices, *but that's a decision that is theirs alone to make.* Architecturally speaking, you may well be right to tell them that they're wrong – but unless they've *asked* you for that advice, it's Not A Good Idea...

As enterprise-architects, how do we carry values and related quality-management into outsourced relationships? That's the concern that we're facing here.

One of the complications is that any outsourced-service is serving two distinct shared-enterprises:

- The enterprise of *the outsourced-service itself* – for example, a security-guard would be in an enterprise revolving around safety and security.

- The enterprise of the *service-client* – for example, the airport does likewise value safety, security, and timeliness, but also friendliness, comfort, and minimal stress.

There may well be values-conflicts and priority-clashes between those two distinct enterprises. Any such conflicts must be identified in the outsourcing-arrangement, and contractual and other mechanisms put in place to manage them.

At first, this might seem straightforward: "just put it in the contract," someone might say. In practice, though, it can be a *lot* trickier than it looks:

- It's about the distinctions between *organization and enterprise*.

- It's about *responsibilities and obligations*; about *perceived boundaries* as well as legal ones.

- It's about *asset-types* and where things happen in the *Service-Cycle*.

- It's about things that we can only *influence*, rather than control through a contract.

It's also about whether we look at the issues from *inside-out versus outside-in* – which, in the Maturity-Model, places us right on the border between Steps 3 and 4, and hence why we need to tackle it at *this* point in this Step.

CHAPTER 10 STEP 3: SET OUT THE STALL

We'll start with a quick reprise on **organization versus enterprise**:

- An **enterprise** is a *social* structure, defined and bounded by vision, values, and mutual commitments
- An **organization** is a *legal* structure, defined and bounded by rules, roles, and responsibilities

The organization is a player within a shared-enterprise. In that role, it has jurisdiction within its own boundaries, and legal responsibilities both within itself and in its immediate transactions and interactions with others. In an outsourced relationship, the respective roles and responsibilities are defined in the contract.

From the organization's perspective, looking from the inside outward, its responsibilities end at its own borders: everything else is the responsibility of the outsourced provider.

However, that *isn't* how others in the broader enterprise might see it, looking inward from the outside. And *that's* where these problems can start to arise.

Probably the simplest way to describe this is in terms of **boundary of identity** versus **boundary of control**. In essence, it's a reflection of the difference between organization and enterprise, and driven by the differences between their respective themes. To put it in real-world legal terms, such as in lawsuits and the like

- The **boundary of control** is where the *organization's* lawyers, looking inside-out from the organization's perspective, believe its liabilities will end.
- The **boundary of identity** is where a *plaintiff's* lawyers, looking outside-in from the broader enterprise, believe that the organization's liabilities end.

As with organization versus enterprise, these boundaries *can* coincide. For example, that would be the case with any legal issues around what happens *inside* an organization. But in a supply-chain context, or wherever there are outsourced relationships, those two different boundaries can separate from each other. This leaves a blurry space where the organization can find itself being blamed for what *others* have done, and where, even if the organization is *contractually* in the right, its reputation and business can be destroyed without warning and without any means of recompense. From a business perspective, that latter fact alone makes this a *very* important architectural concern.

We can illustrate what's going on here with the example of the airport, as shown in Figure 10-19.

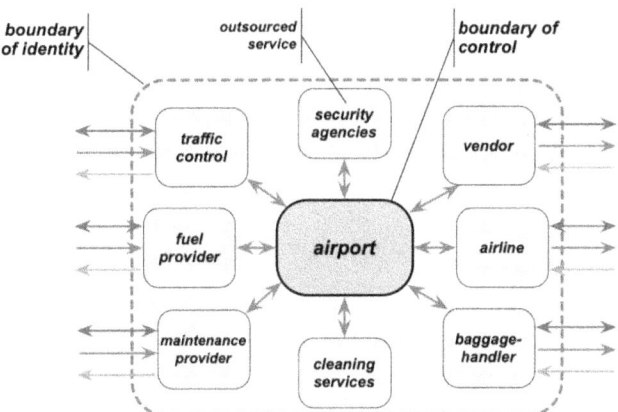

Figure 10-19. *Outsourcing – boundary of identity, boundary of control*

The airport's business-model has a lot of similarity with that of a shopping-mall. The people moving through the airport are not its own customers as such, but the customers of its *actual* customers – the airlines, and the various vendors within airport-landside and airport-airside.

Again, like a shopping-mall, the real organization behind "the airport" is quite small. Its *insourced-services* are things like facilities-management, information-management, operational safety management, and general management. All of that sits inside its boundary-of-control – the part of the context over which it has legal jurisdiction and direct legal liability.

Yet *everything else in "the airport" is outsourced* in some way: to the airlines and vendors, for most of the relationships between people and "the airport"; to direct-outsourced services such as cleaning and security; and to its providers-to-customers, such as baggage-handling, fuel-services, maintenance-services, and traffic-control. As shown in Figure 10-19, all of those outsourced-services sit in a blurry region of *perceived-responsibility* somewhere between the boundary-of-control of the airport-as-*organization* and the boundary-of-identity of the *enterprise* that is "the airport."

To apply this in your own organization's context, ask

- *Is it using your name?* If a call-center makes calls on your behalf, using your organization's name, it's inside the boundary-of-identity.

- *Does it use your signage or branding?* If a delivery-contractor has your organization's logo on their van, or a debt-agency acts on your behalf with your company's name on their letterhead, it's inside your boundary-of-identity.

- *Does it take place on your premises?* To the general public, a janitor or security-guard in your shop or your offices is within your boundary-of-identity.

- *Does it deliver a service that purports to be yours?* Your web-host service, your mail-campaign service, and your social-media response-service will all be perceived as inside your boundary-of-identity.

Whatever it is, and whoever it is that does the work, if it's inside your organization's boundary-of-identity, it's *your* organization's reputation that's on the line.

What can we do about this, as enterprise-architects?

A first step is to **understand which parts of the relationship can or cannot be covered by a contract**, and also help others to understand those distinctions. A key guide for this would be the Service-Cycle, as shown earlier in Figure 10-15, linked to the nature of the *asset-types* in play within the various stages of the cycle. Moving outward from the center-point of the cycle:

- *Real-world actions*, behaviors, and outcomes can be addressed in the contract.

- *Physical-assets* are distinct (have an identity of their own) and alienable (exclusive ownership and responsibility for the asset can be transferred), and hence can be addressed in a contract.

- *Virtual-assets* are distinct, but are non-alienable (cannot be exclusively transferred to another); they can only be covered by a contract via "physical-like" legal-constructs such as intellectual-property and non-disclosure agreements.

- Creation of the *contract* occurs during the "Conversation" stage of the cycle, when the focus is on information and other virtual-assets that underpin the Decision to proceed to the Action.

- *Relational-assets* are non-distinct (exist only between two or more other real-world entities) and non-alienable; these are typically expressed as *feelings* about and/or between the parties, and cannot feasibly be addressed by "physical-like" legal constructs; they therefore *cannot* be covered in a contract.

- *Aspirational-assets* are non-distinct (between real-world and abstract entities) and non-alienable, are typically expressed via shared-vision, shared-values, commitments, and aspirations, and *cannot* be covered in a contract.

The parts of the Service-Cycle that are essential to the outsource-relationship yet cannot be covered in a contract – in particular, the vision, values, principles, and suchlike – must be covered by other means.

Architecturally, we do this via **validation-services**, essentially the same as described earlier in the sections "The Effectiveness of Services" and "From Values to Quality," but customized for use *beyond* rather than within the organization. For example, the airport could embed into the outsource-contract appropriate requirements for "*Develop awareness*" and "*Develop capability*" services to show the outsource-service how to support its own vision and values, but it might be difficult to embed the matching "*Verify and audit*" validation-services, and probably impossible to control the "*Enact*" at run-time within the outsourced-service itself.

Looking at this from the provider's perspective, **many providers of outsourced service base their business-models on economies-of-scale**. This often means that they'll need multiple clients to make the scaling work. Implications here include

- The service-provider needs to balance all of the differing shared-enterprises of their clients.

- The staff of service-providers, and the services themselves, need to be aware of and switch appropriately between each of the respective shared-enterprises for each of the clients.

Given that different trade-offs and different values-priorities may apply in each case, this can be a very real challenge for service-providers.

Much the same applies in the opposite direction with themes such as **auditing and compliance**: the client-organization must demonstrate compliance via the service-provider, but the service-provider may need to demonstrate compliance with multiple and maybe-conflicting standards and audit-schemas.

For the client-organization, alignment with shared-enterprise is a key driver for strategy – which in turn includes themes such as sourcing-arrangements. For the service-provider, this will mean

- Aligning with and engaging with different strategies for different clients, all undergoing different dynamics, different drivers, and different rates of change

- Ensuring that there is no "blur" between clients and their strategies – and especially so where the service-clients are competitors of each other, with all the concomitant concerns around conflicts-of-interest and the like

Most consultancy-providers have had long practice at maintaining "Chinese Walls" between their service-clients. In other types of service-providers, though, the equivalent governance-mechanisms, and even the awareness of the need for them, can be much less common. For example, several cloud-service providers have already fallen foul of "leakage" between clients in not-so-secure online-systems. It needs to be understood that this is **an architectural concern that needs to be addressed at the architectural level** if it is to be appropriately managed – especially over the longer-term.

Into Practice

In the section, "This Goes with That," we explored how to connect everything together, from inside to outside and from strategy to execution, and how to respond to change across the organization and its enterprise. Using what you saw there, apply the same methods and checklists to your own organization.

- In your organization and its architecture, are you able to view *the enterprise as a whole*, or is there some arbitrary focus-theme that is deemed to be "the sole center of everything"? If the latter, what might you be able to do as an architect to counter and mitigate against that pressure? What can you do to expand the scope-awareness for the architecture?

- How would you identify and track the architecture-implications whenever *strategy drives change*? What can you do, as an architect, to ensure that all the issues arising from that strategy are appropriately addressed?

- How would you identify and track the architecture-implications in the opposite direction, when *innovation invokes strategy*? How would you find and assess the value of potential innovations, both from within the organization and beyond?

In the section "Everything's a Service," we explored more about what services are and how they work with each other. Using what you saw there, apply the same methods and checklists to your own organization.

- Do you use a service-oriented approach in your current architecture? If not, what happens when you view your architecture through that lens, in which *the structure of services* provides checklists and cross-checks for completeness? How might that view help in explaining your architecture to others, especially in business contexts such as sales and marketing?

- In your current architecture, how do you identify and model *the flows of services*? What, if anything, do you see differently from before if you use the Service-Cycle as a completeness-checklist for those interactions? How, architecturally, do you help your organization avoid business-traps such as the "quick-profit failure-cycle"?

- In your current architecture, what do you do to ensure the *effectiveness of services*, in terms of the organization's vision, values, principles, and other constraints? How do you connect each service to other services that provide their strategy, tactics, direction, and coordination, and keep it on-track to value?

- In your current architecture-work, how do you guide *the design of services*? How do you guide the transitions from abstract design to development for real-world implementations? Which types of scenarios do you need to identify and address, in order to design appropriate alternative-implementations, trade-offs, and switch-overs for those scenarios?

In the section "Serving the Enterprise," we explored the architectural issues for the organization's value-propositions and quality-promises, and the products and services that it offers to others within its broader shared-enterprise. Using what you saw there, apply the same methods and checklists to your own organization.

- In your organization's business-architecture, how do people understand and distinguish between *promise, service, and product*? How do they choose whether to present a business-offering as a service, and/or as a product? From an architectural perspective, how might you use the explorations in this section to guide the business-conversations about the implications of those choices?

- If your organization's business is oriented toward *products*, in what ways does your enterprise-architecture support that focus? How do you – or might you – use the architecture to explore and improve product-quality, fitness-for-purpose, product-liability issues, maintenance, replacements, and customer-support for products and their use?

- If your organization's business is oriented toward *services*, in what ways does your enterprise-architecture support that focus? How do you – or might you – use the architecture to explore and improve service-quality, value-concerns, service-liability and service-lifetime issues, service and service-level agreements, and customer-support for services and service-use?

In the section "Quality and Compliance," we explored how to identify and address quality-related issues, both within the organization and across outsource-relationships and supply-chains. Using what you saw there, apply the same methods and checklists to your own organization.

- How does your organization do its quality-management, connecting *from values to quality*? Which of the organizational and enterprise values are or are not recognized *as* quality-concerns? Which of those quality-concerns require formal compliance, versus everyday in-house guidance? In what ways, if any, is enterprise-architecture involved in these processes? Would those processes be improved if enterprise-architecture is involved as described in this section? If so, what improvements could be made, and how would you make that happen?

- Does your organization use and/or provide outsourced services, or is it intending to do so? If so, how would the respective concerns about *outsourcing and quality* be managed? Would those processes be improved if enterprise-architecture is involved as described in this section? If so, what improvements could be made, and how would you make that happen?

Do remember to capture into your notebook any ideas and insights that arise from exploring these questions, to include in your final review at the end of the book.

Summary

In this chapter, for Step 3 in the Maturity-Model, we learned how to identify how everything connects with everything else across the organization and enterprise, and how to describe and model the structures, flows, interdependencies, implementations, and trade-offs for services. We also explored the architectural issues relating to the organization's business-products and services, and the quality and compliance issues associated with those business-offerings.

In the next chapter, for Step 4, we'll start to see more about the organization and its business by looking at it from the opposite direction – outside-in rather than inside-out.

CHAPTER 11

Step 4: Interact with the Market

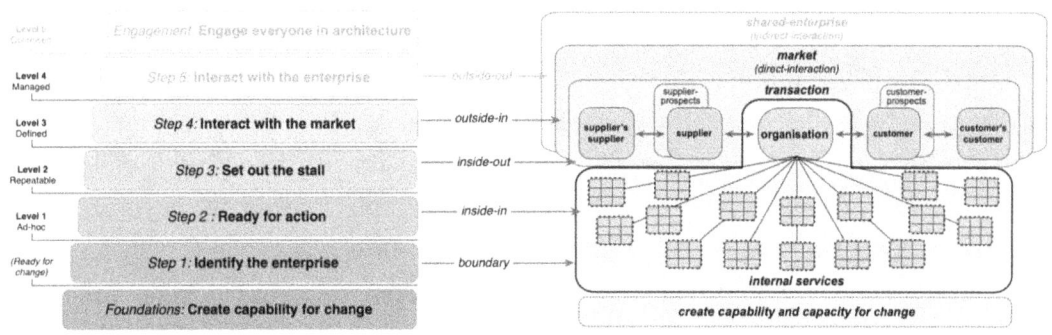

In **Step 1**, we identified the boundaries of the enterprise, and then the boundary between the organization and the enterprise – **the boundary between "inside" and "outside."** We also established the vision, values, and other criteria that would enable our organization to make effective **ad-hoc** decisions.

In **Step 2**, we looked *inside-in*, deep within the organization itself, to identify and design the infrastructures that would enable our organization to do its business in a *repeatable* way.

In **Step 3**, we turned around to look *inside-out*, from the organization to the outside world. We explored how our organization would deliver on its value-proposition to the enterprise, with **defined** products and services, with support-services behind them to help keep our organization on-track to its vision, its promise, and its criteria for success.

But here, in **Step 4**, we now find the enterprise looking *outside-in* at our organization. All those different types of people in the marketplace: potential customers and suppliers, prospects, partners, competitors, regulators, recruiters, trainers, journalists, analysts, and so many more. We've set out our stall of business-offerings, our value-propositions, promises, products, and services. But it's now up to those in the market to choose how *they* will respond to *us*. We need to be able to address this in a ***managed*** way.

Yes, we may perhaps have some *influence* over what happens here. But we're not in *control* anymore – not out here – which, if we've become too used to that comforting sense of certainty and control that we'd had during the previous work within the organization, can feel a bit scary at first...

What can we do about this?

That's what this Step is about. By this stage we already have plenty of tools, methods, and practical experience that we can use here, from the work we did in the previous Steps. This is where we'll also put into use some of the other tools that we learned during the "Step Zero" **Foundations** work: the mode-switching of Context-Adaptive Leadership, for example, and that emphasis on empathy and soft-skills that's more on the "art" side of "the art and science" of enterprise-architecture.

It also helps to remember where we are here, within the broader scheme of things. As indicated in the header-graphic at the start of this chapter, ***we may be beyond the organization here***, but ***we're still in the same shared-enterprise***. Don't worry too much: everyone here should share the same overall vision, values, principles, and success-criteria of this enterprise, and acknowledge the same legal and other constraints that apply in this space. That alone gives us a basis for shared aspirations, relationships, conversations, and commerce with any or all of those people, each in their own distinct roles within this shared story.

In terms of positioning, we're also in the realm where the CALc ***Alchemist*** mode comes to the fore, and where we're likely to find ourselves transiting often through the SCAN ***Ambiguous*** domain.

In CSPAR terms, the main focus will be on the CSPAR ***Action phase***, often moving ***bottom-up*** rather than top-down. However, we'll also need many of the tools from the CSPAR ***Scope phase***, particularly those about framing for sensemaking, and the capability to address emotion-laden "storming" in people-issues and other stakeholder-concerns.

We'll need an ***architecture for flexibility***, to address all of the complexity and variations across the market spaces in which we'll work. We'll also need to learn how to see and understand the meaning of ***quality from the customer's perspective***. For best outcomes, we would aim to build all of this around ***a sense of "being of service"*** to others and to the enterprise as a whole. All of this will also need support from an explicit ***architecture for reputation and trust***.

Once we've tackled all of that, in this Step, the architecture should be able to bring our organization to the **CMMI "managed"** level.

Caution This *isn't* the simple version of "managed" that is all that's needed to make things repeatable in a relatively certain and controllable rules-based context – which is how CMMI v2 seems to define it.

Instead, this is about the CMMI v1 version of "managed," where the organization is able to manage all of those tangled complexities, uncertainties, uniquenesses, and differences of the everyday real-world well enough to get good-enough outcomes every time.

Those two versions of "managed" are not the same, and describe different contexts: don't mix them up!

There's one more task we do need to tackle in this Step, though, and that's to start setting up services to work with the organization's ***investors and beneficiaries***. Although those issues do more properly belong in Step 5, we need to be set up and ready for them by the time we get there.

To address all of those issues above, there are five sections in this chapter:

- *Outside the box*: Learn how to work with that broader enterprise that's looking back at us from outside our box of certainties.

- *Design for flexibility*: Explore how to adapt our offerings to meet those often-ambiguous needs of the market.

- *From qualities to values*: Revisit the previous work on values and quality, but this time from an "outside-in" direction.

- *Service, trust, and responsibility*: Identify the structure, content, and responsibilities of architectural support for the organization's reputation and trust.

- *Investors and beneficiaries*: Extend Service-Canvas to model interactions and relationships with the organization's full range of investors and beneficiaries.

Once again, we'll end this chapter with a brief review of what you've learned during this Step, and how to apply it within your own organization.

CHAPTER 11   STEP 4: INTERACT WITH THE MARKET

Outside the Box

In the previous Step, the **analyst** mode was at the forefront of all of the action, working *inside* a box of our own frameworks, rules, and logic. Yet the moment we step *outside* of that box – as we must do whenever we interact with others – those rules may not hold any more. Knowing which rules to apply, and how to apply them, can be a bit of a challenge here…

We could, of course, hold on to the comforting certainty of the *analyst*-mode and demand that our rules are The Only Rules, That Everyone Else Must Obey. But it's a tactic that rarely works well out here in Reality Department – and especially not over the longer-term.

Instead, we need to switch to the **alchemist** mode, as a bridge across the often-fragile edge between the known-world of the *analyst*, and the unknown-world of the *artist*, one foot in each camp but never fully in either of them. This is a realm of **patterns** and **reframing**, of **analogy** and **metaphor** – and of "*meta-*" in the general sense, too, where things can morph into other things, or act as templates for other things, and where themes such as fractality rule the roost.

Caution   At times there can also be a lot of heat here, especially in that human sense of "storming" and the like. There's a delicate balance to maintain: you'll often have to let things simmer for a while, as need be, but also take care to not let them go so far that they actually go bang!

You'll soon discover that those "soft-skills" will be *really* important here – often much more so than your technical-skills, though you'll need those skills here as well. And you'll need to help others find their own soft-skills, too, through the architecture, through process-design, escalation-design, user-experience design, and any other suitable means that you can create.

We use the term "*alchemist*" to describe this mode, but other labels will work well too: the **sensemaker**, for example. More toward the *analyst*-side of the edge, there's the **designer**, the **engineer**, or the **tool-maker** rather than the tool-user. And over on the other side, more toward the *artist*-mode, there's another label that often also fits well here: the **magician**.

The *artist*-mode is a magician of sorts, often seeming to create something out of nothing at all, jumping from one side to another to create connections that we'd not seen before. The *alchemist*-mode's magician is a bit different from that, with a focus that's more on creating something **useful** from somewhere among that flood of ideas, insights, and experiences. And, to paraphrase Arthur C. Clarke, any sufficiently advanced magic is indistinguishable from technology. Creating a useful technology to work "*outside of the box*" is what we'll start to tackle in this section.

Inside-Out and Outside-In

We're inside the box of our organization's role, holding our organization's offers of products and services, and looking outward toward the market. In turn, the market is looking back at us, from the outside-in. Between the two, there's a gap, an edge, a *liminal space*, where everything happens.

The challenge here is that this liminal-space can often be somewhat blurry, as we saw in the previous Step with the organization's *boundary-of-identity* and *boundary-of-control*. There's all also the sheer range of people in all kinds of different roles, each with their own distinct needs and demands, as we saw earlier above: potential customers and suppliers, prospects, partners, competitors, regulators, recruiters, trainers, journalists, analysts, and so many more. On top of that, we also have to deal with all of the real-world issues around uncertainty, context, uniqueness, and more, across the overall market as a whole.

This creates all kinds of confusions about who is responsible for delivering or doing what, where, how, when, and why, which in turn can lead to all manner of conflicts and overall "storming" in various different forms. And as enterprise-architects, *we* are responsible for creating structures and their stories that would help to keep those "*everyday upsets*" down to a manageable minimum.

One way to make a start on this is to use the distinctions between **transactions** with the organization's suppliers and customers and the various other types of **direct-interactions** we have with others in the market-space. (For now, we'll leave until Step 5 most of the discussion about the *indirect-interactions* that we have with others in the broader shared-enterprise.) The key distinction here is about who gets to go first, and hence whose rules will tend to take priority:

CHAPTER 11   STEP 4: INTERACT WITH THE MARKET

- ***Transactions*** *(organization as supplier)*: The organization makes the offer, presenting its value-proposition and promise for the prospective customer to explore.

- ***Transactions*** *(organization as customer)*: The prospective supplier makes the offer, presenting its value-proposition and promise for the organization to explore.

- ***Direct-interaction*** *(organization as requester)*: The organization asks the market for engagement, advice, or information; the market may choose whether or not to reply.

- ***Direct-interaction*** *(market as requester)*: The market asks the organization for engagement, advice, or information; the organization may often have no choice but to reply.

For example, the organization would be unwise to ignore the regulators, and probably unwise to ignore journalists and the like. Problem-issues arising from further along the supply-chain or value-web, such as from supplier's-suppliers or customer's-customers, would often come via the market rather than direct through the respective supplier or customer.

Figure 11-1 provides a visual overview of those types of relationships between the organization and the others in its broader market-space.

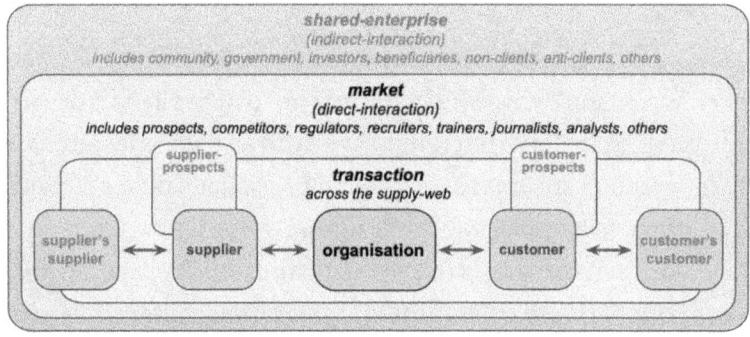

Figure 11-1. Organization and market

412

Example For the airport, its business-model occupies a literal liminal-space, at the boundary between land-transport and air-transport.

At the *transaction* level, it has relatively few direct suppliers of its own: mainly providers of power and data, and various support-services such as maintenance, security, and cleaning. Some of those service-suppliers – particularly border-control staff and the like – will come with the territory, so to speak, and the airport has no choice about that. It *can* change some of the other suppliers, though there is rarely much need to do so.

Its direct customers are the airlines and freight-shippers, and the vendors who lease sales-space within the airport-buildings. It has few opportunities to change those, because everything is constrained by the amount of physical space and the number of boarding-gates available at the airport.

Conflicts would rarely arise with any of these, and there are standard, legally-mandated procedures for doing so if the need does arise.

At the *direct-interaction* level, there will be routine interactions with recruiters, and sometimes with trainers, for changes to the airport's own staff. There'll be interactions with regulators and the like, whom the airport *cannot* ignore. Again, most of these interactions will be relatively straightforward, with standard procedures to follow in case of any conflict. Often the only problem at this level would be from journalists and the like, trying to create imaginary "conflicts" for the sake of a story.

The one *huge* source of problems is in neither of those relationships with the airport, but instead in a relationship-type that's kind of halfway between the two, in a *customer-of-customer* relationship. These people are the *passengers and other visitors*, of course. They fall over or fall ill; they miss their flights, or misplace their passports and boarding-passes; they'll lose their baggage or children or minds or hope; they get drunk in the lounge or spill hot coffee over their clothes; they fail the transit-checks and get into trouble with security; they'll get angry or frightened or collapse in tears, often without warning or reason; and they'll start a fight with *anyone*, including themselves. Trouble aplenty there, in every possible form…

These interactions are rarely about the airport as such. They're not customers of their airport itself: they're customers of the *airport's* customers, the airlines, and the vendors. But because those interactions take place within the airport's space, and because the respective responsibilities are always a bit blurry – somewhat *conveniently* blurry for some, it might seem – then it's often the airport instead that ends up wearing the blame, however unfair it may be.

Given that fact, the airport will need to take a *lot* of care over its architectures for customer-service…

Remember, though, that this is a **pattern of relationships**, about *relative* positioning for types of interactions. Those standard labels of "organization," "transaction," "market," and "enterprise" do all make sense in real-world terms if what we're labeling as "the organization" actually *is* the formal organization as a whole. Yet these labels are just arbitrary placeholders: what the pattern is *actually* about is a set of relationships of **transaction**, **direct-interaction**, and **indirect-interaction** relative to *whatever we've chosen to be* **"the service-in-focus,"** as an "organization" in its own right.

The appropriate labels for the equivalents for "organization," "transaction," "market," and "enterprise" will depend on the context. For example, Figure 11-2 shows the same pattern for an IT-department, which would commonly be called the **"IT-organization"** for a corporation or a government office. For that IT-organization, the transactions with its internal providers and users take place within its **IT-context**. Its direct-interactions with regulators and others in its metaphoric "marketplace" take place within what it calls **"the business."** For that IT-organization, its more indirect shared-enterprise interactions take place with its partners within what *the organization as a whole* would describe as **"the market."** The *organization*'s own shared-enterprise – what we've called "the enterprise" in most of these diagrams – would be one step further out, and for the most part beyond the IT-organization's own scope and remit.

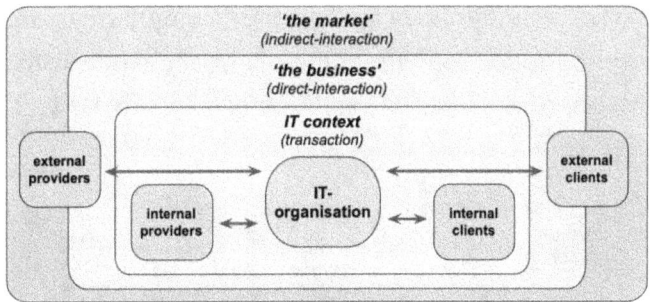

Figure 11-2. "Organization" and "market" for an IT-department

Anyway, there's plenty of space for conflict and confusion, and resolution too, in every interaction the organization might have with anyone else. As we've seen above, these can occur in its transactions, its direct-interactions, and its indirect-interactions with others further out.

From the customer's perspective, this is often referred to as the ***customer-journey***, though from the supplier's perspective it would be fair to describe it as the ***supplier-journey***. Figure 11-3 provides a visual-summary of those experiences, and the perspectives that often underly them.

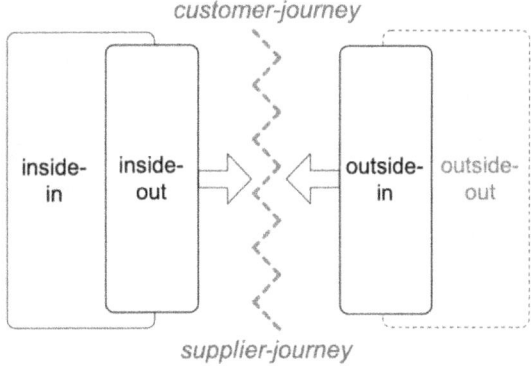

Figure 11-3. Interactions between inside-out and outside-in

It's worth remembering here that each interaction, of any kind, can also be mapped out as a Service-Cycle. As shown in Figure 11-4, the journey would traverse each of the steps in the cycle, back and forth from "enterprise"-type indirect-interaction to "market"-type direct-interaction to transaction to action, and then all the way back out again. Recursively, each of the arrows represents a kind of Service-Cycle in its own right, with an emphasis on the respective part of the context-model shown in the background, but also often with its own multitude of mini-steps. A complete customer-journey or supplier-journey can sometimes take a *very* long time, with a *lot* of steps from end to end.

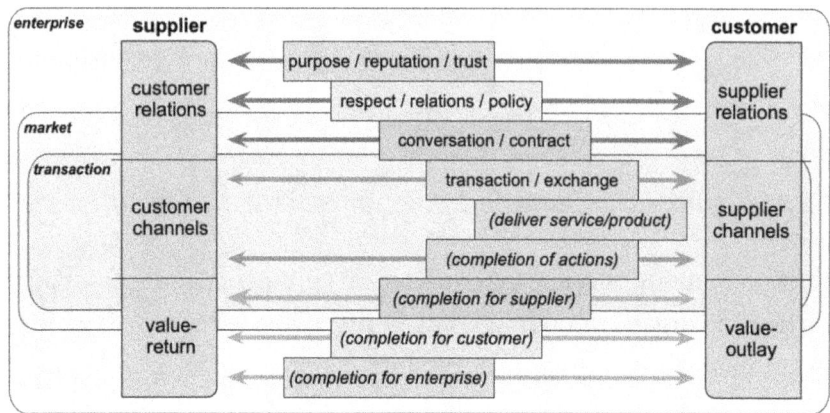

Figure 11-4. *Service-Cycle and Organization-Context layers*

Just as with the Service-Cycle, we'll also need to address the **politics** of "inside-out versus outside-in." We made a start on that issue earlier above with the note about "the key distinction here is about who gets to go first, and hence whose rules will tend to take priority." To say that this can be a fraught topic is definitely an understatement, and we need a fair bit of care about how we tackle it. Rather than rush at it, trying to address it all in one go, we'll need to take this more gently, coming back to it from time to time throughout this chapter, and particularly in the later section here on "The architecture of trust."

Note Another theme that's often a source of those politics-issues is the need to switch between multiple markets or address multiple types of needs. There's a simple tool called SCORE that can help a lot with that, as described toward the end of this section.

Do remember, though, that most business-politics arises naturally from differences in worldview or perspective – such as in this example of "inside-out" versus "outside-in." Simply being aware of the fact that this *will* arise in situations such as operating in multiple markets can help to take much of the heat out of the politics, and good soft-skills will usually take care of the rest. In most cases, the only time when this kind of politics *does* become problematic is when it gets entangled in dysfunctional power-issues and the like: there'll be more on how to tackle those problems in the next chapter, in the section "Facing Hidden Risks."

Managing Uncertainty

Sitting inside the box of our organization's defined rules, roles, and responsibilities can feel comforting and certain. But as soon as we move outside the box – or even *look* outside the box, as we do in this Step – we're thrust into a **VUCA** world: *Volatile, Uncertain, Complex, Ambiguous*. All of those spiky uncertainties shown earlier in Figure 11-3: What if our assumptions aren't right? What if things go wrong? For that matter, what should we do if things go *better* than we expected?

In short, how do we **manage the uncertainty**?

The first requirement is to acknowledge a crucial difference between "*control*" and "*manage*": we can *manage* uncertainty, but we can't *control* it. And to manage uncertainty, we first have to let go of the futile attempts to attempt to control it all.

True, there's a lot of uncertainty that we *can* control, in a "sort-of-control-ish" sense, though *only* if we can reduce that part of the overall uncertainty to a closed logic and an algorithm. For example, we can do that with "reducible-complexity," as we saw earlier in Chapter 7, or by splitting off the "tame-problem" elements from a "wild-problem," as we'll see in the next Step. But even that has limits and constraints, as we saw back in Chapter 3 with Beveridge's warning about "the hazards and limitations of reason" in the sciences and elsewhere.

To put this at its simplest, *"control" is a myth*. The blunt fact is that we *cannot* control everything with rules and algorithms and the like – not in the real-world, anyway. And that fact is not negotiable – no matter how much we might dislike it.

Note There are plenty of mathematical proofs for this, in case you're interested. For example, it's a direct corollary of Ross Ashby's "law of requisite variety", and of Kurt Gödel's "incompleteness-theorems" and other work on decision-problems. In communications-theory, perfect communication is only possible through a connector of infinite size. In chaotic systems, even the smallest variation can cause effects that ripple outward everywhere: everything affects everything else. And so on, and so on.

> Even science itself can't be controlled in a "scientific" way, as Paul Feyerabend showed in his now-classic book *Against Method*. But that kind of stuff tends to lead very quickly into "my brain hurts" territory, so we'd best not go there for now!

Unfortunately, that myth of absolute control and absolute certainty is so desirable, to so many people, that it keeps on coming back, time after time, repeating again and again throughout history. It usually starts with a good idea that does work really well in its original narrow context, and delivers really valuable improvements there. But then someone makes the mistake of thinking that it's "The Truth" that will *at last* provide absolute control everywhere. To give just a few examples:

- **Double-entry bookkeeping** works well within basic accounts-management, but *doesn't* work well when it's misapplied elsewhere as "double-entry life-keeping."

- Frederick Taylor's **"scientific management"** works well as a means to develop incremental improvement for trainee-level tasks, but *doesn't* work well if we pretend, as Taylor did, that it can eliminate all need for any skills on the shop-floor.

- Binary **rule-based IT** works well with the physical world, and with any artificially-constrained virtual-world, but *doesn't* work well with the messy complexities of the human world.

- Current **AI** often works well for decision-*support*, but *doesn't* work so well when it's misused as a substitute for human decision-*making*.

We *need* to understand and acknowledge the role and limits of "control." As in all of those examples above, rules-based methods *do* give useful outcomes in the right place. Yet even there there'll be limits, an often somewhat-blurry transition-region where trying to make rules work everywhere will no longer work. For example, an IT-based rules-engine can be set up to handle an impressive array of decision-rules, but eventually the sheer mass of exceptions-to-exceptions-to-exceptions will bring the whole thing to a grinding halt. When the rules no longer work, we need something else.

Example Several years ago, we were doing some consultancy-work with the state police-authority. At some point, we met up with the executive-board to talk with them about how the work was going. The discussion wandered back and forth across the usual wide range of topics, and eventually we came across the question of decision-making.

How do officers make their decisions out on the street, we asked. "Oh, we have a rule for everything!" they replied, laughing.

What happens when you come across some new type of incident? "We make a new rule for it, of course!". Again, much laughter.

When do you make that new rule? "Uh, after the event, I guess?" said one, eventually, with uncertainty in his voice for the first time.

If you make that new rule only *after* the event, what do you use *during* the event? No answer: just an *interesting* silence...

After a few moments, that silence led into a *really* interesting conversation about the challenges of police-practice in a world that demands absolute certainty from them, even in contexts where there's none to be had. That exploration provided the seeds for what later became the Four-Checklists set and its "checklist for chaos," as you've seen earlier in this book.

The moral of the story, though? When dealing with Reality Department, *don't* try to rely only on having "a rule for everything" – it doesn't work!

Yet even if we can't control every uncertainty through rules and the like, we *can* still manage it, by working *with* that fact of uncertainty.

"Inside the box" is where the rules do apply, or at least *can* apply; "outside the box" is where the rules may not or do not work or make sense. We can model this transition in SCAN, for example, by noting that the "boundary of effective-certainty" is also the boundary between "inside the box" and "outside the box," as shown in Figure 11-5.

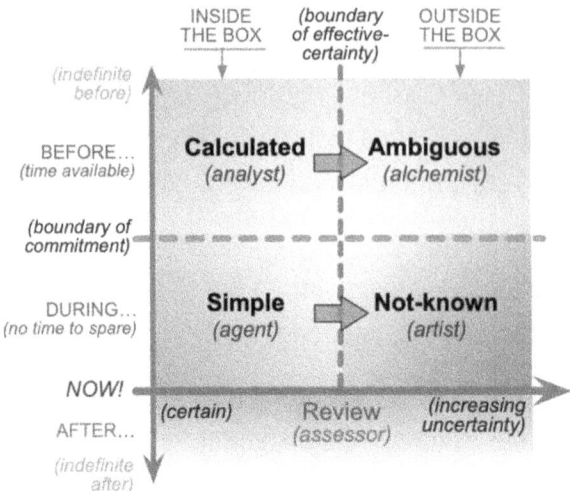

Figure 11-5. SCAN – inside the box, outside the box

In SCAN, as also shown in Figure 11-5, the type of transition from "inside" to "outside" will depend on whether or not we have time available to think. In other words, where we'll end up, and which CALc mode we'll need when we get there, will depend on whether we're still in some kind of planning stage, or deep in the action:

- *Time available*: From SCAN *Calculated* and the *analyst* mode, to *Ambiguous* and the *alchemist* mode

- *No time to spare*: From SCAN *Simple* and the *agent* mode, to *Not-known* and the *artist* mode

Just to complicate things a bit, there are actually *three* transitions along SCAN's horizontal axis that we need to note here, which we could summarize as the differences between *effective*-certainty, *expected*-certainty, and *enacted*-certainty:

- *Effective-certainty*: The level of real-world uncertainty that *can* be absorbed consistently by the system as currently defined.

- *Expected-certainty*: The level of real-world uncertainty that managers and others *expect* the system to absorb.

- *Enacted-certainty*: The level of real-world uncertainty *actually* absorbed when skill is applied alongside the current system.

The position of the *boundary of effective-certainty* depends on how adaptable the system can be. If it's tightly rule-based, the boundary will be more to the left; if it permits flexible interpretation of rules and guidelines, it can be more to the right.

The *boundary of expected-certainty* in principle *should* be in the same position as the boundary of effective-certainty. Unfortunately for almost everyone, managers and others with limited experience of real-world chaos will often place the expected certainty quite a bit further to the right than the system can achieve on its own.

The *boundary of enacted-certainty* indicates what can be achieved when, contrary to the doctrines of "scientific management" and the like, human skills *are* allowed into the picture. The relative position of that boundary can be highly variable, though, and will depend on *skill-level*, as summarized back in Chapter 7:

- *Unsupervised **trainee***: Often to the left of effective-certainty

- *Supervised **apprentice***: At or somewhat to the right of effective-certainty

- ***Journeyman***: At or somewhat to the right of expected-certainty.

- ***Master***: Often far to the right of expected-certainty

Figure 11-6 provides a visual summary of these differences.

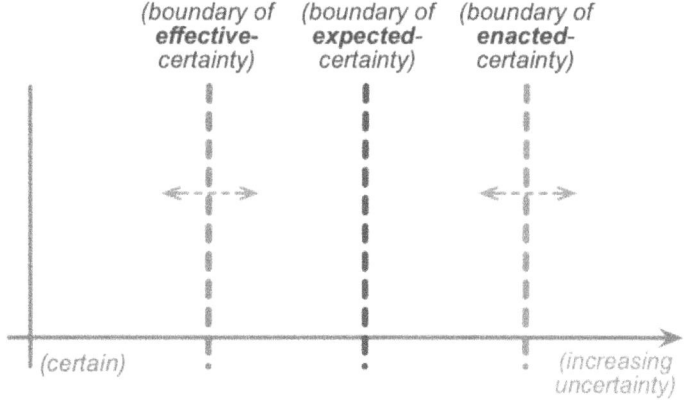

Figure 11-6. *SCAN: Expected, effective, and enacted certainty*

As we can see from the above, in some circumstances a trainee may well give *worse* performance than a machine or IT-based system. Away from the front-line, in planning and the like, that fact can lead us into the **"scientific management" trap** – the mistaken belief that skill itself is the problem, that the supposed "science" is always the answer, and that people should always be removed from the picture as soon as a better machine comes along.

The trap there is that **analytic-certainty only works "inside the box"** anywhere to the left of that boundary of effective-certainty. Trying to use automated certainty-based methods *outside* of that box will usually make things worse. The only methods that *do* work well out there will rely on **human skills** from the *artist* and *alchemist* modes: things like intuition, imagination, experience, and the ability to respond to chance, as we saw way back in Chapter 3. But in "scientific-management," those have been explicitly shut out of the story – and there's also no path available to build the skill-level anywhere beyond that of the trainee. Which means that the automation's built-in level of effective-certainty would probably be the best that anyone *can* get from that system.

The other part of the scientific-management trap is that, as noted above, *the managers' expected-certainty is usually higher than the level of effective-certainty that the system can achieve on its own*. This means that they'll always be somewhat disappointed in the system's performance, and demand *more* automation in the hope that that will make thing better. This can lead to small incremental improvements, but, by definition, still nothing that can handle any uncertainties outside of the box – and the managers' expectations will again rise beyond even those improvements too. Round and round we go...

Another related trap can arise because almost everything outside the box will depend on **probability, not certainty**. It's true that *some* parts of a probability can be very certain, such as a half-life for nuclear fission. But even if that's the case, it doesn't change the fact that *overall* it will still remain uncertain: for example, we may know the half-life for the fission to an extreme precision, but we still can't tell *which* atom will be the next one to split. Probability always remains just that: probable, or not so probable, but never certain.

The catch is that, for many people, their decisions may *depend* on some certainty, even where there's none to be had. For example, the weather-bureau may tell us that there'll probably be rain in this region this afternoon, but cannot say for certain whether that will or won't be the case at the exact time and place where the wedding is due to happen today. This uncertainty can sometimes seem too uncomfortable to bear, and tends to lead people into creating a *semblance* of absolute-certainty within a context that is *inherently* uncertain.

Note This also brings up a related challenge for enterprise-architects and others, around "***defensible uncertainty***" versus "***indefensible-certainty***." There'll be more on that in the next Step.

For example, even in business we'll often come across people who seem to think that high-probability means "will always happen" and low-probability means "will never happen." Mistaking probability for certainty in that way can be very dangerous indeed. For example, it can easily lead into *kurtosis-risk* territory, where a supposedly-tiny risk becomes magnified by repetition – there'll be more on that in the next Step. But wherever people make that mistake, things can go *very* badly wrong, *very* quickly, often seemingly without any warning at all.

Warning It can also be a fatal mistake, too. There was a story about this that we heard around here a couple of years ago. Apparently, a teacher was running an event at a school outdoor-camp, which included a game of throwing peanuts and catching them in the mouth. One student said he was allergic to peanuts, and that it wasn't safe for him to play the game. "That's ridiculous!" snapped the teacher, "That never happens!". He insisted that the boy should join in, or be punished for spoiling the fun for everyone else. The student eventually relented, and, as demanded, did catch a peanut in his mouth – but then went straight into anaphylactic shock, and died from a heart-attack just a few minutes later. *Not* fun, for anyone involved.

Issues such as peanut-allergies may be low-probability, but they can indeed be all too real, with consequences that are all too real as well. Mistaking probability for certainty? Not A Good Idea…

The same issues about managing uncertainty also apply to the "everyday unknowns" of front-line action. In SCAN terms, as shown earlier in Figure 11-5, the transition is from *Simple* and the *agent* mode to *Not-known* and the *artist* mode, but the principles involved are much the same. The catch is that out there there'll be no time to stop and think: whatever the issue may be, it must be addressed on the spot.

CHAPTER 11 STEP 4: INTERACT WITH THE MARKET

Some of these uncertainties can be resolved via real-time escalation, as we'll see later in the section "Design for Escalation." But when there's no-one else around to escalate the issue to, and the issue must be addressed right now, often the only *practical* answer is a **Four-Checklists set** as described in Chapter 7 in the section "The Uncertainties of Change": *Action-checklist* for "known-knowns," *Preventive-checklist* for "unknown-knowns," *Emergency-checklist* for "known-unknowns," and *Chaos-checklist* for "unknown-unknowns." That set of checklists for the respective task needs to be complete *and* immediately-accessible at the point of action – because if they're not, things *will* go wrong out on the front-line.

Example Out on the tarmac at the airport, a young baggage-loader is moving bags from the trolley onto the elevator, for his colleague to load into the baggage-area in the aircraft's hold. In principle it's a straightforward task, and he knows he has to do it as fast as possible because the flight is already running late.

But then he notices that that bag he's just placed on the elevator, and that is already moving up toward the hold, was very warm – hot enough to feel even through his thick work-gloves. Something feels very wrong. Yet his colleague is deep inside the hold at the moment, and there's no-one else around to give him the advice that he needs. How can he decide what to do?

This is where the Four-Checklists set for that task come into the story.

He does have a full **action-checklist**, a manual of work-instructions on how to do each type of task for his work, that he was given after his quite brief training-course. However, it's a thick binder of printed pages, and it's stored in the team-room right now because there's nowhere to put it on the tow-tractor. It's an essential reference for his normal work, of course, but it doesn't cover this specific case of a strangely-hot bag, so it wouldn't be much use here anyway.

He *does* have a **preventive-checklist** on-hand, tucked between the seats on the tow-tractor. It covers all the routine checks he needs to do in his work, such as on the tow-truck (keys, fuel, tires, horn), on the trolleys (all bags secure, not overloaded, gates latched), and out on the tarmac (correct air-gate, correct aircraft, conveyor clear and correctly positioned). Each list points back to the respective section in the *action-checklist* manual. But it doesn't cover this specific question, so again it's not much use here.

He also has an **emergency-checklist**, printed on the reverse side of the *preventive-checklist* on the tow-truck. It covers routine emergencies, such as what to do if a bag has fallen off a trolley and split open, there's been a fuel or oil-leak from the tow-tractor, or if there's been a collision with another vehicle or, worse, an aircraft. But it doesn't describe what to do with a strangely-hot bag, and he's not even sure if it *is* an emergency anyway. Hence, again, not much use here.

His *action-checklist* tells him that he has to load every bag onto the plane, as quickly as possible. But that feeling that something is wrong reminds him that the **chaos-checklist** printed on the back of his security-tag says that security and safety always take priority over everything else. Given that guiding-principle, he stops the conveyor, pulls the bag from the line, and places it off to one side on the tarmac. He then moves back to loading the rest of the baggage into the aircraft.

Moments later, the bag bursts into a ball of raging pink flame, hot enough to melt the tarmac beneath it, and destroying the whole bag in a matter of seconds. That's what a damaged lithium-battery can do. And it would have been devastating if it had done that in the depths of the hold during the flight. Yikes…

Putting the bag aside was the *wrong* decision according to the action-checklists for the expected context, but definitely the *right* decision under the real-world circumstances. That's why it's *essential* to have this layered set of checklists for each task, not just the simple rule-based work-instructions.

Skills and Leadership

This part is more about **organization-architecture**, but since that's part of enterprise-architecture anyway, and often has a lot of the same ambiguities as in the interactions with the market, it does belong here as well.

There's a crucial distinction here between **manager** and **leader**. Although some people may do both, these *are* different roles, and we do need to address them as such. They also have different relationships with "inside-the-box" versus "outside-the-box," and different relationships with skill, too – which is why we do need to address them in this section.

CHAPTER 11   STEP 4: INTERACT WITH THE MARKET

> **Caution**   The key distinction between managers and leaders is right there in the role-names as task-descriptions: **managers *manage*, leaders *lead*.** These are *fundamentally* different roles: don't mix them up!

The **manager** role is relatively new in historical terms, essentially a product of the "scientific-management" era. Its core focus is on managing resources and resource-allocation, and primarily *administrative* – hence "Master of Business Administration" as the preferred professional-qualification for managers. In terms of Context-Adaptive Leadership of change (CALc), its main emphasis is in the *analyst*-mode and the "analyst"-like aspects of the *assessor*-mode, about making and enforcing *rule-based decisions*. In that sense at least, it will tend to work mostly "inside the box."

When we compare the manager-role to the CSPAR phases, as shown in Figure 11-7, we'll see that it doesn't really belong "in" any of them at all. Instead, it's more of a **control-function**, looking on at the real-world work from the outside, to provide **oversight on use of resources**. It has three main focus-areas:

- The classic ***"The Manager,"*** in relation with the *Plan* phase, managing how resources *will be used*

- The classic *supervisor* or ***"man with a clipboard,"*** in relation with the *Action* phase, keeping a tight rein on how resources *are being used*

- The classic ***"bean-counter"*** or *inspector*, in relation with the *Review* phase, keeping track of how resources *have been used*

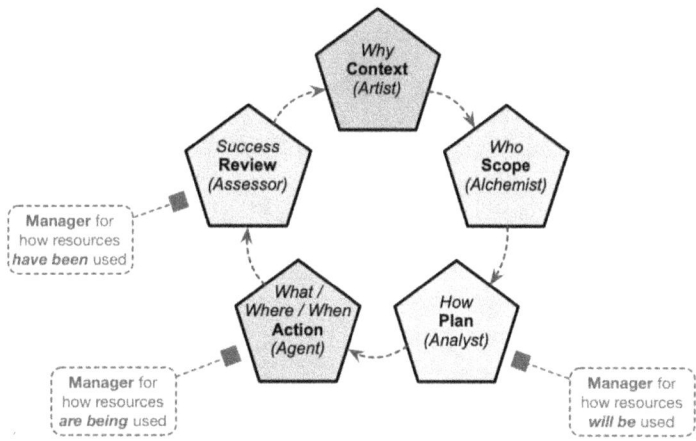

Figure 11-7. Managers and CSPAR phases

In that sense, we would *expect* the manager-roles to **tell others what to do**, but it's mainly telling them that they're "right" or "wrong" in how they're **managing the resources** – including the "resources" represented by the time, effort, skills, and experience of those others themselves.

By contrast, the **leader** type of role is not new at all – it's been around in some form or other since probably forever. Unlike the *manager*-type roles, it's more of a **quality-function**, about **guiding self and others in how to do the work** – in particular, how to do the work *better*, more *effectively*, more *connected*, more *on-purpose*.

In CSPAR terms, there would need to be specific types of leadership that work *within* each of the CSPAR phases, as shown in Figure 11-8. Each of those leadership-types would align with the matching CALc mode: *Artist, Alchemist, Analyst, Agent*, and *Assessor*.

CHAPTER 11   STEP 4: INTERACT WITH THE MARKET

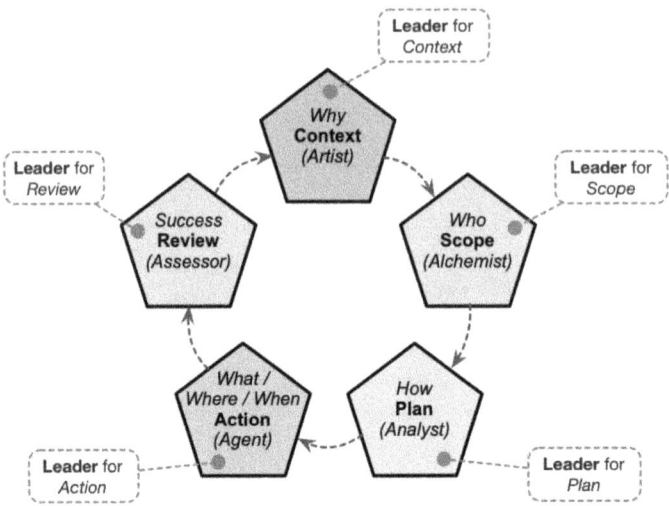

Figure 11-8. Leaders within CSPAR phases

There would need to be another, different set of leadership-types that work *between* each pair of CSPAR phases, to guide self and others through the space "outside the box" from one phase to the next. Another aspect of these roles is to know when it's time to stop working in the respective phase, and move on to the next.

Each of those leadership-types would demonstrate how to *bridge* between the matching CALc modes for the respective CSPAR phases, as shown in Figure 11-9: from *Artist* to *Alchemist*, from *Alchemist* to *Analyst*, and so on.

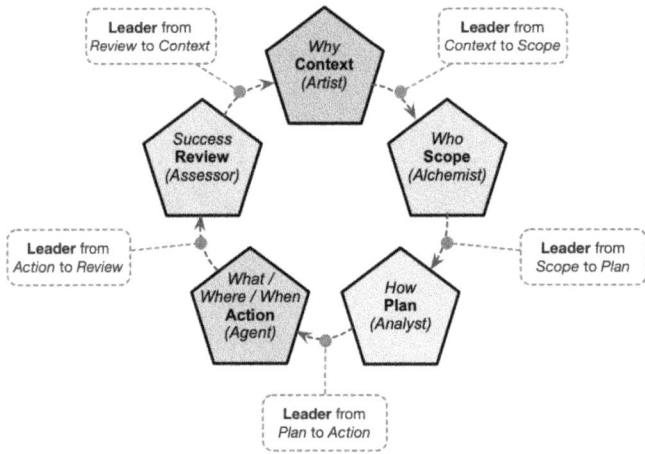

Figure 11-9. Leaders between CSPAR phases

428

And there would also need to be yet another type of leadership to "hold the center" across and between *all* of the CSPAR phases, holding everything in balance, as shown in Figure 11-10. The challenge for *this* leadership is that it demands a solid understanding of all of the other leadership roles, and also the experience and ability to switch between perspectives and between CALc modes at any time, in order to maintain that sense of the "whole-as-whole."

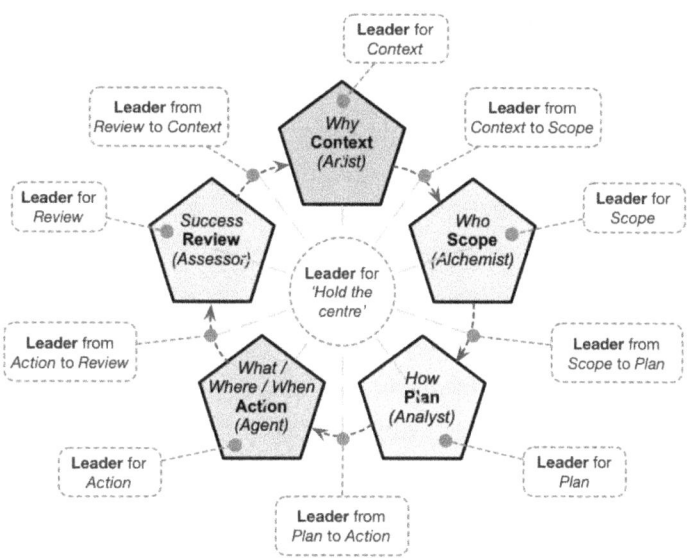

Figure 11-10. Leaders and CSPAR phases

This type of leadership is well understood in our part of the world, perhaps, as it's central to the way that architecture needs to work. Every project or team-lead will be responsible for this kind of leadership. Likewise for the CEO, both in the role as *Chief Executive Officer*, responsible for how everything works together across all of those diverse domains and departments of the organization. And there's also that *other* CEO role as *Chief Encouragement Officer*, responsible for promoting and maintaining the organization's vision, values, and overall success-criteria – "the totem-pole to unify the tribes," as one of our clients put it.

Through mentoring and the like, all of these leadership-roles should also be able to support the organization's **skills-learning pathways**, as described earlier in the section "The Uncertainties of Change" in Chapter 7. It's also not just the supposed "The Leaders" who would do this, because it's probable that *everyone* will need to take on some kind of leadership role, at some time or other, whether for others, or for themselves in self-leadership and/or self-mentorship.

CHAPTER 11   STEP 4: INTERACT WITH THE MARKET

As also mentioned in that same section, there can often be situations at run-time where we have to learn a new skill in a hurry. If there's no master available from whom we can learn that skill, we in effect have to *be* our own "master" – and in those circumstances, some kind of systematic process for self-leadership and self-mentorship will become essential. We *need* our organizational-architecture to be able support those skills-learning pathways, for every type of skill that's relevant within the organization's context.

There are a couple of other **potential traps** here that *need* to be addressed in this organizational-architecture. The first is that executives and others will often say that they want to "develop the leadership," when what they actually mean is that they want to develop new *managers* – which, as can be seen above, is not the same thing at all. If they do make this mistake, there's a risk that they won't do anything to develop any new *leaders* – which, as again can be seen above, would risk crippling the organization's ability to function, especially over the longer-term.

The other trap is the notion of "promotion to manager." If the executives and suchlike think that "manager" is the same as "leader," then it'll look like such a "promotion" would be a good thing all round. And it's no doubt well-intentioned, a real acknowledgment of the person's value to the organization. Yet *it rarely works well*. What happens, far too often, is that the organization *loses* a person who is already highly skilled in their previous domain, who probably *was* a good leader and mentor in that domain. That person is then suddenly thrust into a role whose primary function is resource-management, for which they have neither the skills, the competence, the years of training and experience, the mindset, nor, in many cases, the desire. *Everyone loses* when that happens.

To avoid those traps, the organization needs to **support better understanding of the difference between "manager" and "leader,"** and to ***find better ways to do promotion*** that *don't* involve forcing people into administrative roles for which they're not well-suited in the first place. All of this **needs to be embedded in the organizational-architecture**.

Warning   Those two traps are still frighteningly common in organizations. They often cause enormous damage for almost everyone involved, and for the organization as a whole.

However, do be aware that this one may be seen as *very* "political" – so much so that in some cases it can seem too dangerous to one's career even to suggest it as a topic to discuss. Yet although it can seem scary to challenge these mistakes, the consequences of *not* addressing them are scarier still. Avoiding this issue is Not A Good Idea…

What's the SCORE?

What's a simple frame we can use to help us make sense of issues like these, and support making decisions about what to do?

Perhaps *the* classic starter-tool for this is **SWOT**: Strengths, Weaknesses, Opportunities, Threats. It *does* align well with that distinction between inside and outside the box: Strengths and Weaknesses are issues for the organization, Opportunities and Threats mostly come from the outside. Its main limitation, though, is that we tend to end up with arbitrary lists that rarely provide any real insights on their own, or show us anything new that we didn't already know. It also often feels a bit uncomfortable to face our own supposed weaknesses or external threats – especially when these actually turn out to be neither of those things in the first place.

But we can tweak SWOT into a more useful form, as **SCORE**: *Strengths, Challenges, Options, Responses,* and *Effectiveness*. Relative to an initial concern or focus-question, these five keywords would represent

- *Strengths*: Capabilities, services, support-facilities, and assets or resources of any asset-type that are already available for us to use in this context.

- *Challenges*: Issues in this context for which we do *not* yet seem to have appropriate capabilities, services, and/or assets. (When resolved, these may become Strengths that are available for use in this or other contexts.)

- *Options*: Choices, openings, and affordances, often associated with opportunities and/or risks, that are seen to exist, or could exist, somewhere in the broader-enterprise *beyond* the organization. (Note that, as described earlier, we regard *opportunity and risk as a linked symmetric pair* that should always be addressed together: opportunity implies risk, risk implies opportunity.)

- *Responses*: How the broader-enterprise reacts or responds to what the organization does or does not do, and/or information that we want to receive or have received in response to our questions asked within the broader-enterprise.

- *Effectiveness*: Effective-criteria and/or success-criteria to use in evaluation of "better" or "worse" in relation to Strengths, Challenges, Options, and/or Responses.

As shown in Figure 11-11, we would place *Strengths* and *Challenges* over to the left side of the frame, representing "inside the box" for the respective organization. *Options* and *Responses* are over on the right side of the frame, representing "outside the box." *Effectiveness* sits at the center of the frame, acting as a bridge between "inside" and "outside," and connecting all of the domains together. We always show the initial focus-question somewhere on the frame, to provide a known reference-point to which we can return at any time.

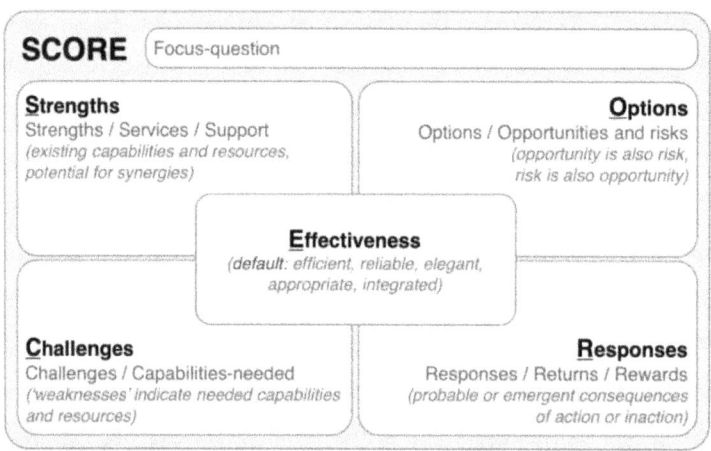

Figure 11-11. Visual-checklist for SCORE

In effect, we use the SCORE frame to **navigate our own interaction-journey** between inside-the-box, on the left, and outside-the-box, on the right.

To **start a SCORE session**, we would

- Specify an initial *focus-question* or concern, to refer back to throughout the session – for example, "What do our customers need from us?"

- Capture any other metadata that would be used later to identify the session.

- Place into the **Effectiveness** box any already-known *effectiveness-criteria*, *success-criteria*, and/or other tests that had been identified in previous phases of the work – for example, "Customers are satisfied".

We can then ***start anywhere*** on the frame. For example, the focus-question itself will often suggest the appropriate keyword to use as a start-point:

- "What's the best use for this new capability?" – start from **Strengths**
- "We want to do *this*, but we don't know how to do it" – start from **Challenges**
- "What risks might we have if we open up in that country?" – start from **Options**
- "We've had a customer-complaint" – start from **Responses**
- "How can we improve our customers' satisfaction?" – start from **Effectiveness**

Whichever start-point we choose, we then use each of the other four keywords as a checklist-item to elicit new ideas, and use the ***dynamics of interconnection*** to guide us toward new insights. For example, given the focus-question "What do our clients need from us?" and an initial effectiveness-criterion of "Customers are satisfied":

- *We start from a **Response**, a real-world complaint*: "Customers say they can't find the information they need about how to use this product."

- *Inquiry about the context of that Response brings us to a **Challenge** that we need to address*: "Our call-center staff don't know enough about how our products can and should be used."

- *When a Challenge is resolved – such as, in this case, ensuring the more experienced staff rotate through the call-center to do training and*

> *tackle real-time escalation – it can then lead to a new **Strength**:* "Our call-center staff can tackle more complex questions and issues about the use of our products."
>
> - *This new Strength becomes available to support new **Options**:* "Our more experienced call-center could now support pre-sales."
>
> - *Being able to address new Options will bring new **Responses**:* "Our new pre-sales advice-service has become very popular, and is helping to improve our conversion-rates."
>
> - *Review of that sequence adds a new criterion for **Effectiveness**:* "Complaints are respected and heard."

Remember to test everything against the *Effectiveness*-criteria, to check the relative importance and value to the organization of each new or suggested Strength, Challenge, Option, and Response.

As we go along, we add each idea, insight, or item of information to the list in respective keyword-box. We then again use the other keywords, and contents of the respective keyword-boxes, as checklists to elicit new insights and the like, and repeat the process until we have enough ideas to use elsewhere, or need to stop and do something else.

However, ***don't just make lists!*** Often the real value here is not just in the items themselves, but in the *connections* between the items that lead from one item to the next. It's often useful to *draw* those connection-lines between items in the different boxes as we go along, so that we can retrieve the meaning of that exploration more easily in a later review.

Example At the airport, the architecture-team want to explore a possible extension to the "people-friendly information-system" that they prototyped back in Step 2. (We described this in the work for the Plan layer in the section "From Architecture to Action" in Chapter 9.) This time they want to look at this for the "Transit Air-to-Air" function, from the perspective of a transit-passenger on an inbound flight. They'd like to use SCORE to help them do this.

They sketch out a SCORE frame, with the focus-question *"What can we do to help make transit easier?"*. They place the airport's "people-friendly" values of *friendliness, comfort, mutual respect,* and *a sense of service* into the Effectiveness box, and add "*keep the panic at bay!*" as an extra success-criterion there. They map out the passenger's perspective as Responses, starting with *"I don't know where to go when I arrive at the airport"* and *"I don't know how long it will take me to get to where I need to go."*

The team set out the Strengths that they have available to address the passenger's Responses. The information-displays at the airport itself already show the time and gate for each flight and, now, how long it will take them to get there. The airport's smartphone-app already has a static map with all gates marked. The passenger should know what their onward flight will be, so once they know the arrival-gate, they'll be able to see where to go, how to get there, and how long it will take.

The team see an Option that can make things easier for the passenger. The arrival-gate will be known as soon as the aircraft lands, so the app could mark this on the airport-map before the aircraft arrives at the gate. The current gates for flights departing from the airport would also be known by then. The passenger could then add their onward flight-number to the map-display, to get the directions and estimated time to go to that gate, all before they disembark from their current flight. All of this could be done from the current Strengths.

There's another Option that could make this even easier for the passenger. The airline and/or previous departure-airport should already know the passenger's next onward flight, and the passenger may also have that information elsewhere in their smartphone, such as flight-bookings and onward boarding-passes. The Challenges for the airport would be to obtain access to that information, and gain the passenger's permission to use it: but if that *is* available, it can be passed to the airport-app, to show the whole "transit air-to-air" route automatically within the app, without the passenger needing to enter the flight-number.

With that functionality available as another Strength, the team could then map out how the airport might be able to help the passenger with their *next* nightmare-scenario: what to do when their flight's running late, and they don't know if they'll make their onward connection in time…

Design for Flexibility

By now we'll have some idea and experience of how to face the world outside of the box, and the architectures that would directly address those issues.

The next task is to work on the architectures to support the run-time process-work of service-delivery and product-delivery. In particular, we'll need to focus on how to enhance the flexibility, adaptability, resilience, and overall value of service-provision.

Note This will depend on and extend the previous work on service-design and service-implementations from Step 2 and Step 3. The more work you've done there, the more value you'll be able to gain here, so you may well find it useful to revisit some of that earlier work while exploring this section.

For this one, we'll draw extensively on the cross-links in the architecture models and repository, and also from the end-to-end process models that would usually be held by the Operations teams. We'll also often need to co-opt the help of service-designers, process-managers, and process-designers, and people such as quality-management teams who have hands-on experience of dealing with the subtle, confusing complexities and chaos of real-world process-delivery.

We'll tackle this in two parts: how to design for run-time *escalations* and how to design for adaptability and *resilience* within real-world action.

Design for Escalation

In the real-world, things go wrong, and things happen that we haven't allowed for in the usual execution of a process. When we're first learning process-design, probably all we'll think about is the standard straight-through process, the "happy-path," how "things ought to go." But as we gain experience – usually the hard way! – we'll need to add many more ways to catch *exceptions*, or what we might call the "expected unexpected."

Caution In most first-level programming-languages, a classic "Hello World!" program is usually just one line of code. Yet by the time its equivalent is usable in a real application, it'll be several hundred lines at least, and in a mission-critical system, it might well have grown to several thousand.

> Designing for an uncomplicated, idealized world is easy; designing properly for the *real*-world is not trivial at all!

An exception usually calls for some kind of **escalation**, which in practice means shifting the task over to a different set of skills and competencies. Externally, it will still be the same *function*, and the same nominal business-service. But internally it will resolve the need by calling on a different *implementation* of that service, using a different *capability*, much as we saw in the section "Everything's a Service" in the previous Step.

Following on from that previous work on services, it should be evident that the escalation will need to respond and report *as if* it's the same service, even though in reality it *is* a different service behind that surface function. The escalation itself is relatively simple in terms of its place in the service-choreography – it's an "upward" or "sideways" move that should automatically return back to the original service that requested the escalation. But the reporting can be quite a bit harder, because the called service will need not only to report in its own right, but may also need to mimic the metrics for the calling service.

The complication here is that, as described in the "Everything's a Service" section, the escalation may need another *type* of implementation. For example, this would often occur when an IT-based process reaches the limits of its analytic competence, and has to hand over to a skilled human operator for guidelines or principles on how to complete the task.

One everyday example of this occurs in mail-sorting. These days, most mail is sorted by machines, many of them with very sophisticated capabilities to read and decipher even hand-written addresses. But when the machine can't cope with some horrible misspelled scrawl, it spits the letter out into a queue for manual interpretation – because humans can still handle that kind of mess better than machines can. And if the routine operator can't handle it, it gets escalated to the *real* interpretation experts at the Dead Letter Office. Given the quality – or lack of it – of many people's handwriting, it's a surprisingly small percentage of the post that ends up on the "undeliverable mail" pile: a real tribute to the way the *overall* mail-sorting service works.

Warning You will *need* appropriate escalation-mechanisms in place for each function – including a "none of the above" service like the mail-service's Dead Letter Office that has ultimate responsibility for the unexpected. If these don't exist, then things can get into a *serious* mess, very quickly indeed.

One of our government clients discovered this the hard way, when they faced a huge outcry in the press about "fundamental failures." In reality, there wasn't any real failure at all, and the ultimate cause turned out to be just a trivial data-design error – specifically, a mandatory key-field requiring date of birth in a "Person" record, but where no date could be given because the respective child hadn't been born yet. The problem was that they had no manual override to resolve that supposedly-impossible-but-actually-real possibility. Because of that, the issue just sat there for several months, quietly festering in the "Too Hard" basket. Until one day, of course, some over-eager journalist spotted it in the performance-metrics on the department's own website, and interpreted it the wrong way. The results were extremely unpleasant for the department, and *very* embarrassing for all of the respective politicians, administrators, and others.

Leave yourself with no means to do a none-of-the-above override? Not A Good Idea…

For each service in scope, we need to explore ***the needs for escalation***:

- What exceptions does the service handle within itself, without needing external escalation? How are these "in-scope" escalations recorded within the service's reporting-metrics?

- What mechanisms does the service have, to identify exceptions that are beyond its competence? To what other services, and how, does it notify this non-competence? What escalation-mechanisms does the service have, to pass these exceptions to other services? How are these "out-of-scope" escalations recorded within the service's reporting-metrics?

- What competences are required to handle these "out-of-scope" escalations? What would these require within the services that handle those escalations? How would these escalations be recorded in the called-service's reporting-metrics? Given that the called service may handle escalations from multiple calling-services, how are these distinctions recorded in the reporting-metrics?

- Via what transactions would the "out of-scope" escalation be passed to the other service? What would need to be returned to the calling service to signal successful resolution or non-resolution of the escalation? What else would need to be returned to the calling service?

- What happens if the called service itself does not have the competencies to resolve the escalation? If further escalated to another service, what needs to be done to ensure that the trail of escalations and returns is maintained intact? What audit-information is required in order to verify that some kind of closure is achieved in each case?

- What capabilities, competencies, and skillsets would be required to resolve a "none of the above" escalation in this context? Are these competencies available within the organization, or in the broader shared-enterprise? If so, how are they made available, and by what means would they be accessed? If not, or if there is no possible resolution, how is this notified to the original service-requestor?

Example For the airport, the team want to work on architecture-support for any medical emergencies that may occur anywhere within the airport's legal boundaries. They'll need to work with the airport's health-and-safety team on this.

The basic escalation-issues seem straightforward enough: identify that the issue exists, and what the issue seems to be; escalate to first-response, including first-aid as necessary; escalate to paramedics, and optionally call for assistance from medical professionals among the passengers and visitors; and then escalate to removal to hospital by ambulance or the like.

There are information-issues here: for example, people will need to know how and who to call for help, and where to find first-aid kits and portable defibrillators (AEDs) for situations where every second will count. These too are relatively straightforward, and for the most part already covered by the health-and-safety team. There may also be other options, though, such as using the airport's display-boards to help in this, in calling for assistance and showing where those people should go.

> The main complications arise from *where* the incident takes place within the airport. On airport-landside, there are no legal access-issues, and everything can proceed as with anywhere in the outside world. Anywhere else in the airport, paramedics and others would need to be able to access there, and do so *fast*. The standard processes may not be equipped to support this, so there'll need to be some means to bypass those controls without actually breaking the law.
>
> The hardest challenges will be in the boundary between airport-landside and airport-airside – particularly in the areas for the "legal-to-travel" and "safe-to-travel" checks. These areas are intentionally somewhat cramped and constrained, to keep tight control on movement there, and hence at times can also be very crowded. This would make it difficult to find the necessary space and privacy to work on a medical-incident there, especially if the patient cannot be moved safely until paramedics and ambulance-crews can arrive. The access-control issues for the latter will be harder, too, because of the tighter legal jurisdictions that apply there. And the staff operating in those areas will usually be outsourced, often by law, and may not be required to go through the airport's own onboarding-processes. The airport will need to ensure that all staff working there do at least know who and where to call for help, and find the respective equipment for initial medical response.

As usual, we would document the results as models and cross-connections in the architecture-repository, and the risks, opportunities, requirements, and so on in their respective registers. We might also need to work with process-designers and service-analysts to outline appropriate projects to address each significant set of risks and requirements.

Design for Resilience

Another aspect of service-adaptability relates to load-balancing and load-switching – which we could think of as a kind of "sideways escalation," because much the same principles are involved.

This draws directly from the trade-off analysis that we did when looking at service-design in the "Everything's a Service" section in the previous Step. There, we were aiming to identify the "best" or optimal implementation for a given set of circumstances.

Here, we do much the same, but we design with the awareness that *the circumstances themselves can change*, and often in real-time, too. What we need for this is that linked set of implementations for the respective abstract-service, and some means to switch between them at run-time as the circumstances change.

To do this, we need to go back to the abstract-service again, but this time paying as much attention to the *service-choreography* as to the services themselves. That's because it would be the choreography's responsibility to monitor the context and handle the switching between service-implementations, in order to control the actual balancing of service-load and service-switching. The service-choreography is itself a service, so we can use much the same assessment approach there as for the main services.

To make sense of *the services balancing-act*, we need to ask the following questions for *each abstract-service in scope*:

- Where does this abstract-service fit, within which end-to-end business-processes? What services drive and govern service-choreography for these business-processes?

- What implementations are available for this abstract-service? What are the trade-offs and design-decisions between them? In what ways do the required or available capabilities and competencies differ between the implementations? What is the availability of each required capability and competence within the respective business unit? In what ways would such availability act as a constraint on the viable performance-throughput and quality for each implementation?

- What are the typical conditions under which each implementation would be the optimal or preferred version? Under which conditions would the implementation be less optimal but still acceptable, and why? Under what conditions, and why, should a specific implementation *not* be used? And how would the service-choreography recognize the respective conditions and switch between implementations accordingly?

- Is it possible to run multiple instances of the implementation in parallel, to increase overall throughput? If so, in what ways would the service-choreography need to change, to manage this? What opportunities, risks, or other issues might arise from such parallel operation?

CHAPTER 11   STEP 4: INTERACT WITH THE MARKET

- Is it possible to run multiple types of implementations in parallel, to increase overall throughput? If so, in what ways would the service-choreography need to change, to manage this? What opportunities, risks, or other issues might arise from such parallel operation? What requirements would this imply for each implementation, and for the service-choreography?

- What impact would implementation-switching and parallel-operation have on the service-level agreements for the abstract service? What performance-metrics would be required to monitor and manage this?

- What impacts would implementation-switching and parallel-operation have on the end-to-end processes? For example, will switching cause bottlenecks in the process-flow on either side of the abstract-service or elsewhere in the end-to-end process? How will such whole-of-system impacts be identified, monitored, and managed?

Example   At the airport, the architecture-team are meeting up with other groups from infrastructure, safety, security, and elsewhere to do a joint lessons-learned exercise about the all-day power-outage at London's Heathrow Airport in March 2025.

At Heathrow, the power went out at about midnight, with almost no fallback. The airport would have been relatively quiet at that time, but there would still have been many passengers there, left in the dark in both a literal and metaphoric sense, with no light and no information. Within quite a short time, even the emergency-lighting went out. As the regular flood of passengers started to arrive for the early scheduled flights, somewhat before dawn, the whole place would still have been blacked-out, in both senses. And it wasn't just the airport that was affected by the outage, but the entire suburban area around it too, so all of the local cell-phone-masts were out of action as well.

Their own airport is at less direct risk of this than at Heathrow, say the infrastructure-team. It's a smaller airport here, and for electrical power they have a fallback path from main-grid to solar to solar-batteries for short-term and backup-generators to take over from there. There'd be less power available in each stage of the fallback, though. There are legal requirements, such as power for emergency-signs and emergency-lighting, but even at the worst stage there'd still be choices about what to do with whatever available power is left over from that.

The architecture-team offer to act as "voice of the customer," looking at the scenario from an "outside-in" perspective. The one constant complaint from every passenger – including themselves, on their own travels – is that whenever something goes wrong, they don't have enough or even any information to help them to decide what to do. There may be occasional announcements over loudspeakers, but nothing on the information-displays other than, at best, a long list of canceled flights all flaring in red.

This suggests three themes that the airport could usefully address. The first is that the displays would need to be kept running, even if only in low-power mode, to explain what's going on and what's being done. There'll also need to be enough power assigned to the airport's information-team to keep the displays updated.

Next, almost every passenger will want to call others to update them on the situation, or to do online-searches to look for alternative options. That would soon swamp the capacity of any cell-phone-masts that are still working and within range. This brings extra urgency to the earlier suggestion about installing smaller cell-phone-nodes throughout the airport, and keeping them powered up during any disruption or emergency.

Lastly, for now, the cell-phone-chargers already installed around the airport need to be included on the list. Passengers will need those to keep their phones charged – if only to use them as personal flashlights, as many passengers had done at Heathrow when all the lights went out.

A lot for the teams to think about already: they'll all continue the discussion later.

As before, we would document the results in the architecture-repositories and registers, and work with process-designers and service-analysts as appropriate to outline any future change-projects.

CHAPTER 11   STEP 4: INTERACT WITH THE MARKET

From Qualities to Values

The aim in this section is to verify the links between the validation-services that promote and support the enterprise values, and the quality-systems and support-services that are already in action in the operations context.

In effect, this is the bottom-up version of the top-down work on compliance and quality that we did for Step 3, in the section "Quality and Compliance" in the previous chapter. What this is really about is completing the chains of relationships for the enterprise "pervasives," and making amendments such that the chains are firmly anchored at each end.

Note   Once again, the overall scope is impossibly huge: you'll probably *never* cover all of it, let alone cover it all in one go. Instead, pick on a theme that is already important to the business – security, perhaps, or compliance to some specific new regulation – and use that as a "trawl-net" to see what comes up. *Always* link it back to a specific business concern and specific business value: for anything else, take a quick yet comprehensive note of what you've found, park the note somewhere such that you know you can find it again – such as in a "for review" section of the architecture repository. Then toss it back into the maelstrom of everyday activity, so that you can fish it out again later when the right opportunity comes around.

To make this work, we'll need to co-opt much the same grizzled crew as before, such as risk-managers, quality-managers, process-managers, and suchlike – people who work with the detail and deep realities of operational quality, security, safety, and so on.

As before, we'll draw extensively on the cross-links in the architecture repository, and on the models developed in the earlier work on compliance and quality. Other key information-sources would include operational procedures and work-instructions on quality-management and the like, and, perhaps even more, the personal experience of the operations practice-specialists.

The business-value of the work would be measured in part by the usual metrics such as customer-satisfaction and response-time, and in part also by broader impacts on overall service-quality and compliance to the enterprise vision, values, effectiveness-criteria, and other "pervasives."

Quality in Practice

So far, much of the discussion about values and qualities has been focused at the top – the problem of POSIWID and so on. Yet the place where most of the crucial quality-issues and quality-actions occur is right at the other end of the scale, down in the detail of service-delivery. There are plenty of people who already work in that space, on quality and qualities: what we need to do now is connect up with them, and create links to them and for them in our architecture.

This is the corollary to the work we did on quality in the previous Step. Here we need to explore operations-level quality-management, and use that to identify and verify the implied values and support for those values, all the way back up to the top level of each of the validation-service trees.

The simplest way to do this is a simple subtraction. If a service is not **delivering** something (a *delivery-service*), **reporting** on something or **managing** something (either as links to a *direction-service* or those services themselves), or **coordinating** something in an end-to-end process (a *coordination-service*), then it's probably about **quality** of some kind (a *validation-service* that's either managing or monitoring the quality itself, or enhancing capability to support that quality). If it's that latter case, about quality, then we need to anchor it to the respective quality-theme or "pervasive" – or identify and model the implied "pervasive" if we haven't done so already.

To **connect to quality**, we need to ask the following questions for *each activity at the operations-level* that is not directly related to service-delivery, management, or coordination of process-execution:

- What does the activity *do*? What role does it play in the operation and effectiveness of the whole?

- What is the business-value and business-purpose of the work? Who or what determines its purpose and value?

- What qualities are enacted or represented within this activity? – for example, security, safety, privacy, trust, efficiency, reliability, maintenance, waste-minimization, or any of the other "-ities" or "-ilities." In what ways and via what means does the activity weave the various qualities together?

- What formal standards, if any, does this activity implement? – for example, ITIL or COBIT for IT, Six Sigma or the ISO-9000 family for the quality of "quality in general," industry-standards such as SCOR for supply-chains or Frameworx for telecoms, or the many ISO and other standards on security, safety, environment-management, and the like. How does the activity verify its own performance against the respective standard?

- In what ways does this link to business-principles, architecture-principles, design-principles, operational principles, and so on? What other guiding-principles are implied in the existence and operation of the activity?

- Who or what does the work of supporting and enacting this quality in practice? What skills, competencies, and capabilities do they need in order to do this? If the quality-support is embedded within the functionality of a machine or IT-application, what skills, competencies, and capabilities are needed in those who create that functionality, and in those who operate it? By what means would you verify that the required skills and suchlike are not only available but applied in appropriate ways?

- In what ways does this activity itself link with the enterprise-pervasives? What validation-services – develop awareness, develop capability, enact, verify, and audit – are implied or required to support those qualities in this activity? By what business processes, if any, are the respective validation-services linked to the activity, to support and enhance the required quality? Via what means does this link back, all the way up the respective validation-services trees, to the "parent" quality in the organizational and/or enterprise values?

- Who is responsible for linking quality in practice to the respective "pervasives"? What skills, competencies, and capabilities are required for such practitioners? How is this work managed and coordinated around the practical concerns of day-to-day service-delivery?

- Are there any aspects of quality within the activity that are *not* currently recorded as enterprise-pervasives, or anchored to such pervasives? If so, what changes would this imply to the ways in which the pervasives are recorded and portrayed in the architecture-repository, and to the implementation of any or all other pervasives?

Example At the airport, the architecture-team apply this checklist to themselves, as proponents of *effectiveness* as a quality-concern.

The architecture-activity promotes and supports continual improvement and adaptation of effectiveness throughout the airport. The team also connects with others doing the same elsewhere in the broader enterprise of air-travel and air-transport.

The business-value of the work would be seen in improved effectiveness, both within individual business-functions and across the airport as a whole, particularly over the medium- to longer-term.

A core part of the task is to weave together and integrate *all* of the organizational and enterprise values and other "pervasives" for the airport, across *a*ll of the airport and into the enterprise beyond.

They support a huge array of formal standards and the authority of standards-bodies, including the international and national standards-authorities for airports and the aviation-industry – their nation's equivalents of the US Federal Aviation Administration or Australia's Civil Aviation Safety Authority. There seem as yet to be few if any formal standards for their own work in whole-enterprise architecture, though they do commit to working with others to create and support such standards.

Their work is strongly aligned with the organization's business principles and its core values for overall effectiveness and commitment to the broader enterprise of air-transport as a whole.

The architecture-team are part of a three-way "checks and balances" relationship with the strategy-team and the change-management group. Each team cross-checks the quality of the others' work, using the respective team's value-propositions as a guide.

In terms of the broader enterprise-values such as *safety*, *security*, *timeliness*, and *management of cost*, particularly in a human sense, the architecture-team refer to the organization's quality-management team for guidance, validation, and audit.

On "quality in practice," everyone in the architecture-team would consider themselves to be *personally* responsible for the quality and business-value of the work. The skills they use do vary wildly, depending on their respective business-focus, but all of them will need significant technical background and solid soft-skills. At the professional level, all of them will have had at least *some* kind of previous architecture-experience, though this too may vary wildly: many of the team have come from solution-architecture or some form of IT-oriented-architecture, of course, or from specific domain-architectures, but one was formerly a naval-architect, and another was involved in the built-environment architecture for the airport itself.

The team also suggest that the organization's additional values of "*friendliness*," "*comfort*," and "*service*" and the aim to *minimize stress* wherever possible could all usefully be extended throughout the rest of the shared-enterprise of air-travel as well.

As usual, we would document in the architecture repository any new items, interdependencies, and cross-links, together with any risks, opportunities, and other issues. If necessary, we would work with quality-managers and others to identify requirements for change-projects that might be needed to support quality-management in any of its forms.

Once again, the architect's primary role here is that of decision-support, not decision-making. All design-decisions and suchlike would be the responsibility of quality-managers and operations specialists.

Service, Trust, and Responsibility

Trust and reputation are arguably *the* most important assets for the entire organization. Without them, the organization won't be able to build or maintain relationships with others in the shared-enterprise, and hence won't be able to do business.

The same applies *within* the organization, too. If we can't trust each other to do what we say we're going to do, there's no chance that the organization will be able to work well in any effective way.

How can we tackle this, from an *architectural* perspective? We'll do this in two parts: map out an **architecture for trust and reputation** and map out the **responsibilities** associated with each entity that's tracked within the overall architecture

The Architecture of Trust

The first task here, as noted above, is that we'll need to map out **an architecture for trust and reputation**.

That might sound like it would be a lot of work. Yet the good news is that *we've already done most of the work for this*, as we'll see later below. All we need to do here is to bring the various elements together into a form that would support this need.

The one part for this that we *haven't* covered yet is **power**. We'll explore those issues in some depth in the next Step, but for now the one essential point is that **trust depends on people "playing fair," and not playing power-games**. To paraphrase that tagline from right back at the start of this book, "things work better when *people* work together, on-purpose." We saw back in Step 1 that no player in an enterprise is inherently "more important" than any other, and that either everyone wins or everyone loses. Those same principles apply to trust as well.

Warning To describe these power-issues as "somewhat political" would be, uh, just a wee bit of an understatement? At present it often seems that "politics" of any kind, within an organization or elsewhere, pretty much *is* people playing dysfunctional power-games with each other…

So yes, even at a purely architectural level, facing these issues is *not* going to be easy. And yet those power-games are a core part of what erodes and destroys the organization's trust and reputation – so we *must* find a way to face them here. Because they cause so much damage, to *everything* in the enterprise, then metaphorically hiding in a corner and refusing to face them even in an architectural sense would *definitely* be Not A Good Idea…

Anyway, on to the architecture itself.

The **purpose** of this architecture will be to ***help the organization manage its concerns around trust***:

- ***Trust*** is an assessment of *personal safety* relative to some other entity such as another person, organization, animal, idea, intent, assertion, place, or the world in general.

- ***Reputation*** is "second-hand trust," an assessment of trust that is held by and obtained from some other third-party.

- ***Trust is created*** when the *actions* or *non-actions* of the other entity *do* seem to align with the desired and/or espoused vision, values, value-propositions, and/or promises.

- ***Trust is lost*** when the *actions* or *non-actions* of the other entity *do not* seem to align with those values and the like.

Here, of course, we're mostly concerned about how *others* view the organization as *the "other entity,"* looking outside-in from their transactions, the market, and/or the broader shared-enterprise. But we may as well tackle this symmetrically, so that the organization can use the same architecture to model and assess *its own trust of others* as suppliers, customers, prospects, and so on.

Architecturally, ***trust is represented as an asset*** – specifically, a composite *virtual*, *aspirational*, and *relational* asset, such as *information or beliefs* about the *intent* of the *other party*, held by an individual and/or a collective group of some kind.

Note that, as implied by that representation via an *aspirational-type asset*, a lot of this is about ***personal perception, not objective fact***. Even if the organization does nothing wrong according to the contract or the formal rules and regulations and so on, trust will still be lost if the other party chooses not to believe that. On the other hand, some people are too over-trusting, or have expectations that are much too high, and the organization will need to find ways to gently rein them back. We *can* sort-of measure trust, through surveys and the like, and we *can* influence it via various means, but we cannot *control* it. In fact, if we *do* try to control others' trust of the organization, doing so will usually make things worse. That's what makes this architecture-work so challenging.

Given that, **how do we do this?**

CHAPTER 11 STEP 4: INTERACT WITH THE MARKET

We'll do it in a step-by-step way, sometimes bouncing back and forth between the steps, but generally following the sequence of this checklist:

- Identify the ***theme*** that the architecture-view will address – ***trust***, in this case

- Identify how trust relates with the ***enterprise and organizational "universals"*** – vision, values, constraints, success-criteria, and effectiveness-criteria, and also the organization's positioning, differentiation, value-propositions, and so on

- Use the *links in the architecture-repositories* and elsewhere to map out ***trails of impact*** for trust, from top to bottom, big-picture-intent to real-world action, and so on

- Follow the *trails of impact* for trust to identify ***potential nodes of impact*** for risks, opportunities, and other issues arising from trust-related interactions, and also any related potential impacts on outputs, performance-indicators, and outcomes

- Cross-map *the nodes for these trails* to identify ***potential intervention-points*** to mitigate risks and act on opportunities related to trust, and ***potential interventions*** to apply at those points

---

Note There'll be a lot of cross-references to other chapters in this section, so we'll keep duplication down by using only the chapter-number preceded by the title of the respective section or subsection. You can derive the Step-number from the chapter-title: references to sections in Step 1 are in Chapter 8, those for Step 2 are in Chapter 9, those for Step 3 are in Chapter 10, and those for Step 4 are in this chapter.

As above, ***trust*** is the overall theme for this architecture and its set of architecture-views.

The ***enterprise "universals"*** – its vision, values, constraints, effectiveness-criteria, success-criteria, and the like – provide the ***ultimate reference-anchor for trust***. We'll need to establish what those "universals" are, to act as that anchor's reference-point.

- How to identify those enterprise "universals": see "Enterprise As Storyworld" in Chapter 8.

CHAPTER 11 STEP 4: INTERACT WITH THE MARKET

We next need to identify the matching ***organizational "universals,"*** and how these connect with and extend those of the broader enterprise, to provide the ***organizational reference-anchor for trust***.

- How to identify the organization's "universals": see "Organization Vision and Values" in Chapter 8.

Before we look at the organization's role in the enterprise, we may first need to know more in general about *enterprise roles, relationships, mutual responsibilities*, and *governance*.

- How to identify those enterprise-roles, and map them out using the Enterprise-Context map and other tools: see "Enterprise Roles and Interactions" in Chapter 8.

For the organization, the **expectations, opportunities, and risks for trust** will depend in part on its chosen *role within the enterprise*, including its *positioning* and *differentiation*.

- How to identify the organization's role, positioning, and differentiation, and to map the relationships with the Organization-Context Map: see "Positioning the Organization" in Chapter 8.

More directly, those expectations would also depend on the organization's *mission*, describing how it intends to serve the enterprise as a whole, and on the organization's high-level *value-propositions*, about how it proposes and promises to deliver value to others in the shared-enterprise.

- How to identify the organization's mission: see "Organization Mission" in Chapter 8.
- How to identify the organization's value-propositions: see "Organization Value-Propositions" in Chapter 8.

As we go deeper into the organization, we'll often need to use *narrative-based techniques* to get at the heart of the respective issues.

- How to select and use those techniques: see "Stories of Change" in Chapter 9.

We'll need to know about the organization's *functional structure*, to provide a base on which to build traceable paths and "***trails of impact***" between the "universals" and other quality-concerns, and the real-world processes and services that deliver those functions.

- How to build a Function-Model to tier-1 and tier-2 level: see "Organization Structure" in Chapter 8.

- How to extend the Function-Model down to tier-3 and tier-4 level: see "Functions and Systems" in Chapter 9.

We'll need to be able to describe the *functional mechanisms* that the organization would use to *link the delivery-services back to the organization's values* and the like, to support values-alignment, compliance, quality-management, and service-effectiveness in real-world action.

- How to do that with the guidance-services and other design-elements in the Service-Canvas model: see "The Effective Enterprise" in Chapter 10.

Given that, we'll then need to be able to create *traceable paths* throughout the architecture, in any appropriate direction, to identify potential ***trails of impact***, and ***potential nodes*** and/or ***intervention-points*** for trust-related issues.

- How to trace from vision through role, mission, goal, plan, and activity to outcome: see "Organization and Enterprise" in Chapter 8.

- How to trace from intent to action: see "From Architecture to Action" in Chapter 9.

- How to trace from value-propositions to actions and outcomes: see "Promise, Service, and Product" in Chapter 10.

- How to use the Service-Cycle to identify traceable paths for individual interactions: see "Promise, Service, and Product" in Chapter 10.

- How to trace from value to delivered-quality: see "From Values to Quality" in Chapter 10.

- How to trace in the reverse direction from quality to value: see "From Qualities to Values" earlier in this chapter.

- How to trace across outsourcing and supply-chain relationships: see "Outsourcing and Quality" in Chapter 10.

To **make sense of trust-issues**, and identify **potential interventions** at those intervention-points identified above, we'll also need many of the methods that we've explored elsewhere in this chapter

- How to identify interaction-types and interaction-journeys: see "Inside-Out and Outside-In" above.

- How to make sense of uncertainty and the risks of mistaking probability for certainty, and to connect and compare expected-certainty and enacted-certainty: see "Managing Uncertainty" above.

- How to use SCORE to map out appropriate responses to trust-concerns: see "What's the SCORE?" above.

- How to design for escalations and resilience in relation to trust-concerns: see "Design for Flexibility" above.

- How to identify and trace paths of responsibility and their relationship with trust: see "The Responsibilities of Service" below.

- How to identify and address trust-issues in the organization's investor/beneficiary-relationships: see "Investors and Beneficiaries" further below.

There'll be more on trust-related issues in the next Step, but for now that's probably enough on which to make a useful start.

But yes, this part of the architecture can be hard – and the higher we go in the organization, the harder it often gets. It can sometimes be surprisingly difficult to get executives to even *begin* to understand what these issues actually *are*, or why they're so important to the organization's business – let alone why we need to take action at the architectural level first, as described above, before we try to do anything else. Yet no matter how hard it might feel at times, we have to do whatever we can to make this work – because without it, the entire enterprise would be put at risk.

Example   Some years back, we were called by the change-management group for that nation's subsidiary of a large multinational bank. They were facing a huge trust-related issue, they said: ***the bank's reputation had plummeted*** in just six months, from the most respected bank in the region, to the least respected and most hated. The executive didn't know what to do about it, and were quietly asking for help. Oh, and we would only have two days at most to do everything. O-kay…

We knew we'd need to take an ***architectural approach*** to this, but we also knew that we couldn't describe it as such. We'd learned the hard way that most executives only want the pain-point fixed, and have no real interest in how to get there.

On the first morning, we met with the executive group – some 30 people, overall – and sat down to ***explore the issues***. The trust problems had grown so bad, they said, that some staff were apparently telling their friends and neighbors that they no longer worked there; otherwise, they themselves would face all the anger and hatred about the bank.

But ***what had caused this?*** The start-point had been a new edict from the parent-bank's international headquarters that *"The only metric that matters is shareholder-value,"* and a demand that everything from now on *must* support that as the only aim. The bank had rushed to comply, but fell into some obvious quick-profit traps such as pushing out new credit-cards everywhere, telling everyone that it was "free money," but somehow failing to warn them about the exorbitant interest-rates that would apply to any remaining debt. Not A Good Idea…

Architecturally, this would have been an issue at a Step 4 or even Step 5 level in the Maturity-Model sense, to tackle the problem at its roots. But the ultimate cause for the entire mess was that edict from headquarters, that no-one would dare to question or challenge. We then discovered that the bank ***had never done any of the Step 1 work*** that would be needed to support any solution to the trust-issues. Our best option, then, would be to start all the way back there.

In the afternoon, we started out with some simple exercises to ***explore the practical difference between organization and enterprise***, about rules and responsibilities versus values and commitments, and the connections between vision, role, mission, and goal. We followed this with another exercise to help them experience **how and why an organization will need different mindsets and perspectives**, and why it's essential to keep those perspectives in balance with each other at all times.

We then moved on to "**get everyone on the same page**" in a literal sense, by building a basic **Function-Model** for the organization as a whole, and show how this could increase trust, respect, and communication across the organization and beyond. We based this loosely on the Service-Canvas, and adapted it as we went along to match their own organization's "inside-in" structure.

Everyone put their own photographs on the model, to show a **personal connection with their business-functions** that they worked in. For many of them, this was the first time they'd been able to see what their colleagues actually did, and how they helped each other to drive the organization's business. There were some good conversations going on between them as they left for the day.

The following morning, our colleague ran an **information-finding session** in a theater, with several hundred front-line and support-staff in attendance. From this we gathered up enough comment-filled flipchart-sheets to cover the entire wall of the executive conference-room, which we duly set up for the executives' afternoon session. The faces of some of the executives turned visibly pale as they at last began to grasp the enormity of **the real problems they faced**, in contrast to the sanitized, over-simplified view that was all that they'd previously seen at their own headquarters.

We talked about that for a while, and then gently introduced the role of an **enterprise-vision**, as a common theme that links everyone in the overall shared-enterprise to increase **trust, respect, and communication** within and *beyond* the organization. Their vision would act as the ultimate anchor for everything that the organization is and does, and upon which their trust and reputation would ultimately depend.

They understood the concept well enough, but had a lot more trouble with the practice. Yet after about an hour of false-starts and flailing around with mission-statements and marketing-slogans, they did eventually arrive at something that would well work enough as a vision: **"better financial futures**." Yes, it's not great: it could have done with at least another half-hour's work to get it into a better form. But we were fast running out of time by then, and we had to make do with what we had.

We showed how the **vision-statement would act as a shared anchor for trust**, and would make sense to every stakeholder. For example, *credit-clients* would want better financial futures for themselves and their families; *business-clients* would want better financial futures for their business; *government* would want better financial futures for its citizens and the country as a whole; and the *bank*, of course, would want better financial futures for itself. Even the bank's many *anti-clients* would agree with it, though they would want the bank to *prove* that it would indeed hold itself to that test.

We then had just enough time to show how that **vision-phrase** "better financial futures" would be used as a core reference-anchor not only to resolve the trust-issues, but also for any subsequent work on *organizational-development*, *market-development*, *community-relations*, *internal architectures*, and more.

They then left for the drinks-party that was the start-point for their main strategic retreat: and that was the end of our part of the task. Although we didn't hear any more from those executives, we *did* hear next day from the change-management group, who were, of course, our *actual* clients there. They were *very* happy, they said: the Function-Model and the vision-statement had been used as the centerpieces throughout those subsequent strategy-sessions, which were, they told us, the first such sessions where the executives *actually* understood what a strategy *was*, and what it needed to achieve. And, from there, to build **a strategy and plan to tackle their problems with trust**.

So yes, this was definitely a successful demonstration of the real power and value of whole-enterprise architectures, in addressing trust-related issues and more.

The Responsibilities of Service

For this section we need to take another slight twist on "service," and review it in human terms as the concept of "*being of service*" to others. This notion is so old that it may seem positively archaic to some, but it actually goes right to the root of "enterprise." If the enterprise is "a group of people coordinating their efforts toward a common mission," then the coordination itself would take place through bonds of mutual service, mutual commitment, and mutual responsibility.

If everything in the enterprise is a service, then not only are all of those services linked together via mutual responsibilities, but each of the assets, functions, locations, capabilities, events, decisions, and composites that underpin them implies a responsibility. What this means in practice is that *someone* should be responsible for each and every entity in the architecture framework: a personal commitment of *personal responsibility* to and with that entity, on behalf of the shared enterprise.

Caution   These commitments are *aspirational assets* – in effect, a declaration by someone that they "belong" to that entity, and hence, via that commitment, also "belong" to the shared enterprise, as "that which is greater than self."

For most architectural purposes, that kind of detail might seem too arcane to be of much concern. Where this *does* start to matter, though, is that responsibility, especially in its literal form as ***"response-ability,"*** is closely coupled with "ability to do work" in any functional sense. When morale is damaged, for example, the aspirational-asset bonds are weakened, the "response-ability" is weakened in turn, and the overall ability to do anything can go down like a brick. If that happens, then critical components may be mislaid, critical activities are not done well or done at all, and problems proliferate throughout the enterprise. Conversely, when morale is enhanced, "response-ability" rises with it – and with that, in turn, the effectiveness of the enterprise. Responsibility *matters*!

Responsibility is the key to the viability, agility, and effectiveness of the enterprise. We explored some of this earlier in Step 1, in the section "Enterprise Roles and Interactions" in Chapter 8. In effect, we need a **RACI matrix** for *each* entity in the architecture:

- *Responsible* or *"accountable"*: The business-owner of the entity. (There should be exactly one person – not just role, but a real person – with this assignment for each entity, at all times.)

- *Assists*: Active stakeholder – those who assist the responsible person in the overall usage or application of the entity (active engagement).

- *Consulted*: Committed stakeholder – those whose opinions may be sought concerning the entity (two-way communication).

- *Informed*: Passive stakeholder – those who need to be kept up-to-date on changes concerning the entity (one-way communication).

Each person referenced in the RACI matrix is a *stakeholder* in the entity – which means that each link will also point to people who will need to be consulted, and at the least informed, about any changes to the entity. Hence in addition to identifying mutual cross-dependencies, as a map of mutual responsibilities across the entire enterprise, this also provides us with the list of stakeholders that we need for architecture-governance or project-governance each time we reference the entity in an architecture-related project.

Note In principle this would mean literally every cross-link of mutual responsibility in the entire enterprise, changing continually at every level of the enterprise from abstract ideals to the moment-by-moment detail of real-time operations. In other words, this is another of these assessment-tasks that's impossibly huge: as enterprise-architects, there's no way we could do it all, and it would be hopelessly out of date even if we did. At first glance, it might seem kind of pointless… and yet we *need* that information.

To get anywhere useful, as architects, we'd need to partition a set of priorities – for which one key source will be the previous work on alternative service-implementations in Step 2 and Step 3. Another approach is to embed the requisite information-gathering within any other architectural work going on at the time – any kind of assessment, right back to reviews of any of the work in the previous steps. If we architects make a habit of collecting the information as we go along, then in time it'll seem as if it collects itself.

But with a serious bit of sideways thinking, we architects wouldn't need to do the information-gathering. Instead, in classic programming terminology, we should include it "by reference," not "by value." It's not really within our remit to do this work, and other people are already doing much of it anyway, in rosters, in team-assignments, and in the myriad of HR detail. It's actually the human analog of a CMDB (Configuration Management Database) that's used to track configurations for software and physical equipment. In that sense, if we can find a way to link in to the respective information-sources – ideally in real-time, as with a typical CMDB – then our responsibility-maps would update themselves.

Either way, as architects we *do* need those "response-ability" maps, especially in the high-priority areas of the architecture. Whichever way round we do it, whether by asking ourselves, asking others, or building some kind of automated self-update, the nominal questions that would be needed are summarized in the lists below.

We need to do this ***responsibility-mapping*** for each entity in scope:

- Who is *responsible* for the entity? – the "responsible owner" who has personal accountability for the appropriate use and application of the entity in its service to the enterprise? If no-one is directly responsible for the entity, is there an implied responsibility, such as by role? If no-one appears to be responsible for the entity, what impact does this have on the effective use or application of the entity in the enterprise?

- In what ways do these "responsible owner" accountabilities intersect with those for equivalent entities in other architecture-layers? – for example, operations responsibility versus those of a scheduler, line-manager, developer, business-unit manager, executive? In what ways do "owner"-responsibilities for a single composite-entity intersect with "owner"-responsibilities for collective sets of the underlying primitives or composites? – for example, responsibility for a specific business-process in which an IT-system is used versus responsibility for all of that type of IT-systems? Given that all of these represent distinct "owner"-responsibilities for what is in effect the same real-world entity, how are the relations between these "owners" managed and resolved?

- Who or what *assists* the "responsible owner" in the use and application of the entity in the aims of the enterprise? In what form is this assistance provided? – for example, in person, by machines, within IT-systems? How and in what ways are these "assists"-responsibilities shared across the enterprise?

- Who needs to be *consulted* on any changes to the entity, or to its use or application in the enterprise? For what reasons do they need to be consulted rather than merely informed? For which changes or uses, and at what timescales? What responsibilities does "consulted" imply and entail in each case?

- Who needs to be *informed* on any changes to the entity, or to its use or application in the enterprise? For what reasons do they need to be informed about such changes? For which changes or uses, and at what timescales? For what reasons should they only be informed rather than actively consulted? What responsibilities does this imply and entail in each case?

- Who needs to be consulted or informed *implicitly* about the entity – for example, in aggregate reports, or as a collective or composite with other entities? For what reasons do they need this relationship with the entity? For which changes or uses, and at what timescales? What responsibilities does this indirect relationship imply and entail in each case?

- Who should *not* be consulted or informed about changes to the entity? For what reasons? – for example, out of scope, or risk of "information-overload"? What *absence* of responsibilities is implied in each case? In what ways does this absence of responsibilities serve the enterprise?

- In what ways, for what reasons, and at what timescales, are each of these responsibilities transferred from person to person? What mechanisms and processes exist to ensure that these transfers do take place? What mechanisms and processes exist to record, monitor, and audit each responsibility and transfer of responsibility?

- Is each person *aware* of the respective responsibility? – for example, is it listed in the duties of a role, but without adequate description of what the responsibilities entail?

- What mechanisms and processes exist to ensure that the respective responsibilities are carried out effectively, in service to the enterprise? In what ways is the effectiveness of the responsibility monitored, measured, and verified?

- In what ways does each of these personal responsibilities represent a service in person to the enterprise?

Caution Do be careful about how you ask these questions! Most of them can have personal overtones, and in the wrong context could be taken as an insult, or even as a threat.

If in doubt, present the more "personal"-seeming questions as something for people to ask *themselves*, rather than as information you're aiming to collect from others.

As usual, we would document the results as attributes for or links between the respective entities in the architecture repository, either by reference or by value. We'll also need to record any related requirements, risks, opportunities, or issues in the respective registers, and, if, appropriate, notify the identified stakeholders for those items about those changes.

For each entity in scope, assess the ***capabilities*** required to support the specified responsibility:

- What capabilities, competencies, and skillsets are required either *as* the entity, *within* the entity, or to *use* or *apply* the entity within the enterprise? In what ways does the capability provide "response-ability" to support or underlie the "owner"-responsibilities and other responsibilities for the entity?

- If required capabilities, competencies, or skillsets are not available to the enterprise in relation to the entity, what would need to be done to obtain or develop them?

- What mechanisms and processes exist to ensure that the respective responsibilities are assigned appropriately? – for example, that each person has the appropriate capability and "response-ability" for the tasks? How and in what ways would changes in that "response-ability" be monitored, and responsibilities re-assigned?

- In what ways are the capabilities and responsibilities "of service" to the enterprise? In what ways does the perspective shift by viewing them *as* services to the enterprise? What are the consequences and implications of that shift in perspective?

As above, we would document the results as attributes for or links to the respective entities in the architecture repository, either by reference or by value. We might also need to advise others of any requirements, risks, opportunities, and issues that we'd identified in this process.

Investors and Beneficiaries

Before we move on to the next Step, we'll need to make a start on our architectures for the organization's relationships with its ***investors*** and ***beneficiaries***, and the issues that can arise with them.

At first glance, this might seem really straightforward. From many people's perspective, it'll probably seem that it's only about shareholders or stockholders, about getting money from them, or sending money to them as dividends and the like. Every commercial corporation would already have an "investor relations" section on their website, and they'll also have a small "investor-relations" department somewhere near the top floor of the headquarters-building. As enterprise-architects, the rest of this is none of our business. That's it, job done.

Unfortunately, it isn't as simple as that. Nothing *like* that simple…

To give an everyday example, your country's tax-authority may refer to you as a *customer*. But if you try to model it as a straightforward customer-relationship, you'll soon discover that there's no way to make it make sense that way. After all, you don't have any choice about being in that business-relationship with them, and you're not buying any products or services from them. It's just money going out into some kind of imaginary black hole or bottomless pit, after which nothing seems to come back, other than further demands and occasional threats.

So no, you're not a *customer* of the tax-authority – not in any normal sense, at least. But what *is* the relationship there?

The answer is that, as a taxpayer, you're an *investor* who's providing a *financial investment* in the workings of the country as a whole. And you're also a *beneficiary* of the country's tax-system, receiving benefits that maybe *won't* be in monetary form, but instead as the use of state-funded roads and bridges, state forests and parks,

CHAPTER 11   STEP 4: INTERACT WITH THE MARKET

emergency-services, regulation of imports, quality-standards, border-control, national-security and defense, and so on. *Everyone* who pays tax is an investor in the country, and also a beneficiary of that country – or *should* be a beneficiary in some way, anyway.

But if these investor and beneficiary relationships are not the same as those for customers or suppliers, where would we place them on the "holomap" or Organization-Context Map? Are they part of the market? – they don't seem to fit there either...

They do have *some* transaction-like interactions with the organization, and *some* interactions that are sort-of direct, as in the market. But most of their interactions are more *indirect*, as in the example of taxpayers receiving benefits such as the use of state-funded roads and bridges, and safety-regulations and the like. This indicates that where they *do* fit best is further out, at the *shared-enterprise* level, as shown in Figure 11-12.

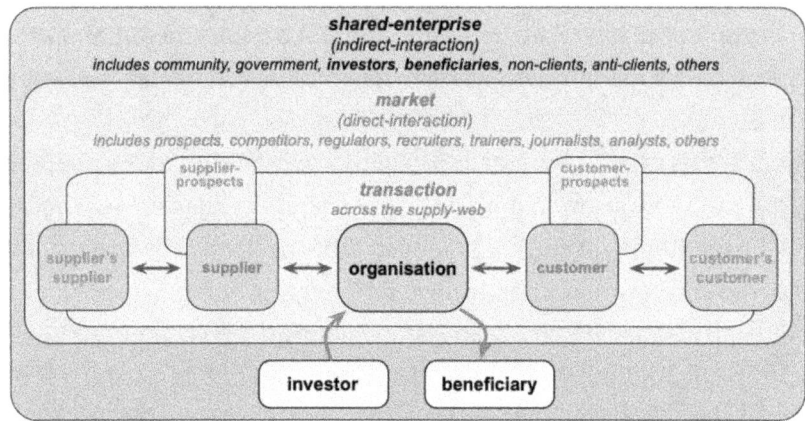

Figure 11-12. *Organization, investor, and beneficiary*

The first catch here, though, is that those labels within that diagram represent **relationship-roles** *relative to the organization*. In that sense, the roles are not fixed, but contextual: those other people and organizations may take on different roles at different times, relative to the organization, depending on the need at that time. For example:

- A ***business-partner*** will be both supplier and customer.

- A ***customer-prospect*** out in the market may become a transaction-customer, and then moves back out into the overall market again once the transaction is complete.

- A ***non-client*** in another country may become a prospect if the organization expands its business out to that market, and vice-versa if the organization withdraws from that market.

- Every ***employee and staff-member*** of the organization is a supplier of services to that organization, a potential customer of the organization, a member of the overall recruitment-pool in the organization's broader market, and lives in a community as a citizen of a government-context within the overall enterprise-space in which the organization operates.

For our purposes here, though, the essential point is this:

- By definition, ***everyone within the overall scope of the shared-enterprise*** will at least have *some* form of investor and/or beneficiary relationship with the organization, either direct and/or indirect.

The other catch is that there can be many different types of investment into and benefit from an organization or service, often with their own distinct form and mix of asset-types. To complicate things even further, the investors and beneficiaries in each case are not necessarily the same people.

It turns out, in fact, that that classic shareholder relationship is almost the *only* straightforward investor/beneficiary pattern that would apply here: they invest money, expect money in return, and it's the same people on both sides of the equation. The other relationship-patterns are often much more complex, and some can be *very* complex indeed, with all manner of embedded hidden booby-traps that may explode on us if we're not careful. To give just a few examples:

- Every ***customer*** who pays more than cost-price for a product is a *financial-investor* in the organization, expecting *non-financial returns* such as quality of product, availability of future repair and maintenance, a continuing relationship with the organization, and perhaps kudos and social-cred for being seen in public with a premium product.

- Every ***supplier*** who offers a monetary discount is a *financial investor* in the customer, perhaps looking for *financial-returns* from future business, but also *non-financial returns* such as reputation, trust, and good reviews on social-media.

- Every ***employee*** invests their commitment, their expertise, and a significant chunk of their life in the organization in the expectation of monetary payment *and* other non-financial benefits such as a safe working environment, training, professional experience and professional reputation, vacation-time, and a sane work-life balance.

- The ***families of employees*** invest their trust in the organization to treat their employees and others fairly, and to support a stable and comfortable-enough life for the family *as* a family.

- The ***local-government authorities*** in the regions where the organization operates will invest a variety of different forms of support, such as roads, infrastructure, planning, grants, and tax-rebates, in the hope of benefits such as jobs and contracts that will support the local economy and communities, and also to not pollute (in any sense of the term) the environment and suchlike in which their communities live.

- The ***national government*** provide investments such as support for national and international trade, national-scale infrastructure, and government contracts, in expectation of social and other benefits such as jobs for taxpayers, good tax-returns from the organization itself, and the organization's behavior as a "good citizen."

- The ***overall enterprise-community*** invests in and is the final arbiter of the organization's "social license to operate."

We *need* to know about all of these different types of interactions, and how to use the architecture to map out appropriate ways for the organization to address them. We already have a basic template for this in that standard structure to manage interactions with financial-investors:

- Acknowledgment that these people *are* investors in the organization

- Acknowledgment that there would need to be appropriate benefits in response to that investment

- Indicate those acknowledgments in public form in places such as the organization's Annual Report and website

- Operate some means to establish and maintain relations with all the various types of investors and beneficiaries

- Operate some means to receive the respective investments and provide appropriate benefits

- Operate some means to manage an appropriate balance between all the different types of investors, beneficiaries, investments, and benefits

- Maintain some means to address any conflicts between the organization, investors, and beneficiaries, such as with ombudsman and arbitration services

Most organizations will already cover *some* aspects of this, though those are often scattered around in almost random fashion across different parts of the organization, and rarely connected together in any systematic, consistent, joined-up way. For example, most larger organizations will have some kind of "**Public Relations**" unit, but few as yet would understand that, for any types of investors who have been parked into a *"none-of-the-above" category*, this is actually *their **investor-relations function***.

Caution As enterprise-architects, the *politics* of these issues will often be challenging, but we *must* take them seriously, and make sure that everyone else in the organization treats them seriously too.

There are *huge* problems that can arise for the organization if the various types and transforms of investments and benefits are not properly understood, or the balance between investors and beneficiaries is not appropriately maintained. At a minimum, it's essential for everyone to be aware that, if not treated with appropriate respect, **any or all of those people out in the shared-enterprise space** may at any moment become **a stakeholder with a sharp-pointed stake!** Only in a metaphorical sense, we'd hope, but maybe literally so if we're not careful enough…

That's what this section is about, and why it *matters*. There'll also be more on how to tackle this in Step 5, in the sections "Facing Hidden Risks," "Wicked-Problems," and "Disruption and Chaos" in the next chapter.

Given all of that, how do we model this in the architecture?

We start by extending the *Service-Canvas* into its **Enterprise-Canvas** form, which, as shown in Figure 11-13, adds checklist-items and links for these *investor* and *beneficiary* relationships. In most cases we would use this Enterprise-Canvas version of Service-Canvas only at or near the whole-of-organization level, because that's usually the only place where we're likely to face these issues about investors and beneficiaries.

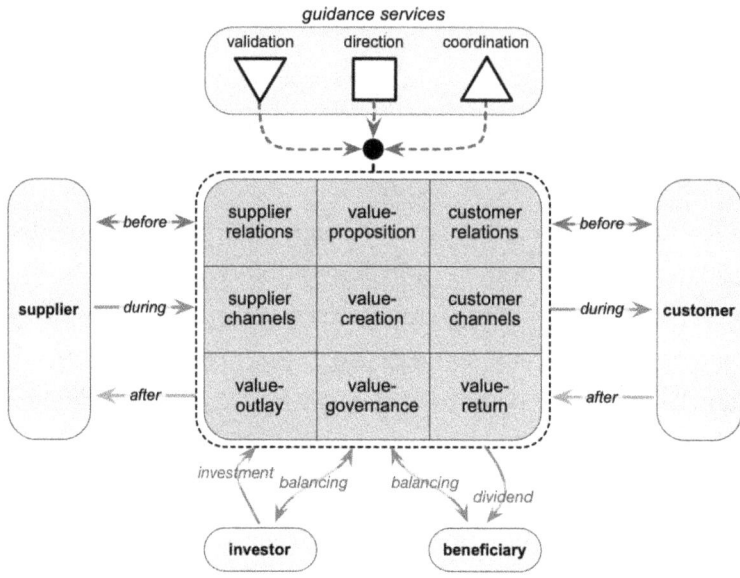

Figure 11-13. *Enterprise-Canvas service-structure for whole-organization level*

Note If you need it, there's also more detail on Enterprise-Canvas and these investor/beneficiary relationships and issues in Tom's book *Mapping the Enterprise*, in it's Chapter 11.

Each of the relationship-types – shown in Figure 11-13 as "*investment*," "*dividend*," and "*balancing*" – would connect through their own version of the Service-Cycle. Regardless of the asset-type mix for the main content – *financial, physical, virtual, relational*, and/or *aspirational* – the Service-Cycle will still follow the same pattern as shown earlier in Figure 11-4, with that pattern of moving from aspirational to relational to virtual to physical, and all the way back again after the main action.

Note We've shown *"financial"* above as it's a separate asset-type. From an architectural perspective, it isn't: it's a merely yet another composite of *virtual* and *aspirational*, in this case an arbitrary number associated with specific societal beliefs about instantiation of value.

But, yeah, people do tend to panic a bit if we describe it that way, particularly if it's about investment and the like. Given that, it's probably best to keep on pretending that it's a unique and special type of asset all on its own, even if that isn't actually true. Oh well.

Notice that we need to model these flows in a different way because they go *in the opposite direction* to the usual supplier- and customer-flows. In the classic shareholder-model, for example, the "*investment*" flow goes from **Investor** to **Value-Outlay** – not Value-Return – because that investment is typically passed onward to a Supplier to help set things up. Likewise, the "*dividend*" flow comes to the **Beneficiary** from **Value Return** – not Value-Outlay – because it's extracted from whatever comes into the organization from its Customer-type relationships.

The organization will also need specific services to manage the balance between investment and benefit, and between all the different types of investors and beneficiaries. In Enterprise-Canvas, we would model those balance-services as part of the **Value-Governance** function, and connected from there to the respective investors and beneficiaries.

Warning If the organization *doesn't* have any means to do this kind of balancing, there'd be nothing to prevent scenarios such as asset-stripping and the like, where all other investments are converted into monetary form and handed solely to the shareholders.

That kind of scenario is illegal in many countries, and would certainly cause legal action to be taken there against the organization's executives. Reputation and trust in the organization would also be likely to collapse within the broader shared-enterprise, leading to the loss of its "social license to operate." In short, failing to manage that balance is Not A Good Idea…

Given that structure shown in Enterprise Canvas for ***investor, beneficiary, and balancing connections***, then ***for each stakeholder-group*** we need to ask the following:

- How would the organization recognize and identify this type of stakeholder, and their expectations for investment and return?

- How would the organization identify and assess the value, values, and value-proposition of the offerings from each investor/beneficiary stakeholder?

- What would this stakeholder invest? What would be the asset-types in this investment, and what form would they take? Through what interactions would this investment take place?

- What would this stakeholder expect as benefit or dividend, in relation to that investment? What would be the asset-types of this benefit, and what form would they take? Through what interactions would this benefit be provided?

- How would the organization show this stakeholder the connections between their investments and benefits, and fairness of the balancing between them?

- What are the mutual responsibilities between the organization and this stakeholder? What are the responsibility-relationships for each stage of the interactions, in terms of responsible, accountable, consulted, and/or informed?

- What laws, rules, regulations, standards, and societal expectations would apply for each interaction, investment, benefit, and balancing with this stakeholder?

- What services will the organization need, to support those interactions for investment, benefit, and balancing with this stakeholder?

Then, for *all* stakeholder-types, as a complete set:

- How will the organization identify and achieve the necessary balancing across all stakeholder-types?

- How will the organization describe and demonstrate, to all stakeholders, the fairness of this balancing across all stakeholder-types?

- What are the mutual responsibilities between stakeholder-groups, and between individual stakeholders, to support and respect the fairness of this balancing? How will the organization support those mutual responsibilities between stakeholders?

- What laws, rules, regulations, standards, and societal expectations would apply for this balancing across all stakeholders and stakeholder-types?

- What services will the organization need, to support this balancing across all stakeholder-types?

Note the questions above about ***fairness*** in relation to "balancing." This is crucial, yet far from simple, because, much like trust and reputation earlier above, perceptions of "fairness" are always going to be somewhat subjective and personal. (Such perceptions of "fairness" are also often deeply entangled in power-relationships and power-dysfunctions, at both an individual and societal level: we'll explore how to tackle those issues architecturally in Step 5, in the next chapter.) There are few easy transforms between asset-types here: for example, we can't really buy commitment or sell a relationship, and despite the commercial-accounting myth of "goodwill," we can't convert business-relationships into monetary form in any honest way.

Finding the right form of fairness for this is always going to be a hard challenge: there are no real standards for any of it, other than for the basic financial-transforms. In a sense, though, don't worry too much about it: often the very fact that the organization is *seen* to be trying to be fair about this, and willing to talk about it, will be enough to provide a solid start-point with many stakeholder-groups. Architecturally, what we *can* do is point to the enterprise-values and the like, and the architecture-work above, as guidelines to help people decide how to do whatever they can to make this work, for everyone.

Example As a commercial organization, the airport has conventional financial-type relationships with banks and stockholders, who provide monetary investment and expect a monetary return.

The regional council provides some financial investments such as grants, and also assistance with planning issues, development, complaints, and more. It looks for returns in the form of local jobs and support for local businesses, the broader income from tourists and other visitors, and the political credibility from having a successful airport as part of their region.

The national government provide similar kinds of investment, though often on a broader scale as part of their support for the air-transport enterprise as a whole. They expect similar returns in terms of jobs, trade, tourism, and the like, but also other returns such as the airport's support for national policies on trade and suchlike and, of course, the tax-revenue to be gained from a large corporation.

Local businesses provide a variety of secondary support-services for catering, engineering, logistics, and more, and look not just for the financial and other related returns, but also the longer-term stability that such work would bring.

The airport's staff and families invest their commitment to the airport, and look for financial and other returns as described earlier above.

The local communities provide less-direct support such as the social context and setting in which the airport's workers live, and hope at least that their voices will be heard by the airport about issues such as pollution, noise, traffic, and other potential disruptions to their lives.

There are also some other less-obvious investment-relationships such as those with the plane-spotters, who may be a bit of a nuisance at times, but do provide their much-enjoyed enthusiasm, and help to spread the airport's fame far and wide!

Into Practice

In the section "**Outside the Box**," we explored the challenges that will arise once the organization's offerings of products and services meet up with the uncertainties of the market. Using what you saw there, apply the same methods and checklists to your own organization.

- How does your organization adapt to that "liminal-space" between *inside-out and outside-in*? How might your architectures help the organization's marketers, salesfolk, and suchlike to thrive amidst the challenges that arise in their interactions with others across that space?

- How might your architectures help the organization in *managing the inherent uncertainties* of this space? How would you use it to dissuade people from holding unrealistic expectations here, or demanding absolute-certainty where none can be had?

- What are your organization's beliefs about *management, skills, and leadership*? What issues or problems might arise from those beliefs? How would you use your architectures to help people address those issues?

- What do you and other people in your organization use to make quick assessments of strategic, tactical, and operational issues? If you currently use SWOT-analysis and suchlike, what happens if you use a *SCORE* approach instead? What do you see differently that you maybe wouldn't have seen before?

In the section "**Design for Flexibility**," we explored how to enhance the flexibility, adaptability, resilience, and overall value of service-provision. Using what you saw there, apply the same methods and checklists to your own organization.

- How does your organization *design for escalation*, to use when things go wrong at run-time? How might you use your architecture to support greater consistency in these escalation-processes, across the organization as a whole?

CHAPTER 11   STEP 4: INTERACT WITH THE MARKET

- How does your organization *design for resilience and adaptability* in run-time action? What service-choreography does it use to guide run-time switching between the respective implementations? How might you use your architecture to support greater consistency in these processes work, across the organization as a whole?

In the section "**From Qualities to Values**," we extended the work we did on quality and compliance in the previous Step, by exploring its bottom-up counterpart, to anchor both ends of the quality-management chain. Using what you saw in that section, apply the same methods and checklists to your own organization.

- What processes does your organization use to support *quality in practice* at run-time? How do you ensure that these will connect correctly with the respective organizational values, constraints, and success-criteria, and any applicable compliance-controls? How might you use your architecture to identify and support those processes, and improve consistency in how they're managed across the organization as a whole?

In the section "**Service and Trust**," we explored the architectural issues relating to trust, and the organization's means to support trust as a business-asset. Using what you saw there, apply the same methods and checklists to your own organization.

- To what extent does your organization have an identifiable *architecture of trust*? As an enterprise-architect, what might you be able to do to improve the organization's ability to manage trust and reputation as business-assets? What issues might you face while working on these concerns, and how would you address those issues?

- How does your organization identify and keep track of the applicable *responsibilities for services*, and for the various types of entities that make up those services? How might you use your architecture to assist in those tasks?

In the section "**Investors and Beneficiaries**," we explored how to identify the organization's investors and beneficiaries, and how to model them and their interactions. Using what you saw there, apply the same methods and checklists to your own organization.

- Who are your organization's *investors*? What do they invest in the organization? How does your organization receive those investments? What does it do with them? How does it keep track of what it receives, and what it does with those investments?

- Who are your organization's *beneficiaries*? What does it provide to them? How does it do so? How are these benefits derived from within the organization or from the broader enterprise? How does it keep track of the benefits it provides? How does it link those benefits to the respective investments?

- How does your organization maintain an appropriate *balance between all of its investors and beneficiaries*? How does it demonstrate that this balance is appropriate and fair?

As always, capture into your notebook any ideas and insights that arise from exploring these questions, to include in your final review at the end of the book.

Summary

In this chapter, for Step 4 in the Maturity-Model, we learned how to manage the complexities and uncertainties within the market and beyond, how to design for flexibility and resilience, and how to connect delivered quality with enterprise-values. We also looked at how to tackle the issues around responsibility, service, and trust, and how to make sense of the organization's relationships with its many investors and beneficiaries.

In the next chapter, for Step 5, we'll explore how to face the harder yet often more urgent challenges hidden deep within the organization and the broader enterprise, including issues such as power, anti-clients, wicked-problems, and the impacts of the everyday chaos of the wider world. And through all of that, as we'll see, we can still always find new ways to optimize the effectiveness of the organization and its enterprise.

CHAPTER 12

Step 5: Interact with the enterprise

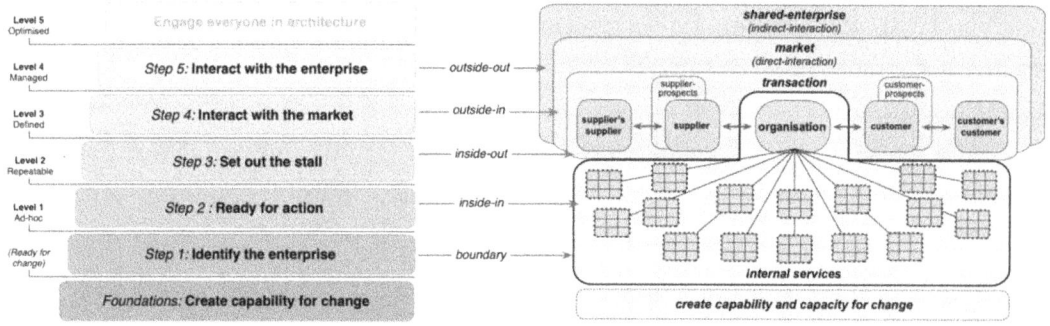

In **Step 1**, we identified the ***boundary between "inside" and "outside"*** for the organization, and established the vision, values, and other criteria that would enable effective ***ad-hoc*** decisions.

In **Step 2**, we looked ***inside-in***, to identify and design the infrastructures that would enable our organization to do its business in a ***repeatable*** way.

In **Step 3**, we looked ***inside-out***, to explore how our organization would deliver on its value-proposition to the enterprise, with ***defined*** products and services.

In **Step 4**, we explored how the enterprise would look ***outside-in*** at our organization and its business-offerings, value-propositions, promises, products, and services, and identified how to use the architecture to address those uncertainties in a ***managed*** way.

Here, in **Step 5**, we complete the pattern by looking ***outside-out***, at the enterprise *as itself*. Much of what happens out there may be beyond the organization's direct reach, but it's still able to affect the organization in many different and disruptive ways, sometimes to the extreme. As enterprise-architects, we *need* to be able to work *with* that chaos to create effective and ***optimized*** outcomes for the organization and for the enterprise as a whole.

This is where top-down plans often *do* come into head-on collision with bottom-up realities, and sometimes in a really big way. This can be very confusing at times: for example, in CSPAR terms, we'll need to keep track of whatever's coming up from **Review** phases, but we'll also need to check each of those against the "universals" that we identified during our focus on overall **Context**, all the way back in Step 1. Much the same would apply if we use a SCORE lens to look at what happens in this Step: the realities arise as *Responses*, yet we'll need to keep checking everything against the criteria for *Effectiveness*.

Throughout this Step, we'll often find ourselves in the SCAN **Not-known** domain, relying heavily on the CALc **Artist** mode to help us find our footing here. All of the other CALc modes will flick in and out of the story too, though, and often in rapid succession in tandem with the matching CSPAR phases, to help us create quick, appropriate, and *effective* responses to each new element of the chaos as it spins past and collides with our organization's aims.

And because so much of what needs to be addressed in this Step sits more in the Not-known, we'll need to play by that domain's rules here. It rarely responds well to the Simple-domain's step-by-step instructions, and to get the best results, we need to let it do things its own way, wandering around somewhat from place to place, idea to idea, insight to insight. Given that, this chapter may feel a bit different from the others: more emphasis on principles and experiences, an approach that's often more exploratory than usual, and fewer bullet-lists and the like.

There *is* structure here, though often more about **meta-structure**, the hidden structure *beneath* what's more easily visible at the surface. At times it'll perhaps need to be more in line with the poet, looping back around itself to show us the same things again from a different direction: "We shall not cease from exploration / And the end of all our exploring / Will be to arrive where we started / And know it for the first time," as T S Eliot put it in the last section of the "Little Gidding" poem in his *Four Quartets*. Like a holograph, a lot of different views into the same space, with each small piece that we add helping to create a richer picture of the whole.

> **Note** In short, if some point here seems to be a bit weird at times, just ride with it for a while until it starts to make sense, such as when you look at it again from a different direction. What happens in this Step is often the exact opposite of the analyst's world, and as you'll see at various points in this chapter, it really *does* need to be tackled that way here.
>
> Anyway, on with the show…

There are two other themes that will keep popping up from time to time throughout this Step, though often in that "arrive where we started" sense of looping back to see them again from a different direction. With both of those, they're not so much separate topics, as connecting-themes that quietly thread their own way through everything that happens here, yet are also important in their own right.

The first of these is that this is where **sustainment-architectures** will come to the fore, perhaps much more so here than in the previous Steps. These architectures provide a big-picture view and a sense of continuity across a broader scope and over much longer timescales, and we'll definitely *need* that here.

The other theme is about the need for "**defensible-uncertainty**" in enterprise-architecture and the like. We've hinted at this a few times already, in some of the previous Steps, but we *need* to tackle this theme in a systematic way at this point, because the inherent uncertainties that we have to address in this Step can make it *much* more of a professional risk than before.

The key point here is about the differences between **effective-certainty**, **expected-certainty**, and **enacted-certainty**, as we saw in the section "Managing Uncertainty" in the previous chapter, on Step 4. The boundary of *effective*-certainty represents the limits of what the system as designed *should* be able to deliver with certainty – in effect, the boundary between "inside the box" and "outside the box." Anything that we can achieve much beyond that point, as the boundary of *enacted*-certainty, will rely on skill and experience.

But for any professional – such as enterprise-architects – there are **two huge catches here**. One is that anything we do *beyond* that box of effective-certainty is, quite literally, an **educated-guess**. That's what skill does: it weighs up the probabilities, assesses the uncertainties, tries out different hypotheses, uses theory as appropriate, and then makes a choice. A good choice, we'd hope. But **it's still only a guess** – and, *by definition*, it *cannot be otherwise*, by the very fact that we're operating beyond the boundary of effective-certainty.

But this is where it collides with the *other* catch: **others' expectations of certainty**, expressed in this type of context as the boundary of *expected* certainty. As we saw in the previous chapter, those expectations can be a long way distant from the *actual* effective-certainty. Even worse, at times they can be barely rational, often giving rise to demands for "***indefensible-certainty***" from us, even where we *know* that no true certainty can be had.

This can put us in a *very* dangerous position, facing huge ***professional, reputational, financial, and legal risks***, without any obvious means for defense. This is where "***defensible-uncertainty***" comes into the picture. We first show that the situation was *inherently* uncertain, beyond the boundary of effective-certainty – which means that the *only* choice we had was to make an educated-guess. We then explain the "educated" part of the educated-guess, showing where the skill and experience come into play, and what we did to identify and mitigate each element of the overall uncertainty. All that's left after that is the true guess, where skill *alone* comes into play, and in which the only way to make a choice was, as Captain Sullenberger described his decision to ditch into the Hudson River, "I eyeballed it."

To address those concerns, we'll explore in this Step a variety of elements that are *not* usually covered in the literature on enterprise-architecture, and show how they may help architects and others when faced with unreasonable demands for "indefensible-certainty."

Caution   Beware in particular of any attempts by others to assert "*retrospective-certainty*," "You should have known," and suchlike – in other words, "certainty in hindsight." Those kinds of attacks are extremely unfair and unrealistic, yet also disappointingly common.

A now-classic example is the assertions made against public-health officials who ordered lockdowns and wearing of masks in the initial response to the COVID-19 pandemic. We'll still see claims that these were a tyrannical overreach by government, an assault on people's freedoms, and the like, with all manner of proof shown that, in the end, the lockdowns and so on weren't as necessary as had at first been thought.

Yes, that had turned out to be true, *in hindsight* – yet *only* in hindsight. Consider instead what was *actually* known at the start – which wasn't much, given that it was, literally, a "Novel Coronavirus," in other words something completely new. All that *was* known was that it was a coronavirus, was highly infective, much more lethal than usual, and with no vaccine available for it. That was it: nothing else. Not even the mode of transmission was known, whether by contact, by air, by water, or whatever. With *that* level of uncertainty, the *only* safe recommendations were isolation to prevent contact, wearing masks to reduce the risk of transmission by air, and social-distancing to minimize the risk of transmission when people could not be isolated.

All of that had been well-established practice for those kinds of new-and-unknown situations – the masks for several centuries, for example, and for more like millennia about the importance of isolation. (That's the origin of the French word "*quarantine*," by the way, literally meaning "forty days" of isolation.) In that sense, they *were* the *correct* choices at the start, when so little was known. Yes, later on, they *could* indeed be eased off, as more became known about the virus, treatments had been found, and vaccines became available. But *only* later on: *not* at the start. That's the crucial distinction there, in that specific case, and why those assertions there are so unfair.

There are many situations, though, where that assertion of "You should have known" would actually be fair – even in enterprise-architecture. Throughout this chapter, you'll see theme after theme that, if you want to reduce your exposure to that kind of risk, you *definitely* need to know about. You'll see the connections to "defensible-uncertainty" as we go along.

To address all of those issues mentioned above, there are four sections in this chapter:

- *Facing hidden risks*: Concerns such as power-issues, anti-client risks, kurtosis-risks, enterprise-hijack, and untested-assumptions
- *Tackling wicked-problems*: Distinguishing between tame, wild, and wicked-problems, and ways to resolve the latter

- *Disruption and chaos*: Themes such as business-continuity and recovery, design for fail-safe and safe-fail, coping with chaos in real-time, and defining an architecture for chaos

- *Enhancing enterprise effectiveness*: Linking to sustainment-architectures and the like, to support longer-term effectiveness

Once again, we'll end this chapter with a brief review of what you've learned during this Step, and suggestions on how to apply it within your own organization.

Facing Hidden Risks

In enterprise-architecture, most of the well-known sources of risk are well documented, and for the most part well understood. "Everyone knows about…" – well, rattle off your own list of what "everyone knows about," really, because it'll depend somewhat on your industry, your preferred focus in the architecture, your own work-context, and so on. But you'll get the idea there, anyway.

Yet there are also some *other*, less well-known sources of risk that are often hidden away in the background, and that can be much more dangerous precisely because we *don't* know about them. In this section, we'll explore five of them: *power-issues, anti-client risks, kurtosis-risks, enterprise-hijack*, and *untested-assumptions*. You can then use what you learn here to help you look for other hidden risks that may apply to your own architecture context.

Note To make this exploration a bit less fraught, do remember that *risk and opportunity are flipsides of each other*: opportunity always implies risk, and risk always implies opportunity. Searching for hidden risks may well turn up some *useful* hidden opportunities too…

A Problem of Power

It's an issue that goes right to the heart of the enterprise and its architecture.
    And yet it's rarely mentioned in any of the literature.
    Why not?
    It's perhaps because this is the *scary* one: **power**.
    Ah…

CHAPTER 12   STEP 5: INTERACT WITH THE ENTERPRISE

Power is a problem. It's *always* going to be a problem, one way or another, for architecture and everything else. The good news, though, is that architecture itself provides perhaps the safest way to tackle these issues, taking the heat out of the situation by quietly shifting the focus away from the personal level, and toward structure, purpose, and the big-picture.

Caution   Architecture may be the safest way to tackle this, but yeah, it's still going to be scary. Almost by definition, these themes can be ***intensely "political"*** – in fact, about as "political" as it can get. "Here be dragons" and all that…

So yes, you *do* need to tread carefully here: those dragons can bite! Yet scary or not, don't flinch from this part of the work: it *must* be addressed somehow; otherwise, there'll be no way for the architecture (or anything else, for that matter) to work well in the real-world.

Yet ***what is power?*** – especially in a human sense?

The usual answer is that it's sort of something kind of blurry and indefinite, that's somehow kind of "out there" somewhere, sort of, that people kind of need to fight about so as to show who's on top and more important than anyone else. Something like that, anyway. And in this view of power, as shown in Figure 12-1, there seems to be only a fixed amount of it, like a pie, sort of, so we each have to compete for our own slice of the pie – even if we don't know what the content of that pie actually *is*.

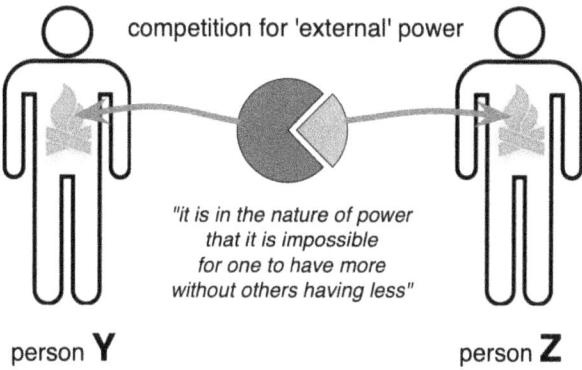

Figure 12-1. The "pie-slice" concept of power

As also shown in Figure 12-1, this often leads to *a belief about power* that's perhaps best summarized in a phrase attributed to Karl Marx, that "it is in the nature of power that is impossible for one to have more without others having less." That can lead to a further belief that all that *we* would need to do to win a bigger slice of the pie is to make sure that *someone else* will lose, and then somehow, magically, their slice of the power-pie will be passed to us. When that type of belief takes hold in an organization, watch the productivity plummet to the floor...

In this case, we're going to need *a definition of power* that's a lot less blurry and indefinite, and one that will actually work.

And there *is* a definition of power that *does* work – literally. We adapt it from the physics definition – that **power is the ability to do work**.

Note To be pedantic, that's the definition for "*potential*," not "*power*": formally, power is *the rate at which energy is expended* in order to do work. For architecture purposes, though, this technically-not-quite-correct-but-good-enough definition is more useful in practice, so that's the one we'll use here.

And for any human context, there's also an important rider that we'll need to add: that *power is the ability to do work*, **as an expression of personal choice and personal commitment**. Without that rider, we can end up with "*arbeit macht frei,*" "work makes freedom" – which in that bleak context at Auschwitz was the one thing that work there did *not* do…

But if "power is the ability do work," then **what is "work"?** The short-answer is that *work is **anything that changes the world in some way***. Think about work in terms of the full set of architectural asset-types – physical, virtual, relational, and aspirational. Digging a ditch is work, but so is solving a technical problem, building and maintaining a relationship, caring for a child or an elderly parent, or reclaiming hope from despair. And all of those consume energy, too – often lots of it, again in terms of all of the respective asset-types.

So where does that power come from, in a human sense? The short-answer here is "*from within the self*" – or **power-from-within**, to use a term from feminist theorist Starhawk.

The catch is that people's access to their own power-from-within can be constrained by issues such as low levels of self-esteem and similar *aspirational-assets* of their own, or by outside sources that can also act on those aspirational-assets. It's hard work to rebuild those kinds of aspirational-assets all on our own. We can, however, work *with* others – as **power-with**, to use Starhawk's term – to help each other work on those aspirational-assets, and improve that access to their own power-from-within. Figure 12-2 provides a visual summary of those power-relationships, with the power-from-within of each individual in the graphic shown as a kind of "inner fire."

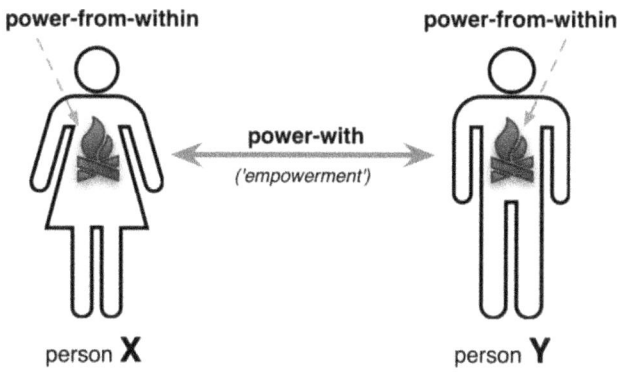

Figure 12-2. Power-with and power-from-within

Note Those terms "*power-from-within*" and "*power-with*" came from Starhawk's books such as *Dreaming the Dark* and *Truth or Dare*. Our usage here is essentially compatible with her original concepts, though adapted somewhat to align with that definition of "power as the ability to do work," and to fit better with the symmetries needed for a context-neutral architecture of power.

There's one important catch here, as illustrated in Figure 12-2 by the term "***empowerment***" shown in quotes under the power-with relationship. In this model, the *only* source of power is from *within the self*: it cannot be *given* by others, via power-with, nor can it actually be "*taken*" by others, as in the "pie-slice" model of power. In that sense, the usual concept of "empowerment," as giving power to someone else, is more than a bit misleading. Even at best, it's just a fancy label for some form of power-with that helps people reclaim *their own power*, and all too often it's only about reducing the active *disempowerment* that currently constrains their power in that context. "Empowerment" is mostly a myth, but disempowerment is all too real…

This brings us back to that *"pie-slice" model of power*: Where does *that* come from? The answer is that it uses the *opposite* definition of power: rather than the ability to *do* work, it asserts that **power is the ability to _avoid_ work**. It's a lazy two-year-old's view of the world, in which "true power" is achieved when they are the sole center of attention, entrapping everyone else into doing all of their work for them.

Note In essence, this view of power is the possessive self-centered temper-tantrum of the two-year-old carried through into adult life. If it's allowed to take hold at a whole-of-context level, anywhere from a family to the whole of an organization or society or nation or beyond, it can easily lead to a *pediarchy*: literally, "rule by, for, and on behalf of the most childish."

Much of that is another topic for another time, but in architectural terms, it's a direct corollary from what's being shown here. As you'll see later here, in the section "Assumptions and Myths," it has *identifiable and measurable impacts* all the way from local (MQ2 level) to fully global (MQ9 level). Given that, it can be useful to apply that kind of architectural lens to make sense of themes such as politics, economics, environment-issues, and international-relations over the past few centuries and more.

In contrast to a **power-with** relationship as above, this is more like "**power-against**." No effort is taken to build one's own power-from-within: instead, all of the effort is placed into trying either to manipulate or force the other into doing the work.

In practice, we'll usually see this "power-against" in two distinct forms. The first, and somewhat less destructive, is **power-under**: any attempt to *evade and offload* onto any other the responsibility for any type of work, without their explicit engagement and consent. The common term for this is "abuse," with all that that implies. In essence, it's about creating and maintaining a slave-culture, though these days it's usually in a somewhat more benign form. For example, we offload physical-work onto machines, or thinking-work onto IT-systems, and then complain that they haven't taken on the full responsibility for getting everything right. We'll also see it sometimes between machines and other systems, such as when an IT-function runs "open loop," offloading the responsibility for overall control onto other parts of the system.

The other, more destructive form is ***power-over***: any attempt to *force* any other to take on the responsibility for any type of work, without any attempt to gain their engagement or consent. Frequently, and particularly in relation to aspirational-type work, we'll see this in some form of "propping Self up by putting the Other down." The common term for this is "violence," with all that that implies too. In essence, it's not so much a slave-culture as an *enslavement* culture, using some or other of the various types of violence to try to enforce the other's compliance: violence against other people, but also violence against machines and the like whenever those don't perform as desired.

In each case, there's a presumed "win-lose" or "transactional" relationship in play here: "I win, you lose," or "I win *because* I make you lose." Figure 12-3 provides a visual summary of these power-relationships.

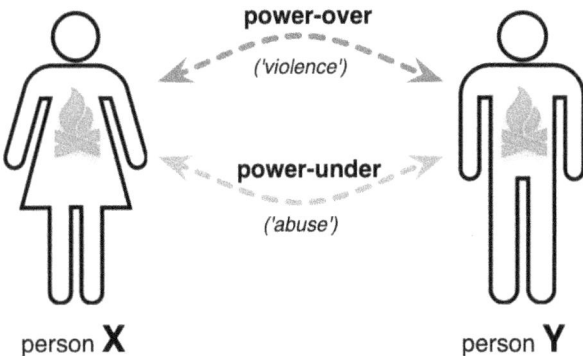

Figure 12-3. Power-against – power-over and power-under

Note There are also "lose-win" versions of these relationships: taking on responsibility *from* another without their engagement or consent, for example, or putting oneself down to prop another up. Unfortunately, well-meant though these may be, they're usually just as dysfunctional as the "win-lose" versions, because all it's doing is enabling the other to avoid work that, often, only *they* can do.

Desirable though this may still seem to so many people, the ***one huge flaw in the "power-against" view of power*** is that ***it doesn't work***: literally so, because its whole aim is to *avoid* work. Whenever power-against comes into the picture, the overall availability of power-from-within will be diminished, as shown by the faded "inner fire" of the characters in Figure 12-3. When more and more people play these "power-games," less and less gets done, and the overall context becomes less and less effective. And once everyone is doing this, then by definition *nothing* can get done, with no possibility for any real effectiveness at all. It really *is* as simple as that.

There are also other ways in which **it not so much <u>doesn't</u> work, but <u>cannot</u> work**. For example, someone else cannot eat for you, or sleep for you, or build a relationship for you, or rebuild your sense of self for you after something's gone wrong in your life. It's often unwise to rely on someone else to make your decisions for you, or tell you what to believe, or what is or is not meaningful to you: you have to do that for yourself. And trying to *force* others to do those things for us doesn't make it any better: it *still* doesn't work. Whether we like it or not, the *only* way to make such things work is to do it ourselves.

The other **huge danger with the "power-against" view of power** is that it's **inherently addictive**. As we've seen above, it does not and often cannot succeed as a means to get the respective work done, especially over the longer-term. But even though it *can't* work "as advertised," it creates a strong belief that it "*should*" work, and that only the *other* person or system is responsible for doing the desired work. The result is that whenever it fails to deliver the desired results, the other person or system is blamed, and the abuse or violence is intensified to try even harder to force the other to do it. This spirals downward from power-under to power-over, and then from bad to worse to catastrophic. And it *still* doesn't work, because it can't. Round and round we go…

Warning   Probably the most common forms of power-against are **blame** and **shame** – blame being a literal example of "offloading responsibility onto the other," and shame being metaphorically "putting the other down." These are not only pointless, because all they do is reduce the other's "ability to do work," but also highly addictive *because* they don't work.

(*Self-blame* and *self-shame* are perhaps almost as common as blame or shame of the other. They might *seem* to help things a bit, by taking out the heat of a tense situation, but in reality they're just the "lose-win" versions of the same thing, and equally pointless and destructive for the same reasons as above.)

In English-language at least, attempts at blaming and shaming are often reinforced by misuse of "**should**." That word is often useful and valid *before* a task, such as part of guidance in a work-instruction – for example, "You should expect to complete this task within no more than six minutes." When used *after* a task, though, it's usually a warning that pointless power-against games are in play. For example, "You should be ashamed!" is a demand that the other should punish themselves, which merely reduces their ability to do work, and "You should have done that!" is an impossible demand that the other go back in time to change what they did.

As enterprise-architects, we do have *some* ways to use the architecture and design to counter against those tendencies: hence, for example, the "No blame!" rule for any After-Action Review. Even so, blaming, shaming, and "should-ing" are often running rampant throughout entire organizations, and the direct cause of enormous amounts of wasteful ineffectiveness everywhere. Not A Good Idea…

In reality, that "transactional" **notion of "win-lose"** embedded **in power-against** always ends up being an **illusory form of "lose-lose"** – and **everyone loses** in some way or other, every time. Trying harder to make that delusion real merely makes it worse, and drives the potential for effectiveness *downward*, every time.

By contrast, the **notion of "win-win"** embedded **in power-with** ends up creating a context in which **everyone wins** in some way or other, every time. Because of that, it drives the potential for effectiveness *upward*, every time.

Note   There's also a useful cross-link here with the concepts in James Carse's book *Finite and Infinite Games*.

People play a **finite-game** to *win*. Power-against might seem appealing there, because of the implication that it might provide easier ways to "win."

But a finite-game only ever exists in the context of an **infinite-game**, which sets the rules for the respective finite-game. People play an infinite-game to *learn*: the real purpose of the finite-games under its rules is to help in that larger process of learning. Power-against *doesn't* work here, whereas power-with does.

And each infinite-game is an enterprise in its own right, in the context of other infinite-games. Ultimately, though, there is only *one* infinite-game that contains all others: the game of life itself.

We don't have enough space here to go into it any more than that, but from an architectural perspective, you may well find it a useful avenue to explore.

And there's **always a choice** about which way to go on this. It's *always* a choice, everywhere, every time, in every context, at every scale from the really-big-picture right down to the smallest fractal level. We can choose

- **Power** as "***the ability to do work***," and *acceptance* of personal responsibility. This leads to constructive **power-with** and power-from-within; ***everyone wins*** in some way or other; the amount of work that can be done goes *up*; and potential effectiveness will *increase*.

Or we can choose

- **Power** as "***the ability to avoid work***," and *avoidance* of personal responsibility. This leads to destructive **power-against**, as power-under or power-over; ***everyone loses*** in some way or other; the amount of work that can be done goes *down*; and potential effectiveness will *decrease*.

That's it. No other choices.

In regard to power and power-issues, there *are* no other choices.

One more thread that we need to add into the mix here is **responsibility**, and its reframing as "**response-ability**," "the ability to choose appropriate responses" in the respective context, which we explored in the previous chapter in the section "The Responsibilities of Service." All of this is tightly interlinked with power, power-issues, and power-relationships. For example, one of those "appropriate responses" would be about making that moment-by-moment choice between power-with and power-against.

Warning   *Never* use the term "*responsible*" as a synonym for "*blame*." As an architect, you *must* do everything you can to prevent that mistake, in yourself and others, because the damage it can cause is enormous.

Wherever that type of power-under does take hold in an organization, no-one can dare to risk taking responsibility for anything. Without the "response-ability" that depends on that respectful acknowledgment of self-responsibility, nothing can get done. And once that happens, any chance of effective outcomes anywhere in the organization will evaporate into a fetid, roiling swamp of finger-pointing, blame, counter-blame, and hopelessness. Not A Good Idea…

There's also the way in which the ability to *access* power as "the ability to do work" also depends on the response-ability that's available in the respective context. This matters, because while power-with can help to *release* an individual's power-from-within, and thence their response-ability, any power-against will *constrain* that response-ability, sometimes to almost nothing. In turn, this can have huge impacts on individual, collective, and overall effectiveness:

- ***Effectiveness*** is driven by personal responsibility, response-ability, and ***power-from-within***.

- ***Power-with*** will *support* more power-from-within, and hence *increase* potential effectiveness.

- ***Power-under*** will *constrain* one's own response-ability, and hence *diminish* potential effectiveness.

- ***Power-over*** will *destroy* everyone's response-ability, and hence *cripple* potential effectiveness.

The classic "***command-and-control***" sits at a kind of neutral mid-point. We may *need* command-and-control as a means to rein in the dysfunctions of power-against. The catch is that in the process, it will *also* rein in the availability of power-with and power-from-within, and hence will limit the maximum potential for power-from-within and higher levels of effectiveness.

In that sense, though, there's an important trade-off here. To achieve maximum effectiveness in any part of its business, *the organization must be able, ready, and willing to relinquish command and control* in those respective areas. However, in some aspects of every business, and in most aspects of any highly-regulated industry, any options to loosen the control may be quite limited, by law, regulations, and more. In effect, command-and-control provides the *best* effectiveness that can be achieved in a context that permits only rule-based "inside the box" decision-making. Yet wherever a choice to loosen the reins does become available, doing so *will* open up new options for the enterprise and its architecture.

Figure 12-4 shows how all of these different elements can be combined together into a single view, as the power-model used in the SEMPER effectiveness-diagnostic.

CHAPTER 12   STEP 5: INTERACT WITH THE ENTERPRISE

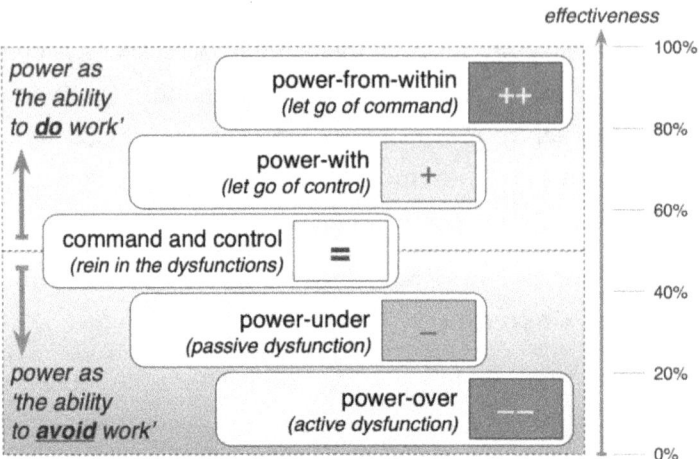

Figure 12-4. SEMPER power-model

A few further notes on that power-model

- The *effectiveness-scale* is rarely quite as linear as that shown in Figure 12-4. The *upward trend* from *power-with*, and especially from fully-supported *power-from-within*, tends to increase exponentially, and likewise the *downward trend* from *power-under*, and especially from *power-over*, increases the damage exponentially as well.

- In practice, *high levels of power-from-within* can be hard to maintain much above the mid-80s in effectiveness, no matter how much *power-with* we might be able to apply. That's because there is *so much power-against embedded in most current social contexts* that it tends to drag everything else down with it.

- In our own work, we've found that organizations typically seem to be *able to survive* with an *effectiveness-level as low as 35%*, or even lower in some cases. Given that effectiveness tends to increase exponentially much above around 50%, this suggests that most organizations can gain a *lot* just by paying attention to those power-issues and the way that they affect overall effectiveness.

- It can be dangerous to attempt to tackle directly any context that's affected by deeply-entrenched *power-over*. As with other types of addiction, its inherent violence can be turned against anyone who tries to intervene in its downward-spiral. Instead, the safer approach is to tackle a nearby context that at worst is only affected by entrenched *power-under*, and as that begins to succeed, allow those effects to seep into the power-over context – easing the inflammation by osmosis, so to speak, rather than by direct action.

Note A quick summary of the SEMPER effectiveness-diagnostic is that it brings together the CSPAR domains and the default effectiveness-criteria into a five-by-five matrix, and then, within each cell in the matrix, uses checklists linked to the steps in the power-model above to provide an assessment of actual effectiveness in that respective part of the context. It also includes a trend-check to provide an estimate of *future* effectiveness there. This not only gives an assessment of *total* effectiveness across the context, but also pinpoints places for potential interventions, and the types of interventions most likely to help in improving effectiveness in each place.

We won't cover that diagnostic in any further detail here, but when you do need to know more about it and how to use it in a business-context, there are full details in Tom's book *SEMPER and SCORE: Enhancing Enterprise Effectiveness*.

Also, for more detail on the relationships between power, responsibility, and "response-ability" in business and beyond, see Tom's book *Power and Response-ability: The Human Side of Systems*.

Given everything above, **how does all of this apply to enterprise-architecture?**

The short-answer is ***everywhere***. Every interaction; every transaction; every decision; with every human agent, but also often with other agent-types too; across every timescale; throughout the entire organization and its business; throughout the entire shared-enterprise, and often beyond. We'll find power-issues of some kind or another threading through every single one of those things.

In other words, power is a *fundamental* aspect of all architectures.

This means we need to stop ignoring it in our architectures, and take it seriously. And get everyone else to take it seriously, too.

So **how do we do that?**

CHAPTER 12   STEP 5: INTERACT WITH THE ENTERPRISE

In essence, we do the same as we did for the issues of *trust*, and for *investors and beneficiaries*: we create an **architecture of power**, as a theme-specific view into the "holograph" of the organization and its enterprise. We build that architecture in the same way as before, using the same sources as described in the previous chapter in the section "Service, Trust, and Responsibility": the *theme* (power, in this case), the enterprise and organizational "*universals*" as an anchor for that theme, the *trails of impact* that connect between the various elements, the potential *nodes for intervention*, and potential *interventions*.

For responsibility and "response-ability," we need to know who has the responsibility for each element in the architecture, so that we know who to contact whenever we come across a power-issue that might affect that element. We'll have already done much of the work for this in Step 4, in the responsibility-mapping process later in that same section on "Service, Trust, and Responsibility" in the previous chapter. The only thing we'd need to add would be a cross-map into the "potential intervention-points" lists in the power-architecture above, to link the responsibilities into an appropriate architecture-view.

The best place to start, though, is perhaps not with the architecture as such, but by **exploring our own experience** of these power-issues. For example, look for situations where you can *see* those two definitions of power at play in real-world action: power as the ability to *do* work, and power as the ability to *avoid* work. Explore what happens when you provide *power-with* to someone – a helping hand, either literal or metaphoric – that enables them to build *their* skills, their *own* power-from-within. Notice the difference when you *engage* someone in a shared task, rather than telling them that they're wrong, or simply telling them to go away. These power-issues are real, *everywhere*: it's useful to gain an *experiential* understanding of them first, *before* tackling the architecture, to prevent us from falling into the trap of trying to be too rational about something that isn't rational at all.

Example   If you travel a lot, like most enterprise-architects do, you'll have plenty of first-hand experience of how these power-issues play out at different airports, and how they impact the overall effectiveness of "the enterprise of air-travel."

For example, look at how the availability and quality of information at the airport affects your own ability to make appropriate choices. When you have the information you need, you can take the right action, quickly, efficiently, effectively, without stress. When you *don't* have that information, particularly when things have gone wrong, the airport has, in effect, offloaded onto *you* all of the responsibility to sort out the mess. When that happens, how does that feel? How does it affect your "ability to do work" for the respective tasks?

Look at your own experiences of the carry-on baggage-scanning area in different airports: some are calm, quiet, respectful; others are, uh, not… What difference does that make to your willingness to cooperate in that *shared* task? What difference do those different approaches to that power-relationship make to the *overall* throughput, efficiency, and effectiveness of the transit through that part of the airport?

If you travel internationally, look at your own experiences of border-control in different countries. Some are, again, calm and laid-back, such as in our late-flight experience in that real example in the "Checks and Balances" section in Chapter 9. By contrast, some are aggressive, threatening, and just plain rude, to everyone. What difference does that make to your willingness to cooperate in that *shared* task? What difference do those different approaches to that power-relationship make to the *overall* throughput, efficiency, and effectiveness of the transit through that part of the airport?

Power-issues can arise *anywhere*, in almost every type of context. To *really* understand what power is and is not, and how it affects overall effectiveness, all you need to do is look at your *own* experiences in situations such as those above…

Anti-clients

By now, we'll know who our organization's clients and suppliers are. We'll know who the prospects are, and all the other players in the market-space. We'll also know about investors and beneficiaries, and some of the other stakeholders in the broader shared-enterprise.

But in Figure 12-5, you'll notice another group out there in the shared-enterprise space that we haven't talked about yet: **anti-clients**. Yet who are they? What's their relationship with the organization? What power do they have? And why do they matter – particularly to the architecture?

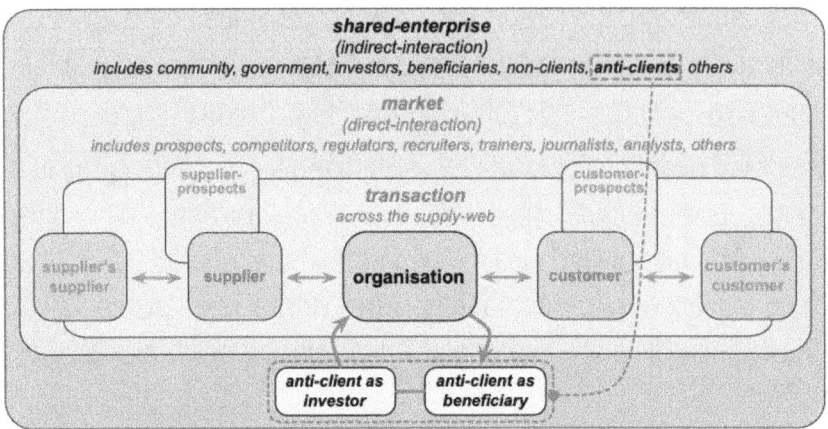

Figure 12-5. Organization, enterprise, and anti-clients

So who are these **anti-clients**? They're *people who are in the same shared-enterprise as the organization, but disagree with how the organization acts within that enterprise*. That disagreement may be about anything at all, and may be based on facts, fictions, or even a total fantasy of some kind – but as long as they hold *some* kind of disagreement about what the organization is or does or represents, they can act in an anti-client role relative to the organization.

As with all stakeholders out there in the broader shared-enterprise, they would typically have only an *indirect* relationship with the organization, much like any other investor or beneficiary. This time, though, they really *are* wielding that metaphoric sharp-pointed stake toward the organization. Their investment would, in effect, be whatever disagreement they have with or about the organization. Their desired benefit would be that the organization offers an apology or some other form of recompense and/or withdraws from that part of the shared-enterprise, or else that the enterprise as a whole will revoke their social-license-to-operate within that enterprise at all.

Example Back about a decade ago, I was at a conference on enterprise-architectures for defense and similar contexts. During one of the conference breaks, I found myself chatting with a very senior officer about business-models. He liked the ideas in Business Model Canvas, he said, and was keen to use it to build a business-model for his own context, but he was struggling to make his context fit into that frame. For example, he said, who *were* his Customer-Segments? Surely, he shouldn't describe the Enemy as a *Customer*, would he?

"No," I said. "The enemy are your anti-clients. You're anti-clients for each other."

He blinked. "What?"

"They're people who are in the same overall enterprise as you, such as a country or whatever, but they fundamentally disagree with what you're doing there." I expanded the description a bit, in much the same way as you'll see below, and scrawled out a rough sketch-version of those relationships shown in Figure 12-5. I added a few extra Service-Canvas-like notes to show how it worked, and to connect it all to what he already knew from Business Model Canvas.

Light-bulb. He stared at the diagram for quite some while, thinking hard, and then let out a long sigh. "Yeah. That fits," he said, nodding his head. "That does work now. Thanks a lot." I gave him the sketch-diagram; he shook my hand, with a smile, and walked off to show his colleagues what he'd found.

Perhaps the simplest way to frame this is that ***anti-clients are part of the enterprise immune-system***. Anti-clients are the metaphoric equivalents of ***antibodies***, the metaphoric white blood-cells for the enterprise-as-organism, protecting the integrity of the enterprise as a whole. The way it works is very similar to an organism's immune-response: some entity within that organism – or, here, the enterprise-as-organism – is somehow identified as a threat, will become surrounded by the organism's "guard-cells" to shield the rest of the organism from its influence, and then either absorbed or pushed out. If enough people *do* interpret the organization as a threat to the enterprise, they can and will eject it from its place in that shared-enterprise.

For an organization, then, ***anti-client activity should be the first warning-bell of a potential immune-response*** against it by the enterprise. Just as in a living body, there'll always be *some* immune-system activity anyway, but alarm-bells should definitely go off as soon as that activity rises much beyond a background level. For its own survival, the organization will *need* to monitor anti-client activity in the enterprise.

There are two distinct types of anti-clients for whom we need to watch: ***inherent-anticlients*** and ***betrayal-anticlients***.

Inherent-anticlients are the anti-clients we'll get automatically from how our organization positions itself within the enterprise, and how it sets out its stall in the market. For example, there'll be people who'll complain to the airport about the noise, or the traffic, or the disruption at night, and so on. Much the same applies if our organization is doing oil-exploration in the Amazon, or doing PR for a political party: by the very nature of that kind of enterprise, there's no way that our organization is *not* going to have someone who vehemently disagrees with what it is and does.

Note At first glance, the organization's ***competitors*** might also seem to be like inherent-anticlients, but the relationship is significantly different. Yes, there are some similarities in terms of interactions, but the organization's relationship with competitors is peer-to-peer in the *market* space, rather than between the organization and its broader *shared-enterprise*.

Crucially, we're also likely to *know* who the competitors are, but anti-clients may be completely unknown, and hence catch us off-guard. That's why anti-clients can be much more of a risk than competitors, and why we need to take special care in the architecture to identify who they might be and how to address those risks that they represent.

Inherent-anticlients tend to **reside in the outer reaches of the shared-enterprise**, often beyond the market-space in which the organization operates. This should be no surprise, because in many cases they'll even reject the validity of the market itself, let alone any one organization that operates within it. They're also relatively easy to identify and to monitor, because in effect "they come with the territory": their opposition is a direct outcome of a ***wicked-problem*** embedded in the core of the enterprise itself. (We'll see more on wicked-problems later on in this chapter.)

This does, however, also mean that there's **no way to eliminate their opposition** as such. That's because it's an outcome of the way that the broader-enterprise defines itself – which is far beyond our organization's control. The best way to ***mitigate inherent-anticlient risks*** is to

- Acknowledge that the clash exists, and that it is *inherent* in the shared-enterprise itself

- Respect the opposition, and the validity of that opposition

- Openly reach out to work *with* the anti-clients, rather than fight against them or attempt to silence or ignore them

That last point about engaging with anti-clients is important, because it provides a way to ***turn anticlient-risk into opportunity***. True, many people will complain just for the sake of complaining: it's a pointless power-game, much as described in the previous section. But the more serious types of inherent-anticlients could be showing us some part of the enterprise-story that we've not yet seen or understood, so we do need to take their complaints a bit more seriously. Rather than the usual struggles with mutual *power-against*, there may be genuine potential there for *power-with*. Once we *do* make the effort to understand what they're telling us, it can sometimes open up a huge opportunity that we'd previously missed, and that could benefit everyone.

Example For years, decades, the retail-giant Walmart had been pestered by activists complaining about sustainability, accusing the company of destroying the world. And for years, decades, Walmart duly ignored them, certain that it wasn't a business issue, and therefore not their concern.

Until one day, much like Ray Anderson at Interface Inc. had done, some senior executive at Walmart finally connected the dots. They didn't make anything themselves, they just sold stuff made by others – so if they didn't have a sustainable supply-chain, they didn't have a sustainable business.

In this case, sustainability *wasn't* something that they could safely ignore: it was a real and urgent business concern that struck right to the core of their business…

And they *knew* that they didn't know what to do about it.

So they took the courageous step: they reached out to the more serious ones among those anti-clients, apologized that they hadn't been listening to them before, and said that they *were* listening now. Would these activists be willing to help?

They were. It took a while to get right, and get it working in real-world action, but yes, it worked out well, for everyone. At the time of writing, it still seems to be working well: much as at Interface Inc., sustainability is shown as a core theme in Walmart's public business-policy, and they run a "Walmart Sustainability Hub" to support long-term sustainability among all of their suppliers and throughout their supply-chain.

By contrast, **betrayal-anticlients** are the anti-clients that *our organization creates* through its actions and inactions. The "betrayal" in this context is ***a perceived betrayal by the organization of the values or promise of the shared-enterprise***, leading to a steep loss of trust in the organization itself – and thence to *active* opposition against the organization.

Sometimes, these are non-clients who don't actually engage in transactions with the organization, but react against what they, as "uninvolved third-parties," perceive as unfairness against others. Sometimes, they can even be the organization's own employees, as we saw in the example in the section "The Architecture of Trust" in the previous Step, with that bank that was facing a collapse of reputation and trust. More usually, though, they are – or *were* – customers of the organization, who now feel *personally* let down or betrayed by the organization. In that sense, betrayal-anticlients tend to start more in the market-space of the enterprise, and then move outward toward the outer reaches of the shared-enterprise.

Unlike the inherent-anticlients, opposition from betrayal-anticlients often seems "unpredictable" – especially if the organization is largely unaware of its impacts on others, or enacts behaviors that can seem cavalier or disrespectful about others. The opposition can also vary wildly in scope and scale, again seemingly "without warning." Yet in practice these "immune-system response" interactions *are* largely predictable: *they arise directly from poor service-design and/or service-execution.*

In the old days, the organization had all the power. There wasn't much that an anti-client could do, other than bore everyone else with their endless complaints, or stand around outside the company headquarters, waving a large placard and looking foolish. But as Doc Searls and his co-authors warned in their 1999 polemic *The Cluetrain Manifesto*, the ubiquity of **social media** and the like has changed all of the dynamics in the situation, ***making anti-clients a much greater risk than before***. The ever-expanding quagmire of malevolent **misinformation and disinformation** on the Internet isn't exactly helping anyone, either.

More worryingly, some organizations even seem hell-bent on making things worse for themselves, with business-models that apparently *depend* on power-under or power-over, in their structures and operations. For example, ***both power-under and power-over are often rampant*** throughout virtually all forms of *so-called "customer-service."* This is definitely not wise, because with social-media's many forms of many-to-many or many-to-one communication, just one seriously-disgruntled betrayal-anticlient really *does* have the power to bring down an entire corporation.

Example Professional-musician Dave Carroll had been an ordinary routine client of United Airlines, until the day that careless baggage-handlers broke his much-loved and very expensive guitar. He asked the airline for compensation to cover repairs, but as he explains in a statement on his weblog, just about everyone at every level at United gave him the run-around, for almost a year.

Yet as he also said on his weblog, "At that moment it occurred to me that ... fighting over this was a waste of time. The system is designed to frustrate affected customers into giving up their claims and [they're] very good at it. However, I realized then that as a songwriter and traveling musician I wasn't without options." He set out to write a song about his experiences, with a goal to get one million people to see his story within no more than one year. He duly posted the song up on YouTube a few months later, complete with its catchy chorus and happily satirical video. It was titled "United Breaks Guitars."

But it didn't take a year to get to a million views: it took just a few *days*. Within a week, the video had gone fully viral, appearing many times on national and then international TV news. At that point, someone at United Airlines finally realized they had a serious PR problem on their hands. And there was nothing they could do to stop it, because it was on a popular public website, with no libel or anything else that any lawyer could reach. They were left floundering in full-on damage-control, their vaunted reputation visibly in tatters as people happily sang the song's chorus-line of "'cos United breaks guitars!" everywhere around the world.

Not a trivial incident at all. The apparent buck-passing games to avoid paying for the repair of the guitar would indeed have saved United perhaps a thousand dollars. But the direct costs they incurred as a result of those games were estimated at around *twenty million dollars* just to address the global PR damage, and untold *millions* more in many other different ways, both direct and indirect.

If that's the amount of damage that just *one* committed anti-client can do to a very large, very powerful corporation, just how much damage could some unnoticed anti-client do to yours? And what could you do to prevent that from happening?

CHAPTER 12   STEP 5: INTERACT WITH THE ENTERPRISE

As enterprise-architects, **what can we do about this**, to identify and engage with the organization's anti-clients?

Perhaps the most crucial requirement is ***a shift in mindset***. It's likely that we, or the organization's executives and others, won't *want* to hear about any complaints, will *want* to pretend that everything will run smoothly just how *we* want, without needing to face any real-world complexities or complications at all. Yet remember that each of these anticlient-complaints is a kind of *immune-response by the enterprise, against the organization*. The risk is real, because it's the shared-enterprise, and *not* the organization, that decides whether the organization's "social-license to operate" will continue to exist. This means that we *must* shift from ignoring or rejecting anticlient-complaints, to *actively* seeking them out and engaging with them.

Given that, the **first steps for action** would include an outline of the overall issues and requirements:

- First, recognize that anti-clients will always exist, and that they can cause very serious problems for the organization.

- Next, recognize that the anti-clients are never going to be under the organization's control. An enterprise is bounded by *shared-commitment*, where control *doesn't* work, but honest negotiation can.

- Recognize that the anti-clients' grievances are real to *them* – and that's all that matters in practice. Whether or not those grievances seem real or fair to *the organization* is almost irrelevant, and arguing about it is not going to work.

- Recognize equally that "giving in" to every complaint is not going to work for *the organization* (nor, ultimately, for the anti-clients either, but they may be too angry to understand that at first). The organization will need to establish common ground where negotiation can take place, preferably *before* it gets to the level of active anti-client action.

- Establish the common-ground between the organization and its anti-clients by identifying the vision and values that provide the common-cause for every player in the shared-enterprise. In effect, these define what quality *means* within the enterprise, and hence within the organization too.

We then need to build a specific *architecture for anticlient-issues*. We'll build this in much the same way as before, but this time combining three previous chunks of architecture-work:

- The ***architecture of trust***, as described in the section "The Architecture of Trust" in the previous chapter

- The additional elements for an ***architecture for investor/ beneficiary relationships***, as described in the section "Investors and Beneficiaries" in the previous chapter

- The additional elements for an ***architecture of power***, as described in the section "A Problem of Power" earlier in this chapter

With that architecture in place, we then use it to guide **continual action** at several levels:

- At the ***sustainment-architecture level***, we would compare and review the organization and its procedures against those values and the vision – starting with any customer-facing activities, but eventually extending throughout every aspect of the organization. Any improvements here will also improve quality within the overall organization and in its relationships with the broader enterprise, which should in turn reduce the risk of creating anti-clients through carelessness.

- At the ***project-architecture level***, we would review all change-projects that might act on services and service-relationships, whether internal or outward-facing. We would look for, and then design-out, any built-in power-dysfunctions that we identify in the structure, story, and operations of those services.

- At the ***tactical level***, the organization would use the enterprise vision, values, and other "universals" as a rallying-point to connect with all of the stakeholders on *their* terms, via the various ways in which they themselves engage with that same vision. In general, this will not *and should not* be linked directly to the organization's marketing.

- At the ***operations level***, the organization will need to maintain an active watch on social-media and the like, such as looking for messages mentioning the organization with a "#fail" tag. The social-media team will need to engage respectfully with all actual or potential anti-clients – for example, it will be useful to view them as allies who can assist in keeping the organization "on-track" toward the vision of the shared-enterprise.

- Repeat indefinitely.

And yes, it *is* challenging. Every anticlient-response is annoying, and tedious, and costly to address, yet it may be *very* expensive to ignore, and may also represent a *real* threat to that social-license-to-operate. On the other side, though, each of those anticlient-responses provides us with information about how we could or should improve the organization and its services, in order to better protect and expand that license-to-operate. And as described earlier about working with inherent-anticlients, there's a lot that *we* can gain from it too, if we turn around and actively engage with our anti-clients.

Kurtosis-Risks

A ***kurtosis-risk***, or *"long-tail"* risk, is a risk that seems to have a very low probability, but very large consequences. As we've seen before, "low probability" does *not* mean "It never happens": for example, it's very unlikely that anyone would be hit by lightning, but it *does* happen, with nasty consequences if they *do* get hit. And if or when a kurtosis-risk does eventuate, it will more than wipe out all of the gains previously made by ignoring that risk – so in a business context, it's a class of risks that we *do* need to take seriously.

That mix of low probability but high impact applies to all types of kurtosis-risks, but there's a special case in which it can get *much* worse:

- There is a low-probability/high-impact risk that applies to each instance of an event.

- There are many instances of that type of event, each with the *same* low-probability but high-impact risk.

- The *effective* probability is cumulative, and hence will increase with each instance of the event.

- Given that cumulative effect, the *effective* risk will change over time *from low-probability* toward *near-certainty*.

- We will not be able to identify beforehand *which* exact instance will cause the risk to eventuate, because each *individual* instance will have the same low probability as every other instance.

Whenever a process with the same "low-probability" risk is repeated many times, the risk shifts from being about low-risk single instances, to a much higher *overall* risk arising from the entire pile of instances, but still with the *same* potential for very high-impact – in short, a ticking time-bomb. If we have one of those risks in our organization's business, we can't know *when* it will explode on us, or *how bad* the explosion will be, but it's pretty much certain that it *will* explode at some point. This makes it kind of important to find them and defuse them *before* it goes up – because ignoring the issue and just waiting around to clean up the mess until *after* it goes up would be *not* much fun.

Rather than a time-bomb, perhaps a better analogy would be something **more like a grenade** being tossed from hand to hand. It's kind of like the metaphoric hot-potato, but worse: if you have a hot-potato, you'll know about it, because it'll burn your fingers when it lands, whereas a grenade feels perfectly safe and ordinary and unimportant until, suddenly, without any apparent warning, you discover that it isn't safe at all…

In business, **the most common kind of "grenade"** is **anything which undermines trust** of that business, whether from customers, suppliers, the market in general, investors, or other seemingly "non-involved" stakeholders further out in the shared-enterprise. To give just a few of the better-known examples:

- So-called "customer-service" whose design, either by default or by intent, denies those who need that service from receiving it

- Kafkaesque policies and procedures that make it all but impossible to obtain service or self-service

- "Prank calls" and other abusive practices, aimed at other employees, customers, or "outsiders"

- Abuses and misuses of monopoly position or status

- Misleading or dubious sales-practices such as unneeded or concealed "payment protection insurance"

- Carelessness with or cavalier attitudes to customer-data and privacy, or outright spying

Given what we've learned so far about trust and power and anti-clients, it should only take a moment or two to recognize that all of these problem-issues above are driven by dysfunctional **power-games**. There's *power-against*, defined as "the ability to avoid work"; *power-under* used to offload work onto others; and *power-over* used to prop themselves up by putting others down, or to blame others for what are actually their own mistakes. They're all there in those examples. And the big challenge here is that, if we're not careful about it in the architecture and in operations, an organization's business-relationships can be riddled with those kinds of power-games – every one of which has the potential to become that kind of metaphoric "grenade."

Caution Far too often, we've seen situations where an entire industry or culture seems to be playing a mutual game of "***pass the grenade***."

True, there'll often be a chorus of "Well, everyone's doing it, so why does it matter?" The reason that it *does* matter is that the pass-it-around game actually makes the risk even worse: it grows in scale and potential impact, and makes it *more* likely that the explosion will happen sooner rather than later.

There may be *some* awareness that the risk is real, but in those cases people are usually either hiding in denial, or in the hope that it will only be someone else – some other company, some other player – who's holding the grenade when it finally explodes. But if the explosion is sufficiently severe to take down an entire industry, that kind of hope isn't much of a defense...

"Everyone's doing it" should *never* be used as an excuse, but instead as a warning-sign that something is seriously wrong, and needs to be addressed!

So **why does this matter?**

It's true that a kurtosis-risk of this type isn't likely to lead to an actual explosion – though that kind of outcome is not unknown. And it's true that each *individual* instance does always remain a low-probability risk, so there's always a good chance that nothing may happen – such as when people become used to poor-quality service, and learn to put up with it as best they can.

But the *collective* risk increases with each instance; and every time it happens, it's yet another chance that that customer will finally snap, scream loudly that "I'm not going to take it any more!" and do something fairly lethal about it. If we're lucky, it'll only be lawsuit-city for a while – and even then, executives and others have been known to go to jail for it. This is not a trivial issue: these are *fundamental* concerns for any organization, and for any viable enterprise-architecture.

In this case, **what do we do about it?**

Unfortunately, there can be a *lot* of challenges around getting others to understand why it's a risk. In a business context, for example, the responses we'll most often see at first will be some variant of the following:

- Pretend that the problem doesn't exist, and do nothing
- Pretend that "It's a tiny risk, so it'll never happen!", and ignore it
- Complain that it will cost too much to do anything, so best to ignore it
- Blame someone else, or try some other way to make it Somebody Else's Problem
- Try to drown it in legalese, to *force* it to be Somebody Else's Problem

Yet none of these "solutions" actually tackle the issue itself. All of them merely make the situation worse, and, in the case of the legal-games, actually put the legal system itself at risk, because the intended outcomes are so obviously unconscionable and unfair.

This means that, often, the only way that *is* going to work will be to **tackle it architecturally**, and build outward from there.

Warning In a business-context, many if not most of the kurtosis-risks will be deeply entangled with dysfunctional power-issues, and hence can be ***intensely "political.***" Do tread with caution here: allowing yourself to get tangled up in that "politics" is Not A Good Idea…

Looking at this architecturally, some themes would be immediately evident. The first is that it's often an issue about ***trust***, which means we'll need to address it via the **architecture of trust**, as described in the section "Service, Trust, and Responsibility" in Chapter 11.

It's also often an issue about ***power*** – or, more specifically, about *dysfunctional* misuses of power – which means we'll need to address it via the **architecture of power**, as described in the section "A Problem of Power" earlier in this chapter.

It's also often a potential or actual **anti-client** problem, which means we'll need to address it via the **architecture for anticlient-issues** as described in the section "Anticlients" earlier in this chapter.

Much of this operates "**outside-in**," not an organization-centric "**inside-out**." As Chris Potts put it in his business-novel *fruITion*, "Customers do not appear in our processes, we appear in their experiences."

Also, be wary about **culture-specific tolerance**, because additional risks apply when one culture's "acceptable norms" are applied to another culture. Any assumptions that may cross cultural-boundaries should be classed as exacerbating elements for any kurtosis-risk.

Most important, though, is that it is a **systemic risk**. Once we understand the nature of the risk, almost everything about it is entirely predictable: often the only point that is *not* predictable is which exact iteration of the system would trigger the eventuation of that risk. The factors in the system risk would include

- **Systemic flaw**, such as implied in each of those examples earlier – dysfunctional or dishonest "customer-service," Kafkaesque procedures, "prank-calls," abuse of monopoly, dishonest sales-practices, and incompetent management of privacy
- **Payoff** *for maintaining the flaw*, such as reduced costs or complexities that the organization will need to deal with, or straightforward power-over "propping Self up by putting Other down"
- **Driver** *for increasing risk-intensity*, usually some form of power-against
- **Potential trigger** *for risk-eventuation*, such as an anti-client with higher leverage, legal action, or social disgust
- **Consequences** *of risk-eventuation*, including legal, financial, social, and so on

The longer that type of flawed system is allowed to run unchecked, the *effective* probability of eventuation will probably increase, because the dysfunctional behaviors that the flaw drives become more and more deeply entrenched. This will also often be coupled with an expectation that the organization will continue to be able to "get away with it" and reap the short-term gains onward into the indefinite future – which merely makes things worse when the risk *does* eventuate.

In this sense, ***management and maintenance of trust*** is a fundamental concern here – and for all forms of enterprise-architecture, for that matter. The relevant forms of trust may vary somewhat according to the scope of the enterprise-architecture: in IT-only enterprise-architectures, for example, we might see trust primarily in terms of privacy, security, and reliability. But whatever the context and scope, the principle remains the same: as shown in Figure 12-6, trust is at the very center of the enterprise – and without it, nothing works.

Figure 12-6. *Trust is at the center of everything.*

Note In Figure 12-6, we've paraphrased the structure somewhat from Nigel Green's VPEC-T pattern (Values, Policies, Events, Content, Trust) from his book *Lost In Translation*. You may well find the original VPEC-T pattern useful not only for tackling kurtosis-risks, but also for any other business issues in which trust may or will be a central concern.

To tackle this, we'll need to do ***trust-mapping***, to identify potential sources, sinks, and leaks for trust. Probably the most useful approach is to apply conventional asset-mapping, regarding "trust in the organization" as an *organizational asset*. Once we do this, we can apply much the same kind of CRUD (Create, Read, Update, Delete) analysis as we would do for other types of assets:

- What processes and activities inside and beyond the organization *create* trust? For example, relationship-building, marketing, value-proposition, and values.

- What processes and activities inside and beyond the organization *read* trust? For example, sales and marketing.

- What processes and activities inside and beyond the organization *update* trust? For example, product-usage, post-service-delivery follow-up, and customer-service.

- What processes, activities, or attributes inside and beyond the organization could *destroy* trust? For example, a mismatch of expectations, perceived non-delivery of, or betrayal of perceived promises.

Note that these dysfunctional processes, activities, and risks may occur *anywhere*. In IT-architectures, for example, they can often occur in the gaps *between* IT-systems, such as where a crude copy-and-paste is required as a kludge to compensate for poor inter-system integration.

Although the mapping and analysis are much the same as for data-assets, it's essential to remember that trust is an *aspirational*-type asset. Unlike a virtual-entity such as data, which can exist in its own right, it exists only *between* a human-entity and some other entity; and unlike physical-assets or, nominally, financial-assets, it is *non-alienable* and *non-possessable*. That means that it *cannot* be managed in the same ways as those other types of assets.

Caution Remember too that while "information *about* trust" may be relatively-easy to model, it's not the same as trust *itself*! The latter is what we need to track – and "information about trust" is only a means to that end. Don't mix them up!

To identify and mitigate other risks of damage to trust, we might also need to do **customer-journey mapping** and **customer-experience mapping** to identify any trust-related issues in those contexts. This should include iterative journey-mapping across journeys, because trust will typically rise or fall around repeat-business or full-completions of journeys. It also needs to be modeled from the *customer's* perspective, not just the organization's perspective.

CHAPTER 12   STEP 5: INTERACT WITH THE ENTERPRISE

It may also be useful to do ***service-cycle mapping***, as per the Service-Cycle. The key concern here is that trust is only reaffirmed and maintained on completion of the *whole* cycle, including the satisfaction of those in the "outer" (non-active) regions of the shared-enterprise – *not* merely the transaction-oriented subset that occurs in the more-visible middle-stages of the cycle.

Similarly – and especially over the longer-term – the service-cycles need to fully encompass the strategic linkage to the shared-enterprise, as well as the tactical and operational concerns that are the more visible concern for the organization. In particular, watch for any tendency in business-models, service-designs, systems-operations, etc., to fall into the classic "quick-profit failure-cycle," where loss of connection back to the more "feeling"-oriented strategic realms also leads directly to loss of trust.

Anything that damages trust – and especially anything that does so in a way that is seemingly-easy to ignore in the short-term – is a potential kurtosis-risk "grenade." Tracking these down, and mitigating their risks, should be a core survival-concern for the organization and its architectures.

Another core system-design criterion here is that ***anything that promotes or condones any form of power-against will represent a systemic risk***. This principle applies at *all* levels of the enterprise, all the way down to automated interactions between individual web-services and the like, but it's most evident, and usually most impactful, at the "big-picture" level.

In present-day business-contexts, most of the more obvious forms of these risks have already been dealt with via legislation and suchlike. For example, we're not likely to be able to run a business-model for long on direct slave-labor or highly-dangerous work-conditions or even on a one-sided monopoly, and we'll likely go to jail if we're caught out in theft or any of the more serious safety-breaches. In short, most of these risks won't eventuate in any *expected* form. Yet *the systemic flaws that create the risk still operate*: so the catch – and the very real danger to the organization and enterprise – is that the risk is therefore most likely to eventuate in some *unexpected* form. In other words, as a supposedly-"unforeseeable" kurtosis-risk.

And it's true that it's rarely about the *people* as such – hence the irrelevance and real unfairness of the "blame-hunts" that so often occur after each incident of this type. Yet even a brief assessment of the context in each case would indicate that the respective incident is a direct outcome of a *systemic* flaw in design, operation, and/or governance –

frequently expressed as *organizational culture*. In other words, it *is* definitely predictable as a *systemic risk*: the only point that is *not* predictable is which exact iteration of the system would trigger the eventuation of that risk.

In terms of **anti-clients**, two key factors need to be assessed here: the *nature* of the anti-client risk, and the increased *leverage* of anti-client-risk afforded by social-media and the like.

The anti-clients we're usually concerned with here are "betrayal-anticlients" – those who feel betrayed in some sense by the organization's behaviors, especially where those behaviors run counter to the organization's own espoused-values. In most cases, an organization may *seem* to be able to sidestep the risk, via attempts to ignore or even ride rough-shod over a "betrayal"-complaint, or even claim to be the victim itself. Yet *some* leverage will always be created, and sometimes on a huge scale in an extreme case or when public anger rises beyond a crucial tipping-point. Present-day social-media provide much greater leverage than in the past for such anger to "go viral" all the way up to a global scale.

The systemic-flaws and concomitant kurtosis-risks may take on any at all of a myriad of possible forms. Yet for purposes of assessment, the key factors behind almost all of those forms can be simplified right down to just one cause: the presence of **unaddressed power-against**. Wherever that occurs in organizations or elsewhere, some form of anti-client risk and/or systemic-failure kurtosis-risk *will* be created: it really *is* as simple as that.

Example   "United Breaks Guitars" was an anti-client incident, but in turn it was also an eventuation of a kurtosis-risk with much the same structure as described above.

The *systemic flaw*, according to Dave Carroll's description, was that the customer-service system seems to have been explicitly designed to frustrate complainants into abandoning their claims.

The *payoff* would have been through keeping customer-compensation-costs lower than they might otherwise have been.

The *driver* was that the system seems to have been designed around systematic power-under "offloading of responsibility" not just onto the complainants but also onto just about *any* Other in the enterprise, such as the baggage-handlers and the airports. There also seems to have been some power-over elements, such as "propping Self up by putting Other down" in a financial sense, and maybe other senses too.

The *trigger* for eventuation was that, unlike most other complainants, Dave Carroll "wasn't without options," and that "as a songwriter and traveling musician" he had the ability to create and publish a song about his experiences.

The *consequence* was that United were faced with significant costs, literally many thousands of times greater than if they had paid the claim in the first place, and also suffered severe long-term reputational damage.

It also had a classic *"pass the grenade" outcome* in that United Airlines found itself bearing the brunt of a lot of blame about similar behaviors by *other* airlines.

Enterprise-Hijack

An ***enterprise-hijack*** occurs when someone, or occasionally something, tries to override the vision and values, or impose someone else's priorities onto the organization or even the entire shared-enterprise. The classic example would be a hostile-takeover or "corporate raid" of a publicly-listed corporation. It's usually done for selfish reasons, though in some situations it can actually be for everyone's benefit.

Warning   For enterprise-architects, the risks here are **not only "political"** in the usual sense, but in some cases can also become entangled in **larger-scale financial, political, legal, and even criminal concerns**. Those more-extreme matters are usually beyond even the organization's own remit, but you *do* need to take care here!

Enterprise-architecture will play a key role in the organization's defenses against enterprise-hijack, so it's likely that you *will* need to be involved in this. But you'll also need to maintain your own defenses – not least because in most organizations, one of the reflex responses when something goes wrong is to go on an immediate hunt for *anyone* to blame, and you won't want to be that scapegoat! Hence, for example, before you tackle any of this, you'll need a solid understanding of "*defensible-uncertainty*," as described at the start of this chapter.

CHAPTER 12   STEP 5: INTERACT WITH THE ENTERPRISE

The role and value of architecture is usually self-evident when the attempted enterprise-hijack is more at the operations level – such as in the airport's examples at the end of this section. There would be few risks for you there. At anything much above that level, though, you *must* remember that your role will be one of decision-support, *not* decision-making: you're there to provide guidance and support for decisions that only *others* can make. Even then, there can be real dangers if it turns out that it's those people themselves who are setting up the attempted hijack: allowing yourself to get tangled up in that kind of mess would *definitely* be Not A Good Idea…

From an architecture perspective, **what is the issue here?**

An enterprise-hijack is an attempt to ***force a change to the core purpose***, priorities, focus, success-criteria, and/or effectiveness-criteria ***for an organization and its shared-enterprise.*** This is often most visible when it's applied from *outside* to a whole organization or enterprise. For example, at a whole-of-company meeting after a hostile-takeover in the late 1960s, the new owners are alleged to have said "So here's a new version of the old golden rule: he who has the gold, rules!", followed by "We're not here to make [the company's product], we're here to make money!" Private profit for the owners became the only imperative for the organization; quality of product went down, along with quality of life for the employees and everyone else.

(The same, of course, could be said for most attempts at colonialism and empire-building throughout history: enterprise-hijack, power-against, and privatization of profit versus socialization of cost, all applied at a whole-of-nation scale.)

It also occurs in **relations between organizations** within the same nominal shared-enterprise: one organization hijacks the relationship to prioritize their own benefit over the needs of the enterprise as a whole. For example, for the past century at least, politicians and others have routinely expressed their concerns about suppliers seeming to have too much control over government organizations, and also seeming to be more focused on their own profit rather than serving the actual needs.

An enterprise-hijack can also be driven ***from within an organization***. The obvious example would be ***embezzling***, where part of the organization's income or other assets become siphoned off for the private profit of one or more of the staff or employees.

Yet it isn't always about money. For example, in the ***Stafford Hospital scandal***, the managers changed the hospital's priorities to place cost-control as a higher priority than the medical needs of the patients. But although those money-issues played a major role in the ensuing disaster, the managers' actual purpose wasn't about private profit, but achieving a specific legal status for the hospital as a whole. In principle, the change was well-intended, but they chose the wrong means to get there – taking the "easy option" of cutting costs, rather than doing the real work to gain greater effectiveness through stronger alignment with the actual enterprise-values.

At an architecture level, one of the most common causes of *unintentional* enterprise-hijack is "**anything-centrism**," arbitrarily placing one particular theme or focus above everything else, and often neglecting or ignoring the rest. For example, we've seen this arise as IT-centrism, business-centrism, money-centrism, shareholder-centrism, and many other themes as well. It also happens when one aspect of the organization is given priority over everything else, such as in sales-centrism or production-centrism. We've also seen it when one specific quality-theme takes priority over everything, such as when people become so obsessed about security or safety that nothing can happen at all.

Another related problem is that senior executives do seem to have an unfortunate tendency to fall prey to "*in-flight strategy*," in which they randomly choose some fad they've read about in an in-flight magazine as "the single most important focus for our entire organization!" This leads to an enterprise-hijack in the form of a "**tail wagging the dog**" syndrome, in which the implementation of support for the fad overrides the organization's existing vision, values, success-criteria, value-propositions, and business-relationships and, all too often, even basic business common-sense. Over the decades, we've seen this in "efficiency" drives, in "business-process re-engineering," in the "dot-com" farce, in the misuse of social-media, and more. At the time of writing, the current "in-flight strategy" is all about computer-based AI and other forms of so-called "artificial-intelligence," but by the time you read this, it'll no doubt be something else. It's very rare that any of these fads work out well in the longer-term.

And **enterprise-architecture itself can also be susceptible to the same hazards and risks**. For example, big consultancies still dominate much of the development for standards and the like, and most EA toolsets still focus on satisfying those organizations' requirements, often preventing any focus on any other part of the actual real-world need. If we're not careful, even the definitions can end up so skewed that they may become worse than useless. For example, up until around a decade ago, business-architecture was still being defined as "*anything not-IT that might affect IT*," with almost no connection at all to the actual business of the organization.

So **why does this matter?**

The real issue is that *enterprise-hijacks always have consequences*, in most cases leading to bad outcomes for some or all of the players in the overall enterprise. For example, according to the subsequent inquiry, the cost-cutting obsession at Stafford Hospital did indeed save some money, but at the cost of the lives of perhaps several hundred patients, and the long-term health of many more.

It *always has impacts on effectiveness*. For example, the existing architecture will have been optimized for one set of values and other "universals," but it will now have to be reoptimized for something else. This will take time, effort, and cost – all of which are anathema to the people pushing for the respective enterprise-hijack. Also, many of those "universals" will have come from the overarching shared-enterprise, and cannot be changed by the organization itself without also changing its entire positioning and value-propositions for the enterprise as a whole – which, again, will require time, effort, and cost, and may also put at risk all of the organization's relationships and reputation with its existing suppliers, customers, and market.

And in far too many cases, the enterprise-hijack will be *driven by attempted power-against* in some form or another, such as for personal profit, evasion of responsibility, and propping self up, by putting others down, or sometimes for stranger reasons such as personal revenge. All of these will create risks around *trust, reputation, power-issues, anticlient-issues, kurtosis-risks*, and more, as we'll have seen throughout this Step and the previous Steps.

In this case, **what do we do about it?**

Remember that *architecture's role here is essentially an advisory one*: we provide information and advice to help guide decisions that *others* will make.

The architecture task here would be to *map out the connections* to identify *potential impacts and costs* that might arise if any given *enterprise or organizational "universal" is threatened or changed*. We may also need to work backward through the same connection-maps to identify which "universals" could have been threatened by actual incidents that have affected specific services and suchlike.

For example, even a simple-seeming case of embezzlement would have costs, governance-impacts, and effectiveness-impacts not just in the specific business-area where the embezzlement occurred, but also in all other business-services below that area, and potentially also in financial-management, reporting, auditing, and fraud-detection throughout many other parts of the organization. And however well-intentioned it might be, *any* change to core values or priorities would have huge impacts, and potentially huge costs as well, that could ripple everywhere throughout the entire organization and maybe beyond.

The one bit of good news here is that ***we'll have already done most of the architecture-work*** that would be needed to set up for this role, because it would build on the existing focus-oriented architectures that we built to tackle that kind of impact-trail mapping for trust and the like. The full worked-example on how to do that is in the section "The Architecture of Trust," in Chapter 11, and further details and examples are in the section on investors and beneficiaries in that same chapter, and in the work on power, anti-clients, and kurtosis-risks earlier in this "Facing Hidden Risks" section. We may need to customize some parts of the mapping to build specific support for enterprise-hijack risks, but otherwise it's essentially the same as before.

Given those impact-trails, we would then prepare advice on what to do to mitigate those actual or potential impacts and risks, both for any specified services, and for any other services that might be affected throughout the organization, in the organization's relationships with others, and perhaps across the broader enterprise as well. Most of that would be the kind of straightforward service-architecture work that we explored throughout Chapters 9 and 10 and also in some parts of Chapter 11.

Example At the airport, the security and safety teams have asked the architecture-team to join them in exploring how to deal with the hazards and problems caused, as one of them drily puts it, by "idiots with drones and idiots with lasers."

Both types of devices are relatively cheap, readily available, easy to operate, and a lethal menace anywhere near an active aircraft. The drones are about the same size and weight as a medium-sized bird, and almost impossible to detect on radar; the lasers can be switched off in an instant, and hidden in a backpack or a pocket. Most of their operators seem clueless about the dangers they cause, and they could be hiding anywhere, outdoors or indoors, within several miles of the airport.

The teams talk for a while about the operational, technical, and architectural challenges of setting up real-time coordination and response across a true whole-of-enterprise scope, including land-operations, air-operations, air-traffic control, airlines, air-crew, airport-security, and civilian law-enforcement beyond the airport itself. Expensive in every sense, and not easy at all.

The conversation shifts to options for prevention. The current laws and regulations do help, but not enough to deter idiots. The country's airports have asked for more help on this, but they've already reached the limit of the trade-off where they start to conflict with the regular lawful usages for those types of devices.

But what about motivation? Why do the idiots do this? There's a power-issue, obviously: "propping themselves up by putting others down" and all that. But what else? The architects suggest it might also be useful to look at it from an enterprise-hijack perspective, about how and why the "idiots" place their own enterprise over others' safety.

For the drone-operators, the challenge is about getting the best and most exciting video of air-operations. That was the cause of the collision between a drone and a firefighting-aircraft in California in January 2025. The danger is that there's a race going on between operators, finding ever more daring ways to show off their expertise and get the most views on YouTube and the like. A YouTuber deliberately caused a train-derailment in Nebraska in April 2024 for that reason. For the operators, the risk of losing their reputation as the "winners" in that race can feel far more important than the risk to others' lives.

For the laser-operators, the challenge is about being able to show that they can hit a fast-moving target at a great distance. There's a similar race to show off their expertise to others, with the further danger that this race happens live and in real-time, passing the laser from one operator to another. That race is far more important to them than the risk of causing a crash – in fact, a crash might almost be seen as a bonus, as it would cement their position in that race forever.

In a culture that has almost no concept of personal responsibility to others, these enterprise-hijacks will be hard challenges to resolve.

Assumptions and Myths

Assumptions provide useful shortcuts in decision-making. If we trust an assumption to be true and valid, it makes decision-making so much simpler, and so much faster. So much more certain, too.

Yet think about that for a while. What **assumptions** underpin your architecture, or your organization's operations and business? What assumptions underpin your own life, or that of your family or friends? What assumptions permeate throughout your community, your culture, your society, its economics, its relations, and so much more?

Just **how many assumptions are there**, of what different types, at what different levels, in what different contexts? Just how much, or how many things or expectations for events, will depend on those assumptions being correct?

But what **if an assumption is wrong**, or out-of-date, or only works with specific people or contexts, and not with others? What happens then? What impact would that have on the validity of the decisions that are based on those assumptions?

In this case, **how do we know that assumptions are correct**? Far too often, we don't. Instead, we make yet another assumption, that that respective assumption is valid, and carry on from there.

Think about that for a while. Think for a while about the *implications* of so many decisions, throughout the business and elsewhere, that are based on assumptions that we don't know are valid and correct.

Yes. That's a *lot* of hidden risk out there, not just in the architecture, but *everywhere*...

To help make sense of that, we'll introduce the concept of a **mythquake**.

The core issue here is about the **use of assumptions to guide decision-making**. If we *do* know, for certain, that the assumption is valid in that context, there's not much of a risk: we can ignore those for now. But if we *don't* know whether or not the assumption is correct or valid in that context, then there's a risk there that we may need to address.

There are all kinds of ways in which assumptions could fail. They may not have been tested for these circumstances, or not even tested at all. They may be out of date, or applied in the wrong context. They may even be *known* to be wrong or invalid, but we want to cling onto them because it makes us feel better if we pretend that they're *not* wrong. For simplicity's sake, let's use a generic term for this type of fragile assumption: a ***myth***.

And when such a myth collides with Reality Department, our world is shaken, rattled, fractured, broken, in what we might call a ***mythquake***.

Example The long-awaited vacation with the family: You'd planned for this for months, but you'd only just managed to scrape enough time away from work to do it right now, before the end of the school recess. Despite your worries, everything's turned out just fine: no problems at the airport, no cancellations or delays, you

CHAPTER 12   STEP 5: INTERACT WITH THE ENTERPRISE

caught the early flight, you're on your way now. The timing will be a bit tight for the connections at the next airport, but it's only a few hours away. All the assumptions were right: you let out a sigh of relief.

And then you hear a voice over the loudspeaker. "This is the captain speaking. We've been ordered to land immediately. We don't know why." He names an airport where you're going to land, some tiny place you've never heard of, out in the middle of nowhere.

When you land, you'll discover that your vacation is gone, you'll be stranded in this place for weeks, and you're now the only surviving member of your New York team. The date is September 11, 2001, and your world is changed forever...

However small it may be, *a mythquake <u>always</u> hurts* – it is *always* painful. It may or may not cause any physical trauma, but it will always cause some level of emotional or psychological trauma, and also often what we might call aspirational or spiritual trauma – a loss of faith in the self, in others, in the world, in anything.

Given that, it should be clear that a mythquake is not merely some theoretical possibility. Rather, it denotes real events with real consequences that *we do need to respect*, and *to care for those who experience them*, whoever they may be.

Note   Much as with risk and opportunity being flipsides of each other, mythquakes are not always a bad thing: there can be "***positive mythquakes***" too. For example, you might have unexpected luck, an important meeting that went much better than you'd expected, or unexpected success in a skill you were certain you couldn't do. It's a mythquake, so there's still a shock, but that's often unnoticed because the outcome is good.

In fact, much of the skills-learning process consists of a continual stream of positive-mythquakes, each causing a shift from "I can't do it..." to "Oh, I can!" A teacher will often use a form of power-with to create positive-mythquakes of this kind that "trick" people into finding their own power-from-within in this way.

And even the higher-level "bad" mythquakes can sometimes be turned into positive opportunities. For example, that kind of perspective is useful to describe the business-opportunities that arose from the mythquake-like "epiphanies" at

Interface Inc. about waste, and at Walmart about sustainability, as described earlier in the book.

We use the term "mythquake" because of the strong **analogies with earthquakes**. The analogy is almost exact, though with layers of assumptions rather than layers of bedrocks as the material being split and broken apart. In that sense, it *does* actually make sense to imagine mythoseismology, fractures in the noosphere, tectonics of the soul, and so on.

The other parallel relates to **metrics** – how we *measure* a mythquake. In earthquakes, it *is* possible to derive a connection between magnitude and intensity, measured respectively by the Richter and Modified Mercalli scales. In mythquakes, though, there's as yet no identifiable correlation between magnitude and intensity: the collapse of some long-held theory or idea may produce no observable effects outside of a narrow group of people, whereas a seemingly small incident somewhere may create huge impacts that ripple right around the world.

Yet what we *can* do is **identify a clear metric** for **mythquake-intensity** or mythquake-impact. It's simple, if perhaps rather bleak at times: the number of people whose lives are affected in significant, often life-changing, and sometimes terminal ways. If we measure this exponentially, in powers of 10, this gives a simple MythQuake or MQ scale from MQ0 representing a mythquake affecting a single person (10^0, or 1), to MQ10 representing an existential-level mythquake that could affect ten billion people (10^{10}, or 10 billion) – more than are currently living on the planet right now.

The **direct cause of a mythquake** could be anything, either natural or man-made. In terms of weather, for example, a damp day might ruin someone's wedding, affecting perhaps ten to one hundred people (MQ1 to MQ2), while an unexpected tempest or tornado might perhaps take hundreds of lives and wreck thousands of livelihoods (MQ3 to MQ4). In terms of man-made mythquakes, though, the potential intensity tends to increase with the degree to which people defend some tightly-held myth that is fragile, brittle, or just plain broken, and which, once the defenses fall, will not survive any final collision with the real-world. From around MQ2 upward, this is almost always the case: an outdated or invalid belief just sitting there like a festering, ulcerated wound, getting worse with every passing day.

So **why does this matter**? In particular, why would this matter to enterprise-architects?

Untested-assumptions are dangerous: even a small mythquake could damage a business, while a larger one could destroy it. That means that this matters in exactly the same way as for any other risk-related concern – in fact, it *is* about risk-management and risk-preparedness, and the architectural challenges that would arise from any other class of risk.

In this case, **what do we do about it?**

Architecturally, this splits into five parts or five stages:

- Mythquake ***risk-identification***, to identify *what* is at risk, and why

- Mythquake ***risk-assessment***, to identify the probable *nature* and *intensity* of the risk, to enable priorities and business-cases to be set out

- Mythquake ***prevention***, for the risks that we *can* and/or are *allowed* to address

- Mythquake ***preparedness***, for the risks that we *can't* and/or are *not allowed* to address

- Mythquake ***response***, to respond when a mythquake eventuates

In every case, it's wise to **practice on the smaller mythquake-risks** before we try to tackle the larger ones.

The latter two parts – ***preparedness*** and ***response*** – are essentially about what we'd do in relation to any other type of larger-scale disruption. We'll look at that later in the "Disruption and Chaos" section further below.

In the ***risk-identification*** part, all we have to do is identify whatever *myths*, in the form of untested or invalid assumptions, might exist within any given context, and why they might create a risk. This *should* be relatively straightforward – in theory, at least, if rarely so in practice. Probably the simplest way to get started with this is to get change-projects to include this as part of their regular risk-assessments, and notify the architecture-team about what they find in that process.

In the ***risk-prevention*** part, we'd need to get projects raised to resolve whatever issues might be implied by the respective myth. We would identify the service that might be affected by the myth via assessment of impact-trails in the architecture models, in the same way that we've done with issues around trust, power, anti-clients, and so on. In this case, we might also want to cross-check the connections in those subsidiary models derived from the Function-Model, such as the Business-Systems Model and

Information-Systems Model described in the "Functions and Systems" section in Chapter 9. Even if we're not allowed to change anything, we can at least ensure that *some* prevention is in place via the **preventive-checklist** and **emergency-checklist** in the Four-Checklists set for the respective run-time tasks.

But it's the **risk-assessment** part that can be hard – sometimes *very* hard. The assessment *itself* shouldn't be all that hard: it's just a regular architecture-assisted risk-assessment, and by this stage of the Maturity-Model, we'll all know what to do and how to do it. The danger is that the ever-unhelpful realm of "***politics***" will often intrude here, and will *not* like what it sees – and then *we* end up being the ones at risk.

Warning You should be safe enough working with anything that has a mythquake-risk below around the *MQ2* level. For anything that even *looks* like it might be above that level, though, you will *need* a solid practical understanding of **defensible-uncertainty** before you start to work on it. At times, the politics of this can be so unpredictable and so extreme that even stumbling upon some higher-level issue by accident could be a career-ending risk.

The only reason why Richard Feynman was able to break the hidden-assumptions logjam of the Challenger Disaster Inquiry, where even astronaut Sally Ride could not safely do so, was that, as a Nobel-winning physicist, he had the clout and credibility to get away with it, and had had plenty of practice at tackling those kinds of "political" risks. For most of us mere mortals, trying to bumble our way through a high-level mythquake-risk, without understanding just how dangerous the "politics" of this can be, would most definitely be Not A Good Idea...

One tool that can perhaps save our hides here is Sohail Inayatullah's **Causal Layered Analysis** (CLA) – for more details on that, see Appendix B. This identifies four distinct modes or "layers" for contextual-exploration that it describes respectively as the everyday *Litany*, the more formal *Social and Structural*, the somewhat-deeper *Worldview*, and the even deeper *Myth and Metaphor*. As shown in Figure 12-7, these layers map well with the four main **CALc** action-modes of *Agent, Analyst, Alchemist*, and *Artist*, and also with the typical social-trigger themes for the MQ **mythquake-scale** levels.

CHAPTER 12   STEP 5: INTERACT WITH THE ENTERPRISE

Litany (Agent mode)	MQ0– *Background Tremors*
	MQ0+ *Everyday Upsets*
	MQ1+ *Everyday Disasters*
Social and structural (Analyst mode)	MQ2+ *Centre of the Universe*
	MQ3+ *I Am What I Do*
	MQ4+ *Whoever You Voted For*
Worldview (Alchemist mode)	MQ5+ *Money Money Money*
	MQ6+ *I Am What I Am*
	MQ7+ *An Illusion of Entitlement*
Myth and Metaphor (Artist mode)	MQ8+ *The Wrongs of Rights*
	MQ9+ *Possession*
	MQ10+ *Wipeout*

Figure 12-7. *Causal Layered Analysis, CALc modes and mythquake-levels*

Even a quick glance at that list of mythquake-themes shown in Figure 12-7 would indicate that it'd take at least another whole book or two to describe what's *really* going on down in that rabbit-hole. Even at this Step in the Maturity-Model, we're not likely to be ready for that yet. But although we don't have enough room here to go into this in any real depth, as enterprise-architects we can get a rough outline of what to do from the following brief summaries.

For myths with a mythquake-potential in the ***MQ0–*** to ***MQ1+*** range

- These risks can trigger events that range from trivial impacts on one person to everyday disasters with life-changing impacts for up to a hundred people. As an enterprise-architect, it should be safe enough to explore these types of risk almost anywhere in almost any business context.

- To assess the underlying social-issues, we would probably need only the CLA ***Litany*** layer: "the voice of the deeper layers of a particular group of people; the unquestioned, the most visible, and obvious beliefs are put into words at this level."

- To tackle the mythquake itself, we would typically use the CALc ***Agent*** mode. For example, in the Four-Checklists set, the purpose of a checklist is to guard against untested assumptions.

For myths with a mythquake-potential in the *MQ2+* to *MQ4+* range

- These risks can trigger events with life-changing impacts on hundreds to thousands of people. As an enterprise-architect, it may only be safe to explore these types of risk when working in that formal role, and often only when working on risk-assessments that have been formally requested by someone with higher authority.

- To assess the underlying social-issues, we would probably need to include the CLA ***Social and Structural*** layer: "the layer of rules, policies, and data analysis is usually articulated by policy institutes and dominates narratives of mass media and social media, often given credibility in not-quite academic journals or think tanks."

- To tackle the mythquake itself, we would typically use the CALc ***Analyst*** mode to create new algorithms and systems-models to address the complexities of the issue.

For myths with a mythquake-potential in the *MQ5+* to *MQ7+* range

- These risks can trigger events with life-changing impacts on thousands to millions of people. As an enterprise-architect, it may only be safe enough to explore these types of risk within a larger organization, and only when working under the authority of a business-unit working on strategy, futures, or suchlike.

- To assess the underlying social-issues, we would almost certainly need to include the CLA ***Worldview*** layer: "the collective norms, standards, and morals that individuals believe they should maintain, most often influenced by religious viewpoints, political allegiances, or professional practices. It is influenced by the myth/metaphor layer to create the collective vision of how they see the world and their place in it."

- To tackle the mythquake itself, we would typically need to use the CALc ***Alchemist*** mode to identify and reframe the respective worldviews and to resolve the structure of any underlying wicked-problems and the like.

For myths with a mythquake-potential in the *MQ8+* to *MQ10+* range

- These risks can trigger events with life-changing impacts on millions to billions of people. As an enterprise-architect, it's probable that it would *only* be safe to explore such types of risk when working within a strategy/futures unit in a government department or a large multinational corporation.

- To assess the underlying social-issues, we would definitely need to also include the CLA *deep-Myth and Metaphor* layer: "the layer that explores the resilience and power of the distinguishing culture of a particular time or place that shapes the identity of a group of people through the historical retelling of archetypical beliefs."

- To tackle the mythquake itself, we would typically need to use the CALc *Artist* mode to recreate and reinvent the context in terms of new deep-myths and deep-stories.

That should be enough to get started with the underlying principles and practice, and from there you should be able to work out for yourself the rest of whatever you might need to make this work.

Example   Heathrow is the largest airport in Britain, and one of the busiest airports in the world. For its power-supply, the management seems to have assumed that it could always rely on the national power-grid, with no need for any alternate backup source.

In March 2025, that assumption turned out to be a myth: the nearby main substation on the grid caught fire, leading to a mythquake in which the power was cut off for the airport and the surrounding region. Heathrow immediately went into blackout, and was forced to shut down for almost a day.

Subsequent news-reports indicated that around 1300 flights were canceled, and many more diverted or canceled at their departure-points. If we use a rough average of around 140 passengers per flight, that suggests that some 180,000 passengers had their journeys disrupted, and probably more than 350,000 including those on incoming flights forced to land in other places or even other countries.

To assess the overall *mythquake-intensity*, the *fatality* rate would have been very low, just above the *MQ0* level: maybe one or two people who were unable to get to overseas hospitals in time for operations, for example, or who succumbed to the stress of the disruption and delays.

There would have been *life-changing impacts* for perhaps 5–10% of the passengers: people who lost a job or opportunity as a result of the delay, for example, or who missed seeing a relative for the last time, or who – as in that previous example – missed their own wedding. For that group, that places it as a mythquake in the mid-range between *MQ4* and *MQ5*.

In terms of *significant impact*, the number of people affected would have been at least twice as many as the passenger-count, including those relying on income from tourism, missed business-meetings, and grandparents unable to meet up with their families. For that group, that's a mythquake almost at the *MQ6* level, with matching impacts on the airport's reputation and more.

For the airlines, the financial cost would have been enormous. Given that airlines typically run their flights at 90% or more of capacity, it would have taken at least ten days to get all of those passengers to their intended destinations. The airlines would be legally liable to negotiate alternate flights and to provide hotels for all of those passengers, the latter for an effective average of at least five days. There were no figures reported for this, but a quick estimate would suggest that the accommodation-costs alone would add up to more than £100 million.

The airport itself reported losses of around £40 million caused by the blackout. That figure is perhaps low enough that the airport might have willingly taken on the *kurtosis-risk* of not building appropriate backup-infrastructure, and might continue that risk onward into the future.

Tackling Wicked-Problems

In this section, we'll aim to identify inherently-intractable **wicked-problems** in the enterprise, and to identify the factors that render those problems intractable. From there, we'll explore how to assist in developing and implementing strategies and tactics to resolve them in practice.

To set this up, it's probably best to start with the list of characteristics for a so-called "wicked-problem," as summarized by Jeffrey Conklin:

- The problem is not understood until after the formulation of a solution.
- Wicked problems have no stopping rule.
- Solutions to wicked problems are not right or wrong.
- Every wicked problem is essentially novel and unique.
- Every solution to a wicked problem is a "one-shot operation."
- Wicked problems have no given alternative solutions.

For the architecture of this work, we'll not only need **solid technical-skills** and a good *practical* understanding of systems-theory and systems-practice, but also some solid understanding and experience of working with "soft-systems" – particularly **the human aspects of complex systems**. We'll also need the trails of links and interdependencies that we've mapped out in the architecture repositories, and some means to use these in architecture modeling, such as described for the "architecture of trust" in the section "Service, Trust, and Responsibility" in Chapter 11.

The other absolute requirement for this work will be **overt support at senior levels**, preferably from the executive-board as a whole. *We cannot do this work without that.* Almost anything we do here will cross organizational boundaries, tramp on much-defended turf, touch on "taboo" topics, and poke into some highly-"political" pain-points. If we don't have the high-level authority and high-level protection to go into those spaces, we're going to find ourselves under full-on attack almost from the moment we start.

Caution   Cultivating a thick skin helps, too. As you'll no doubt discover the hard way, there's a good reason why one well-known list of essential attributes for enterprise-architects not only includes character-traits such as "diplomatic, strong people-skills," but "persistent, enduring" as well. An important warning there!

Expectation-management will also be crucial here. Many stakeholders will no doubt want a fixed, certain "solution" to the problem, but for wicked-problems, no such static, predefined solution can exist, and it's not an achievable "goal" as such. Instead, the best that we will be able to do is an ongoing, ever-evolving *process* of "re-solution" – and it needs to be managed, monitored, and measured as such.

Note Some of the sources we use for this in our own work include the *Fifth Discipline* books by Peter Sengé and others; Gerry Weinberg's classic books *Secrets of Consulting* and *More Secrets of Consulting*; the VPEC-T (values, process, events, content, trust) methodology developed by Nigel Green and colleagues; depth-foresight techniques such as Causal Layered Analysis, developed by Sohail Inayatullah and others; and Tom's research on power-issues, as summarized in the section "A Problem of Power" earlier. You'll find reference-details for all of these in Appendix B at the end of the book.

Tame, Wild, and Wicked

We looked at some of this earlier, about the distinctions between *tame-problems* and *wild-problems*, in the section "The Complexities of Change" in Chapter 7. We need to extend that a bit, by using those distinctions to build a better understanding of wicked-problems and what we can do about them.

Wicked-problems are often contrasted with **tame-problems**. The latter are problems that *can* be formulated before solution, that *do* have a stopping-rule, that *do* have right-or-wrong answers, that *do* iterate in (roughly or exactly) the same way each time, that are *repeatable*, and that in some cases can have whole families of repeatable right-or-wrong solutions. They could be any level of complication, perhaps, but they're always *nice, neat, predictable, well-behaved* problems.

Yet the usual **opposite of "tame"** isn't "wicked." It's "**wild**."

And it's exactly the same kind of contrast as between a tame animal and a wild animal.

A **tame-problem** is one that is predictable. Once we've solved it, and reduced it to a formula, an algorithm, or a predefined process, it stays that way.

A **wild-problem** is "a problem in the wild." It always remains somewhat unpredictable – and often much larger than we are.

It's wild. It doesn't always do what we expect it to – which, for something wild, is what we *ought* to expect.

It's wild. We can perhaps tame it a bit, by understanding it, and by mapping its behavior, context, and drivers.

Yet while a wild-problem *may* have tame elements, it can never be fully reduced to "tame" without breaking it – much like "breaking" a horse, breaking its will, maybe even breaking its sense of self. The act of supposedly "taming" it changes it: it's no longer the same problem as it was in the wild.

Note There's another interesting comparison there, too: people often talk of the "majesty" of a wild animal, often the pathos or sadness, or even loss of soul, of the broken "tamed" one. It might sometimes be useful to think of wild-problems versus tame ones in much the same way...

Another useful cross-map here would be with James P. Carse's concept of *finite and infinite games*:

- ***Tame-problems are like finite-games.*** They have a definite beginning and ending, a "right-or-wrong" answer in terms of its rules or algorithms, and are always subject to – in fact, *defined by* – those rules. We "win" a tame-problem by achieving the right answer.

- ***Wild-problems are like infinite-games.*** They don't have a knowable beginning or ending, and there is no "right answer" – only a "better-or-worse" answer within that specific context. There are sort-of-rules in play, but in practice these are more like "meta-rules" – higher-order rules from which context-specific rules will arise dynamically for a single instance, often or usually different every time. The object of play with a wild-problem is to *learn* – and continually discover something new and different about that problem every time we meet up with it in the wild.

Yet the distinction between "tame" and "wild" is recursive, and fractal. Every wild-problem has *some* tame-problem elements within it. And every tame-problem will *likewise* have wild-problem elements within it – sometimes deeply-hidden, within deeply-improbable-seeming "special-cases," yet somehow, somewhere always there.

Tame-problems are subsets or special-cases of wild-problems. They've had special conditions imposed, much like fences and chains and bridles and the like that are used to "tame" wild-animals. It's in the exact same sense that finite-games exist only as special-cases within an infinite-game.

As we saw earlier, if we look at it in SCAN terms, tame-problems sit over to the left-side of that "boundary of effective-certainty," and wild-problems sit over to the right, as shown in Figure 12-8.

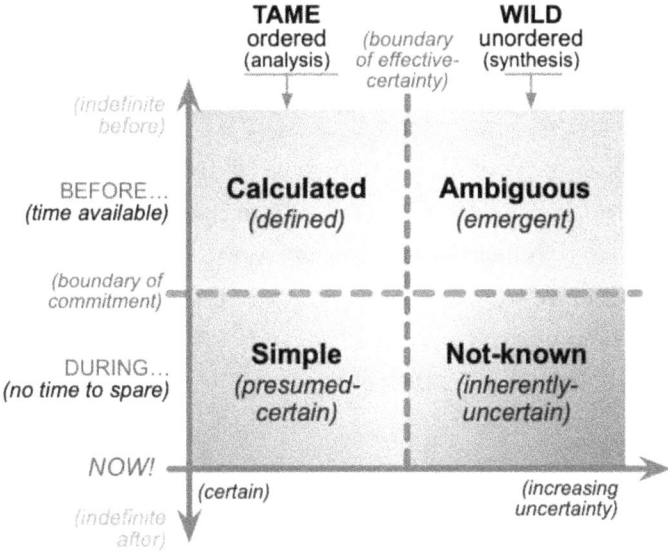

Figure 12-8. SCAN – tame-problems and wild-problems

But let's look again at that list of characteristics for wicked-problems, but perhaps with a more architectural eye:

- Each instance of a wicked-problem is essentially unique.
- A wicked-problem cannot be solved, but only "re-solved" for the context of each unique instance.
- Re-solving a wicked-problem will lead to outcomes that can only be described in terms of "better or worse" rather than a binary "right or wrong."
- There is no identifiable end-point to a wicked-problem.
- Every wicked-problem is a symptom of another unresolved problem.

All fair enough: we see all of those characteristics often enough in enterprise-architecture and the like. Yet notice one really important point: there's no problematic *morality* there, no "bad behavior" or anything like that. **Wicked-problems aren't "wicked" as in bad, naughty, misbehaving** – so why *do* we describe them as "wicked"?

CHAPTER 12   STEP 5: INTERACT WITH THE ENTERPRISE

In practice, **wicked-problems are just another class of wild-problems** that happen to fit that specific set of characteristics above.

In SCAN terms, tame-problems are "inside the box," within the Simple and Calculated domains. They're rule-based, and should be resolvable via a straightforward work-instruction, or a more sophisticated calculation or cross-reference. They're well-suited to machine-based or IT-based solutions, and the way we get to that solution is via *analysis*.

But wicked-problems sit over on the right-hand side of the SCAN frame, within the Ambiguous and Not-known domains, where reality is either emergent or a unique "market of one." Conventional analysis alone will not help us here. For example, *a wicked-problem cannot be solved by IT alone*: attempting to do so is often a core reason why an already-wild-problem turns "wicked." What we need instead is a *synthesis* across of all the conflicting perspectives that are in play in the context, as summarized in Figure 12-9.

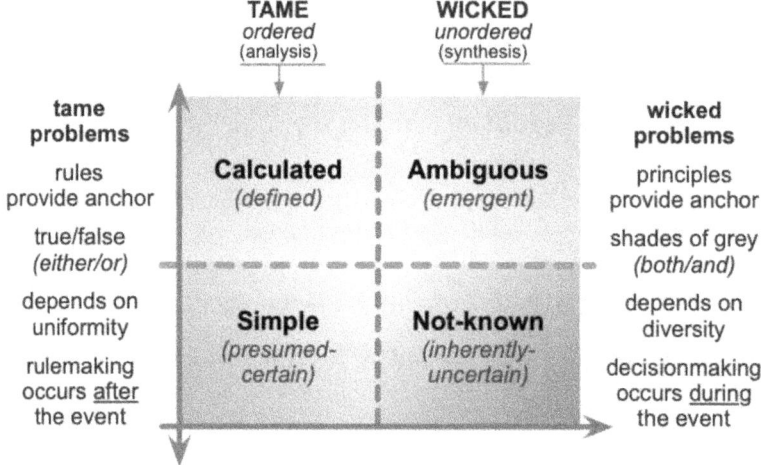

Figure 12-9. Tame-problems and wicked-problems

So let's stop making those supposed "unknown" and "unsolvable" problems even harder to work with by calling them "wicked." **They're wild, not "wicked."** They're just being what they are: *real* problems, out in the wild, without the artificially-imposed constraints of "the tamed." As architects, we need to work *with* that fact, rather than complain unrealistically that it exists.

Working with Wicked-Problems

The issues that we face in enterprise-architecture fall into two fundamentally different categories:

- *"Tame" problems*: Those to which identifiable analytic rules apply – including a so-called "stopping rule" which determines completion and closure – and hence an explicit "solution" which can be identified in advance

- *"Wicked" problems*: Those which are *inherently* dynamic, complex, or chaotic, and for which no stable explicit "solution" can exist

And yes, many of those real-world problems *are* "wicked," rooted in ambiguity, in dynamic uncertainty, tensions of opposites, and clashes of worldviews. There *is* no permanent "solution" to a wicked-problem: indeed, the very act of addressing the problem will, in itself, change the ways in which we experience the problem, and the underlying drivers are themselves changing all the time anyway. The best we can aim for is to create some approach which is *self-evolving*, adapting itself to create a stream of transient, context-specific "re-solutions," each aligned to the overall principles and purpose of the enterprise.

Every wicked-problem is also both a symptom and a cause of other wicked-problems. We can never "fix" a wicked-problem in isolation: everything is connected to everything else, so we can *only* address it at the level of the whole. And because the real-world is inherently complex, it's probable that *most* real business problems are "wicked," or have some significant component of "wickedness" about them.

> **Note** One classic example of a wicked-problem is "***business/IT alignment***" – perhaps more accurately described as the "business/IT divide." One key reason as to *why* it becomes so "wicked" is that the respective worldviews are significantly different, and hence their respective definitions of "success."

There's also a crucial distinction between **technical complexity**, which sits more in the Calculated domain of the *analyst*-mode, and **social complexity**, which sits more in the Ambiguous domain of the *alchemist*-mode. By the definition of "enterprise," organizations are social structures, and social-complexity is an inherent consequence of that – hence the inevitability of wicked-problems in business.

Whenever we're dealing with any kind of social complexity, we're no longer in a predictable, "rational" space. And the only *real* law is Murphy's anyway, as we saw back in Chapter 3. To tackle wicked-problems, we have to start from that fact: be aware of it, acknowledge it, and act accordingly.

Caution   This is not easy, precisely *because* it's not rational, when everyone expects, or even *demands*, that it "should" be rational, predictable, and the rest. Given that, it's best to be ready for the painful fact that tackling any wicked-problem will almost invariably run into "stormy weather": expect ruffled feathers, angry outbursts, screwed-up assumptions, nasty "political" surprises, and lots and lots and *lots* of blame. We've even seen full-on temper-tantrums at times – sometimes aimed at us personally, in classic "shoot the messenger" style. Oh joys…

Gerry Weinberg summarized the architect's agony all too well in his classic *The Secrets of Consulting*: "It seemed that I had only two choices: to remain rational, and go crazy; or become irrational, and be called crazy. For years, I oscillated between those two poles of misery." But as he explains in the book, there *is* a way out of that dilemma: *become rational about the irrationality*. And *that's* the aim here, in this section of the work.

Any "pain-point" in the business will almost certainly be rooted in a wicked-problem of some kind. And the usual reason *why* it's causing pain is because someone's trying to control it. The blunt fact is that **attempts at "command and control" <u>will not work</u> with wicked-problems**. At best, all they'll do is paper over the cracks, making the problems harder to locate, harder to repair, and even more likely to cause a collapse into catastrophic failure.

Yet **it <u>is</u> possible to guide a wicked-problem into a preferred direction**. In his book *The Secrets of Consulting*, Gerry Weinberg describes this as *"the Buffalo Bridle."* A buffalo is *big*, heavy, far too strong to control, and always too much of the wild. But we can make a buffalo go anywhere, as long as *it* wants to go there; and we can keep a buffalo out of anywhere, as long as *it* doesn't want to go there. The trick is not in trying to control it, but in providing conditions such that the buffalo itself decides to do what we want it to do. It's the same with a wicked-problem: we need to understand how it thinks, so to speak, and to work *with* it to achieve the ends we need.

We'll also need to look more closely at the *human* side of systems, because while that may be where the problems lie, it can also be the only place where we're likely to find any real answers. As Gerry Weinberg put it, whatever the problem looks like, and no matter how technical it may seem to be, ***it's <u>always</u> a "people-problem."*** Much of it is about motivation, too: people can go anywhere, do anything, or solve any problem, as long as *they* want to do so. As architects, it's up to us to find the themes of structure and purpose and story that would help them make that choice.

To "solve" a wicked-problem, we need to provide conditions under which an appropriate set of "re-solution" can evolve from the context itself. For example:

- *A wicked-problem is rooted in* **dynamic uncertainty**: Use tools such as the SCAN frame to describe the differences between control and emergence, and the different skills and tactics needed in the complex-domain compared to those used in analysis in the "knowable" (complicated) domain.

- *The uncertainty in a wicked-problem arises from the* **natural tensions between polar opposites**, *such as safety versus agility, or transparency versus security*: Use systems-theory to describe that tension, and model the delays and feedback-loops and other transactions in the overall system.

- *Other tensions in a wicked-problem arise from overt or covert* **clashes of worldviews or value-systems**: Use tools such as Causal Layered Analysis to identify and describe the respective value-systems, and specify "translations" between the respective worldviews and the appropriate leadership tactics to use with each.

- *Some wicked-problems can arise from confusions or disagreements about terminology*: Use the architectural glossary and thesaurus to resolve conflicts by showing relationships between terms, and making it possible to accept multiple definitions as equally "true."

- *A common barrier against resolving a wicked-problem is* **lack of trust** *between stakeholders and stakeholder-groups*: Use the SEMPER diagnostic to measure and monitor the scale and domain of the difficulty; use VPEC-T and other sensemaking techniques to identify the source, and to begin to ease the embedded tension.

But the real key to making wicked-problems manageable resides in **trust**. Anything we can do to help build trust will make wicked-problems easier – if only in terms of easier to bear, easier to accept, easier to live with. For architects, with our uncomfortable "pig-in-the-middle" position in so many inter-silo arguments, this is why diplomacy and dialogue are so important. If we do it right, we literally create and carry that trust with us from place to place within the enterprise.

To **identify** "**wickedness**," a context is inherently "wicked" if any of the following conditions apply:

- Are there any ***direct conflicts*** between any of the major drivers in the context? In particular, are any of the drivers – especially core-values – in *inherent* direct opposition to each other?

- Are there any ***fundamental differences in perspectives and worldviews*** between key groups of stakeholders? For example, management versus operations, or business versus IT?

- Are there any fundamental ***"win/lose" framings of relationships*** that would characteristically enforce a conflict between stakeholder groups?

- Is it ***difficult to define a single "correct" view of the context*** that can be agreed upon by all parties? Are there multiple, conflicting views of the causes of the problem? Is it difficult or impossible to define and agree upon a single set of criteria for "success" in the context?

- Is there evidence of ***inappropriate models or mindsets*** being brought to bear upon the context? For example, issues escalated away from the hands-on knowledge needed to resolve a practical problem?

- Is there a significant degree of ***ambiguity or uncertainty about the context***? Are key data or information-items either missing or inherently uncertain? Is there strong *pressure to deliver a once-and-for-all "solution"* for the context even if there is a high degree of ambiguity?

- Is the context ***highly politicized***, especially with significant amounts of finger-pointing and "other-blame"?

- Are there any strong ***ideological, cultural, or economic constraints*** on the context?

- Is there a high or significant ***resistance to change*** among one or more key groups of stakeholders?

- Do the problems in the context appear to be ***symptoms of other problems*** that seem to be interrelated in ways that are complex and difficult to describe?

- Is the context ***a "pain-point" which never seems to be resolved***, no matter how many attempts have been made to fix it?

We would document the values and their conflicts in the respective parts of the architecture-repository. We would also record any identifiable "wickedness" in the risks-register, and note the context in the issues-register as an item that *will* require regular review.

To **provide architectural support** to **resolve wicked problems**, we'll need to develop a context-specific framework to identify workable "re-solution" for each type of wicked-problem:

- Work with the relevant stakeholders to identify and document the respective drivers as above. (These stakeholders would typically include process-strategists, process-designers, operational change-management teams, and HR specialists as well as representatives of the various players caught up in the wicked-problem itself.)

- Use the respective "pain-point" symptoms to guide us toward a suitable start-point within the architecture, and then spiral-out from there in successive architecture-iterations.

Once a "solution"-framework emerges, we would derive requirements and implementation-designs in the usual way.

Caution Remember always that wicked-problems *cannot* be "solved" in the classic business-analysis sense: they can only be "re-solved" dynamically to match the specific context and conditions that apply in each distinct iteration. Hence, again, do *not* expect to be able to build an IT-only "fit-and-forget" solution for any wicked-problem!

Almost all real-world "solutions" to wicked-problems will require *some* form of people-based intervention, and medium to high skill-levels and competencies in at least some parts of the overall process. You'll also need to work with operational change-management teams and the like to help establish clear guidelines to enable those people to interpret the wicked-problem's boundary-conditions, and to set up "safe-fail" fallback as the tensions between the respective problem-drivers shift within day-to-day practice.

Let's look at ***a real example*** of ours, in an aircraft-research establishment a couple of decades ago. They'd recently brought in a group of test-engineers from another place, and things had started to go wrong very quickly from there. There were huge clashes between the engineers and some of the scientists: "We get a job out in three days," yelled one of the engineers, "and those idiots can't even get a job out in three *years!*" The clashes got so bad that almost all work had stopped.

We mapped out the situation as shown in Figure 12-10, using the CSPAR phases and the CALc modes as the underlying frame.

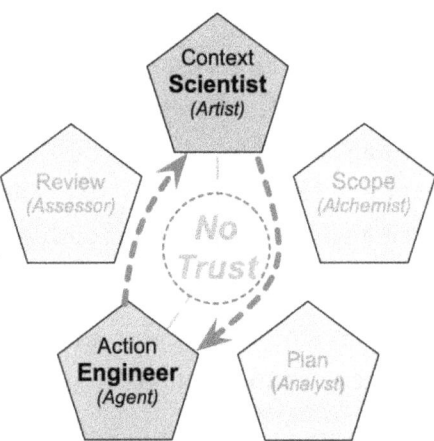

Figure 12-10. *Wicked-problem – clash between scientists and engineers*

Straight away it became obvious that this was a classic wicked-problem: two competing sets of perspectives and worldviews that were so fundamentally incompatible that, in effect, ***the two groups*** had *naturally* become ***anti-clients for each other***. The fight was no-one's fault: it was a *systemic* issue, not a personal one. Both groups were right, in their own way and from their own perspective, and any attempt to force one perspective to be "the right one," and the other "wrong," would only make things worse.

Instead, as shown in Figure 12-11, we described how to use the CSPAR pattern to turn that head-on clash into a "***virtuous circle***," where each phase of the overall research-and-development process would support the next.

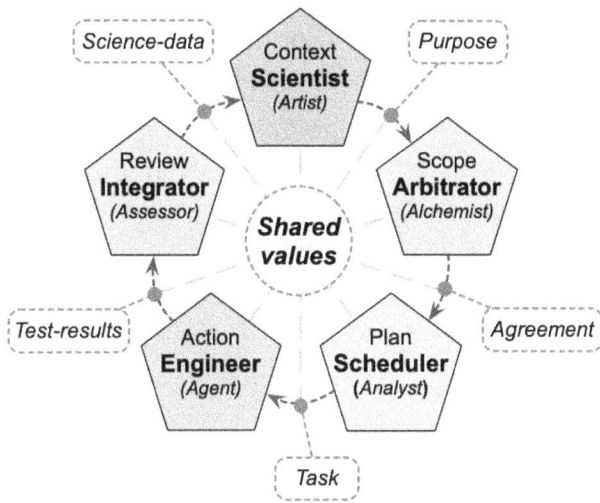

Figure 12-11. *Resolve clash between scientists and engineers*

We started by adding two phases on the "upward" side between the scientists and the engineers. The first of these was an acknowledgment that those clashes would be inevitable in a *systemic* sense, and hence that the two groups would need an "outside" **arbitrator** from elsewhere in the establishment to help them reach a fair outcome in each case. Many of the arguments had arisen over scheduling – the scientists having a tendency to change their entire designs at the last minute – so we added a ***scheduler*** to help the two groups resolve those issues. On the "downward" side, we added an ***integrator*** to help the engineers structure their results in ways that would help their reuse in *other* research projects, and to close the loop back to the science side of the work.

It worked. The clashes did recur from time to time: that would always be the case, by the nature of the system itself. But the anger and heat and blame were gone, the productivity went way up again, and everyone was a lot happier – including the managers who'd asked us to do that piece of social-architecture work.

CHAPTER 12   STEP 5: INTERACT WITH THE ENTERPRISE

Disruption and Chaos

What happens when things go wrong in a big way? How should we respond when those incidents occur? As enterprise-architects, what will *we* need to provide, in terms of structure, story, and suchlike, to mitigate against those risks and to guide the response to that kind of disruption and chaos? That's the theme for this part of this Step.

In terms of people for the task, we're likely to need a lot of help here. We'll certainly need to co-opt from the usual crew of strategists, service-designers, process-designers, quality-teams, and risk-managers. The ones who we'll want most of all, though, are "the old hands" who've dealt with all manner of real-world chaos over the years, and have the bloody-minded cynicism, pessimism, tenacity, and destructive inventiveness of the experienced senior tester.

Note   Some of the people who'll be needed here will literally be "the old hands," because many of the big problems will arise or recur only after long intervals of time. In the preparation for the year-2000 date-rollover problem (often referred to as "Y2K"), there were real challenges in finding enough people who still knew how to work with old, rare, or near-obsolete programming-languages such as COBOL, Forth, and Pick. Much the same is likely to happen again as we approach January 2038, when dates in Unix systems will turn negative, pointing back in time rather than forward.

Sometimes, the timescales that matter can be much longer. Most coastal seawalls on the east coast of Japan had been built during the 1960s and 1970s to a height of 5–10 meters, or around 15–30 feet, because that was the peak height of the 1933 tsunami that had been the highest in living memory there. But the mayor of one small town had lived through that tsunami, and knew that there were stone tablets in the hills above the town that marked the much higher levels that the 1896 tsunami had reached. And there were similar stone records around the region for other earlier tsunamis too, some of them going back more than a thousand years. At his insistence, the town had built its seawall higher than the rest, at around 15 meters. Everyone had mocked him, and complained about the cost, and that it blocked the view of the sea: but in the devastating tsunami that followed the Tōhoku earthquake in March 2011, his town of Fudai was the only one along that entire coastline that survived intact.

We'll again draw extensively on the cross-links in the architecture models and repository, and on end-to-end process models that will usually be held by Operations teams.

Once again, measurement of performance will be difficult here, because the whole point of much of the work is to *prevent* things from happening. Given that, much of the "success" would be measurable only in terms of what *doesn't* happen – which, by definition, is hard to measure. The most usable metrics will probably be around customer-satisfaction, speed of response, and the like. Typical deliverables would include models of failure-and-response scenarios, failure-impact maps, and – co-developed with risk-managers – procedures and work-instructions for "safe-fail" risk-mitigation and risk-recovery activities.

Business-Continuity and Recovery

Planning for ***business-continuity and disaster-recovery*** can present some of the greatest challenges to the architecture, literally testing it to destruction if we don't pay attention to what it shows us. Yet that process itself will show us not only how to make the architecture more robust, but also how to *use* the architecture to guide failure-response, to everyone's benefit.

Strategy and other top-down plans provide an idealized picture of how we want our world to be; constraints coming bottom-up from the operations space tell us what the world really is. Somewhere in the middle, the two forces meet – and often clash, sometimes with ugly consequences. Despite all those nice plans, the real-world is *messy* – and it always will be, whether we like it or not. No matter what the company rule-books may say, the only *real* law is Murphy's: and as we've seen before, Murphy rules supreme...

For this part of the work, though, what we need to know about is what *else* might happen when something "goes wrong," goes "outside of the box." In other words, we need to trace the potential *impact* of an unexpected, unplanned-for event. We always do this from the bottom-up, because the operations-layer is the only place where "the enterprise" touches the real-world. Ideas may begin at the top, but reality exists at the bottom.

In a typical impact-analysis scenario, we imagine that some critical component has suddenly disappeared: there's been a fire, a flood, a break-in, a simple breakdown; we've just lost a server, an underwater cable, a sorting-depot. What happens? What can we now *not* do if that's gone? What *else* won't work? Whose performance figures will be hit, and by how much? How long – if at all – can we keep things going without that item?

CHAPTER 12   STEP 5: INTERACT WITH THE ENTERPRISE

Note   You'll also need to ask what kind of alternative options are available, how long things can keep going on those workarounds, how to recover afterward, and so on. But that comes a little later: for now, we're only concerned with tracing the impact of the event.

This is the same ***impact-trails architecture-mapping process*** that we've used before, for issues around trust, investors and beneficiaries, kurtosis-risks, and more. We use the same information from the architecture-repositories, about what connects with what, and the nature and bindedness of each of those cross-dependencies. All we need to do is follow the trails, and watch the implied impacts ripple outward through the entire enterprise.

First, we ***identify the impact from the bottom-up***. Working with risk-managers, we define a scenario in which one or more key items have been put either temporarily or permanently out of service. We identify the matching items in the architecture repository, first defining appropriate entries for them if required. We then ask

- To what is this item connected? At this level (initially, the Operations layer), what assets, functions, locations, capabilities, events, business-decisions, and their composites depend on this item? What is the business-criticality of each dependency?

- If an "owner"-responsibility relationship exists for the item, how will the owner be notified of the failure? What decisions and actions will the owner need to take? On what would such decisions and actions depend?

- What "owner"-responsibilities can be identified for dependent items connected to the failed item? How will those owners be notified, what actions and decisions will they need to take, and on what will those depend in turn?

- What resource-allocations and performance-metrics will be affected by the failure of this item?

- Overall, what is the business-criticality of this item? What overall impact will it have on business-critical metrics, and on any or all of the enterprise quality-concerns? In what way does the criticality change over time – for example, survivable for one minute, one hour, one day, one week?

- What impact will the failure have on the next level up (initially, the "Implement" operations-planning layer)? What are the assets, functions, locations, capabilities, events, business-decisions, and their composites that will be affected? What dependencies exist from these affected items for items on the next layer down, and so on downward to actual operations? What else will be affected, and what will their knock-on impacts be, as the effects ripple up and down again to the operations layer?

The last set of questions move the exploration up a layer. We then use this to recurse through the questions from the start, moving up another layer at each pass, until impacts can be assessed right the way up to the organizational and enterprise "universals."

We would document any newly-identified items and dependencies in the architecture repository, together with any further risks, opportunities, and issues. Working with risk-managers and others, we would then identify requirements for change-projects to mitigate these risks, perhaps drawing on the previous work here on design for system resilience and flexibility – see the section "Design for Resilience" in Chapter 11. Note, though, that the role of the architect here would again usually be one of decision-support, not decision-making: all design-decisions and suchlike would be the responsibility of risk-managers and operations specialists.

From this, we need to define the **requirements for an impact dashboard**. Following from the previous impact-analyses, we assess what information will be needed at various levels of the enterprise in order to respond appropriately to incidents of varying severity:

- What categories of incidents have significant impacts on the operations and the viability of the organization and its enterprise? In what ways should we prioritize incidents, for which stakeholders, and why?

- For each category of incident, what information will the stakeholders need in order to resolve or mitigate the incident impact? In what timespan would this information be needed, and from which sources would or could it be derived? What transforms would be needed to present this information appropriately and meaningfully for the respective audience?

We would again document, within the architecture-repositories, the requisite metrics and transforms, and their dependencies on the respective assets, functions, and the like. We would also record any identified risks, opportunities, and issues in their respective registers. If appropriate, we would work with system-designers and others to outline requirements for design and implementation of a suitable "impact dashboard."

Example At the airport, the architecture-team and the others are continuing with their "lessons-learned" exercise about the power-failure at London's Heathrow Airport.

Their own airport is at less risk than Heathrow, say the infrastructure-team – it's a smaller airport, for a start, and a newer one as well. In regular use, the systems rely in part on the external-grid, but also on the solar-panels that were installed on most of the buildings right from the start. They also have a large battery-bank, both to reduce costs of buying from the grid, but also as immediately-available backup: there's enough storage in the batteries to run the whole airport at full power for at least a couple of hours, though the teams will want to test and extend that if they can. They have diesel standby-generators to take over at least some of that load, and the ability to call for mobile generators if need be. As each part of that power-system fails or fades out, they can switch automatically to the next.

There's a dashboard that shows the current status of the overall power-system, including the available reserves in the batteries. The dashboard can be accessed by authorized users from anywhere in the airport.

They've tested the system in a variety of simulated conditions, and even run one live-test in the middle of the night when there were no scheduled flights and when any other impacts of failure would be minimal. All seems to have worked well. The one remaining weak-point in the whole system is the mechanism to switch between supply-sources. It *is* possible to do the switchover manually, but that would take several minutes, and may not be reliable or safe under certain weather conditions, so they'll do what they can to find alternative ways to make that work.

Fail-Safe and Safe-Fail

That work above on impact-analysis and impact trails provides us with an effective list of failure-priorities that we can use in enterprise-architecture, solution-architecture, or any other aspect of change-work. Some of the potential failures would be almost trivial, or the respective workarounds fairly self-evident, but some are most definitely not, and we need to design appropriate ways around them. Here, we need to contrast two different approaches:

- *Fail-safe*: No viable alternative – must not fail, because if it does, there may be no possibility of recovery
- *Safe-fail*: Is allowed to fail "gracefully," with fallback to lower-grade alternatives

Fail-safe is the obvious preference, but courtesy of Murphy's Law, it's never actually achievable in practice. The best we can do is deal with the consequences of each failure, and make every effort to learn from those consequences, to extend ever closer toward the "fail-safe" ideal.

Caution   In some cases, the consequences of the failure of a "fail-safe" could well be that someone dies, so this is *not* a trivial matter!

"Lessons-learned" is an essential part of any quality-system, which is why the CSPAR change-process has that explicit "lessons-learned" phase at the end of the cycle. You'll often face a lot of pressure to skip over that "lessons-learned" analysis and go straight on to the next item of work. But it's essential that you resist that pressure, and take at least *some* brief moment to stop, think, reflect, learn – because if you don't, you're literally putting lives and livelihoods at risk. Don't skip it: lessons-learned *matter*.

The aim of ***safe-fail*** is that we *always* have alternatives of some kind. One such option is to use multiple-redundancy in system-design. Aircraft navigation-systems, for example, will use at least two or three systems in parallel, of different vintages and with different technologies, ultimately right back to sextant and compass. If one system fails, we fall back "gracefully" to the next in line, and we can compare between them in case of doubt.

CHAPTER 12   STEP 5: INTERACT WITH THE ENTERPRISE

> **Note**   For test-purposes, another option is to set up circumstances in which failure doesn't matter as long as it can be used as something to learn from. For example, we might set up a simulation or a carefully-isolated "practice field" in which people can develop those parts of skills in which learning only takes place through making mistakes.

This is why the principle of abstract-services versus service-implementations is so important, as we saw back in the section "The Design of Services" in Chapter 10, because it allows us to switch between different implementations without changing the fundamental interface:

- The *parameter-values* in the parameters for the service-level agreement might change – for example, the transaction-volume may drop, or the response-time increase – but the *parameters themselves* should remain unchanged.

- The *interface-details* for the interface may change – for example, if the IT-system fails, we may have to drop back to using paper-based forms, or even just word-of-mouth – but as far as practicable, the *content and structure* for the interface should remain the same.

In essence, it's the same principles as in load-balancing, as we saw back in the section "Checks and Balances" in Chapter 9. By keeping the function-interfaces the same, we can shift the complexity to the service-choreography. And changing the choreography is much simpler to manage – it's already designed for this kind of service-switching, because that's how it handles the existing end-to-end business-processes.

> **Example**   A risk-management colleague working in the banking sector asks executives to imagine that their bank-branch has suddenly ceased to function. Perhaps it's burned down, or been hit by an earthquake, or simply that, as at Heathrow, the power-supply has been cut because the electricity-substation has failed. The reason *why* doesn't much matter here – it's just an example.

The next question: What is the very first department they need to get going again? Answer: *The mail-room* – because communication, even in simple note-form, is the key to coordination. Computer-based IT is important, yes, but it takes *time* to set up – and time is at an absolute premium in any emergency.

To design for fail-safe and safe-fail – to **design for failure** – we need to reassess the abstract-services and the implementations, and the service-choreography that links them together. For each priority failure-scenario, we would ask

- What are the abstract-services in context for this failure-scenario? What are the transactions, resource-requirements, interfaces, service-level agreement templates, and reporting-metrics for each?

- What implementations exist for each abstract-service? What are the characteristics and trade-offs for each implementation? What specific amendments do they each require for the transactions, resource-requirements, service-level agreement templates, and reporting-metrics?

- What are the fallbacks and failure-characteristics for each failure-scenario in which each abstract-service and its implementations are in context? Does the scenario require a fail-safe or safe-fail fallback-response? What transition-management would be required in service-choreography to switch between implementations in a fallback scenario? What additional requirements, if any, will be placed on the service-choreography to satisfy the fallback needs?

- Are all fallback requirements for an abstract-service covered by the existing implementations? If not, what amendments or additional implementations would be required?

If required, we would build models, simulations, and suchlike to illustrate or demonstrate those fallback processes. We would then document any newly-identified items and dependencies in the architecture repository, together with any further risks, opportunities, and issues.

Working with risk-managers and others, we might identify requirements for change-projects to improve fail-safe and safe-fail handling for failure incidents. As usual, though we'd be there solely to provide decision-*support* for system-design, all design-decisions and suchlike would be the responsibility of risk-managers and operations specialists.

Example At the airport, the architecture-team, the infrastructure-team, and the others have gone past the lesson-learned stage: they now need to put what they've learned into action.

Slowly, painfully, it dawns on them that there's no way to make it completely fail-safe: once the power's gone, it's gone. At that stage they'd be limited to getting the ground-operations to lay warning-flares on the runways, and hope that any would-be arrivals would realize that the airport is indeed closed.

But there's a lot that they *can* do in a safe-fail fallback between the moment that main-grid is lost and the time when all the power runs out. And from what exists already, there should be a good chance that they'll never actually reach that latter point. The trick to keeping all of the systems running for as long as possible will be in how they plan out the steps of their "graceful failure," gently cutting back and back until only the absolute essentials are still left until the very last moment. Juggling the priorities and trade-offs is *hard* – but they need to plan it out *now*, because there won't be time to think out how to do it all when the power-failure clock has already started ticking down toward the final time-out.

Right now, they're exploring the switching and connections needed for when the mobile power-generators arrive, to provide secondary backup once the battery-power has run out. Next, they'll need to map out which lights can still stay on in the main lounge-area after the move from second-stage to third-stage low-power mode, and how the respective wiring-blocks will need to be configured to support that change. After that, the next task will be – well, they don't quite know yet, but it'll become clear as they keep moving on.

Back and forth, round and round; detail, detail, more detail… It's a long, slow, tedious process to get it all ready and right, but they know that it *does* have to be done so that things *can* work out all right on the night.

Coping with Chaos

All of this section has been about how to deal with the deeper "unknowns" of the business. In "Business-Continuity and Recovery," we focused on the *"unknown-knowns,"* the preventive work that would underpin the content for the *preventive-checklist* in a Four-Checklists set. In "Fail-Safe and Safe-Fail," we focused on the *"known-unknowns,"* the work that would underpin the respective *emergency-checklist* and the like. Here, we turn to the more challenging *"unknown-unknowns,"* and the work that would not only underpin the respective *chaos-checklist*, but also provide architecture-support in real-time for people who are **coping with the chaos** whenever it hits in real-world action.

Throughout this type of work, we will *need* to maintain "**defensible-uncertainty**." Much of what happens here is *inherently* uncertain, and despite all of the planning, preparation, and prevention-work, things will still go wrong – "The best-laid schemes o' Mice an' Men" and all that. That means that there'll be plenty of blame flying around as soon as anything *does* go wrong, and we *need* to make sure that we don't become the recipients of that blame when it comes our way.

We'll also need to focus on the **sustainment-architectures**. Many of the issues here are longer-term risks, so an architecture-approach that can only support short-term projects may only *create* failure here.

From what we've done earlier in this Step, we know the typical **sources** for that chaos that we're likely to be dealing with here:

- Everyday mistakes, everyday accidents, and everyday disasters
- Misunderstandings, misinformation, and mistrust
- Power-issues, anti-clients, and kurtosis-risks
- Enterprise-hijack, untested-assumptions, and wicked-problems
- Natural disruptions and natural disasters
- Human cluelessness, carelessness, malice, and greed

"Whatever it looks like," as Gerry Weinberg said in *Secrets of Consulting*, "it's always a people-problem." And that's certainly true here: most of that chaos in the list above would seem to be caused by people, one way or another. A lot of power-against flying around in there, for example.

Yet it's always essential to remember that **people** – not just IT-systems or machines – will also often provide us with the only way out of a mess when everything else has failed. Power-from-within is the only real source of the power to make things better, and power-with shared with others is what enables that power to make that happen. Vision, values, and a real sense of shared-purpose will often be the key to that: it provides the way we engage people's help, and keep them going even when things seem to have gone from bad to worse.

In the real-world "Miracle of the Hudson," for example, everyone on Flight 1549 survived because everyone there pulled together in the moment: flight-crew, cabin-crew, passengers, air-traffic crews, helicopter-crews, ferry-crews, emergency-crews, and also those other everyday people all around. They took personal risks, showed personal responsibility, and bent the rules where necessary, all to make it all work in real-time. When things go badly wrong, people's willingness to help will often be the only thing available to make things right again.

Yet **what can we do about this chaos**, as enterprise-architects?

The short-answer is that we create an **architecture of chaos**, in the same way as we've done earlier for power-issues, trust-issues, wicked-problems, and so on. And given that previous work, we'll already know how to do this:

- Map out the **impact-trails** spreading outward from the points of contact, to identify the various services that will need attention

- Use the organizational and enterprise "universals" and other context-specific drivers – vision, values, principles, standards, constraints, success-criteria, effectiveness-criteria, and so on – to guide **priorities for action**

- Use the service-architecture to guide design for **fallback** and **reconfiguration** of services as required, in accordance with those priorities

- Provide **guidance of action** as required

- **Iterate and repeat** all of the above until told that it's safe to stop

It's essentially the same as before. The only real difference is that, in SCAN terms, we do this in two distinct parts:

- **Before** the action, while things are still quiet, we'll switch between the *Analyst*-mode in the *Calculated* domain and the *Alchemist*-mode in the *Ambiguous* domain to explore options and use the architecture to support prevention and preparation for failure.

- **During** the action, when the chaos has already hit, we'll switch between the *Agent*-mode in the *Simple* domain and the *Artist*-mode in the *Not-known* domain, to create new architectures and system-designs in real-time, to serve the immediate need.

We'll only be able to do that real-time architecture *during* the event if we've already done the right preparation *before* the event, when we still had the time available to do so. Without that, we won't have time to take the actions needed to resolve that real-world chaos.

We'll also need to develop those real-time-architecture skills. For that to happen, we'll need to **practice on the small changes, to get ready for the big ones**. And yes, there are plenty of potential sources for the latter that we already know about: the fragility of globalized supply-chains, for example, or increasing constraints on availability of some of the key resources, or, at the time of writing, a return of instability in global-scale geopolitics and the like. Oh well.

Yet large as those challenges may well be, they're still relatively small on the Mythquake Scale: MQ5, MQ6, maybe the higher end of MQ7 in some cases, affecting tens of millions of people. The *really* big ones would be larger again, maybe impacting everyone on the entire planet: for example, natural disasters such as climate-change, sea-level rise, a super-volcano on the scale of Mt Toba or the Deccan Traps, or a megastrike from a passing meteor. And there are also several man-made sources for disasters on that kind of scale, of which, as you can see from the *MQ9+* line in that mythquake-chart back in Figure 12-7, the most dangerous by far is the **deep-myth** of **possession**.

It's been known for decades, or maybe even for centuries now, that *there is no way to make a possession-based economy sustainable*. It can only be made to *seem* sustainable via an illusion of "infinite growth," which is inherently impossible on a finite planet. In practice, it can only be run as a pyramid-game or Ponzi-scheme. When that type of game runs out of room to grow, its only option is to cannibalize itself from the base – and although the collapse would be slow at first, it would keep on going at an ever-accelerating pace until there's nothing left. It's been known since at least the *Limits to Growth* study back in the early 1970s that something like that kind of process seems *already* well underway at a global scale – and ultimately almost no-one would survive that kind of collapse.

That might sound a bit apocalyptic, perhaps, but unfortunately, no, it's real. There's no real doubt about this now: that mythquake is already underway, and the entire possession-economy has to go, as soon as possible, before the collapse goes beyond a point of no return at which there would be no choices left. That's the real challenge that we *all* face right now, not just for a single organization, nor a single enterprise, but for *the* enterprise – the overarching enterprise of life itself.

Fortunately, yes, we do still have *some* time to get ready for this, before the real chaos hits. And fortunately, yes, there *is* a long-proven alternative that not only pre-dates the possession-economy, but is in everyday use in almost every household: a *responsibility-based economy*, built around interlocking mutual responsibilities. If that *is* the direction we go in, it would require literally re-architecting the entire human enterprise – so somewhere in the not-too-distant future, you might well find yourself called upon to use your architecture skills in that global-scale transition. And the methods and tools you've learned in this book would probably be central in your work for that.

For now, though, most of that is still some way into the future. In the meantime, we need to focus on what we *can* do in the present, and practice on improving our architecture-skills on the everyday chaos that comes up in our everyday work. ***To get ready for those big changes, we need to practice on the smaller ones*** – such as the ones in front of us right now.

Example At the airport, later in the year, the lights go out.

Or rather, the lights go out in the city beyond the airport. In the heat of the summer, an unexpected storm-cell had built up without warning, and, just after dark, a lightning-strike had hit the switchgear at the local power-station. It's going to be out of action for at least a day.

But at the airport itself, everything's fine. For now, at any rate. The main power-grid is down, of course, and neither is there any solar-power now that it's after sunset. But the switchover-systems worked; there's enough power in the batteries to last until around midnight. The backup-generators have been started and will be ready to take over, with enough fuel available right now to take the airport through until dawn. Further fuel is already on its way, and the mobile-generators from the next city to the west will be ready to take over within an hour or two if need be.

The airport has started its safe-fail transition toward low-power mode, to conserve energy as much as possible. But it's a "graceful-failure," with no sudden blackouts or cutouts, and using the information-systems at each stage to warn passengers about what's happening and what will happen next. There'll definitely be enough power to continue to receive incoming flights, so there won't be any need for expensive and disruptive diversions to other airports, or aircraft stranded in the wrong places for the next day's flight-schedule.

Outgoing flights should be able to continue for now, though it won't be possible if the airport is pushed into the later stages of low-power mode. There *should* be enough power to avoid that, according to the calculations, but in practice it'll depend on how well the backup power-system holds up under the actual load. Messages have already gone out to warn the passengers for those flights to keep in touch via the airport app, so that they'll know well in advance if their flight is at risk of being canceled.

At dawn, the main grid is still off, but it's a clear day, and the solar-power systems can start to take on some of the load. They're still in a mid-level low-power mode, but everything essential is still working. No incoming flights diverted; no outbound flights canceled or delayed, other than for the usual reasons such as mechanical problems.

When the main grid comes back on, late in the afternoon, the airport's senior management starts to count up the cost. It isn't much: mainly the fuel-bill for the diesel-generators, some extra overtime-pay for emergency-crews, some lost revenue from the airport shops that had to close, but that's about it.

They then count up what the cost *would* have been if the backup-system hadn't been there. It's an eye-watering sum. They'd worried a lot about the cost of that system, and even the need for it, but it's clear now that it's paid for itself many times over in just one day. In their report to the board, the executives single out the architecture-team to thank them for the work they'd done to make this outcome happen.

CHAPTER 12   STEP 5: INTERACT WITH THE ENTERPRISE

Enhancing Enterprise Effectiveness

In this final section for this Step, we need to bring ourselves back to the here-and-now, and reconnect everything we've done here to the role of **sustainment-architectures**. As architects, that's our key tool to keep everything working together, better, always on-purpose, **across the broader scope, scale, and timescales**.

The task here is to explore options to enhance the overall effectiveness of any aspect of the enterprise, by optimizing the trade-offs between the various dimensions of effectiveness. We'll need to do this repeatedly, at least every few months or so, to ensure that the organization can be kept up-to-date and aligned with the continual changes in its own business-context.

As we saw right back at the start, in the initial exploration of the strategic role of architecture, the core business-purpose of all enterprise-architecture is to improve *overall* effectiveness – not just efficiency on its own, for example, but all strands, optimized, in balance, working together across the whole and across all relevant timescales.

By now, the people we'll need to work with here could include *anyone*, with any appropriate skillset, because the trade-offs here between the various effectiveness-dimensions may touch any point or any activity in the enterprise.

We'll again draw on all those cross-links that we've gathered so far in the architecture repositories. We'll use them to trace along those trails of connections, upward, downward, sideways, or wherever, to identify options and opportunities that could enhance any aspect of effectiveness within the scope of the organization and its enterprise.

Caution   This is yet another area where assessments could stretch to infinity! For sanity's sake, always define a cut-off point for the assessment-phases of an iteration, either by placing explicit boundaries on scope, and/or a specific limit on time or budget before you switch over to doing the gap-analysis and requirements for change.

We'll do this through the same old CSPAR cycles and suchlike, working mainly with the checklist below, but dropping in other tools as required. In general, each iteration will require its own business-question, business-purpose, and business-value, though in many cases we'll be able to merge this work into other architecture activities as appropriate.

By this stage of architecture-development, we would not expect this exploration to trigger many, or any, *major* change-projects, because most of those needs should already have been addressed earlier. We should expect, though, that these assessments could well spawn quite a few small- to medium-sized amendments and restructures, especially down toward the operations level. As usual, these too should be managed in accordance with the standard change-governance procedures for all architecture work.

The key success-criteria here are demonstrable improvements in measures of effectiveness in the specified context.

Enhancing Effectiveness

The core of the work here will revolve around that default set of ***five keywords for effectiveness***: *Efficient*, *Reliable*, *Elegant*, *Appropriate*, and *Integrated*. We'll use them as a review-frame across any and every aspect of the enterprise:

- We apply them to *everything*.
- We use them as tests and touchpoints for everything, and as metrics for everything.
- We note how these threads or dimensions interweave with each other.
- We keep coming back to them, again and again.

Note Those default effectiveness-criteria should be enough as a starter-set here. But later on, once you've had some practice with this, do feel free to add your own organization's effectiveness criteria to the checklist below. For example, the airport would include the effectiveness-criteria associated with its values of *friendliness*, *comfort*, *mutual respect*, and *a sense of service*.

We also use those effectiveness-themes to trigger ideas about what we might call ***"emergent outcomes" of effectiveness***: themes such as improved agility, adaptability to change, responsiveness to customers or to suppliers, or shorter product-development cycles. These are likely to vary from one organization to another: for example, a not-for-profit organization dealing with world-wide disaster management may well need high agility, but might not develop any products of its own. The enterprise values and discussions with key stakeholders should indicate which emergent-outcomes are most likely to be relevant in the organization and enterprise.

Overall, it's a very simple checklist, but a surprisingly powerful one. Use it wherever you can in your architecture work, particularly at the sustainment-architecture.

Caution There's one additional proviso here: always remember to anchor that quest for effectiveness back to its anchors in the enterprise and organizational "universals" – vision, values, principles, constraints, success-criteria, and so on. Doing this should be straightforward enough by now, given the sheer volume of links and connections that you'll have gathered into the architecture repository. In a good architecture-toolset, you should even be able to build the requisite models automatically.

But do take care in this, because it's so easy to fall back into thinking only in terms of the immediate scope. That would give us *local* effectiveness – optimized for the immediate context – but probably not optimized for effectiveness *across the whole*, which is our real architectural need. To paraphrase an old slogan that may help us maintain our "ecosystem" here, **"act local, think global"**!

To **review effectiveness** and **enhance agility**, apply these questions to any given context:

- What options exist to enhance and optimize *efficiency* in this context? Are there any means to reduce waste and make better use of the available resources?

- What options exist to enhance and optimize *reliability* in this context? Are there any means to provide more certainty that the context can be relied upon to deliver the required results?

- What options exist to enhance *elegance* in this context – the human factors? Are there any options to augment "elegance" in the scientific sense – to simplify, to clarify, to enhance consistency and reuse? What options exist to develop personal skills and knowledge, to enhance understanding and awareness? What options exist for systems and processes to adapt to and make best use of individual differences and individual skills? For example, ergonomics and accessibility design, self-adapting performance-support systems, and decision-support systems?

- What options exist to enhance and optimize ***appropriateness*** in this context – being more "on-purpose"? Are there any additional means to link this context more strongly to the enterprise vision, values, and principles, such that it could more powerfully support and sustain the overall purpose of the enterprise? What options exist to enhance awareness of, capability for, and monitoring of alignment with each key value in this context?

- What options exist to enhance and optimize ***integration*** and alignment across each aspect of this context? What other options exist to ensure that everything in this context is linked to and supports the integration of the whole *as* a whole?

- What options exist to enhance and optimize any ***other effectiveness-dimensions*** that may apply to this context? What other options exist to ensure that all effectiveness-dimensions work together and support each other across the enterprise as a whole?

- In what ways could any of these options above also be used to enhance ***emergent-outcomes*** such as agility, responsiveness, and reduced time-to-market, both within this context and in areas impacted by this context?

Note That frequent use of the word "*options*" in those questions above would suggest that **SCORE** might well be useful to apply here! The details on that, and how to use it, were back in the previous Step, in the section "What's the SCORE?" in Chapter 11.

We would use these questions to derive content for "what if" scenarios, which should be modeled and documented in the architecture-toolset in the usual way, and used as the basis for further discussion and assessment. As per the *Plan* part of the CSPAR cycle, we would use gap-analysis to derive change-requirements, and then work with the respective stakeholders to expand these requirements into high-level designs, change-projects, and so on.

As usual, we would also need to identify and document any risks, opportunities, and other issues in the respective registers, and ensure that those items are included in any subsequent reviews for this context.

Into Practice

In the section "Facing Hidden Risks," we explored five sources of significant risks that can be hiding in the background of the organization and enterprise: *power-issues*, *anti-client risks*, *kurtosis-risks*, *enterprise-hijack*, and *untested-assumptions*. Using what you saw there, apply the same methods and checklists to your own organization.

- What *power-issues* do you see at play within your organization? What difference might it make if you viewed those issues in terms of a choice between "power as the ability to *do* work" and "power as the ability to *avoid* work"? In what ways might you use the architecture to mitigate against those risks, and reduce the damage that they cause to effectiveness and to the overall success of the organization as a whole?

- Who are your organization's *anti-clients*? How would you identify them, and the issues that drive their antipathy toward the organization? How might you use the architecture to identify and mitigate the risks that they represent, and perhaps turn those risks into opportunities, for everyone's benefit?

- What *kurtosis-risks* might exist within your organization, and in its broader business context such as in customer-services? How would you identify them, and the respective risks? How might you model the underlying systemic-flaw, payoff, driver, and potential triggers such that others might understand the risk and take appropriate action?

- What risks for *enterprise-hijack* can you identify in your own organization's context? For each of those risks, what might the consequences be, from a successful "hijack," or even a failed one? How might you use the architecture to help your organization defend itself against such "hijacks"?

- What *untested, outdated, or invalid assumptions* can you identify within your organization and its enterprise – and in your own context, too? In each case, what might happen if that assumption or *myth* were to collide with Reality Department? What might the consequences of such *mythquakes* be, not just in the immediate context, but rippling out into broader contexts as well?

- What "*positive-mythquakes*" might you find, and how would you use them to improve effectiveness across the enterprise?

- What further challenges might arise with increasing levels of *mythquake-intensity*? What type and maximum levels of mythquake-intensity could you safely discuss and address within your current organization? For the mythquakes that you *can't* safely address, what might be the *overall* consequences for yourself and everyone if and when those risks do eventuate?

- In each case, how will you tackle the *business-politics* that will arise with each of these types of risk? How would you mitigate against the risks to *yourself* and your own career in bringing these issues to others' attention?

In the section "Tackling Wicked-Problems," we explored how to identify and resolve intractable wicked-problems at play in the organization's context. Using what you saw there, apply the same methods and checklists to your own organization.

- Do people in your organization understand the distinctions between *tame-problems and wild-problems*, as "inside the box" and "outside the box"? Do they understand the implications of those differences – for example, that analysis alone won't help us with wild-problems, and that we'll need to call on the Alchemist and Artist modes to distinguish between the elements of a wild-problem that can and can't be tamed? What issues arise when people don't understand those distinctions? What can you do to help prevent, minimize, and mitigate the outcomes of those mistakes?

- Do people understand *wicked-problems* as a class of wild-problems in which some elements will always remain "wild," and cannot be tamed? What happens when people fail to understand those distinctions – for example, trying to build an IT-only "solution" for a wicked-problem? What can you do to help prevent, minimize, and mitigate the outcomes of those mistakes?

- When *working with wicked-problems* in your organization and its business-context, how do you first identify that they *are* wicked-problems? How do you identify the elements that act as its drivers, and that make it into a non-"solvable" issue? If you can extract "tameable" elements that can be managed via IT and the like, how do you integrate those with the elements that can only be addressed by people? What elements might you add into the context to turn it from a constant head-on clash to a mutually-supportive "virtuous-circle"?

In the section "Disruption and Chaos," we explored what to do about things that can or do go wrong in a big way. Using what you saw there, apply the same methods and checklists to your own organization.

- How do you identify which parts of the organization's work will need planning for *business-continuity and disaster-recovery*? How do you do that planning? Who do you need to involve in that planning? How do you implement the outcomes of that planning? How do you *test* that the implementation will work when the expected disruption happens? How do you test it for when an *unexpected* disruption happens? How do you prioritize those risk-issues and failure-responses?

- For each failure-scenario for your organization's business, how do you identify whether the response should be built around a pattern such as *fail-safe* versus *safe-fail*? What elements or factors would you use to guide you in that decision? What would be the consequences, and for whom, if a "fail-safe" design did actually fail? How would you guide a "safe-fail" system through its "graceful failure"?

- How capable is your organization at *coping with chaos and disruption*, whether from within itself, the broader shared-enterprise, or in the wider world? What scale of that kind of chaos could your organization tackle at present? What might you do, within the architecture, to help improve your organization's capability to resist, recover from, and thrive after chaos-events of increasing intensity? What type of *architecture of chaos* will you need, to help you and others identify, address, prepare for, and mitigate against these challenges, and resolve them in real-time actions?

In the section "Enhancing Enterprise Effectiveness," we explored how to use the enterprise and organizational effectiveness-criteria with sustainment-architectures to enhance whole-of-enterprise effectiveness across broader scopes and timescales. Using what you saw there, apply the same methods and checklists to your own organization.

- How would you use your organization's sustainment-architectures to continue to *enhance effectiveness* over the longer-term? What outcomes would you look for from that work? How would you measure the value and success of those architectures – perhaps especially in terms of what *doesn't* happen as much as what does?

As before, capture into your notebook any ideas and insights that arise from exploring these questions, to include in your final review at the end of the book.

Summary

In this chapter, for Step 5 in the Maturity-Model, we explored how to identify a wide variety of risks and challenges hidden away in the depths of the organization and the outer reaches of the shared enterprise, and how to develop architectures to tackle the disruption and chaos that can arise from those sources.

In the next chapter, we'll return to that core theme that *people* are the real core of the enterprise, with a focus on how to engage everyone in the organization in using the architecture to develop *their own ways* to enhance the effectiveness of their enterprise.

CHAPTER 13

Engaging Others in the Architecture

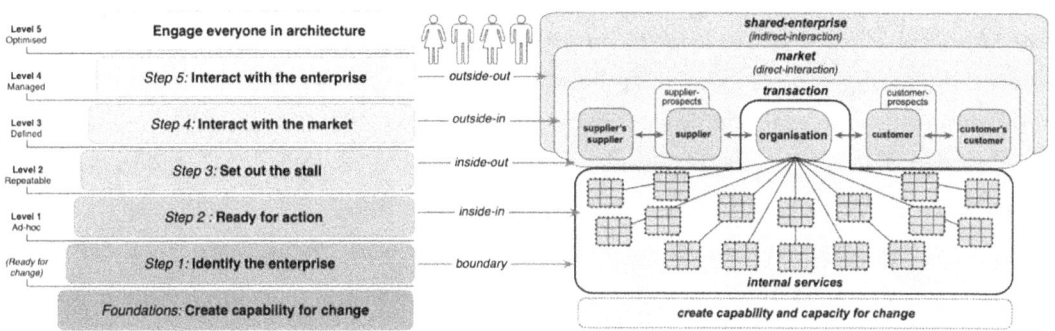

Once we've completed that last Step of the Maturity-Model, we'll have brought our architecture to a point where it should be able to respond to whatever the real-world may throw its way.

Yet there is still more that we can do, of course, to lift that value of enterprise-architecture to even greater heights. We can *always* do better, *always* find new ways to improve the effectiveness of our architectures and our organization as a whole.

If that's the case, then **what's next?**

Short-answer: We refocus on *people*.

There's often so much focus on the technology in current enterprise-architectures that it's easy to forget that the people in the story are just as important. People have skills and experience. People have capabilities that machines and IT-systems don't. People are often the only means that we have to achieve good results outside of the box. And people are everywhere in the enterprise; in an almost literal sense, people *are* the enterprise. We *need* to remember to bring that focus back onto the people.

CHAPTER 13   ENGAGING OTHERS IN THE ARCHITECTURE

The first part of this is that we do need to *engage* people in the architecture, and not just talk *at* them. At first, people won't "get" what we're aiming to do with the architecture and put out all kinds of objections about it, and us. If we want the architecture to succeed, it's up to *us* to engage with them: we need to take their objections seriously, and provide good practical reasons why they would *want* to support and engage with us in developing and maintaining the architecture.

Another "people-related" issue here is that most of what we do in the early stages of architectural maturity is "command and control." For example, we define a reference architecture, and strive to ensure that change-projects comply with it. In the previous Step, though, we saw that as the organization's maturity develops, the architecture needs be able to tackle more and more contexts in which either command or control are the core sources of difficulty – as is often the case in wicked-problems, for example – or where a loosening of mandated compliance is central to solving a problem, as it is in many quality-management contexts. In order to improve effectiveness and resilience, as we also saw in that Step, the organization must be able, ready, and willing to give up command and control in the respective areas of its business.

At this stage, then, we now also need to **apply that same thinking to the architecture itself**. Relinquishing an overly possessive control over the architecture, for example, will permit a shift toward a "hands-off" approach to architecture development that can greatly reduce the day-to-day architecture workload, freeing architects to concentrate on the "big-picture" direction of the overall enterprise. That approach in turn depends on relinquishing command, instead developing the overall architecture through a more intensive and more inclusive emphasis on *dialogue*, with all stakeholders in the architecture as co-equal peers.

To address those issues above, there are three sections in this chapter:

- *Objections and engagement*: How to resolve objections about the architecture, and to support better dialogue about, and engagement in, the architecture.

- *Hands-off architecture*: How to help project-teams and change-management to take over some of the load of supporting and maintaining the architecture.

- *Build architecture-awareness*: How to maintain and enhance the *relevance* of architecture within the everyday working life of the organization.

Once more, we'll end this chapter with a brief review of what you've learned during this Step, and how to apply it within your own organization.

Objections and Engagement

For architecture to be useful, people have to be willing to *use* it. And they'll only be able to use it if they know it exists – which is why it's essential for architects to communicate what they do. Hence the importance of a "communications plan" and the like – and from there, of tools such as wikis and intranet-websites to put that plan into practice.

We do that through **communication and engagement**, as the *other* side of the architect role. The catch is that ***it's mostly about people***, not abstract analysis – and as we've seen throughout this book, that demands a completely different skillset from that we've used so far. For many enterprise-architects, dealing with all of the interpersonal politics and other "people-stuff" is *hard* – but all of the previous work will be in vain unless we *do* tackle it. Yes, all those analyses and models and the like may be the backbone of the work, but the *real* architecture, the place where the architecture is literally "real-ized," is always through people. The dialogue *is* the architecture.

Resolving Objections

People will object to what we do, or how we're doing it: that's a reality here. We need to *expect* that people will tell us that we've "got it all wrong," or worse, will make disparaging comments about our competence, or purported lack of it, of course.

But it's a fact of life here, a normal occupational-hazard for this kind of work, so it's important not to worry too much about it. In practice, we'll need *something* with which to start and guide the architecture-conversation. Yet right at the start of that conversation, the usual response is "I don't know what I want, but I know that isn't it" – or, in short, "you're wrong." Painful though it may feel at the time, though, it's a *natural consequence* of the processes by which people learn in a collective space. Meaning *emerges* from a collective conversation about the "unknown."

Yes, it can be intensely frustrating when other people "just don't get it" in relation to the architecture. But that's *our* problem, not theirs. If we want others to "get it," it's up to *us* to provide conditions under which they *can* "get it," where they *can* see the benefits of working with others in the enterprise in an architectural way.

Yes, we may need to defend our work, but also not *over-defend* it: *the architecture is in the dialogue*, not just in the end-result. When they object, we need to ask for their advice, ask what we could do better. That's how engagement happens. And when others become passionate about the architecture, "owning" what they've co-created with us, that's when we'll know we've succeeded.

These are ***"objections"*** in the classic sales sense, and we'll need to have good answers to each of those objections ready and available for when we need them. Some typical reasons why they don't "get it" might include

- *"This architecture stuff doesn't make sense"* – so *we* need to find ways in which it does make sense for them.
- *"It doesn't apply to our context"* – so *we* need to show where it applies, and why.
- *"It's just theory"* – so *we* need to show how it works in practice.
- *"No-one bothered to ask us"* – so *we* need to show where it *does* take their experience into account.
- *"It's working now, why do we have to change it?"* – so *we* need to justify, in their terms, the requirements behind the change.
- *"We don't have time for this stuff!"* – so *we* need to show why they don't have time to *not* do "this stuff."
- *"Why should we bother to help anyone else?"* – so *we* need to show why it's in their own interest to do so.

Whatever the objection might be – and there'll be many more of them than just that list above – we need to be able to address it and learn from it whenever it comes our way.

Example At the airport, the architecture-team decide to workshop each of those objections above.

"This architecture stuff doesn't make sense" – the team have already proven that tools such as the Function-Model do help people in making sense of where they fit within the organization, and will make more use of this to get the word out about what architecture does.

"It doesn't apply to our context" – again, the Function-Model shows where *everyone's* work-context fits into the overall organization-story.

"It's just theory" – the team show how simple tools such as user-interface templates and standards reduce complexity and cost, and help to make everyone's work easier.

"No-one bothered to ask us" – the team do acknowledge that did happen too often in the past, but can show that they are making deliberate efforts to reach out to front-line staff for their advice and experience.

"It's working now, why do we have to change it?" – the team will explain that in that example, the manufacturer will cease providing support for that system in two years' time, and they need to get ready for that change now.

"We don't have time for this stuff!" – the team can show how the reason for "don't have time" is because the current processes are complicated and time-consuming, and that time taken to simplify things will be more than regained.

"Why should we bother to help anyone else?" – the team use the "things work better when they work together" slogan, the Function-Model and integration-project examples to show how everyone benefits from each item of architecture-work, but that it only works when people do work together.

Enhancing Engagement

We can't make the architecture happen on our own: an enterprise is about *shared* goals, *shared* vision. We need to understand that while we may have nominal *responsibility* for the architecture, we don't *possess* it: it belongs to everyone in the enterprise. The architecture will only happen in real-world practice when those people feel that they "own" it too: not imposed on them from above, but something in which they themselves are its co-authors, its co-creators. That's what engagement is about; that's what it's *for*.

This is one of the reasons why the **Function-Model** is so important: it describes the enterprise in a way that includes *everyone*. Another reason is that it provides a basis for *story* – a story of the enterprise as a whole, as an ecosystem. As we've seen earlier, in the section "Stories of Change" in Step 2, each business-process or use-case is the thread of a story, and each transaction or other interaction is a self-contained story in its own right. With the Function-Model, we can show how these stories literally weave their way across the organization and the enterprise, touching different business functions and services and capabilities, using the enterprise assets in different ways and in different locations, triggering other business events for different business reasons. The architecture *itself* is a story, so to help others make sense of the architecture, we need to tell it *as* a story – a narrative that, in some way or other, includes *them* within that story.

Typical techniques for engagement include

- Publishing models and other artifacts – typically via the architecture-toolset.

- Running your own intranet-website, including wikis and other facilities for feedback – again, some architecture-toolsets will support this requirement "out of the box."

- Seminars and "public" presentations across the enterprise.

- Workshops for engagement with operations staff, particularly those with direct involvement in front-line business processes.

- Maintaining a "watching-brief" relationship with senior staff, strategists, project-managers, and others involved in change-management.

- Building working-relationships with those responsible for other values-related themes such as security, privacy, quality, health and safety, ethics, and environment.

It's unlikely that we would use all of these approaches in a first pass of the architecture. But it *is* worthwhile considering all of the options from the start, as we'll certainly need them later on.

Architecture is a **dialogue**, not a monologue. Perhaps most important of all, **listening is more important than talking**. People are likely to listen to what we have to say only if they feel they too have been heard. This two-way communication creates **engagement** with people; and in turn, engagement creates **governance**. More precisely, it creates the kind of governance in which people *want* to be involved, because the work has meaning to them. And that's what we're aiming for here: enterprise-architecture becomes the architecture *of* the enterprise when the enterprise in general is engaged in every aspect of its creation and use.

Example   At the airport, the architecture-team acknowledge that they do need to improve their communications-skills, and their other soft-skills too. For example, one member of the team said he had first gone into IT because he thought it would help him avoid having to deal with people, and is finding the people-oriented side of his architecture work a real challenge. Another admitted that she was flat-out terrified at the prospect of having to present her work to the executive-board – even though she will definitely need to do that sometime soon. They feel they've failed at this, and doubt that they'll be able to resolve it on their own, so they decide to bring in an outside consultant to help.

Straight away, the consultant puts them at ease. They're not "failures" or anything like that, she says: everyone struggles with this. She gives the example of a professional singer who froze on stage in the middle of a solo-performance after suddenly falling prey to stage-fright. What they *can* do, she says, is get better at it through practice in a "safe-space," and she shows them how to do this.

She leads them through some workshop exercises to show where fears come from, how to identify how they each respond to those fears within themselves, and then learn how to calm the fear so that it won't disrupt the task that needs to be happening at that time. She then leads the team through a set of practices from improvisational theater, such as status-games and how to build a story together in real-time.

Finally, she sets up a simulation where one of the team will do a slidedeck-presentation, and the rest of the team will play-act as the executive audience, variously interested, indifferent, dismissive, or outright rude. There's a lot of laughter here, which helps to ease the tension. The consultant shows them how to use what they've learned about fear-management and real-time improvisation to tackle anything that the audience throws at them, and still be able to get the message across and tackle any objections that might arise. Slowly, the team start to recognize that what she's been showing them is *an architecture of engagement* – and that it's useful for them to think of it that way.

After she leaves, the team also recognize that what they've gone through here has been a kind of "*positive-mythquake*." They'd *assumed* that they couldn't do it, which had made it harder and harder for them to get started. Working with the consultant had shown them that that assumption was wrong, and that they in fact *could* do it, which had then broken them free of the myth. All they need now is more practice, to get better and better at it over time – exactly as with any other architecture-task.

Hands-Off Architecture

When the going gets tough, the tough have the sense to let go of trying to control it all, and turn to a more subtle form of management instead. This is certainly true for enterprise-scale architecture, because we'll find that there suddenly comes a point where

- It's all become too big, too much happening, too fast.
- The architecture-team itself has become too big, too complex.
- Enforcing compliance just takes too much time, too much effort.
- There's an inexorable sense of sliding further and further backward.

That's when we need to shift to ***a "hands-off" approach*** to our architectures, allowing some aspects of the architecture to emerge in a natural way from the complexity itself.

Warning   In the right contexts, with the right kind of backing, and guided by the right kind of experience, a "hands-off" strategy does work extremely well.

Yet do be careful about this, because it will *only* succeed if the architecture and change-management capabilities and processes, and the enterprise itself, are all mature enough to support it. Test the waters first with small, local experiments, and only move on to a full enterprise-wide scale rollout when you *know* that everyone is ready. Do *not* attempt to do hands-off architecture unless the opportunities, risks, and trade-offs are fully understood by all concerned, and addressed appropriately in practice.

> Be aware that if the context isn't right, or the architecture isn't yet mature enough, there's a real risk that it could end up creating chaos in the architecture and elsewhere. We've seen a fair few examples now where people have tried to do it too early – in one case solely as a cost-cutting exercise, which was a bad mistake from the start – and the results have been messy, painful, and expensive. Not A Good Idea…

On the surface, the main reason for using a "hands-off" architecture is to support agility and innovation. But more subtly, it's also about reinforcement of *responsibility* in the overall enterprise. It isn't "our" architecture anyway: we're just its custodians - it belongs to the enterprise, not to us. And now that we've brought the architecture up to this level of maturity, it's time to hand that responsibility back to its true owners.

When done properly, this makes life easier for everyone. The architects no longer have to play the dreaded role of "architecture police," and the architecture-compliance workload shrinks right down to the point where it can be handled by a much smaller team. The domain-architects are freed to go back to their preferred areas of expertise, leaving only a small core to concentrate on longer-term sustainment-architectures at the enterprise-wide scope. Unlike the earlier stages, there's no predefined plan or "blueprint" for the architecture. Instead, the effective architecture is allowed to emerge organically in response to Reality Department and in relation to a set of specific and clearly-enunciated architectural principles, emphasizing overall *effectiveness* for each project in relation to the whole.

In essence it's an extension of the work we did back in Step 2 and Step 3, on guiding change with the broader-scope Program Management Office (PMO) and other parts of the organization's change-management capability. In a "hands-off" approach, most of the responsibility for architectural assessment is passed to project sponsors, domain-architects, and designers. The architecture-team shift mostly to maintaining a watching brief over the projects that pass through the change-management process, and may intervene as appropriate with advice, suggestions, and requests for change, in line with the overall aims for the architecture. The architecture unit also uses the in-progress and completed projects as a source of information for reviews of the architecture itself, at the sustainment-architecture level.

The overall process resembles that for a building-project in a city-planning context

- The "*developer*" is the project-sponsor and project-team.
- The "*regulating authority*" is the Program Management Office.
- The "*planning-authority*" is the architecture unit, maintaining the equivalent of the "city plan."

Just as for a building-project in city-planning, each managed enterprise-project has to pass through a number of go/no-go gateways. At each gateway

- The developer presents to the PMO, as the "regulating-authority," a description of how the project will satisfy any mandatory requirements for the organizational equivalents of "planning-regulations," "building regulations," budgetary constraints, and suchlike.
- The developer also provides to the architecture-unit, as the "planning-authority," a document such as a Project Architectural Description that outlines the project's alignment with architectural principles and the like, for the organization's equivalent of "planning approval."
- If the overall proposal does not satisfy any or all of those requirements, it is rejected and returned to the developer for reassessment.
- If the proposal passes those requirements-tests, the regulatory-authority would publish the description, to allow other sponsors and stakeholders to comment, and optionally collaborate on amending their own projects.
- The regulatory-authority also notifies the architecture unit, as a key stakeholder in all projects, to review the revised proposal and intervene as appropriate – see the "Project-Gateway Notification and Response" section.
- If any disputes or concerns arise from the stakeholders, the overall change-management group would act as a tribunal, with the architecture-team in the role of expert advisor, to arrive at a negotiated agreement on changes to the project.

This process repeats at each project-gateway, dependent on the change-management methodology and the governance-rules in use.

Assuming that the project then passes successfully through each gateway to completion, the sponsor presents a final "as-built" description that summarizes what was actually done over the intervening period. This allows the architecture-team to again review the impact and "lessons learned" for the overall architecture of the enterprise – see the "Project-Completion" section – which then feeds back into the architecture models, principles, and guidelines to be used by subsequent projects.

Preparation for Hands-Off Architecture

Successful hands-off architecture depends on a number of **key items and attributes**:

- A clear set of *principles*, *guidelines*, and *governance-rules* exist and are publicly available to all potential developers: these should be developed and authorized as for the main architecture.

- An explicit set of *reference-frameworks* for the context exist and are publicly available, together with guidance for their use.

- Shared facilities to capture, store, review, and link between *requirements*, *issues*, *risks*, *dispensations*, and the like exist and are generally available.

- Facilities and mechanisms to support *engagement* by and with developers in the architecture are available and generally used.

- Architecture-champions in the enterprise outside of the architecture-team.

Those champions will be important: an individual outside of the architecture-team who understands the architecture is a more powerful and often more credible messenger than anyone from the architecture-team would be.

As with the main architecture preliminaries, we should expect to reassess and, where necessary, update the principles, reference-frameworks, and governance-rules at regular intervals. We should aim to do this at least once each year, and publish any changes through the same mechanisms.

To assess if we're **ready for hands-off architecture**, we need to ask the following questions:

- What engagement do projects already have in the existing architecture? What else would they need in order to take on their responsibilities in a hands-off architecture?

- What reference-frameworks are available and suitable for general use in a hands-off architecture? What scope do they each cover? What governance procedures and processes would they require for general use?

- How much of the existing architecture – particularly principles, guidelines, and reference-frameworks – is published and generally accessible throughout the organization? What other information would be need to be published, and in what forms, to support a hands-off architecture?

- To what extent are projects and change-management ready and able to do their own architectural assessments? What could the architecture-team do to extend that capability? To what scope would a hands-off architecture apply, in which projects and which segments of change-management?

- By what processes and facilities would the architecture-team identify and collect updates for the architecture itself? What governance would be required for this? By what means would the team publicize and promulgate updates for a hands-off architecture?

- From the above, to what extent are the architecture-team ready to run a hands-off architecture? What would the team need to do, or change, to make it more viable? What level of maturity would be needed in the existing architecture to make this happen? What amendments to architecture-governance and project-governance would be required?

- How would the architecture-team describe and present to management the business-case for a hands-off architecture? To what scope within the enterprise would this business-case apply?

Once we're ready, we would present the business-case to executives and others as appropriate. Once approved, we would implement the required facilities and governance-changes to publicize the architecture changes, and then hand over the respective authority to the change-management group.

Project-Gateway Notification and Response

The "hands-off" process is one of management by exception, rather than by routine intervention and control as in the main "hands-on" methodology.

For the architecture-team, the initial trigger for the process is the arrival of a Project Architectural Description or an equivalent document. This is provided by the project sponsor or project-manager via the change-management group, and should describe how the project will conform to the published architectural rules, principles, and reference-frameworks, and also describe any applications or innovations that might be relevant to the overall architecture for the enterprise.

Ideally, the project-team should map the change-project's scope onto the Function-Model, preferably down to tier-3 level on that model. This would then enable to the architecture-team to cross-map the project onto the Business-Systems, Information-Systems, and other overlay-models, and also to check for gaps, overlaps, and potential synergies with other current or planned projects.

Note The architecture-team may well have provided some assistance to the project before this happens, but the whole aim here is that the onus for getting it right should be on the project team rather than the architecture unit – hence "hands-off" architecture.

On receipt of the document, the architecture-team would then carry out a brief review of the description, to assess any possible issues, and then return the results of the review to the project sponsor via the change-management group. Sometimes the issue will be that a project's intentions clash with the architecture or with another project. But it might also be that that project is introducing an innovation that could be valuable elsewhere, and that we would be asking their advice on how best to do this. In other words, it should always be portrayed as a two-way street, not an "edict from above."

The governance-gateways where reviews would take place would always include a start-of-project review, and then others according to the project-governance-model that the change-management group would apply to that context. If there's no explicit governance-model in use, then we would typically do these at the CSPAR layer-boundaries, and , for a larger project, probably the sub-layer boundaries as well.

To do a **project-gateway review**, we would use the following checklist to review the architectural aspects of the content:

- In what ways, and to what extent, does the project comply with the published architecture standards? Where the standards are not mandatory, are the deviations from the recommended or advised standards acceptable? What implications would those variances have for the architecture as a whole?

- If there are significant variances from standards, would an architecture-dispensation be required? For example, what should happen if the mandated or recommended standard is not technically feasible or available in that specific context, or is overruled by local laws and ordinances? If so, how should the dispensation be described and documented, and what conditions and review-periods should be applied to that dispensation?

- Are there direct clashes or conflicts with any other projects, such as each needing exclusive usage or control of the same physical equipment or the same virtual space? If so, what would need to be done by each project to resolve the clash?

- Are there any potential synergies with other projects, such as using the same type of equipment, software applications, or development-tools, or touching the same business-systems or business areas? If so, what changes would be needed in each project to optimize those synergies?

- Is the project introducing innovations of any kind – asset, function, location-category, capability, event-type, business-rule, or composite – which could be applied or reused within the overall architecture? If so, what further information would the architecture unit need from the project in order to do so?

If any issues are identified, we would document the results in an Architecture Position Statement and, if appropriate, an Architecture Dispensation Statement, and return these to the change-management group, together with a request for negotiation with the project if so required. The outcome of this review may include

- Recommended changes to the project or to a group of projects
- A formal dispensation or waiver
- Changes to the architecture itself

These may in turn trigger new architecture-reviews, and sometimes also updates to the published architecture principles and guidelines. We would also update the architecture repositories and the registers for risks, opportunities, issues, and dispensations as appropriate.

Project-Completion

Each project should also create a similar architecture description at the end of the project implementation, as part of their own "lessons learned" review at the CSPAR Review-layer stage. The aim here is to notify the architecture unit about what was actually implemented and delivered – which may not be the same as in the original plan.

Note   There'd probably be no response-document required here, of course, because the project is over and done with, and you can't change that. But what you *can* do is update the architecture, and again let other projects know about any lessons learned from the exercise. It's all part of maintaining stakeholder engagement in the development of the architecture, as an *enterprise-wide* shared resource.

The review here is essentially the same as at the end of any other project for which the architecture unit has provided guidance. In principle the receipt of the Description document should trigger its own architecture lessons-learned review, but in practice the document would more usually be included as part of the content for the next regular review, much as for other types of simultaneous architecture-cycles.

As at the end of the project-gateway review, this may trigger new architecture-related projects, or updates to the published architecture principles, guidelines, and reference-frameworks.

Build Architecture-Awareness

Having relinquished control of the architecture, in hands-off architecture, the final step is to relinquish command of the architecture as well.

As architects we may have a better overview of the organization and its enterprise than most people, but that doesn't make us any more "special" than anyone else. The one area we do know well is enterprise-architecture, as "a body of knowledge about enterprise structure, story and purpose." But we probably don't know much of the fine detail about how the organization *really* works. The people who *do* know that are the specialists and those who work at the "coal-face" out in the operations-space.

So while we may sit up at the top of the tower, sharing the time of day with strategists and senior executives, all that really means is that we, like they, have our own job to do in support of the organization within the enterprise. We have neither right nor reason to "command" others about *anything* – even architecture. And a bit of humility and respect on our part can go a long way in helping the overall cause of the enterprise...

Given that, it'll be useful here to go right back to where we started, to take note of some essentials for the *real* architecture of the enterprise. For example, we'll need to continue to engage with architecture-stakeholders, and acknowledge that all of this is really about the dialogue.

This architecture isn't something we've created on our own: we've *co-created* it with everyone else with whom we've worked. It isn't just "our" architecture: it also belongs to all those domain-architects and designers and project-managers and risk-managers and knowledge-managers and personnel specialists and operations specialists and all the others we've mentioned in the Steps and sections of this book, and no doubt many, many others as well. In essence, **the architecture belongs to everyone in the enterprise**.

We do need to let go at this point; let go of command and control. Instead, we need to commit to **engagement**, commit to **dialogue**, and allow the architecture to evolve and emerge from the enterprise itself.

We've tackled all the basics of this already, such as in the earlier work on engagement back at the end of Step 1. You'll also have built on that base in the meantime, such as with the publishing-facilities built into your architecture-toolset and the like. What we need to do here is to keep extending people's engagement in the architecture. The following sections provide some suggestions about how to take this further, and keep the architecture relevant in everyone's working lives.

Conferences

What are the core architectural issues that people are facing across the enterprise? Much of the time, we don't actually know. We can assess market trends, we can review best-practice inside the organization and elsewhere, we can analyze and assess, often in great depth. But even then, the results may well be little more than a guess...

To find out what's really needed, we have to *ask*. We need to *show* examples, too, because, as in any other form of marketing, people will often only know something when *they* need to know it, will often only know *what* they want when they see it, and also often won't even know *that* they want it until they see it.

Hence a useful tactic here is to organize a regular architecture-conference for the organization, and sometimes also for people beyond the organization as well. This would in part be to promote and explain the role of the architecture and architecture-unit. But it should also aim to engage others at all levels about *their* views on the architecture and where it should be going so as to best serve the needs of the organization and enterprise.

Such conferences work particularly well if they are centered around one or more of the enterprise values and/or quality-concerns, such as

- Security and safety, in any or all of its forms
- Quality – again, in any or all of its forms
- Business-continuity and risk-management
- Privacy and trust
- Customer orientation or service orientation
- Agility and responsiveness
- End-to-end process-integration
- Innovation and experimentation
- The practical meaning and implications of "value"

CHAPTER 13   ENGAGING OTHERS IN THE ARCHITECTURE

In the early stages, it's usually best to set up a formal agenda. But as the architecture-maturity increases, and there is more experience with managing the architecture in a more open and inclusive style, it's useful also to start relinquishing control of the agenda, until the broader enterprise claims full ownership of that as well.

There are a variety of formal models for these more open-format conferences, often described as "Large Group Interventions." Perhaps the best-known of these is Harrison Owen's "Open Space Technology": it draws from the insight that for many people, the most valuable part of a conference is the gap between formal sessions, so Open Space is a type of conference that consists entirely of "gap." There is no formal agenda: instead, attendees take responsibility to present topics that have direct meaning for them. People then "vote with their feet," moving between sessions until they gravitate to a group which has relevance for their own work-interests. The end-result – if it's done right – is a huge outpouring of energy, with active, personal commitment to tackling the self-chosen tasks.

Note   That "if it's done right" criterion is critical here, because the process depends entirely on openness, and on the organizers and the relevant management fully letting go of the agenda to allow it to emerge naturally from the context and from the attendees themselves.

Open Space can sometimes be a bit scary in that regard, because it's impossible to know in advance what the outcome will be. But that almost anarchic freedom and uncertainty is also the key to its real power: any attempt to control it will not only block any possibility of emergence, but will likely also lead to a feeling of betrayal, and an entrenched cynicism and loss of trust that could echo on for months or years. Open Space is probably the most powerful of all the "large group interventions," yet it should *only* be used where there's full support and commitment to the process. If there's any significant risk that the promise of support will be withdrawn – especially in the middle of the process itself – it would be safer to use one of the more "controlled" techniques such as Delphi or Future Search instead.

Communities of Practice

The right kind of conference will also help create the right kind of communities-of-practice that the enterprise needs. Each group of specialists will typically need to form its own explicit community, to share best-practices and worst-practices, to look for advice on how to solve specific problems, to develop each other's skills and the skills of newcomers, and to develop the praxis as a whole.

For the organization and the broader shared-enterprise, each community-of-practice will be a key part of their own knowledge-management: they will *need* those communities-of-practice.

Note The doyen of studies on communities-of-practice is independent researcher Etienne Wenger: "the basic idea is that human knowing is fundamentally a social act." His book *Cultivating Communities of Practice* and Amy Jo Kim's *Community Building on the Web* have both been useful in our work, as has physicist David Bohm's work on communication and dialogue as described in his now-classic book *On Dialogue*.

There are, however, a few practical concerns from the organization's perspective. These include

- Communities of practice succeed *because* they are enterprises in their own right. They intersect with the organization, and support the organization, but do not "belong" to it. The organization can foster them, and support them in turn, but it will risk destroying their value if it tries to control or possess them.

- In most cases, the knowledge underpinning each specialism and skill will extend across almost every kind of border: business-unit, organization, nation, language, culture, whatever. This also means that those conversations *must* be able to cross those borders, which may represent a security-risk in several different senses. Yet closing the borders also limits the knowledge that the organization may gain from the community-of-practice. The trade-offs here are not simple, and need careful management by all parties involved.

- For those reasons above, many communities-of-practice will operate either informally or as a "shadow network." Bringing them out into the light can actually destroy them. Similarly, the organization can rarely create a new community-of-practice to order. Instead, the community develops and evolves from *personal* responsibility and commitment, not formal authority.

As enterprise-architects, we can help in this by identifying capabilities that use or could make use of such communities, and by identifying likely candidates from responsibility-assignments to related architecture-entities. We can use social-network maps and suchlike to identify probable "supernodes" for the communities' social-networks. We can also use the architecture itself to help communities to become more aware of the security risks, and also of other opportunities that could help the community and the enterprise alike. In turn, through dialogue, the communities can feed key information back into the architecture of the enterprise. That way, *everyone* wins.

Communication

Communities-of-practice are extremely valuable, yet they themselves are only one form of communication and organizational learning, as the *other* half of the enterprise's "information technology." This brings us back to a central theme for enterprise-architecture: **the dialogue about architecture is the architecture**.

The architecture-models are useful: but it's about more than just models. Governance-rules are important: but it's about more than just the governance. Change is a key driver: but it's not solely about managing change. *The architecture is the dialogue; the dialogue is the architecture.*

This tells us that we need more than just a "Communication Plan" for architecture. Instead, the multi-way, multi-faceted communication we need is both the source *and* the destination for the architecture. Communication is everywhere; communication is everything.

In effect, enterprise-architecture itself is another of the enterprise "pervasives" or quality-oriented themes. Or, more accurately, the *idea* of enhancing effectiveness via architecture and whole-of-enterprise integration is the real quality-focus here. In that sense, the same practical concerns apply to architecture as for all other quality-oriented themes:

- We need explicit means to *develop awareness of architecture* as a pervasive principle.

- We need to *develop architecture capability* across the enterprise.

- We need to ensure that the *architecture capability is used* throughout the enterprise.

- We need to *verify and audit* that the architecture principles have been applied appropriately in practice.

It'd be fair to say that the last two of these have been our main focus so far. For example, that was the reasoning behind the CSPAR cycle, its "this-applies-everywhere" fractality, and its integration into and with change-management cycles. We now *know* how to do those in a controlled environment. But as we relinquish a rigid control of the architecture and move toward a more open, hands-off approach, we also need much more emphasis on the first pair of concerns: develop architecture awareness, and develop architecture capability. Hence the *need* for dialogue.

Conferences and training-sessions and the like will support the development of capability. That part is relatively straightforward, and we already know how to do that, *if* the awareness and the recognition of the need is already there. But how do we develop that awareness in the first place?

Some of this you'll have had to do already, just to get started with the architecture practice: building the business-case, getting the executives to understand the underlying ideas, and so on. Then there's been all the work around maintaining and publishing the glossary, thesaurus, reference-models, blueprints, roadmaps, and all the architecture-governance rules to go with them. But for most of the current crop of architecture-toolsets, that's still only "one-way," broadcast-style publishing: no interaction, no *dialogue*. And we need that dialogue to happen, and happen *as* a true dialogue.

One way to take this further is to look at how other "pervasives" tackle the same problems – particularly knowledge-management and change-management, who deal with much the same kinds of concerns as our own.

> **Note** Do remember to look outside of enterprise-architecture for tools and techniques to promote and enhance the *human* "information technology" of knowledge-acquisition and knowledge-sharing.
>
> For example, Sengé's *The Dance of Change* and Collison and Parcell's *Learning to Fly* – our source for those notes earlier on the US Army's "After Action Review" process – are both packed with proven examples of how to create engagement and dialogue in practice, across a wide variety of often "difficult" business-cultures. Likewise, Shawn Callahan's *Putting Stories to Work*, on business-storytelling, and Cynthia Kurtz's *Working With Stories*, on participatory narrative inquiry, are useful for developing and improving narrative-based techniques in engaging people in the practical work of architecture development and use..

Yet ultimately, the best way to build awareness in others is to *be* there with them. Tell a story about architecture: perhaps describe a scenario, the value and usefulness of a potential "to-be." We need to tell our *own* story; listen to theirs; work with them to find ways to help the stories align with each other. Often facts alone won't help all that much: what *does* help is the story, the *personal* nature, and personal commitment implied in each story.

The most powerful way to convey the meaning of a principle in practice is not just to "tell" the story, but to *live* it by our own example. If architecture is about creating connections, and integration of the whole *as* whole, then *we* need to be making those connections too, and learning from and with everyone as we go – the architects' equivalent of "management by walking around."

The enterprise *is* its people: those who "coordinate their functions and share information in support of a common mission" will also define what that shared "mission" *is*. Those people are not "assets": it is the *relationship* with each person that is the asset. And it's through those person-to-person connections around ideas of architecture that the awareness and the capability can coalesce.

The architecture is a shared body of knowledge to help the shared enterprise in decisions about its own structure, story, and purpose.

- If some part of the purpose is changing, what changes in structures would we need, to support that change?

- What parts of those structures would change, and how and why would they change, and what else would be affected by those amendments and alterations?

- Given the structures we have, what purpose can we support, for each practical layer of "purpose"? If we lose some part of the structure, what problems might that cause?

- If we change some part of the structure, what new options would that create for the enterprise as a whole?

Architecture helps us to understand how structure and purpose interact, and hence helps us make the right choices for new directions.

We call ourselves "enterprise-architects," but that doesn't mean that we alone create the entire enterprise and its architecture – or any part of either of those, if we're to be honest about it. The reality is that the architecture is something we *co-create* with every other person in the enterprise, both within the organization and often also beyond the organization's own borders, too. For that co-creation to happen, we must let go of command and control of the architecture, share the load, and communicate, communicate, communicate.

The architecture *is* the dialogue; when we do allow the dialogue to become the architecture, the architecture in turn will become the enterprise. That's our real responsibility here: and as architects of the enterprise, it's up to us to make it so.

Into Practice

In the section "**Objections and Engagement**," we explored how to engage people more deeply in the architecture. Using what you saw there, apply the same methods and checklists to your own organization.

- What *objections* do you face when reaching out to engage others in the architecture-work? What do you need to do or explain to *resolve those objections*? How do you turn those objectors into your champions for the architecture?

- What else could you do to *enhance people's engagement* in the architecture, and to help them build a sense that they are *co-creators* of the architecture? What methods do you use for *communicating about architecture* with others? If you're not doing so already, how might you use the Function-Model and other overview-type architecture-models to engage people in the work in a more tactile way?

In the section "**Hands-Off Architecture**," we explored how to engage project-teams to take on more of the responsibility for doing of the input for the architecture as part of their own work. Using what you saw there, apply the same methods and checklists to your own organization.

- How would you *prepare for hands-off architecture*? What principles, guidelines, governance-methods, reference-frameworks, and shared-facilities would you need? What support will you need from senior management, the project-management team, and others to make this work? How would you present the business-case for hands-off architecture? Who would be your *architecture-champions* throughout the organization, and how will you find them and engage them in that task?

- Which project-governance methods does your organization use at present? How would you embed into those methods the *project-gateway notification and response* that you'll need for hands-off-architecture? What content will you need to capture for the architecture within those processes? How will you review that content to identify gaps, overlaps, conflicts, and potential synergies for the architecture?

- At *project-completion*, how will you link project-review to architecture-review? How will you use the outcomes of those reviews to guide the architecture for other change-projects that are either ongoing or in the pipeline? How will these reviews affect the longer-term sustainment-architectures?

In the section "**Build Architecture-Awareness**," we explored how to build a broader awareness of the business role and practice of enterprise-architecture, and also how to support continuous-learning among the architecture-team. Using what you saw there, apply the same methods and checklists to your own organization.

- What events do you run within your organization, such as *conferences*, to engage people's attention and interest in the architecture? If you don't run any such events, how would you do so? What themes and topics would you need to cover? What mix of fixed agenda and free-format discussion would you use in such events?

- What *communities of practice* exist within your organization, and/or connect beyond the organization? What themes or domains of interest do they cover? In what ways do those themes connect with the architecture? How might you engage in those communities to develop and improve the architecture?

- What forms of communication do you use to engage people in the architecture? What content do you provide? In what ways do you adapt that content to fit the respective audience? What might you do to improve your communication, both through media and in how you present in person to others?

As always, capture into your notebook any ideas and insights that arise from exploring these questions, to include in your final review in the next chapter.

Summary

In this chapter we explored how to engage others more deeply in the work of architecture, through tactics such as getting projects more directly involved in maintaining the architecture, and through communication, conferences, and communities of practice.

In the next and final chapter, we'll do a final review of everything you've explored and learned in this book.

CHAPTER 14

Wrapping Up

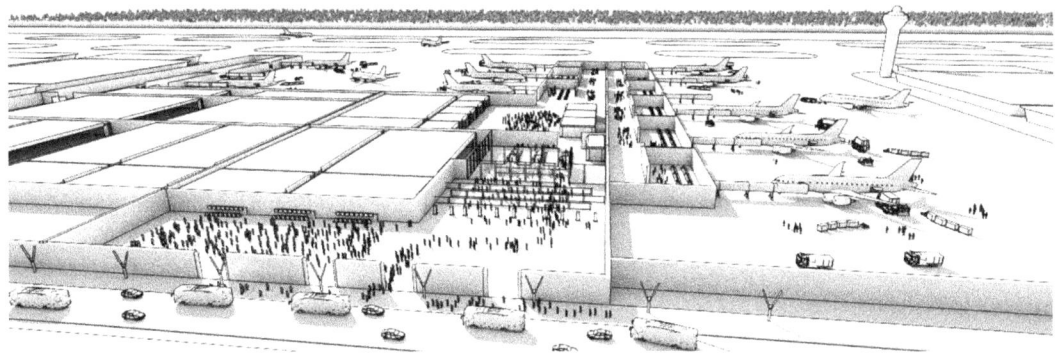

We've now reached the end of this book. So what happens next?

The most important point, perhaps, is to recognize that the development of your architecture doesn't stop here, just because we've reached some magic milestone. It isn't a project: it's a constant quest for new ways to enhance enterprise effectiveness in the face of continual change.

To support that further quest, throughout all of this work you'll have gathered together a versatile set of tools and methods that will help you to guide consistency, change, and effectiveness across the enterprise as a whole. For example, we could summarize many of these **chapter-by-chapter** as follows:

- In **Chapter 1**, we explored the need for ***an "architecture of the enterprise"*** to support enterprise effectiveness, the ***overall scope and content for that architecture***, and, step-by-step, ***how to build that capability for whole-enterprise architecture***.

- In **Chapter 2**, we clarified the ***core requirements for whole-enterprise architecture***, and explored ***key concepts*** such as effectiveness, architecture and design, organization and enterprise, services and systems, fractality, sameness and difference, and the nature of change.

- In **Chapter 3**, we explored the role in change-work of ***observation, imagination, intuition*** and ***chance***, and the ***hazards and limitations of reason***; the range of perspectives, mindsets, and ***action-modes*** that we need in change-work, such as the Artist, Alchemist, Analyst, Agent, and Assessor; and the role and usefulness of ***checklists*** such as the ***Architect's Mantra***.

- In **Chapter 4**, we explored the ***CSPAR change-cycle*** – Context, Scope, Plan, Action, Review – and how to get started in using that pattern consistently within change-work.

- In **Chapter 5**, we explored the detail on how to ***use the CSPAR pattern*** to ***guide the flow of work in a change-project***, at any scale.

- In **Chapter 6**, we explored the detail on how to ***use the CSPAR pattern*** in parallel with ***the action-modes*** to ***guide the flow of work within a single chunk of change-work***.

- In **Chapter 7**, we explored the ***relationships of architecture with other change-roles*** such as strategy and change-management, and the longer-term role of ***sustainment-architectures***, and how to tackle ***inherent-uncertainty***, ***complexity***, and ***scale*** within change-work.

- In **Chapter 8**, we explored how to identify the overall context, content, scope, and storyworld of the broader ***shared-enterprise*** within which the organization will work; how the organization will identify and describe its ***purpose***, ***scope***, ***positioning***, and overall ***value-propositions*** within that enterprise, and its overall ***structure*** to support that purpose; and how to ***set up the architecture capabilities*** to support the organization's purpose.

- In **Chapter 9**, we explored how to identify and model the organization's ***business-infrastructure*** for its chosen role and positioning; how to ***plan, design, build, and implement the services*** for that business-infrastructure; and how to ***test, assess, and improve*** the ***reliability, adaptability, and resilience*** of that infrastructure.

- In **Chapter 10**, we explored how to ***use architecture to connect everything with everything else***; how to ***use a service-oriented architecture*** to define and describe the ***structures, flows,*** *interdependencies, implementations, and trade-offs*; how to *identify and model the organization's choices* about its *value-propositions, promises, products, and services*; and how to *model and maintain values and quality* across the organization and its enterprise.

- In **Chapter 11**, we explored how to *work with the inherent uncertainties of the market*; how to *adapt business-offerings* to meet varying needs in the market; how to *use an "outside-in" perspective* to *support values and quality*; how to *provide architectural support* for *reputation and trust*; and how to *model interactions and relationships* with *investors and beneficiaries*.

- In **Chapter 12**, we explored how to *tackle hidden-risks* such as *power-issues, anti-clients, kurtosis-risks, enterprise-hijack*, and "mythquakes" from *untested-assumptions*; the different tactics needed in *tackling tame-problems, wild-problems, and wicked-problems*; how to *tackle disruption and chaos* of any type, scale, or timescale; and how to use any or all of the above to *enhance enterprise-effectiveness*.

- In **Chapter 13**, we explored how to *engage others in the architecture*, and how to *respond to objections* when "selling" the role of architecture; how to engage others in helping to *run a "hands-off architecture"*; and how to *build and maintain architecture-awareness* over the longer-term.

Next, in relation to **specific tasks**

- How to *develop and maintain "defensible-uncertainty" for your own architecture-work* – see introduction to Chapter 12.

- How to *guide the process of change*, using the CSPAR pattern – for overview, see Chapter 4, section "A Pattern for Change"; at a whole-of-project level, see the **Change-Layers** sections in Chapter 5; for a single chunk of change-work, see the **Change-Cycle** sections in Chapter 6.

- How to *include context-specific content and methods* into the context-neutral CSPAR pattern – see Chapter 4, section "A Pattern for Change."

- How to *engage others in the architecture-work* – as part of architecture setup, see Chapter 8, section "Set Up for Engagement"; for architecture in general, often at larger scale, see each of the sections in Chapter 13.

- How to *identify the role for human skills* in process-design – see Chapter 7, section "The Uncertainties of Change."

- How to *make sense of complexity* in any architectural context – for overview, see Chapter 7, section "The Complexities of Change"; for detail, see the "SCAN" model below.

- How to describe *vision, values, constraints, success-criteria, and other "universals"* – for the overall shared-enterprise, see Chapter 8, section "Enterprise As Storyworld"; for the organization, see Chapter 8, sections "Organization Mission" and "Organization-Vision and Values."

- How to *model the core assets, locations, events, functions, capabilities, services, and decisions* – for the shared-enterprise, at an abstract level, see Chapter 8, section "Elements of the Enterprise"; for the organization, at an abstract level, see Chapter 8, section "Organization Content"; for the different changes and emphases throughout the architecture/design cycle, see the various sections of Chapter 5; for a specific service, see Chapter 9, section "From Architecture to Action."

- How to *create systems for architecture governance* – see Chapter 8, section "The Governance of Change," with other applications and examples appearing throughout the book.

- How to *partition activities into consistent function-models*, business-systems, and their supporting "information-systems" – see Chapter 8, section "Organization-Structure," and Chapter 9, section "Functions and Systems."

- How to **derive business-systems and information-systems models from function-models** – see Chapter 9, section "Functions and Systems."

- How to **optimize across any aspect of a business-system** – see Chapter 9, section "From Architecture to Action."

- How to **use narrative-based techniques to guide inquiry and development** – see Chapter 9, section "Stories of Change."

- How to **guide compliance in the overall process of change** – see Chapter 10, section "Quality and Compliance."

- How to **extend architecture across the whole enterprise** – for overview, see Chapter 1, section "An Architecture for Enterprise-Architecture"; for more detail, see Chapter 10, section "The Enterprise As Whole."

- How to **explore how strategy interacts with change and innovation** – see Chapter 10, section "Innovation Invokes Strategy."

- How to **use service-concepts "top-down" to guide implementation trade-offs** – see Chapter 10, section "From Values to Quality."

- How to **tackle quality-issues in outsourcing-relationships** – see Chapter 10, section "Outsourcing and Quality."

- How to **design for escalation of service-response** – see Chapter 11, section "Design for Escalation."

- How to **design for service-resilience** – see Chapter 11, section "Design for Resilience."

- How to **review and sustain enterprise values from the operations perspective** – see Chapter 11, section "From Qualities to Values."

- How to **make sense of service-relationships and responsibilities** – see Chapter 11, section "The Responsibilities of Service."

- How to **trace from vision through role, mission, goal, plan, and activity to outcome** – see Chapter 8, section "Organization and Enterprise."

- How to **trace from guidance-services back to organization "universals"** – see Chapter 10, section "The Effective Enterprise."

- How to **trace from intent to action** – see Chapter 9, section "From Architecture to Action."

- How to **trace from value-propositions to actions and outcomes** – see Chapter 10, section "Promise, Service, and Product."

- How to **identify traceable paths for individual interactions** – see Chapter 10, section "Promise, Service, and Product."

- How to **trace from value to delivered-quality** – see Chapter 10, section "From Values to Quality."

- How to **trace from delivered-quality back to value** – see Chapter 11, section "From Qualities to Values."

- How to **trace across outsourcing and supply-chain relationships** – see Chapter 10, section "Outsourcing and Quality."

- How to **use architecture to tackle trust-issues** – see Chapter 11, section "The Architecture of Trust."

- How to **use architecture to address issues relating to investors and beneficiaries** and other stakeholders – see Chapter 11, section "Investors and Beneficiaries."

- How to **use architecture to tackle power-issues** in the organization and its enterprise – see Chapter 12, section "A Problem of Power."

- How to **use architecture to tackle anticlient-issues** – see Chapter 12, section "Anti-clients."

- How to **tackle "pain-points" and "wicked problems"** – see Chapter 12, section "Tackling Wicked-Problems."

- How to **guide business-continuity planning and "safe-fail" design** – see Chapter 12, sections "Business-Continuity and Recovery" and "Fail-Safe and Safe-Fail."

- How to **use architecture to address large-scale disruption** – see Chapter 12, section "Coping with Chaos."

- How to **review and extend effectiveness in any context** – see Chapter 12, section "Enhancing Enterprise Effectiveness."

And in terms of specific **models, tools, and methods**

- *Action-modes* (CALc) – for overview and definitions, see Chapter 3, section "Perspectives, Modes, and Mindsets"; for practical use, see all sections in Chapters 5 and 6.

- *Architect's Mantra* as a quick checklist to guide inquiry – see Chapter 3, section "The Awareness of Change."

- *Backbone and Edge* model of system-criticality – see Chapter 9, section "From Role to Infrastructure."

- *Business-Systems Model* (derived overlay from Function-Model) – see Chapter 9, section "Functions and Systems."

- *CALc* (real-time switching between action-modes) – for overview, see Chapter 3, section "Perspectives, Modes, and Mindsets"; for practical use, see all sections in Chapters 5 and 6.

- *CSPAR* task-pattern – for overview, see Chapter 4, section "A Pattern for Change"; for its use as the *Change-Layers* pattern at a whole-of-project level, see all sections in Chapter 5; for its use as the *Change-Cycle* pattern for a single chunk of change-work, see all sections in Chapter 6.

- *Enterprise-Canvas* (variant of Service-Canvas) – see Chapter 11, section "Investors and Beneficiaries."

- *Four-Checklists* for guidance of run-time action – for overview, see Chapter 7, section "The Uncertainties of Change"; for use within process-design, see Chapter 5, section "Plan in the Change-Layers"; for real-time use, see worked-example for a baggage-handler in Chapter 11, section "Managing Uncertainty."

- ***Function-Model*** (organization-structure as abstract-services) – for overview and basic tier-1 and tier-2 models, see Chapter 8, section "Organization-Structure"; for expansion from tier-2 to tier-3 and beyond, see Chapter 9, section "Functions and Systems."

- ***Information-Systems Model*** (derived overlay from Function-Model) – see Chapter 9, section "Functions and Systems."

- ***Maturity-Model*** for the sequence for the development of architecture-capability – for overview, see Chapter 1, section "Building the Architecture Capability"; for practical use, see the content and structure of all other chapters in the book.

- ***Mythquake-Scale*** for the impact of untested and/or invalid assumptions – see Chapter 12, section "Assumptions and Myths."

- ***Organization-Context Model*** ("holomap") – for the generic model as a visual-checklist, see Chapter 1, section "The Architecture of the Enterprise"; for the organization-specific model, see Chapter 8, section "Positioning the Organization."

- ***Power-Model*** of impact of power-issues on effectiveness – see Chapter 12, section "A Problem of Power."

- ***SCAN*** complexity/action map – for overview, see Chapter 3, section "The Shape of Change"; for cross-map with CALC action-modes, see Chapter 3, section "Perspectives, Modes, and Mindsets"; for cross-map with Change-Cycle, see Chapter 4, section "A Pattern for Change," and introduction to Chapter 6; for cross-maps to skills and to Four-Checklists set, see Chapter 7, section "The Uncertainties of Change"; for cross-map to tame-problems and wild-problems, see Chapter 7, section "The Complexities of Change," and Chapter 12, section "Tame, Wild, and Wicked"; for cross-map to "inside the box" versus "outside the box," see Chapter 11, section "Managing Uncertainty."

- ***SCORE*** (sensemaking for strategic options) – see Chapter 11, section "What's the SCORE?"

- ***Service-Cycle*** (pattern of interactions between services) – see Chapter 10, section "The Flows of Services," and Chapter 11, section "Inside-Out and Outside-In."

- ***Service-Canvas*** (default template and completeness-checklist for service-design) – see Chapter 10, section "The Effectiveness of Services."

- ***Service-Content model*** (categories and segments of service-content in the transition from abstract to real-world) – for overview and guidance on which content-themes apply within different Change-Layers in the project-lifecycle, see the Change-Layers sections of Chapter 5; for use to describe the content for a specific service, see Chapter 9, section "From Architecture to Action."

You'll no doubt need to revisit all of those themes from time to time, depending on what's going on in the enterprise and where the flow of change seems to be heading at each moment. It's also important to be proactive, too, and seek out new opportunities to enhance innovation and effectiveness wherever they may be found.

Either way, use those lists above as a menu of options from which you can choose at each point, to keep developing the architecture and embedding it within the enterprise.

Into Practice

This final "Into Practice" section provides you with a space to review the overall set of notes that you captured while reading this book, from the "Into Practice" sections in each of the previous chapters.

At the end of Chapter 1, we invited you to **review your own views and assumptions** about the nature, scope, and role of enterprise-architecture as a discipline and practice. If you did do that exercise, it would have given you a baseline against which to assess your own changes in perspective and more, and the progress of enterprise-architecture practice within your organization.

- When you first started this book, what, to you then, was or was not "enterprise-architecture"? What were the choices and assumptions that guided those decisions?

- Now that you've read the book, what, to you now, *is* "enterprise-architecture"? What is *not* "enterprise-architecture"? What are the choices and assumptions that guide those decisions?

- If you've been re-reading the book after that first time, what do you now see differently as a result of that revisit of some or all of this book's content?

- Between then and now, what differences, if any, have there been to your views about enterprise-architecture? If there have been any significant differences to those views, how will these affect your practice of enterprise-architecture, going forward?

- What do you learn from these comparisons between past, present, and intended future?

Capture some notes to remind yourself of what you've learned from this exercise.

Next, **review your "Into Practice" notes** from all of the previous chapters, in chapter-by-chapter sequence.

- What did you learn from each chapter, according to your notes from your "Into Practice" review at the end of that part of the book?

- What did you learn as you applied the ideas and methods from that chapter into your own organization?

- What, if anything, changed in your understanding of that chapter as you read later chapters in the book, or from real-world practice later on?

- Which sections, if any, would you want to revisit again in a later reading, to further clarify your understanding and practice of that part of the work?

Again, capture any ideas, insights, and experiences that may arise from that review. Then, looking back at all of those notes as a complete set, do one overall *final review*.

- In what ways did your understanding of the role, scope, and practice of enterprise-architecture change as you read through the book?

- What aspects of this book's description of enterprise-architecture will or can you use, or not use, in practice within your own organization?

- Which aspects of this book's description of enterprise-architecture would you *want* to use in practice within your own organization, if you can't do so already? If there are any, how might you make that happen, either now or in the future?

- What other ideas might you have to extend the content of this book in your own way and/or for your own work-context?

- How would you describe to others what you've learned from reading this book? How might you work with others to put this into practice, and extend the practice of architecture itself over the future years?

Capture your notes on those last questions above, as before.

Do keep these notes, and revisit them each time you read the book, to remind you of what you've learned over the intervening time, and to build and extend your practice and experience of doing enterprise-architecture.

Summary

In this final chapter, we provided a list of pointers to where to find practice-oriented themes within the text of the book. We then provided a space for you to review the notes that you'd gathered in response to the "Into Practice" sections in each chapter, to explore what you'd learned while reading the book, and decide what to do next to further develop your skills in enterprise-architecture.

In the appendixes that follow, you'll find brief definitions for key terms that we'd used in the book, and a list of sources and resources for further reading and exploration.

APPENDIX A

Glossary

Term-names are shown in bold; cross-references to other terms are shown in italics.

Abstract (*asset-type*): Non-tangible *asset-type* such as time; can be referenced, but cannot be changed, owned, or transferred.

Action (*CSPAR* phase): Fourth phase in the *CSPAR* change-sequence; cluster of activities within a task, in which the intended *value* and outcomes for the task's *mission* will be delivered, in accordance with the respective *Plan*, *Scope*, and *Context*; loosely associated with the SCAN *Simple* domain.

Action-checklist (*Four-Checklists model*): Part of the *Action-plan* for the *Action* of a task; addresses the *Known-knowns* for that action.

Action-model (*CSPAR*): Template for an *Action-plan*; created during the *Plan* phase of a task.

Action-on (*Service-Content* model): The set of resource-types on which an *agent* of a *Capability* within a *service* will act, to deliver the desired deliverables, outcomes, and *value*; described in terms of *asset-types*.

Action-plan (*CSPAR*): Setup and guidance for a single instance of the *Action* for a task; includes *Four-Checklists* set, start- and end-conditions, sources for inputs and outputs, the means to capture information, ideas and insights arising during the action, and more as required; set up during the first part of the action.

Affordance: An unplanned yet potentially-useful alternative usage for an object, artifact, machine, system, or application.

Agent (*CALc* mode): Mindset and skillset needed to work well with the supposed certainties of real-time action associated with the SCAN *Simple* domain; also associated with the CSPAR *Action* phase and, more loosely, with the *Trainee* skill-level.

APPENDIX A   GLOSSARY

Agent (*Service-Content* model): Person, machine, and/or ICT-application that enacts a *Capability* for a *Service*; described in terms of any combination of *asset-types* (*physical, virtual, relational, aspirational*, and/or *abstract*).

Airport-airside (airport-jurisdiction): A region of any airport-building that is between the *airport-landside/airside boundary* and access to *airside* such as via a departure-gate; contrasted with *airport-landside*.

Airport-landside (airport-jurisdiction): A region between the airport's *landside* boundary and the *airport-landside/airside boundary*; contrasted with *airport-airside*.

Airport-landside/airside boundary (airport-jurisdiction): A boundary between *airport-landside and airport-airside* and/or between *landside* and *airside* that presents the respective access-controls as required by law for that context and usage.

Airside (airport-jurisdiction): In law, anywhere within the region enclosed by an airport's boundary with *landside*; in colloquial usage, any region within the airport-boundary where aircraft may stand, move, or operate; also contrasted with *airport-landside* and *airport-airside*.

Alchemist (*CALc* mode): Mindset and skillset needed to work well with the *soft-systems* complexity, volatility, ambiguity, and uncertainty associated with the SCAN *Ambiguous* domain; also associated with the CSPAR *Scope* phase and, more loosely, with the *Journeyman* skill-level.

Ambiguous (*SCAN* domain): A *domain* of the *SCAN* complexity-map, above the *boundary of commitment* and to the right of the *boundary of effective-certainty*, "outside the box"; focused on experiments, on finding usefulness for new ideas, on identifying and separating *reducible-complexity* from *non-reducible complexity*, and on creating hypotheses or frames for further development "inside the box"; for *CALc*, the part of the task in which the *Alchemist* mode will take priority; also associated with the CSPAR *Scope* phase and, more loosely, the *Journeyman* skill-level.

Analyst (*CALc* mode): Mindset and skillset needed to work well with the *hard-systems* complexities associated with the SCAN *Calculated* domain; also associated with the CSPAR *Plan* phase and, more loosely, with the *Apprentice* skill-level.

Anti-client (also "anticlient"): A person or entity that is within the same *enterprise* as an *organization*, but strongly objects to how that organization does its business within that enterprise; the objection may arise from fundamental differences in *values*, and/or from perceived "betrayal" by the organization.

Artist (*CALc* mode): Mindset and skillset needed to work well with the real-time deep-uncertainty associated with the SCAN *Not-known* domain; also associated with the CSPAR *Context* phase and, more loosely, with the *Master* skill-level.

Apprentice (*skill-level*): Able to use *hard-systems* skills to develop algorithms and processes to manage *reducible-complexity* and uncertainty; will typically need supervision and guidance to reach toward (but not beyond) the respective *boundary of effective-certainty*; associated with the SCAN *Calculated* domain.

Assessor (*CALc* mode): Mindset and skillset needed to work well with the review and continual-improvement processes needed after the "NOW!" in the *SCAN* model; also associated with the CSPAR *Review* phase.

Asset (*Service-Content* model): A *resource* that is used, changed, and/or referenced within a *Service*; described in terms of any combination of *asset-types* (*physical*, *virtual*, *relational*, *aspirational*, and/or *abstract*).

Asset-type (*Service-Content* model): Set of categories for *assets*, and also for *functions*, *locations*, and *events*, and the *agent* or *action-on* of a *capability*; categories are *physical*, *virtual*, *relational*, and/or *aspirational*, or an *abstract* non-changeable resource such as time.

Aspirational (*asset-type*): Connection between people and/or other real entities on one side, and a conceptual or imaginary entity on the other, such as a purpose, symbol, or brand; exists only between entities, non-transferrable, and non-alienable.

Attractor (chaotic-systems): A factor within a *chaotic-system* that supports *pseudo-stability* in that system.

Best-practice: A method or process that is regarded as successful in one context, and is expected to be similarly useful in other related contexts.

APPENDIX A   GLOSSARY

Boundary of commitment (*SCAN*): A point on *SCAN*'s vertical time-axis, indicating a transition between before the action and during the action, relative to the respective "NOW!"; denotes the boundary between *Calculated* and *Ambiguous* domains (above that point on the time-axis) and the *Simple* and *Not-known* domains (below that point).

Boundary of effective-certainty (*SCAN*): A point on *SCAN*'s horizontal-axis of uncertainty, indicating the effective limit of the validity of "true/false" logic and decision-making within that context and task, beyond which modal-logics and probability-based "values"-based decision-making must be used; denotes the boundary between *Calculated* and *Simple* domains (to the left of that point on the uncertainty-axis) and the *Ambiguous* and *Not-known* domains (to the right of that point).

Business-model (in CSPAR *Plan* phase): Description in abstract terms of the elements in a context, and the relationships and interactions between those elements; contrasted with *Logical-model* and *Physical-model*.

CALc (also ***CAL***): See *Context-Adaptive Leadership*.

Calculated (*SCAN* domain): A *domain* of the *SCAN* complexity-map, above the *boundary of commitment* and to the left of the *boundary of effective-certainty*, "inside the box"; focused on simplifying *reducible-complexity*, and on developing rules, algorithms, and checklists for real-time action; for *CALc*, the part of the task in which the *Analyst* mode will take priority; also associated with the CSPAR *Plan* phase and, more loosely, the *Apprentice* skill-level.

Capability (*Service-Content* model): Ability of a *service* to act on *assets* to deliver its desired deliverables, outcomes, and *value*; typically described in terms of the *agent*-types that will do the respective work, the *action-on* set of types of resources and assets to be used and changed in during the action, and the *skill-level* and experience needed to achieve the desired outcomes.

Chaining (in *task-tree*): Relation of dependencies between tasks or sub-tasks at the same *level* within a *task-tree*, in which the tasks are connected together such that one task in the chain will begin as the previous task ends.

Change-Cycle: *CSPAR* change-pattern used in "horizontal" form to guide a single chunk of change-work, typically at a single change-*layer*; each CSPAR *phase* will usually be coupled with the respective *CALc* change-mode.

Change-Layers: *CSPAR* change-pattern used in "vertical" form to guide the sequence of activities for an entire change-project.

Change-Mapping: Framework of methods and templates to guide change-work, using the *CSPAR* pattern in both *Change-Layers* and *Change-Cycle* forms, and tracking all activities of and in a *task-tree*.

Chaos-checklist (*Four-Checklists model*): Part of the *Action-plan* for the *Action* of a task; addresses the *Unknown-unknowns* for that action.

Chaotic-system: Context with high levels of *non-reducible complexity*, uncertainty, and uniqueness, typically maintained in a dynamic state of *pseudo-stability* by its *attractors*; when the system is stressed beyond the limits of its attractors, it moves into a deeply-unstable chaotic state until its attractors can bring it back into a new (and usually different) pseudo-stability.

Child (in *task-tree*): Relation of a sub-task to a *parent* task or sub-task within a *task-tree*.

Complexity: An element of a context that can, may, or will render some or all aspects of that context unpredictable or uncertain; may be usefully divided into *reducible-complexity* versus *non-reducible complexity*.

Constraints: Limits and boundaries such as physics, geography, laws, standards, and regulations that are imposed upon a task from beyond the *mission* itself; usually non-negotiable, and typically identified and established for a task during its CSPAR *Context* phase of activities.

Context (*CSPAR* phase): Initial *phase* in the *CSPAR* change-sequence; cluster of activities within a task in which its *mission*'s broader context, *vision*, *values*, *constraints*, and *success-criteria* can be established; also loosely associated with the SCAN *Not-known* domain.

Context-Adaptive Leadership of change (CALc): Systematic method for switching between modes/mindsets during change-work, to match the needs of the respective part of the change-task; based on the *SCAN* complexity-map; modes are *Artist*, *Alchemist*, *Analyst*, *Agent*, and *Assessor*; used to guide change-work, particularly in the *Change-Cycle*.

Contextual-awareness: During *action*, a continual state of maintaining awareness of purpose, the big-picture, the governing rules and guidelines, *values*, *success-criteria* and *effectiveness-criteria*, and the boundaries for action.

APPENDIX A   GLOSSARY

CRUD (*information-systems*): Acronym for Create, Read, Update, Delete.

CSPAR: Pattern of distinct yet interdependent *phases* of activities in change-work, linked together as a *chained* sequence of sub-tasks; phases are *Context, Scope, Plan, Action,* and *Review*; used in *Change-Mapping* and the *Change-Layers* and *Change-Cycle* task-guidance patterns.

Decision-type (*Service-Content* model): Set of decision-modes used to guide decisions within the activities of a *Service*; decision-types are rule-based, algorithm-based, pattern-based, and principle-based; aligned with *SCAN* domains (respectively, *Simple, Calculated, Ambiguous,* and *Not-known*), and loosely associated with *asset-types* (respectively, *physical, virtual, relational,* and *aspirational*) and *skill-levels* (respectively, *Trainee, Apprentice, Journeyman,* and *Master*).

Dispensation: An architecture-record that identifies a deployed solution that does not meet architectural standards and that implies *technical-debt*; the record should include details on what needs to be addressed, why the non-compliant solution was allowed, and review-dates or review-conditions to reassess that solution. (Note: In this context, "dispensation" is also a synonym for *waiver*.)

Domain: A bounded region of focus or interest within a description or map of some context, such as in the partitioning created by the *boundary of commitment* and *boundary of effective-certainty* in the *SCAN* complexity-map.

Effectiveness: Assessment and/or metric of alignment of change-outcomes with the respective *effectiveness-criteria*.

Effectiveness-criteria: Set of criteria used to assess *effectiveness*; derived from the applicable *vision, values, principles, constraints, success-criteria,* and definition of *value* for that context; typical default criteria would include *efficient* (minimizes waste), *reliable* (can be relied upon to deliver the desired value), *elegant* (supports simplicity and human-factors), *appropriate* (on-purpose), and *integrated* (all elements linked together, dynamically).

Emergency-checklist (*Four-Checklists* model): Part of the *Action-plan* for the *Action* of a task; addresses the *Known-unknowns* for that action.

Enacted-value: A *value* that is actually applied throughout a given context; often contrasted with *espoused-value*.

Enterprise: Denotes a purposive *storyworld* or "ecosystem-with-purpose," within which interactions related to that purpose will take place between various *agents*, *organizations*, and/or *services*; bounded by *vision, values*, commitments, and intentions (classically described as "the animal spirits of the entrepreneur"); enterprises may enclose, be enclosed by, overlap, and/or intersect with other enterprises. (Note: The term "enterprise" should not be used as a synonym for "organization.")

Enterprise Canvas: Instance of a *Service-Canvas* in which the *organization* as a whole is viewed as a service or set of services, in context of the respective overarching *enterprise*.

Espoused-value: A *value* that is claimed or purported to apply throughout a given context; often contrasted with *enacted-value*.

Event (*Service-Content* model): An identifiable "something that happens" within or for the activities of a *service*; the trigger for an event may incorporate any combination of *asset-types* (*physical, virtual, relational, aspirational*, and/or *abstract*).

FAQ: Acronym for "Frequently-Asked Questions," or a support-service of some kind that provides answers to such questions about an organization's *products* and/or *services*.

Four-Checklists model: Set of guidance-checklists for the *Action* of a task, consisting of the *Action-checklist, Preventive-checklist, Emergency-checklist*, and *Chaos-checklist*; developed during the *Plan* phase for the task.

Fractal: A pattern in which part but not all of the structure, activities, and/or parameter-set for entities will repeat, creating a set of entities that are "self-similar" but not identical with each other, and at every scale; contrasted with *recursion*, in which all entities are nominally identical with each other.

Function (*Service-Content* model): External interface for a *service* (hence may seem to be synonymous with the service when seen from outside); includes parameter-set, action-events, inputs and outputs, service-description, and service-level agreement; parameters, events, inputs, and outputs described in terms of any combination of *asset-types* (*physical, virtual, relational, aspirational*).

APPENDIX A   GLOSSARY

Hands-off architecture: A tactic for *sustainment-architecture* information-management in which most of the information about the architectural reach and scope of a change-project is maintained by project-teams rather than the architecture-team.

Hard-systems skills: Techniques and methods for calculation that may be used to establish certainty, predictability, and control in a given context; will be reliable only if the context has no *non-reducible complexity* or, in *SCAN* terms, is solely on the left side of the *boundary of effective-certainty*; often contrasted with *soft-systems* skills.

Journeyman (skill-level): Able to use experiments and *soft-systems* skills to identify *reducible-complexity* and develop patterns and methods to manage *non-reducible uncertainty*; will typically need supervision to work beyond, and extend, the respective *boundary of effective-certainty*; associated with the SCAN *Ambiguous* domain.

Known-knowns (uncertainty): Types of elements for a task that can be presumed to be known and certain prior to or during the execution of the *Action* of that task; addressed by the task's *Action-checklist*.

Known-unknowns (uncertainty): Known types of failure-conditions that may occur during the execution of the *Action* of a task; addressed by the task's *Emergency-checklist*.

Landside (airport jurisdiction): Anywhere outside of the *airside* boundary; legally, everywhere beyond the airport's boundary-fence, including anywhere up to but outside of the airport-building's doors; see also *airport-landside and airport-airside*.

Layer (*Change-Layers* model): Within an overall project, a cluster of activities associated with a single *CSPAR* phase.

Level (in *task-tree*): Location of a *task* within the hierarchical *nesting* of a *task-tree*.

Linking (in *task-tree*): Arbitrary non-hierarchical relationship between tasks and/or sub-tasks within a task-tree, often between different branches of the task-tree, or even between different change-projects.

Location (*Service-Content* model): An identifiable position of some kind that is relevant within or to the activities of a *service*; may be described in terms of any combination of *asset-types* (*physical, virtual, relational, aspirational,* and/or *abstract*).

Logical-model (in CSPAR *Plan* phase): Description in real but implementation-neutral terms of the elements in a context, and the relationships and interactions between those elements; contrasted with the *Business-model* and *Physical-model*.

Maturity-Model: Step-by-step metric for, and/or (as in this book) guidance on how to improve, the ability of a *capability* and/or *organization* to support *effectiveness*, in accordance with the respective *effectiveness-criteria*.

Master (*skill-level*): Able to use skills and experience in real-time to address any challenges within scope; will typically need little to no supervision to work beyond, and extend, the respective *boundary of effective-certainty*; associated with the SCAN *Not-known* domain.

Mission: Literally a "sending"; describes and represents the purpose, question, and/or concern to be addressed by a given change-project, task, or sub-task. (Note: The term "mission" should not be used as a synonym for "*vision*.")

MoSCoW: Acronym for Must-have, Should-have, Could-have, can-Wait, as a set of descriptors for relative-priorities of *requirements*.

Nesting (in *task-tree*): Hierarchical and recursive set of *parent*-to-*child* relationships within a *task-tree*.

Non-reducible complexity: Elements of complexity within a given context, such as in a *wicked-problem*, that cannot be reduced to *hard-systems* formulae and algorithms; contrasted with *reducible-complexity*.

Not-known (*SCAN* domain): A *domain* of the *SCAN* complexity-map, below the *boundary of commitment* and to the right of the *boundary of effective-certainty*, "outside the box"; focused on real-time sensing and sensemaking to explore and/or resolve issues that are "outside the box"; for *CALc*, the part of the task in which the *Artist* mode will take priority; also associated with the CSPAR *Context* phase and, more loosely, the *Master* skill-level.

OODA (Observe, Orient, Decide, Act): Sensemaking/decision-making, action-learning loop to guide real-time adaptation and action developed by John Boyd, originally for combat fighter-pilots.

Organization: Denotes a bounded structure of *agents*, *resources*, *capabilities*, and other *service-elements* that collectively present *services* to other organizations in context of one or more *enterprises*; bounded by rules, roles, responsibilities, and

APPENDIX A   GLOSSARY

obligations; organizations may contain, be contained by, overlap, and/or intersect with other organizations, creating composite structures such as departments, alliances, and consortia. (Note: The term "organization" should not be used as a synonym for "enterprise.")

Parallel (in *task-tree*): Sub-task that is at a similar *level* to a given sub-task in a *task-tree*, but is in a different branch of that task-tree (i.e., does not share the same *parent*).

Parent (in *task-tree*): Task or sub-task within a *task-tree* that has at least one *child* sub-task.

PDCA: Acronym for "Plan, Do, Check, Act," the sequence of steps in the Deming/Shewhart quality-management cycle.

Phase (*CSPAR*): Cluster of activities within a change-project or task, associated with one specific part of the *CSPAR* sequence (*Context*, *Scope*, *Plan*, *Action*, or *Review*).

Physical (*asset-type*): Tangible "thing"; separate, transferable, and alienable (passed in entirety from one agent to another).

Physical-model (in CSPAR *Plan* phase): Description in implementation-specific terms of the elements in a context, and the relationships and interactions between those elements; contrasted with *Logical-model* and *Physical-model*.

Plan (*CSPAR* phase): Third *phase* in the *CSPAR* change-sequence; cluster of activities within a task to identify, in accordance with *Scope* and *Context*, how the *Action* should proceed, in order to deliver the desired outcomes and *value*; loosely associated with the SCAN *Calculated* domain.

POSIWID: Acronym for a test-phrase coined by cybernetician Stafford Beer, that "the Purpose Of a System Is [expressed in] What It Does."

Preventive-checklist (*Four-Checklists model*): Part of the *Action-plan* for the *Action* of a task; addresses the Unknown-knowns for that action.

Principle: An actionable version of one or more *values*, packaged as a decision and/or priority-guidance for trade-offs, with an associated rationale and description of what success would or would not look like when the principle is applied in real-world practice.

Product (in *Service-Canvas* model): An *asset* that is transferred and/or amended between *agents* of *services*, via the interactions of a *Service-Cycle* between those services.

Pseudo-stability (chaotic-systems): State or status of a *chaotic-system* that can make it seem to be a simple rule-based system, but whose apparent stability is in reality actively maintained by the dynamic tension between its *attractors*; if any of the attractors are taken beyond their maximum limits, the apparent stability will collapse into a fully chaotic non-predictable state.

RACI: Acronym for "Responsible, Accountable, Consulted, Informed"; descriptor of mutual-responsibility relationships between players and/or roles within an *enterprise*.

Recursion: A pattern in which of the structure and/or parameter-set for entities will repeat, creating a set of entities that, other than in their parameter-values, are identical with each other, and at every scale; contrasted with *fractal*.

Reducible-complexity: Elements of complexity within a given context, such as in a *tame-problem*, that can be reduced to *hard-systems* formulae and algorithms; contrasted with *non-reducible complexity*.

Relational (*asset-type*): Connection between people and/or other real entities; exists only between entities, non-transferrable, and non-alienable.

Requirement: Description of a desired outcome for a task; identified in the *Scope* phase of the *CSPAR* change-sequence, to guide decisions and developments in the *Plan* phase for the task.

Resource: A proto-*asset*; a potential asset for which responsibility has not yet been acquired or asserted by any *organization* or *service*.

Review (*CSPAR* phase): Final *phase* in the *CSPAR* change-sequence; cluster of activities within a task to establish the benefits-realized and lessons-learned from the outcomes and/or deliverables of the preceding *Action* phase, in relation to the applicable *Plan, Scope* and *Context*; outcomes from the review are used to guide continuous-improvement of overall effectiveness.

Rule: A predefined decision that is presumed to apply within a given type of context or *Action*.

APPENDIX A   GLOSSARY

SCAN complexity-map: A two-axis matrix of time relative to an arbitrarily-chosen "NOW!" or moment of action, versus the level of perceived or actual *complexity*, unpredictability, uncertainty, and/or uniqueness; typically partitioned into *domains* relative to a *boundary of commitment* on the time-axis, versus a *boundary of effective-certainty* on the complexity-axis; resultant domains from that partitioning are *Simple, Calculated, Ambiguous,* and *Not-known*, plus a review-domain that applies after the "NOW!"

Scope (*CSPAR* phase): Second *phase* in the *CSPAR* change-sequence; cluster of activities within a task in which its *mission*'s scope, *stakeholders*, and *change-requirements* should be established, in alignment with the *vision, values, constraints,* and *success-criteria* identified in the *Context* phase; loosely associated with the SCAN *Ambiguous* domain.

Scope-creep: Expansion of project scope, requirements, and/or designed functionality beyond the range previously specified and agreed in project-governance.

Serious play: Using playfulness to support a serious purpose, such as through role-play, storytelling, simulation, low-fidelity prototyping, and other *Artist*-mode techniques; typically used in the CSPAR *Context* phase and SCAN *Not-known* domain, though also, in more people-oriented form, in the *Scope* phase and *Ambiguous* domain.

Service: A facility within an *organization* (or *stakeholder* in that role) that delivers *value* to and/or receives value from another service; alternatively, an instance of execution of the processes of that service; the *service-elements* for the service are defined by its *Service-Content* model; typically described via a *Service-Canvas* (or, for the organization as a whole, an *Enterprise-Canvas*), with interactions between services described in terms of the *Service-Cycle*.

Service-Canvas: A template and visual-checklist for design of a *service*, of which the core is a matrix of activities before, during, and after an interaction, relative to the inputs, processes, and outputs of that service, all linked to guidance of those activities for that service; interactions between services are described in terms of the *Service-Cycle*.

Service-Content model: Partitioning of the content for a *service* into six categories: *Asset, Function, Location* and *Event* (defined in terms of *asset-types*), *Decision* (defined in terms of *decision-types*), and *Capability* with its three subcategories of *agent* and *action-on* (defined by *asset-types*) and *skill-level* (defined by *decision-types*).

Service-Cycle: A sequential pattern and visual-checklist of typical sub-interactions within a broader interaction and exchange of *assets* between *services*; sub-interactions are partitioned into sets that align with the "before, during, after" structure of the *Service-Canvas*.

Service-element: An element or component of a *service*, as described by the *Service-Content* model.

Sibling (in *task-tree*): Sub-task within a *task-tree* that shares the same *parent* as another sub-task.

Simple (*SCAN* domain): A *domain* of the *SCAN* complexity-map, below the *boundary of commitment* and to the left of the *boundary of effective-certainty*, "inside the box"; focused on delivering the desired outcomes and *value* for the task, in accordance with the specified *action-plan*, yet also maintaining *contextual-awareness*, *task-awareness*, and *situational-awareness*; for *CALc*, the part of the task in which the *Agent* mode will take priority; also associated with the CSPAR *Action* phase and, more loosely, the *Trainee* skill-level.

Situational-awareness: During *action*, a continual state of maintaining awareness of what's happening in the broader context while doing the work of the task.

Skill-level (*Service-Content* model): Competence, capability, and adaptability of a given *agent* (*Service-Content*) for a given type of context and/or task; partitioned into *trainee*, *apprentice*, *journeyman*, and *master* skill-levels; in *SCAN*, determines the *boundary of effective-certainty* for that agent, relative to the respective task.

Social-license-to-operate: An informal constraint on an organization's viability within its shared-enterprise, typically determined by criteria such as social opinion and reputation; loss of social-license-to-operate may cause the failure of the organization, even if it has nominal financial or other forms of viability.

Soft-systems skills: Techniques and methods that may be used to establish some useful level of certainty and predictability (though not "control") within a context that incorporates elements of *non-reducible complexity* such as *wicked-problems*; in *SCAN* terms, will typically be used on the right side of the *boundary of effective-certainty*; often contrasted with *hard-systems* skills.

APPENDIX A   GLOSSARY

Stakeholder: Person and/or system that has a concern ("stake") in the execution and/or outcomes of a task; identified during activities of the *Scope* phase in the *CSPAR* change-sequence.

Step (*Maturity-Model*): A set of tasks and activities defined within a *Maturity-Model* that are intended to raise the competence of the *capabilities* and *services* of that *organization* to the next level in the respective maturity-models metrics.

Storyworld: A context within which interactions take place between *organizations* and their respective *services*, to support the overall shared-*vision* of the respective *enterprise*.

Sustainment-architecture: The aspect of enterprise-architecture that addresses the long-term for the organization's architectures, covering a broader scope and timescale than that of any single change-project or business-transformation.

Tame-problem: Context that has no apparent *non-reducible complexity*, and is amenable to solution via rules, algorithms, and other *hard-systems* methods; contrasted with *wild-problem*.

Task: A set of activities intended to deliver the desired outcomes and *value* for a given *mission*.

Task-awareness: During *action*, a continual state of maintaining awareness of what is being done, right here, right now.

Task-tree: Hierarchical, recursive partitioning of a *task* into sub-tasks and sub-sub-tasks.

Technical-debt: Implied costs of various kinds incurred when an expedient or short-term solution, and/or a solution contrary to architectural or other standards, is deployed into an operational context; must be documented in an architectural *waiver* or *dispensation*, and addressed in rework as soon as practicable to minimize metaphoric "interest" on the debt building up over time to unmanageable levels.

TOGAF: Acronym for "The Open Group Architecture Framework," a well-known framework for IT-oriented enterprise-architecture.

Trainee (*skill-level*): Able to use (but not develop) predefined algorithms and processes in real-time action; will typically only be able to work within a narrow *boundary of effective-certainty*; associated with the SCAN *Simple* domain.

Unknown-knowns (uncertainty): Known types of elements for a task that can only be identified immediately-prior to or during the execution of the *Action* of that task; addressed by the task's *Preventive-checklist*.

Unknown-unknowns (uncertainty): Previously-unknown, unexpected, unprecedented, or unique elements or types of failure-conditions that may occur during the execution of the *Action* of a task; addressed by the task's *Chaos-checklist*.

Value: A desirable outcome, or state or status of an *asset*, typically described in terms of some kind of metric.

Value-proposition (business): How an *organization* proposes to deliver *value* to others within the same *enterprise*.

Values (*asset*): The plural of *value*.

Values (*mission* and/or *enterprise*): A set of descriptions about the meaning of "*value*" within a given context such as a *mission* or broader *enterprise*, often expressed as *aspirations*; made actionable as *principles*; often implied by or derived from the enterprise *vision*, and applicable to all missions or tasks associated with that enterprise; typically identified and established for a task during its CSPAR *Context* phase of activities.

Virtual (*asset-type*): Data, information, or other intangible *asset*; separate, transferrable, but non-alienable (can only be transferred by making a copy).

Vision (for *enterprise*): A description of the overarching purpose of an *enterprise*, such as in the form of a three-part descriptor for the "what," "how," and "why" for that enterprise; will typically imply specific *values*, *principles*, *constraints*, *success-criteria*, and *effectiveness-criteria* that should apply throughout the respective context; aligns with the ISO9000 definition of "vision" for a quality-system.

Vision (for *task*): A description of the intended results or outcomes of the successful completion of a given project or task; aligns with the Business Motivation Model definition of "vision."

VUCA: Acronym for Volatile, Uncertain, Complex, Ambiguous.

Waiver: See *dispensation*.

APPENDIX A   GLOSSARY

Wicked-problem: A specific type of *wild-problem* that, for example, has no clear end-condition, in which each instance is in some way unique, and where each iteration changes the nature and/or content of the problem itself.

Wild-problem: Context that either includes or may include *non-reducible complexity*, and hence is not or may not be amenable to solution via rules, algorithms, and other *hard-systems* methods; contrasted with *tame-problem*.

APPENDIX B

Sources and Resources

This appendix is split into two sections: "Sources" and "Resources."

The "Sources" section provides details on books that we referenced in the text.

The "Resources" section provides a list of pointers to further details on people referenced in the text, and other topics and themes that came up during the text. Most of these point to the respective Wikipedia pages: those are only summaries, of course, but they do each present a useful overview, and in most cases do provide links to more authoritative sources.

Weblinks were valid as of May 2025.

Sources

William Ian Beardmore Beveridge, *The Art of Scientific Investigation*, Heinemann, 1950; see also the Internet Archive at https://archive.org/details/artofscientifici00beve for legal full-text download in multiple formats.

Stafford Beer, *Brain of the Firm* (2nd edition), Wiley, 1995; see also the Internet Archive at https://archive.org/details/brain-of-the-firm-reclaimed-v-1 for legal full-text download of the original 1972 edition in multiple formats.

David Bohm, *On Dialogue*, Routledge, 2013.

Shawn Callahan, *Putting Stories to Work: Mastering Business Storytelling*, Pepperberg Press, 2016.

Andrew Campbell, Mikel Gutierrez et al., *Operating Model Canvas: Aligning operations and organization with strategy*, Van Haren, 2017.

James P. Carse, *Finite and Infinite Games: A Vision of Life as Play and Possibility*, Ballantine Books, 1967.

Chris Collison, Geoff Parcell, *Learning to Fly: Practical Lessons from one of the World's Leading Knowledge Companies*, Capstone Publishing, 2001.

APPENDIX B   SOURCES AND RESOURCES

Paul Feyerabend, *Against Method: Outline of an Anarchistic Theory of Knowledge*, Verso, 1975.

Atul Gawande, *The Checklist Manifesto: How to get things right*, Henry Holt, 2010.

Tom Graves, *Power and Response-ability: The human side of systems*, Tetradian Books, 2008.

Tom Graves, *SEMPER and SCORE: Enhancing enterprise effectiveness*, Tetradian Books, 2008.

Tom Graves, *The Enterprise as Story: The role of narrative in enterprise-architecture*, Tetradian Books, 2012.

Tom Graves and Joseph Chittenden, *Change-Mapping: Connecting business tools to manage change*, Tetradian Books, 2020.

Tom Graves and Joseph Chittenden, *Tools for Change-Mapping: Expanding the Change-Mapping tool-set*, Tetradian Books, 2021.

Tom Graves and Joseph Chittenden, *Advanced Change-Mapping: Exploring, resolving and addressing issues of any size and complexity*, Tetradian Books, 2022.

Tom Graves, *Making Sense of Services In EA: Structure, design, governance and value-flow*, Tetradian, 2022. (Available only in ebook format: see `https://leanpub.com/tp-easervices`)

Tom Graves, *Everyday Enterprise Architecture: Sense-making, strategy, structures, and solutions* (2nd edition), Apress, 2023.

Tom Graves, *The Service-Oriented Enterprise: Learn enterprise architecture and its viable services* (2nd edition), Apress, 2023.

Tom Graves, *Mapping the Enterprise: Modeling the enterprise as services with Enterprise Canvas* (2nd edition), Apress, 2023.

Dave Gray, Sunni Brown, and James Macanufo, *Gamestorming: A playbook for innovators, rulebreakers and change-makers*, O'Reilly, 2010.

Dave Gray and Thomas Vander Wal. *The Connected Company*, O'Reilly, 2012.

Dave Gray, *Liminal Thinking: Create the Change You Want by Changing the Way You Think*, Two Waves Books, 2016.

Nigel Green and Carl Bate, *Lost in Translation: A handbook for information systems in the 21st century*, Evolved Technologist Press, 2007.

John Hagel, John Seely Brown, Lang Davison, *The Power of Pull: How Small Moves, Smartly Made, Can Set Big Things in Motion*, Basic Books, 2010.

Michael Henderson and Dougal Thompson, *Values at Work: The invisible threads between people, performance and profit*, HarperBusiness, 2003.

IDEO Group, *The Field Guide to Human-Centered Design*, IDEO.org, 2015.

Sohail Inayatullah and Ivana Milojevic (eds.), *CLA 2.0: Transformative Research in Theory and Practice*, Tamkang University Press, 2015.

Keith Johnstone, *Impro: Improvisation and the theatre*, Eyre Methuen, 1981.

Amy Jo Kim, *Community Building on the Web: Secret Strategies for Successful Online Communities*, Peachpit Press, 2000.

Cynthia Kurtz, *Working with Stories in Your Community or Organization: Participatory Narrative Inquiry*, Kurtz-Fernhout Publishing, 2014.

Rick Levine, Christopher Locke, Doc Searls, David Weinberger, *The Cluetrain Manifesto: The end of business as usual*, Perseus Books, 2000; also full-text and notes at https://cluetrain.com/

Alexander Osterwalder, Yves Pigneur et al., *Business Model Generation: A Handbook for Visionaries, Game Changers, and Challengers*, Wiley, 2010.

Alexander Osterwalder, Yves Pigneur et al., *Value Proposition Design: How to create products and services customers want*, Wiley, 2014.

Chris Potts, *fruITion: Creating the Ultimate Corporate Strategy for Information Technology*, Technics Publications, 2008.

Suzanne Robertson, James Robertson, *Mastering the Requirements Process*, ACM Press/Addison-Wesley, 1999.

Peter Sengé, *The Fifth Discipline: The Art and Practice of the Learning Organization*, Random House, 1990.

Peter Sengé, Art Kleiner, Charlotte Roberts et al., *The Fifth Discipline Fieldbook: Strategies and tools for building a learning organization*, Nicholas Brealey Publishing, 1994.

Peter Sengé, Art Kleiner, Charlotte Roberts et al., *The Dance of Change: The challenges of sustaining momentum in learning organizations*, Nicholas Brealey Publishing, 1999.

Marc Stickdorn, Adam Lawrence et al. (eds.), *This Is Service-Design Doing: Applying service-design thinking in the real world – a practitioner's handbook*, O'Reilly, 2018.

Gerald M. Weinberg, *Secrets of Consulting: A guide to getting and giving advice successfully*, Dorset House Publishing, 1985.

Gerald M. Weinberg, *More Secrets of Consulting: The Consultant's Tool Kit*, Dorset House Publishing, 2002.

Etienne Wenger, Richard McDermott, and William M. Snyder, *Cultivating Communities of Practice: A Guide to Managing Knowledge*, Harvard Business School Press, 2002.

APPENDIX B   SOURCES AND RESOURCES

Resources

After-Action Review: see Wikipedia at https://en.wikipedia.org/wiki/After-action_review

Air France Flight 447: see Wikipedia at https://en.wikipedia.org/wiki/Air_France_Flight_447

Ray Anderson and Interface Inc: see Interface Inc's "Mission Zero" at https://www.interface.com/GB/en-GB/sustainability/our-mission.html

Archi free and open-source enterprise-architecture-toolset: see https://www.archimatetool.com/

W. Ross Ashby: see Wikipedia biography at https://en.wikipedia.org/wiki/W._Ross_Ashby

Asset-stripping (enterprise-hijack): see Wikipedia at https://en.wikipedia.org/wiki/Asset_stripping

Stafford Beer: see Wikipedia biography at https://en.wikipedia.org/wiki/Stafford_Beer

Bohm Dialogue: see Wikipedia at https://en.wikipedia.org/wiki/Bohm_Dialogue

Causal layered analysis: see Wikipedia at https://en.wikipedia.org/wiki/Causal_layered_analysis

Corporate raid (enterprise-hijack): see Wikipedia at https://en.wikipedia.org/wiki/Corporate_raid

Decision-problems in computability-theory: see Wikipedia at https://en.wikipedia.org/wiki/Decision_problem

Escrow: see Wikipedia, particularly the section on intellectual-property, at https://en.wikipedia.org/wiki/Escrow

Richard Feynman and Rogers Commission Report (Challenger disaster): see Wikipedia at https://en.wikipedia.org/wiki/Rogers_Commission_Report

Goodwill (accounting): see Wikipedia at https://en.wikipedia.org/wiki/Goodwill_(accounting)

Incompleteness-theorems (Kurt Gödel): see Wikipedia at https://en.wikipedia.org/wiki/G%C3%B6del%27s_incompleteness_theorems

ISO-9000 standards for quality-systems: see Wikipedia at https://en.wikipedia.org/wiki/ISO_9000_family

ISO-14000 standards for environment-management systems: see Wikipedia at https://en.wikipedia.org/wiki/ISO_14000_family

ISO-27000 standards for information-security: see Wikipedia at https://en.wikipedia.org/wiki/ISO/IEC_27000_family

Kurtosis-risk: see Wikipedia at https://en.wikipedia.org/wiki/Kurtosis_risk

"Limits To Growth" report, 1972: see Wikipedia at https://en.wikipedia.org/wiki/The_Limits_to_Growth

"Little Gidding" (poem, part of TS Eliot's "*Four Quartets*"): see full text at https://www.columbia.edu/itc/history/winter/w3206/edit/tseliotlittlegidding.html; for the "Four Quartets," see Wikipedia at https://en.wikipedia.org/wiki/Four_Quartets

Donella Meadows: see Wikipedia biography at https://en.wikipedia.org/wiki/Donella_Meadows

Mercalli scale (earthquake-intensity): see Wikipedia at https://en.wikipedia.org/wiki/Modified_Mercalli_intensity_scale

Noosphere: see Wikipedia at https://en.wikipedia.org/wiki/Noosphere

OODA (Observe, Orient, Decide, Act): see Wikipedia at https://en.wikipedia.org/wiki/OODA_loop

Participatory Narrative Inquiry: see https://www.workingwithstories.org/ and https://cfkurtz.com/

PDCA quality-cycle: see Wikipedia at https://en.wikipedia.org/wiki/PDCA

RACI responsibility-categories: see Wikipedia at https://en.wikipedia.org/wiki/Responsibility_assignment_matrix

Scientific management (Frederick Winslow Taylor): see Wikipedia at https://en.wikipedia.org/wiki/Scientific_management

Serious play: see Wikipedia at https://en.wikipedia.org/wiki/Serious_play

Claude Shannon (information-theory): see Wikipedia biography and links at https://en.wikipedia.org/wiki/Claude_Shannon

"Somebody Else's Problem" responsibility-avoidance: see Wikipedia at https://en.wikipedia.org/wiki/Somebody_else%27s_problem

Stafford Hospital scandal: see Wikipedia at https://en.wikipedia.org/wiki/Stafford_Hospital_scandal

Starhawk (Miriam Simos) (power-model): see Wikipedia biography and links at https://en.wikipedia.org/wiki/Starhawk

"*Sully*" movie (US Airways Flight 1549): see Wikipedia at https://en.wikipedia.org/wiki/Sully_(film); see the film's depiction of the period from the bird-strike to the ditching on YouTube at https://youtu.be/wLdNcFlkYSY; see Wikipedia for the event itself at https://en.wikipedia.org/wiki/US_Airways_Flight_1549

APPENDIX B   SOURCES AND RESOURCES

Sustainability at Walmart: for policy on sustainability, see https://corporate.walmart.com/purpose/sustainability; see also the Sustainability Hub at https://www.walmartsustainabilityhub.com/

SWOT analysis: see Wikipedia at https://en.wikipedia.org/wiki/SWOT_analysis

Frederick Winslow Taylor: see Wikipedia biography at https://en.wikipedia.org/wiki/Frederick_Winslow_Taylor

Toy-theatre: see https://www.pollocks-coventgarden.co.uk/categories/toy-theatres/

Tuckman Group Dynamics: see Wikipedia summary at https://en.wikipedia.org/wiki/Tuckman%27s_stages_of_group_development

"Twelve Leverage Points" (Donella Meadows): see Wikipedia at https://en.wikipedia.org/wiki/Twelve_leverage_points

"*United Breaks Guitars*": see song-video on YouTube at https://youtu.be/5YGc4zOqozo; see Wikipedia on the song and its background at https://en.wikipedia.org/wiki/United_Breaks_Guitars

Variety and "requisite variety" (W. Ross Ashby): see Wikipedia at https://en.wikipedia.org/wiki/Variety_(cybernetics)

Viable System Model (Stafford Beer): see Wikipedia at https://en.wikipedia.org/wiki/Viable_system_model

VPEC-T analysis: see Wikipedia at https://en.wikipedia.org/wiki/VPEC-T

VUCA (Volatile, Uncertain, Complex, Ambiguous): see Wikipedia at https://en.wikipedia.org/wiki/VUCA

Wicked-problem: see Wikipedia at https://en.wikipedia.org/wiki/Wicked_problem

Year 2000 problem ("Y2K"): see Wikipedia at https://en.wikipedia.org/wiki/Year_2000_problem

Year 2038 problem (Unix dates): see Wikipedia at https://en.wikipedia.org/wiki/Year_2038_problem

Index

A

Action architecture, 269
    action model, 311, 312
    business-infrastructure, 269
    change-cycle model, 289
    context layer, 291–294
        core elements, 292
        effectiveness, 291
        functions/systems, 291, 292
        roles/relationships/responsibilities, 293
    document-repositories, 288
    functional-decomposition, 290
    governance, 288
    layers/sub-layers, 288
    plan layer
        action-model package, 310
        asset types, 304, 306
        backbone-and-edge, 301
        benefits, 308
        capabilities, 304
        categories, 304
        content-segment types, 306
        coordination/process-choreography, 303
        decisions, 305
        deliverables, 307
        deployment-model, 309
        design-model, 302, 303
        development-model, 307, 308
        domestic *vs.* international path, 300
        events, 305
        function/locations, 304
        function-model, 299
        information-systems, 307
        interaction-model, 299, 300
        layer details, 299
        operations-procedures, 302
        policies and procedures, 302
        procedure/policy, 301
        redundancy and duplication, 308
        repositories, 308
        requirements, 298
        respective repositories, 303
        service-providers, 303
        valid/legal/safe-to-travel, 307
        vision, 301
        work-instructions, 301, 302, 310
    real-world enterprise, 288
    review layer, 312, 313
    scope (*see* Scope management plan)
    scope layer
        conflicts-of-interest, 298
        development exercise, 298
        function-specific form, 295
        gateway governance-check, 298
        preferred methods, 297
        realizable/understandable, 297
        requirements, 294
        scope-boundaries, 295
        storming phase, 296, 297
        sub-layer, 296
        tier-3 business-function, 294
        translations, 295

Action architecture (*cont.*)
   sections, 271
   service building (*see* Service building enterprise)
   service-content model, 290
   significant organization, 270
   stories
      creation/execution, 320
      larger story, 319
      mini-figures, 316
      operational-view diagram, 314
      people/process/technology, 314, 317
      scene content, 318
      scents, 315
      stage, 319
      structured approach, 317
      technical/non-technical diagrams, 315
      theater-metaphor, 318
      visual-checklist, 317, 320
   sustainment processes, 288–291
Architectural process
   ad-hoc decisions, 252
   capabilities
      domain-architectures, 256
      enterprise-architecture, 256
      mission, 253
      module/solution, 255
      positioning process, 258
      professionals, 255
      project/technical-lead, 256
      project-type/sustain-type, 254
      requirements, 257
      research-lab, 255
      setup, 254
   communication/engagement, 265, 266
   continuity, 259
   distinct parts, 253
   documents/repositories
      management themes, 264
      planning and preparation, 263
      stages, 263
      users of documents, 264
   function-model, 260
   governance, 260–262
   methods/checklists, 266–268
   respective scope, 260
   sustainment-type, 259–261
   tasks, 259
Architectural process maturity-model, 252
Architecture-awareness
   command/control, 578
   communities-of-practice, 581–585
   conferences, 579, 580
   organization overview, 578
   practical concerns, 581
   quality-concerns, 579
   quality-oriented themes, 583
   shared enterprise, 584

B

Betrayal-anticlients, 500, 512
Business-continuity/disaster-recovery
   architecture repository, 542
   impact-analysis scenario, 541
   impact dashboard, 544
   infrastructure-team, 544
   mapping process, 542
   Murphy rules, 541
   requirements, 543
   responsibilities, 542
   strategies, 541
   system resilience and flexibility, 543
   universals, 543

INDEX

C

CAD, *see* Computer-Aided Design (CAD)
CALc, *see* Context-Adaptive Leadership of change (CALc)
Chaos-checklist
    architecture, 550
    defensible-uncertainty, 549
    information-systems, 553
    mechanical problems, 553
    Mythquake Scale, 551
    people power, 550
    real-world action, 549
    responsibility-based economy, 552
    SCAN terms, 550
    sources, 549
    sustainment-architectures, 549
    switchover-systems, 552
CMDB, *see* Configuration Management Database (CMDB)
Complexities change
    characteristics, 191
    customer-service system, 194, 195
    dimensions, 189
    inherently-uncertain, 193
    key concepts, 188
    planned-events, 193
    pseudo-stable system, 190
    reasonable-uncertainty, 193
    scale (*see* Scale changes)
    SCAN frame, 191, 192, 196
    surgical-operation, 192
    tame *vs.* wild-problem, 190, 197
    unplanned-events, 193
    wicked-problem, 191
Computer-Aided Design (CAD), 106
Configuration Management Database (CMDB), 459
Context-Adaptive Leadership of change (CALc), 426
Context/scope/plan/action/review (CSPAR)
    awareness, 74
    change-cycle pattern, 70
    change-layers/change-cycle, 71
    change-layers pattern, 70
    checklists, 73–75
    complexity, 188–197, 203
    context-neutral core, 68
    cycle (*see* Cycle patterns)
    dependencies, 69
    horizontal form, 71
    layers (*see* Layer pattern)
    mapping methods, 72, 73
    method/framework, 71
    mid-range task, 69, 70
    outcomes, 74
    practice process, 201–204
    roles (*see* Role changes)
    scale, 197–201, 204
    uncertainties, 182–188, 202
Create, Read, Update, Delete (CRUD), 509
CRM, *see* Customer Relationship Management (CRM)
CRUD, *see* Create, Read, Update, Delete (CRUD)
CSPAR, *see* Context/scope/plan/action/review (CSPAR)
Customer Relationship Management (CRM), 22, 306
Cycle patterns
    action phase, 163–166, 172
    CALc modes, 146, 147
    change-cycle phases, 153
    completion, 173

625

INDEX

Cycle patterns (*cont.*)
    context phase, 153–156, 170
    context-specific standards, 145
    core structure, 143
    fractality, 136–143
    horizontal pattern, 135
    inputs, 150
    interactions, 150
    iteration, 144
    key points, 146
    mode-switching, 149
    outputs, 151
    parent-task, 152
    plan phase, 159–163, 171
    relationships, 147, 148
    respective layer, 145
    review phase, 166–169, 172
    scope phase, 156–159, 171
    single fractal-instance, 149, 150
    single/sub-layer, 144
    source-phase, 151
    structure-template/checklist, 169–173
    task-content, 144
    themes, 146
    uncertainty-domains, 147
    visual relationship, 152

D

Disruption/chaos
    methods, 560
    checklists, 560

E

Engagement system
    architecture-awareness, 578–585
    communications plan, 565
    executive-board, 569
    function-model, 568
    governance, 568
    hands-off approach, 570–578
    methods/checklists, 585–587
    objections, 566–568
    positive-mythquake, 570
    slidedeck-presentation, 569
    techniques, 568
Enterprise-architecture
    airport's architecture, 4
    architectural enterprise, 2–5
    business model, 5
    capabilities
        CMMI maturity-model, 11
        development skills, 14
        engagement, 14
        foundations section, 13
        increments, 12, 13
        maturity-model, 10–12
        practice sections, 15–17
        respective dependencies, 9
        roadmap, 9
        role/purpose/function of, 8, 9
    chapter summarization, 589–591
    command and control, 564
    complexity, 6
    effectiveness, 1, 2
    methods/frameworks, 3
    models/tools/methods, 595–597
    people, 563
    perspectives, 6–8
    practice section, 597–599
    regulatory environment, 5
    sections, 564
    security, 6
    specific tasks, 591–595
    term-names, 601–616

whole-enterprise architecture, 4, 5
Enterprise-hijack, 513–518
Escalation design
    complications, 440
    fundamental failures, 438
    implementation, 437
    information-issues, 439
    learning process-design, 436
    legal-to-travel/safe-to-travel checks, 440
    manual interpretation, 437
    mechanisms, 437
    models and cross-connections, 440
    service, 438, 439
    service-choreography, 437

F, G

Facing hidden risk
    anti-clients, 495–504
        antibodies, 497
        architecture-work, 503
        betrayal-anticlients, 500
        business-models, 496
        competitors, 498
        continual action, 503
        customer-service, 500
        immune-system response, 500
        indirect relationship, 496
        inherent-anticlients, 497–499
        operations level, 504
        organization/enterprise, 496
        project-architecture level, 503
        requirements, 502
        sustainment-architecture level, 503
        tactical level, 503
        Walmart, 499
        weblog, 501, 502
    wicked-problems, 498
    assumptions/myths, 518–527
    enterprise-hijack, 513–518
    kurtosis-risk, 504–513
    power problem
        architecture, 483
        aspirational-assets, 484
        blame and shame, 488, 489
        command-and-control, 491
        effectiveness, 491
        empowerment, 485
        finite-game, 489
        fractal level, 490
        fundamental aspect, 493
        infinite-game, 489
        investors and beneficiaries, 494
        literal/metaphoric data, 494
        mapping process, 494
        physics definition, 484
        pie-slice concept, 483
        power-issues, 495
        power-over/power-under, 487
        power-with/power-from-within, 485
        respective tasks, 495
        responsibility, 490
        SEMPER power-model, 491, 492
        transactional relationship, 487
    sources of, 482
Foundations section
    CSPAR, 65
    patterns, 65–79
    science
        awareness, 60–62
        concepts/definitions, 33, 34
        elements, 34–42
        elements/SCAN domains, 47–60
        practice, 62–64

INDEX

Foundations section (*cont.*)
    shape of change, 42–46
    sense of change
        capabilities, 19–21
        key term and concepts, 23–30
        requirements, 21–23
Fractal analytics
    action-learning loop, 142
    alchemist mode, 141
    arbitrary framing, 141
    assessor-mode, 139
    assumption, 142
    back-and-forth conversations, 138
    back-to-front aspect, 141
    categories-error, 142
    context-space mapping, 140
    detail-level, 139
    different contexts, 136
    frameworks, 143
    horizontal-axis, 136
    metadata-parameters, 137
    metametamodel, 140
    planned *vs.* unplanned aspects, 139
    same-and-different perspectives, 138
    same/different mapping, 140–143
    types of, 137

H

Hands-off approach
    architecture unit, 571, 573
    building-project, 572
    city-planning context, 572
    completion, 577, 578
    domain-architects, 571
    enterprise-scale architecture, 570
    gateway review, 576–578
    governance-gateways, 576
    key items/attributes, 573–575
    responsibility, 571
    strategies, 570

I, J

Identity enterprises
    ad-hoc decisions, 407
    architectural perspective, 208
    architectural work (*see* Architectural process)
    broader shared-enterprise, 206
    business-architecture, 205
    business-offerings, 332
    context, 208, 209
    core capabilities and services, 269, 331
    core context/scope, 205
    differences/boundaries, 331
    essential tasks, 207
    maturity-model, 331
    ongoing strategic capability, 332
    practical value, 207
    shared-enterprise content, 209
    storyworld (*see* Storyworld enterprise)
    unwise approach, 206
Inherent-anticlients, 497–499
Interactions (outside-out), 477
    CALc modes, 478
    defensible-uncertainty, 479
    differences, 479
    disruption/chaos, 540–553
    effectiveness
        appropriateness, 557
        architecture-development, 555
        dimensions, 557
        emergent-outcomes, 555, 557

integration and alignment, 557
keywords, 555
review/enhance agility, 556
strategic role, 554
sustainment-architectures, 554
universals, 556
expectations, 480
fail-safe/safe-fail
abstract-services *vs.* service-implementations, 546
approaches, 545
fundamental interface, 546
graceful failure, 548
lessons-learned analysis, 545
Murphy's Law, 545
navigation-systems, 545
priority failure-scenario, 547
risk-management, 546
switching and connections, 548
indefensible-certainty, 480
isolation, 481
meta-structure, 478
novel coronavirus, 481
retrospective-certainty, 480
review phases, 478
risk (*see* Facing hidden risk)
sections, 481
significant risks, 558–561
sustainment-architectures, 479
wicked-problems, 527–539
Investor/beneficiaries pattern
architectures, 463
classic shareholder relationship, 465, 466
concepts, 465
fairness, 471
financial investments, 463, 472
financial-investors, 466
interactions, 464
investment/dividend/balancing, 468
investor relations section, 463
local businesses, 472
local communities, 472
local-government authorities, 466
organization, 464
public relations, 467
relationship-roles, 464
stakeholder-types, 471
structure, 470
value-governance function, 469
whole-organization level, 468

K

Kurtosis-risk
assets types, 509, 510
betrayal-anticlients, 512
business-context, 507
challenges, 507
consequences, 504, 513
CRUD analysis, 509
customer-service, 505
dysfunctional misuses, 507
dysfunctional power-games, 506
eventuation, 513
fundamental concerns, 507, 509
grenade, 506
journey-mapping, 510
low-probability, 504, 505
service-cycle mapping, 511
solutions, 507
system-design criterion, 511
systemic flaws, 508, 511, 512
trust, 509
VPEC-T pattern, 509

INDEX

L

Layer pattern
    action phase
        abstract terms, 119
        accept/reject options, 121
        agent mode, 120
        assessment, 118
        conceptual overview, 119
        content, 119
        outputs, 122
        role of, 118
        sub-layers, 121, 122
        task-tree, 120
    action plan/sub-layers, 133
    action process, 88
    awareness, 89
    classic change-layers, 83
    conceptual trap, 83
    context phase, 87, 90, 130
        artist mode, 91
        brainstorming, 92
        child-tasks, 91
        context-neutral methods, 95, 96
        core elements, 91
        effectiveness, 93
        elements, 94
        inputs, 92
        outputs, 95
        role of, 90
        sub-layers, 94
        sub-tasks, 93
    different models, 82
    fractal approach, 88
    fractal-instance, 84
    fundamental difference, 84
    generic context-neutral pattern, 81
    higher levels, 90
    plan layers/sub-layers, 131
    plan phase
        abstract process, 110
        action-model, 115–117
        activity-architecture, 113, 115
        agent-types, 111, 112
        analyst mode, 107
        assumptions, 117
        complexities, 118
        content development, 106
        coordination/process-choreography, 111
        deployment-architecture, 113
        design model, 111
        documentation, 112, 114
        documents, 109
        entity-type, 105
        goal-based/continuing change, 106
        infrastructure model, 114
        inputs, 107
        installation-model, 114
        interaction-model, 110
        outputs, 117
        planning-process, 104
        qualitative constraints, 109
        real-world equivalents, 109
        redundancy and duplication, 114
        regulations/standards, 113
        scope/action, 104
        segment-types, 105
        service-oriented approach, 116
        small-scale/large-scale disruptions, 105
        structure, 108
        sub-layers, 109
        task/sub-task, 104

plan stage, 85
representation, 84
review phase, 88
   after-action review, 126
   assessor mode, 125
   benefits-realized, 127
   content, 123, 124
   effectiveness, 123
   governance-issue, 128
   inputs, 125
   lessons-learned, 127
   machine-learning, 124
   outputs, 128
   rules, 126, 127
   sub-layers, 126
   task-tree, 123
   themes, 125
review plan/sub-layer, 133
scope phase
   alchemist mode, 99
   child-tasks, 98
   complexity, 103
   content development, 97
   inputs, 99
   outputs, 102
   requirements, 96, 97
   stakeholders, 103
   sub-layers, 100, 101
   task-specific form, 101
   task-tree, 98
   vendor-driven architectures, 103
scope plan, 87
   sub-layers, 130
structural-checklist, 129–134
task/sub-task, 85, 86, 89
vertical form, 81, 82
whole-of-project level, 87
Long-tail risk (*see* Kurtosis-risk)

M, N

Marketplace interaction, 407
   alchemist mode, 408
   CMMI managed level, 409
   different types, 407
   flexibility design
      abstract-service, 441
      architectures, 436
      escalations, 436
      exceptions, 436–440
      resilience, 440–443
      service-choreography, 441
      trade-off analysis, 440
   investors and beneficiaries, 409, 463
   methods and checklists, 473
   outside (*see* Outside box)
   practice section, 473–475
   qualities/values
      architecture repository, 444
      business-value, 447, 448
      compliance, 444
      cross-links, 444
      formal standards, 447
      issues/actions, 445
      process-execution, 445–447
      subtraction, 445
   trust and reputation, 448–463
Murphy's Law, 322

O

Observe, Orient, Decide, Act (OODA), 42
OODA, *see* Observe, Orient, Decide, Act (OODA), 42
Organization enterprise
   content and structure, 230
   content process, 246, 247
   mission-statement, 236–238

INDEX

Organization enterprise (*cont.*)
    positioning terms
        context map, 232, 233
        cross-check questions, 231
        differentiation, 233, 234
        fundamental types, 230
        roles and interactions, 231, 232
    strategic anchors, 229
    structure, 247
        alchemist-mode, 249
        artist-mode, 249
        business-context/scope, 252
        context-space, 249
        function-model, 248, 249
        nested hierarchy, 248
        organization positions, 251
        tier-1 function-model, 249, 250
        tier-2 function-model, 250, 251
    value-proposition, 241
        classic business-model, 241
        responsible/accountable, 245
        role-relationships, 242–244
        roles and interactions, 241, 245
        shared-enterprise, 241
        source-information, 244
        transaction type, 242
        vision/constraints, 244
    vision/role/mission/goal, 229
    vision/values
        actual-values, 239
        architecture-risks register, 240
        business-purpose, 239
        espoused-values, 239
        gap-analysis, 239
        POSIWID, 239
        refinements, 238
        required-values, 238
        shared-enterprise, 237, 238
        Stafford Beer, 239
Outside box
    alchemist mode, 410
    analyst mode, 410
    inside-out/outside-in, 411–417
        appropriate labels, 414
        business-politics, 416
        challenges, 411
        customer-journey, 415
        customer-of-customer, 413
        direct-interactions, 411, 413
        indirect-interactions, 411
        interactions, 414, 415
        IT-organization, 414
        organization and market, 412
        politics, 416
        service-cycle/context layers, 416
        standard labels, 414
        supplier-journey, 415
        transactions, 411, 413
    manage uncertainty
        absolute control/certainty, 418
        action-checklist, 424
        chaos-checklist, 425
        checklists set, 424
        differences, 420, 421
        effective-certainty, 421
        emergency-checklist, 425
        enacted-certainty, 421
        expected-certainty, 421
        high-/low-probability, 423
        human skills, 422
        mathematical proofs, 417
        planning stage, 420
        preventive-checklist, 424
        rules-based methods, 418, 419
        SCAN, 419, 420
        scientific management trap, 421, 422

VUCA management, 417
SCORE, 431–435
skills/leadership
    control-function, 426
    CSPAR phases, 427–432
    leadership-types, 427
    manager/leader, 425
    organization-architecture, 425
    potential traps, 430
    scientific-management, 426
    skills-learning pathways, 429

P, Q

Pattern changes
    change-method, 66
    completeness-checklist, 77
    consistent method, 65
    CSPAR tasks, 68–72
    different kinds, 76
    Gantt-chart, 66, 67
    lower-level task, 78
    real-world work-context, 76
    task-begin and task-end gateways, 67
    task-tree, 66
    type task, 67

R

RACI, *see* Responsibility Assignment Matrix (RACI)
Resources section, 617–619
Responsibilities service
    architecture framework, 458
    aspirational assets, 458
    assessment-tasks, 459
    capabilities, 462, 463
    concepts, 457

mapping, 460, 461
programming terminology, 459
RACI matrix, 458
response-ability, 458, 460
Responsibility Assignment Matrix (RACI), 224, 225
Role changes
    architecture and design, 178, 180
    architecture-work, 179
    change-layers, 180
    change-management, 178
    connect-architectures, 180
    consistent method/frame, 175
    content, 180
    deliverables, 181
    distinct roles, 176
    fractal-instances, 180
    planned/unplanned-change, 181
    practical implications, 178
    relationships, 177
    respective roles, 177
    role-switching, 178, 179
    strategy-and-tactics, 177
    sustainment-architecture, 180
    themes, 177

S

Scale changes
    ambiguous-mode assessments, 198
    compound-delay effects, 199
    e-commerce application, 199
    emergent effects, 198
    emergent risks, 200
    information-system, 200
    interactions, 198
    non-reducible elements, 198
    situational-awareness, 200

Scale changes (*cont.*)
  source of, 197
  strategies, 199
SCAN (simple/calculated/ambiguous/
    not-known)
  agent mode, 56–58
  Alchemist mode, 53, 54
  Analyst mode, 55, 56
  artist mode, 50, 52, 53
  assessor/mentor, 48
  assessor mode, 58–60
  change-modes, 49
  comfort-zone mode, 50
  distinct modes/mindsets, 48
  hypotheses/experiment, 47
  intuition/chance, 48
  mode-perspectives, 49
  observation/imagination, 47
  preparation, 47
  real-time checklist, 51
  strategy/reason, 47
  time and uncertainty, 46
Science architectures
  awareness, 60–63
  concepts and definitions, 33, 34
  contextual-awareness, 61
  defensible uncertainty, 34
  feel of change
    chances, 38–40
    core limitation, 40
    formal-reasoning, 40–42
    imagination, 35
    intuition, 36–38
    observation, 35
  perspectives/mode/mindsets, 63
  SCAN domains, 47–60
  self-awareness, 61
  shape of change
    action-learning loop, 42
    change-cycle, 43
    fractality, 44
    horizontal-axis, 44
    insanity definition, 44
    SCAN frame, 46
    sense, make-sense, decide, act, 43
    sensemaking and decision-
      making, 45
    skill-level and decision-level, 45
    vertical axis, 42
  situational-awareness, 61
  task-awareness, 61
Scope management plan
  business-infrastructure, 271, 276
  methods and checklists, 328
  narrative-oriented methods, 277
  practice section, 328–330
  role infrastructure, 271
    abstract level, 273
    architectural perspective, 271
    backbone and edge, 274
    backbone/median/edge, 275
    business-offerings, 276
    edge-developments, 276
    functional structure, 273
    function/service, 272
    service-oriented approach, 272
    workflow/process, 272
  setup setting, 276, 277
SCORE, *see* Strengths, Challenges,
    Options, Responses, and
    Effectiveness (SCORE)
Sense of change
  capabilities, 19–21
  concepts/principles
    architecture/design, 24
    business motivation model, 29

context-neutral/specific parts, 27
continuous-change, 28
effectiveness, 24, 25
fractal patterns, 27, 28
frameworks/standards, 29
goal-based change, 28
organization/enterprise, 25
planned-change/unplanned-change, 29
requirements, 23
service-as-system, 25, 26
structure aspect, 24
vision/mission, 28
core requirements, 21–23
discipline/rigor, 30, 31
Service building enterprise
business-infrastructure, 277
functions/systems
abstract verbs, 279
airport's test-run, 280
business processes, 278
business-systems, 282, 284, 285
identify business-systems, 283
individual business-systems, 285
information-systems model, 282, 286, 287
responsible agency, 284
service-category-type, 283
tier-2 function, 278
tier-3 functions, 279, 281–284
test (*see* Testing services)
Sources section, 617–619
Storyworld enterprise
central success-criterion, 215
constraints, 213, 214
effectiveness-criteria, 215
elements, 220–222
enterprise-vision, 212
essential/characteristic elements, 221
interaction, 210
principles/values, 216
core-principle, 217
explicit/implicit, 218
interpretation, 216
principle via keywords, 218
requirements/content, 218
satisfaction, 217
transparency *vs.* privacy, 218
whole-enterprise architecture, 219
priorities, 213
real-world constraints, 214, 215
roles/interactions
benefits, 229
business-context, 228
context map, 224
governance, 225–227
mutual-responsibilities, 226
relationship categories, 223
responsibilities, 223–225
responsible *vs.* accountable, 225, 227
shared-enterprise, 228
shared-enterprises, 211, 212
themes, 210
vision-statement, 211, 213
Strengths, Challenges, Options, Responses, and Effectiveness (SCORE)
appropriate keyword, 433
connections, 434
effectiveness-criteria, 433
information-system, 434, 435
interaction-journey, 432
interconnection, 433
keyword representation, 431
strengths and weaknesses, 431
visual-checklist, 432

INDEX

Strengths, Weaknesses, Opportunities (SWOT), 431
SWOT, *see* Strengths, Weaknesses, Opportunities (SWOT)

T

Testing services
   business-infrastructure, 321
   checks/balances, 328
      alignment, 327
      capabilities, 325
      circumstances, 326
      end-to-end process, 326
      events, 325
      lifecycle, 327
      transformation, 327
   services *vs.* processes
      boxes/lines, 323
      differences, 321
      function-model, 324
      international passengers, 322
      monolithic chunks, 322
      vertical layer, 323
      workflow process, 324
Trust architecture, 449
   architectural approach, 455
   architectural level, 449
   aspirational-type asset, 450
   business-functions, 456
   change-management, 455
   checklist/methods, 451
   elements, 449
   enterprise-vision, 456
   functional structure, 453
   function-model, 456
   information-finding session, 456
   intervention-points, 454
   maturity-model sense, 455
   narrative-based techniques, 452
   organization, 450
   positioning and differentiation, 452
   real-world action, 453
   rules/responsibilities, 455
   shareholder-value, 455
   trust problems, 455
   trust-related issues, 453
   universals, 451
   value-propositions, 452
   vision-statement, 457

U

Uncertainties change
   action-checklist, 187
   agents, 185
   artist/alchemist-modes, 184
   change-cycle, 182
   chaos-checklist, 188
   checklists set, 186, 187
   definition, 182
   effective-certainty, 183
   emergency-checklist, 187
   preventive-checklist, 187
   productivity, 186
   SCAN frame, 184
   skill-levels, 185
   skills-development-path, 185

V

Values, process, events, content, trust (VPEC-T) methodology, 529

W, X, Y, Z

Wicked-problems
   architecture modeling, 528
   characteristics, 528
   expectation-management, 528
   methods and checklists, 559
   requirements, 528
   solid technical-skills, 528
   tame-and wild-problems
      characteristics, 531
      contrast, 529
      conventional analysis, 532
      distinctions, 529
      finite and infinite games, 530
      SCAN terms, 531, 532
      unknown/unsolvable problems, 532
   VPEC-T methodology, 529
   working process
      aircraft-research establishment, 538
      business-analysis, 537
      business/IT alignment, 533
      CALc modes, 538
      categories, 533
      context, 535
      dynamic uncertainty, 535
      identify wickedness, 536
      isolation, 533
      natural tensions, 535
      pain-point, 534
      real-world problems, 533
      real-world solutions, 538
      re-solution, 537
      scientists/engineers, 538, 539
      shared values, 539
      technical/social-complexity, 533
      value-systems, 535
      virtuous circle, 539

GPSR Compliance

The European Union's (EU) General Product Safety Regulation (GPSR) is a set of rules that requires consumer products to be safe and our obligations to ensure this.

If you have any concerns about our products, you can contact us on

ProductSafety@springernature.com

In case Publisher is established outside the EU, the EU authorized representative is:

Springer Nature Customer Service Center GmbH
Europaplatz 3
69115 Heidelberg, Germany

www.ingramcontent.com/pod-product-compliance
Lightning Source LLC
LaVergne TN
LVHW081344060526
838201LV00050B/1702